# BRINGING OUTSIDERS IN

# BRINGING OUTSIDERS IN

TRANSATLANTIC PERSPECTIVES
ON IMMIGRANT POLITICAL
INCORPORATION

*Edited by*

**Jennifer L. Hochschild**
*and* **John H. Mollenkopf**

Cornell University Press  *Ithaca and London*

An earlier version of Chapter 3 appeared in Rainer Bauböck (Ed.),
*Migration and Citizenship: Legal Status, Rights and Political
Participation.* IMISCOE Reports, Amsterdam University Press, 2006.

First published 2009 by Cornell University Press
First printing, Cornell Paperbacks, 2009

Printed in the United States of America

*Library of Congress Cataloging-in-Publication Data*

Bringing outsiders in : transatlantic perspectives on immigrant
political incorporation / edited by Jennifer L. Hochschild and
John H. Mollenkopf.
    p. cm.
  Papers originally presented at a conference held Apr. 22–23, 2005 at
the Radcliffe Institute for Advanced Study.
  Includes bibliographical references and index.
  ISBN 978–0–8014–4811–9 (cloth : alk. paper) —
  ISBN 978–0–8014–7514–6 (pbk. : alk. paper)
  1. North America—Emigration and immigration—Political
aspects—Congresses.   2. Europe, Western—Emigration and
immigration—Political aspects—Congresses.   3. Immigrants—North
America—Political activity—Congresses.   4. Immigrants—Europe,
Western—Political activity—Congresses.   5. Political participation—
North America—Congresses.   6. Political participation—Europe,
Western—Congresses.   I. Hochschild, Jennifer L., 1950–
II. Mollenkopf, John H., 1946–   III. Title.

  JV6351.B75 2009
  325.73—dc22

2008053441

Cloth printing        10  9  8  7  6  5  4  3  2  1

Paperback printing    10  9  8  7  6  5  4  3  2  1

# Contents

# Acknowledgments

This volume began as a conference at the Radcliffe Institute for Advanced Study on April 22–23, 2005. Our first debt of gratitude is to the outstanding scholars who worked long and traveled far to that event for little but the intrinsic rewards of scholarly exchange. Old friendships were reinforced by this process and new ones formed. The co-editors planned the conference, with the help of a cluster of visiting scholars who had previously been in residence at the Institute for a year. In addition to the two of us, the cluster included Richard Alba, Luis Fraga, Riva Kastoryano, Reuel Rogers, and Mary Waters. We are grateful for our ongoing stimulating conversations with them on the topics analyzed in this volume, as well as many others. Luisa Heredia provided invaluable assistance in identifying excellent and appropriate scholars for the conference—many thanks to her.

Neither the cluster nor the conference would have occurred without the energy and leadership of Katherine Newman, then the social science dean of the Radcliffe Institute and now a professor at Princeton University. We owe an equal debt of gratitude to Drew Faust, then dean of the Radcliffe Institute, for creating such a fantastic intellectual environment, and to the staff of the Institute, particularly Phyllis Strimling and Liz Maguda, for handling the logistics of the conference with competence, grace, and good humor.

We are extremely grateful to the Andrew W. Mellon Foundation and Harriet Zuckerman, its executive vice president, for providing the financial support needed to plan the cluster and to develop and underwrite its activities. The Mellon Foundation's willingness to stay with this project, and its confidence in the book and its many authors, has sustained us over periods when the project looked as though it might falter.

It has been a pleasure working with Peter Wissoker of Cornell University Press to bring the volume into being. He believed in it from its earlier and rougher incarnations and has been very helpful in pushing us to push the authors to make a good book even better. We also thank Emily Zoss and Julie F. Nemer for all the essential support necessary to produce a volume worth looking at and reading.

At Harvard University, members of the undergraduate Research Assistance Collective (RAC) provided astonishingly good research assistance in many languages and through multiple sources of information. Andrea Blankmeyer, Idriss Fofana, Emina Kobiljar, Edlira Nasi, Rares Pamfil, and Ipek Yakupog will go far in life, and we have been pleased to know them in their formative years. Many thanks to the Weatherhead Center for International Affairs for organizing and supporting the RAC. Jacqueline Chattopadhyay proved to be a superb editor and critic. She shaped chapters, drafted the part introductions, gave wise comments and suggestions on our own chapters, and fostered the enterprise in countless ways. Anne-Marie Zapf-Belanger used her sophisticated editorial skills to whip the bibliography into shape, despite the idiosyncratic referencing styles of over twenty recalcitrant authors. At the Graduate Center of the City University of New York, the staff of the Center for Urban Research provided constant support and encouragement.

Finally, as always, our spouses and children continued to love and support us despite our tendency to go to a lot of meetings, send endless e-mails, and get distracted by our focus on issues that, however important, were removed from family life. We are blessed to live with such understanding people. They are (for Jennifer Hochschild) Tony Broh, Eleanor Broh, and Raphael Broh and (for John Mollenkopf) Kathleen Gerson and Emily Mollenkopf.

J. L. H. and J. H. M.

# PART I

# FRAMEWORKS

# CHAPTER ONE

# Setting the Context

*John H. Mollenkopf and Jennifer L. Hochschild*

Over the last six decades, millions of immigrants have arrived in the wealthy democracies of Western Europe and North America. Despite increasing restrictions, the volume of arrivals remained high as families reunite, asylum seekers find safe havens, undocumented workers cross borders, and residents of the new accession states of the European Union travel west. The current economic crisis may slow these flows, but they will resume with recovery. Immigrants come from many different countries and have diverse motives: finding economic opportunity, escaping political conflict, and following kinship networks. Groups concentrate in specific places: Mexicans in California, Cubans in Florida, Turks in Germany, South Asians in England, West Indians in Canada, and Moroccans in France. Although foreign nationals generally make up no more than one-eighth of the European populations, they and their children have a large presence in urban areas, sometimes a majority. According to a recent projection, immigrants and their children are expected to account for 82 percent of the population growth in the United States between 2005 and 2050 (Passell and Cohn 2008). Similarly, Eurostat reports that fertility rates are well below replacement levels in the European Union (Giannakouris 2008) so immigrants and their children will soon be a disproportionate share of young and working-age EU residents.

Although the term *assimilation* has fallen further out of favor in Europe than in the United States, native-born elites and wider public opinion in both settings nonetheless want immigrants to become productive members of their societies.[1] However, North America and Western Europe both face great challenges in achieving the cultural, economic, social, and political incorporation of the new populations. On the one side, they have afforded a mixed welcome to immigrants. Many Westerners appreciate immigrants' hard work and contributions to the host country cultures, but many, perhaps more, also express great concern about how immigrants and native-born citizens will adjust to one another, what will happen as immigrants' children grow to adulthood, and whether their country is changing too much or in the wrong direction (Fetzer 2000; Citrin and Sides 2006). On the other side, immigrants are also ambivalent; they remain attached to their home countries even as they form new lives and communities in host countries. They want their children to succeed in western jobs and cultures, but they are not at all sure that they want their children to become western. They want to influence host countries' public policies, but they typically find host country political processes confusing, unappealing, and unwelcoming.

The counterpoise between assimilation and exclusion deeply challenges liberal democracies (Hollifield, Hunt, and Tichenor 2008; Carens 2000). Their electoral systems deprive foreign-born noncitizen residents of the formal right to participate (although some allow voting in local elections), their cosmopolitan political cultures have difficulty dealing with illiberal beliefs, their national ideals and party systems may be predicated on refusing to recognize racial and ethnic differences, their avenues for economic mobility may be constrained by labor market regulations designed to protect native workers, and native-born citizens may not be happy about sustaining immigrants in generous social welfare systems. Immigrant political actors usually find local-level politics to be more vibrant, varied, and responsive—but that arena is contentious, often fractured, unable to deal with basic problems, and resource-poor. In coming decades, North America and Western Europe will have to work out these tensions if they are to reach the goal consistent with their underlying political values—enabling new immigrants to become integral parts of their national political communities.

This book seeks to make sense of these multiple and intersecting dimensions: assimilative and exclusionary trajectories, socioeconomic and political arenas, liberal democratic and nativist values, local and national venues, and immigrants' agency and established structures. In this chapter, we first explicate the main reasons for and paths of immigration across Western Europe and North America and describe the current patterns of economic and social incorporation of immigrants and their children. We then turn to our chief concern—immigrants' political incorporation in western liberal democracies.

## Pathways to Immigration

After World War II, immigrants arrived in Western Europe and North America from nearby less-developed countries to perform jobs for which there were no ready takers among the native-born. Two patterns framed this migration: (1) the residents of former colonies moved to the metropoles of former colonizers and (2) temporary guest workers were recruited from poor nations of southern Europe, North Africa, and the Middle East. The first were prevalent in the United Kingdom and France; the last two were most prevalent in Germany, Austria, Belgium, and the Netherlands. At first considered a temporary presence both by the foreign workers and their hosts, guest workers settled down and brought their families from home or formed families in the host countries. Their oldest children have now entered adulthood and have children of their own. To paraphrase Max Frisch, these countries wanted workers but got people—and families—instead (Garson 2004; Hansen 2003; European Commission 2006).

As de-industrialization and rising global competition reduced the demand for factory workers in the West and as the global economy encountered oil crises and instability, Western European countries began restricting further immigration through these channels in the 1970s. Nevertheless, the provision for family reunification, acceptance of refugees and asylum seekers, increasing numbers of undocumented workers, demise of the Soviet Union, and expansion of the European Union into Eastern Europe have all generated additional population flows into Western and southern Europe since the 1980s.

Immigrant entry to the United States has had a different rhythm. Apart from those who lived in territories conquered or purchased by the United States, Mexicans had informally entered the United States to work since the nineteenth century. Many participated in the federally regulated bracero program—which was, roughly speaking, a guestworker program—from the 1940s until its dissolution in the early 1960s (Montejano 1987; Ngai 2004). Ironically, immigration of western hemispheric residents to the United States was not subject to numerical limits until the adoption of the 1965 Hart-Celler Act, but migration to the United States surged after the act was passed (Zolberg 2006; Tichenor 2002). Although subsequent legislation has sometimes made incorporation or upward mobility more difficult for immigrants, the volume of net new migration to the United States has remained high since the 1970s, in many years reaching 1 million or more.

The trajectory of immigration to Canada has been roughly similar to that of the United States, although Canada liberalized admissions earlier than the United States, puts more emphasis on admitting immigrants with labor market qualifications, and created more immigrant-integration programs (Bloemraad 2006).

Several demographic trends resulting from this history are clear—or at least as clear as possible given the different national definitions of *immigrants* and *citizenship* (Bauböck 2006). First, the actual number and population share of the foreign-born varies a good deal across the countries of Western Europe and North America; columns 2 and 3 of table 1.1 show the range (see also Münz 2006).

Second, different immigrant groups settle in different countries. Not surprisingly, most immigrants to a given country come from nearby countries—in many cases, from within the European Union. With a few exceptions (concern over migration from Poland, for example), movement within the European Union causes little stir. But in all Western European and North American countries, members of at least one of the three largest immigrant groups comes from a geographically—and, more important, culturally—more distant country. They tend to be the objects of anxiety about immigrant incorporation. Table 1.2 shows this patterns. Turks, the largest immigrant group in Europe, are concentrated in Germany, although they are also present in the Netherlands, Belgium, Austria, and France. North Africans, the second largest group, are concentrated in France but also reside in Spain, Italy, the Netherlands, and Belgium. Citizens of the new accession states are a rapidly growing presence in Western Europe, particularly in Germany and the United Kingdom. People from the former Yugoslavia are particularly prevalent in Germany and Austria. Any cross-national comparisons must take account of these concentrations, with all of their implied religious, cultural, social, economic, linguistic, and political particularities.

Third, most western countries include postcolonial migrants, such as the Congolese in Belgium and the Indonesians and Surinamese in the Netherlands. These groups tend to have a different relationship to the state and politics of the host country than

**Table 1.1** Foreign-born population, 2006, and acquisition of nationality, 1996–2005

| [1]<br>Country | Foreign-born population, 2006 | | [4]<br>Average proportion of foreign-born<br>acquiring nationality per year,<br>1996–2005 (%) |
| --- | --- | --- | --- |
| | [2]<br>Percentage | [3]<br>Number | |
| Luxembourg | 33.4 | 152,100 (estimate) | 0.5 |
| Switzerland | 23.8 | 1,772,800 (estimate) | 2.0 |
| Canada | 19.1 | 5,895,900 (estimate) | 2.9 |
| Austria | 13.5 | 1,100,500 | 3.9 |
| United States | 12.9 | 38,343,000 (estimate) | 2.3[a] |
| Germany | 12.9 | 10,620,800 (estimate)[b] | 1.8 |
| Sweden | 12.4 | 1,125,800 | 7.2 |
| Belgium | 12.1 | 1,268,900 | 4.4 |
| Netherlands | 10.6 | 1,734,700 | 7.1 |
| United Kingdom | 9.7 | 5,841,800 (estimate) | 3.7 |
| Norway | 8.2 | 380,400 | 5.6 |
| France | 8.1 | 4,926,000 | 4.6[c] |
| Denmark | 6.5 | 350,400 | 4.5 |
| Spain | 5.3 | 2,172,200[d] | 2.0 |
| Finland | 3.4 | 176,600 | 3.8 |
| Italy | 2.5 | 1,446,700[d] | 0.9[e] |

*Sources:* For foreign-born population, Organisation for Economic Co-operation and Development (OECD 2007, table A.1.4); for nationality, OECD (2007, table A.1.6) and Migration Policy Institute (n.d.).

*Notes:* The table includes all EU-15 countries plus selected other Western European nations, the United States, and Canada. Note that some foreign-born residents might not be permanent immigrants.

[a] Based on data for 1991–2001.
[b] Based on data for 2003.
[c] Based on data for one year.
[d] Based on data for 2001.
[e] Based on data for nine years.

do economic migrants, often having language skills, cultural capital, and political knowledge useful for integration. Finally, table 1.2 shows that few immigrant groups in Europe are as important a part of the national population as Mexicans are in the United States. Almost 15 percent of the U.S. population is Hispanic; of this group, two-thirds are of Mexican descent. Two-fifths of U.S. Hispanics are foreign-born; most of the rest are the children or grandchildren of immigrants (U.S. Bureau of the Census 2007).[2] The only European groups that approximate the importance of this group are the people from the former Yugoslav states in Austria and the Portuguese in Luxembourg.

## Arenas and Trajectories of Immigrant Incorporation

Given these pathways to and patterns of immigration, how are immigrants and their descendents being incorporated in the social, economic, and cultural arenas? Let us briefly consider each arena in turn.

Social incorporation is slow but mostly linear across generations. Except for migrants from former colonies, first-generation immigrants are seldom fully comfortable in the host-country language. In some of the largest immigrant-receiving U.S.

**Table 1.2** Country of origin of three largest immigrant groups and their share of total foreign-born population, 2001–2006

| Country | Immigrant group and percentage of foreign-born population | | |
| --- | --- | --- | --- |
| | Largest | Second largest | Third largest |
| Austria (2005) | Former Yugoslavia, Bosnia & Herzegovina 27.6 | Turkey 13.0 | Germany 12.5 |
| Belgium (2005) | France 12.3 | Morocco 11.7 | Italy 9.9 |
| Canada (2001) | United Kingdom 11.1 | China (excluding Taiwan and Hong Kong) 6.1 | Italy and India 5.8 (each) |
| Denmark (2005) | Turkey 8.9 | Germany 6.6 | Iraq 6.0 |
| Finland (2005) | Former Soviet Union 22.8 | Sweden 16.7 | Estonia 7.1 |
| France (2005) | Algeria 13.7 | Morocco 12.6 | Portugal 11.5 |
| Germany (2006) | Turkey 16.5 | Russian Federation 6.2 | Poland 5.6 |
| Luxembourg (2001) | Portugal 28.8 | France 13.0 | Belgium 10.2 |
| Netherlands (2005) | Turkey 11.3 | Surinam 10.9 | Morocco 9.7 |
| Norway (2005) | Sweden 8.9 | Denmark 5.9 | Pakistan 4.1 |
| Sweden (2005) | Finland 16.3 | Former Yugoslavia, Bosnia & Herzegovina 11.4 | Iraq 6.4 |
| United Kingdom (2006) | India 9.9 | Ireland 7.2 | Pakistan 4.8 |
| United States (2006) | Mexico 30.4 | Philippines 4.4 | India 4.0 |

*Source:* OECD (2007, table B.1.4); for Germany, Statistiches Bundesamt (2008), "Bevoelkerung und Ewerbs-taetigkeit" (March, table 2).

states, including Texas and California, for example, over two-fifths of the foreign-born have limited or no proficiency in English (Grieco 2003). The slow acquisition of the national language is also an issue in Europe, particularly where the national language community is small, as in the Netherlands. In addition, immigrants who arrive as adults seldom wholeheartedly embrace the host-country culture, and they retain strong ties to their countries of origin (Kastoryano 2002).

Most seriously, immigrants' educational attainment—a route to social as well as economic incorporation—remains comparatively poor. The parental generation often arrives with low levels of prior education, and their children have widespread difficulty in school, especially in Europe. The 2006 survey of the Organisation for Economic Co-operation and Development (OECD) Programme for International Student Assessment (PISA) found that, on average, 15-year-old immigrants to European countries score approximately 8 percent lower than their native peers in science, reading, and mathematics; immigrants to the United States score almost as poorly on science and mathematics[3] (Organisation for Economic Co-operation and Development [OECD] 2006, tables 4.2c–e). These educational gaps are especially large in Austria, Belgium, Switzerland, and Germany; they are small in Ireland and Canada.

Economic challenges occur in all immigrant-receiving countries, although their nature varies according to the structure of particular labor markets and social welfare systems. Consider table 1.3, which shows clearly that, across Europe (with the exception of Spain), most members of the low-skilled non-European guestworker generation have been pushed out of the labor force and on to various social supports. Conversely, in the comparatively open labor market of the United States, most first-generation immigrants continue to work in low-wage service sector jobs and the immigrant employment rate is just as high as the native-born employment rate. As a result of these dynamics, foreign-born men and women in Europe have consistently had higher unemployment rates than native-born populations since the mid-1990s (in some cases, twice as high or even higher); in contrast, in the United States, immigrants had a lower unemployment rate in 2005 and the same rate a year earlier (OECD 2007a, annex table I.A1.4).

Complicating immigrants' efforts to enter their new societies is the fact that many residents, even descendents of immigrants, usually treat newcomers with suspicion or even downright hostility. Across fifteen European nations, 58 percent of respondents to the 2003 International Social Survey Programme (ISSP) agreed or agreed strongly that "people who do not share [Country's] customs and traditions" cannot "become fully [Country's] nationality]" (ISSP 2003 National Identity II Survey Question 8a). Three-fifths or more of respondents in the former East Germany, Austria, the Netherlands, Hungary, Norway, France, Denmark, and Finland thought that immigrants

**Table 1.3**  Employment rates for native-born and immigrant men and women, ages 15–64, in Western Europe and United States, 2003 or 2004 (%)

| Country | Total | Nationals | EU-15 immigrants | Non-EU-15 immigrants |
|---|---|---|---|---|
| Austria | 66 | 68 | 71 | 55 |
| Belgium | 60 | 61 | 56 | 38 |
| Canada[a] | 79 | 83 | 76 | |
| Denmark | 76 | 78 | 74 | 48 |
| Finland | 69 | 69 | 68 | 48 |
| France | 63 | 64 | 69 | 44 |
| Germany | 65 | 66 | 68 | 49 |
| Netherlands | 74 | 75 | 76 | 45 |
| Spain | 61 | 60 | 64 | 68 |
| Sweden | 73 | 74 | 68 | 49 |
| United Kingdom | 72 | 73 | 70 | 61 |
| United States | 69 | 69 | 69 | 69 |

*Sources:* For European countries, British Council Brussels (2005); for Canada, Statistics Canada, 2001 Census; for the United States, *Current Population Survey,* March 2004.

*Notes:* This table reflects data gathered before the accession of twelve new countries into the European Union in 2004 and 2007.

[a] Data for 2001.

had to learn to share the host-country customs and traditions, compared with approximately one-half in the former West Germany, Great Britain, Ireland, Sweden, Spain, and Switzerland. Only one-third of Americans and two-fifths of Canadians made the same demand. Nevertheless, even the United States has recently experienced controversy over whether "cultural America is under siege" from excessive Latin American immigration, which might "divide the United States into two peoples, two cultures, and two languages" (Huntington 2004, 12).

ISSP respondents express economic and social, as well as cultural, anxieties. In the same fifteen European nations, 32 percent of respondents agreed that "immigrants take jobs away from people born in [Country]," and a whopping 57 percent agreed that they increase crime (ISSP 2003 National Identity II Survey Questions 10a and 10c). Respondents in the United States were even more likely to concur on the jobs issue (43 percent), although fewer (27 percent) on agreed about a link between immigrants and crime (analysis of Zentralarchiv für Empirische Sozialforschung an der Universität zu Köln, ZACAT, data).[4]

The specter of terrorism further complicates social incorporation. The September 11, 2001, attacks on the World Trade Center by a mostly Saudi group organized from Hamburg, the March 2004 Madrid train bombings by Moroccan residents of Spain, the killing of Theo van Gogh in Amsterdam in November 2004 by a Dutch man of North African ancestry, the July 2005 London transit bombings by young Britons of immigrant backgrounds, the rioting by young people of North African descent in Clichy sous Bois in October 2005, and the more recent arrests of Muslim converts for suspected terrorism in Germany all suggest limits to assimilation and lead some native-born citizens to conflate immigration with terrorism and concern for security.

A 2002 survey by Worldviews asked respondents "whether you favor or oppose restricting immigration" in order to "combat international terrorism." About three-quarters of respondents in Great Britain, the United States, and Italy favored restriction, as did seven-tenths of respondents in Poland and three-fifths in France and the Netherlands. Only in Germany did a minority (44 percent) favor restriction (www. worldviews.org). The association between immigration and terrorism has since declined, at least in the United States; about 40 percent of U.S. respondents agreed in 2007 that both legal and illegal immigration increased the threat of terrorism (the sample was split so that respondents addressed only one form of immigration) (CBS/ *New York Times* Poll, May 2007). (No comparable recent data are available for European nations.) But two-fifths is still a large fraction of the population, especially six years after the attacks on the World Trade Center and Pentagon.

Finally, political incorporation is uneven and halting, for reasons explored in greater detail throughout this book. As column 4 in table 1.1 shows, relatively few foreign-born residents of any Western European country acquire the nationality of the host country in a given year. Not surprisingly, therefore, their electoral or public presence ranges between slim and nonexistent, except for sporadic protest activity. In the United States, up to 60 percent of legal permanent residents have acquired citizenship over the past few decades (U.S. Department of Homeland Security 2007; see also Bergeron and Batalova 2008; Castles and Davidson 2000). Their political impact is gradually growing, although nowhere commensurate with their numbers.

In the end, the first-generation experience cannot settle the question of whether a group is assimilating (or integrating). By definition, most adult members of the first generation spent their formative years outside the host country and resocialization as an adult can be difficult and painful. Their children, the immigrant 1.5[5] and second generations, have much greater potential for incorporation. The trajectory of immigrant assimilation therefore depends on whether the children in the second generation can close their parents' gaps in achievement and participation and fully join their host societies, adding their own flavors, or whether they will also be blocked from opportunities and will turn into angry, alienated, and troublesome ethnic or racial minorities.

A full answer to this question must await comparisons from studies that are now underway, such as The Integration of the European Second Generation (TIES) project, the Immigrant Second Generation in Metropolitan New York (ISGMNY) study, and the Immigration and Intergenerational Mobility in Metropolitan Los Angeles (IIMMLA) study—and more time. Nevertheless, based on the partial evidence currently available, the United States and Canada appear to be doing a better job than most of the Western European countries in affording opportunities for upward mobility and the political incorporation to the children of immigrants (Alba 2005; Silberman, Alba, and Fournier 2007; Waters and Alba 2008). We can see this disparity in several arenas; here we consider only two.

Education may be the key to all other forms of social, cultural, and economic incorporation. Some second-generation Europeans enter universities and find professional jobs. Most, however, still leave school without university qualifications and are shunted into low-skilled jobs or are unemployed. In the 2006 PISA, the gap in reading, science, and math scores between the children of immigrants and the children of host-country nationals was at most only marginally smaller than that between adult immigrants and their host-country counterparts. (The United Kingdom and Canada were exceptions to that generalization; OECD 2006, tables 4.2c–e). Second-generation immigrants have, on average, gotten further in the more loosely structured U.S. educational system; in PISA, the gap in math scores between second-generation and native-parentage Americans is about one-third smaller than it is between immigrant and native-born young people (OECD 2006, tables 4.2c–e).

Political incorporation usually comes later than other forms of assimilation, but it is crucial to giving immigrants a stake in their new country and in enabling them to shape its policies and practices. But, like their parents, second-generation immigrants in Europe usually lack citizenship and have little involvement in conventional politics. In contrast, native-born children of immigrants to the United States are U.S. citizens by definition, with full legal access to the political system. The 1.5 and second generations move into the political arena at about the same pace as native-born U.S. youth with native-born parents. Young adult immigrants who came to the United States as children are nearly three times as likely to become naturalized as are older immigrants; they report high levels of trust in the government and endorse individualism; they are no less likely to volunteer in civic associations, contact a government official, or participate in a rally or march than are native-born youth. Only the rates of identification with a political party vary substantially with immigration status. Native-born young citizens are also more likely to register and vote than are naturalized young adults, but that gap disappears once controls for socioeconomic status are introduced (Setzler and McRee 2005). The Canadian Ethnic Diversity Survey of 2002 found similar patterns (Statistics Canada 2003, 1).

It is not surprising, given these legal and participatory differences, that immigrant groups and their descendents have more political representation in the United States than in most countries of Europe. At the local level, elected officials of recent immigrant ancestry serve as mayor of Los Angeles and comptroller of New York City. Immigrants or the children of immigrants hold five of the fifty-one seats on the New York City Council. A few European cities match or exceed these proportions: the forty-nine-member city council of Amsterdam has approximately seven members from immigrant backgrounds, in part because legally resident immigrants can vote in local elections. And Brussels has by far the most representation of people descended from non-Europeans—twenty (22.5 percent) out of eighty-nine total seats in the Brussels Parliament. But these cities are exceptions; the twenty-five-member London Assembly has only three members of non-UK origin. The 163-member Conseil de Paris has only a few members who appear to be from immigrant backgrounds. An analysis of 90 French municipal elections in 2001 found that 173 (5.6 percent) of the 3,062 elected officials were of foreign origins, judging by their names (Geisser and Oriol 2002). The 149-person Berlin Parliament includes 9 non-European members (of whom 8 were born in Turkey).

At the national level, the United States is even more distinctive. Eleven members of the 435-person U.S. House of Representatives were born outside the United States; others, such as Brooklyn's Yvette Clarke, are the children of immigrants. In total, twenty-seven Hispanic and seven Asian members serve in the House (Amer 2007). The House of Representatives has one Muslim member (he is not an immigrant or immediate descendent of immigrants). As we write, the son of an African Muslim has become president of the United States. In contrast, the United Kingdom 635-member House of Commons includes four Afro-Caribbean members, ten South Asian members, and one member of African ancestry, in total just over 2 percent. The United Kingdom has a proportionately smaller minority population than the United States, but this rate of representation is still well below that of the U.S. Congress. Only 6 of the 577 members of the French National Assembly are from non-European backgrounds (and one of these was appointed rather than elected); the 331-seat Senate has 3 elected members from non-European backgrounds. Of forty elected senators in Belgium, two are of non-European descent; of the 150 members of the Chamber of Representatives, only 6 are descended from non-Europeans (2 were appointed). Similarly, the 614-member German Bundestag has 7 members from outside Western Europe (for more on Muslim elected officials in Europe, see Klausen 2005). The Netherlands has somewhat more representation, proportionally, of non-nationals; its 150-member Parliament had 15 members of non-European origin in 2003. In the Dutch Senate, three of the seventy-five members in 2007 were of non-European origin. These are low numbers of representatives with non-European ancestry, despite many decades of immigration.

Obviously, much more needs to be said to fully describe the variation across countries, arenas of incorporation, and immigrant groups. Nevertheless, we have enough preliminary information at this point to be able to consider factors that shape these patterns.

## Political Opportunity Structures for Immigrant Political Incorporation

Immigrants bring resources, needs, and desires into the political arena, and they are met by political institutions, practices, and commitments (see Hochschild and Mollenkopf, chap. 2 in this volume). The interaction among those forces shapes the patterns of political incorporation, which the chapters in this book illuminate. This can be described as the relationship between a political opportunity structure (Eisinger 1973; Tarrow 1994; Koopmans and Statham 2000c) and the capacity to take advantage of opportunities.

### Immigrants' Resources

The resources, tangible and intangible, that immigrants bring to a host country are a key component of that capacity. Because selection plays an enormous role in positioning first-generation groups vis-à-vis the native-born, we must understand the differences in the composition of the groups that began arriving in the rich democracies half a century ago. Many European migrants (except for those moving from Eastern to Western Europe) are adherents of Islam, and the common parlance of the native majority has sometimes deemed them to be members of a distinct ethnicity even when they are phenotypically white. In contrast, recent immigrants to the United States have been predominantly Christian, largely Catholic, or they have not included religion as a central element of their identity. Although most were or are considered to be only marginally white, they generally were granted higher status than the disvalued native population of blacks. Furthermore, a higher proportion of first-generation migrants to Europe were rural dwellers with traditional values and little or no formal education than has been the case for immigrants to North America.

In the United States and Canada, largely because of their immigration policies, many new groups contained some well-educated members who could provide the kernels of group with upward mobility and political leadership. For example, whereas 27 percent of native-born Americans are college graduates or have an advanced degree, fully 49 percent of immigrants from South and East Asia and 44 percent of those from the Middle East have the same level of education (Pew Hispanic Center 2008, table 22). Not surprisingly, the same groups enjoy higher household incomes than do native-born Americans (Pew Hispanic Center 2008, table 32).[6] The same pattern holds for the postcolonial migrants to European nations, but they have not been very politically or socially salient.

Thus, immigrants to some countries have been more positively selected than those in others. These characteristics make incorporation into the political opportunity structure somewhat easier in the United States and Canada than it is in Western European states.

### Politically Relevant Circumstances

The social and economic context is correspondingly more favorable for immigrants' political incorporation in the United States than in most of Europe. First, as we have noted, the highly regulated labor markets and strong social welfare states of northern Europe meant that migrants faced restricted job opportunities and could be constructed into a dependent class once they had been pushed or kept out of the labor market. Other features of Western European states confounded that problem; in response to the horrors of Nazism and based on their commitment to civic republicanism, officials in many states have been reluctant to permit racial or ethnic categorizations. Such reluctance, along with the absence of a visible native minority category with some political clout, has made it difficult for European authorities to recognize and measure racial or ethnic differences. So without much official realization, immigrants settled in (or were confined to) old inner-city working-class neighborhoods and suburban social housing, creating a degree of ethnic segregation that, in turn, led to low levels of language acquisition and cultural change. Some of these neighborhoods have become problematic as the purported sites of crime or "no go" areas for natives.

Many European national education systems are also highly stratified, both in terms of neighborhood elementary schools (with a considerable degree of "white flight" from immigrant-rich schools) and selection mechanisms for higher levels of schooling (with national sorting tests for entry to gymnasia, lycees, and universities). Immigrants and their descendents have had a great deal of difficulty passing through the filter of the sorting tests (Alba and Silberman forthcoming).

In contrast, the weakly regulated, open labor markets and thin social welfare state in the United States have meant that immigrants *had* to work to survive and could not rely on public assistance as an alternative to even exploitative low-wage jobs. Ironically, given the stringent U.S. laws—the 1996 welfare reform law denied to noncitizen immigrants eligibility for social welfare benefits—the lack of citizenship has also made it harder to construct the first generation as a dependent class. At the same time, U.S. settlement patterns differ from those of Western Europe. As in Europe, many immigrants initially settled in highly concentrated first-generation areas. But, in part because they are largely excluded from public housing, many others did not and the first generation has in any case diffused away from the initial zones of settlement into more predominantly white suburban or rural communities throughout the United States (Frey 2006; Singer, Hardwick, and Brettell 2008; Jones-Correa 2008). As a consequence, although many second-generation children go to low-performing, segregated, inner-city schools (along with native minorities) and have little opportunity to advance, a large proportion do not.

U.S. immigrants' children also benefit from affirmative action mechanisms that were set up decades ago to help native-born minorities attain higher education or training for some public service jobs. More generally, the diffuse structure of American higher education has provided the children of immigrants with greater access to post-secondary schooling because they can use general equivalency diploma (GED) programs, community colleges, branches of state universities, and the City University of New York as first- and second-chance mechanism. In fact, "about 31 percent...of the second generation 25 and older have completed a four-year college degree or higher compared with 27 percent...of the foreign born and 28 percent...of the third-and-later generation" (Migration Policy Institute 2006).[7]

Furthermore, as we noted previously, the political opportunity structure leading to full citizenship is easier to negotiate in the United States than in many European countries. Given the stringent citizenship laws (Weil 2001), naturalization levels of first- and even second-generation immigrants are lower in most European states than in the United States (Minkenberg 2003a). Naturalized Americans register to vote and vote at lower rates than do native-born citizens, but they are available for mobilization, and political parties are slowly beginning to take notice.

Finally, too often the second generation in Europe is in the process of being constructed as a new and disfavored minority group (the situation is more ambiguous in Canada). This is occurring as some native-born Europeans attribute immigrant groups' lack of labor market success; residence in poor, segregated communities; and higher rates of crime to an apparent lack of abilities that are construed to come naturally to natives. Those abilities include command of the host-country language, comfort with cultural forms, educational attainment, liberal and democratic norms, and familiarity with industrial and service-oriented job contexts. In contrast, in the United States, the second generation is most frequently positioned as a "third group" between black and white, with Asians and Middle Easterners being more successful than Latinos. Even immigrants with African ancestry, such as West Indians or Dominicans, especially those with darker skins, enjoy some preference from the larger society over their native minority counterparts (Waters 1999).

Relations among African Americans, various immigrant groups, and native-born European Americans can be tense and difficult, to put it mildly. But from the vantage point of immigrants and the second generation, the presence of a highly visible native-born minority that has been subordinated for centuries provides them, ironically, with a more favorable role than their European counterparts have. Native-born whites may not see U.S. immigrant groups as fully white, but the groups are not the descendents of slaves; European immigrant groups have no major native-born minority group to do better than.

In sum, it might initially seem that second-generation immigrants would do better in Europe than in the United States because Europe lacks the U.S. tradition of racial subordination and provides social citizenship rights independent of nationality, thus buffering immigrants and their children from the worst outcomes. But, in fact, Europe may be creating new forms of distinction and discrimination and the political incorporation of second-generation immigrants may prove harder, slower, and less complete than in the United States. This, at any rate, is what the evidence suggests so far.

# CHAPTER TWO

# Modeling Immigrant Political Incorporation

*Jennifer L. Hochschild and John H. Mollenkopf*

By definition, immigrants have always been included in some fashion or other in the states to which they permanently migrate. In some countries and at some times, immigrants have been granted or have seized a route from the political margins to the center, at least across generations. They have protested, voted, engaged in informal politics, and on occasion been welcomed and influential.

So there is variation along several dimensions, many illuminating case studies, and a plethora of important outcomes—but few systematic or theoretically elegant analyses of the modes and trajectories of immigrant political incorporation (however, see Marco Martiniello, chap. 3, and Lorraine C. Minnite, chap. 4, in this volume). Fostering such a systematic analysis, largely through appropriate comparisons, is the purpose of this book. We begin with our own model of immigrant political incorporation; if it works as we hope, it will permit analysts to understand how and where the particular phenomena on which they focus fit into the overall process of bringing outsiders in. No single model, of course, can encompass all cases and circumstances, and as one reader of an earlier version of this chapter (Christian Joppke, pers. comm.) insisted, "your hope for a more generic model of political incorporation is, in my view, fundamentally misguided. There can't be such a model, and if you could formulate one, it would have to be at such a high level of abstraction to be vacuous." That may turn out to be correct; nevertheless, we are immodest enough to hope that the model proffered here addresses most of the important cases and contexts. The proof of the pudding will be in the eating.

Recent discussions of immigrant political incorporation show common threads. Martin Shefter describes "full [political] incorporation" very generally, as "gain[ing] a position in the regime that is secure" (1986, 90). Rufus Browning, Dale Marshall, and David Tabb develop this point a bit more fully, defining incorporation as "the responsiveness of the [political] system to the interest of inclusion and substantial authority and influence" or more simply as "the extent to which group interests are effectively represented in policy making" (1986, 25). Picking up on this definition,

Ricardo Ramírez and Luis Fraga describe political incorporation as the "extent to which self-identified group interests are articulated, represented, and met in public policymaking" (2008, 64). Michael Jones-Correa points to an array of possible definitions, ranging from "at the least, the process of naturalization" through "participation in electoral and nonelectoral forms of politics" and representation to, at the most, "how immigrants' interests are reflected in political outcomes and policies" (2005, 75–76).

These initial definitions already cover substantial analytical ground. It is also important to underscore that in our view incorporation is a process in which individuals or groups move from less to more (or vice versa) or from early stages to later ones rather than a particular moment or threshold. Thinking of incorporation in this way enables us to describe immigrants or groups as more or less incorporated or as incorporated in some ways but not in others or as moving away from rather than toward further incorporation. (Note that Minnite, chap. 4 in this volume, makes much the same claim for similar reasons.) This is a much more flexible and useful framework than a simple dichotomy between incorporation and its absence, or exclusion. In addition, we can distinguish stages of incorporation, moving from entry into the political arena of a host country to influence over its actions and institutions. So the process of bringing outsiders in is linear, at least in its ideal form, rather than cyclical or random.

Even given this shared starting point, immigrant political incorporation can be understood in different ways. Ramírez and Fraga focus on "self-identified group[s]" with "interests"—not on individuals with particular demographic characteristics or emotions, attitudes, and perceptions. Browning, Marshall, and Tabb pay closer attention to changes in policy outcomes than do the others. Jones-Correa's understanding of incorporation ranges most widely, from simply an individual's law-abiding residence in a polity to full engagement with "the *process* of democracy" (2005, 77; emphasis in original). Shefter emphasizes that "the process through which new social forces gain a secure position in…politics is simultaneously a process of political exclusion," involving "defeat of potential leaders who are regarded as unacceptable by the established forces" (Shefter 1986, 50–51; see Minnite, chap. 4 in this volume, for a different treatment of exclusion).

Given our ambitions for the model, we take the broadest approach to these initial definitions—addressing individuals as well as groups, attitudes and beliefs as well as interests, processes as well as outcomes, exclusion as well as inclusion, and change caused by immigrants' actions as well as changes in those actions. We treat the move from less to more incorporation as an empirical proposition to be tested rather than assuming that it is linear. Figure 2.1 shows our starting point. It depicts incorporation as (1) a process (2) for individuals or groups, (3) encompassing views as well as interests, (4) involving various forms of political activity, and (5) including changes caused by as well as changes to immigrants' political activity.

However, the model in figure 2.1 is too simple because it says nothing about context, feedback, incorporative failure, nonlinearities, or exclusion. We therefore expand the basic model into the full model in figure 2.2. After first explicating the elements of the full model, we then consider how the whole system might work in a given country or for a given immigrant population.

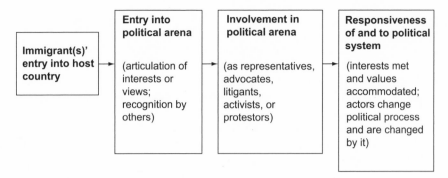

**Figure 2.1** Basic model of successful immigrant political incorporation.

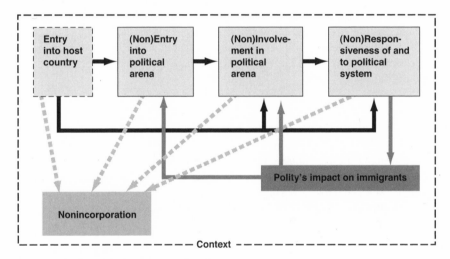

**Figure 2.2** Full model of immigrant political incorporation.

## Entry into the Host Country

As we discuss in chapter 1, the conditions under which immigrants move into a host country affect the terms and ease with which they can pursue incorporation. Our starting assumption is that immigrants want to be politically incorporated into their host country and that the host country is willing to provide some sort of channel for incorporation. We will relax both of these assumptions later in the analysis.

At the level of individuals, every state has various categories for classifying immigrants' legal standing, with distinct criteria for each. They can be clustered roughly into (1) legal permanent residence, (2) legal temporary residence, (3) short-term stay, (4) political exceptionalism, and (5) illegal entry (see Peter Schuck, chap. 11 in this volume). Only for people who enter in or can move into the first category (and possibly the fourth) is there the possibility of full political assimilation, although people with other statuses can and do become politically engaged.

At the level of groups, many countries used to distinguish among nationalities in their citizenship laws. Most no longer do so, perhaps because of their commitment to liberal universalism (Joppke 2005), but a few still do. Until 1953, the United States did not permit people from most Asian nationalities to become citizens. Germany grants automatic citizenship to most children whose parents are German citizens, regardless of where the children were born; a complicated set of laws governs whether, when, and how people of other nationalities, even if born in Germany, may become German citizens. Ethnic Germans from the former Soviet Union have a right of return to Germany, although other residents of the former USSR do not. Children born in France of foreign-born parents must request citizenship on reaching adulthood, with the exception of French-born children of parents from former colonies; under certain conditions, they automatically receive French citizenship. Israel's law of return distinguishes between Jewish and non-Jewish immigrants, and the former acquire citizenship more readily than the latter. Noncitizens in all these and in similar countries can still be politically active, but with a few exceptions (such as some local elections in the United States and the Netherlands), they cannot vote or hold office.

## (Non)Entry into the Political Arena

Moving to a new country is necessary but hardly sufficient for becoming politically incorporated in it. Entry into the political arena can be slow, uneven, and truncated, or it can be rapid, effective, and complete. The characteristics of individuals, groups, political practices, and institutional structures all affect that trajectory.

### Individual Characteristics

Traits well beyond a person's legal immigration status affects his or her ability to enter, and likelihood of entering, the political arena. For example, even if both are legal permanent residents of the host country, an English-speaking South Asian with a college degree moving to Canada under its point system is much more likely to be politically incorporated than is a Hmong refugee with less than a high school education moving to the United States as part of a family reunification plan. More analytically, researchers find, not surprisingly, that many demographic traits associated with political activity among native-born people are also associated with immigrants' political activity. Such traits include race, gender, education, homeownership, occupation, language ability, marital status, and age. They also find characteristics that are distinctive of immigrants—such as nationality, parents' immigration status, duration of stay, date of entry, age of entry, the level of democratization of the home country, and perceptions of nativist threat—to be politically relevant (Ramakrishnan 2005; Lien, Conway, and Wong 2004; Janelle Wong and Adrian Pantoja, chap. 17 in this volume). Moreover, factors that influence the actions of the native-born may have different impacts on immigrants, or even none at all.

As with native-born residents, immigrants' attitudes and values affect how likely they are to enter the political arena. Religious commitments, for example, might enable a person to connect with a particular protest movement, moral crusade, or candidate for office (Heredia 2008; Tariq Modood, chap. 15 in this volume). Immigrants who relate to the ideological assumptions underlying their host country's partisan politics will understand more readily what is at stake in a given election than will those from a radically different political background. Some immigrants will see political engagement as a channel for getting a job, improving a child's schooling, or attaining social services—or simply making friends in a strange community. Transnational ties may inhibit (Jones-Correa 1998) or facilitate involvement in a new country's affairs (Eva Østergaard-Nielsen, chap. 13 in this volume; Levitt 2003). Perceptions of discrimination may push people into or out of political activity. Thus, background characteristics and interests will surely facilitate (or inhibit) entry into the political arena, but they are not the only or even the dominant reason for getting involved.

## Group Characteristics

A person's shared status also affects the likelihood of his or her entry into the political arena. Consider the political resources that attach to nationality, independent of a given person's resources. Groups from former colonies of the host country may feel a stronger tie to host country politics, whether positively or negatively, and may be given special access. Groups from countries bordering on the host country (such as Poles in Germany) may feel differently about entering a host country's politics than do groups from far away (such as Chinese in Canada). In the European Union, nationalities from other EU countries may be more (or less, in some cases) welcomed into the polity than are nationalities from another continent.

The size of a group and its geographical distribution can also affect its members' ability to join the political arena. Large, spatially concentrated groups, as long as they are not isolated, have more political resources and internal channels of communication than do small groups thinly scattered among the native-born or people of other nationalities. The perceived size of a group may itself be a matter of political choice as well as an influence on political impact. For example, some groups may have a stronger commitment to or find it easier to practice pan-ethnic unification than others. Similarly, some groups may find it easier to see "people like them" already exercising political power in the host country, whether because co-nationals have in fact attained descriptive representation or because the group's members have a fairly elastic definition of who counts as "people like them."

Local political entrepreneurs or organizations may already be working on behalf of some groups but not others (Ramakrishnan and Bloemraad 2008). Thus, if they choose, Mexicans moving to Los Angeles or Dominicans moving to New York City can move into vibrant politicized communities that will teach them about the U.S. political system so they can protest, become naturalized citizens, or join labor unions. At times, they see elected officials speaking and working on their behalf; and, if they experience discrimination or unfavorable living conditions, they can more readily join others in mobilizing to work for change.

Twice in 2006, for example, documented and undocumented immigrants alike marched together with many nonimmigrants in cities across the United States to protest a congressional bill that would have deemed unauthorized immigrants felons subject to deportation (see Luis Fraga, chap. 12 in this volume). Conversely, Moroccans moving to Paris find a sparse environment of political parties, civic networks, and advocacy groups with which to connect. Many are residentially isolated in small suburbs without political clout; they are sufficiently separated from labor markets and schools to have a hard time linking with people outside their own communities. They may find engagement with home-country politics or religious activities more rewarding than efforts to break into a strange and hostile political process. There are few elected officials who share their ethnicity or feel politically accountable for their well-being, and their social and political networks are thin. In these circumstances, it is very hard to enter the political arena. We can thus expect immigrants with similar personal but different group characteristics to have widely different likelihoods of beginning to become politically incorporated.

## Political Actors and Practices

Rather than entering the political arena on their own, people are usually brought into it though mobilization by those already politically active (Verba, Schlozman, and Brady 1995; Rosenstone and Hansen 1993). For newcomers to a political system, these mobilizers are especially important. Mobilizers may affect how as well as whether immigrants join the political process. Advocacy groups typically facilitate naturalization to enable people to vote and also encourage protest and claims to rights, perhaps through litigation. Political parties focus on those who are already citizens, trying to get them to join parties, register if necessary, and vote for the party's candidates. Religious organizations, labor unions, schools, and civic or neighborhood organizations foster membership and participation in civic or group activities. Home-country associations emphasize nationality-specific celebrations, remittances, and politics in the country of origin, all of which might encourage rather than undermine political engagement in the host country. Government agencies may be mandated to acclimatize newcomers to the host country and thereby may provide some of the resources needed for them to become politically involved (Bloemraad 2006; Pickus 2005; Ramakrishnan and Lewis 2005).

Some political actors will be much more effective mobilizers than others. Ironically, despite the aspirations and assumptions of democratic theory, political parties are frequently reluctant to bring in newcomers until pushed to do so, because they must balance their current constituencies against possible future ones (Erie 1988; Thompson 2005; Reuel Rogers, chap. 7 in this volume). Electoral calculations may even pull parties toward nativism rather than toward the incorporation of new voters (Minkenberg, chap. 10 in this volume). If the number of possible new voters becomes sufficiently tempting, however, parties may suddenly discover the virtues of mobilization (see Fraga, chap. 12 in this volume, on varied party strategies). More broadly, governing coalitions can change, and occasionally do so, from a stance of protecting existing constituencies and keeping outsiders at arm's length, to one of incorporating newcomers and thereby shifting political and policy directions (Stone 1989; Orr 1999; Thompson 2005; Burns 2006).

The stance of schools, labor unions, and neighborhood associations similarly ranges from hostility toward those who seem too foreign or might vie for scarce resources to enthusiastic welcome for new recruits. Advocacy groups and civic organizations are perhaps most likely to believe that they can best fulfill their traditional goals by bringing in newcomers, at least as followers if not as leaders (Wong 2006). Rights-oriented groups may be searching for appropriate litigants, protest organizers want participants, and religious leaders generally work hard to bring newcomers into the practice of their faith.

## Political Institutions

Finally, features of the political system itself shape immigrants' entry (Martiniello, chap. 3, and Richard Alba and Nancy Foner, chap. 18 in this volume). As we note in chapter 1, the concept of political opportunity structures elegantly captures the idea that political institutions encourage some forms of action and some actors while deterring others (Eisinger 1973; Tarrow 1994; Koopmans and Statham 2000c). Opportunity structures affect all political actors, of course, but they may particularly affect immigrants in the shape of laws for attaining citizenship or the franchise (Waldrauch 2003), rules for joining a party, and residency or language requirements for formal political participation (Gianni D'Amato, chap. 5 in this volume). Whether electoral structures favor or penalize small minorities, the importance of residential concentration (great for single-member districts; slight for elections based on party lists), the number and array of offices for which people can vote in local elections (John Mollenkopf and Raphael Sonenshein, chap. 6 in this volume), the penalties attached to political protest, the accessibility of the judicial system—all these structural features of a given political system affect how immigrants use personal resources, how groups can position themselves, and how extant political actors mobilize newcomers.

## Involvement in the Political Arena

Once immigrants have legally entered a host country and later joined its political system as voters, protesters, or civic actors, the next step toward full incorporation is political activity. As with the earlier stages, this one has many possible variants; we focus on those most relevant to immigrants.

## Forms of Representation

Winning elective office is the most obvious, and perhaps most important, form of immigrants' political involvement. Immigrants' first elective office is typically in local government (pace Arnold Schwarzenegger)—an arena that is relatively accessible to small groups of newcomers even though it can also be fractious and fragmented. Election to local office can socialize a newcomer to the subtleties of political practice in the host country while enabling him or her to gather political resources needed for attempting a higher office. It can also give the new politician practice in navigating a classic dilemma of newcomers: a representative from a disfavored group is expected to work on behalf of his or her whole group, regardless of whether its members are part of that person's constituency, whereas constituents outside the group want their elected representative to show no racial or ethnic favoritism. Every politician has to deal with cross-pressures, of course, but this may be an especially difficult one to learn how to manage.

Elective office is only one form of direct political activity. Group leaders may bring needed resources—funds, volunteers, information networks, transnational ties—to an interest-based alliance or a pan-ethnic coalition. Group members may, unfortunately, be well suited to act as named plaintiffs or witnesses in an anti-discrimination lawsuit. Individual immigrants or immigrant groups may participate in or even organize protests, both about broad concerns common to many (globalization, unemployment, school quality) and about issues specific to immigrants or even to just their group (such as wearing headscarves in schools, deportation of illegal immigrants, more slots for would-be refugees or asylees, or relations with religious leaders from the home country). Immigrants may revitalize neighborhoods with festivals and sports leagues, new congregants in churches or mosques, and volunteers in schools or civic associations (Sandro Cattacin, chap. 16 in this volume; Jones-Correa 1998). Possibly just an increasing density of energetic young families in a run-down neighborhood can be seen as a form of political involvement or, at least, as a precursor to it. Immigrants may begin moving into public-sector jobs and thereby change the ways in which police departments, hospitals, libraries, and social service agencies deal with clients. They may eventually attain appointive office as, for example, judges, officials in regulatory agencies, or educational administrators—thereby obtaining a chance to change the rules of the game as well as to apply them to individuals or groups.

## Nonlinearities

We should not assume a straightforward increase in the amount or direction of political involvement. Between 1966 and 1979, for example, Hispanic representation on city councils in California rose sharply and then declined to almost the same level at which it had started (Browning, Marshall, and Tabb 1986, 28). Nor should we assume that local government is more accessible than higher levels of government; just as black Americans found the federal government to be more amenable to change than were state and local government, so it is possible that migrants to or within Europe will find more opportunity at the EU level than in localities or states. Immigrants may move back and forth among civic activity, protest, and voting without seeing one activity as more "incorporated" than another. And involvement in the politics of the country of origin may sometimes reinforce and sometimes substitute for political activity in the host country.

More broadly, there is no necessary linearity in the process of incorporation as a whole. Figure 2.2 moves horizontally across the four squares, suggesting advancement to greater and greater political incorporation. But a person or group may skip one or another stage of the outlined "normal" incorporation, as the lower set of black arrows in figure 2.2 indicates. Cuban exiles to the United States in the early 1960s, for example, encountered a highly responsive state before almost any had become naturalized citizens, voters, or political activists. Spokespeople for would-be refugees or asylees in France can be understood as representing a particular immigrant group even before some members of that group have actually entered the host country, never mind become citizens or political participants.

Having immigrants' interests met and values accommodated by the polity is theoretically the next stage in bringing outsiders in, to which we now turn. But whether and when political activity generates good results from the immigrants' perspective need to be treated as empirical questions and not presumed.

## Responsiveness of and to the Political System

Despite our cautions about nonlinearity, a plausible starting point is to posit a link between descriptive and substantive representation. Once immigrants are politically involved, they are able to shape outcomes that are more to their liking than had hitherto been the case. Of the many ways in which we could map the responsiveness of the political system, here we focus on whether change is relatively superficial or broad and deep.

### Policy Change

Immigrants, like everyone else, enter political life to achieve goals—interests, as in Ramírez and Fraga's formulation; claims to respect and recognition; or values and norms. One measure of successful incorporation is the promulgation and implementation of policies to meet a reasonable share of these goals. For example, some extant policies were designed to satisfy interests and promote the recognition of native-born disadvantaged minority groups; immigrants might be added to their target populations. Such policies could include affirmative action, majority-minority districting, in-state tuition rates, multicultural school curricula, state support for religious schools, exemption from certain laws, and bilingual education. Or immigrants might obtain new policies to advance their interests or respond to their values, such as single-sex gym classes for Muslim students in public schools, adult education classes to teach the host-country language and social practices, state subsidies for religious organizations or activities, inclusion of particular nationalities in censuses or other official documents, and so on.

Service agencies such as libraries, hospitals, and police departments might change their agendas or procedures, perhaps with substantial budgetary and personnel shifts, to help new clients (Jones-Correa 2008). National policies toward the state from which immigrants came might be made more friendly or accommodating, for example by permitting dual citizenship or easing restrictions on remittances or travel across borders. The array of possible policy changes that would signal full immigrant political incorporation is indeed extensive; understanding which policies are promulgated and how deeply they are embedded is a crucial element of studying whether outsiders are truly being brought in.

## Change in Institutions and Practices

Important as policies are, political incorporation might not stop with them; it could encompass alterations in the institutions and practices that shape the political opportunity structure. Here, too, a variety of changes can be imagined. Laws affecting the composition of the country's population and the conditions for and meaning of citizenship can be changed. For example, recently arrived immigrants may be made eligible for naturalization after serving in the armed forces, or noncitizens may be granted the franchise in certain elections, or quotas for particular types of immigrants might be relaxed. Rules may be eased to permit the native-born children of noncitizens to attain citizenship, as recently occurred in Germany and France.

Political practices might be revised. Immigrants and their allies could form new political parties or new voting blocs within existing parties. Immigrants might be included in the population base to determine majority-minority voting districts, to decide whether voters had encountered discrimination, or to reapportion congressional seats. Party lists for election to local, regional, or national assemblies may be reconstituted or candidates' location on the list shifted upward. Parties or legislatures may impose quotas or targets for immigrant candidates or representatives (Htun 2004).

A polity's practices with regard to rights and values might even change. Courts could, for example, recognize a right to wear headscarves or turbans in what had been a secular public arena. Legislatures may permit *shariah* to govern Muslims' family practices. Religious or celebratory holidays might be added to the state's official calendar, with implications for workers and students. Local versions of *mestizaje* might become culturally prominent and institutionally sanctioned, for example, through multicultural school curricula (Jan Willem Duyvendak, Trees Pels, and Rally Rijkschroeff, chap. 9 in this volume, describe how this has *not* happened in the Netherlands). Host countries might decide that all residents should be bilingual and should be taught more of the history and culture of immigrants' home countries; countries might reconsider their self-image and the presentation of their colonial past or their current imperialistic tendencies in textbooks, museums, or national symbols.

There is no necessary end to the changes that could follow full immigrant political incorporation. The United States, Canada, and Australia, after all, are totally different entities than they would have been had there been no immigration or had its influence been curtailed after particular waves. Nevertheless, most western countries are now so firmly established that the type and amount of deep structural or normative change produced by immigrants' political involvement are likely to be sharply limited, at least in the foreseeable future.

## The Impact of the Polity on Immigrants

Arguably immigrants are likely to be more changed by political incorporation than they will be able to change the political system, perhaps despite their own preferences and efforts. After all, immigrants' children quickly learn the host country's language, and the third generation may have lost that of the home country altogether.

Immigrants' descendants also intermarry, change their religious affiliation, move away from ethnic enclaves, and become immersed in popular culture.

As in society, immigrants are changed by as well as changing the polity, as the feedback arrows in figure 2.2 indicate. Immigrants (or more likely, their children) may develop political loyalty if one party provides material benefits or expresses symbolic commitment to immigration or group-based values. And once attached to a party, immigrants—like native-borns—may permit partisanship to change or shape their norms or views on various subjects (Goren 2005). Immigrants may begin to align their values and ideological commitments along the conventional left-right dimension of many Western European nations and the United States. They may begin to classify themselves and others along the racial lines of their host (rather than home) country. They may shift their political attention to the host country and away from the politics of their country of origin. They may take on the coloration of the labor unions, civic groups, advocacy organizations, or other entities that they have joined.

In short, political incorporation of immigrants, or at least of their children, is a two-way street, when it works. Incorporation may, however, be partial, halted, or even reversed—processes to which we now turn.

## (Non)Entry into or (Non)Involvement in the Political Arena, and the (Non)Responsiveness of the Political System

As these awkward phrases indicate, immigrant political incorporation can be curtailed at any point along the model's pathway. We need not point out all the ways in which the process can go awry; basically, the absence of any of the key features that foster incorporation can be said to discourage it. Thus, immigrants may enter a host country but not be mobilized into political engagement, a group may become politically engaged but be too small to attain representation, or sets of immigrants may be politically represented but have none of their interests met or norms validated. In addition, it is at least theoretically possible that the political system is responsive to some group interests or values but that the group is not changed at all by this connection to politics. In short, not only is incorporation not linear or temporally predictable, but also there is no guarantee that the process will continue once it has started (see Minnite, chap. 4 in this volume, for more on this point).

### Nonincorporation

We represent a more active form of failed immigrant political incorporation with the term *nonincorporation* (and box with dotted arrows in figure 2.2). By this we mean not just that engagement fails to develop further at some point in the process but that immigrants are intentionally excluded from, or choose to remove themselves from, political incorporation.

Active nonincorporation can happen at any stage of the model of immigrant political incorporation. Would-be immigrants may be denied entry into a host country, may enter illegally with no path toward amnesty, or may enter with a legal status that provides no path to citizenship. They may be deported or "voluntarily" repatriated. After entry into a host country, immigrants can be kept out of the political arena in many ways. They may be isolated in separate neighborhoods, schools, and workplaces with no party or organization seeking to make connections with them. Fear of harsh treatment may intimidate them into shunning protests or litigation. Antagonism from native-born minority groups, established political parties, or xenophobic public opinion can push immigrants out of the political arena.

Conversely, immigrants may themselves reject any move toward incorporation. They can have many reasons: they see themselves as sojourners, they want to keep their children and culture unchanged, they feel deep hostility to the host country, or they fear harm from the police or immigration agency. Immigrants may misunderstand or reject the norms of western liberal democracy, with its insistence on tolerance of hated views, acceptance of electoral defeat, frequent compromises over interests, shifting political allegiances among groups, separation of religion and state, gender equality, and national self-perception as the benefactor rather than exploiter of weaker countries.

Nonincorporation at the third stage, direct political activity, depends more on the dynamics of governance than on the behaviors of individual immigrants, groups, or the citizenry in general. Here the question is how groups can be involved in the political arena but still remain powerless. A robust literature on racial politics answers that question (Pinderhughes 1987, 2003; Browning, Marshall, and Tabb 1990; Rogers 2006; Hero 1992). For example, a group may have token representation within powerful institutions, but its representative has little credibility or power to affect policy. The group and its representative may be victims of covert racism, may not have the political resources that other actors need, or may have goals that are too far outside of mainstream politics. Native-born citizens may vote against an immigrant representative, or established organizations or actors may not include the representative in genuine political deliberations. Representatives of immigrant groups may even serve as scapegoats in electoral campaigns or in efforts to promote new policies—thus making political involvement a step toward nonincorporation rather than a contradiction of it.

Alternatively, immigrant representatives may themselves seek to avoid incorporation into "politics as usual"; they may use their new insider status to criticize or even disrupt the political process or an organization's standard operating procedures. Less dramatically, they may pursue outcomes that are not politically feasible or use tactics that get in the way of political alliances or policy success. None of these forms of nonincorporation is unique to immigrants or immigrant groups. But they could be especially salient for people who come from outside an ongoing political process; are visibly and aurally different from the mainstream; and may bring with them distinct, even antagonistic, values and interests.

Nonincorporation can even occur at the final stage of paradigmatic immigrant political incorporation, the point at which policies or practices are changed in response to immigrants' desires. Most simply, policies may not be changed; legislatures, courts, service agencies, interest groups, civic organizations, and so on may refuse to modify their practices or adjust their services to meet immigrants' needs or values. There may even be hostile legislation, judicial decisions, agency treatment, or advocacy group protest (Duyvendak, Pels, and Rijkschroeff, chap. 9; Christian Joppke, chap. 8;

and Minkenberg, chap. 10 in this volume). Immigrants, in turn, may resist standard practices, break laws, make untenable policy demands, or otherwise refuse to permit the political system to influence them. At this point, we can expect interacting and escalating hostility, such that the nonincorporation of immigrants even after they are fully involved in the political arena will be a sign of deep and possibly intractable societal divisions. Immigrants may be radicalized; host country natives may become xenophobic; violence can occur.

## Context

All these dynamics occur within an environment and set of circumstances—the large, framing box in figure 2.2 that we label "context." Perhaps the most useful taxonomy for political context focuses on its scale: local, national, or international. Local context includes the demographic composition of an area, its economic base and level of well-being, the nature and quality of schools and social services, the structure and practices of local governance, the location of municipal boundaries, the permeability of neighborhoods, and transportation and communication channels. Less tangible features of a local context can be just as important, including native-born elites' and opinion leaders' explicit statements and implicit tone with regard to immigrants and immigration; local religious leaders' capabilities and commitments; the robustness and agendas of civic organizations and community associations; the availability of sports and other casual recreational facilities; and the degree of welcome from schools, workplaces, agents of the criminal justice system, and health-care workers.

National context includes laws, regulations, and judicial rulings on immigration and treatment of immigrants. It also includes laws and regulations regarding minority individuals and groups, relations between religious organizations and state, public involvement in employers' practices, rules and practices of criminal justice, eligibility for social welfare, and rules determining military service. Broad demographic trends—the trajectory of immigration, the size and origins of particular nationalities, birth rates, marital patterns, and family structures—are part of the national context. Economic circumstances matter, including inflation and unemployment rates, links to global markets, the robustness of the manufacturing and service sectors, the organization of the agricultural sector, and the accessibility of banking services. In addition to the many features of the political context already discussed, we include the salience of immigration to electoral politics, the legitimacy of nativist political movements, public opinion with regard to immigration and its consequences, and the country's self-image as a settler or ethnically rooted society. Political structures that ostensibly have little to do with immigration, such as federalism, the nature of the electoral system, the degree of subsidiarity of public decision making, and competition among a country's regions, shape the political opportunity structure. Relations with native-born minority groups are crucially important.

The international context includes alliances and treaties, both with immigrant-sending states and in regional arenas such as the European Union, North American Free Trade Agreement (NAFTA), and Central America Free Trade Agreement (CAFTA) (Gallya Lahav, chap. 14 in this volume). Antagonisms and wars matter as well. The country's involvement in international trade, international financial and labor markets, and cultural exchanges affect how immigrants are received and their impact on domestic policymaking. Finally, a country's size and location—whether it shares a border with an immigrant-sending state, its accessibility to desired or undesired nationalities, its sense of security with or threat from other countries—affect whether and how outsiders are brought in.

## Putting the Pieces Together

With the elements of a coherent structure for understanding immigrant political incorporation in place, we can think more synthetically about its implications.

### Boundaries

A useful starting point is a different framing of modes of immigrant incorporation from our own.

> Collective identity formation…usually…involves self-conscious efforts by members of a group to distinguish themselves from whom they are not, and hence it is…a dialectical process whose key feature is the delineation of boundaries between "us" and "not us." The process of incorporation can be thought of as the negotiations in which hosts and immigrants engage around these boundaries. (Zolberg 1999, 8)

If both groups agree that boundaries between insiders and outsiders are fixed, there is no negotiation and no incorporation of immigrants. But if boundaries can in principle be changed, Aristide Zolberg identifies three distinct patterns of negotiation. The first is "individual boundary crossing, without any change in the structure of the receiving society.…This is the commonplace process whereby immigrants change themselves by acquiring some of the attributes of the host identity" (1999, 8). An analysis of how individual immigrants enter a country, join its political process as a consequence of their political capacity and commitments, and perhaps even become political actors fits this understanding of boundary negotiation. Governor Schwarzenegger of California and President Nicolas Sarkozy of France are highly visible examples of boundary crossing, but there are millions of others throughout all immigrant-receiving countries.

The second form of negotiation occurs through "boundary blurring." This type of incorporation "affects the structure (i.e.[,] the legal, social, and cultural [and political] boundaries of the receiving society. Its core feature is…the overlapping of collective boundaries hitherto thought to be separate and mutually exclusive" (Zolberg 1999, 8–9). In our model, boundary blurring occurs when nationality groups, not just individuals, enter the political arena and become political actors and when the new immigrant participants both change political outcomes or structures and are, in turn, changed by them. In figure 2.2, boundary blurring is represented by the combined paths of the two sets of solid arrows.

The third form of negotiation is "boundary shifting." It "denotes a reconstruction of a group's identity, whereby the line differentiating members from nonmembers is relocated, either in the direction of inclusion or exclusion" (Zolberg 1999, 9). In our model, boundary shifting moves toward inclusion as immigrants become more and more fully incorporated, to the point where they become an unremarked part of normal political operations and an element of the context for the next round of immigration. Thus, former colonial subjects from Algeria are now, at least in principle, considered French when North African incorporation becomes a political issue. And Irish and Italian Americans are now merely whites in the eyes of most Americans, whereas a century ago the dominant view held that they could never become full democratic citizens and that a Catholic neither could nor should become president (Alba Forthcoming). Conversely, boundary shifting moves toward exclusion in our model if nonincorporation predominates at any point along the pathway. If immigrants are kept in the status of illegal aliens, if they are scorned by parties and ignored by civic organizations, if their representatives have only token status or are treated as scapegoats, if their policy preferences are seldom met, and if they have no impact on political institutions and vice versa, then the boundary between us and not-us is clearly marked even if immigrants continue to reside in the host country.

We have examples in this book of all three types of incorporation (or all four, if we treat boundary shifting as two distinct and opposite phenomena). Individual assimilation, or boundary crossing, is the old U.S. and current French model of immigrant incorporation. Mutual transformation, or boundary blurring, is now the preferred model for some Americans and was the goal of Great Britain and the Netherlands until recently. Arguably, boundary shifting toward exclusion characterized the German treatment of Turks until recently (Alba 2005) and now (increasingly?) characterizes the U.S. treatment of undocumented immigrants (Fraga, chap. 12). Further systematic characterization of boundary formation and transformation in countries on both sides of the Atlantic would be of great benefit to both analysts and activists.

## Modes of Political Action

We can also parse the model of immigrant political incorporation through a focus on immigrants' modes of political activity. An analysis of the roughly 1,000 Latino/a participants in the 1999 National Longitudinal Survey of Freshmen found three stances with regard to mainstream U.S. society. All survey participants are in some sense already successfully incorporated because they were first-year students at one of twenty-eight elite private colleges and universities in the United States. But they saw their situation differently, in ways that map usefully onto our framework.

Assimilationist students (26 percent of the sample) are essentially Zolberg's boundary crossers, or our individual immigrants moving through the standard stages of political incorporation. They see themselves as similar to their white peers, operate comfortably in mainstream society, and perceive little or no discrimination against their group. They are presumably more or less as politically active, and for the same reasons, as any white native-born person; like most native-borns, they engage with politics mainly through conventional electoral participation.

Accommodationist students (32 percent of the sample) perceive discrimination against minority groups, including their own, but believe that with hard work they can overcome all barriers. When they compare themselves to relatives in Latin America, "the immigrant experience provide[s] a source of optimism along with an awareness of discrimination" (Mooney and Rivas-Drake 2008, A37; see Rivas-Drake and Mooney 2007 for the complete analysis). We expect them to be more closely associated with strategies for group-based political incorporation and to be more committed to policies favoring immigrants than the assimilationists will be. Accommodationists might also be more willing to engage in protest or other forms of unconventional politics to help their group or to demonstrate their loyalty to it.

Finally, resister students (43 percent of the sample) perceive a lot of discrimination against their group, feel distant from white students, and are deeply skeptical of the claim that a person can attain success through hard work. They are likely to be highly sensitive to blockages along the path toward immigrant political incorporation, to expect more active efforts toward nonincorporation, and to find it hard to develop alliances with native-born whites or other mainstream political actors. They are the most likely to participate in protests, rights-based litigation, or advocacy group activity. Whether they are changed by political incorporation as much as they seek to change the polity of their host country remains an open empirical question (see Modood, chap. 15 in this volume, on resisters in Great Britain).

## Conclusion—and Starting Point

Even with these or other efforts at synthesis, no single researcher or team can address all the elements of our model of immigrant political incorporation. Nor will all elements matter equally and in the same way for all groups, countries, time periods, political structures, or goals. We quoted one skeptic about this enterprise at the beginning of the chapter; we close by quoting another (Jan Willem Duyvendak, pers. comm.), whose reasons differ but whose sentiment is equally clear.

> The modeling is very inspiring—though we hope that it won't be misunderstood as if every country has its own model of immigrant political incorporation. Countries don't have models but messy combinations of pragmatic policies, some ideological notions, imitation and copying behavior, et cetera; thinking in terms of coherent country models is one of the biggest obstacles in our field, we think.

Some of this disbelief is surely warranted; no country fits completely and tidily into any analytic framework. Nevertheless, the chapters in this book show that countries do differ in predictable ways—an immigrant to Germany would not mistake that country for the United States, nor would someone moving to Sweden think that he or she had landed in Switzerland. Theoretical elegance and parsimony have their place in characterizing incorporative regimes, if only to set up the arguments to come that explicate the complexities of immigrant-receiving countries and cities on both sides of the Atlantic.

# PART II

# EXPLORING IMMIGRANT
# POLITICAL INCORPORATION

What *is* immigrant political incorporation? How does it differ from the political incorporation of minority groups or uninvolved native-born individuals in the majority population? Does political incorporation resemble economic or social incorporation? Does political inclusion take varied forms, follow different routes, or get blocked at predictable points along the way? Is political exclusion simply the mirror opposite of political incorporation for immigrants? For immigrant political incorporation to advance as a field of study, scholars must answer these questions; we need at least a rough consensus on what is distinctive about political (dis)incorporation for immigrants, what aspects of it are well and poorly understood, and what theories will deepen our understanding.

In part I, we (Jennifer Hochschild and John Mollenkopf) offered our own initial model of bringing outsiders in. Our model is intended to be broad enough to cover most groups in most western nations and flexible enough to permit differentiation among different routes to, degrees of, and forms of incorporation. We see successful immigrant political incorporation as a two-way process; immigrants receive some political and policy outcomes that they want and thereby change some elements of the host country at the same time that they themselves are changed through their participation in the political arena.

The chapters in part II offer further frameworks for answering the urgent questions that follow from recognizing the importance of bringing outsiders in. In chapter 3, Marco Martiniello focuses on immigrants in the European Union. He rejects the claim that they are and should be quiescent, and he substitutes for that view a typology of types of immigrant political participation. The typology has two main dimensions: "the geographical-political level of action" (that is, the level of government at which participation occurs) and "the contrast between state and nonstate politics" ranging from electoral politics to participation in labor unions.

Analyzing key components of each dimension yields an extensive matrix of arenas for political action—although Martiniello assures the reader that not every one of these "has been, can be, or should be studied separately." Instead, he provides a framework for making sense of the range and variation of immigrants' participation in the politics of their new country of residence. Martiniello emphasizes that differences in attitudes and policies with respect to immigration in European countries make it unlikely that immigrants will behave similarly across the European Union, and he stresses the need for more systematic research.

In chapter 4, Lorraine Minnite focuses on immigrants in the United States. She too presents various definitions of immigrant incorporation—but in this case focusing on definitions by previous scholars that she finds seriously deficient. Too often, in her view, scholarship on immigrant inclusion engages in "concept stretching," that is, terms, assumptions, and empirical strategies developed to study the black civil rights movement are inappropriately used to study immigrants' actions. Most scholarship also evinces theoretical gaps, such as insufficient analyses of how self-conscious groups come into being or "how national legal and transborder regulatory regimes... may fragment groups in ways that are inimical to [immigrant incorporation]." The extant literature is also, she argues, riddled with inconsistencies and competing rationalities, and it too seldom considers whether immigrants gain or lose through incorporation into the U.S. social and political system.

To remedy these errors, Minnite calls on scholars to examine the distinctive origins of immigrants' political mobilization, the segmented and conditional manner through which inclusion proceeds, and contextual factors responsible for this segmentation and variation. In short, we need new models of incorporation, not retrofitted old ones, to understand new populations and conditions.

Both chapters call for more attention to the interaction between political opportunity structures in the host country and immigrant groups' political commitments and resources. Both emphasize that state conditions may block as well as nurture immigrants' strategies for accessing political power. Finally, both call for attention to how immigrants' ties to their countries of origin and links across state boundaries affect their political behavior. When and how, Martiniello asks, do immigrants mobilize in their new countries to push for political changes in their old, as well as in their new, homes? Later parts of *Bringing Outsiders In* take up all these points.

# CHAPTER THREE

# Immigrants and Their Offspring in Europe as Political Subjects

*Marco Martiniello*

Academic, political, and policy debates have offered many insights about the position of immigrants and of their offspring in Europe. As Jennifer Hochschild and John Mollenkopf (chap. 2 in this volume) have outlined, the themes raised about immigrants depend on the local, national, and international context, in particular the orientation of those in power toward immigrants and the mobilization of the immigrants themselves. Since the 1980s, migration has been at the top of the political agenda in the European Union and North America. This politicization has led to an overdramatization, and sometimes a media saturation, of the issue, because many societies see migratory flows as a cause of insecurity and even as a real threat.

The media and conservative populists often present immigrant populations as a threat to native economic well-being. Immigrants and their offspring are often accused of taking jobs from nationals or of taking unfair or fraudulent advantage of the social welfare systems in rich countries. Immigrant populations are also presented as a threat to law and order, and are associated with the rise in transfrontier organized crime (drugs, prostitution, arms dealing and human trafficking mafias, etc.). The children of immigrants are also associated with the rise in urban criminality affecting many towns and suburban areas of Europe. Consequently, their presence is sometimes presumed to be linked with the rise of extreme-right parties. In this way, immigration finally appears as a threat to democracy and immigrants as internal enemies who jeopardize our social benefits, our relative economic well-being, and even our cultural and national identity. Since the September 11 attacks, debates have focused on terrorism, Islam, and Muslim minorities. According to an alarmist view displayed in the media and sometimes in politics, Europe is suffering from galloping Islamization, which threatens European cultures and values, including democracy and human rights.

To be fair, many observers present more positive views of migration and multiculturalism. They present immigration as a solution to the demographic decline of European countries and a way to save the European social security systems. Immigrants are offered as an answer to the graying of the population and as a necessary condition for economic advancement in the framework of the Lisbon agenda. Increasingly, European politicians stress the need for migrant labor to foster the economic development and competitiveness. The same holds for diversity. Whereas many politicians and other opinion leaders favor neo-assimilationist policies and aim at abolishing ethnic diversity, urban sociologists, economic geographers, and city planners increasingly identify diversity as key for economic growth. Fractions of the general public also value their contribution to their social lives and consumption patterns, as illustrated by the success of ethnic food and world music in most European cities (Martiniello 2005).

One major recent development is the transnationalization of the debates and policies, as evidenced by the partial Europeanization of immigration and integration policies. Not so long ago, these policies were exclusive competences of nation-states. Each nation-state could decide autonomously whom to let in for how long and with which legal status. Each nation-state also developed its own approach to integration. There are various national narratives of citizenship, integration, and multiculturalism across Europe. In France, the republican conception of national integration and citizenship underlines the divisive effects of a public recognition of cultural diversity. This view takes multiculturalism to be a new tribalism that might balkanize France and, in the end, threaten its conception of citizenship. In Britain, there are conflicting views on multiculturalism but they discuss the issue and are open to accommodating diversity in the public sphere. In Germany, a *multikulti* trend coexists with a more exclusive conception of citizenship, despite the liberalization of German citizenship. Belgium takes no single approach to the issue. The differences among the regions of a given country can sometimes be significant (Bade 2003). Increasingly, debates on integration, diversity, and multiculturalism also take place at the supranational level, even if the EU member states want to retain sovereignty over these matters. This explains why progress is slow at the supranational European level in the field.

However, the European Union has, in fact, created a European institutional framework for immigration and asylum policy. The regulation of foreigners' entry, freedom of movement, and right to stay in the European territory are the focal points of legal and political debates within European and national institutions, but nations continue to exercise sovereignty over the integration of foreigners, specifically in terms of citizenship rules. Nevertheless, in this area as well, some convergence has taken place, notably in the generalization of *jus soli*. In fact, the issue of immigration and integration in Europe is characterized by a national differentiation against a backdrop of European convergence.

EU countries are at different stages in the migratory process. Some countries are mainly concerned with the settlement of recent arrivals and the control of their borders. Others find themselves in both a migration and a postmigration situation, having already faced several waves of immigration in the past five decades (Martiniello 1993). It is therefore difficult to compare the political participation of immigrants across European countries. The political mobilization and participation of immigrants are not high on the political and academic agendas of the newer target countries of immigration. Political authorities often focus on identifying spokespeople for immigrants groups and on getting to know the immigrants' needs and expectations.

In the older target countries of immigration, political mobilization, participation, and representation of immigrant ethnic minorities have become topical issues, especially at the local and metropolitan levels. In many places, immigrant politicians have been elected in various political assemblies. Some hold positions in the local and even national government, although this varies even in countries with a long experience of immigration. In France, immigrant political participation became an issue in the 1980s, but sank into oblivion when the *Beur* movement (comprising young North Africans born in France) ran out of steam. Few people openly questioned the voting behavior of the French of foreign origin in the 1990s and the early 2000s as the representation and election of immigrants and their offspring began to occur within the French political system. The 2007 presidential election revived these debates. A second-generation Hungarian immigrant, Nicolas Sarkozy, was elected president of the French Republic and he appointed three women of immigrant descent as members of government: Fadela Amara, Rachida Dati, and Rama Yade.

In Great Britain, the position of ethnic minorities in the political process has, since the 1980s, become a recurrent theme in academic literature and political debates (Anwar 1994; Geddes 1993; Saggar 1998b; Solomos and Back 1995). The ethnicization of British local and parliamentary politics has become a legitimate object of research and debate. The debate has focused on the "black sections" within the Labour Party, the emergence of ethnic minority members of Parliament (MPs) such as Bernie Grant, Diane Abbott, and Paul Boateng, and the political influence of Indo-Pakistani citizens in some cities.

This chapter focuses specifically on the political participation, mobilization, and representation of immigrants and their offspring throughout the European Union. It provides a qualitative overview of recent trends and presents some perspectives to be explored in future research. Although we now have a reasonably good knowledge of immigrants' political activities, some gaps remain. The first section of the chapter discusses the first major thesis to be found in the literature, namely that of political quiescence of immigrants. The second section focuses on explanations of the various forms of immigrant political participation. The third section presents a typology of the various forms of immigrant political participation. This typology constitutes a map for locating further research areas. The fourth section discusses the issue of transnational political participation, and the fifth identifies gaps in the literature that new research should address. The chapter concludes by assessing the political participation of immigrants and their offspring in their European countries of residence.

## The Thesis of Immigrant Political Quiescence

For a long time, immigrant political mobilization, participation, and representation were not considered important issues in either academia or politics. Immigrant workers were not considered to be potential citizens or simply political subjects. They were not supposed or expected to be politically active. As guests, they were even expected to observe a *devoir de réserve* (duty not to interfere). In other words, they were invited not to get involved with their hosts' political and collective affairs. Migrants just played an economic role in the host society—to work and produce.

The thesis of political quiescence, or passivity, of immigrants was logically the first to emerge in the European literature on immigration, and it was dominant for a long time. Migrant workers were considered to be apolitical and apathetic (Martiniello 1997; Miller 1982). The empirical point of departure was correct. In many countries, migrant workers had virtually no political rights. They could not take part in elections or be elected. They did not enjoy any form of direct political representation within political institutions. According to some scholars, exclusion from the electoral process prevented migrants from playing any relevant political role and explained their apathy (Castells 1975). Apart from seeing migrants as being formally disenfranchised, the literature also saw them as strongly oriented toward short-term economic goals and thus not interested in political participation. Analysts also often thought that migrants were politically passive because they lacked democratic values and skills, due to the authoritarian or only recently democratized regimes of their countries of origin.

The first explanation, put forward mainly by Marxists, is partially correct, but is flawed in two ways. First, we cannot reduce all relevant forms of political participation to electoral participation. Migrants are capable of other important forms of participation—within trade union politics, voluntary associations, and community organizations. Many studies show that immigrants have always had such involvements. Second, the explanation tends to consider the migrant only as a factor of production whose life is totally determined by macroeconomic and macrosocial structures. It leaves no place for agency or autonomy and, in this respect, dehumanizes migrant workers. Many Marxist scholars were more interested in emphasizing how capitalists used migrants to divide and demobilize the working class than in studying immigrants' political activities.

The second explanation, mainly put forward by non-Marxist scholars, reflects a simplistic culturalist and paternalistic approach. An early work by Jan Rath (1991) illustrates this perspective for the Dutch case. It viewed migrants as less culturally developed than local workers and therefore less politically active. This problematic interpretation ended up being clearly refuted by the facts. In many cases, migrant workers had actually been politicized in their country of origin before departure and they had used migration as a way to escape dictatorship. Illustrations of immigrants arriving with a strong political culture and democratic aspirations include migrants from Italy during fascism, from Spain during Franco's rule, and from Greece during the colonels' regime.

Furthermore, both explanations seem to confuse quiescence or passivity with apolitical attitudes. Being politically passive does not always indicate a general disinterest in politics. Passivity can sometimes be a form of resistance and defense. When political opportunities are limited and avenues of political participation restricted and controlled, passivity can mean a transitional waiting position before better opportunities for participation.

In any case, subsequent trends threw both variants of the migrant quiescence thesis into question. Migrants have always been involved in politics either outside or at the margins of the political systems of both their countries of origin and residence. More recently, migrants and their offspring have become increasingly involved in mainstream political institutions. This process has been facilitated by an extension of voting rights to foreigners in several countries and by a liberalization of nationality laws in others. But just as migrants are not more passive than other citizens, their involvement should not be exaggerated into "an emerging political force" (Miller 1981) or as the vanguard of a new global proletariat, as some leftist approaches tend to portray them.

## Explaining the Forms of Immigrant Political Participation

Political science and political sociology have tried to explain political participation in many different ways. Theories of political participation abound and each gives a different answer to the question of why people participate in politics. Traditionally, there has been a dispute between the rational choice and identity approaches to political participation. Nowadays, social capital approaches to political participation have become quite fashionable in North America and in Europe. Over the past two decades, scholars have also tried to explain the general decline in democratic political participation. The question of political participation (or lack thereof) is complex.

This is also true for migrant populations and the subsequent generations. If we accept the idea that immigrant populations always display some degree of political participation, we can concentrate on what factors explain the variation in participation. This focuses attention on such questions as whether migrants are mobilized within the political mainstream or outside of it; what explains the intensity of participation; how immigrants spread their political attentions among the host society, the country of origin, and global political space; why and how some individual migrants may pursue a career in politics; what role unions play in immigrant political mobilization; and whether some elements of immigrant communities are more inclined than other groups to opt for violent political behavior, such as terrorism.

Many scholarly observers employ a political opportunity structure approach to answer such difficult questions. This political opportunity structure is defined by the inclusion-exclusion mechanisms developed by the states (both of residence and of origin) and their political systems (Martiniello 1998). By granting or denying voting rights to foreigners, facilitating or impeding access to citizenship and nationality, granting or constraining freedom of association, ensuring or blocking the representation of migrants' interests, and establishing or not arenas and institutions for consultative politics, states open or close avenues of political participation for migrants and provide them with either more or fewer opportunities to participate in the management of collective affairs.

Whether immigrants and their offspring seize these opportunities in this changing institutionally defined framework depends on several more or less classical factors in political science. These include political ideas and values; previous involvement in politics (including political experiences in the country of origin), the degree of "institutional completeness" of the immigrant ethnic community (Breton 1964), whether they regard their sojourn as permanent or temporary, their feelings of belonging to the host and/or home society, their knowledge of the political system and institutions, the social capital and density of immigrant associational networks, and all the usual individual determinants of political behavior such as education, linguistic skills, socioeconomic status, gender, and age or generational cohort.

Recent academic interest in immigrant political participation is connected to a renewed interest in citizenship. This interest is clearly not the same in all EU member states and in the United States. A lot of work has been done in France on the extra-parliamentary mobilization of second-generation immigrants during the 1980s and the role of ethnicity in politics. Sylvie Strudel's (1996) work on Jews in French political life considers the existence of a Jewish vote. Vincent Geisser (1997) undertook one of the first studies on immigrant local councilors in France. One of the most prolific authors on immigrants and politics in France is Catherine Wihtol de Wenden (1988). Siméant (1998) studied the *sans-papiers* movement of the 1990s. The religious-political mobilization around the Islamic headscarf and the evolution of secularism (*laïcité*) has also attracted attention in France and other European countries (Broughton and ten Napel 2000).

In the United Kingdom, the issue of the electoral power of ethnic minorities—as well as the political color of each ethnic minority—is discussed in every election. West Indians and Asians have historically been largely pro-Labour, but they have recently distributed their votes a little more evenly across the parties. The issue of the representation of minorities in elected assemblies has also been studied by scholars such as Andrew Geddes (1998) and Shamit Saggar (1998a, 1998b). Jean Tillie (1998) and Maritta Soininen (1999; Soininen and Bäck 1993) have undertaken detailed studies on the electoral behavior of immigrants in the Netherlands and Sweden in the 1990s. In Sweden, the decline of immigrant voter turnout during the past decade has attracted a lot of attention from policymakers. In the Netherlands, Jean Tillie, Laure Michon, and Anja Van Heelsum undertook three exit polls in the 1990s to explore why immigrant-origin voters tend to have a lower electoral turnout than other Dutch citizens (Bauböck 2006, 89).

## A Typology of Political Participation by Immigrants and Their Children

We can create a typology that covers legal forms of political participation but excludes terrorism, political violence, and corruption.[1] We can distinguish different types of ethnic or immigrant political participation according to the geographical-political level of action and the contrast between state and nonstate politics.

### The Geographical-Political Level of Action

The nation-state is certainly an imperfect and vulnerable form of political organization. It currently faces both internal and external problems. On the one hand, internal regionalisms and subnationalisms seem to be on the increase in some European states. Italy, the United Kingdom, Spain, and Belgium face such difficulties, although with variable intensity. On the other hand, new supranational forces are emerging to challenge to the nation-state in its present form. The European Union, transnational corporations, and mass telecommunication systems and other new technologies stimulate debate about the possible demise of the nation-state. Despite these problems, the nation-state remains a crucial setting for political action. We can envisage immigrant political participation both in the country of residence and the country of origin. Political action also takes place from the neighborhood to the region. The expression "local politics" has a different meaning in each country, although all countries present local opportunities for participation and mobilization.

The 1992 Maastricht Treaty provided a new impetus for the construction of a European political union. The unfinished debate about the EU Constitutional Treaty shows that there are many problems still to be solved, but migrant political action certainly occurs at the EU level (see Gallya Lahav, chap. 14 in this volume). Furthermore, there is no reason why the European Union should constitute the geopolitical limit for such action. It can eventually extend to the world level, for example in the antiglobalization movement or when pro-immigrant groups tend to reach out to the Organisation for Economic Co-operation and Development (OECD) or the United Nations (UN).

## State Politics and Nonstate Politics

*State* is used here to refer to the formal political institutions that frame executive, legislative, and judiciary powers. Beyond the state, the polity is also made up of other institutions and actors who—at least in a democracy—take part in defining and managing the society's collective affairs in some way.

### STATE POLITICS

Three main forms of state ethnic participation and mobilization can be distinguished: electoral politics, parliamentary politics, and consultative politics.

*Electoral Politics*    Nearly all European states reserve full electoral rights for the countries' nationals, although some have enfranchised aliens at the local level. The United Kingdom is exceptional in extending voting rights in national elections to all Commonwealth and Irish citizens. Legal obstacles to immigrant electoral participation are therefore essentially determined by *jus soli* or naturalization.[2]

The first relevant issue is the electoral turnout of immigrants once they have the right to vote. Not many studies have dealt with this issue in Europe. Norway is probably the only European country offering official statistics on the electoral turnout of immigrants. The figures recently presented by Statistics Norway indicate a lower electoral turnout of immigrants compared to other Norwegian citizens at the municipal and county elections of 2007.[3] Lise Togeby (1999) tries to explain why the immigrant electoral turnout was higher in Denmark than in Sweden, for which Anthony Messina (2006) has compiled electoral turnout data. He shows that immigrant electoral turnout decreased in Sweden between 1976 and 2002 but that Swedes also tended to vote less. In the Dutch case, Van Heelsum (2000) documents that immigrants are less inclined to vote in the local elections than are Dutch citizens. In the United Kingdom, Saggar (1998a) examines the registration and electoral turnout of different ethnic minorities and concludes that Indians are the most participatory South Asian group. Studies have not been conducted for other European countries, so it is hard to make solid generalizations. Available studies show that immigrants participate less than nonimmigrant citizens and that their participation seems to have decreased with time, which is often also true for nonimmigrant citizens. Finally, the various immigrant groups also seem to have different turnout rates.

Whom do immigrants support when they do vote? The authors cited here suggest that immigrants are attracted to progressive and green parties. Recently, the issue of the ethnic vote has attracted attention in some EU countries and even provoked a political and media panic. U.S. political scientists have extensively studied racial and ethnic voting patterns, especially after the 1965 Voting Rights Act removed discriminatory barriers for African Americans and other "protected classes." In Europe, the Community Relations Commission carried out a study of the importance of the "black vote" during the British general elections of 1974 (Solomos and Back 1991). Since then, political parties have shown increasing interest in gathering support from ethnic and black communities, but few studies have been done. Tillie (2000) examines the ethnic dimension of the immigrant vote over twelve years in Dutch local elections. Surprisingly, the issue has not yet seemed to catch the interest of Danish and Swedish political scientists.

In any case, the ethnic vote should always be treated as a contingent phenomenon, not as a presumed ethnic block vote. Researchers must identify the factors and circumstances likely to promote specifically ethnic electoral behavior, in this case voting by people of immigrant origin. The interplay of two sets of factors influence this: (1) residential concentration, density of social networks, shared experiences of discrimination, and the formation of political elites within an immigrant population, and (2) features of the electoral system (such as voter registration rules, majority or proportional representational voting systems, and rules for determining electoral districts) that create differential incentives for various kinds of groups to participate.

In a first meaning, the *ethnic vote* refers to the votes cast by individuals who belong to the same ethnic group as one or several of the candidates or for a political party that lists candidates of this same group. In this case, the voter considers these candidates or political parties as her or his automatic representatives due to their shared ethnic belonging. This may be sufficient to win votes irrespective of the political program proposed. In a second and broader meaning, the *ethnic vote* appears when a substantial number of a given ethnic group decides to support a specific candidate or party irrespective of ethnic belonging.

This collective or block vote may be subjected to some degree of bargaining between the immigrant electorate and the candidates who promise to give a particular advantage to them in exchange for their support. This vote can also result from the subjective awareness of the group that one of the candidates or parties really understands their concerns and is therefore more likely to defend their interests. This distinction may not reflect a real difference. It is easy to imagine cases in which the vote could be ethnic in both senses simultaneously. It should nevertheless be stressed that a voter from a specific ethnic group does not necessarily—by nature—cast an ethnic vote, in either of these two senses.

The potential emergence of an Islamic immigrant vote has recently been prominent in Europe, although we do not know precisely how immigrant-origin Muslim citizens actually vote in many settings. Although there are many Islamic associations, the Islamic parties, such as the Parti des Musulmans de France (PMF) in France, the Parti des Jeunes Musulmans (PJM) in Belgium, the Islamic Party of Britain (IPB), or the Dutch Islamic Party have not so far been able to gain seats in parliamentary elections or local elections. To date, Muslim citizens have mainly voted for traditional mainstream social democratic or conservative parties, perhaps because the Muslim parties are not led by popular Muslim community leaders.

*Parliamentary Politics*   The representation of ethnic minorities in central government, parliament, and local government is also an increasingly important issue, especially in those countries that have long-established immigrant populations, such as the United Kingdom, Belgium, France, and the Netherlands. It is quite remarkable that a second-generation Hungarian immigrant, Nicolas Sarkozy was elected president of the French Republic. As mentioned earlier, he appointed three women of immigrant descent as members of his government. In some districts of Brussels, there seems to be an overrepresentation of immigrant-origin local councilors in the city councils (Martiniello 2007). In Germany, there are German-Turkish politicians in the Bundesrat. And in the United Kingdom, the issue of ethnic representation in elected local government was studied already in the early 1990s (Geddes 2003).

Political philosophers and normative theorists consider whether ethnic minorities have claims to special representation to offset disadvantages they face as discriminated groups in society or as permanent minorities whose concerns risk being consistently overruled in majority decision making. The well-established descriptive representation model holds that representative assemblies should mirror the composition of the wider society (Pitkin 1967; Phillips 1995). Political scientists study how ethnic diversity affects the internal workings of parliamentary assemblies and parties, that is, the emergence of ethnic caucuses or cross-party voting on ethnic issues. Sociologists examine the role of immigrant and ethnic minority politicians and ask to what extent they differ from mainstream politicians their agendas and their modes of functioning.

Two relatively recent studies deserve specific attention. Garbaye (2005) compares the local ethnic representation in Lille and Roubaix with a British city, Birmingham. He shows that cooptation strategies of the party in power explain why immigrant ethnic representation diverged in the three city councils. In another comparative study, Karen Bird (2005), the Canadian political scientist, examines the political representation of visible minorities in France, Denmark, and Canada. In her view, citizenship regimes, institutional features, and interest constellations are central to understanding the different levels of representation of immigrants in elected assemblies. These factors interact to shape the political opportunity structures for immigrant political representation.

*Consultative Politics*   Some states have created consultative institutions at the periphery of the state to deal with ethnic groups and immigration problems. These bodies usually have little power. Among the earliest examples are the Belgian Conseils Consultatifs Communaux pour les Immigrés (Local Consultative Councils for Immigrants), established in the late 1960s in several cities (Martiniello 1992).

Political scientists have criticized the idea of special consultative bodies as leading to a further marginalization of immigrants while giving them the illusion of political participation (Martiniello 1992). Davide Però talks about the comedy of participation in his research on consultation practices in southern European cities (Bauböck 2006). However, a recent Council of Europe initiative puts the issue back on the table (Gsir and Martiniello 2004). As hundreds of consultative bodies sprout up across Europe, the Council of Europe seeks to develop common consultation principles and guidelines.

NONSTATE POLITICS

As far as nonstate politics is concerned, four main avenues of ethnic and immigrant political participation and mobilization can be distinguished: involvement in political parties, involvement in unions, involvement in other pressure groups, and the direct mobilization of ethnic communities.

*Political Parties*    Political parties are located at the intersection between civil society and state institutions. They translate societal interests and ideologies into legislative outputs, and they train and select personnel for political offices. Party politics is therefore an element of conventional politics. But democratic parties are also voluntary associations, not state institutions that exercise legitimate political authority. Moreover, not all political parties are represented in legislative assemblies. Some stay at the margin of the political system where they often campaign for more radical political change.

Ethnic involvement in political parties first emerged as an issue in Britain with the debate about the black section of the Labour Party in the 1980s (Kalbir 1998). On the continent, the development of France Plus gave another dimension to the problem, which then became a sensitive issue in other countries. France Plus sought to encourage immigrants to join all democratic parties and negotiate their electoral support on the basis of the advantages promised by each of the parties (Baillet 2001). In other countries, some parties also established special structures for immigrants. In Germany, the liberal Freie Demokratische Partei (FDP) hosts a Liberale Türkisch-Deutsche Vereinigung.

As a matter of fact, few continental European studies have explored the participation of immigrants in political parties or the party strategies for attracting immigrant membership. One study (Fanning et al. 2007) looks at one of the newest country of immigration in the European Union, Ireland. Bryan Fanning and colleagues (2007) examine the specific measures taken by the most important Irish political parties to encourage members of immigrant ethnic groups to become party members.

*Union Politics*    Immigrant presence in the unions is an older and better-known phenomenon. We could say that union politics is the cradle of immigrant political participation. In Italy, a relatively new country of immigration, the mobilization of immigrants was initially supported by the trade unions, although the contrary has been the case in Greece. The various European unions have had different responses to ethnic and immigration issues (Penninx and Roosblad 2000). Some unions organized specific institutions for migrant workers, whereas others refused to do so in the name of the unity of the working class. In any case, the decline of unions all over Europe is a crucial dimension of studying ethnic participation and mobilization.

*Other Pressure Groups*    Like other citizens, immigrants also get involved in all kinds of pressure groups and movements that defend a wide variety of interests. In this context, it is relevant to mention the *sans-papiers* (undocumented migrants) movements across Europe, which used several unconventional types of action, such as hunger strikes and occupation of churches. Barbara Laubenthal (2007) has examined the emergence of the collective action of undocumented immigrants in France, Spain, and Switzerland since the mid-1990s. Étienne Balibar (2001) claims that the movement of the undocumented migrants in Europe has fostered the development of active citizenship through the solidarity it generated between them and a fraction of the local population. Immigrants have also been involved in environmentalist movements, animal rights groups, and similar initiatives, just like any other group of citizens.

*Ethnic Community Mobilization*    In order to promote and defend political interests or to exert political influence, immigrant groups can operate as collective actors along ethnic, racial, or religious lines. The mobilization of Muslim immigrants around religious concerns has received considerable attention, even though it is only one form of ethnic political mobilization. Joel Fetzer and Christopher Soper (2004) have recently examined the mobilization of Muslims in Germany and the United Kingdom by looking at the resource mobilization process, the political opportunity structures, and the question of ideology.

## Summing Up the Typology

Combining the geographical-political and the state and nonstate levels of action (the seven avenues of mobilization in conventional and nonconventional politics) generates numerous arenas for political action. Not every aspect has been, can be, or should be studied separately. The goal of this typology is, rather, to indicate the scope and variety of immigrant participation within the host countries of the European Union.

## Transnational Political Participation

Transnational political activities can take many different forms. Migrants can mobilize in their country of residence to produce a political impact in their country of origin. Party leaders from the country of origin can travel to the countries of residence to gather electoral support in transnationally active migrant communities (Lafleur 2005). Countries of origin also try to use immigrant communities to intervene in the host countries to defend their interests. Sociocultural transnational activities can be numerous and diverse. Examples of this include the selection of expatriate beauty queens to compete in home-country contests and tours of folk music groups from the country of origin to perform for migrants in their country of residence.

At a higher level of abstraction, these transnational practices reveal that a crucial change has occurred with the globalization of the economy, namely the passage from the national to the transnational condition (see Eva Østergaard-Nielsen, chap. 13 in this volume). Not long ago, migrants were considered to be an anomaly within the nation-state framework. With the acceleration of globalization, transnational politics has emerged as a new phenomenon linking immigrant groups in advanced countries with their nations of origin and hometowns. This transnational process is "composed of a growing number of persons who live dual lives: speaking two languages, having homes in two countries, and making a living through continuous regular contacts across national borders" (Portes, Guarnizo, and Landolt 1999, 217). Insights into transnational politics are based on the fact that immigrants' integration or incorporation into the host country and transnational practices can occur simultaneously. But more research is needed both at the theoretical and empirical levels to make sense of the impact of transnationalism on immigrants' political participation.

## Research Perspectives

This review suggests that the literature on immigrant political participation has several gaps, despite its having made dramatic progress over the past decade. Our knowledge remains fragmented and largely confined to specific national contexts. The gender dimension of immigrants' political participation has also not sufficiently been explored. Attempts to produce comparative data, both qualitative and quantitative, with an integrated theoretical framework are still in their earliest stages. It would be interesting, for example, to design cross-EU electoral surveys or exit polls to better understand how citizens with an immigrant or ethnic minority background vote. We have yet to examine their political attitudes in detail. We do not even know who votes for ethnic minority candidates in the various member states of the European Union and who does not. In short, we need studies on at least three main topics.

1. *The implications of transnational political participation of migrants and their offspring in Europe.* Both theoretical and empirical discussions are needed on the links between immigrant transnational political participation and citizenship in the country of origin and the country of residence. What happens when immigrants who have acquired legal citizenship (nationality) in their country of residence participates politically in their country of origin? How does that affect the common understanding of nationality? Can an individual be an active citizen in more than one polity? What impact does double participation have on identity and belonging? These questions have already been raised and researched in some countries for specific groups of immigrants, but much work remains to be done.

2. *The links between religion and political participation in postmigration situations.* New Islamic parties have recently been formed by immigrant-origin citizens or local converts in several EU member states. These parties have not yet had any dramatic electoral success. Nevertheless, in the present context they reveal new developments concerning the links between religion and politics for immigrants and their offspring.

3. *The rise of virtual ethnic and immigrant political communities.* The Internet has opened up new channels of political mobilization across state boundaries. The new electronic media may be a potent resource for immigrants engaged in transnational political activities across different host countries or between countries of residence and or origin. We do not know the extent to which immigrants use the Internet for political purposes, however. More attention has been paid to the use of the Internet for global terrorism than to its use for nonviolent purposes.

## Assessing the Political Participation of Immigrants and Their Offspring

Several difficulties must be overcome in constructing the kinds of indicators of political participation of immigrants and their offspring that would allow for comparison across the European Union. The variety of citizenship (nationality) laws and policies complicates matters. Rules of access and loss of citizenship directly affect immigrant opportunities to participate in formal political life and determine which institutions are open to immigrants and their offspring. Where access to citizenship is easy, it may be easy for immigrants to take part in political life, but many may still choose not to naturalize and thus remain excluded. Where access to citizenship is difficult, immigrants are restricted to nonconventional forms of political participation. Similarly, regulations concerning the political rights and opportunities for noncitizen residents are important. Several EU member states grant local voting rights to all foreigners, whereas others limit them to EU citizens. These different legal frameworks make it difficult to compare immigrant political participation across states.

The EU countries are also at different stages of the migratory process. Some countries are more concerned with the settlement of recent arrivals, whereas others have many decades of experience and more developed institutions of integration. The older immigration countries in northwestern Europe have spent a long time discussing issues that the newer immigration countries in southern Europe and eastern Europe are currently (re)discovering.

Finally, the group "immigrants and their offspring" is not a homogeneous group in terms of political attitudes and behavior. Some immigrants are highly politicized and were politically active in their country of origin, from which they often escaped for political reasons. Others, like many native citizens nowadays, are not interested in politics at all.

All this is complicated by the unequal availability of adequate statistical data in the EU member states. For comparative analysis, we need data on foreign nationality and on country of birth in addition to the year of immigration and ethnic self-identification. This is not available in many settings, where only foreign nationality is recorded in the official statistics. In other countries, the statistical apparatus is much more developed and it is easier to access data concerning the voting behavior of ethnic minorities.

Having said this, we can still suggest some practical steps for studying the political participation of immigrants and their offspring based on the distinction between conventional and less conventional forms of political participation. When using these indicators, we must bear in mind that they reflect responses to political opportunity structures prevailing at a given time and place.

In the field of conventional political participation, answers to at least five questions will provide good indicators of political participation of immigrants and their offspring.

1.  Where immigrants and their offspring are enfranchised, what is their electoral turnout compared to that of nonimmigrant citizens?
2.  Where immigrants and their offspring are distinguished on electoral lists and in elected positions, and possibly in representation in legislative and executive offices (from the local level to the European level), what is their level of representation?
3.  What is their rate of membership in political parties, and what activities do they undertake within those parties?
4.  Where immigrants and their offspring have formed their own political parties based on a religious or ethnic agenda and stand for election, what has been the experience of those parties?
5.  In states, regions, or cities that have created specific consultative institutions at the margin of the political system to specifically deal with ethnic and immigration issues, how extensive has participation been in those institutions and with what effect?

In the field of nonconventional political participation, at least three questions will provide indicators of political participation of immigrants and their offspring that are promising.

1.  To what extent are immigrants active in trade unions, either as supporters, activists or members of the executive?
2.  Where immigrants and their offspring have organized along ethnic, racial, national, cultural, or religious lines, to what extent have claims-making immigrant associations emerged and with what impact?
3.  To what extent do immigrants participate in pressure groups and movements (these can defend a wide variety of interests, such as humanitarian movements, environmentalist movements, neighborhood committees, and customers' associations)?

This set of possible indicators is far from exhaustive but nevertheless points research in promising directions.

Before trying to compare immigrant political participation across Europe, we must also place it in the context of participation by nonimmigrant citizens. Clearly, the road to transforming immigrants from political objects into political subjects is long and difficult. Many European countries have made significant progress on it; in others, everything is still to be accomplished. A crucial challenge facing Europe is, thus, whether it will be able to develop a European model of political incorporation of immigrants that will enhance the development of an active European citizenship. Only time will tell.

# CHAPTER FOUR

# Lost in Translation?

## A Critical Reappraisal of the Concept of Immigrant Political Incorporation

*Lorraine C. Minnite*

The return to high levels of immigration to the United States over the last forty years has generated a familiar concern for how immigrants are changing U.S. society. Sometimes this concern is motivated by a prickly nativism, a lingering anxiety about what "they" are doing to "us" and how much we might have to change to include, accommodate, or simply tolerate "them" (Huntington 2004). More broad-minded people who retain their faith in the power of democratic institutions to "make citizens" nevertheless worry that these institutions may not be up to the task of integrating so many more newcomers from so many different places (Benhabib 2004; Putnam 2007).

Interestingly, compared to research on the economic and social impacts of immigration on host societies, scholars of the new immigration have paid less attention to the political dimensions of immigrant integration. This is especially surprising given the national state's monopoly over the flow of people across borders and in regulating those people once they arrive.[1] Analysts of the U.S. case have addressed this question when they have employed the metaphor of *incorporation,* by which they usually mean the extent to which immigrants have become citizens and mobilized their interests within the political system. The dominant notion of immigrant political incorporation, which looks for evidence in electoral politics, representation, and policy responsiveness, is largely borrowed from older research on minority groups in U.S. urban politics. Is this research paradigm suitable for understanding immigrant politics today?

Before we go too far down this road, it is worth reappraising the concept of political incorporation, as some analysts of immigrant political behavior have already begun to do. For example, Michael Jones-Correa describes how scholars using this concept meander from a notion of pathways to integration shaped by local contexts to one of end states resulting from "events" such as naturalization or electoral participation. "What is striking," he comments, "is that we know so little about the variation along any one of these dimensions, much less how variation in one dimension might affect outcomes in other dimensions" (Jones-Correa 2002, 2).

Similarly, Janelle Wong argues that the concept is so diffuse that the resulting research agenda lacks coherence. Some analysts look at mechanisms of immigrant political participation, others at rates of participation, and still others at measures of a political system's openness to new groups. "Maybe all of these activities and concepts should count as political incorporation," she notes, "but should they all count in exactly the same way?" (Wong 2002, 1). The lack of conceptual cohesion, she argues, makes it difficult to specify the directions of causality among these different indicators. Is membership in a civic organization a determinant or only an indicator of political incorporation?

These are sound criticisms, but the usefulness of the incorporation paradigm can be challenged further. To do so, we need a deeper examination of the ways the incorporation metaphor's assumptions and values shape the research questions we ask about immigration and politics. Let us consider, then, three basic issues: (1) that the many divergent meanings that scholars have attached to political incorporation render it a conceptual muddle, (2) that theories of incorporation borrowed from U.S. ethnic and urban politics may not be suitable for explaining immigrant political behavior, and (3) that we might do a better job by paying more attention to what is missing from incorporation theories. The conclusion to this chapter argues that the incoherence of the concept of political incorporation limits its utility and highlights the need for theoretical development. We need a more careful, contingent, and grounded approach to the study of how immigration and immigrants are changing U.S. society and, especially, urban politics.

## What Is Political Incorporation?

Martin Shefter argues that political incorporation, viewed as the study of how new social forces enter the political system, is a central theme in the study of U.S. political development. As a theory of emergent groups in the polity, it is at the center of longstanding investigations of party systems and partisan realignment and of analyses of ethnic succession in urban politics (Shefter 1986).

As such, most theories of political incorporation generally fit into two groups, one emphasizing inclusion and the other stressing absorption. The differences between these categories are not large, but it is still useful to make the distinction. To include is to embrace, comprise, or contain, sometimes as a subordinate element; to absorb is to swallow up, to take a thing in until the loss of its separate existence. The former refers to the putting together of groups in specific ways, whereas the latter implies that the state of amalgamation changes the groups and the polity as a whole. Inclusion theories accommodate what Arthur Bentley says is "the process of [mutual] adjustment of a set of interest groups" (Bentley 1908, 260), or how the self-styled pluralist genius of the U.S. political system successfully manages and balances a proliferation of groups and their demands. Absorption, on the other hand, shifts the focus from the equilibrium-seeking dynamics of the group process to how new groups change as they interact with and merge into the political system. Inclusion theories emphasize the mechanisms through which the political system expands, how it balances competing claims and accommodates new political forces to return to equilibrium, whereas absorption theories emphasize endogenous processes in the recalibration of the political order when new political forces threaten instability.

The most recent and influential inclusionary theory of political incorporation derives from the entry of blacks and Latinos into U.S. urban electoral coalitions beginning in the 1960s. Rufus Browning, Dale Rogers Marshall, and David Tabb's seminal 1984 book *Protest Is Not Enough* set the agenda for the analysis of coalition politics in U.S. cities. They use the term *political incorporation* "to refer to the extent to which group interests are effectively represented in policy making" through inclusion of minority group representatives in a dominant electoral coalition (Browning, Marshall, and Tabb 2003, 11). Incorporation is treated as both a process and an outcome. Browning, Marshall, and Tabb identify a simple sequence of causality from mobilization to incorporation to policy responsiveness, with two possible paths for minority group mobilization: the "protest strategy" and the "electoral strategy," both of which can converge on local political institutions to produce policy outcomes favored by the new groups. Thus, incorporation occurs in stages measured by the degree to which a formerly excluded group is represented in a coalition that dominates city policy making on issues that concern them.

Emergent groups may stake claims but have no representation in a governing coalition, or they can have a degree of representation on a city council or local governing body and, therefore, some incorporation. At the highest levels of incorporation, the group is a dominant player in a governing coalition, thereby achieving substantial influence over policymaking. Although Browning, Marshall, and Tabb attempt to account for the influence of nonelectoral minority protest movements, theirs is essentially a theory about the dynamics of biracial electoral coalitions and the terms under which they become—or fail to become—governing coalitions. They conclude that protest alone does not produce results but that protest combined with the formation of minority-led bi- or multiracial insurgent political coalitions may. From their studies of ten northern California cities, they conclude that minority political incorporation depends as much on whether white liberals become coalition partners as it does on the electoral aspirations and coalition-building skills of blacks and Latinos. Without white allies, they argue, minority groups cannot forge successful governing coalitions.

Because Browning, Marshall, and Tabb develop easily quantifiable measures of incorporation, their book launched a cottage industry of studies replicating their approach in different urban contexts.[2] Subsequent work went far to expand the insights of *Protest Is Not Enough.* The studies of several anomalous big-city cases have particular value in that they point out ways to revise the original model to account for barriers to minority incorporation, including interethnic competition for coalition leadership and power, elite strategies for developing policies that coopt minority challenges, and modes of representation that do not lead to empowerment (see, especially, the essays by DeLeon, Mollenkopf, Pinderhughes, and Sonenshein in Browning, Marshall, and Tabb 2003). Yet these studies do not challenge the core values and conceptual coherence of the original model of incorporation. In the process of stretching the meaning of *political incorporation,* they reduce it to its empirical content.

## Political Incorporation as Concept Stretching

*Protest Is Not Enough* set out to account for minority political mobilization in cities in the 1960s and 1970s and to theorize a link between mobilization and policy. More recent treatments have applied the Browning, Marshall, and Tabb model to the study of immigrant politics (Lien 2001; Mollenkopf, Olson, and Ross 2001; Ramakrishnan and Espenshade 2001).[3] For example, Luis Fraga and Ricardo Ramírez define the *political incorporation* of Latinos in California as, "the extent to which self-identified group interests are articulated, represented, and met in public policy making" (2003, 304). In these studies, incorporation is both a process and an outcome, a catch-all concept describing a wide range of complex behaviors and end states, from levels of group identity, mobilization, and participation to representation and influence over policy-making. Incorporation manifests itself in degrees along the continuum first set out by Browning, Marshall, and Tabb.

Not all scholars of the new immigrant politics, however, apply the concept so broadly. Those writing from a social movement perspective tend to emphasize the role of agency and self-organization over policy outcomes as the best measure of immigrant incorporation. For example, distinguishing between incorporation and assimilation, Nhu-Ngoc Ong and David Meyer write, "...by political incorporation, *we mean the development of the capacity to mobilize effective political action in response to perceived political opportunities in a host country*" (2004, 4; emphasis in original).

But political scientists usually retain the electoral framework (DeSipio 1996; DeSipio and de la Garza 1992; Mollenkopf, Olson, and Ross 2001; Ramakrishnan 2005). In a thoughtful and wide-ranging exploration of the meaning of political incorporation, Jones-Correa argues that the concept of incorporation could be taken to mean (1) naturalization leading to participation in formal electoral politics, (2) living within the polity as a law-abiding citizen, and (3) participation in organizational life. Immigrants, he points out, can be incorporated as individuals and as groups. Immigrant group incorporation may be reflected in the number of immigrant co-ethnics elected to office, appointed to administrative positions, or employed in government; beyond representation, incorporation "may be best measured...by how immigrants' interests are reflected in political outcomes and policies" (Jones-Correa 2005, 76), moving the analysis back toward Browning, Marshall, and Tabb.[4]

Because Latinos dominate the immigrant population both nationally and in many U.S. cities, data on immigrant political behavior are often aligned with ethnicity and connected to theories of ethnic group political behavior. The degree to which that behavior is affected by immigrant status, identity, culture, and collective action per se sometimes gets lost behind familiar patterns of ethnic group differentiation and minority group politics.[5] For example, immigrant Latinos become co-ethnics, distinguished from other native-born Latinos only by their legal status. Following this line of reasoning, a growing number of immigrant advocates argue for extending local voting rights to noncitizen residents to speed their incorporation.[6] They seem to believe that, given the opportunity, immigrants will integrate by voting themselves into the polity.[7] Irene Bloemraad, one of the few scholars to "bring the state back in" to studies of immigrant political integration by showing how state intervention can foster integration through efforts to strengthen immigrant organizations, nevertheless sees incorporation mostly as a product of agency and self-mobilization, as well (Bloemraad 2005).

Absorption theories applied to immigrant political incorporation are similar to sociological theories of assimilation. They assess incorporation as a measure of the degree to which cultural and political attitudes among the foreign-born and native-born converge. In other words, with absorption theories, the dimensions of difference are reduced and the immigrant disappears. So, for example, Rodolfo de la Garza, Angelo Falcon, and F. Chris Garcia (1996) measure incorporation in terms of support among immigrants for core U.S. values such as patriotism and economic self-sufficiency. Scholars measuring absorption rely mainly on survey data, which tend to be thin on this topic, leaving us with little real knowledge of the political ideologies and attitudes of the foreign-born. To the extent these approaches mirror traditional assimilation models, however, they are outdated.[8]

To summarize, as worked out in the context of minority group political incorporation, inclusion and absorption approaches emphasize alternative dynamics of political integration. Inclusion implies that vestigial distinctions binding the emergent group together will persist beyond incorporation and may even convert to positive resources for the group in the political system. Absorption approaches usually measure integration between the new group and the incorporating body differently. Instead of focusing on political behavior, levels of group representation, or policy responsiveness to group needs and demands, analysts focus on patterns of partisan identification, political attitudes or ideology, and public opinion and evaluate levels of convergence and change the dominant culture.

But scholars applying either of these approaches to the contemporary political incorporation of immigrants may be guilty of what Giovanni Sartori once called "concept stretching" (Sartori 1970). When a concept is extended to cover a set of conditions, subjects, cases, or circumstances that lie somewhat outside the class of things on which it was originally based, the properties, meanings, or attributes that identify or define the concept in the first instance can get distorted. Stretching a concept too far, Sartori argues, does not produce a more general concept but, instead, a counterfeit through "simple terminological camouflage: things are declared alike by making them *verbally* identical" (Sartori 1970, 1052; emphasis in original).

Both inclusion and absorption theories of immigrant political incorporation require a critical reappraisal on these grounds. Immigrants today are not like blacks and Latinos in urban politics in the 1960s and 1970s. Indeed, immigrants are often exploited in the labor market; nevertheless, they do not share the history of oppression that structured labor-market inequalities in the first place and gave the civil rights movement its distinctive character, forms, targets, demands, and promise. The nascent immigrant rights movement is much more fragmented and diffuse and is not producing the kind of collective identity forged in the struggles of African Americans, in particular, for the right to vote. In fact, the demand for the right to vote was central to the earlier movements of African Americans, whereas it is nearly absent in the mobilizations of today's immigrant groups. This means that immigrant politics probably are not on the path to incorporation through electoral participation as conceptualized in Browning, Marshall, and Tabb's minority group model. The ill fit of this model is producing gaps, inconsistencies, and distortions in the ways political scientists approach questions of immigrant political incorporation and the impact of immigration on U.S. politics, particularly urban politics.

The conceptual stretching of political incorporation from urban minority group electoral fortunes to diverse immigrant group politics is producing a counterfeit. The distortions are evident in current research on immigrant politics. In reappraising political incorporation, it may not be possible to move up the "ladder of generality" (Collier and Mahon 1993, 846) in applying the minority group model to immigrants. The conceptual problems run deeper than the sort identified by revisionists of Sartori's framework; they cannot be resolved by conceptual refinement using more flexible criteria such as family resemblances and radial categories to amend the framework. The problem is rooted in the fundamental attachments of the concept to electoral representative institutions as incorporating mechanisms. Outside this framework, the application of political incorporation models to other cases makes little sense. Moreover, beyond what might appear to be workable problems of conceptual extension and intension, the very assumptions underlying political incorporation are weakening through the pressures of economic globalization and unfettered market capitalism. The next section discusses these problems.

## Assumptions

In abstract terms, political incorporation is a classical liberal trope descended from the traditions of the French Revolution. *To incorporate* means to unite into one body, to mix thoroughly together, to put into or include in the body or substance of something else—to form one integral body. The social contract establishes the conditions for political combination, for the merging and forging of a political community, for political incorporation. To join the polity, individuals give up some autonomy in return for greater protection. In modern democratic states, one aspect of this exchange involves individuals' surrendering exclusive control over their identity and subordinating it to a universal, totalizing concept of citizenship and a primary identity as citizen (Young 1989). Thus, the unfulfilled promise of citizenship for black Americans excluded from the universe of citizens by racism and the Jim Crow state not only heightened black identity but gave the civil rights movement a good deal of its moral force.

On the other hand, the merging is never complete, nor should it be. William Kymlicka argues that while multiculturalism recognizes group differences it is compatible with liberalism because it assumes immigrants will adopt core liberal values (Kymlicka 2001). Liberalism's universalism and optimism assume that, given the opportunity, all will choose to integrate into the liberal polity through the mechanism of active citizenship. Not to do so is irrational because this would represent a rejection of enlightened self-interest. So the first liberal assumption of political incorporation is that all outsiders can be converted into insiders; the second assumption is that outsiders want to be included in the liberal polity.

Democratic institutions provide the mechanisms of conversion. Constitutions, elections, representative legislatures, elected leaders, voluntary organizations, and many other, more informal venues for participation make the polity by involving and enveloping (incorporating) citizens. When functioning properly, these institutions reduce unregulated conflict by ordering citizens' demands and preferences, bestowing legitimacy, and serving as the mechanisms of self-government. According to early elaborations of U.S. pluralism, the U.S. political system, "with all its defects...nonetheless does provide a high probability that any active and legitimate group will make itself heard effectively at some stage in the process of decision" (Dahl 1956, 150). For these reasons, incorporation is the expected outcome of the pluralist model of politics. It both presupposes and generates a pluralistic society.

In the logic of incorporation, it follows from these assumptions that new immigrant groups have no rational basis for remaining outside the liberal polity. Those who do, whether by misguided design or choice, are presumed to be dangerous to the survival of liberalism. This more punitive strand of thinking weaves through warnings about the dire consequences of a failure to integrate; these include mounting concerns about the bifurcation of the liberal order into separate and unequal spheres, predictions of more racial or sectarian violence fed by the rage generated by exclusion, and a growing fear of unending threats to "our way of life." Incorporation is seen as a bulwark against political inequality, deformed citizenship, unregulated social and political conflict, and other undifferentiated threats to the liberal order.

That political incorporation into the liberal polity is always rational and protects against unregulated societal conflict, however, is not something we should simply assume. The experience of immigration in the liberal democracies of the West, including the United States, over the last forty years suggests that our assumptions could be wrong. In fact, the liberal state has sometimes incorporated groups in very different ways than those assumed by the minority group model; moreover, incorporation theories generally cannot account for reversals and disincorporation, as evidenced in the failure to protect immigrants from exploitation in the labor market; in the ongoing erosion of community bonds and the physical environment; and in the decomposition of the electorate, where minority and working-class voters have lost the most. The political incorporation of the working class and of the racial and ethnic minorities that make up large swaths of it, in fact, has not always delivered what it promised. For immigrants, it may not be such a rational choice after all. Instead, to the un-incorporated, the rhetoric of incorporation may sound the dominant society's ambivalence toward full inclusion and sharing the benefits that inclusion is supposed to bring.

## What Is Missing from Political Incorporation

Political incorporation theories are also missing a number of important ingredients extending beyond the unexamined and perhaps unwarranted liberal premises on which they are based. Applied to the question of immigrant impacts, they are plagued by theoretical gaps, internal inconsistencies, and historical distortions of fact.

## Theoretical Gaps

Political incorporation theories may address group dynamics in the political sphere, but they have nothing to say about the prior question of what makes a group a group in politics. As Susan Clarke and others note, the minority group model does not contend with variations within racial and ethnic groups (Clarke 2005, 224). Instead, emergent political groups appear already formed and internally coherent on the assumption that processes of group formation are prepolitical.

This assumption is weak when it comes to immigrants. Theories of political incorporation in urban politics were largely about ethnic and racial succession and, significantly, the travails of African Americans in their quest for equality. But are the immigrants of today like the blacks in the urban United States during the 1970s and 1980s? Do they share a cultural legacy, a consciousness, and history of segregation and discrimination? Have they engaged in disruptive social movements or forged a collective identity through political action against racial exclusion? If we define immigrants only as people who are born in one country but reside in another, we obscure the distinctions among them that result from the different timings of their migrations, the different conditions under which they migrate, the different legal regimes under which they are admitted to their host countries, and the different host country communities into which they are inserted—not to mention, of course, the race, class, and gender differences among immigrants and between them and the native-born.

The hyperdiversity of the New York City immigrant population makes this clear. At 36 percent of the population and 43 percent of the city workforce, the New York foreign-born population share rivals that of a century ago. Today, however, the population of the city is twice what it was. Although the largest contemporary immigrant groups—Dominicans, Chinese, Afro-Caribbeans, and refugees from the former Soviet Union—would constitute small cities on their own, no one national origin group makes up more than 13 percent of the foreign-born population. This diversity has strong class dimensions. Dominicans and Mexicans are far below the city median in education and earnings, whereas Filipinos and Indians are far above it. High rates of homeownership coexist with high rates of overcrowding within immigrant groups. For example, although 42 percent of the Chinese live in owner-occupied housing (compared to a citywide rate of 30 percent), they also suffer from higher than average rates of overcrowding (34 percent, compared to 15 percent of all households citywide) (Lobo and Salvo 2005). Nearly one-half of Chinese Americans living in Bayside, Queens, are professionals; 42 percent have degrees above the college level and average annual incomes of $69,000. Only 14 percent of the Chinese living in Manhattan's Chinatown are professionals, only 7 percent have degrees above the college level, and the average annual household income is $24,000 (*World Journal* 2003). Under these circumstances, we cannot assume common immigrant group identities, especially when U.S. citizenship practices continuously attempt to erase them.

Second, because political incorporation theories have been worked out in the context of specific groups with coherent political identities (mainly racial groups formed in specific urban contexts), they ignore how national legal and transborder regulatory regimes affect immigrant incorporation and may fragment groups in ways that are inimical to it.[9] Absent strong linkages to the U.S. racial order, national legal, and political practices may overdetermine immigrant political identity.

This is demonstrated by the experiences of immigrant groups that have not yet negotiated their place within the racial order. The ordeal of South Asian Muslim immigrants in New York City following the terrorist attacks of September 11, 2001, provides a case in point. Over the previous two decades, South Asian immigrants had flooded into the city. Bangladeshis were too few to count in 1980, but by the end of the 1990s, for the first time, Bangladesh, Pakistan, and India were among the top ten sending countries to New York City. South Asian immigrants rapidly expanded their numbers in the city through heavy use of the diversity visa or visa lottery system. Between 1992 and 2002, 14 percent of the more than 100,000 immigrants arriving to New York City on a diversity visa came from Pakistan or Bangladesh. Because immigrants arriving through the diversity visa program are akin to traditional sojourners, they are more likely to be young and single or with young families, and less likely to join established communities with dense networks of family and friends. Moreover, the diversity visa program requires visa holders to have a high school education or at least two years of work experience in a career or occupation requiring at least two years of training; because they are not emigrating on work visas to particular jobs, diversity visa holders often end up doing menial work or in employment for which they are overqualified. This can further contribute to their isolation.

The way immigrants arrive in the United States creates the context for their reception, and that context, in turn, shapes immigrant communities in ways that are important for immigrant politics. Despite the fact that no South Asians were shown to be connected with the terrorist attacks in any way, their vulnerability allowed them to be singled out for detention and deportation during the post-9/11 federal criminal investigation (Minnite 2005). The government's assault on their civil liberties stimulated an activist-oriented politics that has made allies of unlikely partners among the city's established civil liberties and human rights legal advocates, with implications for city politics. A theoretical approach that looks only at naturalization rates, immigrant attitudes toward U.S. civic values, or participation in local electoral politics misses this important development.

## Inconsistencies

Is incorporation a process or an outcome? It is studied as both, but most treatments fail to make a distinction between the two. Cast as a process, studies of immigrant political incorporation might focus on identity dynamics, collective action, or community-building. Conceptualized as an outcome, the focus might be on the political behavior of immigrants, broadly conceived; policy responsiveness; institutional change; and changes in values and norms.

It is more consistent with its general meaning to define incorporation as an outcome, but this is difficult because incorporation must stand in relation to migration as a process that unfolds unevenly over time. We generally think of an outcome as a steady state, but the sequencing and layering of immigrant groups in politics are more likely to look unstable at any point in time. If it is unstable, can we then accurately call it incorporation? When more conservative whites replaced the black mayors of Los

Angeles and New York and mostly neglected the needs of their black constituents and excluded black political leaders from their governing coalitions, minority incorporation scholars reevaluated the minority group model. Raphael Sonenshein has paid particular attention to the disincorporation of blacks in Los Angeles following the election of Richard Riordan in 1993 (Sonenshein 2003a). But his work has not led to a full-scale revision of the incorporation concept. Instead, Sonenshein himself argued that the model should give greater emphasis to the role of ideology and leadership in fashioning coalitions that led to minority incorporation.[10]

Examples of disincorporation should not be so easily dismissed. If, as Louis De-Sipio and others have shown, immigrants are entering the electorate through the same channels of class that bias political participation in the United States, at a time when those at the lower end of the social hierarchy are increasingly marginalized, then immigrant disincorporation might be more the norm than the exception (De-Sipio 2001).

## Distortions

Rogers Smith and others have shown that liberal democracies have relied on various forms of exclusion to define boundaries of belonging and rights (Smith 1997; see also Zolberg 2006). Past struggles to expand the franchise in the United States have shown that the greatest value of the vote was the value the disenfranchised placed on it. Similarly, today, as the state is "hollowed out" and liberal institutions of self-government erode (Jessop, quoted in Clarke 2003, 30), citizenship is increasingly made meaningful by what it is not, that is, by alienage.

Globalization is accelerating the movement of people across borders, causing liberal states to re-assert their prerogative to decide who belongs to the nation. A number of analysts have pointed to how the free international flow of capital, technology, and information stands in contrast to restricted flows of people. James Hollifield (1992) terms this contradiction the "liberal paradox" of modern states, whereby practices of exclusion are becoming more important than those of inclusion in defining the liberal political order. If we conceive of political incorporation as only a one-way process of inclusion or absorption, then we ignore these important exclusionary practices and their effects.

The standard model of political incorporation also often fails to highlight how processes of inclusion can be selective or uneven, changing both the emergent political group and the larger body. It neglects the way struggles for inclusion serve as sites for bargaining agreements between established and emergent political forces. As Shefter (1986) has shown, the local electoral incorporation of fractions of the working class in New York during a period of great instability in the 1940s was accompanied by the extrusion of the most radical political elements vying for representation and power. This process made New York City the largest and most generous local welfare state, but it realigned working-class politics along axes of race and ethnicity rather than (multiracial) class. A central question for the emerging movement for immigrant rights, then, is how the movement will negotiate its identity within the U.S. racial order. Is this movement simply another chapter in the struggle for Latino empowerment, or is it something else? As a group interacts with the established order to fashion a new, incorporated political identity, whose politics will be excluded as its acceptable leaders become included?

## Competing Rationalities

Finally, the standard model cannot account for rational opposition to integration. According to some, this is one element of the Islamic challenge in the West (Huntington 1996; but see Haddad 2002). What little data we have on why immigrants choose to naturalize suggest that the post-1965 cohort's relatively low (but rising) naturalization rates may not be a product of irrational thinking (DeSipio 2001; Jones-Correa 2001a, 2001b). Using survey data, Harry Pachon and Louis DeSipio (1994), for example, found that approximately one-third of Latino immigrants were not interested in becoming U.S. citizens. Greta Gilbertson and Audrey Singer (2000) found rational instrumental reasons for naturalization among Dominicans but not the usual ones associated with the liberal polity. Some of the Dominican immigrants interviewed for their study, for example, said that they naturalized so that they could maintain control over their U.S.-based businesses after they retired to the Dominican Republic.

Jane Junn (2000) agrees that more political participation by immigrants and traditionally disadvantaged minorities is desirable if it increases the voice of systematically excluded groups. But it may not be justified if the price of participation in the political process means acceding to a process that produces inequality by privileging certain groups or ideologies over others. She argues that, for those who differ from the cultural norm of what it means to be a "good citizen," which in the U.S. context means having the resources to participate in the electoral process and voting, assimilating to a norm of citizenship that denies difference is not rational.

The concept of incorporation does not account for host society fragmentation and the ways that immigrants can be integrated or stratified at varying scales and levels (i.e., fully in the labor market, partially in society, and not at all in the polity; see Andersen 2008; Clarke 2005). Nor can it be stretched far enough to account for transnational social spaces that may provide some protection for immigrants, changing their calculus of belonging (Smith 2001; Kivisto 2003; Pantoja 2005).[11]

Jones-Correa's pioneering work notwithstanding, political scientists have not systematically investigated how transnationalism affects the political incorporation of immigrants. Indeed, the incorporation model takes no account of how the simultaneity and multiplicity of ties across borders may affect different areas of social action. Instead, transnational ties have been treated as incompatible with U.S. political incorporation because they create a transient mentality among immigrants, causing them to devalue naturalization and political participation. Research on whether this is actually the case has produced mixed findings. Some scholars have found evidence of a negative relationship (Waldinger 1986; Dwyer 1991), whereas others have concluded that most immigrants are not transnational (Jones-Correa 2001b; Itzigsohn and Giorguli-Saucedo 2002). Jones-Correa (1998), for example, found that dual nationality facilitated naturalization in the United States, whereas Yang (1994b) found the opposite.

Transnational social spaces are real, both as physical and social phenomena and as elements in the capacity of groups to imagine a bond with others as subjects

(Buttimer, in Kivisto 2003).[12] Any theory of how immigrants incorporate into the polity of their host societies must take into account how immigrants construct these spaces and the institutions that make them durable.

Finally, although the minority group model includes mobilization, the applications of the model to immigrant politics neglect it. Many of these studies look for incorporation in the dearth of evidence of mobilization as a prior condition to immigrant incorporation.[13] In the absence of any guidance on the question of what constitutes a group in local politics, standing incorporation theories are a poor fit for the study of immigrant politics.

### The Way Forward

We need to radically rethink the incorporation metaphor as a basis for studying the dynamic impact of immigration on U.S. politics. As a theory of ethnic succession in urban politics and of the conditions under which African Americans were able to extend the gains of the civil rights movement to achieve government and policy responsiveness at the local level, Browning, Marshall, and Tabb's insights of twenty years ago present a coherent framework for the analysis of U.S. urban politics. But as globalization and large-scale immigration diversify and diffuse urban populations, their construction is less viable.

Incorporation is not a wholly wrong framework for research on immigrants and politics, but we should not uncritically adapt it for this purpose. We cannot simply tinker with the incorporation models or go up the ladder of generality to address their causal specificity, their overemphasis on electoral politics, and their inability to account for differences within racial and ethnic groups. We need both broader and more intensive investigations of comparative immigrant politics across different contexts that go beyond electoral participation and go backward into the mobilization process as well as forward into the contingent, segmented, and reversible nature of incorporation (Jones-Correa 2005; Clarke 2005).

New kinds of case studies will help in this task. If we look anew at dynamic patterns of immigrant political behavior, we will move away from the older static notions of incorporation and generate fresh questions for research. This would include asking when and how immigrants become groups that are important to politics and how they fashion their identities as political subjects. It would also include asking how the institutions and policies of the liberal nation-state shape immigrant identities and contribute to their differentiation, segmentation, and uneven development. It would ask how most immigrants are enmeshed in the restructuring of the global working class and the reshaping of racial, class, and gender categories under various globalization regimes. Finally, a new lens would ask what the emergence of new immigrant minority groups means for social justice and the future of democratic politics.

# PART III

# IMMIGRANTS' LOCAL POLITICAL OPPORTUNITY STRUCTURES

Whereas national laws govern the entry, legal status, and naturalization of immigrants to a host country, more local arenas shape their lives. The neighborhoods, cities, and regions in which immigrants live; the schools their children attend; the libraries they frequent; the police they encounter; and other civic services they use are, as they are for the native-born, the political entities most important in immigrants' day-to-day activities. Localities can offer immigrants opportunity for participation in labor unions, neighborhood associations, school councils, public-sector service jobs, religious organizations, and town governance; they sometimes even grant local suffrage to noncitizens. Communities can harbor zones in which immigrants from the same country of origin live together, create a common identity, and help even more recent immigrants gain economic and linguistic footing. Conversely, local laws, practices, geography, and people can push newcomers away rather than bring them in. Localities may isolate immigrants, sharpen their differences from the native-born, discourage their political participation and civic socialization, and, in some countries, even bar their naturalization.

Part III of *Bringing Outsiders In* focuses on the roles of local polities. In chapter 5, Gianni D'Amato provides a detailed and fascinating account of the consequences of Swiss municipalities as gatekeepers to naturalization. It is an unusual, perhaps unique structure of (non)inclusion, and it generates a complicated politics, mixing views about immigration and immigrants with jockeying for position and power among competing political parties and levels or regions of governance. Many old and cherished Swiss norms and practices of local decision making, partisan mutual accommodation, and regional coordination are under attack by Christoph Blocher's radical-right Swiss People's Party (SVP). Blocher is an aggressive and brilliant policy entrepreneur, and strong public support for his party's hostility to immigration and immigrants may transform national and regional, as well as municipal, politics, to the severe detriment of immigrants and would-be citizens. D'Amato's chapter necessarily ends in the middle of the story, and he can conclude only that "This struggle is ongoing."

The other two chapters in this part examine how the political institutions of cities, particularly their electoral rules, structure immigrants' ability to attain representation in the comparatively stable United States. From John Mollenkopf and Raphael Sonenshein's comparison of Los Angeles and New York in chapter 6 and from Reuel Rogers's comparison of New York and Hartford, Connecticut, in chapter 7, we learn that immigrant groups living in cities with large voting districts (Los Angeles) or at-large electoral systems (Hartford) have a strong incentive to form coalitions with other non-Anglo groups to achieve their political interests. When successful, these efforts ease tensions with whites in those cities and pave the way for immigrants to rise to the highest levels of local political office—but the number of immigrants who actually win elections is low. In contrast, the electoral system of the highly partisan, centralized city with district elections (New York) enables immigrants to elect many more of their members to the city council, but hampers immigrants' ability to build the wide-ranging coalitions needed to realize tangible political benefits and attain higher elective offices.

Part III, then, pushes us to debate what strategies immigrants should choose, as individuals and as members of a group, if they seek to enter into the political fabric of their receiving localities. Should a person settle in a neighborhood dense with his or her co-ethnics and unite with them in political activity, or should that person downplay his or her ethnicity in order to participate in an electoral coalition that already has some power and influence? Should an immigrant group seek political representation for itself, or durable coalitions with other groups in the city? Mollenkopf and Sonenshein and Rogers agree that coalition-building is the better option.

All three chapters, however, underscore the fact that immigrants may have little choice in their political strategies. In the United States, electoral systems, the many offices available, and partisan competition have a long and deep history that can be changed only slowly and by insiders. In Switzerland and (by implication) elsewhere, the racial and ethnic groups that already inhabit a city, its native-born residents' attitudes, and the rules that govern immigrants' admission to citizenship and legitimated political participation all condition the possibilities for bringing outsiders in.

# CHAPTER FIVE

# Swiss Citizenship

## A Municipal Approach to Participation?

## Gianni D'Amato

"The Federal Council [Swiss Government] is directly responsible to the people. The sovereign has decided. Its vote should be applied and there is nothing else to be added." With these words, Christoph Blocher, former minister of justice, endorsed the Swiss voters' September 2004 defeat of measures that would have widened access to citizenship for the immigrant second generation and introduced *jus soli* principles for the third generation (D'Amato and Skenderovic forthcoming). This was contrary to Swiss tradition, under which members of the government are supposed to indicate feasible solutions in their areas of responsibility and build bridges to those who have lost such a popular referendum. But this case was different. Just nine months before, Christoph Blocher, the charismatic leader of the radical right-wing populist Schweizerische Volkspartei (SVP; Swiss People's Party) had already broken the "magic formula" of Swiss concordance (under which the older parties shared power) to become part of the government. Given his party's strong opposition to such measures before he entered government, he had little inclination to back a fundamental reform of migrants' rights that he had inherited from his predecessor.

Indeed, mobilizing anti-immigrant sentiment was one of the main ways that the SVP attracted electoral support. In previous years, the SVP had mounted several attempts in the German part of Switzerland to shift decisions about naturalization from their customary location with local officials to popular referenda. Only an order from the Federal Supreme Court that municipalities should prohibit arbitrary procedures and argue their final decisions on citizenship applicants thwarted these efforts. The SVP thereafter attacked the Federal Supreme Court and central government as wanting to centralize the process of granting citizenship in order to sell Swiss nationality to undeserving immigrants and disempower the municipalities from making naturalization decisions. The party immediately started a political campaign to overthrow the new ruling of the Federal Supreme Court.

The failure of this attempt to reform the Swiss citizenship law was rooted both in the tensions between different levels of government and the ways in which Swiss citizens have historically valued citizenship. As a federal system—a "sister republic" of the United States, as Benjamin Franklin once called it (Abegg and Verein Migrationsmuseum Schweiz 2006)—municipalities have an unusual degree of influence over citizenship and naturalization, making it both a "natural experiment" and an interesting contrast with other European experiences.

## Immigrants as Political Actors

Social scientists have tended to see immigrants as workers, neighbors, parents, or school pupils but not as political subjects who influence our political communities or carry legitimate political and social claims. Because we see them move about discretely and almost unnoticed in our public spheres, only rarely do we become aware that they may have claims. Many are perceived to be demanding asylum or seeking protection from oppressive political regimes. As an expression of global crises, it may seem we are being surrounded by migrants who are menacing our economic and cultural equilibrium, an impression often reinforced by the media. The long-time residents from traditional countries of emigration who arrived after World War II, by contrast, no longer seem to be immigrants, but have become "invisible" in the public sphere of European states (Giugni and Passy 2006).

How do migrant populations define their relation to the political communities of their host countries? How do their political mobilization and claiming of rights contribute to the quality of our democracies? These questions have not been prominent in the literature (Miller 1981, 1999). Instead, the focus has been on sociostructural, socioeconomic, and demographic trends (see, e.g., Castles and Kosack 1973; Castles, Booth, and Wallace 1984; Miles 1982, 1986; Miles and Phizacklea 1977). Although these studies sometimes discuss how the state regulates admission or how public policy affects immigrant integration, they devote little attention to the mobilization of migrants themselves. They are seen instead as passive nonactors being influenced by these policies.

Some studies have considered the relationship between immigrants and ethnic minorities on one side and the native white majority on the other (see, e.g., Foner 1979; Royce 1982; Banton 1985; Rath 1988b; Etienne 1989). A few have focused on political participation and collective action of migrants. According to Ireland (1994), one school of thought analyzes mobilization through the lens of class theory, reducing race and ethnicity to class relations. They are characterized by a certain economic determinism that neglects the role of a political process in which migrants may shape the debates on migration and their social and political situation. A second school points to the impact of ethnic and racial identities on the political agenda. This substitutes a kind of cultural determination for the economic determinism of the neo-Marxist theorists. It also neglects the relation between the immigrants and their surrounding political and institutional contexts.

A third school of thought seeks to fill this gap by focusing on the political institutions of the host country (Ireland 1994). This approach emphasizes the importance of public policies and citizenship laws in shaping the situations of immigrants and the nature of ethnic relations. According to this approach, the mobilization of the immigrants and their possible alliances with native-born groups reflects not class divisions or ethnic identities but, rather, how migrants relate to the institutional context and the political process (Koopmans and Statham 2000a). In particular, the citizenship framework helps to channel political claim making.

## The Significance of Citizenship

A number of scholars have advanced the idea that national incorporation models shape the process of social inclusion (Soysal 1994; Castles 1995; Koopmans and Kriesi 1997; Favell 2001; Joppke 1998, 1999a; Brubaker 1992; Giugni and Passy 2002). According to Rogers Brubaker's seminal work (1992), citizenship has two critical qualities: universalism and social exclusion. It is universal in the sense that every citizen shares the same rights and duties; it is exclusive because noncitizens are not admitted to these rights. In other words, not all inhabitants of a state are citizens, indeed not all human beings have a state, which is always the state of a particular nation.

Citizenship allows access to a territory and regulates a person's interactions within the state. The rights of noncitizens are limited and never unconditional. Even privileged noncitizens can be excluded under certain circumstances. Given the dual authority of naturalization to grant full rights to immigrants and to facilitate their acceptance, it is a powerful tool through which nation-states secure social closure. There are only two possible ways of receiving citizenship: by ascription or by acquisition.

States govern access to citizenship in different ways. France has granted automatic citizenship to the second generation of immigrants since 1889, whereas Germany maintained until very recently a deeply rooted descent-based policy. In Switzerland, a nationalist renewal movement prevented the introduction of *jus soli* in this plurilingual republican nation at the turn of the last century. This reflects a distinction between *Staatsnation* and *Kulturnation*, the competing patterns of nation-building featured in France and Germany (Meinecke 1919). The French concept *Staatsnation* presumes a state-centered and assimilationist understanding of the nation, whereas German nationhood stems from the Romantic and the Prussian reform movements, both influenced by the French occupation of Germany in the nineteenth century. The Romantic Movement understood the nation to be a body of historically rooted, organically developed individualities, united by a distinctive *Volksgeist*. This was diametrically opposed to the French model, in which political unity was a precondition to, and the cultural unity was an expression of, the nation. The German tradition fundamentally offered aliens no option of incorporation (Brubaker 1992, 115).

However, Brubaker's dichotomist and formalist reduction of naturalization principles to *jus soli* and *jus sanguinis* does recognize ways that nation-states actually provide citizenship to immigrants. Marco Giugni and Florence Passy (2003) outline the dimensions of integration policies. Some nation-states demand full assimilation and require applicants to subordinate themselves to the ruling culture in order to gain citizenship. They base their national self-understanding on the seductive term *cultural nation* and call their program cultural homogeneity. Other host states accept the cultural norms of immigrants and demand only that they integrate into the public aspects of the dominant culture, often through various forms of civic participation. Giugni and Passy assign France to the civic assimilationist model because new French citizens must share republican values. They allocate Germany to the ethnic assimilationist model (although changes to its naturalization law in 2000 shifted it toward the French model). But where does Switzerland belong?

## Swiss Citizenship: A Local Affair?

The nineteenth-century French philologist Ernest Renan (1993) missed the point when, in a famous speech at the Sorbonne, he described the Helvetic Confederation as a nation founded on pure civic-political will. Swiss nation-building has certainly developed an approach to citizenship that remains distinct from the German and French models (Centlivres and Schnapper 1991, 149–61). However pluralist and accepting of national differences among the German-, French-, and Italian-speaking parts of Switzerland it may be at federal level, it remains as exclusionist and assimilationist at the local level as Germany and France.

Although Switzerland is said to be seven hundred years old, the contemporary federal state can be traced back to the Federal Constitution of 1848. The victory of the liberal, mostly Protestant cantons over the secessionist, Catholic-conservative cantons of the Sonderbund ("confederation apart") during the Civil War of 1847 established, for the first time, a permanent federal government that abolished the annual meetings of a loose confederation. Claiming political hegemony in the new state, the liberals learned from the failures committed by the first centralist Helvetic Republic (1798–1803) installed by the French occupation army. The new Federal Constitution respected the linguistic, religious, economic, and political cleavages of the new nation-state (Linder 1998, 8) and used federalism to shield the Catholic and French-speaking cantons from the unitary thrust of the central government. At the same time, the liberal founders used patriotic associations and shooting matches rooted in the founding myth of 1291 and other heroic battles against foreign oppressors to form a common national identity based in a liberal-republican political ethos (Braun 1970). Membership in the federal state thus had a dual nature: a national identity rooted in a liberal-republican political culture and a local identity rooted in membership in a cantonal municipality. Nation as a political category referred only to the republicanism of the state, whereas cantons and municipalities were decisive for everyday life. The political vocabulary of Switzerland uses *nation* carefully and sparingly. The only political institution claiming the attribute national is the Nationalrat, the chamber of representatives.

Naturalization is currently governed by the "Federal Law relative to Acquisition and Loss of Swiss Citizenship" (September 29, 1952), in a version modified in 1990. It requires that candidates prove they are worthy of being naturalized by showing they have adopted Swiss culture, which means local culture. It requires a minimum residence of twelve years, counting the years between ages 10 and 20 double. It grants the authority to determine whether candidates are worthy to the cantonal municipality. Local, not national, political actors thus determine access to membership and political rights in Switzerland. The federal office only initiates the process and receives the decision made by the canton. The local legislative body makes this decision, and the different cantons apply different procedures. Each candidate must pass an aptitude test demonstrating integration into the local community and demonstrate that he or she has observed local laws.

Cantonal citizenship commissions often use this aptitude test to filter out undesired candidates, for example those who are not cooperative or do not participate in local associations or events. Although the federal administration does not require an explicit assimilation, many municipalities and cantons, particularly in the German part of Switzerland, stress this. They require not only knowledge of laws and citizenship rights but also a more subjective embracing of cantonal culture. They look for an interiorization of local customs and habits that cannot be learned through socialization alone.

## Institutions Channeling the Opportunity Structures in Switzerland

Access to the political system, the level of state repression, configuration of power, and state capacity to implement decisions are the key aspects of the political opportunity structure and strongly shape and constrain the ways in which immigrant actors engage in political participation (see John Mollenkopf and Jennifer Hochschild, chap. 1, and part IV in this volume). In Switzerland, their key institutional features include federalism, municipal autonomy, and consociational and direct democracy.

### Federalism

Federalism has been the primary way in which the country has succeeded in accommodating its cultural and religious diversity. Switzerland is a confederation of twenty-six cantons, each of which has a great deal of autonomy in such policy fields as education, police, and taxes. The Swiss Parliament has two chambers, the National Council (*Nationalrat*, representing the people) and the State Council (*Ständerat*, representing the cantons). New laws must pass both chambers, but can be immediately vetoed by a popular referendum.

The mechanisms of influence are complex. The Swiss population does not directly elect the members of the government, the Federal Council; this is a prerogative of the parliament. The seven members of the Federal Council hold office for four years, during which the Parliament cannot hold a vote of no confidence. This gives the government a certain amount of autonomy, but it is restricted by two instruments of Swiss direct democracy: the referendum and the popular initiative. The popular initiative enables citizens to amend the constitution if a measure attracts the signatures of 100,000 voters within eighteen months. If 50,000 citizens request such an action within one hundred days of the publication of a federal law, it is also subject to a referendum. The passage of a veto requires both a majority of the popular vote and a majority of the cantons. Voters can also launch initiatives and referendums about cantonal laws at the cantonal and municipal levels.

Federalism has a great impact on many aspects of immigrant admission and integration, with education being the paradigmatic case. Not only does the education system allocate access to higher education, legitimating the unequal distribution of life opportunities (Moser and Berweger 2003; Organisation for Economic Co-operation and Development [OECD] 2004; Zahner 2005), but it is a key tool for social mobility and social integration. The cantons organize the Swiss educational system and want immigrants to adapt to the dominant cantonal language and culture. During the 1970s, cantonal education systems showed little respect for social and cultural differences and could not guarantee equal educational opportunities (Schuh 1987). Problems of school segregation persist; however, the federal education authorities (Schweizerische Erziehungsdirektorenkonferenz, EDK) regularly publish recommendations for the better integration of immigrant children. Some cantons have provided better support for immigrant children and sought their better integration into the school system (Truniger 2002b), but others have not implemented these recommendations and continue to be unfriendly toward migrant children. The more rural, German-speaking cantons have tended to set up separate schools for immigrant children (Truniger 2002a), whereas the French- and Italian-speaking areas of Switzerland have integrated all children in mainstream institutions.

## Municipal Autonomy

A relatively strong urban network has arisen within the larger Swiss political fragmentation (see Sandro Cattacin, chap. 16 in this volume). Municipal autonomy plays a key role in questions of citizenship and nationhood. The naturalization procedure involves a three-stage application: first municipal citizenship, then cantonal citizenship, and finally federal Swiss citizenship. Whereas the Federal Constitution requires only that foreigners live legally in Switzerland for more than twelve years, be familiar with Swiss culture, and comply with the laws, cantons and municipalities may impose additional requirements with regard to residence, finances, and fees. Their criteria quite often show a local ethnic logic, as demonstrated in the different approaches of the German- and the French-speaking cantons. The French have more formal procedures, but many German cantons require the demonstration of local political participation, which often transforms the question of citizenship into dislikes and prejudices (Helbling 2008). Small towns in the German part of Switzerland have used the Eastern European or oriental origins of the applicants as negative markers (Leuthold and Aeberhard 2002; Ehrenzeller and Good 2003). So, in many parts of the country, naturalization is built on local ethnicity.

Since the Federal Supreme Court decreed in July 2003 that public votes on naturalization are unconstitutional, a new debate has emerged on judicial authority over naturalization between those who favor the rule of law and those who see the granting of citizenship as a sovereign act of the citizenry. The Standing Committee on the Political Institutions of the Council of States (the upper house of parliament) argued in favor of the right of municipalities to hold votes on individual citizenship applications before the Federal Supreme Court. Nevertheless, it did ask that localities provide a justification for refusing naturalization to an applicant, even if the decision was taken by ballot.

## Consociational and Direct Democracy

Consociational democracy and direct democracy are more important for the understanding of integration *politics* than integration *policies*. As Hans Mahnig and Andreas Wimmer (2003) have lucidly stated, they have heightened the politicization of migration issues in Switzerland and helped to exclude migrants from political participation. *Consociational democracy* refers to the proportional representation of linguistic, political, and religious minorities in federal institutions and the use of measures other than simple majorities to balance competing political forces (Linder 1998). Positions in the government and higher administration are allocated as a proportion of their party affiliation ("magic formula") and of their linguistic and regional origins; representatives in turn are supposed to engage in a permanent process of compromise-building. The preparation of legislation involves a consultation procedure that enables the cantons, parties, associations, and sometimes also other interested groups to review the draft legislation. People who are not invited to take part in the consultation procedure can also state their views. All these views and possible objections of the cantons, parties, and associations are evaluated also with regard to the potential veto power of those who might reject a reform. The Federal Council debates the draft legal act in the light of this consultation and passes the main consensus points on to the parliament.

*Direct democracy* stems from the provisions for popular initiative and referenda at the federal and local levels. According to some observers, direct democracy led to the consociational system because all laws voted in parliament need the support of large alliances within the political elite to survive the potential threat of popular rejection (Neidhart 1970). This leads to long periods of non–decision making whenever the constituent parts of the system hold divergent views or find bargaining to be too sensitive, which has been the case with immigration. At the same time, political actors can also use the instruments of direct democracy to force political elites to address questions they have been avoiding. Since the 1960s, radical right-wing populist parties have used immigration to gain public support by claiming that the high number of immigrants are overforeignizing Swiss society. These xenophobic movements launched eight popular initiatives and several referenda to veto liberal government reforms and curb the presence of the foreigners. Although none of them passed, they have influenced public opinion and pushed the Swiss government toward more restrictive admission policies.

In recent years, the right-wing populist SVP, led by Christoph Blocher, has used an anti-immigrant agenda to push the federal government to adapt its policies to SVP political goals (see also Michael Minkenberg, chap. 10 in this volume). The SVP political campaign focused on the costs of immigration and the need for control, security, and restriction of immigration. It emerged as the strongest party in parliament, winning the biggest shares of votes in both the 2003 and 2007 general elections. Since Blocher took responsibility in the national party and started to campaign against immigrants, Europe, and the *classe politique* (to which he belonged), the SVP increased its electoral share from 11.9 percent (1991) to 26.7 percent (2003) and 28.9 percent in the 2007 election.

The 2003 SVP victory had already upset the traditional consociational system, which, since 1959, had distributed the seven seats in the Federal Council among the four leading political parties (the Liberal Radical Party, Social Democratic Party, Christian Democratic Party, and SVP). Following the elections, the SVP forced the parliament to accord them one more seat (at the cost of the Christian Democratic Party) in the Federal Council and to elect Blocher as a member of government. The historic leader of the SVP became minister of justice and police in charge of migration and asylum questions. The strengthened position of the SVP in the government let it to approve several of Blocher's restrictive proposals on illegal migration, undocumented workers, asylum law abuses, and unsatisfactory international cooperation with regard to the readmission of rejected asylum seekers (D'Amato and Skenderovic forthcoming).

In the 2007 electoral campaign, once again immigrants were made responsible for social disorders, criminality, youth violence, and welfare abuses. The posters accompanying the launch of the initiative to deport criminal immigrants, showing a white sheep throwing a black one out of country, attracted worldwide attention. The *New York Times* reported, that the "subliminal message of this campaign is that the influx of foreigners has somehow polluted Swiss society, straining the social welfare system and threatening the very identity of the country" (October 8, 2007).

Amazingly, the end of the campaign was—unusual for Switzerland—heavily focused on the figure of Christoph Blocher. The party wanted his position in the Federal Council to be strengthened through a larger share of the SVP in parliament. The strategy worked, and the party booked another incredible success in the October 21 election, displacing the Social Democrats and the Liberal Radical Party to the second row. The strengthened presence of the SVP in the Federal Council since 2003 put it in a win-win situation in which the party can set the agenda for the parliamentary debate and, if it fails, can launch a veto against any reform it opposes through a referendum. The tools of direct democracy enable them to highlight issues in ways that parliament cannot contain.

Even though a large minority of the electorate appreciated this double game between the government and the opposition, members of parliament increasingly disapproved and opposed the dysfunctional role played by Blocher, who refused to be merely one member among others of a consociational government; the cooptation and integration of Blocher into the federal government had failed. In December 2007, the parliament voted in Evelyn Widmer-Schlumpf, a moderate SVP representative, as new member of the Federal Council, manifesting their disapproval of the populist anti-parliamentarian strategy and style of Blocher and his party.

The style of Blocher's party convinced a wider constituency than just the people who had lost in the modernization of the rural, German-speaking, Protestant parts of the country, mainly men and traditional professionals. Since the 1990s, the SVP has enlarged its electorate in practically all social strata, particularly in the middle classes and urban areas. But decisive for its success was its ability to penetrate the French-speaking and Catholic cantons previously politically controlled by the Liberal Radical Party and the Christian Democrats. Surprisingly, even though the SVP electorate has nearly tripled in the last sixteen years, the share of those members opposing more opportunities for immigrants has not changed. Moreover, the leaders of the SVP have been able to mobilize that proportion of the population that, since the 1960s, has voted for xenophobic issues at popular referenda but elected other political parties (Skenderovic and D'Amato 2008).

The direct democratic possibilities of intervention offered by the political system, therefore, make it quite likely that the SVP will be able to use migration policy to reinforce its oppositional role in the coming years because controversial questions can never be contained in parliament alone. Other European countries may be able to adopt policies "behind closed doors" to extend political and social rights to migrants (Guiraudon 2000), but this is impossible in Switzerland. But even such a determined strategy may not always find popular support. An important point of reference is the defeat of the SVP in the balloting on June 1, 2008. A vote on "democratic naturalizations" was evoked by the desire of the party to use popular initiative to abolish national guidelines for the acquisition of Swiss citizenship, permitting municipalities once again to make arbitrary decisions about this matter. Its failure proved that even a strong and resolute party cannot always gain support, especially when its arguments offend the people's sense of equal and just access to rights.

## (Local) Citizenship as a Contested Political Field

Until the 1960s, immigrants in Switzerland mostly oriented their political activities toward their homelands. The Swiss political opportunity structure restricted the scope of action for immigrant elites to this activity (Kriesi 1995, Kriesi et al. 1995). For example, Italian immigrants lobbied consular, party, and union contacts in Italy. The public debate in Italy then moved from the domestic to bilateral and international arenas, transforming the immigrant rights debate into an issue between Italy and Switzerland. The renewal of a bilateral agreement in 1964 granted Italian immigrants increased civil and social rights in Switzerland. This induced Switzerland to make similar concessions to citizens of other countries, but it also mobilized the right-wing populist parties, which proposed a referendum to expel immigrants. Immigrants, in turn, reacted strongly against the referendum, focusing this second wave of immigrant politicization toward Swiss domestic politics. They formed alliances with solidarity organizations and got support from Swiss business organizations opposed to the nativist referendum. This higher level of support from established Swiss interest groups in the 1980s reinforced the shift of immigrant elites toward the Swiss political system (Cerutti 1992, 1994, 1995).

Since the 1980s, Switzerland has experienced three major waves of immigrant mobilization. Each focused on achieving political rights—specifically local voting rights, dual citizenship, and easier access to citizenship. Immigrants promoted the first two issues themselves. Although the last was part of a government project aimed at facilitating the integration of young immigrants through naturalization, immigrant groups actively supported it. Nativist resistance led to the defeat of the local voting rights and citizenship access measures, but the dual citizenship proposal was, surprisingly, successful. By the end of the 1980s, immigrant social-movement organizations considered themselves a stable minority in Swiss society, not transient guests. Consequently, they focused their campaign on making Swiss society more aware of their cause, as well as on helping their community become less isolated. The final goal of these demands was the political equality of foreigners (D'Amato 2001, 236).

The Swiss Federal Constitution allows foreigners to have political rights (Thürer 1989). Each canton has the prerogative of including foreigners in its political processes. For example, the cantons of Neuchâtel and Jura allow foreigners to vote in local elections. During the 1990s, referenda in several German-speaking cantons showed, however, that native citizens were not willing to concede political rights to foreigners, even long-term immigrant residents (Koopmans and Kriesi 1997). This happened only in Appenzell-Ausserrhoden, also the late-runner in granting political rights to women (at the end of the 1980s!). But, in the French-speaking west, Geneva, Vaud, and Fribourg joined Neuchâtel and Jura in granting political rights to foreigners.

Conservative voters have shown ample ability to deter such measures. In 2004, the federal government tried to make it easier for second-generation residents to become citizens and to introduce *jus soli* for the third generation, which would have benefited more than 400,000 second- and third-generation immigrants (Wanner and D'Amato 2003). Both a majority of the voters and a majority of the cantons rejected these measures in September 2004. The right-wing populist parties campaigned aggressively against the measures as a devaluation of Swiss citizenship and a diminution of local sovereignty (Kaya 2005). Voting patterns showed slight majorities in favor of the measures in the larger central cities, especially in the French-speaking part of the country, and heavy opposition in the suburbs, small towns, and rural areas, particularly in the German-speaking cantons.

The Swiss Parliament did approve dual citizenship in 1990. Many members of parliament remarked that the Swiss found it obvious that one should not lose one's original nationality when taking on another—as when Swiss became U.S. citizens. This decision did not face a popular referendum. Representatives of all the parties accepted the idea of dual nationality to improve the integration of young immigrants and to allow them to express their multiple loyalties. Unions and business associations both heavily favored the measure. The Swiss political elite was also generally open to European integration at the beginning of the 1990s and saw the political integration of European immigrants as a positive sign for Brussels.

The Swiss case, therefore, supports the idea that referenda are not helpful to immigrants when political rights are at stake. Switzerland and its immigrant population have, nevertheless, developed practices by which many immigrants acquire dual citizenship and Swiss political rights without having to make too many logistical or emotional sacrifices. As a result, the number of naturalizations has been growing (Wanner and D'Amato 2003).

## Conclusion

The granting of local voting rights to immigrants, dual nationality, and greater naturalization have not proceeded evenly in Switzerland, a multilevel state. The French-speaking part in the west has facilitated naturalization procedures and provided local voting rights, transforming this linguistic area into a sort of transnational democracy; in contrast, the dominant German-(and also the Italian-) speaking remainder of the country has moved in the opposite direction, constructing an ethnically bounded democracy (Peled 1992). As a result, only native-born citizens are entitled to universal liberal rights, whereas immigrants enjoy only a reduced form of these rights, mainly in the social and (to a lesser degree) civic sphere. Voters in many parts of the country maintain a deeply rooted skepticism toward newly arrived immigrants, whom they suspect are not trustworthy and whose loyalty to the society and state they cannot take for granted. In rural and periurban Switzerland, established political actors feel committed to a deeply Rousseauean belief in republican traditions. For them, democracy can work only within conditions of strong cultural homogeneity and deep communal bonds reflecting a strong faith in common values.

This position stands in deep contrast to the principles embedded in the Swiss constitution and may ultimately lead the country to a future conflict between the partisans of the (national) rule of law and supporters of (local) popular sovereignty, as embodied in reactions to the declaration of the Federal Supreme Court that popular balloting of naturalization was unconstitutional. The Federal Supreme Court judges signaled that, even though foreigners may find themselves outside the procedures of legitimate decision making, they are nevertheless protected by the constitution. The powerful devotees of an absolute and unlimited sovereignty interpreted that decision as an attack on the traditions of direct democracy and as a devaluation of Swiss citizenship. This struggle is ongoing.

The case of Switzerland thus shows that sovereignty can never be absolute if we are to prevent democracy from drifting toward an unbound, democratic form of "totalitarian" rule (Lübbe 2004). Switzerland is still a long way from this situation, but the deep conflict over citizenship rights for its large immigrant population raises the possibility that the country will move toward it. The possibility of a transnationalization of citizenship is confronted by the risk of renationalization through xenophobic politics. Both sides are highly mobilized, and both have strong conceptions of citizenship. It remains to be seen whether Swiss civil society will favor the enlargement of its democratic base, as has already happened in the western part of the country, or will continue to see it through the calculus of advantage by the native majority.

# CHAPTER SIX

# The New Urban Politics of Integration

## A View from the Gateway Cities

*John H. Mollenkopf and Raphael Sonenshein*

Major population shifts have always affected local politics first in the United States, having an impact on national politics only after a long and winding trail. When a large number of people reach new destinations, established residents often react unfavorably to their arrival, which perturbs local politics. In time, the new entrants find their way into local politics through some combination of organizing themselves, being organized by others, challenging the status quo, and allying with established groups. The 36 million mainly European immigrants who migrated to the United States between 1840 and 1930 literally built its great cities and were deeply implicated in the rise of urban political machines and the transformation of local government structures and functions. During and after World War II, the great migration of African Americans from the South into the industrial cities of the East, Midwest, and even the Pacific Coast states set off political tremors that led to a new racialized politics of city, state, and nation.

Since 1965, millions of immigrants from Latin America, the Caribbean, and Asia, as well as Eastern Europe and the Middle East, have once more transformed urban America. Most have settled in the biggest cities of New York, New Jersey, Florida, Illinois, and California, but they are now spreading beyond these traditional receiving areas. New York City, now (as then) a great magnet for immigrants and a major point of arrival, has been joined by southern California as a new major gateway and destination. By 2005, New York City had 8.1 percent of the nation's foreign-born and Los Angeles County had 9.8 percent. Together with their surrounding metropolitan areas, these two regions accounted for almost one-third of all immigrants to the United States.

Although the role of immigrants in politics has long been a theme in scholarship on New York City, it is just emerging in the study of Los Angeles. Comparing the political impacts of immigration in the two largest cities will go a long way toward clarifying how the new immigration will affect the United States as a whole. Both cities have advanced service economies derived from their position as major nodes in the global urban system. Both have dynamic and complex populations in which new immigrants are rapidly gaining ground on older native-born populations, including African Americans. But the two cities have diametrically different local political systems and political cultures. Los Angeles is highly reformed, fragmented, and nonpartisan, whereas New York is highly partisan and centralized. This pairing allows us to ask how the variation in political structure, dynamics, or culture might affect the political progress of old and new immigrant minority groups in the two cities. The fact that New York and Los Angeles have economic and demographic similarities but political differences has led to a small cottage industry of comparative studies (Halle 2003; Kaufmann 2004; Logan and Mollenkopf 2003; Mollenkopf, Olson, and Ross 2001; Wong 2006). Each city has, of course, generated many studies of its political development, including works by the authors of this chapter, who each keep a "weather eye" on the other city (Sonenshein 1993, 2004; Mollenkopf 1992, 2003).

The highly diverse residents of the first and second largest U.S. cities have generated some of the most interesting local U.S. politics. In 1950, both cities had predominantly white populations with new and growing African American and native Hispanic minority populations; in subsequent decades, these groups struggled to achieve representation within the white-dominated systems. By the early 1990s, white Catholic Republicans, Richard Riordan and Rudolph Giuliani, had succeeded the first—and only—black mayors elected in the two cities, Tom Bradley and David Dinkins, despite heavily Democratic Party registrations and dwindling white populations. Finally, after term limits forced Riordan and Giuliani out of office, Latino candidates waged impressive mayoral campaigns in 2001 and 2005. Los Angeles and New York thus both illustrate the problematic nature of minority and immigrant empowerment in the polyethnic cities of the post–civil rights era.

Although white candidates won the mayoralties over candidates with minority support in both cities in 2001, Antonio Villaraigosa became the first Mexican American mayor of Los Angeles in 2005; however, Fernando Ferrer failed for the second time to become first Puerto Rican mayor of New York. The major immigrant heritage groups have gained representation in both city councils. Four members of the fifteen-person Los Angeles City Council are Mexican American (although none was an immigrant), another has partial Mexican-American ancestry, and three are African American. The New York City fifty-one-person council has three West Indian, two Dominican, one Chinese, nine Puerto Rican, and ten African-American members. Although immigrant and minority representation on the New York City Council appears a bit more diverse, council members in Los Angeles are individually more powerful than their counterparts.

This chapter addresses one relatively simple and a second more complex question. The simple question is, what do recent mayoral elections in New York and Los Angeles teach us about where the rising new immigrant minority groups fit within the larger constellation of racial and ethnic politics in the two cities? With whom do they align and how much influence do they exercise as a result? The more complex question is, how do the political arrangements of the two cities encourage or retard the political empowerment of new immigrant groups? Does the larger, stronger, more partisan, more centralized political system of New York City provide a more capacious political opportunity structure for immigrant groups than the smaller, weaker, less partisan, more fragmented system of Los Angeles (Eisinger 1973; Tarrow 1994; Koopmans and Statham 2000c)? And do the institutional dynamics work the same way at all levels of political participation, from voting to attaining legislative office to playing important roles in mayoral coalitions to winning the mayoralty? Before returning to these questions, however, let us begin by setting the demographic and political stage in the two cities.

## The Arrangement of Local Political Institutions

Los Angeles is the quintessential fragmented metropolis. The city of Los Angeles is only one of eighty-eight municipalities within Los Angeles County. The city provides such property-related services as police, fire, zoning, and planning, whereas the county government provides health and welfare services. Water and power are delivered by a semi-independent authority, and the public schools are also run by an independent body, although Mayor Villaraigosa won direct authority over a few high schools. Los Angeles city politics is both formally and substantively nonpartisan. It has relatively few city council members—fifteen for a population of almost 4 million people—who are elected for staggered four-year terms. Los Angeles City Council districts are the largest in the nation for a city with members elected by district.

Although most candidates for city office in Los Angeles are Democrats, the Democratic Party is weakly organized at the city and county levels and does not strongly influence the nonpartisan primaries for local office. Many city agencies are overseen by commissions whose members are appointed by the mayor for relatively lengthy terms, thus buffering them from direct mayoral control. A new city charter in 1999 began to erode some of that independence, giving mayors the authority to unilaterally remove most city commissioners (Sonenshein 2004). The LA city budget for the year ending in 2006 was just under $6 billion, or approximately $1,500 per resident. (Other levels of government, such as the Los Angeles departments of Water and Power and the Harbor, and the Los Angeles Unified School District, not to mention the Los Angeles County government, also spend comparable amounts of money. When the proprietary departments are included, the city budget doubles.)

New York City government, on the other hand, is highly centralized and politicized, with persistent machine politics. New York City encompasses five counties, whose borough presidents have only residual and largely symbolic powers. The mayor exercises virtually untempered authority over a wide range of services. The current mayor, Michael Bloomberg, even won administrative control of the New York City school system. Virtually all local governmental functions, save the mass transit system, the Port Authority, and the city university, are under the mayor's purview. The city council is one of the largest in the nation, with fifty-one members, or about 70 percent more council members per capita than Los Angeles. Local elections are partisan, Democratic Party nominees win most of the contests, and regular Democratic Party organizations exercise significant influence over party primaries. Regulars frequently use arcane election regulations to knock challengers off the ballot. The city budget for the fiscal year ending in 2006 was $54 billion, or roughly $6,750 per resident, almost five times larger than the Los Angeles city budget.

## Immigration and Ethnic Politics:
## An Uncertain Connection

The study of minority (and immigrant) political incorporation builds on the idea that new population groups can ultimately translate their demographic growth into political influence, however many obstacles they face and however long it takes, by mobilizing their base, attaining political representation, contending to be part of the governing coalition, and finally forming administrations that will adopt public policies responsive to their interests (Browning, Marshall, and Tabb 1984). The European migrants of the late-nineteenth and early-twentieth centuries and the African Americans who migrated to the large U.S. cities in the mid-twentieth century both followed this trajectory.

The nineteenth-century immigrant groups mobilized, shifted old alliances, and created new coalitions. Their progress turned urban politics into ethnic politics, not immigrant politics. As Max Weber reported after visiting America in 1906, a new creature was invented in its immigrant-industrial cities: the professional politician who derived his livelihood from organizing the vast European immigrant populations that had accumulated in them. They transformed the dominance of economic elites into party-based, mass-organized systems of power. Similarly, the gradual incorporation of African Americans and, to a lesser extent, native Latino groups after World War II converted urban ethnic politics into racial politics. Whatever the frustrations, blockages, conflicts, compromises, and disappointments, we can say that ethnic and racial incorporation took place in both sequences.

Today, the new waves of immigration from Asia and Latin America face local political systems in which parties and political organizations have atrophied in the face of candidate-centered, money-driven elections and in which nonparty organizations, such as industry interest groups, labor unions, and racial and ethnic hierarchies, play more important roles (Gerstle and Mollenkopf 2001). It will take a long time for this new wave of immigrants to have as much impact on urban politics as did the European immigrants and African Americans, but their partial success implies that we should not be too quick to say the newcomers will never have such an impact.

The political incorporation of the new immigrants is likely to take a different path than that of African Americans. The new immigrants are not a distinctive race. African Americans started out city life as a relatively homogeneous group, often characterized as having a "linked racial fate" (Dawson 1994, 10) approach to politics. Immigrant groups arrive from many national origins and do not cohere into a single people. Usually, they start out by defining themselves in national terms (e.g., Korean American), although some political elites may embrace wider pan-ethnic identities (e.g., Asian American). These disparate groups vary in the recency of their arrival, their socioeconomic characteristics, their propensity to naturalize, their voter participation, and their partisanship. All the African Americans who came to northern cities had the right to participate in elections, at least on paper. Although faced with racial discrimination, the barriers to their collective political action were far lower than those confronting the new immigrants. Discrimination made African Americans more politically cohesive, although, like any group, they had more internal differences than the "shared racial fate" perspective often acknowledged (Cohen 1999).

As immigrant communities in New York and Los Angeles have grown in size, naturalized, and begun to vote, they have gradually become potentially important political constituencies, now constituting one-third of the voting-age citizens in both places (combining naturalized adults with their native-born adult children). As their numbers grow and factions within the political system find advantages in gaining their support (or blocking their ascent), immigrant communities become politically relevant even if they are slow to form into ethnic voting blocks.

With other observers (Skerry 1993; Barone 2002), we hypothesize that, in contrast to black involvement with racial politics, ethnic politics will shape the incorporation of immigrant groups. In other words, immigrants from different national origins will not coalesce into one large voting block but will be drawn, instead, into the existing ethnic voting alignments made up of people who are their ethnic nearest neighbors. In time, new arrivals may bolster the size of these groups, which began with earlier immigrants, sustaining their political force. Within these alignments, under the right circumstances, we may also see a certain degree of pan-ethnic identity emerge, such as Latino or Asian American.

In other words, immigration does not so much create a politics of immigration as it enlivens and modifies the preexisting ethnic politics. It seems likely to us that the immigrant communities will achieve representation and enter into the larger political system in this way. Of course, acquiring citizenship is a key part of the transition from immigration to ethnic politics. Although local practices inhibited African Americans from enacting their rights for a long time, the civil rights era definitely widened the scope for black voting. The most recent immigrants to the United States face a taller barrier—many lack the most basic resources for political participation, creating major gaps between who lives in a city and who can vote in its elections. That Mexican Americans in Los Angeles and the West Indians and Dominicans of New York have managed to generate significant political representation despite the large numbers of noncitizens from these backgrounds testifies to the strength of an immigrant-enhanced ethnic politics.

## Evolving Political Demography

Although both cities have been growing overall, the populations of native whites have been declining, although more rapidly in the population than the eligible electorate. From the 1950s through the 1980s, they were being replaced by native-born minority groups (African Americans and Puerto Ricans in New York; African Americans and Mexican Americans in Los Angeles). From the 1980s to the present, new immigrants have been supplanting native-born minorities as well as whites, and immigration has become the force driving population growth in the two cities (Frey and Liaw 2005). As shown in table 6.1, as of the 2000 census, more than one-half the people in Los Angeles lived in households headed by a foreign-born person and the voting-age citizens in these households made up one-third of the eligible electorate of Los Angeles. Table 6.2 shows similar patterns for New York City.

Such large demographic shifts ultimately lead to the reorganization of political cleavages, especially when they change the active electorate. In the immediate

**Table 6.1**  Major immigrant-origin groups in Los Angeles, 2000

| Region or country of origin | Immigrant-origin population | | Immigrant-origin voting-age citizens | |
|---|---|---|---|---|
| | Number | Percentage of total | Number | Percentage of total |
| Mexico | 945,196 | 45.4 | 181,341 | 30.7 |
| Central America | 448,708 | 21.6 | 86,310 | 14.6 |
| Middle East (including Iran) | 95,766 | 4.6 | 51,246 | 8.7 |
| Philippines | 95,515 | 4.6 | 47,043 | 8.0 |
| Korea | 85,032 | 4.1 | 31,009 | 5.2 |
| Western Europe | 66,741 | 3.2 | 48,692 | 8.2 |
| Former Soviet Union | 66,741 | 3.2 | 29,349 | 5.0 |
| Other Asia | 63,120 | 3.0 | 27,500 | 4.7 |
| China | 40,022 | 1.9 | 21,029 | 3.6 |
| Total immigrant origin | 2,081,833 | 100.0 | 590,768 | 100.0 |
| Total in Los Angeles | 3,613,154 | 57.6 | 1,771,192 | 33.4 |

*Note:* Classified by foreign nativity and birthplace of head of household.

**Table 6.2**  Largest immigrant origin groups in New York City, 2000

| Region or country of origin | Immigrant-origin population | | Immigrant-origin voting-age citizens | |
|---|---|---|---|---|
| | Number | Percentage of total | Number | Percentage of total |
| NH Caribbean | 806,816 | 21.8 | 335,225 | 24.9 |
| Dominican Republic | 524,060 | 14.2 | 157,031 | 14.2 |
| West Europe | 483,074 | 13.0 | 269,317 | 13.0 |
| China | 319,438 | 8.6 | 132,039 | 9.2 |
| Ecuador, Colombia, Peru | 288,517 | 7.8 | 90,968 | 6.4 |
| Former Soviet Union | 222,174 | 6.0 | 95,191 | 6.7 |
| Other Asian | 177,400 | 4.8 | 48,615 | 3.4 |
| Mexico | 159,522 | 4.3 | 14,206 | 1.0 |
| Africa | 123,901 | 3.3 | 36,722 | 2.6 |
| India | 87,467 | 2.4 | 28,256 | 2.0 |
| Korea | 83,998 | 2.3 | 26,221 | 1.8 |
| Total immigrant origin | 3,703,559 | 100.0 | 1,428,626 | 100.0 |
| Total in New York | 8,004,759 | 46.3 | 4,687,337 | 30.5 |

*Note:* Classified by foreign nativity and birthplace of household head. NH, non-Hispanic.

post–World War II period, when the minority populations of both cities were small relative to native whites, intrawhite cleavages dominated the politics of the two cities. Protestant Republicans competed with Catholic and Jewish Democrats in Los Angeles, and Catholics and Jews competed within the Democratic Party in New York. Los Angeles had a Republican mayor between 1953 and 1961. He was succeeded by a conservative Democrat, Sam Yorty, who served between 1961 and 1973. In New York, the post-war mayors were white Catholic Democrats (William O'Dwyer, Vincent Impellitteri, and, for three terms, Robert Wagner). All were more or less aligned with the regular Democratic organizations (McNickle 1993).

As their native minority populations grew into the electorate but could not break into the cadre of elected officials, the intrawhite politics evolved as bi- or multiracial challenges to the white political establishment emerged, aiming to place African Americans, Puerto Ricans, Mexican Americans, and white liberal reformers into offices where they could exercise more power. From the late 1960s through the 1980s, the civil rights era was marked by these struggles in cities across the country (Browning, Marshall, and Tabb 2003). Even though they did not achieve everything that the civil rights activists wanted, they nonetheless made quite real gains.

In Los Angeles, a coalition of African Americans and liberal whites (especially Jewish Democrats living on the west side) elected Mayor Tom Bradley, that city's first African American mayor, for five terms between 1973 and 1993 (Sonenshein 1993). African Americans and Mexican Americans slowly joined the city council and Los Angeles County Board of Supervisors. (Mexican Americans remained highly underrepresented compared to their presence in the population, even during Bradley's heyday.) The 1992 riots enabled a white Republican, Richard Riordan, to succeed Bradley for two terms, keeping the biracial minority coalition at bay. But the question of its future came back on the table in 2001 and 2005.

Results were even more mixed in New York. Only in 1989, for one term, was a coalition of African Americans, Puerto Ricans, and liberal whites able to elect a black mayor, David Dinkins (Mollenkopf 1992). In all the other years between 1977 and the present, relatively conservative mayors held office, including four successive victories by white Republicans between 1993 and 2005. At all other levels of office holding, however, native minority groups made gradual but steady progress in terms of gaining seats in the city council, state legislature, borough presidencies, and city comptroller. Somewhat out of political sight, however, immigration was already shifting the ground underneath the tension between native whites and native minority groups.

Los Angeles and New York have attracted immigrants from many national origins, but in different mixes. Mexicans dominate the migration to Los Angeles, as table 6.1 indicates, followed by Central Americans and a host of smaller groups. New York has drawn more broadly from the West Indies and Haiti, the Dominican Republic, China, South America, India, Korea, and elsewhere in Asia, as table 6.2 indicates. Table 6.3 gives the overall picture of all the racial groups by immigrant origin. Los Angeles clearly has far more Latino immigrants, whereas New York City has more native-born Latinos (primarily Puerto Ricans who, even though they migrated from a Caribbean Island, are U.S. citizens). The African American share is roughly comparable, but the black population of New York is bolstered by a substantial number of those living in immigrant-headed households, whereas the black population of Los Angeles is almost entirely native stock. Both cities have comparable Asian immigrant populations, although tables 6.1 and 6.2 show that the Chinese are much more prominent in New York and the Filipinos and Koreans are much more prominent in Los Angeles. Finally, both cities have fairly substantial white immigrant populations, although Iranians

**Table 6.3**  Race and nativity in New York and Los Angeles (%), 2000

| Group | Total population | | | Voting-age citizens | | |
|---|---|---|---|---|---|---|
| | New York City | City of Los Angeles | Rest of Los Angeles County | New York City | City of Los Angeles | Rest of Los Angeles County |
| NHW NB | 24.6 | 21.9 | 26.6 | 35.4 | 38.0 | 39.8 |
| NHW FB | 10.4 | 7.6 | 4.8 | 9.1 | 8.0 | 4.7 |
| NHB NB | 14.4 | 9.7 | 7.8 | 17.3 | 14.2 | 9.9 |
| NHB FB | 10.0 | 1.0 | 0.5 | 7.4 | 0.8 | 0.4 |
| Latino NB | 11.9 | 7.6 | 12.6 | 13.4 | 9.5 | 14.3 |
| Latino FB | 15.2 | 39.2 | 31.1 | 7.7 | 15.9 | 15.3 |
| NHA NB | 0.9 | 1.5 | 1.8 | 1.0 | 2.6 | 2.6 |
| NHA FB | 9.4 | 8.1 | 11.0 | 5.9 | 7.2 | 9.4 |
| Other NH NB | 1.0 | 1.7 | 2.0 | 1.2 | 2.3 | 2.2 |
| Other NH FB | 2.4 | 1.8 | 1.8 | 1.5 | 1.5 | 1.4 |
| Total number | 7,822,712 | 3,613,128 | 5,736,374 | 4,527,490 | 1,771,897 | 3,068,344 |

*Source:* 2000 U.S. Census 5% Public Use Microdata Sample.
*Note:* People living in households classified by head of household. FB, foreign-born; NB, native-born; NH, non-Hispanic; NHA, non-Hispanic Asian; NHB, non-Hispanic black; NHW, non-Hispanic white.

play a fairly prominent role in Los Angeles whereas immigrants from the former Soviet Union gravitated toward New York City.

In the city of Los Angeles, people of Mexican descent made up 45 percent of those living in immigrant-headed households in 2000. The next biggest groups were Salvadorans, Guatemalans, Armenians, Iranians, Filipinos, Koreans, residents of the former Soviet Union, and Chinese, although no group after the Central Americans accounted for as much as 5 percent of the immigrant origin population. The Mexican migration to Los Angeles has been so long-standing that many Mexican Americans are third generation and beyond; at the same time, very recent migration from Mexico has been massive. Thus, the Mexican-origin population in Los Angeles includes highly assimilated people whose parents were born here as citizens along with people who arrived just yesterday. This has sometimes created a level of cleavage between the two groups (Acuña 1996; Gutiérrez 1998). Although the comparison is hardly exact, third-generation Mexican Americans in Los Angeles might be compared to Puerto Ricans, whereas recent Mexican immigrants may have more in common with other recent immigrants from Latin America.

Yet all Mexican immigrants to Los Angeles can connect with, or be connected with, the existing ethnic politics networks. Because of the size of the Mexican community and its historic location on the city's east side, new immigrants bolster the populations required for forming city council districts during reapportionment even if they cannot vote. By contrast, the new Salvadoran immigrants have often flocked to South Los Angeles, historically an African American area. With their low level of citizenship and their lack of a previous ethnic bloc in the area, whose numbers they might bolster, these new immigrants find themselves at political sea, outvoted by African Americans and cut off from the Mexican-dominated Latino political structure. Similarly, West Indians in New York have gravitated toward the peripheries of existing African

American neighborhoods, whereas Dominicans have established a major zone of arrival in the Washington Heights neighborhood of northern Manhattan.

As noted, New York has a more diverse immigrant population that is not dominated by any one group, as is the case in Los Angeles. Indeed, table 6.2 shows that the biggest single national origin group in New York, Dominicans, makes up only 14 percent of the population in immigrant households, although West Indians are larger (21.8 percent) if we put all the island nations together. Those whose families hail from Colombia, Ecuador, and Peru are also a significant presence, and the New York Mexican-origin population has also been growing rapidly in recent years. Asian groups are also large, with the Chinese leading (8.6 percent), followed by Indians (2.4 percent), and Koreans (2.3 percent). Finally, like the Armenians and Persians in Los Angeles, a large immigrant population from the republics of the former Soviet Union (6.0 percent) is in New York. (Los Angeles has also attracted this group, although in smaller numbers.) Both cities also have remnants of the traditional European immigrant groups, although they are more numerous in New York.

One clear difference between the two cities is that Mexicans and Central Americans dominate the immigrant population of Los Angeles to such an extent that they could reasonably claim to speak for the interests of most immigrants. And Latino ethnic politics in Los Angeles has largely been Mexican American politics. No similar group can lay claim to representing the diverse immigrant population of New York. Both cities have growing Asian communities that, like the Latino communities, stand ambivalently between blacks and whites but do not fit comfortably into either. The Asian groups are quite heterogeneous, but they tend to have high rates of human and financial capital accumulation and some detachment from U.S.-style ethnic and racial politics (Wong 2006). Despite having nearly a half million Asian American residents, only one Asian person, Michael Woo, former council member, has ever been elected to public office in Los Angeles. (He ran for mayor against Richard Riordan and lost.) Similarly, New York has only elected one Asian member to the city council.

The vast differences among immigrants in terms of class, culture, communal organization, and political heritage suggest, as we have argued, that they will make a fragmented, varied, and perhaps halting progress toward political empowerment. The bottom right-hand cells of tables 6.1 and 6.2 show, nevertheless, that immigrant-origin voters have come to be a substantial part of the eligible electorates of the two cities. In Los Angeles, those living in households headed by Latino immigrants make up 16 percent of the voting-age citizens and Asians make up almost 8 percent. As Wong (2006) has recently explored, a critical question is how they are mobilized in relationship to whites and blacks and how the two groups will relate to one another. (Clearly, blacks and Asians have experienced tension in Los Angeles, particularly after the 1992 riot, but this tension has also sparked significant efforts to build new working relationships between the groups.) The potential electorate of New York also has substantial shares of immigrant Hispanic and Asian people but with the added feature of a large black immigrant population (Rogers 2006). The 2001 and 2005 mayoral elections provide some interesting evidence of how these groups have lined up.

## Recent Electoral Competition

We can use the lens of the 2001 and 2005 mayoral elections to look at these questions. In 2001, term limits forced out popular incumbents in both cities—Mayor Richard J. Riordan in Los Angeles and Mayor Rudolph W. Giuliani in New York. Both might be considered anomalous for their settings. Born not far from Giuliani's birthplace in New York City, Riordan was a wealthy white Catholic Republican attorney who was elected in the wake of the Los Angeles riots of 1992 to succeed long-serving African-American mayor Tom Bradley. Similarly, Giuliani, a white Catholic Republican former federal prosecutor and Reagan administration official, displaced a black predecessor, incumbent Mayor David Dinkins. Both were determined to return government to its basics, lower taxes, promote development, and reassert law and order after periods in which a more liberal coalition had held sway. Both succeeded in these missions. At the same time, their political momentum seemed to have run its course by the 2001 elections, permitting new forces to emerge. Given how demographic change had altered the potential electorates of each city, the time seemed right to alter political representation patterns.

### The 2001 Mayoral Elections

The 2001 mayoral elections were momentous in both cities. In Los Angeles, the charismatic Antonio Villaraigosa, a past speaker of the California Assembly, was seeking to become first modern Latino mayor of that city. Villaraigosa's father was a Mexican immigrant and his mother was California-born of Mexican descent. In the nonpartisan primary, in which all candidates run on the same ballot, he faced another Latino and several whites, including a popular city attorney, James Hahn, whose father had long represented the black neighborhoods of Los Angeles on the County Board of Supervisors.

Villaraigosa came in first during the primary, but lost the general election run-off to Hahn. According to the *Los Angeles Times* exit poll, whites cast a bare majority of the votes in this general election, with blacks accounting for 17 percent and Latinos 22 percent of the total. The great majority of Latinos favored Villaraigosa, as did a minority of whites, but four-fifths of the black voters favored Hahn; along with three-fifths of the white voters, that was enough to put him in office (Sonenshein and Pinkus 2002).

Clearly, however, something was moving under the surface. Villaraigosa's chances had been bolstered by an immigration-driven increase in the ethnic bloc potential of Latinos. In 1993, Latinos cast only 8 percent of the votes in the mayoral election. After the passage of the anti-immigrant Proposition 187 in 1994, a major increase in Latino citizenship and voter registration occurred, concentrated in the greater Los Angeles area. Immigration was being transformed into ethnic politics. In the 2001 run-off election, Latinos cast 22 percent of all votes, according to the *Los Angeles Times* exit poll.

Table 6.4 shows the outcome of these two elections, summing the vote by classifying each precinct in terms of its predominant racial group. Note that the open

**Table 6.4** Primary and general election results for 2001 and 2005 by racial majority of precincts, Los Angeles

|  | White | Black | Latino | Asian | Total |
|---|---|---|---|---|---|
| **2001 primary** |  |  |  |  |  |
| Total votes | 194,151 | 34,822 | 158,925 | 5,915 | 393,813 |
| Villariagosa (%) | 33.7 | 19.4 | 48.5 | 37.5 | 38.5 |
| Hahn (%) | 23.9 | 83.7 | 29.6 | 37.3 | 31.7 |
| **2001 general** |  |  |  |  |  |
| Total votes | 281,277 | 48,297 | 229,891 | 8,263 | 577,699 |
| Villariagosa (%) | 41.7 | 22.1 | 57.5 | 43.4 | 46.5 |
| Hahn (%) | 58.3 | 77.9 | 42.5 | 56.6 | 53.5 |
| **2005 primary** |  |  |  |  |  |
| Total votes | 213,853 | 33,344 | 152,272 | 6,335 | 405,804 |
| Villaraigosa (%) | 26.6 | 21.5 | 46.1 | 31.8 | 33.6 |
| Hahn (%) | 25.5 | 18.9 | 22.1 | 40.0 | 23.9 |
| **2005 general** |  |  |  |  |  |
| Total votes | 239,860 | 38,629 | 206,869 | 7,705 | 498,709 |
| Villaraigosa (%) | 51.5 | 57.5 | 67.5 | 48.0 | 58.6 |
| Hahn (%) | 48.5 | 42.5 | 32.5 | 52.0 | 41.4 |

*Note:* Absentee ballots allocated to precinct totals.

nonpartisan primary draws relatively fewer voters than the general election. As the multicandidate field was narrowed down to two in 2001, Villaraigosa gained across the field, but Hahn gained even more, attracting votes that had gone to other white candidates, holding his commanding lead in black neighborhoods, and doing surprisingly well in Latino precincts. Table 6.4 shows that immigration does not create its own constituency, at least in the case of Asian Americans, who were fairly evenly split during the primary but who clearly shifted away from the immigrant-origin candidate in the general election.

The prospect of electing a Latino mayor in New York City also emerged in 2001 but for different reasons. In the months leading up to the Democratic primary election, slated to be held on September 11, 2001, candidate Fernando Ferrer, the Puerto Rican former borough president of the Bronx, built relatively strong support among African-American elected officials and public opinion. This was based partly on his having participated in the protests against the murder of Amadou Diallo; partly on black leaders', particularly Reverend Al Sharpton, protesting against the U.S. Navy's use of the Puerto Rican island of Vieques as a bombing range; and partly on the desire among black leadership to supplant the Giuliani administration with a minority-friendly administration in which they had a large hand in putting in office.

Ferrer's leading opponent, Mark Green, the Public Advocate, had historically received support from black voters in his previous campaigns. A well-known white liberal, he had served as consumer affairs commissioner in the Dinkins administration before becoming public advocate. The presumptive Republican nominee, a billionaire former Democratic businessman, Michael Bloomberg, had never held public office. Yet he had growing support from the relatively conservative constituencies that had supported Mayors Giuliani and Edward I. Koch and an unlimited amount of money to spend on the campaign.

**Table 6.5**  Primary, run-off, and general election results for 2001 and 2005 by racial majority of precincts, New York City

|  | White | Black | Latino | Asian | Total |
|---|---|---|---|---|---|
| **2001 primary** |  |  |  |  |  |
| Total votes | 340,629 | 229,057 | 184,320 | 22,229 | 780,396 |
| Ferrer (%) | 13.4 | 57.4 | 64.8 | 30.0 | 35.8 |
| Green (%) | 35.7 | 35.3 | 17.6 | 29.6 | 31.1 |
| **2001 run-off** |  |  |  |  |  |
| Total votes | 346,853 | 224,547 | 192,790 | 20,796 | 790,019 |
| Ferrer (%) | 22.5 | 66.3 | 76.7 | 45.8 | 49.0 |
| Green (%) | 87.5 | 33.7 | 23.3 | 54.2 | 51.0 |
| **2001 general** |  |  |  |  |  |
| Total votes | 840,719 | 325,702 | 255,491 | 52,509 | 1,519,303 |
| Green (%) | 35.9 | 73.5 | 55.0 | 45.7 | 47.9 |
| Bloomberg (%) | 62.4 | 24.6 | 43.0 | 52.7 | 50.3 |
| **2005 primary** |  |  |  |  |  |
| Total votes | 212,205 | 135,132 | 121,167 | 12,316 | 493,459 |
| Ferrer (%) | 25.0 | 40.3 | 64.1 | 43.6 | 39.0 |
| Weiner (%) | 48.5 | 13.8 | 10.5 | 28.4 | 28.2 |
| Fields (%) | 7.5 | 33.3 | 10.6 | 8.9 | 15.4 |
| **2005 general** |  |  |  |  |  |
| Total votes | 671,162 | 295,181 | 269,269 | 44,661 | 1,289,919 |
| Ferrer (%) | 22.9 | 51.3 | 66.3 | 35.7 | 39.0 |
| Bloomberg (%) | 73.6 | 47.1 | 32.1 | 62.0 | 58.4 |

*Note:* Percentages do not sum to 100 due to minor candidates.

The September 11 attacks threw the primary and general election season into a fair degree of chaos and changed the political dynamics of the city (Mollenkopf 2005). During the two weeks when the primary was postponed, Ferrer continued to consolidate his black-Latino coalition and finished first but not with enough votes to avoid a run-off. His strongest base was among voters in Latino areas, but he also drew strong black support (table 6.5). Between the primary and the run-off elections, this trend continued. Thus, unlike Villaraigosa, Ferrer had some initial success in moving beyond the ethnic politics of Latino empowerment into a coalition with African Americans. In the process, he got strong support as well from Dominican and West Indian voters in 2001.

In response to Ferrer's strong showing, Green tacked furiously to the right, playing on concerns among the so-called Giuliani Democrats that a Ferrer victory would bring greater political influence to people like the Reverend Sharpton. Green narrowly won the run-off, mainly with white votes and diminished support from black voters. But in the general election, many white Democrats who had voted for him over Ferrer chose instead to support Republican Mike Bloomberg, who loosed an overwhelming and effectively crafted media blitz in the days running up to the general election and won narrowly.

In short, neither mayoral election in 2001 produced the new form of Latino-led minority political empowerment, built on increased immigration, that some had anticipated. The valence of African-American voters and the state of the black-Latino coalition played major roles in both elections. In Los Angeles, black voters helped the white candidate that they overwhelmingly favored to defeat the Latino challenger. In New York, black voters joined Latino voters in the Democratic primary to support a candidate who lost to one supported largely by white voters and then gave more tepid support than originally expected to the white candidate of the party they normally favored by lopsided margins. In both cities, the white liberals who might have supported a minority challenger did not play a central role. They were divided in Los Angeles between Villaraigosa and Hahn and backed a candidate in New York who could not quite pull together the traditional liberal coalition, in no small part because he had just defeated the minority candidate in the primary election. In 2001, therefore, two cities in which the 2000 census had just revealed that native-born whites were a small minority of the population and indeed probably less than half of the voting-age citizens elected native-born white mayors.

## The 2005 Mayoral Elections

The political trajectories of Los Angeles and New York diverged even more sharply in the 2005 mayoral elections. Villaraigosa and Ferrer both attempted to achieve in 2005 what they could not manage in 2001. Villaraigosa had run a successful campaign to displace an incumbent and gain a seat on the Los Angeles City Council in 2003 and carefully positioned himself to broaden his constituency, particularly developing an even stronger relationship with labor unions that had immigrant constituencies.

Mayor Hahn, who had been elected in large part because of strong support from black voters, fired the Los Angeles African-American police chief, Bernard Parks, and put former New York City police commissioner William J. Bratton in his place. Parks turned around and won a city council seat as well in 2003, becoming a thorn in the mayor's side. Hahn also played a major role in organizing voters against the secession movement in the San Fernando Valley; the defeat of this initiative also may have soured some conservative white voters who had supported him in 2001 (Sonenshein 2004).

In the 2005 mayoral race in Los Angeles, therefore, the incumbent was perceived to be facing some degree of political trouble. In addition to Villaraigosa, the challengers to Hahn in the 2005 primary included councilman Parks, a second Latino candidate, and a popular Jewish candidate, the last two from the San Fernando Valley. As table 6.4 shows, Villaraigosa once more emerged with a somewhat narrow lead from this crowded field, with 33 percent of the vote. The pattern of support was roughly similar to that in the 2001 primary, although he did less well in white neighborhoods and a little better in black ones. Because the race featured candidates who appealed to every component of the electorate, the vote was fairly fragmented. Because many black voters gravitated to Parks and many white valley voters gravitated to Hertzberg, Hahn's electoral base from the 2001 general election was sharply undercut.

In the 2005 general election between Hahn and Villaraigosa, many black and white voters clearly shifted from "their own" candidates to Villaraigosa rather than reverting to Hahn, and Villaraigosa handily won the general election with 59 percent of the vote (table 6.4). Compared to the 2001 general election, he made huge advances across the board, particularly in black neighborhoods (a gain of 35.4 percentage points) and white neighborhoods (a gain of 9.8 percentage points), particularly in the valley.

Although his strongest base remained among Latino voters, whose turnout surged, all the other constituencies also shifted his way (Sonenshein and Pinkus 2005). In short, a hard-working and attractive challenger managed to pick up all the pieces of the incumbent's delaminating electoral coalition between the primary and general elections and make them into a liberal, multiracial coalition. Strikingly, Latinos cast 25 percent of all votes in the run-off election. With nearly one-half the population of the city, Latinos were now casting one-quarter of all votes. As leaders of the largest single voting bloc in the city, built on a base of hundreds of thousands of immigrants, Latino-elected officials could only imagine how Los Angeles politics would look if citizenship moved faster.

Just the opposite happened in New York in 2005. Mayor Bloomberg proved to be an effective leader in his first term. He reached out to those who had been disappointed by Ferrer's defeat in 2001, met with Ferrer himself, and made a point of creating far friendlier relations with black leaders than had been the case under his Republican predecessor, Mayor Giuliani. He faced the economic downturn and fiscal stresses of 2002 by raising taxes rather than laying off unionized city workers, kept the crime rate down even while reducing the size of the police force, and eliminated the Board of Education and took direct control of the school system.

Meanwhile, on the Democratic side, Fernando Ferrer once more seemed to be the presumptive nominee. He faced three other candidates—C. Virginia Fields, the African-American Manhattan Borough president; Gifford Miller, the impressive young white city council speaker; and, late in the day, Anthony Weiner, a Jewish candidate from Brooklyn and congressman, who emerged as a favorite of many white Democrats who had defected to Republican candidates in previous elections. None of the three was as widely liked or as experienced in citywide elections as Ferrer. The relative weakness of the field reflected not only Ferrer's prominence but the judgment among many political insiders that any Democratic nominee was going to have a hard time beating the incumbent.

Ferrer ran a relatively low-key primary to avoid alienating any constituencies he would need in the general election, as Green had done. Whatever the merits of this strategy, a late surge by Anthony Weiner plus the presence of a black candidate drained from Ferrer votes that he had been able to attract in the 2001 run-off. As table 6.5 shows, he led the low-turnout primary with a bare 39 percent of the vote. After thinking overnight about making a race of it, the second-place candidate, Anthony Weiner, withdrew and proclaimed that Ferrer had the 40 percent of the vote necessary to preclude a run-off.

As in Los Angeles, the Latino candidate thus emerged as the challenger from a racially divided field. Unlike Villaraigosa's success in Los Angeles, however, Ferrer was unable to bring together the elements of a challenging coalition between the primary and the general elections. The odds may well have been stacked against him; Mayor Bloomberg increasingly consolidated support among white Democrats, African Americans, and immigrant constituencies as well as his (small) core of white Republicans.

In one of the few aspects of the election over which he had some control, Ferrer made one move that had a lingering adverse impact on his campaign. In March, Ferrer remarked to a meeting of the police sergeants union that he did not think the police shooting of Amadou Diallo was a crime and that it had been "over-indicted." This produced a furor, with many African-American leaders criticizing his words (Cardwell, Hicks, and Archibold 2005). Although many in the black establishment ultimately endorsed Ferrer, the remark clearly had a negative impact on his standing in black public opinion. In the primary, black support for Virginia Fields eroded Ferrer's position compared to the 2001 run-off election (a decline of 26 percentage points). Despite receiving many endorsements from the black political establishment, he was never able to re-create the same degree of mass support he had had in 2001.

The general election became a blow-out of historic proportions for Mayor Bloomberg. He won 58.4 percent of the 1.3 million ballots cast (again, a relatively low turnout), having spent a new campaign spending record of $84 million, or almost $112 for every vote he received. Although no traditional exit poll was mounted, it appears that Mayor Bloomberg won almost three-quarters of the white vote, nearly half the black vote, more than half of the Asian vote, and a surprisingly large minority of the vote in Latino areas, many of whose voters were immigrants. Ferrer's base was largely restricted to Puerto Rican neighborhoods, with a somewhat broader reach in the Bronx.

Whereas the Latino challenger triumphed in Los Angeles by adding support from white and black voters disaffected by the incumbent mayor to his mobilized Latino base, the Latino challenger in New York failed to attract those black and white supporters and failed even to energize his own base. In a telling sign, Mayor Villaraigosa withheld an endorsement of his friend Ferrer, perhaps thinking that this would improve his relations with the man who would be sitting in the City Hall "bull pen" for the next four years. It also helped dissipate any perception that a nationally oriented alliance of Latino political forces was being mounted at the moment when Villaraigosa was poised to win power in Los Angeles.

We conducted a fine-grained statistical analysis of the vote, looking at class, ethnicity, and other factors. We cannot provide all the details here, but, even after we control for income, homeownership, education, and family form, voters living in different racial and ethnic contexts voted differently from one another. Voters in whiter areas were consistently less favorable to the Latino challengers in these races, and voters in black and especially Hispanic areas were more favorable. In New York City, Ferrer was much more likely to be the candidate chosen by the dependent poor than was Villaraigosa in Los Angeles.

Second, as the previous discussion has underlined, blacks were the main swing constituency in these two cities between 2001 and 2005. In New York, they swung away from the Latino challenger and toward the white incumbent (although blacks were still far less likely to vote for him than whites), whereas in Los Angeles they swung away from the white incumbent and toward the Latino challenger. Third, the larger racial categories hide important differences within their component groups. Although broad racial categories are useful, perhaps unavoidable, for analysis, specific national origin groups provide the detailed story.

Most crucially, massive immigration did not lead to a broad coalition or alignment of immigrant origin groups in either city. Although those who resented and feared the change to the streets of their city by new immigrants might lump all immigrants together, the actual politics of immigration became ethnic politics. Latino candidates in each city managed to be competitive in a critical citywide election, but found that another immigrant group, Asian Americans, favored native white candidates rather than the candidate from the immigrant background. Relations between the Latino candidates and African American voters were volatile but also pivotal in both instances, deeply affecting the electoral outcomes.

## The Impact of Differences in Political Institutions and Culture

Our analysis of how different groups of voters contributed to the 2005 mayoral elections in the two cities produced some expected and some surprising results. The biggest difference is that Latino empowerment took a major leap forward in Los Angeles with the election of Antonio Villaraigosa, whereas Fernando Ferrer fell short in New York City. But in neither case did Latino immigrants determine the outcome. Newly arrived Mexicans and Salvadorans in Los Angeles and Dominicans and South Americans in New York remained small components of the electorates. They leaned toward the Latino candidates, but did not achieve the same levels of political mobilization and candidate support that their proximal ethnic voters—Mexican Americans and Puerto Ricans—did. (Class differences clearly count; Ecuadoran and Colombian voters were significantly less likely to support Ferrer than were Puerto Ricans and Dominicans.) Other recent immigrant voters, such as Iranians or Armenians in Los Angeles and Russians in New York, were even less likely to favor these immigrant-origin candidates. On the other hand, New Yorkers have elected West Indians, Dominicans, and a Chinese American to the city council, yielding a level of immigrant representation that appears to be a long way off in Los Angeles. The two cities present a paradox—a system that seems to deter immigrant ethnic representation on the city council (Los Angeles) nevertheless elected a Mexican-American mayor.

On the face of it, we would have assumed that the greater importance of partisan affiliation and partisan activity in New York, combined with the overwhelming enrollment of the voters in the Democratic Party and the fact that the dominant party put forward a Latino nominee in 2005 for the first time, should have produced a greater groundswell of support for this candidate, all other things being equal. Of course, all other things are not equal. In particular, Mayor Bloomberg had broad support, was perceived to be doing a good job, and had effectively unlimited campaign resources, whereas Mayor Hahn had alienated some key constituencies, particularly African Americans and, to a lesser extent, white valley voters. Another confounding factor was that white voters in New York generally appeared to have more strongly negative feelings toward a Latino mayoral candidate than they did in Los Angeles. Last but not least, there are simply more Latino voters in Los Angeles than in New York.

An analysis of Villaraigosa's election suggests that the New York City partisan structure, if grafted onto Los Angeles, might paradoxically have *increased* the chance of a white candidate's winning in 2001 and 2005 because it would have guaranteed a general election contest between the Latino candidate and a native white candidate. Raphael Sonenshein and Mark Drayse (2006) examined the coalitions behind all the candidates in those elections and found a sleeper coalition rallying behind moderate white candidates, Steve Soboroff in 2001 and Bob Hertzberg in 2005. The absence of party primaries meant that Soboroff and Hertzberg each had to come in second behind the leading candidate to be in the two-person run-off. Had either been able to go directly to the general election as the Republican nominee (with Democrat Hertzberg doing a Bloomberg-like party switch), each would then have faced a battered Democratic nominee, either Hahn or Villaraigosa.

Our chapter began by noting how their differences in political institutions and cultures may contrast with the economic and demographic similarities of the two cities. New York City is a complex political organism with numerous opportunities for office holding, high levels of public interest in local politics, and strong mayoral authority. At least until recently, Los Angeles has been a simpler political setting with fewer political opportunities and with a more horizontal division of authority among elected officials. (This may be changing as term limits on the state legislature expand the number of political opportunities for local politicians; Sonenshein 2006).

How do these differences play out in the two cities? Although both cities have diverse populations and electorates, New York City politics reflects that diversity with far more fidelity than does Los Angeles politics. Despite the image of Los Angeles as the most diverse city in the United States, ethnic distinctions seem to have a lower profile in Los Angeles. New York has experienced clear political competition between African Americans and Afro-Caribbeans, as evidenced in the primary election for Brooklyn's Eleventh Congressional District, in which the son of the sitting African-American congressman lost to a second-generation Jamaican-American woman whose mother was the first West Indian woman elected to the city council. Despite the presence of a great many Salvadorans and Guatemalans in Los Angeles, they have not (yet) asserted themselves as a distinct group with respect either to the Mexican-American establishment or the African Americans who hold office in the neighborhoods where they live. Meanwhile, Dominicans have generated their own candidates for legislative office and are quite distinct from the Puerto Rican political establishment.

These differences in sensitivity to and ability to reflect ethnic differences may be related to the differences in citywide outcomes. The extraordinarily rich range of political opportunities for emerging ethnic groups in New York City, with its fifty-one-member council and numerous state legislative offices, encourages relatively small but residentially concentrated immigrant ethnic groups to organize for access. (Indeed, a Russian American was recently the first to be elected to the New York Assembly.) This may reinforce ethnic distinctions that currently do not seem to matter in Los Angeles, perhaps because only the big groups can hope to influence its council or mayoral politics. By contrast, the large council districts in Los Angeles provide minority groups with an incentive to conceptualize themselves as broadly as possible. The Los Angeles City Council has perhaps four Latino seats of fifteen. The two Hispanic politicians who hold citywide office today in Los Angeles are seen as Latinos, not Mexican Americans, even though Mayor Villaraigosa presents himself as being more liberal than Rocky Delgadillo, the city attorney. Both have won many votes in non-Latino neighborhoods.

Asian Americans have also been more successful in gaining small-scale representation in New York, encouraging their mobilization, than in Los Angeles. With such large council districts and their lower rates of residential concentration, Asian

Americans have had little success in winning office in Los Angeles. The only Asian American ever elected to the city council, Mike Woo, represented a diverse and not predominantly Asian Hollywood district. Today, no Asian American holds elected office in Los Angeles. Even with their definition as a pan-ethnic group (Asian American rather than Chinese or Japanese or Korean), Asian Americans have been unable to overcome the structural barrier created by large districts.

New Yorkers were more amenable to increasing the size of their city council in a 1989 charter reform than were Los Angeles voters in 1999. Indeed, a primary aim of the 1989 New York City charter reform was to make the city council more representative by increasing its size from thirty-five to fifty-one. In 1999, Los Angeles voters voted two to one against two charter amendments that would have increased the size of the city council (the first to twenty-one; the other to twenty-five), despite voting in favor of a more general charter reform on the same ballot (Sonenshein 2004).

Paradoxically, the institutional and cultural factors that helped create the fine-grained political diversity of New York City elections may limit the ability of minority and immigrant communities to reach the summit of urban power because they heighten ethnic and racial cleavages. After all, the same question arose decades ago when conservative Los Angeles elected a black mayor with a stable coalition relatively early in the civil rights era and the more liberal New York City was unable to do so (Sonenshein 1993; Mollenkopf 1992).

A complex system with numerous opportunities for partial incorporation and strong party organizations can pick off and absorb new leaders, making it hard for emerging immigrant ethnic groups to attain citywide political success. Furthermore, the mayor's great strength in relation to other officeholders may greatly enhance the concern that white voters—still the plurality in both cities—have about which group will be perceived to hold that office. Los Angeles puts fewer eggs in the mayoral basket. Even to get to the main event, a candidate has to win an immensely powerful council seat representing a quarter of a million people. That seems to be an easier jump to make than from a New York borough presidency or other citywide office. If aspiring Los Angeles politicians from immigrant communities need to subordinate their national identities to pan-ethnic identities to attract the widest range of voters, they may indeed have a wider appeal and face fewer interethnic liabilities.

This may also contribute to the greater white unity against immigrant minority empowerment in New York City than in Los Angeles. In general, whites in Los Angeles, perhaps apart from Jews, do not see themselves as members of ethnic groups, and their political behavior does not divide along strongly ethnic lines (Waldinger and Bozorghmehr 1996). They are divided more by ideology than ethnicity. Villaraigosa made broader inroads into the white vote in Los Angeles than either Dinkins or Ferrer did in New York.

## Conclusion and Implications

The ethnic and racial politics confronting today's immigrants to the great U.S. cities are not blank slates. They have been already shaped by waves of previous newcomers who have established enduring patterns of intergroup conflicts and alliances. These preexisting narratives can seem hard for immigrants to join in midstream. Clearly, the growth of immigrant communities has altered how established residents see the political lay of the land. Whites divide, as usual, along ideological lines. African Americans have a more poignant reaction because their history leads them to believe in equality for all groups of color but their established positions may be threatened by the new immigrants. As a result, black voters end up as the principal audience for the political aspirants whose main base is in communities whose growth depends on immigration. This dance of trust and mistrust between immigrants and native minorities is likely to shape urban politics for years to come.

We therefore conclude that political structure and political culture matter. Quite simply, cities ruled by machine politics, with highly evolved political systems, break immigrant groups up into smaller pieces, all the better to digest them and partially incorporate them. But these fine ethnic divisions may come at a political cost, namely the distance they create between partial victories and citywide power. Reform government places many barriers to immigrant minority access, beginning with the smaller number of offices available and the lack of partisan organizations to mobilize working-class and minority communities. Yet reformed structures also provide large openings for those who can mobilize effectively on a citywide basis.

Immigration will continue to reshape urban politics. As new immigrant communities and their children and their grandchildren demonstrate their ability to organize and vote, other leaders of ethnic groups will increasingly seek them out. Some political actors may seek to demonize them to build conservative populist coalitions, but an energetic coalition politics across ethnic and racial lines will ensure that new immigrants have the opportunity to prevail within the particular culture or structure of each city.

# CHAPTER SEVEN

# Political Institutions and Rainbow Coalitions

## Immigrant-Minority Relations in New York and Hartford

*Reuel Rogers*

Immigration has reshaped the demography of the metropolitan United States in the last half century. Cities, once largely a mix of blacks and whites, are now decidedly multiracial, with rapidly increasing numbers of immigrants from Asia, Latin America, and the Caribbean. There are countless questions about how these demographic shifts will change the urban political landscape. One of the most important is whether these immigrants will engage in coalition building or conflict with native-born groups. Intergroup dynamics typically have had significant implications for the political-incorporation patterns of urban minority populations, such as African Americans, whose prospects for inclusion often hinge on their relations with whites. Presumably then, the ability of recent nonwhite immigrants to forge relationships with one another and with native-born groups will figure heavily in their incorporation prospects as well (see Jennifer Hochschild and John Mollenkopf, chap. 2 in this volume).

It is difficult to say whether those relations will generate conflict or coalition building. First, relatively little is known about how immigrants' policy preferences and political proclivities compare with those of native-born groups. Nor is it clear how the peculiar protocols of racial categorization in this country will stamp these immigrants. For instance, will Latinos, like African Americans, be consigned to a permanent racial minority status fraught with stigma and disadvantage, or will they retrace the path of twentieth-century European immigrant groups, like the Irish, who became white and now enjoy all the attendant privileges of that status (Jacobson 1998; Ignatiev 1996)? Do these newcomers share enough racial affinity or political common ground with African Americans or whites to allow for a stable alliance with either of these groups? Researchers are still sorting out these questions (e.g., Joyce 2003; Kim 2000; Hochschild and Rogers 2000).

Second, for better or worse, theories of intergroup relations and coalition building on this side of the Atlantic often are heavily informed by assumptions drawn from the distinct history of blacks and whites: the legacy of slavery, the strange career of Jim Crow, economic tensions between blacks and poor whites, racial attitudes among liberal and conservative whites, and so on (Key 1949; Browning, Marshall, and Tabb 1984). It is unclear whether some of the basic premises of these established theories will apply to the increasingly multiracial realities of many cities in the United States. Evidence from the 1970s and 1980s suggested that minorities were most likely to achieve incorporation in cities when they allied with liberal whites. This has certainly been the case for African Americans, who joined with white liberals to elect the first generation of African American mayors. But it is not at all clear whether the same formula will be necessary or relevant for Latinos, Asians, and Afro-Caribbeans.

Despite these uncertainties, forecasts about relations between immigrants and native-born groups hardly have been in short supply. The vast majority in the 1980s and 1990s heralded a grand rainbow coalition among the immigrants and native-born African Americans (Jennings 1997; Marable 1994). The expectation was that this new minority-majority demographic would translate into black-brown coalitions and minority political ascendancy in local elections. Observers believed that the racial minority status, vulnerability to discrimination, and material disadvantages shared by these immigrants and African Americans would become a sturdy basis for political cooperation (Marable 1994).

But the predicted rainbow coalition has proven elusive. Rainbow and black-brown alliances have been rare and short-lived in local politics. Conflicts between these groups have been more common (Vaca 2004; Joyce 2003; Kim 2000; Meier and Stewart 1991; Oliver and Johnson 1984). Hostilities between African Americans and nonwhite immigrant groups over housing, jobs, and other socioeconomic resources are well documented. Recent big-city elections in New York, Miami, Los Angeles, and Houston grimly demonstrate that conflict over political power among these groups is equally intense. "[African Americans], Latinos, [and Asians] rarely rally behind one another's candidates" (Kaufman 2007, 80). Decidedly bleaker outlooks thus have replaced the once optimistic forecasts for minority coalition building.

The looming question is why these groups have had such difficulty fashioning stable coalitions. The absence of sustainable rainbow or black-brown alliances may be especially harmful to African Americans, who, after three decades of significant advances in big cities, lately have seen many of their policy goals blocked and electoral ground lost. The most dramatic examples of such reversals have come in cities, such as New York and Los Angeles, where African American mayors were supplanted by conservative white mayoral regimes in the 1990s (Mollenkopf 2003; Sonenshein 2003a). African Americans may find it difficult or impossible to address some of their more challenging policy needs in the current climate if they fail to cultivate alliances with the growing nonwhite immigrant populations in these cities (Gay 2006).

Latinos, Asians, and Afro-Caribbeans currently lag behind African Americans in sheer political power because many of the rank-and-file in these heavily immigrant constituencies are still noncitizens. But with increasing numbers, citizenship rates, and organizational capacity, all three are on the upswing of their political trajectory, enjoying recent big-city electoral successes. In the case of both Latinos and Afro-Caribbeans, some gains have come at the expense of African Americans (Kaufman

2007; Rogers 2006). These recent advances, coupled with the continuing elusiveness of stable interminority coalitions, have raised the specter of foreign-born nonwhites bypassing African Americans and leaving them in grim political isolation (Mollenkopf 2003). Yet Latinos, Asians, and Afro-Caribbeans also ultimately might confront a political glass ceiling in their bids for incorporation, particularly as they move beyond symbolic goals, such as descriptive representation, and try to find solutions to more difficult problems, such as unemployment and educational disadvantage. They too eventually might need to enlist African American support to ensure future political progress.

Coalition building is thus a do-or-die fact of political life for both African Americans and their nonwhite immigrant counterparts. African Americans and Latinos have demonstrated their capacity for forging biracial coalitions with whites (Kaufman 2004; Browning, Marshall, and Tabb 2003). But alliances with whites, even those who have decidedly liberal leanings, have not been effective vehicles for satisfying the more redistributive policy needs of minorities (Kaufman 2007; Mollenkopf 2003). It thus remains to be seen whether interminority coalitions might do any better at pursuing such aims. On their face, black-brown alliances seem more amenable to these goals because the principal partners—African Americans, Latinos, and other nonwhite populations—have overlapping needs and direct stakes in these areas. The often-tense relations between African Americans and recent immigrants are all the more worrisome, then, if black-brown coalitions remain the one last hope or unexplored avenue for advancing minority interests. Determining why these groups have been unable to forge stable alliances thus seems critical to their respective future political fortunes.

This chapter argues that city-level electoral institutions have a significant influence on the prospects for coalition building and conflict among minority groups. The established literature points to a number of factors—economic conditions, population shifts, interest divergence, and ideological incongruities—to explain why African Americans and nonwhite immigrant groups have had difficulty forging stable coalitions. But researchers have paid less attention to the role that institutions play in shaping intergroup political dynamics. In the first section of the chapter, I briefly review the existing research and make the theoretical case for paying more attention to institutions. In the rest of the chapter, I provide a comparative overview of interminority dynamics and a closer analysis of relations between African Americans and Afro-Caribbeans in two cities with very different electoral systems: New York and Hartford.

At first blush incommensurable cases, these two northeastern minority-majority cities have experienced similar demographic, economic, and political trends over the last several decades. In each city, a once largely biracial population split between African Americans and whites has become multiracial due to the influx of immigrants from Asia, Latin America, and the Caribbean. Accompanying the demographic changes in both cities have been periods of fiscal difficulty that have generated serious hardships for African Americans and some of the immigrant groups. Finally, after enjoying decades of significant electoral success, African Americans in New York and Hartford have suffered political setbacks. Their population numbers have not kept pace with those of the foreign-born; the new groups have raised the specter of political encroachment; and the white liberals, who were once reliable political allies, have drifted rightward or have left for the suburbs.

These developments have made conditions ripe for conflict and minimized the prospects for coalitions between African Americans and nonwhite immigrants in both cities. This bleak scenario is certainly in keeping with predictions derived from existing theories of group conflict and coalition building in the literature. But interminority dynamics in the two cities actually have been quite different. Electoral conflicts have undermined minority group relations in New York for decades. The political clashes between African American and Latino New Yorkers and their continuing inability to forge a stable black-brown coalition, for example, are well known (Mollenkopf 2003; Falcón 1988). Although African Americans and nonwhite immigrants in Hartford also have had their share of disagreements, these groups have had notably more success in forging electoral alliances. The following analysis suggests that differences in electoral institutions go a long way to explaining why minorities in Hartford have had more coalition-building success than their counterparts in New York.

## Theories of Coalition Building and Group Relations

Existing research has tended to highlight two sets of factors that are believed to influence the odds of conflict or coalition among groups. First are the groups' interests, ideological values, attitudes toward one another, and leadership (Sonenshein 2003b; Mollenkopf 2003; Oliver and Wong 2003; Hochschild and Rogers 2000). Shared values, favorable out-group attitudes, and the presence of bold leadership are all important bases for building coalitions and minimizing conflict among groups. But interests seem to matter most of all. Not only does the convergence of interests among groups appear necessary for a coalition to gather and sustain political momentum, it also seems to be sufficient to overcome limitations or weaknesses in any of the other bases (Carmichael and Hamilton 1967). Likewise, coalitions appear more prone to collapsing when interests begin to diverge, even if the other important girders remain in place. This was the case, for example, when the long-standing biracial coalition between African Americans and liberal whites in Los Angeles broke apart in the early 1990s (Sonenshein 2003a).

The other factors thought to influence intergroup relations are contextual. In particular, relative numbers and material conditions often determine whether groups regard one another as potential allies or competitors (Gay 2006; Oliver and Wong 2003; Oliver and Mendelberg 2000; Key 1949). When one group expands relative to another under conditions of economic or political vulnerability, competition is likely to ensue and prospects for coalition building are likely to recede. It is thus perhaps no surprise that tensions ran high between African Americans and nonwhite immigrants in several big cities during the economic and political hard times of the 1980s and early 1990s (McClain and Tauber 2001; Johnson, Farrell, and Guinn 1997; Johnson and Oliver 1989). Add to these factors the cultural chasms and historical differences between these groups, and it is easy to see why rainbow and black-brown alliances were elusive.

## The Missing Institutional Link

Taken together, then, the main variables emphasized in the literature—interests, ideology, leadership, numbers, and material conditions—help explain the absence of sustainable interminority coalitions. But they do not provide the full picture. Although the alignment of these variables creates the potential for either coalition or conflict, politics turns these possibilities into realities. One factor with powerful direct influence on political action has garnered only limited attention in the literature—the institutional environment.[1]

Institutions constitute and structure the strategic political environment in which groups and their leaders operate, often influencing how these actors perceive and frame their interests, ideological commitments, and other political factors that shape the odds of coalition building. They create a web of incentives that shape the strategic decisions of leaders and their constituents, including whether to make common cause or compete with other groups.

Two sets of institutions are particularly influential. The first are those that make up the electoral system: the style of elections, party configurations, number of representative offices, and so on (Rogers n.d.). The second set of institutions are civic and organizational networks, which often serve as a staging ground for mobilization and interactions among groups in a city (Joyce 2003). (See the concluding section of this chapter for more discussion on the influence of civic institutions on intergroup relations.)

An emphasis on electoral institutions, in particular, yields formal predictions about how they each might affect interminority relations. First, open electoral institutions tend to reduce the potential for intergroup conflict in cities (Hajnal 2005; Mollenkopf, Olson, and Ross 2001). Cities that offer considerable opportunities for group representation, say through district elections or numerous elective offices, tend to see fewer intergroup conflicts (Hajnal 2005; Joyce 2003).[2]

Electoral institutions also might influence interminority relations by the extent to which they encourage political coordination among groups (Rogers n.d.). Consider the difference between at-large and district elections for city council seats. Insofar as nonwhite groups constitute numerical minorities and suffer resource deficits in many cities, they often have difficulty electing leaders from their own ranks to public office. At-large elections exacerbate this difficulty because they make campaigns more expensive and allow simple majorities to dominate city council election outcomes. District elections facilitate minority representation because they enable smaller groups that are residentially concentrated to elect their own representatives. Yet district elections also may tutor minorities to go it alone, leaving more room for intergroup conflict.

Institutional variations across cities therefore may help explain why African Americans and recent nonwhite immigrants have been unable to forge sustainable alliances in some cities. Specifying these institutional variables and testing for their effects on group relations require a great deal of methodological care and more empirical evidence than I can muster in this chapter. The following analysis focuses on electoral institutions. The differences in interminority dynamics in New York and Hartford illustrate that these institutions matter a great deal and deserve more serious empirical consideration.

## Minority Group Relations in Two Cities:
## Black Meets Black

New York City

Race certainly has the potential to be a great unifier for native- and foreign-born minorities in New York City. Although the divisions among these groups are hardly trivial, their similarities and the looming racial realities of economic and political life in the city would seem to provide considerable impetus for them to form the kind of rainbow coalition many observers long have envisioned.[3]

Socioeconomic disparities between whites and nonwhites have persisted for several decades, even during periods of relative prosperity when black, Latino, and Asian New Yorkers have enjoyed gains in income, education, homeownership, and business activity (Lewis Mumford Center 2002; Falcón 1988). (See table 7.1.) Minority populations have made notable political advances in recent decades. All three groups—blacks, Latinos, and Asians—have won City Council and state legislature seats. Blacks and Latinos have held borough presidencies and made inroads in the Democratic Party leadership, which has long dominated New York City politics. Despite these gains, minorities have had considerably less influence than whites over both legislative and executive policymaking decisions. Their bids to consolidate and expand their political power have almost routinely stalled or lost ground to the prerogatives of the city's more numerous, active, and influential white voters (Mollenkopf 2003),[4] despite the fact that the number of whites in the general population has declined relative to those of minorities.

The political and economic disadvantages that black, Latino and Asian New York City populations have in common appear to give them a set of shared interests, perhaps the most crucial girder for coalition building. These groups also all lean toward the Democratic Party, and each has developed to varying degrees its own cadre of leaders. In short, African Americans and foreign-born minorities in New York have all the building blocks for a sturdy multiracial coalition: interest convergence, a measure of ideological compatibility, and available leadership. Yet these incentives have failed to translate into a sustained alliance. There have been some encouraging developments, to be sure. Black and Latino leaders, for instance, have established a caucus

**Table 7.1** Neighborhood characteristics for racial and ethnic groups, New York, 1990 and 2000

|  | Median household income | | College educated (%) | | Homeowners (%) | |
|---|---|---|---|---|---|---|
|  | 1990 | 2000 | 1990 | 2000 | 1990 | 2000 |
| Non-Hispanic white | $49,001 | $51,343 | 29.6 | 37.6 | 38.6 | 39.7 |
| Non-Hispanic black | $32,495 | $32,885 | 13.1 | 16.2 | 24.3 | 27.7 |
| Hispanic | $30,019 | $31,176 | 14.0 | 16.9 | 17.8 | 20.1 |
| Asian | $40,596 | $41,492 | 22.9 | 27.9 | 29.1 | 32.8 |

*Source:* Lewis Mumford Center for Comparative Urban and Regional Research.

in the state legislature. The three minority groups, with liberal whites, put together the coalition that elected the city's first African American mayor, David Dinkins in 1989. The groups also have joined to support high-profile Democratic candidates, such as Hillary Clinton, for state and city offices.

But these instances of political cooperation have been ephemeral. The coalition that elected Dinkins derailed after one term; white conservatives have controlled the mayoralty since 1993. Minority political figures as varied as Al Sharpton and Fernando Ferrer have tried unsuccessfully to resurrect a Dinkins-style multiracial alliance with blacks and Latinos at the forefront. During the most recent effort, a 2005 mayoral bid by Latino Democratic nominee Ferrer, almost half of blacks who went to polls crossed party lines and voted for Republican incumbent Michael Bloomberg. Ferrer lost by a gaping twenty-point margin (Healy 2005). In light of these failed efforts, some observers have actually dismissed the prospect of a race-based coalition among African Americans, Latinos, and Asians as untenable, insofar as it underestimates the political significance of differences in culture, history, and even racial perceptions among the groups (e.g., Sleeper 1993).

The difficulties of fostering and maintaining such a coalition, however, also have surfaced between African Americans and Afro-Caribbean immigrants. As blacks, the two groups share an obvious history, a racial minority status, and vulnerability to similar forms of discrimination. As the two most residentially segregated groups in the city, they frequently live in close proximity to one another and share many of the same neighborhood problems, especially in Brooklyn and the Bronx: failing schools, poverty, and crime. (See table 7.2.) Both have had their share of racially charged neighborhood conflicts with whites and city police. Finally, both are the most reliably Democratic voters in the city, and both groups' leaders—especially the African American leaders—have a firm foothold in the party establishment.[5]

These commonalities have translated into numerous instances of political cooperation between the groups. The African American–led street protests against police brutality in the mid-1990s drew significant numbers of Afro-Caribbeans (Rogers 2006). In 2001, Caribbean-born Kendall Stewart won the Forty-fifth District City Council seat from Brooklyn with the backing of two African American congressmen and African American voters, despite the presence of an African American candidate in the field (Logan and Mollenkopf 2003).

**Table 7.2** Neighborhood characteristics for African Americans, Afro-Caribbeans, and Africans, New York, 1990 and 2000

|  | Median household income | | College educated (%) | | Homeowners (%) | |
|---|---|---|---|---|---|---|
|  | 1990 | 2000 | 1990 | 2000 | 1990 | 2000 |
| African-American | $30,914 | $31,159 | 12.4 | 15.7 | 22.9 | 25.6 |
| Afro-Caribbean | $38,319 | $37,684 | 14.9 | 17.5 | 29.8 | 34.2 |
| African | $37,493 | $33,101 | 21.6 | 19.1 | 21.4 | 22.0 |
| Black ethnic total | $32,510 | $32,898 | 13.1 | 16.2 | 24.3 | 27.7 |

*Source:* Lewis Mumford Center for Comparative Urban and Regional Research.

But for every instance of political cooperation between African American and Afro-Caribbean New Yorkers, there also have been episodes of conflict, most focused on political turf and representation (Rogers 2006). Consider the 2001 Democratic primary contest for Brooklyn's Eleventh Congressional District between Major Owens, the long-time African American incumbent, and Una Clarke, a Caribbean-born former city councilwoman. The highly contentious race was rife with interethnic tension. Clarke characterized the incumbent as anti-immigrant, and Owens, who ultimately won, complained that his opponent and her ethnically focused campaign were undermining greater black empowerment (Rogers 2004). Similar tensions surfaced in the 2006 contest for the same seat. The crowded field included a white city councilman, an Afro-Caribbean city councilwoman, and two African Americans— one a state senator and the other the retiring incumbent's son (Hicks 2006). Black leaders worried that the three black candidates would produce an ethnic split in the black vote, clearing the way for the white opponent and threatening the loss of a congressional seat occupied by a black politician since 1972. The Afro-Caribbean councilwoman ultimately won the seat for the majority-black district. But the election dust-up showed how fragile the racial ties between Afro-Caribbeans and African Americans can be and how much their intergroup dynamics matter for overall black political progress in the city.

Existing theories on intergroup relations might point to material factors to explain the recurrence of such conflicts. The socioeconomic disadvantages that these minority populations share compared to whites may not be a basis for minority racial unity; rather, they may be cause for mutual suspicion and competition. African Americans might be troubled by the specter of striving Afro-Caribbeans opening businesses, taking over their neighborhoods, and bypassing them to catch up with whites. But there is little support for the economic threat hypothesis in this case. Although Caribbean New Yorkers have a slight socioeconomic edge over African Americans, there is little evidence of economic competition between the groups. Although each constitutes a significant presence in government jobs, they mostly gravitate to different parts of the New York City labor market (Waldinger 1989; 1996). What is more, none of the political conflicts between the two has focused on economic, labor market, or even neighborhood issues. Nor have there been any of the violent street-level conflicts associated with minority economic frustration in other cities.

But if Afro-Caribbean immigrants do not pose an economic danger to African Americans, they certainly present a potential political threat. African Americans are the most politically dominant minority group in New York City by virtue of their numbers in the electorate, level of political engagement, office holding, and influence in the Democratic Party. Yet they have been unable to convert their political resources into consistent policy influence, have failed to regain the mayor's office, and have seen their numerical and electoral advantage over foreign-born minority groups shrink. Their political vulnerability to Afro-Caribbeans is especially pronounced. Although the immigrants' share of the pool of voting-age citizens is less than their proportion in the total population, they and other foreign-born groups have been closing that gap in recent years with increasing rates of citizenship, registration, and voting.

More important, Afro-Caribbean leaders have been capitalizing on the population's increasing numbers and political resources to make serious bids for elective office.

With African Americans and Afro-Caribbeans concentrated in many of the same election districts, however, Afro-Caribbean leaders often face African American incumbents or candidates in these contests. This increasingly common scenario explains why most recent conflicts between the two groups have centered on political representation and turf. The stakes of such battles involve not only political office but also the government jobs and material rewards that come with it (Rogers 2004).

The question this development begs is why the competition over political offices between Afro-Caribbeans and African Americans has centered on ethnicity or nationality rather than some other cleavage. Why have these electoral contests not focused on the much-rehearsed and sometimes overstated cultural and socioeconomic differences between the groups? The basic institutional design of New York's electoral system places ethnicity at the center of political organizing and competition. Electoral jurisdictions—Community Board, City Council, and New York State Assembly seats—roughly coincide with the outlines of the quilt pattern of ethnic neighborhoods in the city. This overlap between electoral districts and ethnic neighborhoods is no accident. The districts are drawn specifically to reflect the contours of these ethnic enclaves. The neighborhood-based district seats of the City Council, in fact, were adopted in the late 1980s to facilitate the election of ethnic and racial minorities (Macchiarola and Diaz 1993).

This institutional arrangement influences how leaders and their constituents frame their political aims, mobilize at election time, and relate to other groups. "The most obvious [and efficient] way for an aspiring politician…to build a constituent base…is to…mobilize voters in ethnic neighborhoods" (Rogers 2004, 305). The electoral system is designed to reward political candidates who follow this ethnically based approach to political competition. Making ethnic or racial group appeals to galvanize voters has become a strategic norm for New York politicians.

This has certainly been the case for Afro-Caribbean New Yorkers. As population shifts and political redistricting have given Afro-Caribbeans a numerical edge or at least a critical mass in districts in Brooklyn and Queens, many Caribbean politicians have employed this ethnic strategy. Since the early 1980s, the vast majority of Afro-Caribbean candidates for city and state offices have employed ethnic appeals to rally their constituents to become citizens and voters. Their efforts actually have helped crystallize and heighten pan-ethnic identification among immigrants from the Caribbean region to New York. This last point is worth underscoring because it highlights an important dimension of the immigrant incorporation process—politicians socialize newcomers to emphasize their ethnic group attachments in their electoral choices.[6]

But even as New York City district elections give politicians incentives to make racial or ethnic appeals, they increase the likelihood of intergroup conflict. Ethnic or racial group cues in campaigns create a political context in which voters are motivated to elevate ethnic or racial group considerations in their decisions.[7] Although this is an almost surefire strategy for mobilizing minority groups, especially those lacking the resources that typically lead to political engagement (Chong and Rogers 2005; Leighley 2001), the heavy emphasis on racial or ethnic group identification risks sparking group-based countermobilization by other candidates and voters (Kaufmann 1998, 660). Existing research in public opinion and group psychology has shown conclusively that strong group identification not only fosters in-group favoritism but also generates out-group antagonism or competition (Gibson and Gouws 2003; Bobo and Hutchings 1996).

The battles between Afro-Caribbeans and African Americans in New York over descriptive representation appear to be a case in point. When Afro-Caribbean candidates make ethnically targeted appeals during campaigns for seats in districts they share with African Americans, they not only rally their Caribbean constituents; they also run the risk of engendering conflict with African American politicians and their base (Rogers 2004, 306). African Americans tend to become concerned about losing ground to their foreign-born black counterparts and defensive about their own group interests. Conflict couched in in-group and out-group terms then ensues. Many recent City Council and congressional races in districts where the two groups predominate have fit this pattern of interethnic bickering over descriptive representation, including the 2006 contest for the Eleventh Congressional District seat in Brooklyn. Many of the conflicts between African Americans and Latinos similarly center on which group should lead or represent multiracial or minority constituencies. In sum, New York's district-based electoral system does not just make racial and ethnic group identities and attachments salient for leaders and their constituents; this institutional design also heightens the potential for intergroup friction.

This neighborhood-based electoral arrangement nonetheless has obvious benefits. The district-based system provides so many opportunities for elective representation that immigrant and minority populations probably have less reason to resort to violent, street-level conflicts or other costly extra-systemic activities to pursue their interests or grievances (Hajnal 2005; Mollenkopf, Olson, and Ross 2001). The problem, however, is that, by encouraging politicians and constituents to frame issues in racial or ethnic terms, this institutional design increases the likelihood of intergroup conflict in the electoral arena. Moreover, to the extent that the city's district-based electoral map makes racial or ethnic group appeals a strategic norm for politicians, it also renders coalition building for citywide elections more difficult, even when there are strategic incentives to do so.

For example, attempts to build broad-based, multiracial alliances for mayoral campaigns in New York often have been frustrated by the unwillingness or inability of political leaders and voters to get past their particular group interests and focus on larger goals. There are numerous instances of blacks or Latinos signaling ambivalence or opposition to the prospect of an electoral alliance because a leader from their own group was not at the helm. Consider the recent campaigns by Ferrer, the Latino mayoral candidate, in which he had admitted difficulty rallying black support. Although black-brown electoral alliances have been difficult to engineer in a number of big cities, they have seemed especially elusive in New York. The group identification encouraged by the electoral system is accompanied by an in-group bias that leaders and voters seem hard pressed to abandon. Instead, broader goals are overshadowed by anxieties and disputes about which groups are entitled to lead or follow and which stand to gain or lose most from prospective coalitions.

## Hartford

With its surprisingly strong record of politically constructive group relations be-tween African Americans and immigrants, Hartford offers a marked contrast to New York City. Nonwhite groups in the small New England city have their share of common problems, mutual interests, and political similarities—all of which provide incentives for race-based coalition building. On average, blacks, Latinos, and Asians in Hartford live in neighborhoods with lower median incomes, higher poverty rates, fewer home-owners, and smaller numbers of college-educated residents than their white counter-parts. (See table 7.3) The thirty-two-school public education system was ranked one of the worst-performing in the country in 2002 (Zielbauer 2002). With a student popula-tion that is 95 percent black and Latino, these problems have fallen disproportionately on minority populations in Hartford.

In addition, blacks and Latinos in the city both have had a history of conflict with whites. There were riots by Puerto Ricans and blacks in the heavily minority North End and South Green neighborhoods in the late 1960s (Cruz 1998). Although few and far between, such episodes have deepened resentment between whites and non-whites, contributed to residential segregation, and spurred white flight. Add to these socioeconomic woes, the significant political similarities that African Americans and nonwhite immigrants in Hartford share. Black and Latino Hartforders both have long-standing attachments to the dominant Democratic Party, although Puerto Ri-cans and Afro-Caribbeans have voted for Republican candidates in a handful of city council elections.

These commonalities would seem to augur well for coalition building. But the New York City case proves that similar racial interests and partisan affinities are hardly enough to ensure a stable, rainbow-style alliance and can in fact become a basis for hostility and competition in difficult economic conditions. Hartford then ought to be hotbed of interminority conflict. Once among the wealthiest cities in the country, it has suffered a drastic decline in fortunes in the last half century. Consider this litany of grim economic statistics culled from the last census. With roughly one-quarter of its residents living below the poverty line, Hartford ranked as one of the ten most destitute cities in the country in 2000. Population loss, middle-class exo-dus, deindustrialization, business relocation, and the concomitant tax-base erosion

**Table 7.3** Neighborhood characteristics for racial and ethnic groups, Hartford, 1990 and 2000

| | Median household income | | College educated (%) | | Homeowners (%) | |
|---|---|---|---|---|---|---|
| | 1990 | 2000 | 1990 | 2000 | 1990 | 2000 |
| Non-Hispanic white | $41,284 | $40,281 | 22.3 | 25.0 | 39.0 | 44.3 |
| Non-Hispanic black | $30,084 | $27,208 | 10.8 | 12.3 | 27.9 | 30.6 |
| Hispanic | $24,659 | $24,902 | 12.3 | 11.5 | 16.8 | 22.4 |
| Asian | $34,173 | $33,070 | 20.9 | 21.7 | 27.6 | 31.6 |

*Source:* Lewis Mumford Center for Comparative Urban and Regional Research.

all have contributed to deepening poverty in the city (Zeilbauer 2002; McKee 2000). To the extent that its minority populations have borne the brunt of these economic problems, it may be difficult for them to view one another as anything other than competitors for dwindling resources. African American and immigrant populations in Hartford thus might each elect to go it alone and shore up its own fragile status rather than trying to engineer coalitions. They might be expected, in fact, to have considerably more conflict than their counterparts in New York, where economic conditions have been less dire. As it turns out, however, African Americans and nonwhite immigrants in Hartford actually have had far better results in building alliances.

Consider the evidence of their success. While minority politicians in New York City were lamenting Ferrer's loss in 2005, those in Hartford were enjoying a series of unprecedented gains under the Puerto Rican–born Democratic mayor Eddie Perez, the first Latino mayor both in Hartford and in New England, elected in 2001. Outpolling his white opponent by a margin of four to one in a landslide victory, Perez assembled a rainbow-style electoral coalition, including large numbers of Latinos, blacks, and whites. Much like Ferrer in New York, Perez garnered endorsements from most of the black and Latino leaders in Hartford. But the Hartford mayor managed a notable feat that Ferrer was unable to accomplish—Perez actually mobilized Latino and black voters in significant numbers. That he registered and brought 2,000 new, mostly Latino voters to the polls was perhaps to be expected on account of the symbolic ethnic significance of his candidacy (*New York Times* 2001). More surprising was the fact that Perez was able to overcome potential opposition and fears about political displacement from African American leaders and voters.

As in New York and other cities, African Americans in Hartford have enjoyed more political power than Latinos and other nonwhite immigrants over the last several decades. Yet they have worried about losing their fragile political advantage to these groups, especially Puerto Ricans (Cruz 1998). Their concerns have increased as these immigrant populations have grown in number and electoral muscle. With their own share of the population dwindling, African Americans understandably might have been hesitant to support Perez. Yet he managed to draw African American leaders and voters into a multiracial electoral alliance with his Latino base.

In contrast to the short-lived or politically impotent rainbow alliances that have emerged in other cities, the Hartford coalition headed by Perez has shown both traction and a capacity for substantive policy influence. Perhaps one of the most striking instances of political effectiveness was its success in passing a charter reform referendum in 2002 to replace the weak-mayor, council manager form of city government with a strong-mayor system. When Perez and his coalition won the mayoralty in 2001, they were in danger of claiming an all-too-familiar hollow prize. The first Latino mayor of Hartford assumed office with the city at the nadir of its decades-long economic slide. This conjunction of minority political ascendance and central city economic decline has been a common scenario throughout the United States in recent decades (Kraus and Swanstrom 2001; Friesma 1969). Institutional limitations compounded the problem in Hartford; the weak-mayor form of government relegated Perez to a ceremonial role without the policy levers to attempt the reforms needed to help his disadvantaged minority constituents. Several of his mayoral predecessors, both black and white, had attempted unsuccessfully either to circumvent these institutional constraints or abolish the weak-mayor form of government (Zielbauer 2002; McKee 2000). Perez, however, managed to win citywide approval for charter reform and enlarge his official powers in 2002 (Stowe 2002).

Although the political successes of the Perez regime are partly due to his unique leadership abilities, the multiracial alliance that supports him is no anomaly. Despite the long-standing tensions between African Americans and Latinos, Hartford minority voters over the years have managed to put aside their differences and forge workable rainbow-style electoral coalitions to advance their political fortunes. The city elected its first African American mayor, Thirman Milner, in 1981—eight years before Dinkins was elected in New York. Although Milner's triumph was assured by an overwhelming black vote, he also drew support from heavily Latino precincts and some liberal white neighborhoods (Levine and Douglas 1981).

An alliance of black, Latino and white liberal Hartforders elected the country's first big-city African American female mayor, Carrie Saxon Perry, in 1987. Perry's three-term tenure amply demonstrated the coalition-building proclivities of minority populations in the city. Strong support from the mostly black North End and the white liberal West End fueled her first two triumphs. Her third was the result of an independent campaign outside the Democratic Party with her own slate of candidates (McKee 2000, 38). She activated not only black support but also Latino voters and leaders. Although Perry's three terms in office were marked by considerable political acrimony and severe economic hardships for the city, she still managed to increase the presence of blacks and Latinos in government and to keep racial tensions at bay. When many other cities erupted in racial disturbances in the wake of the Rodney King trial in 1992, for instance, Hartford stayed calm (Johnson 1993).

Perry floundered in her 1993 reelection bid to Mike Peters, a white Italian Democrat who had lost to her in the primary but petitioned his way on to the general election ballot. The contest between the two, however, was nothing like the racially polarized mayoral race between Dinkins and Giuliani in New York City the same year.[8] Unlike Giuliani, who had almost no support among black voters, Peters drew up to 25 percent of the vote in several predominantly black districts in Hartford (Johnson 1993). Peters won with a bipartisan slate balanced by race, ethnicity, gender, and neighborhood representation (McKee 2000, 40). This is not to say that there were no racial or minority intergroup tensions during these various mayoral regimes. The larger point, however, is that these groups identified compelling incentives and effective strategies for transcending these divisions to make electoral common cause.

The success that Hartford minority groups have had in overcoming differences and forging workable alliances is reflected in relations between the African American and Afro-Caribbean residents of the city. Much like their counterparts in New York City, African Americans and Afro-Caribbeans in Hartford have between them grounds for both coalition building and competition. Recent census data show that African American and Afro-Caribbean enclaves in Hartford have practically identical socioeconomic profiles with many of the same problems and deficits.[9] (See table 7.4.) On the other hand, the grim economic environment of the city may overshadow these shared interests and turn them into a basis for competition.

**Table 7.4** Neighborhood characteristics for African Americans, Afro-Caribbeans, and Africans, Hartford, 1990 and 2000

| | Median household income | | College educated (%) | | Homeowners (%) | |
|---|---|---|---|---|---|---|
| | 1990 | 2000 | 1990 | 2000 | 1990 | 2000 |
| African-American | $29,123 | $26,828 | 10.6 | 12.2 | 26.5 | 29.5 |
| Afro-Caribbean | $34,535 | $28,612 | 11.6 | 12.3 | 34.6 | 35.1 |
| African | $35,817 | $30,908 | 21.7 | 21.9 | 28.2 | 27.0 |
| Black ethnic total | $30,084 | $27,208 | 10.8 | 12.3 | 27.9 | 30.6 |

*Source:* Lewis Mumford Center for Comparative Urban and Regional Research.

There are also grounds for electoral conflict. Afro-Caribbeans in Hartford have yet to attain the levels of political mobilization and representation achieved by their Caribbean counterparts in New York City. But in the last decade and a half the group has begun to make serious bids for political office as their numbers in the population and citizenship rates have increased. Many Afro-Caribbean leaders contend that the group has been underrepresented in the electoral arena for too long, despite the fact that so many of the immigrants are homeowners, local retailers, and a notable presence in the government workforce (Noel 1996). With this rallying cry, calls for prominent co-ethnics to run for office, and campaigns encouraging the rank-and-file to register and vote, Afro-Caribbeans in Hartford and surrounding towns began to make bids for elective office in the 1990s (Rogers n.d.). Although these mobilization efforts could pose a political threat to African Americans, there has been little evidence of outright electoral conflict between the two groups.

One of the most notable and telling instances was the successful campaign run by Veronica Airey-Wilson, Hartford City Council member and former deputy mayor. In 1993, Airey-Wilson became only the second Afro-Caribbean and the first woman from the ethnic group to be elected to the council. Her campaign easily could have triggered significant conflict between the Afro-Caribbean and African American populations. Airey-Wilson and the Afro-Caribbean community leaders who drafted her to run met with chilly resistance from the African American Democratic establishment when they broached the idea of the party's endorsing her for one of the nine at-large seats on the council (Rogers n.d.).[10]

She and her backers then decided to try to run under the Republican banner for one of the three seats on the council reserved for minority parties by the city charter.[11] Running as a Republican posed two serious political risks for Airey-Wilson—both of which had potential ramifications for relations between Afro-Caribbean and African American Hartforders.

First, the decision threatened to jeopardize Airey-Wilson's assumed electoral connection to Afro-Caribbeans. Most Afro-Caribbean voters in Hartford are registered Democrats. For example, the ratio of registered Democrats to Republicans in the most heavily Afro-Caribbean voting district was roughly twenty-four to one in 2005. To carry her ethnic base, then, Airey-Wilson would have to persuade Afro-Caribbeans to abandon their usual electoral habits and cross party lines to vote for a Republican co-ethnic. She therefore needed Afro-Caribbeans to put ethnic loyalties over their partisan attachments. This kind of electoral strategy typically requires outright appeals to ethnic identity that risk the disaffection or group-based countermobilization of other segments of the electorate. An Airey-Wilson campaign that played mostly to Afro-Caribbean ethnic solidarity might have triggered opposition from African Americans in particular; recall similar efforts by Caribbean leaders have done so in New York City.

As a black woman running as a Republican candidate, Airey-Wilson also tempted questions from opponents about her racial credentials as a minority politician. In a city where nonwhite voters are mostly Democrats, taking up the Republican banner obviously might prompt serious or even mischievous questions about a candidate's connection to a minority base, especially from overwhelmingly Democratic African Americans keen to raise doubts about her racial authenticity to score political points.

Airey-Wilson managed to avoid these pitfalls in 1993. She made broad appeals to the entire Hartford electorate—blacks, whites, and Latinos alike (Rogers n.d.). Although she mobilized Afro-Caribbean immigrants, she balanced these efforts with outreach to other groups. There was no serious backlash or campaign by African American leaders to challenge her candidacy, despite their resistance to putting her on the Democratic slate. Airey-Wilson ultimately drew votes from both Afro-Caribbeans and African Americans in the North End and from liberal whites in the West End.

The Airey-Wilson election is quite consistent with the history of multiracial coalition building at the mayoral level. The successes African Americans and nonwhite immigrants in Hartford have had in moderating intergroup conflict and forging alliances are a considerable contrast to the more fractious history of minority group political relations in New York City. The differences in electoral institutions between the two cities may help account for these contrasting intergroup political dynamics. Unlike the district-based City Council elections in New York, the Hartford at-large council races do not provide much of a strategic incentive for politicians to make racially or ethnically targeted appeals to groups in the electorate. Rather, the at-large elections actually encourage candidates to fashion broad campaigns pitched to the city population as a whole.

Of course, the relatively small size of the total electorate in Hartford might prompt some candidates to stake their election hopes on a single ethnic or racial group, especially if these constituents are residentially concentrated.[12] Candidates might be inclined to disregard the strategic incentives of the electoral system and eschew broad-based citywide campaigns in favor of less costly and more efficient targeted appeals to a reliable core of ethnic or racial constituents. It is conceivable that a candidate for City Council could win one of the at-large seats by garnering an overwhelming share of the votes from a single racial or ethnic group.

The danger in this strategy, however, is that it risks sparking countermobilization from other groups in the electorate, as the New York case demonstrates. Airey-Wilson possibly might have alienated or angered a large number of African Americans in the North End if she had appealed only to her Afro-Caribbean co-ethnics in the 1993 campaign. An ethnically targeted strategy might have spurred African American leaders to oppose her outright in the election and rally the larger number of African American voters behind an alternative candidate. But Airey-Wilson followed the institutional logic of the at-large system and ran a broad-based, ethnically inclusive campaign.

At-large city council elections favor broad, citywide campaigns and discourage strictly group-based mobilization. These electoral institutions probably have helped to make broad-based, or at least balanced, campaigns a strategic norm among Hartford politicians. It is perhaps no surprise, then, that the African American and nonwhite immigrant groups in Hartford have had more success forging workable electoral coalitions at the mayoral level than their counterparts in New York City. The New York electoral environment encourages politicians and constituents to calculate and organize their political interests in terms of their specific ethnic or racial group attachments, which can be difficult to suspend even when alliance building is at stake. Hartford politicians, on the other hand, are accustomed to making broader calculations and fashioning appeals that span racial and ethnic lines. The strategic imperatives of the at-large electoral environment have made this more encompassing approach the norm in City Council elections in particular. But it stands to reason that this strategic norm applies also to mayoral elections, where there is only one electoral prize and alliance building or other forms of group coordination are even more critical for success.

## Conclusion

Institutional configurations in New York and Hartford appear to influence the odds of electoral conflict and coalition building among native- and foreign-born minority groups. District-based City Council elections in New York seem to increase the chances for intergroup friction and complicate coalition building by inducing leaders and their constituents to elevate their racial or ethnic attachments above other political considerations. The at-large system of elections in Hartford appears to do just the opposite—it encourages politicians to downplay identity-based politics or at least balance such group-centered efforts with broader appeals, which in turn minimizes intergroup conflict and facilitates alliance building across racial and ethnic lines. Although at-large systems may furnish more strategic incentives for intergroup coordination, they historically have hampered the electoral prospects of minority populations saddled with numerical and resource disadvantages, such as African Americans and Latinos. The same populations tend to do better in cities with district-based electoral systems.

This might appear to pose a practical political dilemma for these groups. But electoral rules are hardly the only institutional arrangements that shape groups' political choices and opportunities for representation. For instance, it is well established that new groups have better prospects for inclusion in competitive two-party systems than in electoral environments in which a single party dominates (e.g., Erie 1988). The Airey-Wilson case in Hartford demonstrates that even a weak multiparty system can provide alternative routes to representation for politically disadvantaged groups.

Minorities are not at all doomed to exclusion in at-large systems, then, if other institutional arrangements can help bolster their odds of achieving representation.

Moreover, the impediment that at-large systems pose to minority group representation may be overstated in the literature. Institutional arrangements, such as rules stipulating at-large elections, are hardly ironclad. Political actors do not always follow such requirements to the letter. Indeed, they often seek to bend the rules—without overturning them completely—to achieve various ends. For example, politicians in some cities have pushed for hybrid electoral systems that mix both at-large and district city council seats to address minorities' demands for descriptive representation without undermining opportunities for group coalition building.

We need not frame the difference between district and at-large elections as starkly as one between more or less representation for minority groups as long as there are other institutional routes for achieving this goal. By this light, the coalition-building benefits of at-large elections are worth taking seriously above and beyond their impact on minority prospects for descriptive representation. At-large systems may be better for interminority alliance building, and district elections may enhance individual group opportunities for elective representation. But to the extent that native- and foreign-born minority groups have common problems, forging coalitions is a critically important challenge. Alliances furnish organizational sites for these groups to clarify shared issues, fashion consensus around potential policy solutions, and identify promising leaders to pursue mutually endorsed agendas. Building sturdy alliances may be imperative, then, if African Americans and nonwhite immigrants are to move beyond purely descriptive representation and secure substantive policy influence to address the problems they have in common.

The problems these groups share often have not been rallying causes; rather, they have become flashpoints for conflict and mutual suspicion. But the severity and reach of the challenges that these groups face are not purely objective empirical facts—they are also significantly matters of perception. At-large electoral systems, such as the one in Hartford, provide a strategic incentive for politicians to identify and target such crosscutting issues because they are more likely to appeal to a broad swath of the electorate and engage a number of different groups across a city. Hence, at-large elections help to clarify the problems that groups have in common by inducing politicians to fashion broad encompassing agendas that address the interests of wide range of constituencies. To the extent that district-based elections encourage narrower targeted appeals to discrete groups, they are not nearly as likely to prompt politicians to identify such issues or mold an agenda around them.

Of course, formal electoral institutions are hardly the only ones that matter. Civic organizations outside government are an important staging ground for mobilization and alliance building as well. Organizational networks connecting different minority groups in New York City, for instance, have offered the most promising glimpses of intergroup political cooperation. Emerging research suggests that African American, Afro-Caribbean, and Latino public employees are using the unions in New York, with some success, to reach a common political vocabulary and identify new leaders (Greer 2007; Foerster 2004; Wong 2006). This kind of political and social learning across racial and ethnic lines lays the foundation and creates the impetus for coalition building (Rogers 2006).[13] Organizational sites not only serve to identify leaders and shared issues; they also help build trust and norms of reciprocity among these groups, which in turn can become important political capital for alliance building, especially at election time. Several Afro-Caribbean leaders in Hartford, for instance, trace their support for Mayor Perez to their work with him in several North End community organizations. Perez himself attributes his success in appealing to black voters to his work with these neighborhood groups.

The evidence of the impact of electoral arrangements on intergroup relations in New York City and Hartford catalogued in this chapter is only suggestive. But it is an invitation to researchers to devote more serious empirical attention to how institutional configurations influence the odds of coalition building and conflict among racial and ethnic groups in cities in the United States. Recent studies on the often-tense relations between African Americans and nonwhite immigrants have considered a range of possible causal factors, from economic insecurities to ideological incompatibility to failures of leadership within these populations. Less attention has been paid to the formal and informal political institutions and organizational networks that guide the political behavior of these groups and their leaders. To the extent that institutions induce political actors to make particular choices—such as whether to emphasize common causes or highlight differences from others—they are bound to have an impact on group relations. Researchers studying intergroup dynamics in Europe have been pursuing this analytic path for some time now and turning up significant empirical results (Dancygier 2007; Ireland 2004; Horowitz 1985). Scholars trying to make sense of the shifting tides in relations between African Americans and recent nonwhite immigrants in cities in the United States might gain new insights by adopting a similar focus on the role of institutions.

# PART IV

# IMMIGRANTS' NATIONAL POLITICAL OPPORTUNITY STRUCTURES

We turn next to the national level. The interest groups, electoral system, political party incentives, statutory and constitutional structures, and cultural traditions of a country all emerge as critical influences on immigrants' political incorporation. Both immigrants and native-born political actors have an array of choices to make and strategies to consider. Nevertheless, as at the local level, elites who support immigration and immigrants' inclusion lack a free hand to foster their goals. They are constrained not only by deeply embedded laws and institutions but also by a fluctuating and occasionally uncontrollable hostility to immigrants that emerges from an interaction between an anxious or nativist public and political actors with their own agenda.

Christian Joppke and Jan Willem Duyvendak, Trees Pels, and Rally Rijkschroeff present a paired set of chapters that examine, from contrasting vantage points, the relationship between the willingness of states to accommodate distinct immigrant cultures and immigrants' socioeconomic success. Not surprisingly, given their topic, both chapters discuss symbolic or literal exclusion as well as integration. In chapter 8, Joppke shows how France and Germany have shied away from a formal embrace of multiculturalism, choosing instead state neutrality among cultural practices or a more assertive national particularism. Joppke argues that these states reject multiculturalism for two reasons: multicultural policies have demonstrably failed to bring about immigrants' economic integration, and in a post–September 11 world, elites are more strongly asserting liberal values and seeking to imbue immigrants with them. On balance, Joppke endorses the rejection of state-sponsored multiculturalism. Nevertheless, he cautions that its abandonment risks promoting immigrant disincorporation, encouraging young Muslims to identify with a transnational Islamic movement at the expense of engagement with their country of residence.

In chapter 9, Duyvendak, Pels, and Rijkschroeff take direct issue with Joppke's claim that states determine their cultural accommodation policies in light of their success at achieving economic incorporation. They insist that immigrants were, in fact, making economic and educational progress under the recently eliminated Dutch policy of at least partial multiculturalism. In these authors' view, the Dutch abandoned the policy not because it ostensibly failed but mainly because their highly progressive monoculturalism was, in fact, intolerant of genuine cultural pluralism. Duyvendak, Pels, and Rijkschroeff share Joppke's concern that, although the abandonment of multiculturalism might help integrate some immigrants, it is likely to push others even farther from the mainstream, with harmful impact on themselves and possibly on their state.

In chapter 10, Michael Minkenberg examines political movements that genuinely do seek to push immigrants out of the mainstream (albeit not into religious or political radicalism). He shows that since the 1970s, politicians and state actors in several European countries have responded to the growing organizational strength of radical right-wing, anti-immigrant elements by adopting and legitimizing some of their demands. In turn, some parties of the new radical right have developed a much more sophisticated and appealing argument by "replacing attacks on the democratic order as a whole with a mobilization of populist and ethnocentric campaigns to foster a rightist, value-based, New Politics cleavage." Minkenberg provides an elegant analysis of the nativist right in six European states by analyzing the recent history of each in terms of three elements: "the organizational strength and party and nonparty forms of the radical right, its ability to mobilize support, and its capacity to force a response from and recalibration of the larger political environment." The result is a frightening portrayal of increasing xenophobic violence and political influence, with some movement into policy responsiveness.

The United States and Canada, Joppke indicates, have done better than European states in keeping Muslim immigrants from being lured into radical movements by including them in higher education and the economy. Peter Schuck concurs. More than any other author in *Bringing Outsiders In,* Schuck offers, in chapter 11, a prescription for how states should incorporate their immigrants. He comes closer to Joppke than to Duyvendak, Pels, and Rijkschroeff in his attitude toward multiculturalism: a state has a legitimate interest in maintaining its national culture and thus cannot make ethnic and cultural difference a public goal. It should instead be "liberal" (in Tariq Modood's sense of the term; see chap. 15 in this volume). That is, a state should *protect* privately expressed cultural diversities from discrimination and monopoly, and should import diversity through its immigration policy. But it should not take a more active role such as mandating, certifying, or promoting diversity, which is more properly a function of civil society. Appropriately designed public policies and a public education system will help assimilate immigrants into the linguistic and economic mainstream. Political involvement will eventually follow.

In addition to his prescription, Schuck provides a comprehensive review of U.S. immigration law and policy over the past few decades, public opinion with regard to immigration, and the role of structures such as federalism, policies such as affirmative action, and cultural norms of assimilation in shaping immigrant inclusion. The breadth of his vision provides a fine counterpoint to Luis Fraga's close look at U.S. arguments for and against immigration and immigrants over the past few years.

In chapter 12, Fraga is skeptical of any claim that opposition to undocumented immigration is significantly different from opposition to immigration per se; in his view, both positions are similarly "driven by a heightened sense of the need to maintain traditional notions of national identity and, at this point in time, to largely exclude noncitizens from full participation in U.S. society." Proponents also do not sharply distinguish between legal and illegal immigrants; supporters of expanded immigration or the regularization of undocumented immigrants' status "say that even immigrants without legal papers contribute to U.S. society, and so should be part of the U.S. community." Fraga analyzes an array of claims on each side of the immigration debate and shows how they have operated in the recent abortive efforts by the U.S. Congress to pass legislation on immigration.

Comparing Minkenberg's and Fraga's chapters supports Joppke's suggestion that the U.S. political system resists xenophobic political movements more effectively than do most European systems. Even Fraga notes that, despite the failure of comprehensive immigration reform, four political factors are likely to constrain opponents of immigration: (1) the many people who can be mobilized to publicly support immigrant rights; (2) Latinos' capacity to be pivotal voters for Democrats in California and elsewhere, and possibly for Republicans in Florida; (3) the growing tendency of state and local governments to form their own immigration policies in light of federal inertia, thus relieving pressure on federal legislators; and (4) the possibility that tighter border enforcement would actually increase unauthorized immigration from Mexico.

Part IV of *Bringing Outsiders In* is dense with new arguments and evidence, but it nevertheless leaves us with as many questions as answers. Minkenberg shows how political opportunity structures interact with right-wing opposition to immigration in Europe, and Fraga suggests a parallel dynamic in the United States—but we still lack clarity on how national political systems connect to immigrants' aspirations and assets. Does multiculturalism help or hurt integrative efforts? Should states distinguish between private and public arenas? Must states exclude some in order to build a sense of community among others? Can political parties tame xenophobia by incorporating it, or do they just make it stronger? How should states react to immigrants who do not value inclusion? Finally, how do parts III and IV of *Bringing Outsiders In*—that is local and national opportunity structures—interact?

# CHAPTER EIGHT

# Successes and Failures of Muslim Integration in France and Germany

*Christian Joppke*

If we compare immigrant integration in Europe and the United States, we immediately hit a paradox. In Europe, religion and how to deal with Muslim immigrants are indisputably the major topics. By contrast, in the United States the main problem seems to be language and how to deal with Hispanic immigrants (Zolberg and Woon 1999; Huntington 2004). This is despite the fact that it is the United States that has waged major wars against groups and regimes that are Islamic in claim or origins. The country that lamentably has become, together with Israel, the most hated country in the Islamic world ("the Great Satan") is not known to have any particular problem with integrating Muslim immigrants—no problems here with mosque-building, dietary restrictions in public kitchens, exemptions from certain parts of the public school curriculum, or dress codes. Accordingly, when a U.S. "veil affair" seemed to be in the making in an Oklahoma school in March 2004, the federal Department of Justice promptly intervened, arguing that "religious discrimination has no place in American schools" (BBC News 2004).

An explanation of this striking paradox is beyond the scope of this chapter. Let me only mention three sets of factors that are likely to be involved in it. First, and at the risk of stating the obvious (which does not therefore make it less true), church and state are more thoroughly separated in the United States than in Europe. Among other factors, this is due to the denominational fragmentation of the dominant Protestant religion in the United States, which rendered impossible any privileged rapprochement between state and any one church (as happened between the state and the Catholic Church in notionally laicist but factually corporatist, group-recognizing France).

A second, much less commented on factor is the different social profiles of Muslim immigrants in Europe and the United States, poor and undereducated in the former but relatively privileged and with high skill levels in the latter. Europe, *grosso modo,* took in poorly educated postcolonial peasants whose likewise marginalized or unemployed children and grandchildren are now receptive to the protest ideology of a transnational Islamic movement. In fact, if we look for a parallel in the United States to the group of postcolonial immigrants in Europe, it is not Muslim immigrants but the nonimmigrant African Americans, who arrived involuntarily as slaves and some of whom have adopted a variant of politicized Islam, the Nation of Islam. By contrast, for Muslim immigrants in the United States, Islam mostly is not an issue because of their high social status. For instance, the well-to-do Iranian immigrants that we find in larger numbers in southern California have little interest in public prayer calls and the like because most of them are refugees from a regime that takes a keen interest in precisely such things. Overall, a recent survey found that, much in contrast to their socioeconomically marginalized European peers, U.S. Muslims are "solidly middle-class and solidly integrated with their non-Muslim neighbors" (Ackerman 2005, 18).[1]

Third, and in an interesting counterpoint to a comparatively incomplete separation between state and church in Europe, European societies are highly secular societies, whereas U.S. society has not only remained stubbornly religious but, in striking deviation from most other western societies, has become even more religious in recent years. There is a contrast in Europe between churches that are empty and mosques that are full. We may well argue that religious claims by Muslim immigrants are more difficult to accommodate in secularized societies such as those in Europe than in a society, such as the United States (to the limited degree that religious Muslim claims are raised here at all), where religion is more of a lived reality and common experience and thus not exotic to the same degree. As a young U.S. Muslim expressed his experience, "When I go out to Bush Country, it is true that, for some people, the way I pray is peculiar. But they don't think I'm hallucinating when I say, 'It's prayer time'" (quoted in Ackerman 2005, 20). By contrast, in Europe, it is not so much a religious society as, at best, the Christian churches that support Islamic claims, and we cannot help the impression that this is the solidarity of the underdogs.

The very fact that Islam *is* an issue in Europe but not in the United States casts doubt on the often-made argument that there is something inherent in Islam that makes it incompatible with western ways. Ernest Gellner, among many others, summarized it in the notion that "Islam is the blueprint of a social order" (1981, 1), and one that does not allow for the distinction between public and private, the political and religious spheres, which has become the mark of secularized Christianity (and which is inherent in the proclivity of Christianity to "(r)ender...unto Caesar the things which are Cesar's"; see Lewis 2003, chap. 5). This view, a common stance in the Clash of Civilizations discourse that has become the hallmark of the post-2001 era, paints an unduly monolithic view of Islam, obscuring its many internal schisms and reform tendencies. It is particularly silent on less secularized versions of the Christian and Jewish branches of monotheism. What about Hassidic Jews in Nablus and Brooklyn who applauded the killing of a dovish Israeli prime minister? What about Christian fundamentalists who bomb abortion clinics in the United States? The weirdoes are just next door.[2]

The specificity of Islam is probably more to be found in its current transnational mobilizing capacity than in its cultural content. The context of a worldwide operating Islamic movement is central to understanding why very similar politico-religious claims are raised by second-generation Muslim immigrants or ethnics across Europe but, strikingly, not by adherents of other immigrant religions (Hindus, Sikhs, Buddhists, etc.; see Statham et al. 2005). And if young Muslims in the United States and Canada are mostly unresponsive to the global Islamic movement, this is because of the fabled assimilatory capacities of these societies. North American Muslims are simply too busy making it through college and they have become too American or too Canadian in too many ways to perceive themselves as Muslims only. As a U.S. federal government official explained the absence of politicization among U.S. Muslim immigrants, "It's the American dream. American Muslims are living that dream" (quoted in Ackerman 2005, 19). Furthermore, note that upon the characteristically pro-active approval of *shariah*-based Muslim tribunals of family law by the Canadian provincial government of Ontario, it was mostly (female) Muslims throughout Canada who protested loudly against this move (*Toronto Star* 2004).[3]

Conversely, European societies are facing, in their politicized Muslim youngsters in the French *banlieues* and in the decrepit industrial towns of northern England, their failure to make postcolonial immigrants well-to-do members of their societies. Whereas there is not known to be an unemployment problem for U.S. Muslims, Muslim unemployment is disproportionately high in Europe. For instance, British Pakistani men have a 15 percent jobless rate, three times above that of British white men, and some French, heavily Muslim-populated *banlieues* show 40 percent unemployment, which is more than four times higher than the national unemployment rate. Overall, what is often characterized as a conflict of cultures or of religions is at heart a failure of socioeconomic integration.

The French-government-commissioned Stasi Report (2003), which launched the recent legislative ban on veiling (and on other "ostentatious" religious symbols) in public schools, interestingly noted the socioeconomic root cause of politicized Islam very clearly.

> It has been signaled to the Commission that in seven hundred urban quarters, all of which comprise numerous nationalities, the difficulties accumulate: unemployment exceeding 40 percent, acute schooling problems, social alarm signals that are three times stronger than in the rest of France. The inhabitants of these abandoned quarters have the sentiment of being victims of a social relegation that condemns them to withdraw amongst themselves. This is especially the case with the young. Thirty-two percent of this population is under 20 years—what a disaster for these people and for the Republic. (Stasi Report 2003, sec. 3.3.1)

It is all the more remarkable that this otherwise very sensitive and probing document still got fixed on the cultural terrain, fighting a perceived "permanent guerilla war against *laïcité*" (Stasi Report 2003, sec. 3.2.2).

In addition to the push factor of socioeconomic marginalization, which has made young Muslim ethnics receptive to the lure of the transnational Islamic movement, there is also a domestic pull factor that has conditioned and framed recent conflicts in Europe over Muslim immigrants in general and over the veiling of Muslim women in particular—a fatigue with, if not retreat from, multiculturalism (see Joppke 2004). Advocates of multiculturalism have long presented as a logical *sequitur* that an increasingly multiethnic and multicultural reality should be reflected in multicultural recognition policies of the state (in its most serious formulation, Kymlicka 1995, this logical *sequitur* is presented as a matter of liberal justice). This logical *sequitur* is under fire today, at the level of theory (Barry 2001) and at the level of policy, in Europe and elsewhere. In turn, a long-discarded alternative to multicultural recognition policies of the state—state neutrality—is having a revival. State neutrality and the privatization of religion were actually *the* solution to the first wave of multicultural conflicts in Europe, the religious wars of the sixteenth and seventeenth centuries, and it is the formula that gave birth to modern liberalism. The state neutrality position argues that, precisely because society is divided by many creeds, the state should not take sides in this but leave creedal, ethnic, and life-style matters to the realm of private rather than public action.[4]

## Resurgent State Neutrality

The veil has become a contested issue also because the state neutrality response is gaining ground over the official multiculturalism response to multiculturalism as social fact. Incidentally, the notion of state neutrality features prominently in the Stasi Report (reflecting, of course, that in terms of *laïcité* it has a long pedigree in France). And it has been central in recent court rulings on the veil in Germany, interestingly both in rulings that prohibited and in rulings that allowed the contested symbol to be exhibited by teachers in public schools (for more details, see Joppke 2007b). The argument in both cases was that the neutrality mandate of the state was gaining more importance precisely because society was becoming more culturally and religiously diverse—and not the other way around, that a plural society requires a plural stance-taking "recognition" state, as advocates of multiculturalism have claimed.

The reasons for the withering of official multiculturalism and the resurgence of state neutrality as a way of regulating multiethnic societies are themselves complex and multiple. First, multicultural policies have failed to bring about the socio-economic mainstreaming of migrant ethnics, feeding instead their separation into marginal parallel societies. This factor has been prominent in the Netherlands's recent move from official multiculturalism toward civic integration, which stresses Dutch language competence and other host-society skills and knowledge. Second, European societies are currently preparing for a new wave of large-scale immigration, wanted both for economic and demographic reasons. The downscaling of multiculturalism is seen by political elites (including by those who once were sympathetic to multiculturalism, as in the British Labour Party) as a price for making this opening acceptable to insecure and anxious natives (a prime document demonstrating this reasoning is Home Office 2002). Finally, since the terrorist attacks of September 2001 there has been a stronger assertiveness that liberal values should be accepted by newcomers. As Charles Taylor (1994, 26) once put it, liberalism is also a "fighting creed"; and this potential has surely been released by this epochal event. An example of this is the new kind of civic integration policies that screen newcomers and applicants for naturalization for their acceptance of liberal-democratic values, in addition to their required mastery of the host-society language (for an overview, see Joppke 2007a).

Next to multiculturalism-in-crisis, however, there is a second competitor to state neutrality in dealing with migrant diversity—national particularism. If we compare the veiling debates in France and Germany (for more details, see Joppke 2007b), a major difference between them is that in France the positions of state neutrality and national particularism tend to overlap whereas they are starkly apart in Germany. As the French constellation of these stances is described by a Republican intellectual, with characteristically overdrawn pathos: "The French particularism is universalism" (Todd 1994, 228). The principle of *laïcité* is nevertheless open to conflicting interpretations and incarnations. It may be either a particularistic, almost sacralized condition of assimilation *à la française* (as it appears in the Stasi Report and the subsequent anti-veiling law) or a liberal principle guaranteeing religious freedoms to everyone, Muslims included. This is why *laïcité* is defended by everyone in France, even by the Muslim organizations that may find fault with the particularistic incarnation that is found in the anti-veiling law.[5] And, shortly after the passing of this law in 2004, the spontaneous solidarity after two French journalists had been taken hostage in Iraq and French Muslims' distancing themselves from a hypermilitant branch of transnational Islam show the emergence of a French Islam. It affirms that the taking of a neutral stance toward religion by the state is not just a smokescreen for discrimination but potentially protective of Muslims.

Although state neutrality and national particularism thus tend to overlap in France, both stances are clearly separate, even opposite, in Germany. The Federal Constitutional Court, in its September 2003 landmark ruling in the *Ludin* case (discussed further later in this chapter), and then Federal President Johannes Rau, in a high-profile intervention in the political rush toward banning the veil that was spurred by this court ruling,[6] have taken the state neutrality position—to treat all religions equally. Combining state neutrality with a headscarf ban, warned Rau, would in effect amount to the introduction of French-style *laïcité* in Germany and depart from the German tradition of "open and encompassing neutrality" (*offene und übergreifende Neutralität*) (Böckenförde 2001, 725), according to which all religions are equally invited into public space (e.g., schools, media, or the health sector). So, if Germans wanted to ban the headscarf in public schools, the constitutional equality principle (invoked by court and president) commanded the banning of *all* religious symbols, including the Christian or Judaic ones that so far no one had found fault with. Many would not like this outcome, as the deeply religious President Rau clearly did not. But—if equality was to be respected—*laïcité* became inevitable once the ball started rolling against wearing the veil. In the words of President Johannes Rau: "I am in favor of liberty [*Freiheitlichkeit*], but I am also in favor of treating all religious confessions equally. If the veil is considered a religions confession, an [impermissible] missionary cloth, then this must apply also to the monk's dress [*Mönchkutte*] or the crucifix" (2004).

However, the laws that were introduced in 2003 and 2004 by conservative Länder governments, especially in the German south, Hesse, and northern Lower Saxony, were in blatant violation of the equality principle. They sought to reinforce a national particularism untainted by any liberal neutrality constraint in targeting the veil only and explicitly allowing the display of Christian and Jewish wear by public school teachers. The argument was that the German nation was Judeo-Christian, and that the state representing this nation had the license to be partial and discriminatory against religions that were not traditionally a part of it. Interestingly, this stance, which in France is relegated to Le Pen's National Front and thus is outside the political mainstream, constitutes the conservative mainstream in Germany. A prominent former constitutional judge coolly responded that all state laws singling out the veil for prohibition were in violation of the equal religious liberty clause (Article 4) of the Basic Law; accordingly, if one counted on the safe intervention by the Constitutional Court, these state laws—against their own intention—would pave the way toward the introduction of *laïcité* in Germany (Böckenförde 2004).

In sum, because in Germany national particularism collides with the norm of fundamental equality that the contemporary liberal-constitutional state is morally committed to and even legally bound by, the national particularism stance has no viable future here, despite its considerable presence in the political mainstream.

## Inclusive Trends in Muslim Integration

The presence of national particularism in the veiling debate deflects from the generally inclusive stance that Germany—like all western liberal states since the 1960s (see Freeman 2004)—has taken toward its immigrant minorities, Muslims included. Because this is a topic that has notoriously been distorted by hyperbole and polemics, it deserves further scrutiny. What is inclusive? It is rejecting the idea of assimilating immigrants, in a kind of hands-off de facto multiculturalism that even France has not been able to deny, while essentially inviting immigrants into the citizenry by means of liberalized (as in Germany and most other European states) or historically inclusive (as in France) citizenship laws. It is true that in Germany this inclusive stance had long been blocked by its division into two states and by the West German self-definition as an incomplete nation-state geared toward unification with the eastern state (see Joppke 1999b, chap. 6).

It was this geopolitical circumstance, and not some alleged ethnic nationhood tradition, that made Germany different from other western states for a while. Proof of this is that exactly since unification some old mantras, such as the notorious "we are not an immigration country," have crumbled (Green 2004, chap. 5); that ethnic migration (of *Aussiedler*) has been severely restricted, even stopped in principle (Joppke and Rosenhek 2002); and that Germany is now a country with one of the most liberal nationality laws in Europe, with a conditional *jus soli* provision and some 150,000 naturalizations per year (Minkenberg 2003a).

How do Muslims fare in this generally inclusive picture of German immigrant integration? There are about 3 million Muslims in Germany today out of some 7 million immigrants and offspring. Most of them are Turkish. Here lies an important difference from France. French Muslim immigrants mostly originate from the former French colonies in North Africa and (as in the case of Algerians) often carry resentment that dates back to colonial times and the struggle for independence. This has made them receptive to the lure of transnational politicized Islam. At least since the mid-1990s bombing of the Paris Metro by Algerian extremists, the specter of politicized Islam, which might bring the distressed, heavily Arab-origin-populated *banlieues* to the brink of revolt, has haunted the French state, motivating also the recent anti-veiling law. By contrast, Turkish immigrants, who cannot look back to a similar history of colonialism, conflict, and resentment, are less likely to use Islam as a political weapon against the German state.

The two politicizations that we find among Turks in Germany are intra-ethnic and not directed against the German state or society: (1) Kurdish minority nationalism, which, as the hypermilitant Maoist Partiya Karkerên Kurdistan (PKK, Kurdistan Workers' Party), has been notoriously present in Germany, often through the asylum venue, and (2) Turkish Islamic groups or parties, which until recently were forbidden in a strictly laic Turkey and which have vicariously acted out Turkish domestic politics on German territory. In contrast to France, the German state did not really fear a politicization of Turkish Muslims that could be directed against the German state but, instead, the violent playing out of Turkish domestic politics on German territory, motivating also a strong opposition to dual citizenship (which has no parallel in France) or to granting protected minority status to Turks.

Of course, since the great reform of the nationality law in 1999, there has been a marked turn of Turkish organizations to domestic German issues, most notably the fight against discrimination and xenophobia. It is interesting to observe that Turkish organizations have adopted the Jewish analogy in this respect, seeing both Turks and Jews as repressed minorities (see Yurdakul and Bodemann 2006). And after September 11, 2001, there was a striking display of Turkish-Jewish solidarity, along with a joint distancing of Turks from Arabs, who are now associated with terrorism (this distancing certainly is not as new as it seems; it has a long pedigree in the Kemalist, Western-oriented Turkish state, which has always been pro-Israel and anti-Arab).

How have specifically Islamic claims been dealt with by German policy and jurisdictions? These claims are, overall, the same as elsewhere in Europe, and they have been similarly resolved (or not). Among the three most important of them are (1) religious education, (2) ritual slaughter, and (3) dress codes in public spaces.

## Religious Education

A long-standing demand by Turkish Islamic organizations has been to have Islam recognized as official religion, on a par with Christianity and Judaism. This would give them a license to tax their members (and to have the state collect these taxes on their behalf) and to teach Islam in state schools. This demand has long been rebuffed because of the nonchurch structure and the fragmentation of Islam in general and of Turkish-German Islamic groups in particular. In contrast to the recently created Conseil Français du Culte Musulman (CFCM) in France, there is not yet an organization that can credibly speak for all Muslims in Germany. Certainly, in April 2007, three major Islamic organizations in Germany—the Arab-dominated Central Council of Muslims, the Milli-Görüs–based Islam Council (Islamrat), and the Diyanet İşleri Türk İslam Birliği (DITIB, Turkish-Islamic Union for Religious Affairs; representing Turkish state Islam in Germany)—overcame old rivalries to found the Coordination Council of Muslims (CCM) with an eye on achieving the highly coveted status of *Körperschaft des öffentlichen Rechts* (corporation of public law). However, the German state has refused to acknowledge the new organization as representative of German Muslims, arguing that it speaks, at best, for 15 percent of German Muslims and for the extremely conservative factions at that, those that, among other things, propagate the Islamic headscarf and gender separation in physical education in public schools.

At the same time, this state reservation is wearing thin for two reasons. First, the refusal of the state to grant Islam the same privileges that Judaism and Christianity already enjoy stands against an irrefutable equality claim (protected in Article 4 of the Basic Law) made by what is now the second strongest religion in Germany. Second, as throughout Western Europe in the post-2001 era, there is also a pragmatic state interest in creating a nationalized form of Islam that is immune to the siren song of global Islamism.[7] Even though there is no publicly recognized central organization of Islam yet, some Länder (such as Berlin and North Rhine-Westphalia), partially forced by administrative court rulings, already allow Islamic instruction in state schools. Showing again the pivotal importance of considerations of public order in incorporating Islam, for some ten years there has already been a cross-party consensus for allowing Islam instruction in schools. The reason is that it is preferable to have state-controlled Islamic instruction, in the German language, than to leave this instruction to the obscurity of Turkish-language Koranic schools.

Much has been made in the literature of the diametrically opposed models of state-church relations in Germany and France—strict separation between the two in France versus their "concordatarian" rapprochement in Germany, whereby public status is assigned to the main religions in society—and both distinguished from a third model of a national church that we find in England and Scandinavia (see Ferrari 1995). In reality, these institutional differences are at best tangential to the accommodation of Islam. In all three regimes, there have recently been similar advances toward creating nationalized forms of Islam, arguably most pronounced in the regime where we would least expect it, laic France.

From the point of view of claims-making Muslims, however, there is a preference for church-state regimes in which religion plays an official role in public life, which is more the case in the concordatarian and national church regimes. Accordingly, Muslim intellectuals in Britain, such as Tariq Modood, have endorsed the Anglican establishment regime, only advocating pluralizing it in a multifaith direction (see König 2003, 185). In this vision, which is also the one held by the likely successor to the current monarch, the head of state would advance from being the "defender of *the* faith" to become the "defender of faith" in general. The Christian churches in the concordatarian and national-church regimes have often supported the Muslim quest to be included on equal terms. This is because the alternative to upgrading Islam is the downgrading and loss of privileges of the established religions. Therefore the archbishop of Canterbury's recent, rather spectacular advocacy of *shariah* in Britain. Whatever the state-church regime may be, at the formal level of laws and institutions there is a strong pull to accommodate Islam on equal terms with the already established religions.

## Ritual Slaughter

A German constitutional court ruling in 2002 granted Muslims an exemption from animal-protection laws that prescribe the stunning of animals before killing them.[8] Such an exemption already existed for Jews, so it could not be denied to Muslims.

This suggests a larger point about the political opportunity structure of Muslim integration—wherever there is a Jewish precedent or analogy, there is bound to be smooth sailing. By contrast, where no such Jewish precedent or analogy exists, there is likely to be resistance. This may be *one* reason why the Muslim veil is so contested— the Jewish *kippah* is too different in appearance and connotation to serve as analogy, although its removal from public spaces is very often the price that must be paid for targeting the veil.

The 2002 German court ruling further held that the production of *halal* meat via ritual slaughter was a matter of professional freedom (*Berufsfreiheit*) and of religious freedom, both of which are guaranteed by the Basic Law. This ruling thus suggests a second larger point about Muslim integration, this time with respect to its legal mechanisms—the protections of individual rights in the constitutional state are a potent mechanism for accommodating cultural difference, obliterating the need for further maximalist calls for group rights and cultural recognition (on this, see also Grimm 2002). And such integration is achieved precisely by being agnostic about the content of the cultures that are to be accommodated, leaving their definition, instead, as a matter of subjective interpretation and certainly no business of the state. Note here that a previous rejection of religious slaughter by the Federal Administrative Court[9] had been based on an *objective* evaluation that there was no absolute prescription of ritual slaughter to be found in Islam. The Constitutional Court overruled this decision, arguing that it was not up to the state to decide what a religion prescribes or is but that this had to be left to the subjective views shared by the members of that religion.

This suggests a third, larger point about Muslim integration, which is really about the symbolic dimension of accommodating cultural difference in the liberal state—if such accommodation succeeds, it is hands-off with respect to the meaning of the signs and practices to be accommodated, stressing instead their polyvalence and inherently subjective properties. By contrast, such accommodation fails when objective meanings are assigned to these signs and practices. With respect to the veil, its rejection by state agencies is usually in reference to its alleged objective meaning of female subordination and rejection of the West. And when the German Constitutional Court left the veil in place, it stressed its inherent polyvalence and multiplicity of meanings, which—in principle—could not be evaluated and adjudicated by the neutral and agnostic state.

However, the toleration of religious slaughter is bound to be contested to the degree that the moral principle and social movement of animal protection gains strength. This notably has happened in Britain, when the government-appointed and -funded Farm Animal Welfare Council concluded, after a four-year study, that Jewish and Muslim methods of slaughter were "inhumane," causing unnecessary suffering to the animals (*The Times* [London], May 15, 2003). In Germany, the opponents of the court-ruled Muslim exemption, in a shrewd political move, promptly pushed for the granting of constitutional status to the principle of animal protection and achieved this in an amendment to the Basic Law in 2002. Now there is a clash between two principles of equal constitutional value, religious freedoms versus animal protection. This development puts at risk one of the most significant legal successes of Muslim integration in Germany so far.

## The Veil, Again

As in most other European countries, with the exception of France, the veil had largely been a non-issue in Germany. It was first brought up by a German-naturalized female teacher of Afghan origin, Fereshta Ludin, who had been denied a civil service job in the conservative-ruled state of Baden-Württemberg on the grounds of her refusal to take off her headscarf in the classroom. In a highly publicized ruling in September 2003, the Federal Constitutional Court decided in her favor, overruling the verdict of the Federal Administrative Court on this matter.

The ruling goes a remarkably long way toward dispelling public fears and prejudices surrounding the veil and specifically rejects the idea (usual brought forward by headscarf opponents) that a single objective meaning can be assigned to the wearing of the headscarf, namely that the headscarf is in itself a sign of the oppression of women by men in Islam. "(I)n the face of the multiplicity of motives (attached to it), the veil cannot be reduced to a sign of the societal oppression of women (in Islam)," argued the court.[10] Since Nilüfer Göle's (1996) ethnography of veiling by young female university students in Turkey (which was cited with approval by some members of the Constitutional Court in the Ludin decision), this has become a sociological commonplace. It also corresponds to a larger trend of ethnicity in the liberal state as being subjective and self-defined rather than objective and other-defined (see Kertzer and Arel 2002; Joppke 2005, chap. 1).

The court also took seriously, however, the argument on the opponents' side, that in light of an increasing cultural and religious diversity in society the neutrality mandate of the state was gaining in importance. This might legitimize a prohibition of religious wear by teachers who represent this state. But, for such prohibition, the court concluded, legislation at the Land level was necessary. Without Land legislation, and as of September 2003 there had been no such legislation, the exclusion of the plaintiff from civil service was without legal basis and violated her constitutional right of equal access to public office, according to Article 33 of the Basic Law. This ambivalent, and on the central issue of the permissibility of the veil evasive, court ruling opened up a flurry of legislative initiatives in various Länder, from Christlich-Soziale Union (CSU, Christian Social Union)–ruled Bavaria to Sozialdemokratische Partei Deutschlands (SPD, Social Democratic Party)–ruled Berlin, for prohibiting teachers from wearing a veil in public schools.

Two fundamental differences between the French and German veiling conflicts are central to any meaningful comparison. First, the ban of the veil in France applies to all students in public schools, in an expansion of the original scope of *laïcité* (which had applied only to teachers, not to students) and indicating the predominance of a "sacral" over a "liberal" variant of *laïcité* (for a brief overview of the evolution of *laïcité*, see Baubérot 2004). By contrast, in Germany the ban applies only to teachers; the right of students to wear the veil has never been in question here.

This is an important difference. Teachers are not *Lumpenproletariat* in Germany but highly paid and privileged civil servants (*Beamte*). Proponents of banning the headscarf argued that the price for this privileged status was the restriction of certain individual rights if they contradicted the neutrality or educational mandates of the state. It is still an open question whether a teacher executes the sovereignty (*hoheitliche*) function of the state, which might require or legitimize the restriction of his or her individual rights, or whether the state's educational mandate, on the contrary, is not better served by exposing students in the classroom to the full variety of the diverse creeds and life styles that make up a complex and plural society (Böckenförde 2001).

Whatever stance you take on this, it is incontrovertible that the freedom-restricting implications of the veiling ban are more severe in France than in Germany because in France it is the state that is intruding uninvited into the private choices of individuals. By contrast, in Germany the individuals in question (aspiring teachers) are "seeking a special nearness to the state" rather than the state "invading" society— this was the reasoning adduced by three minority justices in the 2003 Constitutional Court ruling, who voted against the court majority and in favor of banning the head-scarf, even without specific legislation.[11]

Liberal values are nevertheless potentially more impaired in Germany than in France by the ruling, which points to a second difference between both cases. This is because of the mentioned selective targeting of the veil in most Länder laws in Germany, which is in blatant contradiction to the constitutional equality principle and the very Constitutional Court opinion on this issue. This raises a larger issue that transcends the scope of this paper: Is it still possible for a liberal-constitutional state to engage in particularistic nation-building, which is meant to be different here than elsewhere? My hunch is "no." Witness that at the EU level all references to "God" and "Christianity" (which in the veiling conflicts are in themselves universalistic code words for taking sides and being discriminatory) were erased from the (eventually aborted) draft constitution. In an age of human rights, Europe cannot but define itself in a universalistic way, and liberal-constitutional constraints push its member states (Germany included) in much the same direction.

## Socioeconomic Marginalization
## and the French Riots of 2005

To be distinguished sharply from the cultural accommodation of Islam, which has been fairly successful in Europe, at least at formal institutional level, is a persistent socioeconomic marginalization of Muslim immigrants and ethnics, which affects the latter not qua Muslims but qua immigrants or ethnics. This can be illustrated by the French Riots of 2005. The tragic electrocution, after a police chase at night, of two teenagers of North African origin in late October 2005 triggered the worst social turmoil that France had seen since the student unrest of 1968, with over 9,000 torched vehicles and 3,000 people arrested in nearly three weeks of continuous rioting. With an eye on the absence of Islam as a factor in the unrest, *The Economist* rightly spoke of an "angry rebellion of a beardless, Nike-wearing teenage underclass" (2005, 24).

The socioeconomic background to the "beardless rebellion" is obvious—at 23 percent, French youth unemployment is the highest in Europe; in the riot-struck "sensitive urban zones," populated mostly by immigrants and ethnics of North African origin, it is a staggering 40 percent(*Economist* 2005). The combination of unemployment and ethnic segregation in the dreaded *banlieues* is a major factor explaining the French riots.

In addition, because of a long-standing domestic preoccupation with Algerian terrorism, France was the only European country that had responded to the terrorist attacks of September 2001 in New York and of March 2002 in Madrid with tough counterterrorism measures. Under Interior Minister Nicolas Sarkozy, special police cells were built up in all twenty-two regions of France, with stepped-up surveillance of mosques, Islamic bookshops, long-distance phone facilities, *halal* butcheries, and ethnic restaurants. "Today," writes Robert Leiken, "no place of worship is off limits to the police in secular France" (2005a, 120). This ultra-repressive policing, introduced in 2002 under Sarkozy, has even been indicted by Amnesty International (International Crisis Group [ICG] 2006, 21). "If your skin color is not right, you are permanently harassed (by the police)," says a young Frenchman of Turkish origin (quoted in *Frankfurter Allgemeine Zeitung* 2005a, 3). That the tragic electrocution of the two teenagers of North African origin occurred in the context of yet another instance of repressive policing was an important factor in transforming long-simmering discontent into open violence.

For many, the French riots are a dramatic indication that immigrant and ethnic-minority integration in France, if not in Europe, has failed. But consider that only a few months later privileged Sorbonne students staged a protracted street-level protest against an employment reform that was specifically meant to ease access to jobs for the unemployed in the *banlieues*. From this we must conclude that the riots actually testify to the progress, not the breakdown, of French-style integration. In the words of Emmanuel Todd: "It is very French if a marginalized social group takes its grievance to the street. France is the land of revolts. Since 1789" (*Frankfurter Allgemeine Zeitung* 2005b, 39).

Whatever meaning we attribute to the French riots, as proving or disproving the effectiveness of French-style integration, perhaps the most important lesson to draw from them is that the successful accommodation of Islam is not a recipe for the successful integration of Muslim immigrants and ethnics. A detailed report investigating the causes and the context of the French riots by the International Crisis Group (ICG) found that "the presence of a quiet and controlled Islam is no guarantee against the radical temptation [of *jihad*] nor against street-level violence" (2006, 26). In fact, for the ICG, echoing Olivier Roy's analysis of "globalized Islam" (Roy 2002), the French riots occurred precisely because of the "exhaustion of political Islamism" and "depoliticization of young Muslims" (ICG 2006, i).

Within the ambit of the state-created Muslim federation CFCM, for instance, the Union des Organizations Islamiques de France (UOIF), an offshoot of the Egyptian Muslim Brothers and the previous flagship of a more militant political Islamism in France, has recently taken a softer, clientist stance toward the state, speaking for the educated middle class of Muslim origin in France but losing touch with the rougher reality of the *banlieues*. A *fatwa* of the UOIF not to participate in the riots notably failed to calm the situation. Tariq Ramadan, the iconic French Muslim leader, admitted the failure of organized Islam to be heard by the predominantly Muslim (but nonreligious) rioters: "The Islamic organizations, including myself, are incapable of reaching the banlieues and their declassed populations" (ICG 2006, 12). The disjunction between organized Islam and the nonreligious *banlieue* has a sociological grounding in the split between the *blédards,* the first-generation North Africans (mostly students of middle-class background) who staff the Islamic organizations, and *beures,* the declassed, French-born second- and third-generation Muslim ethnics who are stranded in the *banlieues* and who instigated the riots of 2005 (ICG 2006, 9).

Even religious practice among young French Muslims is increasingly outside organized Islam and more influenced by Saudi-based salafism. This is an apolitical, nonviolent, and purist Islam that incites its practitioners to *hijra* (exodus to Arab countries). Salafism is the Islam of the upwardly professional "new young orthodox urban Muslim" (ICG 2006, 16), who is individualistic, discrete in appearance, and consumerist—the preferred *hijra* destination being not austere Saudi Arabia or Yemen but the lusher Emirates or Dubai.[12]

As the 2006 ICG report further outlines, into the political vacuum of a withering political Islamism and individualistic salafism have stepped terrorist *jihad,* on the one side, and the revolt of the *banlieue,* on the other side. Whereas old-style political Islamism had been a territorial cause, seeking power in an Arab state (Lebanon in 1986 or Algeria in 1995), *jihad* is the deterritorialized fight against the enemies of the global *ummah,* stepping into the anti-imperialist legacy of militant third-worldism (see Roy 1992). As is known from the biographies of prominent *jihad*ists, rather than growing out of a Muslim community, *jihad* usually grows out of a radical rupture with family and community.

It is therefore incorrect, as French political elites are prone to, to depict the conflict as one between republican individualism, on the one side, and ethno-religious *communautarisme,* on the other side. In fact, the influences are the other way around—the new protests, both the *jihad* and riot variants, are individualistic and are certainly decoupled from Mosque-based organized Islam; by contrast, communitarianism is more accurately the inadvertent result of French state policy.

An example for state-furthered communitarianism is the ethnic distribution of social housing, in which the desirable inner sections of the cities are reserved for the white ethnic French and the North Africans are shuffled together in the peripheral *habitations à loyer modéré* (HLMs, rent-controlled housing) (ICG 2006, 24). Moreover, because of the chase after the Muslim vote or the attempt to resolve communal grievances, ethnic clientism is rampant at the local level. As a community leader of a Parisian *banlieue* describes the local scene, "nobody defends the inhabitants of the *cité,* but the *Comoriens* of *the cité* or the *Maliens* of the *cité,* etc." (ICG 2006, 24). Finally, there is a paradoxical tendency of French state authorities to engage the authorities of the country of origin in the resolution of domestic conflicts. For example, in March 2005 the mayor of the French city of Dreux asked the Moroccan consulate to resolve a conflict between an unpopular imam and young *beurs* (ICG 2006, 25).

The uncomfortable message of the ICG in-depth investigation into the context of the French riots is clear: "(T)he territories of radicalization are less and less religious in nature" (ICG 2006, 26). Accordingly, the creation of a French Islam, which has been the intention of the French state over the past decade or so, is at best tangential to and at worst perversely implicated in the creation of terrorist *jihad* and street-level violence. Instead of continuing this policy, the 2006 ICG report recommends a solution that resonates with the thrust of this volume—open channels for the political participation of Muslim youngsters within the established political parties. Consider that of 8,424 candidates in the 2002 national election there were only 123 *beurs* or blacks, most of them within the ambit of small sectarian parties on the extreme left. Here, in combination of course with combating socioeconomic exclusion, lies the frontier of more successful Muslim integration in the future.

## Conclusion

In the European imbroglio surrounding Muslim integration, the fundamental distinction between cultural and socioeconomic integration tends to be ignored. With respect to cultural integration, the accommodation of Islam has made huge strides across European societies, irrespective of divergent nationhood and church-state legacies. By contrast, the unresolved problem is the persistent socioeconomic marginalization of the children and grandchildren of Muslim immigrants. This marginalization has no religious roots—it meets Muslims not qua Muslims but qua immigrants. But it has often found a religious expression in that global Islam provides an idiom of protest and identity for excluded Muslim ethnics.

To the degree that religion is causally involved in the production of marginality, it is less as the cause of discrimination than as a factor in cultural withdrawal. The notion Islamophobia, invented in mid-1990s Britain, has obscured the real causes of Muslim disadvantage, which have little to do with a behavioral or institutional animus against Islam and everything to do with the demographic profile of this minority (see Joppke forthcoming). On the contrary, when we consider how much the confrontation with Islam has historically shaped the Christian identity of Europe, we should be surprised at how flexible its laws and institutions have proved to be in accommodating the former "enemy" in cultural and religious terms.

Assertive Muslim identities, for which the headscarf, above all, stands today, unfortunately contributed to deflecting attention away from the crucial socioeconomic problems to more peripheral cultural and religious issues, for which a solid constitutional and statutory framework exists. By the same token, a firm stance on cultural integration, as in the French anti-headscarf law, may well be a prerequisite for fighting socioeconomic marginalization more effectively. It is wrong to argue that the French headscarf ban was a "delusional 'fix' given the much larger set of social problems that needed to be addressed," as Joan Scott argues (2007, 115). Instead, in a kind of lexical ordering, French lawmakers first brought Muslims into the national fold by asking them—like all French citizens—to abstract from their origin features in public space. Once this was done and the Frenchness of French Muslims was assured, the struggle against discrimination (*lutte contre la discrimination*) could start in earnest, with a robust push toward Anglo-Saxon-style ethnic counting and positive discrimination under current President Sarkozy. Once the headscarf chapter was closed, diversity, that is, the idea that the key positions in society and polity should mirror the racial and ethnic composition of society, took hold in France much as it has throughout Europe, and this is the French and European Muslims' best hope for the future.

# CHAPTER NINE

# A Multicultural Paradise?

## The Cultural Factor in Dutch Integration Policy

*Jan Willem Duyvendak, Trees Pels,*
*and Rally Rijkschroeff*

Western European countries heatedly debate the issue of how much and what kind of cultural differentiation is to be allowed in the public domain. Many have witnessed the rise of right-wing populist parties that see migrants as a threat to social cohesion and national identity (Van Kersbergen and Krouwel 2003; Michael Minkenberg, chap. 10 in this volume). Whether the integration policy in the past has stressed accommodating immigrants' cultural or religious identities, as in the Netherlands and Great Britain, or cultural monism or uniformity, as in Germany and France, the culture debate continues to rage widely (e.g., Brubaker 2001; Favell 2001; Benhabib 2002; Commission on Multi-Ethnic Britain 2000; Joppke 2004).

Much of the debate focuses on Muslim minorities, who form the majority of the migrant population in Western Europe. The building of mosques, the call to prayer, the use of religious symbols such as the headscarf, gender inequality, anti-integration pronouncements by ultra-orthodox imams, and Islam-inspired political extremism are all popular subjects in the media (e.g., Christian Joppke, chap. 8 in this volume; Verhaar and Saharso 2004; Uitermark, Rossi, and Van Houtum 2005). Citizens from the majority population are increasingly coming to fear Islam (European Monitoring Centre on Racism and Xenophobia 2002; Scheepers, Gijsberts, and Hello 2002).

This certainly applies in the Netherlands, where the Islamophobic Lijst Pim Fortuyn (LPF) party took second place in the 2002 elections, despite the murder of its leader, Pim Fortuyn. "These events did not fit the Netherlands's global image...as a wealthy, tolerant, and perhaps excessively liberal society" (Van Der Veer 2006, 212). This chapter examines the retreat from multiculturalism in the Netherlands, one of its supposed standard-bearers in Europe. According to Christian Joppke (2004; chap. 8 in this volume), the Dutch abandoned their pluralistic policy for two reasons. First, the whole approach of allowing designated minority groups to emancipate themselves within their own parallel institutions allegedly fueled segregation and separation from mainstream society. Second, the Dutch pluralist integration policy did not remedy the most pressing problems among immigrants and their offspring—unemployment and economic marginalization—and may even have worsened them. In Joppke's view, "under the shadow of official multiculturalism, an 'ethnic underclass' had been allowed to emerge" (2004, 248). Other scholars agree that Dutch multiculturalist integration policy has had pernicious effects on the cultural and economic integration of migrants (Koopmans and Statham 2000c; Koopmans et al. 2005; Ireland 2004; Sniderman and Hagendoorn 2007).

The Dutch debate on "the multicultural drama"[1] led, in 2002, to the establishment of a parliamentary committee of inquiry. This committee requested that the authors of this chapter evaluate the objectives and results of the Dutch integration policy between 1970 and 2002 (Rijkschroeff, Duyvendak, and Pels 2004; Rijkschroeff et al. 2005). Our study leads us to conclude that Dutch integration policy did not, in fact, fail, nor was it all about pluralism. We acknowledge that migrants still face many serious and persistent problems; however, they nevertheless seem to have been fairly successful in economic terms, as evaluated by the standards set by Dutch policymakers. The sociocultural results are more mixed, however, as are the cultural policies of the Dutch government.

This leaves us with a puzzle: If integration policies did not produce negative outcomes, why has the pluralism debate been so heated in the Netherlands? What has really motivated the repudiation of multiculturalism and the demand that immigrants become, in Gans's terms, "like non-immigrants culturally and socially" (2007, 154)? Despite the characterization of the Dutch majority population and Dutch integration policies as pluralist and tolerant, we believe that the Dutch cultural mainstream in fact is strongly monoculturalist and intolerant of pluralism. In other words, it is our claim that the Dutch progressive liberal cultural consensus actually contributes more to the current intolerance of cultural and social differences than the alleged failures of Dutch integration policies.

## Our Evaluation of Dutch Integration Policy

Our study of Dutch integration policy began with several key questions: What were the actual policy objectives? How coherently and consistently were they pursued? To what extent were they achieved? We began by mapping out all the objectives stated in the relevant recommendations, memoranda, and Dutch parliamentary debates and linking them with the specific policy measures adopted to advance them. Analyzing these data enabled us to draw some conclusions about the coherence and consistency of the Dutch integration policy in the period under study.

With regard to actual policy outcomes, we used two approaches. First, we summarized prior evaluations of the effectiveness of the policy measures adopted. Second, we examined the relevant empirical data on immigrant outcomes using the various systems established since the mid-1980s for monitoring the socioeconomic position of the Dutch integration policy target groups (see Guiraudon, Phalet, and ter Wal 2005). These two sources of information enabled us to assess the success or failure of the Dutch integration policy and its constituent parts.[2]

## Phases of Dutch Integration Policy

Large-scale immigration to Holland began with the recruitment of guest workers during the 1950s and 1960s and migration from former Dutch colonies, particularly Indonesia, in that same period. The migration of former colonials was not particularly problematic because many had been part of the Dutch civil service; they had Dutch citizenship, spoke the language, and understood the culture. It was assumed at that time, however, that most migrant workers would stay in the Netherlands only temporarily and that they would return to their country of origin once they had fulfilled their economic goals.

The 1970s saw the start of the follow-up migration of partners, children, and other family members of the original guest workers. Nevertheless, it was still assumed that these people's stay would only be relatively short. At this point, integration policy focused on maintaining group cohesion with only peripheral attention to integration into Dutch society. Policy in the 1970s focused on managing labor migration, encouraging the guest workers to return to their country of origin, and regulating family and marriage migration.

The assumptions about the temporary nature of the migrants' stay were gradually abandoned in the 1980s. This was the era of the minorities policy. Migrants with a low social position were deemed to be the target groups of the new minorities policy. As expressed in the slogan "integration while maintaining one's identity," this policy focused both on combating social deprivation (particularly in education, the labor market, and housing) by strengthening the legal position of migrants and opposing their unequal treatment and on creating spaces for preserving "one's own" culture, religion, and language.

The 1990s saw the arrival of integration policy, inspired above all by the persistent educational deprivation of the children of migrants compared with their counterparts in the majority population, together with an increased demand for more highly educated labor and the concomitant higher unemployment levels among poorly educated migrants. The integration policy sought to foster increased educational attainment and labor market participation. The emphasis shifted to the socioeconomic integration of the individual. Attention to collective emancipation through cultural distinctiveness faded into the background.

Finally, after the mid-1990s, citizenship policy became a predominant motif. It emphasized the rights and duties of the individual citizen. The government abandoned the institutionalization of ethnic diversity as a policy objective. What did remain was attention to improving the accessibility of mainstream facilities, developing the social and cultural capital of migrants to further their socioeconomic participation, and stimulating interethnic contact.

## Socioeconomic Outcomes

Although developed in phases, government policy showed considerable consistency in seeking to improve the socioeconomic position of migrants and ethnic minorities in the core institutions of Dutch society: education, the labor market (work and income), and housing. An important question is whether, after taking relevant background characteristics into account, members of ethnic minorities are now at the same position as the Dutch majority. This is called the proportionality objective (Van der Laan and Veenman 2004, 15). Moreover, we want to know if a minority group middle class is developing.

## Education

Ethnic minority pupils start primary education at a disadvantage. On completing their elementary school, Turkish, Moroccan, and Antillean children are still behind their native counterparts in the Dutch language and, to a lesser extent, math. Surinamese pupils perform better than the other minority groups, but they too lag behind Dutch majority pupils. Studies show, however, that minority group pupils are gradually performing better at school over the last two decades, resulting in a reduction of their deficit relative to majority pupils (Dagevos, Gijsberts, and Van Praag 2003; Gijsberts and Herweijer 2007). These studies show that in secondary education immigrants Surinamese and Antillean pupils are almost as likely to reach higher school levels as pupils from the Dutch majority, whereas Turkish and Moroccan pupils are more likely to reach lower secondary school levels than pupils from the majority population.

Wendy Van der Laan and Justus Veenman (2004) analyzed the educational positions of the four large minority groups on the basis of the 2002 survey of Social Position and Use of Facilities by Members of Ethnic Minorities (SPVA). They find that, although these ethnic minority groups lagged behind the Dutch majority, the differences diminished greatly after controlling for social background. After they had adjusted for such factors, the entire Surinamese population and Antilleans/Arubans between ages 15 and 65 achieved parity. Although significant differences remain for the other two groups, they have been making progress as well. Furthermore, if we look only at second-generation youngsters—born and raised in the Netherlands and therefore socialized in the Dutch educational system—they generally perform more equitably. More recent data clearly corroborate these trends (Turkenburg and Gijsberts 2007).

It is surprising that the gap between disadvantaged ethnic minority pupils and children from the Dutch majority has narrowed in recent years, whereas the gap between disadvantaged native Dutch children and the majority has widened. Turkish and Moroccan pupils who started in year 4 (grade 2) in 1994 and 1996 made much more progress in both language and arithmetic than disadvantaged pupils from the majority population (Meijnen 2003; Gijsberts and Herweijer 2007). Wim Meijnen concludes, "it is not the foreign origin that is the most important reason why many ethnic minority children lag behind but, their socio-economic background, in this case their parents' education" (2003, 14).

Although the average educational level of minority pupils has increased over the past decades, only up to half of them leave the educational system with at least the minimum level of qualifications required by the labor market,[3] compared to 77 percent of the majority pupils. Again, however, the performance of second-generation minority pupils tells a more successful tale—between 46 (Turkish pupils) and 78 percent

(Antillean pupils) of the second-generation youth leave school sufficiently qualified for the labor market (Turkenburg and Gijsberts 2007). With respect to those who are in school now, the picture becomes even more positive. "This group of the second generation performs remarkably well. More than forty percent of them are in higher education" (De Valk and Crul 2007, 63).

## Labor Market and Income

Generally speaking, Dutch minorities have long had a poor position in the labor market (Penninx 1988; Veenman 1994, 1999). We can look at how they have been faring in terms of unemployment and the types of jobs held by the working-age population using data from the 2002 SPVA survey (Van der Laan and Veenman 2004).

Overall, the picture of unemployment is predominantly positive from the standpoint of achieving background-adjusted proportionality with the majority Dutch population. Not only have young people from the second generation gained an equal position compared with their native counterparts who have the same background characteristics, but the total population of 15- to 65-year-olds have also done so. Although it remains true that the immigrant population generally has higher unemployment levels than the native Dutch population, this can be traced back to their less favorable background characteristics in most cases. Generally speaking, proportionality has been achieved.

The total population of people of immigrant origin between the ages of 15 and 65 has not achieved equality with the Dutch population in the types of jobs held. In 2002, the percentage with a middle or higher occupational level ranged from 13 (Turks) and 15 percent (Moroccans) to 32 percent (Surinamese and Antilleans), against 49 percent (native Dutch). Nevertheless, thanks also to the increasing flow of ethnic minority members into higher occupational and scientific education, we do observe a fast rise of the middle class. The proportion of 15- to 65-year-olds reaching middle or higher job levels doubled in 2002 compared to 1991 (Dagevos and Gijsberts 2005). In addition, we observe proportionality as far as the average job level is concerned among second generation young people from ethnic minorities—which is mainly due to improvements in educational attainment and language proficiency (Euwals 2007). The most recent yearly trend report on the integration of Dutch minorities confirms the gradual improvement of their position on the labor market. The proportion of working members of ethnic minorities is higher now than it was ten years ago and the unemployment rate has decreased. "A substantially higher percentage of second than first generation Turks and Moroccans in the age group 25 to 35 years of age have paid work" (Heering and ter Bekke 2007, 79). Although minorities, on average, still lag behind the native Dutch labor force, they unmistakably have fared better over the years. Caution regarding their future prospects is necessary, however, because their labor market position appears to be relatively vulnerable to conjunctural fluctuations (Dagevos 2007).

The net hourly wages of minority groups have not achieved proportionality. To the contrary, the situation has deteriorated, mainly since 1998. These unfavorable findings apply to both the total population between 15 and 65 years of age and the 15- to 30-year-olds belonging to the second generation (Van der Laan and Veenman

2004). Bearing in mind the positive developments surrounding job levels, this is a surprising finding; even when migrants have the same or similar characteristics (including the same job level), they receive lower net hourly wages than indigenous residents. This might be because migrants work in different industries than their indigenous counterparts with the same characteristics.

On the brighter side, young migrants between the ages of 15 and 30 do show proportional rates of benefit dependency. This implies that they are much less likely to claim unemployment benefit (WW), invalidity benefit (WAO), or social assistance benefit (ABW) than usually assumed. Apart from the Surinamese, the total population of 15- to 65-year-olds has not, however, achieved parity on benefit dependency in spite of favorable developments over the past years (Dagevos 2007).

## Housing

Our review reveals that the housing situation of migrants (Veldboer and Duyvendak 2004) has improved considerably since their arrival in the Netherlands. Compared with thirty years ago, the quality of accommodations has clearly improved and immigrants are particularly well integrated in public-sector rental housing (Amse and Faessen 2000), which is of quite high standard in the Netherlands.

Nevertheless, immigrants have not achieved proportionality in the housing market. Deprivation tends to apply in particular to Turkish and Moroccan people. Compared with the indigenous population, the Surinamese, and the Antilleans, the upward housing mobility of Turkish and Moroccan people has been slow. One reason has been their sluggish income growth, but their (young) age structure also has played a role. Over the past decade, however, the housing quality for people of Turkish and Moroccan descent has increased at a relatively high pace (Kullberg 2007). "The second generation occupied somewhat more often single-family dwellings than the first. Especially the Turkish second generation showed more often owner-occupancy than the first [generation]" (Van Praag and Schoorl 2007, 42). Although it is not clear how the entire second generation (15- to 30-year-olds) will experience the housing market in the future, these facts leave room for some optimism.

These findings lead us to conclude that mobility patterns may differ highly between and within immigrant groups but that these groups are, on the whole, coming closer to achieving social equality. Because educational success offers the key to further integration (Odé 2002), the positive results in this area offer hope for the future, even though attaining an identical educational level still does not guarantee equal job opportunities for members of ethnic minorities compared with the Dutch majority.

Labor market discrimination appears to be the main obstacle to progress. Opportunities for better jobs and higher incomes enable people to find better housing and break away from housing segregation (i.e., white and black neighborhoods) (Rijkschroeff, Duyvendak, and Pels 2004). The persistently low income of many ethnic minorities does deter them from moving to more favorable districts; however, we do not find that large groups of permanent drop-outs have been left behind in the disadvantaged neighborhoods.

Most of the data show that immigrants or their children have reached a status that is proportional to that of natives after adjusting for socioeconomic background. But can we detect tendencies that the differences in socioeconomic background themselves are disappearing? Are migrants becoming more equal to the native-born Dutch in nominal terms as well? Is a middle class developing? Recent data suggest that this indeed is the case (Dagevos and Gijsberts 2005, 2007). The most recent report on second-generation immigrants draws the following conclusion regarding the development of a middle class among people with an immigrant background:

> The TIES [The Integration of the European Second Generation survey] findings on this are quite optimistic. About a third of the second generation is either studying in higher education, or has already finished higher education. They will be the future elite of their communities. They can be found in high level jobs, are owner of their own business or are active as representative of immigrant and religious organizations. Those who entered the labor market already make good salaries....The children of these parents will grow up in financially steady middle class families and have good prospects for the future. (Crul, Groenewold, and Heering 2007, 139–140)

These data do not allow us to draw unequivocal conclusions about the extent to which public policies have contributed to the socioeconomic achievements of the immigrant-origin populations. Some of the successes may have resulted from factors other than policy. It is also hard to demonstrate causal relationships between policies and outcomes. Nevertheless, we think some credit should be given to the fact that integration policies started out with the goal of socioeconomic parity, held this goal over the long term, and sought to achieve it on a consistent basis. Our report led the Parliamentary Committee of Inquiry (2004) to conclude that the facts did not corroborate the popular belief that socioeconomic integration had failed. On the contrary, many migrants were either fully or partially integrated, as the committee concluded.

## Sociocultural Integration Policy

Policies that focused on the sociocultural position of immigrants were characterized by far more variety than many accounts suggest. The Netherlands had no specific policy regarding this particular issue in the 1970s, the central tenet being that guest workers should maintain their identity with a view to their eventual return home. In the early 1980s, policy tended to concentrate on helping ethnic groups maintain their cohesion. In addition, emancipation within an immigrant's own circle was considered to be conducive to strengthening the societal position of minorities. This ideal of group empowerment as a tool for emancipation built strongly on the legacy of the pillarization[4] that characterized Dutch social structure well into the 1960s (Richard Alba and Nancy Foner, chap. 18 in this volume). This policy emphasis, however, has already faded into the background by the late 1980s as the objective of fully individual socioeconomic integration and participation gradually took center stage.

As a result, central government policy toward sociocultural integration manifested little consistency. It evolved from focusing on achieving group emancipation through the retention of group culture to an approach that accentuated individual integration. More recently, policy has insisted that migrants adjust to "Dutch" norms and values in order to avert the impending danger of insufficient social cohesion.

These changes in policy emphasis make it difficult to assess the extent to which Dutch integration policies have achieved their sociocultural objectives. The many changes and recent toughening of the sociocultural objectives indicate disagreement about what policy should actually try to achieve, a disagreement that continues today. Whereas many of the Dutch majority population currently support the idea of migrants' adopting "Dutch" norms and values, migrants aspire to cultural development that they themselves define (Phalet, Van Lotringen, and Entzinger 2000).

Given the many signs of socioeconomic progress among immigrants and their children, it is difficult to understand why Dutch majority elites came to believe that tolerance for cultural differences among immigrant minorities had somehow produced bad results instead. Moreover, a review of sociocultural policy shows that Dutch integration policy has not been characterized for long periods of time by a commitment to pluralism. Finally, even if it had, it is hard to understand how or why that might obstruct the socioeconomic progress of immigrants. Thus, the interpretation offered by Joppke (2004; chap. 8 in this volume) and Ruud Koopmans and colleagues (2000c, 2005) seems to be ripe for revision.

Although Koopmans and colleagues label the Dutch situation as culturally pluralist, or even as being increasingly pluralist (2005, 73; see also Minkenberg, chap. 10 in this volume), this seems an exaggeration of what government policies were actually promoting. As Koopmans and his colleagues acknowledge themselves, tolerance for the *religious* practices of immigrants had little to do with national integration policies. They observe:

> To an important extent, the extension of multicultural rights to minorities in the Netherlands is based on the heritage of pillarization...and was meant to accommodate cultural conflicts between native religious groups. Muslims and other minorities have made use of this available institutional framework to claim their own schools, broadcasting rights, and other cultural provisions. (Koopmans et al. 2005, 71)

Thus, the development of specific cultural provisions for migrants was due to the general Dutch institutional framework.[5] Insofar as this provided a basis for creating migrant religious and cultural institutions, it had nothing whatsoever to do with pluralist integration policies (Rath et al. 1999; Duyvendak et al. 2004). Instead of favoring the development of a new (Islamic) religious pillar, most politicians were decidedly reluctant to support such a development. As one of the most secularized countries in the world, the Netherlands showed little inclination to accommodate new religious institutions. In fact, from the 1970s onwards, local governments tried to prohibit immigrants from claiming their rights as Dutch citizens to set up Muslim schools (Feirabend and Rath 1996).

Should we take tolerance for the emergence of religious self-organization among immigrants as a sign that Dutch integration policies actively promoted pluralism? The answer again must be in the negative. Islamic organizations did not receive support from Dutch integration policies, nor even from the pillarized institutional framework. In part, this unwillingness to support such activities reflected the diminishing importance of religious organizations in a depillarizing country and the continued importance of the separation of church and state. Yet policymakers were also convinced that religious organizations were ill equipped to help immigrants form a bridge to the larger society. Religious organizations were assumed, after all, to keep people in isolation. Even though such organizations did help some people acquire social capital (Fennema et al. 2000), according to the dominant view (Sunier 2000; Tariq Modood, chap. 15 in this volume) they mainly served as a tool for keeping an eye on one's own supporters.

To sum up, the dominant idea in the scholarly literature and public opinion (Kramer 2006)—that multicultural policies somehow caused the integration of migrants to be "a total failure"—is empirically wrong. The cultural integration policies of the Netherlands were less pluralist than is often assumed and, more important, even though serious problems remain, the socioeconomic integration of migrants has been far less negative than is often claimed. Still, the Dutch are desperately in need of a better understanding of the deep crisis in the multiethnic Netherlands. We think the explanation can be found in the exact opposite direction than the one in which authors such as Joppke and Koopmans are looking.

## Intolerance of Pluralism in the Dutch Mainstream

Matters of culture are so prominent today not because the Dutch adopted culturally pluriform policies but precisely because the Netherlands has rapidly become more culturally homogeneous—as far as the majority population is concerned. Whereas majority opinion is divided on gender, family, and sexuality in many other countries, including the United States, the entire political spectrum of the Dutch majority population supports progressive values on these matters. After a period of intense cultural polarization during the "long sixties," the majority has developed remarkably uniform, progressive ideals according to the Eurobarometer, European Social Survey, European Values Study, International Social Survey Program, and the Continuous Tracking Survey (as recapitulated in, e.g., Uitterhoeve 2000; Duyvendak 2004; Halman, Luijkx, and van Zundert 2005).

More than anywhere else in Europe, the Dutch majority population believes that divorce is acceptable and homosexuality nothing out of the ordinary. It also disagrees most with the propositions that "women have to have children to be happy," that "a child should respect its parents," and that "we would be better off were we to return to a traditional way of life." Finally, the Netherlands has less of a value gap on these questions between more and less highly educated people and is now one of the three least culturally polarized European countries (Achterberg 2006, 55). To the extent that any native Dutch do hold conservative positions, they are not strongly politically articulated.

It appears that the Dutch demand that migrants share these values reflects a strong consensus within the majority population. In this respect, the Netherlands is similar to Denmark. This progressive consensus evidently requires policy to enforce the acculturation of those who are assumed to fall outside of it. A liberal country need not esteem diversity (Wikan 2002).

Thus, Dutch society appears to be losing its ability to cope with cultural differences. As Ian Buruma has observed, "Tolerance, then, has its limits even for Dutch progressives. It is easy to be tolerant of those who are much like ourselves...It is much harder to extend the same principle to the strangers in our midst, who find our ways as disturbing as we do theirs" (2006, 128).

The growing consensus around progressive values has created a bigger value gap between the native majority and Muslim migrants than in countries with less progressive majority cultures. As Peter Van der Veer puts it, "For the Dutch, Muslims stand for theft of enjoyment. Their strict sexual morals remind the Dutch too much of what they have so recently left behind....In a society where consumption and especially the public performance of sexual identity have become so important, the strict clothing habits of observant Muslims are an eyesore" (2006, 119–20).

## Conclusion

How has the progressive monoculture of the Dutch majority affected integration opportunities for minorities? Even though survey results (Dagevos et al. 2003; Dagevos, Schellingerhout, and Vervoort 2007) show increasing support for so-called western values among Dutch migrants, the value gap between Muslim groups and the majority population is nevertheless greater than in other countries. Froukje Demant (2005) shows, for instance, that the majority-immigrant distance in value orientations is lower in Germany than in the Netherlands on such dimensions as community spirit, (equality in) gender roles, and sexuality.

Evidently, culture does matter. Cultural differences can make the immigrant integration process more problematic even as acculturation and assimilation have a complex relationship to social mobility (see Gans 2007). Our review suggests that the supposed esteem of Dutch integration policy for cultural or religious differences has had little impact on the socioeconomic achievement of the minority groups. It is the cultural homogeneity of the Dutch mainstream, not its acceptance of cultural diversity, that helps us to understand the sociopolitical crisis in the Netherlands. Of course, the Dutch majority population may be rightly proud of the unique nature of its progressive cultural consensus. But the paradox of recent years is that the majority has deployed it to exclude Islamic migrants (Harchaoui and Huinders 2003) instead of encouraging them to emancipate themselves further—something that many women and girls are already doing (Pels and De Gruijter 2006). If the majority population of the Netherlands does not become more reflective about these matters, instead of being a paradise of multiculturalism, the Netherlands may become an unsettled society of monoculturalists.

What broader implications could the current gap between liberal secular westerners and more conservative minorities have? One question is whether the conservatism of the relative newcomers will affect progressive Dutch morale. Will women's emancipation slow down and homosexuals be forced back into the closet? It is hardly to be expected that a rather small minority will have such an enduring impact on mainstream culture (e.g., Phalet and Andriessen 2003).

What we see happen, however, in the Netherlands as elsewhere, is a defensive and contorted reaction to ethno-cultural diversity, threats to democracy by violent extremism, and globalization (Brubaker 2001; Joppke 2004). The Dutch idealize the past days of supposed unity and uniformity (although, in fact, the Dutch are now-adays much more uniform in their opinions and attitudes than in the pillarized past). The recent efforts to include a national cultural canon within the school curriculum and to found a museum of national history, as well as the installing of a Dutch cabinet in which Christian parties are heavily represented, are all exemplary of this nostalgic trend. It is very questionable, however, whether this politics of nostalgia offers any answers to today's problems, let alone to those of the future.

Perhaps the most worrying development is that the claim to superiority of the native Dutch culture has quite effectively silenced migrants' voices in the debate, except for those former Muslims who depict Islam and its followers as being backward. Cultural paternalism, however, is not exactly the best approach to finding common ground.

# CHAPTER TEN

# Anti-Immigrant Politics in Europe

## The Radical Right, Xenophobic Tendencies, and Their Political Environment

*Michael Minkenberg*

$T$oday's European societies are characterized by socially and economically marginal immigrant communities. Political elites—largely divided on this issue—respond mainly when the media report or public outcries push them, rarely in immigrants' favor. More established parties compete with old and new radical right parties, which now regularly strive to push the political agenda on immigration and multiculturalism in many countries to the right, sometimes with violence.

This chapter examines the rise of radical right-wing anti-immigrant politics and violence in several European democracies, and their impact on established parties, mainstream debate, and public policies affecting immigrant political incorporation. It underscores how established political actors have sought to preempt or coopt radical right mobilizations, thus granting them new legitimacy and, hence, engaging in a politics of exclusive (rather than inclusive) boundary shifting toward immigrants that highlights the differences between "us" and "them" (see Jennifer Hochschild and John Mollenkopf, chap. 2 in this volume).

After the 1970s, a new radical right emerged in Europe that replaced attacks on the democratic order as a whole with populist and ethnocentric campaigns to foster a rightist, value-based, New Politics cleavage (Minkenberg 2000, 2002; Ignazi 2003). The impact of deindustrialization and globalization on traditional party alignments assisted this effort (Downs 2001), as did the role of public opinion as a resonance chamber for anti-immigrant politics (Minkenberg 1998, chap. 9; 2002; see also McAdam 1982; Rucht 1994). In short, to understand the emergence and impact of radical right parties, we must look at how right-wing radical mobilization interacted with the larger political environment. Three elements are of particular interest: the organizational strength and party and nonparty forms of the radical right, its ability to mobilize support, and its capacity to force a response from and recalibration of the larger political environment.

Membership figures and votes are only two indictors of organizational strength. The degree of organizational consolidation within the radical right is also relevant, as are effects of violence and protest. Given a particular public climate, right-wing violence by nonparty actors can make radical right parties appear "moderate." The strength of radical right parties thus lies partly in their connections to nonparty organizations and partly in their supporters' sociodemographic characteristics. The extent to which immigrants pose real or perceived cultural and interreligious challenges to the nation also conditions these interactions.

The chapter begins with an overview of the research on radical-right policy impact that informs this model. It then applies the model to a general mapping of radical right actors across Western Europe and uses these analytic elements to explore six case studies. In Germany and the Netherlands right-wing parties are marginal; but in Germany, acts of right-wing anti-immigrant violence took on a high profile. In France and Belgium, radical right parties are strong but have remained pariahs. The radical right in Austria and Denmark became a partner in the government.

## State of the Research on Radical Right Impact

Many studies have looked at the ideologies and electoral fortunes of radical right-wing parties (see overview in Kitschelt 2007; Mudde 2007); very few have paid more than cursory attention to their impact on the larger political environment in general and on immigration issues in particular. When studied at all, these effects are framed as agenda setting, not as influences on immigrant political incorporation. The analysis of these effects remains an academic lacuna that this article does not claim to fill but does narrow with a systematic cross-country study of these effects.

A pioneering article by Martin Schain (1987) demonstrates clear agenda-setting effects by the French Front National (FN) on the attention of other parties and their voters to immigration and security in the 1980s, but it does not address policy effects per se. A study showing how immigration-related legislation increased in volume with the rise of the radical right in Austria, France, and Germany likewise fails to causally link radical right performance and legislative output (Williams 2006). Some tightening of immigration and immigrant policies was observed where parties or individuals of the radical right held executive offices (Minkenberg 2001; Heinisch 2003; Zaslove 2004). But, again, the focus was more on the general policy direction than on immigrants' political participation and inclusion. Moreover, as shown with regard to Austria (Minkenberg 2001; see also Mudde 2007, 281; Zaslove 2004, 114), immigration policies have sometimes tightened before the radical right has held formal power. To assess the impact of the radical right on immigration policies and immigrant incorporation, then, it is less important to study the few cases in which the radical right participates in national or local executives and more important to study the interaction between the radical right and its political environment.

## Patterns of Right-Wing Radical Mobilization in Western Europe

With regard to political and policy effects, three radical right variants can be distinguished: powerful anti-immigrant parties (the cases of Austria, Belgium, Denmark, and France), powerful extra-parliamentary anti-immigrant movements (Germany), and weak anti-immigrant parties and movements (the Netherlands). Table 10.1 summarizes their electoral fortunes by country.

These trends in electoral strength reveal several important insights. First, voting support increased markedly between the 1980s and the 1990s in all six countries. Second, the countries fall into two categories. In the first category, Austria, Belgium, Denmark, and France, right-wing parties are strong and they consolidated in the 1990s. In the second category, Germany and the Netherlands, the opposite was the case (the rise of the Dutch Lijst Pim Fortuyn in 2002 being a flash phenomenon). In some countries, support for radical right parties slumped after 2000, especially in 2004, and especially in Austria, where the participation of the Freiheitliche Partei Österreichs (FPÖ) in the government evidently yielded widespread disillusionment. In Denmark and Belgium, the radical right continued to attract support in the new millennium.

Explanations of these patterns typically involve such demand- and supply-side factors as voters' preferences; the type of electoral system; the convergence or divergence of mainstream right and left parties; and the ideology, organization, and leadership of the radical right (Kitschelt 2007; Mudde 2007; Rydgren 2007). This chapter identifies a slightly different set of factors, concerning the political and cultural context of the mobilization of the radical right and its potential effects on immigration issues in particular, as opposed to overall effects or law-and-order effects in the European Union.

A first set of factors concerns immigrants' inflow and presence in their host countries. Table 10.2 presents data from United Nations and EU statistical sources. It is quite clear that there are significant differences in these six countries regarding the size and share of the foreign-born population (numbers here include EU nationals), with Austria topping the list, followed by Germany. On the other hand, Germany joins the Netherlands and Denmark in having a low level of net migration, whereas Austria and Belgium are at or above the EU level. Similar variations exist in the rate

**Table 10.1** Election results for radical-right parties in national parliamentary elections in selected Western European countries, 1980–2004 (average per 5 years), and in the European Parliament, 2004 (%)

| | 1980–1984 | 1985–1989 | 1990–1994 | 1995–1999 | 2000–2004 | European Parliament, 2004 |
|---|---|---|---|---|---|---|
| Austria | 5.0 | 9.7 | 19.6 | 24.4 | 10.0 | 6.3 |
| Belgium | 1.1 | 1.7 | 6.6 | 10.9 | 13.8 | 17.1 |
| Denmark | 6.4 | 6.9 | 6.4 | 9.8 | 12.6 | 6.8 |
| France | 0.4 | 9.9 | 12.7 | 14.9 | 12.4 | 9.8 |
| Germany, Federal Republic of | 0.2 | 0.6 | 2.3 | 3.3 | 1.0 | 2.8 |
| Netherlands | 0.8 | 0.7 | 2.9 | 0.6 | 11.4 | 2.5 |

*Sources:* Minkenberg (2003a); Minkenberg and Perrineau (2005); Veugelers and Magnan (2005).

*Note:* The following parties were included: Austria: Freiheitliche Partei Österreichs (FPÖ); Belgium: Vlaams Blok/Belang, and Front National; Denmark: Fremskridtsparti, Dansk and Folkeparti; France: Front National and, Mouvement National Républicain; Germany: Republikaner, Deutsche Volksunion (DVU), and National-demokratische Partei Deutschlands (NPD); Netherlands: Center Party, Centrum Democrats, and Lijst Pim Fortuyn. Data for Germany from 1980 until 1989 are Federal Republic only.

**Table 10.2** Population data in selected European democracies

| | Population, January 2005 (in thousands) | Size of foreign-born population, 2005 (in thousands) | Foreign-born population (% of total population) | Net migration rate per 1,000 in population | Number of asylum applications, 1989–1998 (in thousands) |
|---|---|---|---|---|---|
| EU-25 | 459,488 | n.a. | n.a. | 3.7 | n.a. |
| Austria | 8,207 | 1,234 | 15.1 | 7.4 | 131 (0.016) |
| Belgium | 10,446 | 719 | 6.9 | 3.2 | 153 (0.015) |
| Denmark | 5,411 | 388 | 7.2 | 1.4 | 71 (0.013) |
| France | 60,561 | 6,471 | 10.7 | 1.7 | 327 (0.005) |
| Germany | 82,501 | 10,144 | 12.3 | 1.2 | 1906 (0.023) |
| Netherlands | 16,306 | 1,638 | 10.1 | −1.2 | 296 (0.018) |

*Sources:* Münz (2005); Mudde (2007, 212).
*Note:* Values in parentheses are asylum applications per 1,000 in population. n.a., no data available.

**Table 10.3** Trends in religious pluralism in selected European democracies, ca. 1980 and 2000 (%)

| | Catholics | Protestants | Orthodox | Jews | Muslims | Other/ none | Pluralism index, ca. 1980 | Pluralism index, ca. 2000 |
|---|---|---|---|---|---|---|---|---|
| Austria | 73.6 | 4.7 | 1.9 | 0.1 | 4.2 | 15.5 | 0.15 | 0.41 |
| Belgium | 80.9 | 1.7 | 0.5 | 0.3 | 3.8 | 12.8 | 0.05 | 0.21 |
| Denmark | 0.6 | 88.5 | 0.0 | 0.1 | 2.8 | 8.0 | 0.07 | 0.23 |
| France | 78.8 | 1.6 | 0.3 | 1.1 | 8.5 | 9.7 | 0.08 | 0.40 |
| Germany | 32.1 | 31.8 | 1.1 | 0.1 | 3.7 | 30.3 | 0.54 | 0.66 |
| Netherlands | 34.5 | 30.1 | 0.0 | 0.2 | 5.7 | 29.9 | 0.62 | 0.72 |

*Source:* Minkenberg (2007, 898–99).

of asylum applications. Germany and the Netherlands top the list, whereas France is at the bottom. The relationship between influx and asylum application rates and the electoral support for the radical right is unclear (see table 10.1).

Another compilation of data demonstrates growing internal diversity of these countries in terms of culture and helps interpret the significance of the size and composition of the foreign population. Table 10.3 shows some significant trends in religious pluralism. In historically homogenous Belgium, France, and Denmark, Islam is the second largest religion. In Austria, Muslims are on the verge of pulling even with Protestants. From around 1980 to 2000, religious pluralism increased in all European democracies (except for Sweden; see Minkenberg 2007, 898–99), from historically high starting points in countries such as the Netherlands and Germany and from much lower levels in others.

Against this backdrop, the European mass public have shown widespread, but not majoritarian, intolerance for immigrants, minorities, and a multicultural society, with some significant exceptions. A 2000 Eurobarometer survey showed that in Greece, followed by Belgium, Denmark, France, and Germany, intolerance clearly exceeded the EU average. Austria and the United Kingdom were close to the EU average, whereas

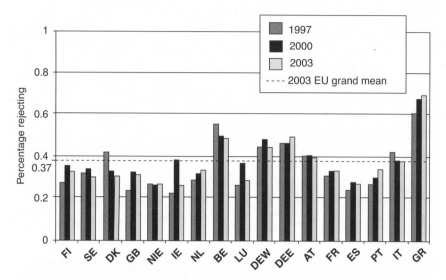

**Figure 10.1** Resistance to a multicultural society in the EU-15. AT, Austria; BE, Belgium; DEE, East Germany; DEW, West Germany; DK, Denmark; ES, Spain; EU, European Union; FI, Finland; FR, France; GB, Great Britain; GR, Greece; IE, Ireland; IT, Italy; LU, Luxembourg; NIE, Northern Ireland; NL, Netherlands; PT, Portugal; SE, Sweden.
*Source:* European Monitoring Centre on Racism and Xenophobia (EUMC 2003b, 42).

Sweden and Finland were below it. Likewise, a survey analysis by the European Monitoring Center on Racism and Xenophobia (EUMC) (see figure 10.1) shows that resistance to a multicultural society lies at or above the EU mean in Greece, Belgium, East and West Germany, Austria, and Italy. Spain, Portugal, Ireland, the Netherlands, and Great Britain are below average in resistance to multiculturalism. With the exception of Germany and France, resistance to a multicultural society is strongest in Catholic societies where Islam is a strong minority. This is surprising given that French elites have opposed multiculturalism and that the major parties have attempted to coopt the radical right.

Intolerance is actually not associated with voting for right-wing or far-right parties, despite some congruence in the cases of Belgium, France, and Denmark (Minkenberg 2007, 898–99, 20–23; see table 10.1; Minkenberg 1998, chap. 5; Norris 2005, 180). How, then, do these patterns of cultural diversity, xenophobia, and voting strength relate to movement strength and more structural context factors? Here, we use information on right-wing violence, organizational membership, and size of skinhead milieus as proxy measures of radical right strength (Koopmans 1995; Koopmans et al. 2005; Anti-Defamation League 1995; Minkenberg 1998; European Commission 2004b). We conceptualize structural context as the degree of polarization or convergence between the major parties, the level of voting along a value-based New Politics cleavage, the response of the states and major parties to the radical right, and the type of electoral system (for details, see Minkenberg 2003a). Cultural factors are configured with regard to the dominant understanding of national identity (in ethnic, cultural, or political terms), the share of foreign-born population, the level of resistance to multiculturalism, and the religious landscape (the historically dominant confessional patterns and the strength of Islam).

Table 10.4 suggests that some countries have strong radical right-wing parties and weak movements, whereas others have weak radical parties and strong movements. Certain contextual factors seem to bear on this pattern. Three of the four cases in which radical right parties scored high in the 1990s are Catholic countries. In all countries where Islam is the second largest religion, the radical right parties gathered strong

**Table 10.4** Party strength and movement strength of the radical right and context factors in selected European democracies, ca. 2000

**A.**

| | Culture | | | | | Structure | | | | Actor | |
|---|---|---|---|---|---|---|---|---|---|---|---|
| | 1a | 1b | 1c | 1d | 1e | 2a | 2b | 2c | 2d | Party strength | Movement strength |
| Austria | 0.5 | 1 | 0.5 | 1 | 0.5 | 1 | 0.5 | 1 | 1 | High | Low |
| France | 0.5 | 1 | 0 | 1 | 1 | 0 | 0.5 | 1 | 0.5 | High | Low |
| Denmark | 1 | 0 | 0 | 0 | 1 | 0.5 | 1 | 0.5 | 1 | High | Medium |
| Belgium | (0) | 0 | 1 | 1 | 1 | 1 | 0 | 0.5 | 1 | High–medium | Medium |
| Germany (West) | 0.5 | 1 | 1 | 0.5 | 0 | 0.5 | 1 | 0 | 1 | Low | Medium |
| Germany (East) | 1 | 1 | 1 | 0 | 0 | 0 | 0 | 0 | 1 | Low | High |
| Netherlands | 0 | 1 | 0 | 0 | 0 | 0 | 1 | 1 | 1 | Low | Low |

**B.**

| Context factors | | Explanation | |
|---|---|---|---|
| Factor 1: Culture | | | |
| 1a | Nation type | Ethnocultural nation 1 | Political nation 0 |
| 1b | Share of foreign-born population | High 1 | Low 0 |
| 1c | Level of resistance to multicultural society | Above EU level 1 | Below EU level 0 |
| 1d | Predominant religious tradition | Catholic 1 | Protestant 0 |
| 1e | Second largest religion | Islam 1 | Other 0 |
| Factor 2: Structures | | | |
| 2a | Cleavages | Convergence 1 | Polarization 0 |
| 2b | Cleavages: New Politics voting | Strong 1 | Weak 0 |
| 2c | Political opportunity structures: state and party | State and parties' latitude 1 | Exclusion/repression 0 |
| 2d | Political opportunity structures: electoral system | PR electoral system 1 | Majority 0 |

*Sources:* Minkenberg (2003a, 166; 2007, 898–99; 2008); European Commission (2004b).
EU, European Union; PR, proportional representation.

support. We might conclude that a new Islamic presence in homogenous Catholic or Protestant countries feeds radical right support (Anderson 2003; Bruce 2006). This notion clearly does not apply to movement mobilization, however, because Catholic countries exhibit comparatively weak radical right movements or, as far as comparable data are available, racist violence. These figures seem highest in Protestant countries.

Such cultural factors as national identity, foreign population share, and resistance to multiculturalism appear even less significant. For example, party strength is high regardless of the proportion of foreigners. Electoral system type also seems only marginally relevant, whereas the convergence of established parties may be more relevant for the breakthrough of radical right parties than for their consolidation (Kitschelt 2007; Schain, Zolberg, and Hossay 2002).

State and political actors appear more significant. Where these actors shifted from excluding the radical right to partial collaboration, radical right parties seem to have benefited (Minkenberg 2002). The radical right has suffered when established parties have actually brought it into government, as in Austria and briefly the Netherlands. Where established parties and the state have stood rigid against the radical right, its parties have not flourished, but its movements have. This larger analytic map reinforces the importance of seeing the organizational strength of radical right parties as conditional on the larger political environment, particularly the behavior of established parties and the state. The cultural context of each country, in turn, affects the impact of the radical right on immigration policy and immigrant incorporation.

## The Pivotal Case Studies

### Germany

Germany is a clear example of a country where right-wing radical parties and violence pushed the established parties to the right in a national context unfavorable to open immigration and multiculturalism (Minkenberg 2003b). Germany has several radical rights, with some distinct east-west differences. As seen in table 10.5, overall political party membership declined significantly after 1993, the year of the asylum compromise of the Bundestag parties Christlich Demokratische Union–Christlich-Soziale Union (CDU/CSU), Freie Demokratische Partei (FDP), and Sozialdemokratische Partei Deutschlands (SPD). The more extreme Nationaldemokratische Partei Deutschlands (NPD), however, has had a steady membership of around 5,000 members. Membership in the eastern radical right parties was underdeveloped until the mid-1990s, and then grew within the NPD. Five years after the failed government attempt to ban the NPD, this party is the strongest of the radical right, with a heavy concentration in the eastern *Länder*.

By contrast, the number of militant and violent right-wing extremists has risen steadily since the unification of East and West Germany and reached a record level of 10,000 at the beginning of the new decade, accompanied by a dramatic increase of right-wing violence (Minkenberg 1998, 306; Stöss 2005, 150–57). Here, the center of gravity has always been in the east (see the right column of table 10.5).

**Table 10.5** Membership in radical right organizations in Germany

| | Total members | REP | DVU | NPD | Other organizations | Subcultural milieus |
|---|---|---|---|---|---|---|
| 1992 | 61,900 | 20,000 | 26,000 | 5,000 | 4,500 | 6,400 |
| | (16.2) | (15.0) | (11.5) | (14.0) | (11.1) | **(43.8)** |
| 1993 | 64,500 | 23,000 | 26,000 | 5,000 | 4,900 | 5,600 |
| | (14.2) | (15.2) | (6.9) | (11.5) | (10.9) | **(49.4)** |
| 1994 | 56,600 | 20,000 | 20,000 | 4,500 | 6,700 | 5,400 |
| | (12.9) | (13.0) | (5.9) | (11.3) | (8.4) | **(45.8)** |
| 1995 | 46,100 | 16,000 | 15,000 | 4,000 | 4,900 | 6,200 |
| | (15.1) | (12.5) | (5.3) | (10.8) | **(16.1)** | **(47.6)** |
| 1996 | 45,300 | 15,000 | 15,000 | 3,500 | 5,400 | 6,400 |
| | (14.5) | (10.2) | (5.1) | (12.6) | (15.3) | **(46.9)** |
| 1997 | 48,400 | 15,500 | 15,000 | 4,300 | 6,000 | 7,600 |
| | (14.6) | (9.0) | (3.2) | **(27.7)** | (14.6) | **(41.5)** |
| 1998 | 53,600 | 15,000 | 18,000 | 6,000 | 6,400 | 8,200 |
| | **(17.4)** | (6.9) | (10.0) | **(36.7)** | (12.3) | **(42.8)** |
| 1999 | 51,400 | 14,000 | 17,000 | 6,000 | 5,400 | 9,000 |
| | **(18.6)** | (6.4) | (11.8) | **(32.7)** | (14.5) | **(43.7)** |
| 2000 | 50,900 | 13,000 | 17,000 | 6,500 | 6,400 | 9,700 |
| | **(19.0)** | **(16.8)** | (5.1) | **(25.4)** | (14.6) | **(43.8)** |
| 2001 | 49,700 | 11,500 | 15,000 | 6,500 | 7,100 | 10,400 |
| | **(19.9)** | **(16.9)** | (5.3) | **(20.9)** | **(19.4)** | **(43.3)** |
| 2002 | 45,000 | 9,000 | 13,000 | 6,100 | 7,000 | 10,700 |
| | **(19.4)** | **(18.4)** | (4.9) | (15.9) | (12.5) | **(44.3)** |
| 2003 | 41,500 | 8,000 | 11,500 | 5,000 | 7,600 | 10,000 |
| | **(19.0)** | **(18.3)** | (3.5) | (14.5) | **(16.5)** | **(41.9)** |
| 2004 | 40,700 | 7,500 | 11,000 | 5,300 | 8,100 | 10,000 |
| | (n.a.) | (n.a.) | (n.a.) | **(28.3)** | (n.a.) | (n.a.) |
| 2005 | 39,000 | 6,500 | 9,000 | 6,000 | 8,100 | 10,400 |
| | (n.a.) | (n.a.) | (n.a.) | **(35.3)** | (n.a.) | (n.a.) |
| 2006 | 38,600 | 6,000 | 8,500 | 7,000 | 8,000 | 10,400 |
| | (n.a.) | (n.a.) | (n.a.) | **(33.9)** | (n.a.) | (n.a.) |
| 2007 | 31,000 | *a* | 7,000 | 7,200 | 8,400 | 10,000 |
| | (n.a.) | | (n.a.) | **(36.0)** | (n.a.) | (n.a.) |

Sources: Stöss (2005, 104); for 2004–2007, Bundesministerium des Innern, *Verfassungsschutzbericht* (2006, 51; 2008, 48); various East German *Länder* reports on the protection of the constitution (including Berlin).

Notes: Values in parentheses are proportions of members in the eastern *Länder;* values in boldface are those above average. DVU, Deutsche Volksunion; GDR, German Democratic Republic; n.a., not data available; NPD, Nationaldemokratische Partei Deutschlands; REP, Republikaner.

*a*In 2007, the "Republikaner" (REP) were no longer classified as right-wing extreme by the Federal Office and was taken out of the annual report.

Electoral trends illustrate the east-west difference. Before 1998, radical right parties, in particular the Republikaner, scored higher in *Land* and national elections in the west than in the east. At the turn of the century, the reverse was true. By 2006, the radical right had representatives in three of the five East German state parliaments, but—contrary to the 1990s—none in West Germany. (The radical right has failed to gain representation in every national and European Parliament election since German unification.)

Since the rise of the Republikaner in 1989, the radical right vote has been disproportionately among manual workers and, in the new *Länder,* the unemployed

(Minkenberg 1998; Stöss 2005). In cultural and religious terms, in the southern regions where Catholicism is prevalent and conservative parties more deeply rooted, right-wing party formation, especially with the Republikaner, has advanced, but right-wing violence is limited. In the northern and especially eastern (former German Democratic Republic, GDR) regions, where left-wing and working-class parties have historically dominated, right-wing mobilization and violence advanced during the 1990s despite weak radical right parties. Voter support for the radical right in the east has increased for the more extreme DVU and NPD parties, which combined their movements and party strategies. Only recently did some West German regions (for example, around Bremen or in the Ruhr area) follow up (Stöss 2005, 107–8).

This eastern overrepresentation in the presence of organized Nazi groups, violent right-wing extremist milieus, and, more recently, electoral successes is connected to the structural consequences of German reunification. The effort to transplant western institutional and labor market patterns to the east while protecting the West German social order has overloaded the eastern welfare state and created new quandaries in its labor market, producing record (and stable) levels of unemployment and regional impoverishment (see contributions to Kitschelt and Streeck 2004). This institutional transfer hid adaptation problems in various sectors. The helpless maneuvers of local authorities and police in the face of xenophobic riots in Hoyerswerda in 1991 and Rostock in 1992 are cases in point (Schmidt 2002).

The social consequences of unification led to a rapid growth in East German resentment. According to a 2003 survey, 23 percent of East Germans exhibit a right-wing radical attitude profile compared to 14 percent of West Germans. This difference has a marked class aspect, with 37 percent of the East German lower classes and 22 percent of the West German lower classes showing right-wing radical potential (Stöss 2005, 68). Similarly, 53 percent of East Germans preferred spending cuts in benefits for foreign asylum seekers, compared to only 13 percent of the West Germans (Roller 1999, 27). East Germans are much more likely than West Germans to oppose immigration by labor migrants. In 1996, half of East Germans favored a complete prohibition of labor migrants from non-EU countries—a clear sign of widespread anxieties about the labor market situation in the new *Länder* and an expression of welfare chauvinism (Roller 1999).

These patterns of opinion and organizational mobilization significantly shape the efforts of the mainstream parties to control the German radical right. Amid the asylum crisis of 1992–1993, the established parties felt compelled to raise discourse on the abuse of asylum and the foreigners' alleged criminality. Radical right pressure from the streets and the polls put the governing CDU/CSU in a position to play the radical right card against the SPD, pressuring it to conform to the government approach. A grand coalition of the CDU/CSU, Free Democrats, and Social Democrats agreed in late 1992 to amend the Basic Law asylum article, making it virtually impossible for a foreigner to ask for asylum in the Federal Republic because of the "third-country" rule (Joppke 1999b, 93–94). This SPD shift reflected a consensus among party elites and activists, for principled or practical reasons, in favor of an ethnic notion of German nationhood.

From the 1994 Bundestag campaign until the end of the decade, the CDU/CSU emphasized its opposition to immigration, its limited support for integration, and its increasing devotion to law and order. The SPD has also tried to instrumentalize these issues. Hence, the issue of asylum helped delegitimize the entire project of multiculturalism and integration; asylum seekers were linked to rising rates of crime und unemployment. When the CDU/CSU found itself in the opposition after the federal elections of 1998, it continued its hard-line approach against the reforms of the Schröder government. In Hesse, Roland Koch engineered a signature campaign against the new nationality code. The resulting compromise eliminated the option of dual citizenship for immigrants' children born in Germany, restricting their political incorporation as envisaged by the reforms (Minkenberg 2003b, 231–32).

## The Netherlands

The Dutch case reveals how right-wing mobilization and violence can radicalize the national agenda even when radical right parties attract little support (except for the brief intermezzo of the Lijst Pim Fortuyn) and right-wing movement violence is comparatively absent—with the spectacular exception of the murder of Theo van Gogh. Other than the Centrumpartij in the 1980s and its successor, the Centrumdemocraten, which pulled 2 percent of the vote in 1994, the Netherlands had no radical right party until the rise of the populist Lijst Pim Fortuyn. In 2002, experts estimated that extreme right-wing groups had only 650 members, with an active core of about 55 to 125 people (see table 10.6).

The spectacular rise of Fortuyn's party proved short-lived. After being expelled from the Leefbar Nederland in February 2002, Fortuyn had founded his own party, the Lijst Pim Fortuyn (LPF). In the wake of his killing, the LPF won twenty-six seats in the parliamentary elections of May 15, 2002 (17 percent of the vote), becoming the second largest party (Evans and Ivaldi 2002). The party joined the Balkenende governing coalition (CDA-LPF-VVD) in July 2002. But the constant scandals and conflicts among the coalition partners and the LPF (with the exit of Winnie de Jong and Cor

**Table 10.6** Membership and active core of extreme right-wing groups in the Netherlands, October 2002

| Category | Group | Number of members/ followers | Active core |
|---|---|---|---|
| Political parties | NNP | 300 | 20–25 |
| Extreme right-wing organizations (National Movement) | LANS, NSE, etc. | 100 | 10–20 |
| Neo-Nazi groups | ANS-NVU-FAP | 150 | 15–20 |
| | cluster | 100 | 10–20 |
| | Stormfront Netherlands | | (together 25–40) |
| Total | | ~650 | 55–125 |

*Source:* Van Donselaar and Rodrigues (2004, 13).

*Notes:* ANS, Aktiefront Nationale Socialisten; FAP, Fundamentalistische Arbeiderspartij; LANS, Landelijk Actieplatform Nationalistische Studenten; NNP, New National Party; NSE, Nationalistische Studenten Eindhoven; NVU, Nederlandse Volksunie.

Eberhard, members of parliament, MPs, to form their own faction) caused the government to fall in October 2002 (after only eighty-six days). The January 2003 elections left the LPF with only eight seats. The LPF experienced further fragmentation in August 2004 when the whole LPF parliamentary group resigned from the party but continued using its name as an independent faction. In the most recent elections in November 2006, a new far-right alliance formed under the leadership of deputy Geert Wilders (the Party of Freedom, or Partij van de Vrijheid), and gained nine seats.

Despite the rapid demise of the LPF and the weakness of other far-right groups, these events dramatically changed Dutch attitudes toward immigration. Racism and intolerance had been largely taboo in Dutch society (Koopmans et al. 2005). By 2005, however, half of the Dutch (as well as half of the German) population expressed unfavorable views of Muslims, well above the levels in France (34 percent) and the United Kingdom (14 percent) (European Commission 2006b, 35). Violence among racist young people, called Lonsdale youth, proliferated, especially after Van Gogh's murder in 2004. Experts believe that 125 groups with a radical right-wing orientation, varying in size from five to fifty people, now operate (Van Donselaar 2005, 2).

Elite positions on the radical right also shifted quite dramatically during this period. Although both major parties adopted a *cordon sanitaire* against the Centrumpartij and the Centrumdemocraten in the 1980s and 1990s, this collapsed after 2001 (Fennema and van der Brug 2006). In the 1980s, the Dutch state supported antifascist organizations that sometimes employed violent means to keep adherents of the Centrumpartij from meeting (Fennema 2000). By 2000, the situation was quite different. Pim Fortuyn was never persecuted (Fennema and van der Brug 2006); and mainstream parties have hardened their policies on alien integration and terrorism.

In 2004, the minister for immigration and integration proclaimed that Dutch residents and foreigners born outside the European Union and Dutch nationals who received their nationality after April 1, 2003 were obligated to integrate themselves. Since March 15, 2005, people wanting to move to the Netherlands (except from other EU states, the United States, Canada, Australia, and Japan), have had to demonstrate Dutch language ability and knowledge of Dutch society (Browne 2005). At the request of populist MP Geert Wilders, the Dutch government considered banning the *burka* "in specific situations" on grounds of public safety before the elections in November 2006. Two parties in the governing coalition and the LPF supported the proposal, but the coalition lost the election. The new government, again headed by Prime Minister Balkenende, proposed a more restricted ban in early 2008. As in Germany, the Dutch case shows that the rise of far-right political activism can induce established parties to shift toward more restrictive stances on immigrants. It is particularly noteworthy that the initial conditions seemed far less conducive to such a shift in the Netherlands than in Germany. Radical right mobilization has altered what was once considered the model case of a European multicultural society (Koopmans et al. 2005).

## France

France presents a case in which a radical right party arose out of nowhere and established itself as a permanent fixture. Unlike Germany and the Netherlands, where radical right groupings are fragmented, various groups and organizations strongly clustered around the FN. Before a split in early 1999, the FN had approximately 70,000 members and normally attracted approximately 15 percent of the vote in national elections. And even after Bruno Mégret's Mouvement National Républicain (MNR) split from the FN in 1999, party division existed only among the party elites, delegates, and activists, not the voters. In the first round of the 2002 presidential elections, Jean-Marie Le Pen scored a historic 16.9 percent of the votes. Whether the drop in its electoral support in the 2007 elections signals the beginning of the end for the FN, remains to be seen.

The FN had adopted a mass party organization by constructing subcultures (Birenbaum 1992). FN leaders deny links with the militant right-wing subculture, but it seems that members of the Front National de Jeunesse (FNJ, the FN youth organization) belong to such violent groups as the student organization Groupe Union Defense. Moreover, skinheads and FNJ members have been growing more radical (Marcus 1995, 192).

To strengthen its position as a working-class party, since the late 1980s the FN has coupled its anti-immigration message with hostility toward free-market capitalism, globalization, free trade, the European Union, and the United States (Mégret 1996, 131–56; Minkenberg 1998, 279–80; Minkenberg and Schain 2003). In 2002, this strategy enabled the party to draw disproportionate support among lower-income groups and the unemployed (Ivaldi 2002, 139). In 2004, 38 percent of FN voters were working class (compared to 31 percent of the socialist voters, 25 percent of the communists, and 11 percent of the Union pour un Mouvement Populaire (UMP) electorate, according to Pascal Perrineau (2005, 33). Almost one-third of party followers claim to be close to a union (Schain 2006, 281–82).

The FN working-class vote, welfare chauvinism, and alternative vision of French nationhood have shaped the established political elites' response. Before the breakthrough in 1984, they hardly interacted with the FN. After 1984, the emergence of the FN caused the two established political poles to react in very different ways (Schain 2006, 23). As the FN consolidated, national leaders of the Gaullist RPR (Rassemblement pour la République) and the moderate-right UDF (Union pour la Démocratie Française) vehemently opposed an alliance with the FN, but did not stigmatize the party. The RPR and UDF also made local and regional tactical alliances with the FN in 1986 and 1988 (Marcus 1995, 136–43). This linkage continued until 1992, when the RPR leadership enforced a strict demarcation. The cooptation of part of the FN anti-immigration agenda by the right did not roll back the FN but, rather, changed the center of gravity of the national debate. The restrictions in the nationality code and immigration policy in 1993, the immigration and naturalization proposals in 1997, and the more recent hard-line immigration and law-and-order policies of Nicolas Sarkozy, then minister of interior and now president, reflect policy shifts by the political right that were explicitly or implicitly designed to reduce FN electoral support and win back some voters (Schain 2006, 282–83).

## Belgium

Despite the unique role of regional cleavages in Belgium, it shares with France the rise of a radical right that prospered in isolation. A striking difference, however, concerns the role of the state—the Belgian legal system targeted the entire far-right party. After a long legal battle, the Court of Cassation found the Vlaams Blok (VB) guilty of breaching the Belgian law against racism in November 9, 2004, costing the party its state financing, and forced it to rename itself on November 14 the Vlaams Belang (Flemish Interest). The name change was the last in a series of reforms the party undertook to make itself more mainstream for the 2006 elections; although, VB leader Filip Dewinter stated that the changes had "nothing to do with content but everything to do with tactic," since "nothing ha[s] changed in the party program" (quoted in Erk 2005, 498).

Traditionally a Flemish nationalist party striving for independence, the VB put immigration at the top of its agenda in 1988 when Filip Dewinter became the leader of the VB faction in the Antwerp city council. Its seventy-point program of 1992 proposed seventy measures to combat immigration (De Winter 2005, 104–7; Swyngedouw and Ivaldi 2001). Despite the 2004 VB facelift, the seventy-point program remains its platform, updated with an emphasis on the need for foreigners to assimilate (see interview with Dewinter in *De Standaard,* March 29, 2000). VB rhetoric also ties law-and-order matters with immigration by arguing that foreigners feed crime (Fisher 2002, 3). In the French-speaking part of Belgium, the VB sibling, the Front National, advocates a more statist program and opposes Flemish separatism (Ignazi 2003, 129–31).

The VB steadily improved its electoral support from 6.6 percent in the 1991 national election (10.4 percent in Flanders), to 7.8 percent in 1995 (13.1 percent in Flanders), 9.9 percent in 1999 (15.9 percent in Flanders), and 11.6 percent in 2003 (18.8 percent in Flanders) (De Winter 2005, 97–103). Despite the legal battle and name change in 2004, the VB continued its upward trend and received 12.0 percent of the vote in the most recent elections in June 2007. A postelection survey by TNS Media-Dimarso for the Vlaamse Radio- en Televisieomroep (VRT) and *De Standaard* after the June 2004 regional elections revealed that 313,000 voters had shifted from the mainstream parties Christen-Democratisch en Vlaams (CD&V; Christian-democrats), Vlaamse Liberalen en Democraten (VLD; liberals) and Socialistische Partij anders (SP; socialists) to the VB, many angered by the granting of local political rights to foreigners. VB voters were also the most loyal (93 percent) (Vaes 2004).

So far, Belgian authorities and parties have strictly contained the radical right. Although the VB is currently the largest Belgian party, it has never participated in the government because the democratic parties signed a *cordon sanitaire* agreement in the Belgian Parliament on November 19, 1992, rejecting VB participation in any coalition (Center for Equal Opportunities and Opposition to Racism 2004, 16, 112–14; Downs 2001). This has changed somewhat since the 2004 regional elections. Yves Leterme, Flemish Christian Democrat chief, held talks with VB leaders "out of respect for the party's one million voters" (Harding 2004). Some voices in the VLD have argued against maintaining the *cordon sanitaire.* Hugo Coveliers did not rule out cooperating with the VB in the 2006 municipal elections if it softened its statements, and Jean-Marie Dedecker advocated for a VLD vote on reconsidering the *cordon* (Harding 2004; De Muelenaere 2004).

The VB has clearly pulled the political center toward the right in Flanders (Erk 2005, 499; see also Downs 2001). A case study on how the mainstream parties reacted toward the VB in Antwerp in 2000 showed that many of their representatives (40.0 percent of the VLD, 52.4 percent of the Christelijke Volkspartij (CVP; Christian-Democrats, now CD&V), 50.0 percent of the Volksunie (VU; conservatives), and 14.3 percent of the socialists (SP) favored coopting VP policies. Moreover, 19.1 percent (CVP), 50.0 percent (VU), and even 14.3 percent (SP) favored a direct collaboration with the VB (Downs 2001, 36). And even though the VB has had to take the extremist edge off some of its policies, mainstream Flemish parties are increasingly adopting its discourse (Erk 2005, 500).

## Denmark

In Denmark, a radical right party has become a key element of a minority national governing coalition. The seed of this situation was planted in 1973, when the Uafhængig Fremskridspartiet (UF; Danish Progress Party), led by Mogens Glistrup, surprisingly won seats in the Danish parliament. The party was originally not anti-immigrant, but had sharply criticized the government tax policy. By the mid-1980s, however, Glistrup began campaigning against immigrants, copying from the French FN (Meliss and Sund 2003, 121; Bjørklund and Andersen 2002, 107–10; Rydgren 2004, 480). Gilstrup's fundamentalists led a group of pragmatists, headed by Pia Kjærsgaard, to split away to from the Dansk Folkepartiet (DF; Danish People's Party) in the early 1990s (Widfeldt 2000, 489–90). After the split, the UF vote decreased continuously during the 1990s and failed to surpass the 2 percent threshold in 2001; four years later, it did not run for election at all. The increasingly radical rhetoric of the UF and its 2001 election campaign for a "Mohammed-free Denmark" evidently positioned the party too far to the right (Rydgren 2004, 487).

The DF, however, became increasingly more successful, winning 7.4 percent in 1998, 13.2 percent in 2005, and 13.9 percent in 2007. It attracted even more support in public opinion polls (Widfeldt 2000, 486). Built on "the core of ethno-nationalism" (Rydgren 2004, 480), the DF rejects immigrant integration and favors a strict quota on access to citizenship (Bjørklund and Andersen 2002, 113). In 2001, the DF issued a book listing fourteen pages of crimes by immigrants against native Danes (Rydgren 2004, 485). The growing success of the DF coincided with the emergence of smaller anti-immigrant organizations in the November 2005 regional elections. Shortly after the Muslim community joined with local authorities to make plans for building a mosque and a Muslim cultural center in Århus in 2004, the DF candidate for Århus, Niels Brammer, told the *Jyllands-Posten* that Islam was a fascist ideology and that Danes should oppose the building of the mosque.

In contrast to the other countries, established parties in Denmark have tried to neither isolate the DF nor adopt a *cordon sanitaire*. The October 2001 elections resulted in a minority government led by Prime Minister Anders Fogh Rasmussen, a coalition of Venstre (V; liberals) and Det Konservative Folkeparti (KF; conservatives). It needed, and got, DF support on crucial questions of legislation (Roberts and Hogwood 2003, 172–73). The impact of the party increased after the 2005 elections because the minority governing coalition lost two more seats. Many adherents of fundamentalist religious groups such as the Danish Association and New Era—some of whose founding members are judges, chief police inspectors, and local administrators—have become

DF members (Rydgren 2004, 483). Conversely, Søren Krarup, Pia Kjærsgaard, Søren Espersen (writer for *Danskeren* and public relations person for DF), Jesper Langballe, and others have been members of the Association. The fact that Scandinavian radical right-wing parties are less anti-system compared to other Western European parties of that family might explain the relatively high degree of willingness to cooperate with the governing parties (Widfeldt 2000, 499; see also Heinisch 2003).

And, in tandem with these developments, populist anti-immigrant rhetoric found its way into the mainstream political discourse during the 1990s. Liberal (V) and conservative politicians (KF) began to adopt more right-wing rhetoric from 1997 onward (Rasmussen 2001, 109). Even Social Democratic candidates adopted a strong emphasis on Danish virtues and norms and their strong differences with those of immigrants, typical DF rhetoric, in the 2001 election campaign. All parties, including the Social Democrats, put forth plans to restrict further immigration, reduce development aid, ban Muslim prayer in workplaces, and repatriate immigrants (Meliss and Sund 2003, 126).

Today, the DF has acquired a "normal status" in the party system and is accepted by some other parties (Meliss and Sund 2003, 126–27). In 1998, it drew 49 percent of its vote from the working class; this increased to 56 percent in 2001 (490). Prime Minister Anders Fogh Rasmussen regards the DF as a possible coalition partner; only public opinion and perhaps conservative pressure prevent him from officially bringing it into government. After the fourth so-called integration meeting (*integrationsmøde*), the prime minister stated that he did not want to isolate the DF just because it did not like all the government immigrant policies (*Politiken,* March 22, 2006).

## Austria

This process played out even more thoroughly in Austria. Unlike Germany and Italy, and very much like Denmark, the party had no formal connection to the fascist past. It evolved from a neoliberal critique of the welfare state toward a moderate ethnocentrism that has facilitated its move closer to the centers of political power.

As figure 10.1 shows, Austrians resist multiculturalism more than the European Union as a whole and are also more likely than the EU average to believe that Austria has reached the limits of multicultural society, that immigrants should have only limited civil rights, and that many should be repatriated (European Commission 2003b, 3, 84). These beliefs emerged against the backdrop of a rather large foreign-born population and the biggest jump toward religious pluralism of all six countries considered here (see table 10.3).

These sentiments have fostered, and been fostered by, Jörg Haider's rise as leader of the Freiheitliche Partei Österreichs (FPÖ; Freedom Party of Austria). When Haider took over in 1986, he engineered a sharp right turn, increasing party membership from around 37,000 to 53,000 by 2000 (Höbelt 2003, 231), crowding out or absorbing smaller rightist groups. One of Haider's confidants, Andreas Mölzer, has been a long-time editor of such right-wing extremist publications as the monthly of fraternities, *Aula,* and has links to Nazi individuals in Austria and Germany (Dokumentationsarchiv des österreichischen Widerstands 1993, 119–26; see Höbelt 2003, 75–76). Before Haider, the FPÖ free-market orientation attracted mostly middle-class support, especially from business people and the self-employed. Under Haider, it turned toward the working class and protectionism (Prantl 2005). Only after prolonged membership in the government and growing tensions within the party did its electoral support drop significantly in recent elections.

The FPÖ had a long track record of parliamentary activities, even when it was excluded from government (Minkenberg 2001; Heinisch 2003). The FPÖ delegates introduced one hundred bills in the 1995–1999 session of the Vienna Nationalrat Parliament, which adopted many, including proposals to lower the number of legally employed foreigners (1997), revise the citizenship law to include the passage "Österreich ist kein Einwanderungsland" ("Austria is not an immigration country") (1997), and tighten the asylum law (1998). In the October 1999 elections, the FPÖ achieved its apogee in electoral support, leading the conservative Österreichische Volkspartei (ÖVP) to form a government with it in 2000, following a long, drawn-out negotiation. Their agreement yielded the FPÖ as many ministerial posts as the ÖVP (Pelinka 2005), led the European Union to freeze most of its relations with Austria, and led Haider to resign the FPÖ chairmanship in favor of Vice Chancellor Susanne Riess-Passer but, nonetheless, remain the de facto FPÖ strongman (Luther 2003, 137). The new government embraced some new, largely FPÖ-inspired proposals. The most striking included reducing immigration to zero, establishing an employment preference for nationals, and creating a new Austrian National Foundation to protect Austrian culture.

For its part, the ÖVP embraced the FPÖ as a coalition partner to win over former FPÖ voters, keep the FPÖ supporting the government, and prevent it from gaining further strength. ÖVP Interior Minister Ernst Strasser told the *Kleine Zeitung* in December 2002 that "there must be no room to the right of the ÖVP for a right-wing populist party" (Luther 2003, 148). This strategy was successful in fragmenting the FPÖ. As a result of these internal conflicts and the pressure by the coalition partner, the FPÖ lost nearly two-thirds of its 1999 voters in the early elections in November 2002, winning only 10 percent of the total. Still, in this campaign, both major parties aimed to win over as many previous FPÖ voters as possible.

In its weakened condition, the FPÖ was still a more attractive coalition partner for the ÖVP than the Sozialdemokratische Partei Österreichs (SPÖ; socialists) or greens, and a much-chastened FPÖ returned to the government in February 2003 and remained a much-weakened part of the government until the 2006 elections returned the old grand coalition of SPÖ and ÖVP under a social-democratic chancellor to power.

In the meantime, Jörg Haider had broken away from the FPÖ and formed his own Bündnis für die Zukunft Österreichs (BZÖ, Alliance for the Future of Austria). With its positions not very different from those of the FPÖ, it was remarkable that the September 2008 elections witnessed a sharp rise in electoral support for both FPÖ (17.5 percent of the vote) and BZÖ (10.7 percent)—a triumph for Haider, which he, however, was unable to savor because he died in a car accident just two weeks after the elections. Paradoxically, Haider's death may usher in a new era of radical right politics in Austria, since he was seen by the FPÖ as the major obstacle to the reunification of both parties.

The Austrian case thus diverges sharply from those of France or Germany, and even Denmark, both because of the size of the FPÖ and its omnipresence on the right and the ÖVP determination to win over FPÖ voters and marginalize it as a populist opponent by bringing it into government. Although this tactic did indeed weaken the far-right opposition, it did so by making the far-right platform the center of government policy. Moreover, it failed in the longer run to marginalize the radical right.

## Conclusion

This chapter has shown that established European political (and state) actors have reacted to the growing organizational strength of the radical right by adopting and legitimizing some of its elements. This trend represents a major shift from earlier patterns in which established actors ostracized such positions.

Political violence in the Netherlands shifted public sentiment and party politics against immigrants, and government policy hardened into a less liberal approach even though the organized radical right could not consolidate its political position. In Germany, by contrast, the growing integration of violent right-wing subcultural milieus into the NPD helped it gain a position in the party system, at least in some parts of East Germany—but with little effect on policymakers. The organizational and electoral consolidation has progressed even further in France and Belgium. Efforts by conservative parties in Denmark and Austria to coopt the electoral rise and relative pragmatism of the radical right led to a greater legitimacy for these parties. Although these tactics did indeed "tame" the far-right parties, they came with newly hardened anti-immigrant policies.

Overall, however, the effects of the radical right on immigrant incorporation must be seen as limited. In fact, a comparative analysis of integration policies, as measured by the recognition of (immigrants') cultural group rights, shows an expansion rather than a contraction over time. Following the five-country study by Koopmans and colleagues (2005), these group rights were identified as allowances for religious practices outside of public institutions and cultural rights and provisions in public institutions. During the rise and consolidation of the radical right, in none of the six

**Table 10.7** Group rights of minorities in selected European democracies, 1990 and 2002

|  | Religious rights | | Cultural rights | | Average religious rights and cultural rights | |
|---|---|---|---|---|---|---|
|  | 1990 | 2002 | 1990 | 2002 | 1990 | 2002 |
| Austria | −0.66 | 0.33 | 0.50 | 1.00 | −0.08 | 0.67 |
| Belgium | 0.00 | 0.00 | −0.20 | −0.20 | −0.10 | −0.10 |
| Denmark | 0.00 | 0.00 | 0.00 | 0.66 | 0.00 | 0.33 |
| France | −0.33 | 0.00 | −0.60 | −0.60 | −0.47 | −0.30 |
| Germany | −0.33 | 0.00 | −0.60 | 0.00 | −0.47 | 0.00 |
| Netherlands | 0.66 | 1.00 | 0.60 | 0.80 | 0.63 | 0.90 |

*Source:* Minkenberg (2008, 65).
*Note:* Values indicate the level of recognition of group rights from very low (−1) to very high (1).

countries under review were these cultural and religious group rights curtailed (see table 10.7). Only in Belgium (and France in the realm of cultural rights only) did the recognition of these rights stagnate. In all other countries and instances, substantial gains were made, in line with the general trend in all western democracies toward an enhanced policy of integration (Minkenberg 2008).

# CHAPTER ELEVEN

# Immigrants' Incorporation in the United States after 9/11

## Two Steps Forward, One Step Back

*Peter H. Schuck*

The last decade has been momentous for immigrants to the United States and for the course of their integration into U.S. society. If we look for a smooth trajectory, we will be sorely disappointed. Instead, immigrants' path to integration has been characterized by forward progress interrupted by setbacks and new obstacles. The bitter debate over immigration legislation that has roiled the U.S. Congress since 2005 might seem evidence of another sharp detour in this path.

At a deeper socioeconomic level, however, the powerful U.S. assimilatory machine has continued to churn out millions of new citizens and legal permanent residents (LPRs) who identify with the nation, embrace its ideals, and participate in its social, civic, and political life pretty much as actively as did their predecessors—despite the unprecedented conditions surrounding their migration and settlement here. The United States has also attracted an estimated 12 million undocumented migrants as of 2008, whose status raises difficult political and policy questions. If we wish to understand these developments, we must attend both to the eye-catching, headline-grabbing events and to the more opaque, profound, and powerful continuities.

### The Policy Debate: 1994–2008

The history of U.S. immigration policy is long, complex, and pervaded by paradox (Zolberg 2006). This chapter focuses on the tumultuous period beginning in 1994 with the passage of Proposition 187 in California, a frontal assault on access to social benefits by millions of undocumented aliens in our largest state. The battle over Proposition 187 erupted only four years after the Immigration Act of 1990 had seemed to strike a stable, sustainable policy equilibrium (Schuck 1998). In 1995, a House of Representatives committee held hearings on proposals to reduce legal immigration levels, to withdraw birthright citizenship from the native-born children of illegal aliens, and to strengthen enforcement against undocumented, out-of-status, and criminal aliens.

A year later, Congress enacted two laws—the Antiterrorism and Effective Death Penalty Act of 1996 (AEDPA) and the Illegal Immigration Reform and Immigrant Responsibility Act of 1996 (IIRIRA)—that imposed tough new restrictions on noncitizens convicted of crimes in the United States or of immigration law violations. These acts were the most radical reform of immigration law in decades—or perhaps ever (Schuck 1998, 143). A third statute—the Personal Responsibility and Work Opportunity Reconciliation Act of 1996 (PRWORA, or "welfare reform")—made many LPRs, not to mention undocumented aliens, ineligible for certain federally subsidized public benefits, including cash assistance and many in-kind transfers. The number of states, already a majority, with English-only rules for government business and communications continued to grow.

Just because most Americans support the removal of criminal and undocumented aliens does not mean that they are hostile to immigration (Schuck 1998, chap. 5). The goal of these removals, after all, is to prevent the blatant violation of our laws, a goal shared not only by virtually all citizens but also by the vast majority of LPRs who benefit from law enforcement and who, more than Americans generally, are disadvantaged by competition and negative stereotyping resulting from illegal migration. (LPRs are likely more ambivalent about the 1996 welfare reform law because many disabled and elderly LPRs received Supplemental Security Income (SSI), checks under the pre-1996 rules, and many immigrant families include members who are LPRs, undocumented or otherwise removable, and U.S. citizens.)

In any event, the political pendulum soon began to swing back toward easing legal restrictions on immigrants. In 1997, the U.S. Commission on Immigration Reform submitted numerous policy recommendations to Congress designed to promote *Americanization,* defined as integrating immigrants while respecting their cultures of origin, increasing family-based immigration in the short-term by focusing on nuclear family reunification, and returning to the level of family admissions that prevailed in the 1980s (U.S. Commission on Immigration Reform 1997). Congress also restored many of the SSI and related benefits to those who had been eligible before 1996 and to the newly disabled and President Bill Clinton vowed to restore food stamps for immigrant families with children, which Congress eventually did. California, New York, New Jersey, and other high-immigration states filled some of the remaining gaps with their own funds. (This refuted predictions that immigrants were so politically friendless that the states would engage in a headlong "race to the bottom" to cut benefits to induce them to return home or move to other jurisdictions.)

Congress enacted amnesties for an estimated 155,000 Nicaraguans and Cubans, many Haitians, and 240,000 Guatemalan and Salvadorans who were in the United States illegally in 1997 and 1998. In December 2000, Congress enabled about 400,000 illegal aliens, who had been ruled ineligible for earlier amnesties, to obtain green cards. The new George W. Bush administration twice mobilized Republicans in Congress to extend the application deadline. In March 2001, the administration gave temporary legal status to 150,000 undocumented Salvadorans. Bush then began a campaign for another large amnesty for Mexican agricultural workers. Congress expanded the number of temporary H-1B visas available to technical workers, many of whom would later adjust to LPR status. Finally, between 1999 and 2001, LPR admissions increased from 646,568 to 1,064,318, the highest level since 1914, not including the Immigration Reform and Control Act of 1986 (IRCA) amnesties (U.S. Department of Homeland Security 2005, table 1). Almost half of these LPR "admissions" were of people already in the United States, many illegally.

This expansive policy was convulsed by the destruction of the World Trade Center on September 11, 2001, an event that transformed—and in some ways, *de*formed—that policy. Stephen Legomsky has described the immediate impact:

> In immigration as in other areas of public life, everything changed. Proposed immigration liberalizations were suddenly off the table. Taking their place were the USA PATRIOT Act of 2001, the Homeland Security Act of 2002 (transferring almost all functions of the former INS [Immigration and Naturalization Service] to multiple agencies in the new Department of Homeland Security, controversial new Justice Department regulations intensifying the investigation, apprehension, and detention of non-citizens, the President's Order subjecting various categories of non-citizens to criminal trials before military tribunals without the usual constitutional constraints, and the REAL ID Act of 2005. (2005, vi)

The administrative processing of nonimmigrant and LPR visas, as well as naturalizations, slowed considerably. But by 2005, legal immigration returned to record levels, 1.12 million LPRs and 604,000 naturalizations; in 2006, the numbers increased further to 1.26 million and 702,000, respectively. (Both numbers declined in 2007, to 1.052 million LPRs and 660,000 naturalizations, with a huge increase in the backlog of pending naturalization petitions, to 1.13 million.) A similarly sharp decline in student visas after 2001 was reversed after intense protests by university leaders and scientific researchers dependent on the flow of talented foreigners to their institutions. By some measures, enforcement increased. Formal deportations (now called "removals") are at record levels (319,000 in 2007). The immigration enforcement agency manages one of the largest detention operations in the federal government (exceeding 25,000 beds, with thousands more authorized). The agency has engaged in high-profile enforcement actions against street gangs with undocumented members, some workforces, and at least one large employer, although the number of employer sanctions imposed overall is negligible. President Bush's administration budgeted a huge expansion in border and interior enforcement and in detention capacity in 2008 and future years, assigning thousands of National Guard troops to assist with border enforcement.

At the same time, the policies of Congress and the Bush administration for the monitoring, identification, apprehension, detention, interrogation, prosecution, and removal of immigrants suspected of links to terrorism have been subjected to growing and sometimes bipartisan criticism for their ineffectiveness, doubtful legality, and threat to the civil liberties of immigrants and citizens alike. The courts, including the U.S. Supreme Court, have rebuked and rejected certain aspects of some of these policies (*Hamdi v. Rumsfeld,* 542 U.S. 507 [2004]; *Rasul v. Bush,* 542 U.S. 466 [2004]; *Hamdan v. Rumsfeld,* 126 S.Ct. 2749 [2006]; and *Boumediene v. Bush,* 128 S.Ct. 2229 [2008]). Other challenges are still being reviewed by the courts.

This chapter is not the place for a policy-by-policy assessment of the so-called war on terrorism, nor are scholars yet in a good position to conduct such assessments.

The sad truth, inherent in the nature of this unprecedented campaign, is that the publicly available information about how this war on terrorism is being waged and with what consequences remains radically incomplete. To be sure, the abstract values at stake in the conflict between conducting the war effectively and protecting the civil liberties of citizens and noncitizens seem clear enough. But we lack the crucial information needed to know the actual terms of this trade-off so that we can then assess its legal, moral, and political acceptability.

The courts, properly mindful of their limited constitutional role and expertise in national security matters, have entered this debate—but only at the edges and mostly to preserve their own jurisdiction and to insist on observing minimal standards of due process. The Justice Department and the Pentagon have already conducted a number of internal investigations that have identified some highly disturbing patterns of both fecklessness and lawlessness under both domestic and international legal standards (U.S. Department of Justice 2003).

Other widely criticized practices targeting particular immigrant groups, such as profiling, may in principle be more justifiable if conducted with appropriate safeguards against invidious discrimination and unnecessary invasions of privacy (Schuck 2006, 140; Viscusi and Zeckhauser 2003). Most of the USA PATRIOT Act was reauthorized in March 2006.

The antiterrorism measures being adopted in almost all European countries, particularly in the wake of the murder of the Dutch activist Theo Van Gogh and the July 7, 2005, bombings in London, appear to be moving almost entirely in the direction of tougher controls on immigrants and citizens alike. In June 2008, for example, the British Parliament approved legislation extending the period of time during which suspected terrorists can be held without a judicial hearing.

Still, we can easily be misled by the asserted crisis surrounding immigration policy and enforcement in the post-9/11 period (examples include Cole 2003; *University of California at Davis Law Review* 2005). In fact, this period is just as remarkable for what has *not* happened as for what *has* happened. Just as Sherlock Holmes gained a pivotal clue from the dog that didn't bark, we can advance our understanding of immigrant incorporation in the United States by attending to its deeper, more structural, and often unremarked regularities that the changes wrought after 9/11 have interrupted but not essentially altered. My analysis of these systemic patterns proceeds in five sections: (1) public attitudes toward immigration, immigrants, and the diversity that they bring to U.S. life; (2) the role that affirmative action and other public benefits play in the incorporation of immigrants; (3) the role of federalism in this incorporation; (4) emergent notions of citizenship; and (5) the nature and extent of immigrant assimilation.

## Public Attitudes toward Immigration, Immigrants, and Diversity

Americans hold four different kinds of restrictionist views (Schuck 1998, 4–11): xenophobia (an undifferentiated fear of foreigners or strangers as such), nativism (a more discriminating belief in the moral or racial superiority of the indigenous stock), principled restrictionism (the belief that current levels of immigration inevitably threaten particular policy goals or values advocated by the restrictionist), and pragmatic restrictionism (the belief that such policy and value conflicts are contingent, not inevitable). Most Americans are probably pragmatic restrictionists— they favor lower levels of immigration (almost regardless of what the current levels are, which the public misestimates), but they remain open to argument and evidence about what those levels should be and about the actual effects of immigration. Like the public attitudes toward race-oriented policy issues that Sniderman and Piazza (1993) found notably responsive to counterarguments, public views on immigration levels are, within limits, fluid.

According to survey data (with the usual caveats about sensitivity to the wording of questions and other factors), Americans like immigrants more than they like immigration, favor past immigration more than recent immigration, prefer legal immigrants to illegal ones, prefer refugees to other immigrants, support immigrants' access to educational and health benefits but not to welfare or Social Security, and feel that immigrants' distinctive cultures have contributed positively to U.S. life and that diversity continues to strengthen U.S. society today. At the same time, they overwhelmingly resist any conception of multiculturalism that discourages or impedes immigrants from swiftly learning and using the English language.

Americans treasure their immigrant roots yet believe that current immigration levels are too high—and, the data indicate, they always have. New immigrant groups have always raised anxiety about immigration, a tendency that a 1982 Gallup poll places in a revealing historical light. When asked about its views on the contributions of particular immigrant groups, the public gave the highest scores to precisely those groups that had been widely reviled in the nineteenth and early twentieth centuries; the lower-scoring groups were the newer arrivals (at that time, Cubans and Haitians). Rita Simon has captured this ambivalence in an arresting metaphor: "We view immigrants with rose-colored glasses turned backwards" (2003, 44). Recent poll results support this finding (Bowman 2006).[1]

The optimist might infer that seventy-five years hence, the public will view today's newcomers—who by then will be old, established groups—with the same solicitude and admiration now generally reserved for Italians, Jews, Slovaks, and other well-assimilated groups. The pessimist, of course, will reject this "postdictive prediction," insisting that things really *have* changed for the worse. (Some immigration scholars find support for this more pessimistic view.) Recent national polls (Connolly 2006) find high levels of opposition to illegal aliens, an unsurprising view that has propelled almost universal demands for more effective enforcement.

Public attitudes toward demographic, ethno-racial, religious, gender, and other diversities have nevertheless become far more liberal since the 1960s. This liberalization is strikingly evident in the election of multiracial Senator Barack Obama for the presidency and in the evolving views of openly gay relationships and lifestyles by a society that harshly repressed them and to an extent still does (Schuck 2003, 4). Immigration law has shifted from the exclusion of a category interpreted to include homosexuals (upheld by the Supreme Court in *Boutilier v. INS*, 387 U.S. 118 [1967]) to its elimination by Congress as grounds for exclusion in the Immigration Act of 1990 (Legomsky 2005, 259–60; Eskridge 1990). This liberalization helped to produce the landmark 1965 immigration reform that, in turn, utterly transformed the face and culture of the United States. Canadian immigration policy experienced a comparable—by some measures, an even greater—liberalization during this period.

In sharp contrast, however, even the most liberal European states, such as Denmark, are experiencing enormous difficulties absorbing a far lesser degree of diversity. As Michael Minkenberg (chap. 10) and Gianni D'Amato (chap. 5 in this volume) show, right-wing parties with harsh anti-immigrant ideologies have gained strength in almost all of them. The December 2005 riots that convulsed France and the Europe-wide violence two months later in response to the publication in a Denmark newspaper of cartoons offensive to many Muslims, may well be harbingers of bitter conflicts to come. Unfortunately, for a variety of reasons, these states seem comparatively ill-equipped to manage such conflicts (Foner and Alba 2008).

In sum, Americans tell survey researchers that they favor legal immigration and cultural diversity in principle but want less of it in practice. Research also indicates that racial and ethnic diversity reduces social capital within and between communities (Putnam 2007; Schuck 2007b). Americans harbor deep concerns about the impact of immigration and diversity on specific aspects of U.S. life—since 9/11, on the risk of terrorism in particular—and also worry about how quickly and completely the newer immigrant groups can be assimilated. These same anxieties troubled earlier generations as well (King 2000; Tichenor 2002; Zolberg 2006). But anti-Muslim incidents—conduct that President Bush sought to forestall by affirming solidarity with law-abiding Muslims in the United States and elsewhere in his first public address after the terrorist attacks—seem to have declined substantially since the spate of local harassment immediately after 9/11, The tension between Muslims and non-Muslims in the United States is far lower than in France or the Netherlands, where the Muslim population is proportionately larger, more socially isolated, and more sympathetic to Islamic radicalism (Roy 2004; Pew Research Center 2007).

The survey data prompt an intriguing question: If Americans are ambivalent about immigration and desire even less legal immigration, how can we explain the notably liberal immigration policies of the last decade (Tichenor 2002)? (On a similar situation in Europe, see Lahav 2004a.) The IRCA, much-heralded as an example of a "get tough" policy, turned out on balance to be expansionist, legalizing almost 3 million out-of-status workers, while its employer sanctions have never been strongly enforced. The expansionist Immigration Act of 1990 has persisted through two economic recessions and even after 9/11. Large amnesties were also enacted during the late 1990s, Congress and the major immigrant-receiving states restored most of the benefits withdrawn from LPRs under the 1996 welfare reform law, and restrictionist measures have focused almost entirely on criminal and undocumented aliens rather than on the vastly larger number who are in legal status. In May 2006, the Senate rejected the strong enforcement bill passed by the House of Representatives in December 2005—which would not have restricted legal immigration—in favor of large new amnesty and guestworker programs and an expanded quota for employment-based permanent visas. As the failed effort at comprehensive reform in spring 2007 suggests, any bill that emerges from Congress is likely to increase immigration even as it also contains tougher enforcement provisions.

Three factors go a long way toward explaining this strong tendency to expand immigration even in the face of public opposition to it: the distinctive political economy of immigration policy; immigration federalism; and the remarkably successful assimilation of many immigrants, particularly the Asian groups whose numbers have increased rapidly since the late 1960s. (For a more extensive explanation, see Schuck 2007a).

The political economy of almost any important public issue consists of interests that are starkly opposed to one another, often from more than two directions. In the last few decades, rapid technological change, increased foreign trade and global competition, the decline of private-sector labor unions, a better-educated and more diverse population, a differentiation of product and service markets, a proliferation of nonprofit organizations, and many other factors have increased and diversified the number of interests affected by most public policies, immigration included. Political rhetoric aside, the classic struggles of capital versus labor, rural versus urban, importers versus exporters, agriculture versus industry, producers versus consumers, military versus civilian, national versus local, and ethno-racial majority versus minorities have largely gone the way of carbon paper. These traditional dualisms fail to capture the actual dynamics of today's far more complex political pluralism.

What is so unusual and significant about immigration politics is the extent to which its many vectors converge to press for more expansionist policies. The manifest failure of the leading restrictionist lobby (the Federation for American Immigration Reform, FAIR) to mobilize the latent unorganized public opposition to immigration expansion illustrates this point. Primary support for FAIR comes from population-control interests along with some environmental and labor groups. The small but resolute restrictionist caucus in the House, led by Tom Tancredo of Colorado (he claimed 101 members, almost all Republican from strongly Republican districts), served mainly to increase the already significant pressure on the Bush administration to increase enforcement. The restrictionists' long-standing efforts to eliminate birthright citizenship for the native-born children of undocumented aliens has little public support.

Although this political disconnect has in the past produced a more expansionist policy than the public says it wants, this may not continue. Whenever the underlying social values or facts change but a policy itself does not, the widening disjunction ripens political opportunity for the opponents of the policy. This is what drives much fundamental policy change. In the immigration context, this dynamic may take the form of a harsh political backlash by voters frustrated by what they see as a recalcitrant, unresponsive political establishment, an impulsive reaction that may be extreme and misguided rather than merely striking a new, more desirable equilibrium. Some examples of crude policies resulting from a backlash against a political disconnect that had grown too wide include Proposition 187, IIRIRA, the Arizona Proposition 200 of November 2004, and the REAL ID Act of 2005. The enforcement-only bill adopted by the House in December 2005 was a similar overreaction; it would have made felons of anyone, including clergy, who assist such immigrants.

Despite the failure of comprehensive reform in 2007, surveys show many in the public have reached a balanced and realistic view about the prospects for effective immigration enforcement. In October 2005, a new poll of eight hundred registered "likely" Republican voters indicated that 72 percent favored an earned legalization proposal combined with tougher border security and employer sanctions. An even higher share (84 percent) agreed that it is not possible to deport all illegal aliens

(Manhattan Institute for Policy Research 2005). (Of course, this proposition is so obviously true that we might have expected 100 percent agreement!)

## Affirmative Action and Other Public Benefits for Immigrants

The issue of immigrants' eligibility for affirmative action and many other public benefits has long been controversial in the United States, particularly during the last decade, when strong political, legal, and ideological challenges have been mounted, some successfully, against even citizens' access to such benefits (see Schuck 2003, chap. 5; 2006). Nonetheless, the continuing availability of many public benefits—even to undocumented aliens—suggests that immigrants today are treated less as a "discrete and insular minority" than at perhaps any time in our history.

Opposition to affirmative action, defined as quotas or preferences, runs deep. The vast majority of Americans, including more than one-third of blacks and more than 70 percent of Hispanics, oppose racial preferences in hiring and promotion, with the level of this opposition having grown somewhat over time. Rightly or wrongly, opponents view preferences as inconsistent with the ideals of equal opportunity and merit that almost all strongly endorse. Opponents of affirmative action are strengthened by the little-known fact that four out of five immigrants—by definition, individuals without a history of victimization in the United States—become automatically eligible for affirmative action benefits the moment they arrive (Graham 2002, 192). Immigrants' eligibility for affirmative action may help to explain, for example, why almost 20 percent of the black faculty at the University of Michigan were immigrants, as were more than half of the "Asian-Pacific Islander" (a census category) faculty. Professors Henry Louis Gates and Lani Guinier have lamented the fact that a high percentage of black students at Harvard are from immigrant or biracial families (in Rimer and Arenson 2004)

Immigrants' eligibility for and use of affirmative action benefits may fuel resentment from many Americans who might otherwise sympathize with their cause, particularly low-income blacks with whom many immigrants compete for jobs and other resources. When U.S. blacks claim a preferential entitlement for themselves as a group, it spotlights their underlying claims about uniqueness, desert, opportunity, and performance. Earlier immigrant groups, now largely and comfortably assimilated, who may feel disadvantaged by the preferences, may also feel that their *own* feelings of uniqueness, desert, opportunity, and performance are not getting due respect or may resent the fact that they managed to assimilate without the benefit of costly bilingual programs put into place for later immigrants. Some of the bitter intergroup clashes in urban areas surely reflect feelings of moral superiority and animus inspired by intergroup comparisons

Immigrants' eligibility for other public benefits has a long history that cannot easily be disentangled from the complex histories of the welfare state and of constitutional federalism. Suffice it to say that states and localities often barred even LPRs from claiming such benefits, particularly in the years before the Great Society, when programs, dollars, and beneficiaries were far more limited. Courts generally upheld these restrictions if the government could show that they would promote "a special public interest" (Spiro 1994). In *Graham v. Richardson,* 403 U.S. 365 (1971), the Supreme Court held that the Equal Protection Clause prohibited states from conditioning their welfare benefits on citizenship, and in *Plyler v. Doe,* 457 U.S. 202 (1982), the Court held that states could not bar the children of resident undocumented aliens from attending their public schools. The Court was unclear about whether these invalidations of state restrictions on benefits for noncitizens were based on equal protection principles or, instead (or in addition), on the federal power to preempt state law regulation in the immigration field. For example, in *Mathews v. Diaz,* 426 U.S. 67 (1976), the Court upheld federal law restrictions on immigrants' eligibility for Medicare benefits, distinguishing its 1971 decision by citing the difference between congressional and state authority in this area.

The 1996 welfare reform statute made many LPRs and other legal immigrants ineligible for important cash and in-kind benefits using federal funds such as SSI and food stamps. These restrictions constituted an important source of the deficit-reduction compromise negotiated by Congress and President Clinton, along with severe new limits on benefits for U.S. citizens. Although immigrants did not receive means-tested benefits more than did demographically comparable Americans, some subgroups (e.g., elderly noncitizens on SSI and refugees on welfare) received them at much higher rates.

During this period, George Borjas, a labor economist, and his associates were reporting relatively high welfare and SSI utilization rates by certain immigrant groups, including Dominicans, refugees, the elderly, and some others. Legal immigrants are admitted under the explicit condition that they have jobs or citizen sponsors who promise to support them if and when necessary. Given this fact, voters might well believe that low-income citizens have a stronger claim to shrinking resources than immigrants admitted on condition that they not become public charges on pain of possible deportation, a condition now enforced by stiffer, legally enforceable affidavits of support from their sponsors. Assuming that we accept the legitimacy of requiring the financial independence of entering immigrants, it seems a fair and prudent compromise, not evidence of anti-immigrant animus, to use the resources gained by denying nonemergency public benefits to noncitizens in order to preserve benefits for destitute U.S. citizens.

As noted earlier, Congress and the states subsequently restored many of these withdrawn benefits. The Republican governor of New York, George Pataki, used state funds to restore Medicaid assistance not just for legal immigrants whose benefits had been repealed by the 1996 federal law but also for pregnant illegal aliens; other high-immigration states followed suit. In 2002, California, New York, and some other states extended their much lower in-state tuition rates to illegal aliens who graduate from state high schools and apply for legal status. (These benefits are now being challenged in the courts as illegal under a provision of IIRIRA intended to bar them.) Sympathy for immigrants, regardless of legal status, was evident when the federal 9/11 Victims Compensation Fund, with much publicity but little opposition, extended benefits to undocumented immigrants. So many high-immigration states authorized drivers licenses for undocumented aliens that enforcement-minded Republicans in Congress had to enact the REAL ID Act of 2005, limiting the uses that could be made of the license—yet protests by the states persuaded Congress to delay the implementation of that law. New York City forbids its public hospitals and other agencies to inquire about or disclose the immigration status of those with whom they come into contact. Other states and localities, in contrast, have cracked down. In general, however, recent political developments demonstrate that immigrants, both legal and undocumented, enjoy considerable public support (Schuck 2007c).

## The Role of Federalism in Structuring Immigrant Incorporation

The role of the states in defining the rights of noncitizens in the United States has a complex history (Schuck 1998, 194–97). The question is how fair treatment of noncitizens can be assured when the national government bears the primary responsibility for regulating them but the states, which may have stronger fiscal and political incentives to discriminate against them, define and carry out many relevant public services, such as education.

The Supreme Court has held that Congress remains free as a matter of policy to delegate some of its plenary power over immigration policy to the states by authorizing, or perhaps even requiring, them to act in ways that would be impermissible had Congress remained silent. In recent years, Congress has prescribed only a very limited affirmative role for the states in immigration policy—primarily, to provide federally mandated social services for refugees. Indeed, the REAL ID Act of 2005 requires the states to tailor their regulation of drivers' licenses to federal immigration enforcement priorities. The tight restriction of 1996 welfare reform on the power of the states to provide federally subsidized social services to nonqualified aliens is the clearest example of federal preemption of a field, public benefits, in which states have traditionally played a central policymaking role.

Nothing in the nature of immigration policy requires that it be an exclusively national responsibility. Although immigration control is a national function in all countries, subnational units in the federal systems of Canada, Germany, and Switzerland exercise important policymaking functions with respect to immigration. If Congress were to assign the states a more affirmative role in immigration policy and the courts sustained it, how would this alter the nature and process of immigrant incorporation? The vast majority of immigrants tend to live in a handful of state and metropolitan areas, and the distribution of those who are undocumented is even more skewed. However great the economic and other benefits of immigration to the nation as a whole may be, the costs imposed by immigrants' use of schools, hospitals, prisons, and other public services are highly concentrated in these high-impact states and localities.

For these communities, the cost of providing these services to immigrants is as salient as any policy area with which they deal. A recent U.S. Government Accounting Office (GAO) study documented this fiscal mismatch in the incarceration of criminal aliens (U.S. Government Accounting Office [GAO] 2005a). Under the Justice Department's State Criminal Alien Assistance Program (SCAAP), the federal government is supposed to reimburse state and local governments for a portion of their costs of incarcerating some, but not all, criminal aliens who are illegally in the country. The *number* of incarcerated immigrants has increased significantly in recent years, although immigrants have much lower, and declining, incarceration *rates* compared with comparable native-born Americans (Butcher 2006). Despite this, federal SCAAP reimbursements declined by approximately half between 2001 and 2004, representing only 25 percent or less of the estimated incarceration costs. California estimated that it spent $662 million in fiscal year 2006 alone to jail unauthorized aliens but received only $107 million in SCAAP funds.

Recent moves to increase the role of state and local criminal justice officials in enforcing federal immigration laws raise the question of immigration federalism in a specific and controversial context. The 1996 law authorized the federal government to negotiate agreements with states and localities that would, in effect, deputize their law enforcement officers to assist in the apprehension and detention of aliens who violate the immigration laws. This prospect is attractive to federal officials. After all, state and local police often apprehend criminal and undocumented aliens, albeit for nonimmigration offenses, and immigration officials must rely on local law enforcement agencies for criminal records and other data, access to local detention facilities, temporary custody arrangements, and other cooperation (Schuck and Williams 2000). In summer 2005, an unofficial Minuteman project had volunteer civilians patrolling areas of the border between Arizona and Mexico, and it claimed that it had 15,000 volunteers ready to patrol the entire Mexican-U.S. border. Responding to this pressure, Arizona and New Mexico declared an immigration emergency at their borders and demanded that the federal government provide special assistance. Governor Arnold Schwarzenegger of California, who praised the Minuteman campaign, has resisted political pressure to do likewise. In May 2006, President Bush began sending National Guard troops to help patrol the southern border. When all of this dust clears, one suspects that the federal government will feel compelled to delegate somewhat more enforcement authority and funds to the states. There are good reasons why it should do so (Schuck 2007c).

## Emergent Conceptions of Citizenship

The admissions system is not simply a gateway to the United States; it is also a gateway to becoming an American. Once immigrants enter as LPRs, they will in all likelihood be eligible to naturalize. In effect, the demographic diversity of the citizenry resembles that of the admitted immigrants, at least over time, although different immigrant groups naturalize at very different rates. Mexicans and Canadians, for example, are less likely to naturalize, and take longer to do so, than many Asian groups, reflecting greater geographic proximity and more enduring ties to their homelands. Also, members of some groups are more likely to have entered the United States without documents and subsequently gained legal status, which lengthens their time to naturalization as well. Regardless of the parents' legal status, a child born on U.S. soil becomes a U.S. citizen at the moment of birth under the rule of *jus soli* (law of the soil), which dates back to sixteenth-century English common law (Schuck and Smith 1985). This rule, of which the U.S. version is probably the most liberal in the world, may increase the incentive of undocumented aliens to enter illegally. (A May 2004 U.S. Census Bureau report estimated that the 14 million U.S. residents living in households with an undocumented head or spouse included 3.1 million U.S.-born children.)

U.S. naturalization requirements, although roughly comparable to those of Canada, are easier to satisfy than those of Europe and much easier than those of Japan.

Although this has been true since 1790, important and shameful exceptions to this openness have existed for long periods of time (Zolberg 2006; Smith 1997): ideological restrictions during much of the period; exclusion of U.S. blacks until 1870; exclusion of the Chinese and races indigenous to the Western Hemisphere until the 1940s; exclusion of all other nonwhites (other than those of African descent) until 1952; and provisions that automatically denationalized U.S. women who married any alien (from 1907 to 1922) or an alien ineligible (usually for racial reasons) for naturalization (until 1931).

Today, the English language and literacy tests are notoriously easy to pass—the statute mandates a "simple" literacy test and exempts many disabled individuals and older immigrants who are illiterate in English from having to take it (McCaffrey 2005). The U.S. history and government test requires only rote responses. Indeed, making these requirements a bit more rigorous might actually strengthen the political support for immigration, just as the 1996 welfare reform statute limiting immigrants' access to welfare benefits may have had the unanticipated effect of undermining a traditional argument for restricting immigration—welfare utilization by immigrants.

Although the immigration statute disqualifies from naturalization those individuals deemed subversive or "not attached to the principles of the Constitution," this bar has been considerably narrowed by statute and judicial interpretation since the 1960s. The risk of denationalization due to the commission of "expatriating acts" has been practically eliminated. Although the "good moral character" requirement is now interpreted quite generously with respect to noncriminals, it does flatly bar "aggravated felons," a category that Congress introduced into the law in the 1980s and has steadily expanded. Finally, in *Kungys v. United States,* 485 U.S., 759 (1988), the Supreme Court narrowly interpreted the legal authority for rescinding the citizenship of those who procured their naturalization through fraud or misrepresentation.

This inclusive naturalization regime has produced impressive numerical results. More than 1 million people naturalized in 1996, the highest number ever, and naturalizations have remained quite high since then, despite a post-9/11 slowdown in processing that produced large backlogs in some regions. As noted earlier, 660,000 immigrants naturalized in 2007. Especially striking is the source-country diversity of those naturalizing. About 36 percent were from Asia, 36 percent from North America (including Canada and Mexico), and only 13 percent from all of Europe (U.S. Department of Homeland Security 2008).

Dual nationality—the consequence of international marriages, legal changes in other countries, and a softening of traditional opposition by the United States and other governments—is a growing component of U.S. citizenship law (Spiro 2008). Nearly 90 percent of legal immigrants to the United States today come from states that allow dual citizenship. Indeed, our largest source country, Mexico, now actually *promotes* it for the U.S.-born children of its nationals, and some other Latin American states either now do so or soon will.

## Immigrant Assimilation

The term *assimilation* is controversial. Alan Wolfe, sociologist, notes that assimilation "is a form of symbolic violence. Like the actual violence of war, assimilation is disruptive and heartless, the stuff of tragedy" (2004, 11), a theme central to the creative writing on this topic. Nathan Glazer, for example, reports that most of his Harvard students (an elite group, to be sure) react negatively to the term, that "[n]either liberals nor neoliberals, conservatives nor neoconservatives, have much good to say about assimilation, and only a branch of paleo-conservatism can now be mustered in its defense" (1993, 123). For these reasons, some prefer the term *integration,* thinking that it carries less of the ideological baggage of Anglo-conformity (Gordon 1964) or that it imposes obligations on both the immigrant and the receiving society. In truth, *integration* is no more than a euphemism for the kind of deep disruption that Wolfe describes. Because Anglo-conformity is largely discredited and assimilation, no less than integration, denotes a two-way process of transformation, we might as well use the traditional term.[2]

How well the assimilation process is working has been much debated in recent years. In its 1997 report to Congress, the U.S. Commission on Immigration Reform issued a call for the "Americanization" of new immigrants, invoking this affirmation by the commission chair, the late Barbara Jordan: "That word earned a bad reputation when it was stolen by racists and xenophobes in the 1920s. But it is our word, and we are taking it back" (U.S. Commission on Immigration Reform 1997, 26). The commission went on to define *Americanization* as "the process of integration by which immigrants become part of our communities and by which our communities and the nation learn from and adapt to their presence. Americanization means the civic incorporation of immigrants through the cultivation of a shared commitment to the American values of liberty, democracy, and equal opportunity" (U.S. Commission on Immigration Reform 1997, 26–27). Seeking to go beyond these lofty but vague sentiments, the commission urged that all levels of government commit resources to orienting newcomers to their communities, educating them in English language skills and core civic values, and enhancing the attractiveness of naturalization.

Other commentators, however, lament that we have abandoned this benign notion of cultural exchange. This view is nicely, if oversimply, captured in the title of John Miller's 1998 book, *The Unmaking of Americans: How Multiculturalism Has Undermined the Assimilation Ethic* (see also Salins 1997; Chavez 1991). Such critics think that affirmative action, bilingual education, and other policies that seek to preserve immigrants' customary loyalties and social systems have retarded assimilation and emptied it of civic meaning. Such measures, they say, encourage immigrants to imagine that they can avoid the sacrifices necessary to become thoroughly Americanized and can instead cling to their values, languages, and practices of origin even when they are inconsistent with those prevalent in the larger U.S. society.

Both sides agree that assimilation would be a good thing. The traditionalists believe that assimilation provides newcomers with the civic values, social skills, and cultural capital that they must have in order to succeed in the United States and thus reinforces the national fabric of ideals and institutions, generates democratic participation and consent of newcomers, and enhances their future prospects. Most multiculturalists (for want of a better term) agree that these ends are desirable but think that immigrants can best achieve them by maintaining their cultures of origin while gradually navigating their way into the U.S. mainstream. Still other multiculturalists, surely only a small minority, reject much of U.S. culture and wish to construct and preserve ethnic enclaves in which their members can enjoy parochial comforts with a minimum of normative conflict and cultural stress.

Every modern state has its own way of obsessing about its own political identity and destiny. And many of these states have much to worry about (Schuck 2000). Still, among the relatively few with a secure and unchallenged national unity, the U.S. preoccupation is among the most insistent. Whereas the unity of most other states is based on sturdy, indeed primordial, commonalities such as language, religion, and ethnicity, the unity of the United States is founded on a potentially more fragile allegiance to universal civic ideals accessible, in principle, to all of humanity. These ideals—individualism, democracy, the rule of law, pragmatism, the spirit of compromise, respect for differences, equality of opportunity, social mobility, love of freedom, capitalism, and openness to newcomers—constitute a civic nationalism or ideology suitable to what Ben Wattenberg calls "the first universal nation."

In practice, of course, these cultural ideals are imperfectly realized. Even as stated, they are highly abstract and can mean many things to different people. Indeed, their openness to interpretation is part of their enduring strength. But they can also be rhetorically hijacked and politically compromised, leaving their defenders without a fixed authoritative standard to which they can appeal. This robust national culture may be less unique and autonomous than it was in the past, perhaps weakening its ability to serve as the core of a U.S. political identity that boasts exceptionalism (or at least distinctiveness) (Schuck and Wilson 2008). Today, many other states cherish these same values, although balancing them in different, sometimes more egalitarian ways (Alesina and Gleaser 2004) and implementing them through different institutions.

This national culture faces greater challenges to its unity today than at any time since the Civil War. Many immigrants live in enclaves that are so large and self-sustaining that it attenuates their economic, linguistic, and cultural integration with the larger community, at least in the short run. Reduced transportation and communication costs enable many immigrant families to maintain strong transnational ties. With the greater acceptance of dual citizenship, naturalized immigrants can retain (or regain) their old nationalities. And now, as in the past, immigrants without democratic traditions in their home countries—Haiti and Pakistan, for example—may find U.S. political values hard to comprehend and practice.

The absence of conventional war, a military draft, external threats, a strong communitarian ethos, robust public rituals, or other solidarity-enhancing experiences may make being American seem less central to citizens' self-definition than in the past. Although 9/11 temporarily heightened this political solidarity, it may be atrophying under the polarizing pressures of subsequent events and partisanship. Citizenship demands little of Americans, and remarkably, there have been few calls after 9/11 to make naturalization requirements more demanding. In short, the mere fact of citizenship may contribute less to forging a U.S. identity. Finally, globalization is exerting new pressures on our national culture. Our borders are more porous than ever and remittances to developing countries dwarf U.S. foreign aid. For some analysts, these developments prefigure an inevitable retreat of national sovereignty and the loss of cultural distinctiveness. But even those who find such predictions overblown must acknowledge a diminution in both the autonomy of national cultures and in the freedom of action of states in pursuing them.

By almost any definition, however, immigrants are rapidly integrating into U.S. life, although at group-specific rates (Vigdor 2008). Immigrants have a far higher rate of employment than in European economies. Market pressures magnify immigrants' intense desire to learn English. Most studies (summarized in Schuck 2003, 110) find that the immigrant generation acquires fluency at roughly the same rate as earlier waves did, that the "one-and-a-half generation" (who arrived as children) and second generation (the U.S.-born children of immigrants) learn it at school and strongly prefer it to their parents' native language, that 98 percent of the second generation speak it proficiently by the end of high school, and that the third generation is largely monolingual in English and likes it that way. This optimistic picture is marred by the estimated 3 million or more U.S.-born students with limited English proficiency (LEP) despite—perhaps because of—bilingual education programs. Indeed, 10 percent of LEP students are third-generation Americans, and the 1990 census found that almost 8 million households, 8.3 percent of the U.S. total, were "linguistically isolated," meaning that no person fourteen-years-old or older spoke English well.

The rates of interethnic marriage are high, particularly among Asian women and Hispanics, and the residential integration of those groups into white-majority urban and suburban communities is growing rapidly (Schuck 2003, 208). Other important agents of integration are the allure and ethnic diversity of a powerful mass media and popular culture (including minority-dominated sports teams) and the receptiveness of U.S. religious communities to newcomers, who are reinvigorating and often transforming them (Schuck 2003, 337–46).

Some sociologists of immigration (Portes and Rumbaut 2001) worry about downward or segmented assimilation, when young immigrants and young children of immigrants adopt dysfunctional norms and conduct all too common in the United States that may impede their future mobility and integration. Desiring healthy assimilation by their children, immigrants try to use the cultures of origin to inoculate them against these dangerous aspects of U.S. life, providing a cultural shelter and breathing space in which their youngsters can flourish. Some groups are more successful at this daunting task than others (Portes and Zhou 1993). Among at least some immigrant groups, these authors argue, the best academic achievers assimilate more *slowly* to U.S. culture, whereas the delinquent youngsters are *quicker* to abandon their ethnic heritage.

A particularly worrisome challenge to the assimilation project is the amount of criminal activity engaged in by immigrants, both documented and undocumented. GAO (2005a, 2005b) reports suggest the magnitude of the problem. The number of aliens incarcerated in federal facilities increased from approximately 42,000 in 2001 to approximately 49,000 in 2004. The percentage of all federal prisoners who are aliens is approximately 27 percent, accounting for approximately $1.2 billion in federal costs in 2004. These statistics do not include the large number of aliens in state prisons and local jails. In a study of more than 55,000 illegal aliens in federal prisons, GAO found that the average alien had approximately eight arrests (for thirteen offenses); 26 percent had eleven or more arrests. Approximately 45 percent of the offenses committed by this population were for drug or immigration crimes, but 12 percent were for violent crimes such as murder, robbery, assault, and sex-related crimes, and 15 percent were for property-related crimes.

These statistics reflect the high levels of immigration in recent years; they do *not* mean that immigrants are more prone to crime. In fact, precisely the opposite is true (Rumbaut et al. 2006). Incarceration rates for foreign-born men ages eighteen to thirty-nine are much lower than for native-born men (in 2000, 0.7 percent vs. 3.5 percent); moreover, this difference has increased substantially since 1990. Indeed, if we exclude island-born Puerto Ricans, who have far higher crime rates but are citizens, the foreign-born rate is even lower and the difference correspondingly greater. The incarceration rates of the U.S.-born children of immigrants, however, are higher than those of their parents or of non-Hispanic white citizens, and their incarceration rates generally increase with the length of time in the country.

Some immigration scholars, such as John Mollenkopf and Raphael Sonenshein (chap. 6), Reule Rogers (chap. 7), and Sandro Cattacin (chap. 16 in this volume), emphasize the extent to which immigrant assimilation depends partly on the political structures and styles that prevail in particular communities. Peter Skerry's (1993) rich comparison of Mexican-American incorporation in San Antonio and Los Angeles argues that the ways in which politicians tried to shape immigrants' political identities had an impact on their assimilation. The different leadership styles, party systems, interest-group coalitions, community organizations, media tactics, and mobilization strategies in those cities influenced the political techniques and self-understandings of politicians, voters, and civil society institutions. Overall, one recent analysis of Mexican economic assimilation concludes that "The progress of second-generation Mexican men and women exemplifies 'assimilation' but only if one defines it in absolute terms. Relative to…whites, there remains a very substantial gap" (Waldinger and Reichl 2006). Other groups exhibit equally intricate and multifactored patterns (Jones-Correa 1998; Waters 1999).

## Multiculturalism

Multiculturalism, a perennial *casus belli* in the culture wars, also affects the nature and process of immigrant assimilation in an ethnically diverse society. Its salience has increased as immigrants' transplanted cultures have grown more diverse and as group demands for recognition and protection have become legally and politically more strident. K. Anthony Appiah, referring to the educational context, explains why:

> [Multiculturalism] is now used…to cover an extraordinary range of educational practices from the anodyne insistence that American students should be taught something of the history of all the world's continents to the kooky suggestion that they should learn that the Africans who built the pyramids did so by telekinesis. But because the word has become a term of ritual abuse for some conservatives and a banner for many on the left, there is not much hope of agreement on its core meaning. (1997, 30)

Today, multiculturalism is perhaps best understood as a set of ideas whose common theme is respect and toleration for cultural differences—globally, nationally, locally, and individually. Its common claim is that a nation should accommodate (to some extent) most (if not all) of the distinctive values and practices of culturally diverse groups in its midst. Multicultural policies are of many kinds; they may facilitate the integration of group members into the national culture, recognize their cultural identity as a vital end in itself, or even help groups wall off their cultures from the mainstream.

Such policies can instantiate a wide range of values—liberal, communitarian, or even conservative—depending on how they are defined, and they may be pursued through a wide range of methods. Will Kymlicka's (2001, 163) illustrative list includes affirmative action, reserved seats in public institutions, revised public school curricula, religious accommodation in secular settings, revised dress codes, programs to encourage toleration, antiharassment codes, diversity training for officials, efforts to reduce ethnic stereotyping, public funding of ethnic festivals and programs, multilingual social services, and bilingual education.

The seminal analysis of contemporary multiculturalism in the United States is historian David Hollinger's *Postethnic America* (2005), an avowedly Americocentric essay on cultural diversity. His vision of U.S. cultural identity resembles the robust "new nationalism" advanced in Michael Lind's book, *The New American Nation* (1995). Both reject a fixed, state-regulated, state-fostered structure of ethno-racial identity in favor of a more fluid, individualistic, voluntary, and privatistic set of affiliations. They are committed to what Alan Wolfe describes as a "soft multiculturalism [that] is the friend of civic nationalism, not its enemy" (2001, 33). My own view takes this position farther by rejecting the claim made by many multiculturalists that the government should facilitate immigrants' cultural diversity. It is perfectly natural for immigrants to want to maintain their cultures and that may be fully compatible with the level of assimilation that Americans have a right to expect of them. Such cultural maintenance, however, is not an appropriate public goal; it should be a private matter for immigrant families to pursue (if they wish) at home or in their ethnic communities, not in the public schools (Schuck 2003, 121–23).

Immigrant cultures, indeed *any* cultures, are difficult for outsiders to comprehend. The problem is not that the state must be rigorously neutral in cultural matters. In reality, that is neither possible nor desirable. The state is necessarily in the business of maintaining the dominant culture—here, an English-speaking one—and it properly insists that newcomers wishing to become citizens must demonstrate some English language ability, a basic knowledge of U.S. political institutions, and a commitment to certain civic principles. These tools are necessary, although not sufficient, for successful assimilation. Today's immigrants, desperately eager to learn English, understand no less than their (now-)admired predecessors. Government has a vital interest, often neglected in practice (especially with adult immigrants), in helping them to do so.

The United States, which consigns cultural maintenance to civil society, permits children to wear or display private religious symbols in public schools, whereas France, which also emphatically protects the free exercise of religion, rigidly proscribes this conduct in the name of secularism and the protection of Muslim girls from harassment by Islamists in their communities (Weil 2004; Foner and Alba 2008). One possible explanation is that the United States is less insecure than France about the durability of its national identity when faced with such challenges. This explanation might seem paradoxical in light of the far greater, more strident secularism (*laïcité*) of

French society, but this trait may magnify the risk posed to French self-understanding by prominent religious displays in the very schools designed to cultivate its secular ideology. In contrast, Americans, who are more comfortable with diversity and more solicitous of individual rights of self-expression, see little social harm in it unless and until it engenders significant conflict.

The U.S. relative openness to immigrants, even during the nineteenth century when racism and nativism were rampant, has been remarkable. If past is prologue, immigrants to the United States will shed some aspects of their ethnic identities as they live here. This molting process will be particularly rapid for the second and certainly the third generations. The melting pot metaphor, then, is not altogether inapt, even today when many immigration advocates and scholars deride it or prefer other images such as a mosaic or a salad bowl. The kind of identity-stifling assimilation demanded by some in the Americanization movement that thrived amid the nationalist passions stoked by World War I, was often paternalistic, bigoted, and coercive. Despite these abuses (or perhaps because of them), it was quite effective at a time when the stakes of rapid assimilation were high. The nuanced, well-designed, sensitively implemented, and diversity-friendly version of Americanization recommended by the U.S. Commission on Immigration Reform would be welcome today.

# CHAPTER TWELVE

# Building through Exclusion

## Anti-Immigrant Politics in the United States

*Luis Ricardo Fraga*

In January 2004, President George W. Bush called for comprehensive immigration reform in launching his reelection campaign. Immigration became a high profile issue in U.S. national politics in late 2005, received unprecedented attention in spring 2006, and remained significant through parts of the 2008 presidential election. Usually, this pattern happens during major economic downturns but this focus on immigration occurred well before the economic meltdown of September 2008. Nor was there a major immigration scandal, albeit there were some arguments that several of the 9/11 perpetrators had overstayed their visas.

No one predicted, however, that the House of Representatives would adopt Representative James Sensenbrenner's (R-Wisconsin) H.R. 4437 in December 2005, a bill that deemed unauthorized immigrants felons subject to immediate deportation. Equally surprisingly, no one predicted the mass demonstrations against the bill in March and May 2006, during which upward of 3 million people took to the streets in major cities throughout the country. Finally, in the wake of the shift of control of Congress from the Republicans to the Democrats in November 2006, few predicted that immigration reform would reemerge in 2007 through a small bipartisan group in the House and the Senate seeking to craft a compromise that included border enforcement, new legal status for the undocumented, and a shift in selection criteria from family connections to skills.

Immigration politics has always made strange bedfellows in the United States (Zolberg 2006). Few issues so consistently defy the logic of a liberal-conservative continuum or even simple partisan differences (Wong 2006). Recent debates have put major employers on the same side as immigrants' rights advocates, put low-wage workers together with cultural conservatives, and put a majority of congressional Democrats with a minority of Republicans. These debates have featured both a labor-market component (the desire of employers for low-wage or high-skilled immigrant workers) and an ethnic identity component (the claim of immigrants' rights organizations and native-born minority groups that the civil rights agenda has not yet been fulfilled).

Polls of U.S. adults consistently reveal that 51–65 percent support a path to citizenship for unauthorized workers currently living in the United States, if they meet a criminal background check, pay a fine and back taxes, and learn English (National Immigration Forum 2007; PollingReport.com 2008). Yet strong and vocal subsets of the electorate opposed to reform often seem to have an unusually significant impact in structuring the public discourse regarding immigration policy.

This chapter explores how the recent anti-immigrant impulse in U.S. politics reflects a propensity to strengthen national identity and gain partisan advantage by excluding some from the body politic. I refer to this pattern as the *identity-community trade-off*. It also outlines the main threads of the current immigration debates with special reference to the undocumented, illuminating the ways in which advocates on both sides talk past one another. This nonengagement explains why members of Congress and the White House provided the key to identifying what common ground might make immigration reform possible; but it also explains why these public officials have not yet been able to build legislative coalitions to enact comprehensive immigration reform. I outline the major components of immigration legislation considered in 2005–2007 to further examine this failure.

The chapter concludes by considering the inevitable risks that arise when the nation writes off part of the population in positioning itself on the identity-community trade-off. As the United States pursues its interests in an increasingly globalized world, choices about who belongs to the nation and who does not will have dramatic consequences for U.S. democracy and the moral position of the United States in the world.

## Citizenship, National Identity, and the Evolution of Community

Rogers Smith (1997) argues that the U.S. polity gradually, at times painfully, assigned full citizenship rights to new segments of the population because it was simultaneously denying these rights to other groups. Expansions of citizenship have never included all who might want it. The notion that inclusion involves exclusion helps us begin to understand anti-immigrant politics in the United States today.

Smith suggests that three fundamental civic myths have animated the expansion of who is fully part of the United States. The first, individual liberalism,[1] holds that not only do individuals have certain inalienable rights and liberties but that government can only legitimately limit these rights under very unusual circumstances. The second, civic republicanism,[2] holds that U.S. citizens share a linked fate[3] that may require individuals to sacrifice for the common good at critical moments of nation-building.

The final civic ideology is ascriptive inegalitarianism,[4] which argues that the most durable understanding of who is American depends on a clear sense of who is not. For example, the removal of property ownership as a condition for suffrage did not lead to the inclusion of women or even free blacks. Enfranchisement for former slaves during Reconstruction did not include black women. The extension of the vote to women in 1920 occurred precisely when the former states of the Old Confederacy were actively denying the franchise to African Americans.

Political leaders today arguably gauge the balance of these civic myths in order to gain office and change the group bases of national identity (Smith 1997, 31–33). Stated differently, we can view the current immigration debate as an exercise in using the explicit exclusion of some to build winning coalitions of voters who believe that individual rights and linked fate belong only to current citizens. What makes the identity-community trade-off an effective mechanism through which to structure immigration politics is the evolution of the "illegal alien" in U.S. law in the first quarter of the twentieth century (Ngai 2004).

## Dimensions of Contemporary Anti-Immigrant Politics

A range of interests and concerns motivate arguments for stricter immigration policy. Some are normative, others are driven by perceived tangible costs, and, others, rarely discussed, may involve racial prejudice. Here, we review seven such arguments: (1) the law-breaking nature of unauthorized status, (2) terrorism and security threats, (3) criminality among the unauthorized, (4) the cost of social services, (5) labor market competition with the native-born, (6) dilution of American culture, and (7) racial prejudice. Although each is distinctive, all these arguments are driven by a heightened sense of the need to maintain traditional notions of national identity and, at this point in time, to largely exclude noncitizens from full participation in U.S. society.

The most widely accepted argument is that many immigrants have violated or ignored U.S. laws in gaining entry. Although this category has been part of national law at least since the Alien and Sedition Acts of 1798–1801, few unauthorized noncitizens were deported during the nineteenth century. In 1891, however, legislation created a one-year limitation to allow a person to be deported because of becoming a public charge; this was extended to five years in 1917 (Ngai 2004, 58–61). The Immigration Act of 1924 allowed deportation at any time; also Congress established the Border Patrol at this time (Ngai 2004, 60). A 1927 Immigration Report on the smuggling of unauthorized people into the United States observed "[w]hatever else may be said of [the bootlegged alien]: whether he be diseased or not, whether he holds views inimical to our institutions, he at best is a law violator from the outset" (quoted in Ngai 2004, 62). The Federation for American Immigration Reform states that "illegal immigration is a crime. ... Each year the Border Patrol makes more than a million apprehensions of aliens who flagrantly violate our nation's laws by unlawfully crossing U.S. borders. Such entry is a misdemeanor, but, if repeated, becomes punishable as a felony" (Federation for American Immigration Reform [FAIR] 2005). The American Patrol (2007) makes similar arguments, and respondents to polls and newspaper op-eds often contain similar views (Petaluma Argus-Courier 2006; de Silva 2007).

The unprotected U.S. borders have also become a prominent argument for stricter immigration policy since 9/11. One critic notes,

> The terrorists are foreigners, most or all of whom should not have been allowed to live in our country. As [former] FBI [(Federal Bureau of Investigation)] Director Robert Mueller admitted, at least some of the hijackers were "out of status," i.e., they had

no proper immigration documents. It should be repeated over and over again: The terrorism threat is from illegal aliens who are allowed to live in our midst—and this is a failure of our immigration laws and our immigration officials. (*Phyllis Schlafly Report* 2001)

Similar arguments circulate in a variety of venues (Perrazzo 2002; Camarota 2002). An organization known as We Need a Fence refers to those who threaten the United States as "other than Mexicans," (OTMs) and indicate that "[w]ithin the last year, over 450 OTMs have been apprehended illegally entering the U.S. from... Afghanistan, Angola, Jordan, Qatar, Pakistan, and Yemen" (2007).

Immigration opponents also allege that immigrants perpetrate crime. The journal of the Manhattan Institute recently carried an article entitle "The Illegal-Alien Crime Wave: Why Can't Our Immigration Authorities Deport the Hordes of Illegal Felons in Our Cities?" (MacDonald 2004). Jerry Seper of the *Washington Times* writes, "About 80,000 illegal criminal aliens, including convicted murderers, rapists, drug dealers and child molesters who served prison time and were released, are loose on the streets of America, hiding from federal immigration authorities" (2004). An organization named Immigration's Human Cost (2007) lists the stories of twenty alleged victims of crimes perpetrated by unauthorized immigrants on its website.

Undocumented immigrants are also criticized for the costs of the social services they use. Few would argue that we should not provide the children of the unauthorized with educational services or emergency health services; federal law, in fact, mandates the provision of such services. Nonetheless, state and local officials rightly argue that they have to pick up the costs of services to people who might not be present if the federal government better enforced its immigration laws.

Madeleine Cosman (2005, 6) argues that serving unauthorized immigrants has bankrupted at least eighty-four hospitals in California. Congressman Gary Miller's (R-California) website includes a section entitled "How Much Do Illegal Aliens Cost U.S. Taxpayers?" (Miller 2005). The website for Immigration Counters (2007) provides a running tally of the number of real-time "illegal immigrants in country" and of the estimated cost of "social services for illegal immigrants since 1996," "illegals in K-12 since 1996," and "incarcerations since 2001."

That immigrants, especially unauthorized immigrants, lower wages and take jobs away from U.S. workers is one of the most contentious claims by advocates for more restrictive policies. Among the early respected economists to make this claim was George J. Borjas in *Heaven's Door: Immigration Policy and the American Economy* (1999). The titles of two recent articles reflect its persistence: "Bush Administration Pushes for Illegal Alien Amnesty Again! Devastating Effects for American Workers, Taxpayers and Citizens" (Carrying Capacity Network 2005) and "Dropping Out: Immigrant Entry and Native Exit from the Labor Market, 2000–2005" (Camarota 2006).

Competition between lesser-skilled African American workers and undocumented workers is often mentioned. Some have begun to argue that competition also exists at higher skill and education levels with other types of immigrant workers. Lorinda Bullock writes in the *Baltimore Times,* "As the Black community debates whether Hispanic immigrant workers create competition for jobs with low-income African-Americans, the president of the Coalition of Black Trade Unionists says too little attention is being paid to educated immigrants taking high-tech jobs away from middle- and upper-class African-Americans" (2006).

The capacity of immigrants to culturally integrate into U.S. society appears in current anti-immigration politics. Tom Tancredo (R-Colorado) recently stated in response to the question "What is your greatest concern as to the impact of illegal immigration?":

> I believe that we are becoming balkanized. I believe this is not a fault of immigration, it is exacerbated by it. The radical multiculturalism we have witnessed over the past forty years in America, I call it a cult of multiculturalism. It has, I think, been successful in destroying the ties that hold us together as Americans.... We're losing sight of who we are. (quoted in McMahon 2006)

This same type of view makes up a substantial part of Samuel Huntington's book *Who Are We?: The Challenges to America's National Identity* (2004). In a chapter entitled "Mexican Immigration and Hispanization," he argues that current Mexican immigration is different from immigration from other countries, and especially from immigration during earlier periods of U.S. history (Huntington 2004, 222–30). Huntington cites high Spanish language use, low levels of formal education, lower-status occupations and resulting incomes, low rates of naturalization and out-group intermarriage, and low "identification with American values" as evidence of a low desire and resulting slow assimilation by Mexican immigrants into U.S. society (230–43). Thus, Huntington critiques the possibility that Hispanics might develop their own version of the American Dream (256).

A final dimension of arguments in favor of a more restrictionist policy involves race (Center for American Progress 2007). An intelligence report of the Southern Poverty Law Center (2001a, 2001b) identifies a series of comments made by a range of anti-immigration organizations from which we can see that race-related concerns are paramount.

- The Council of Conservative Citizens states, "[T]he meaning of this massive increase in non-white and non-Western populations groups within U.S. borders is that the United States is not only ceasing to be a majority white nation but also is ceasing to be a nation that is culturally part of Western Civilization."
- The National Alliance states, "America becomes darker—racially darker—every year, and that is the direct result of our government's immigration policy.... We White people, we descendants of the European immigrants who built America, will be a minority in our own country. ... [M]alicious aliens [European Jews] came into our land and...spread spiritual poison among our people, so that our spirits became corrupted and our minds became confused."
- The National Association for the Advancement of White People writes, "Unless stopped now, massive illegal immigration from the Third World will surely make America more like the Third World than the nation of our forefathers....Forced integration and unrestrained immigration destroy schools, neighborhoods, cities and ultimately nations."

- The National Organization for European American Rights comments, "the very underpinnings of America are being gnawed away by hordes of aliens who are transforming America into a land where we, the descendants of the men and women who founded America, will walk as strangers.... Unless we act now... we will be helpless to halt the accelerating dispossession of our folk."
- An organization known as Voices of Citizens Together states, "The Mexican culture is based on deceit. Chicanos and Mexicanos lie as a means of survival. Fabricating false ids is just another extension of that culture... [, which] condones everything from the most lowly misdemeanor to murder in the highest levels of government."
- The White Aryan Resistance states, "[even] beyond immigration, legal or illegal, the very numbers of non-Whites already here, and their high birth rate, are enough to plunge North America into a banana republic status within two decades or less.... [After the United States is split up into racial mini-states, if] an area like Florida wanted to accept the dregs of the Caribbean, let them, with the understanding that the second this mud flood oozed into the sovereign state of Georgia, it would be 'lock and load' time."

Each of these seven arguments characterizes unauthorized immigrants as outsiders to the U.S. nation-state and, in fact, threats to U.S. identity, workers, and culture. The proponents of these arguments have a very clear vision of where they would like to see the balance in the identity-community trade-off.

## The Counterimage: Pro-Immigrant Advocacy

Ironically, the dynamic of building national identity through group exclusion also helps explain arguments in favor of greater rights for immigrants, often including the unauthorized. These advocates say that even immigrants without legal papers contribute to U.S. society and so should be part of the U.S. community. Their presence stems from the underlying needs of the U.S. economy, promotes the living standards of the vast majority of Americans, and reflects the inevitability of labor migration in a global world. As workers, illegal immigrants should have a right to fair wages, fair working conditions, social services, and a bureaucratic route to becoming legal permanent residents, and, over time, even naturalized citizens. If they challenge aspects of U.S. cultural practices, the United States can benefit, according to this view, by accommodating difference and building a more inclusive community.

Pro-immigration arguments have six dimensions: (1) the tradition that the United States is an immigrant nation, (2) immigrants' desire to contribute to and integrate into U.S. society, (3) human rights, (4) civil rights, (5) Latinos' importance to current and future party politics, and (6) transnational labor migration and economic growth as driven by global capitalism. The following examples allow us to appreciate the language used to characterize immigrants and immigration in these arguments and to see the identity-community trade-off reflected in these views.

The argument that the United States is a land of immigrants is so commonly accepted as part of U.S. heritage (however inappropriate this characterization may be in specific historical eras) that we can argue that it is part of the American creed (Schle-singer 1991; Zolberg 2006). Interestingly, among the most powerful statements of this aspect of the U.S. polity was made by President George W. Bush when he challenged the nation to reform current immigration law. He stated,

> As a nation that values immigration, and depends on immigration, we should have immigration laws that work and make us proud. Yet today we do not. Instead, we see many employers turning to the illegal labor market. We see millions of hard-working men and women condemned to fear and insecurity in a massive, undocumented econ-omy. Illegal entry across our borders makes more difficult the urgent task of securing the homeland. The system is not working. Our nation needs an immigration system that serves the American economy, and reflects the American Dream. (2004)

The Reverend Jesse L. Jackson Sr. recently characterized the argument this way: "Now is the time to put an end to the vicious cycle of pain and blame, to fulfill the prom-ise of the Statue of Liberty and the fundamental notion that all people have 'an in-alienable right' to life, liberty and the pursuit of happiness" (2006). In critique of Huntington (2004), the Mexican American Legal Defense and Educational Fund (MALDEF) and the League of United Latin American Citizens (LULAC) write "The United States is a nation of immigrants from around the world. In the U.S., individual accomplishment is valued" (Mexican American Legal Defense and Educational Fund [MALDEF] 2004).

A related line of argument is that immigrants, even the unauthorized, value mak-ing contributions to U.S. society and even desire to be meaningfully integrated within U.S. society. Again, President Bush's comments clearly capture this position:

> As a Texan, I have known many immigrant families, mainly from Mexico, and I have seen what they add to our country. They bring to America the values of faith in God, love of family, hard work and self reliance—the values that made us a great nation to begin with. We've all seen those values in action, through the service and sacrifice of more than 35,000 foreign-born men and women currently on active duty in the United States military. (2004)

The Pew Center reports that "Hispanics in general, and Hispanic immigrants in par-ticular, are more inclined than blacks or whites to take an upbeat view about one of the most enduring tenets of the American dream—the idea that each generation will do better in life than the one that preceded it" (Pew Hispanic Center 2006).

As further evidence of the desire of immigrants to integrate into U.S. society, recent reports have noted the long waiting lists all across the country for adults who want to learn English. A survey conducted by the National Association of Latino Elected and Appointed Officials (NALEO) in 2006 "found that in twelve states, 60 percent of the free English programs had waiting lists, ranging from a few months in Colo-rado and Nevada to as long as two years in New Mexico and Massachusetts, where the statewide list has about 16,000 names" (Santos 2007, A1). Data from the recent Latino National Survey (LNS), the largest state-stratified survey of all Latinos in the United States, found that in 2005–2006 Latino adult respondents in each of the first, second, third, and fourth generations ranked the importance of learning English very strongly by overwhelming majorities of just over 90 percent (Fraga et al. 2006).

Yet a third argument made in support of immigrants is that even if current U.S. law does identify the unauthorized as illegal, it is important to understand that these individuals still have basic human rights. President Bush also made this argument:

> Their [immigrants'] search for a better life is one of the most basic desires of human beings. Many undocumented workers have walked mile after mile, through the heat of the day and the cold of the night. Some have risked their lives in dangerous desert border crossings, or entrusted their lives to the brutal rings of heartless human smugglers. Workers who seek only to earn a living end up in the shadows of American life—fearful, often abused and exploited. When they are victimized by crime, they are afraid to call the police, or seek recourse in the legal system. They are cut off from their families far away, fearing if they leave our country to visit relatives back home, they might never be able to return to their jobs.... This situation I described is wrong. It is not the American way. (2004)

Among the most forceful advocates of the need for the United States to recognize the human rights of unauthorized immigrants have been U.S. churches and their religious leaders. The Roman Catholic Church was among the first to openly make this argument, starting with Cardinal Archbishop Roger Mahony of Los Angeles, who was later joined by public statements from Red de Pastores Latinos del Sur de California (Network of Latino Pastors and Leaders of Southern California), which represents 1,200 Latino protestant churches, and the National Christian Leadership Conference, a group representing Latino evangelicals (Mangaliman 2006).

A report by the Southern Poverty Law Center entitled "Close to Slavery: Guest-worker Programs in the United States" (2007) refers to the operation of the current H-2 visa guestworker program that allowed an estimated 121,000 workers to come to the United States legally in 2005. The reported harsh, and at times, inhumane treatment of these workers supports those who claim that the current system of U.S. immigration law violates fundamental human rights.

> Bound to a single employer and without access to legal resources, guestworkers are: routinely cheated out of wages; forced to mortgage their futures to obtain low-wage, temporary jobs; held virtually captive by employers or labor brokers who seize their documents; forced to live in squalid conditions; and denied medical benefits for on-the-job injuries. House Ways and Means Chairman Charles Rangel recently put it this way: "This guestworker program's the closest thing I've ever seen to slavery." (Southern Poverty Law Center 2007, 2)

Another argument made in support of immigrants, especially unauthorized immigrants, is that despite their legal status they still have civil rights in the United States that cannot be violated. The long-held practice of immigration agents' conducting unannounced raids on workplaces is often noted as a violation of workers' civil rights, not so much because of the raid itself as because of the subsequent treatment of the workers and its consequences for their families. A recent example of this concern was expressed in a joint press release by MALDEF, LULAC, the National Council of La Raza (NCLR), and NALEO. In response to immigration raids conducted in December 2006 at a number of Swift and Company plants, they stated:

> Various news reports and accounts from members of the community have claimed that racial profiling was used to single out workers for questioning; furthermore, we have reports that lawful permanent residents were detained. Furthermore, we understand that authorities prevented family members, clergy, and legal representatives from communicating with those detained, including in situations which could affect the health and safety of their family members. We are especially concerned for the children of those detained. (National Council of La Raza [NCLR] 2006b)

The American Civil Liberties Union (ACLU 2004) has recently renewed its commitment to protecting the civil rights of immigrants through its Immigrants' Rights Project (IRP). Some speculate that the larger issues associated with unauthorized immigrants provide a foundation for a new civil rights movement in the United States (Mangaliman and Rodriguez 2006; Democracy Now 2006).

Yet another argument made against more restrictive immigration policies directly refers to the costs that could be imposed on the political party that champions anti-immigration measures. This argument is driven by an understanding of the growth in the Latino population in the United States and the way that this growth can translate into a type of ethnic politics that will punish the party and its leaders who want to punish unauthorized Latino immigrants. The basis for this argument is an interpretation of what happened in California after 1994 when incumbent Governor Pete Wilson embraced Proposition 187, an initiative that restricted access to social services, health care, and education for undocumented immigrants. Although Governor Wilson effectively used Proposition 187 to enhance his reelection, it is generally understood that it pushed many Latinos in California to vote and identify as Democrats. The metaphor used to characterize this potential is the sleeping giant. The protests that occurred in March 2006 against what became known as the Sensenbrenner Bill are understood to be the catalysts to this new sense of political empowerment by Latinos (Oppenheimer 2006; Aizenman 2006; *The Nation* 2006; NCLR 2006b).

The final set of arguments made in support of immigrants is based on an understanding of the inevitability of labor migration in an increasingly globalized economy. The argument has at least two distinct tracks. The first focuses on understanding that among the primary causes of legal and unauthorized immigration to the United States is the increasing growth and privatization of developing economies around the world and, especially, in Latin America. The inability of workers to find sufficient employment in their home countries is largely undisputed. But a more nuanced understanding of this reality is that job growth does not keep pace with job demand in developing countries precisely because job loss occurs in traditional areas of employment as industries become more efficient and competitive in the global marketplace. In *Beyond Smoke and Mirrors: Mexican Immigration in an Era of Economic Integration,* Douglas Massey, a sociologist, and his colleagues state, "no nation has yet undergone economic development without a massive displacement of people from traditional livelihoods.... in the vast majority of cases a large fraction of these people have ended up migrating abroad" (2002, 144). Massey and colleagues provide considerable evidence of how this pattern has directly affected the waves and magnitude of immigration from Mexico to the United States since the 1970s.

It is also argued that undocumented consumers have become major markets for some businesses in the United States (*Business Week* 2005). In testimony before the Senate Judiciary Committee in 2006, Benjamin Johnson, director of the Immigration Policy Center of the American Immigration Law Foundation stated that "[t]he economic benefits of immigration extend beyond increasing the available labor supply. As immigrant workers spend and invest their earnings, new jobs are created, demand for labor increases, and wage levels rise—offsetting any decline in wages that might have resulted from the introduction of more workers in the labor force" (Johnson 2006, 3). Citing figures from the Selig Center for Economic Growth at the University of Georgia, he noted that Latino purchasing power was estimated at $736 billion in 2005 and was expected to increase to $1.1 trillion by 2010. Asian purchasing power was estimated at $397 billion in 2005 and expected to increase to $579 billion in 2010. Moreover, he quoted from the 2005 *Economic Report of the President* that "more than half of undocumented immigrants are believed to be working 'on the books,' so they contribute to the tax rolls but are ineligible for almost all Federal public assistance programs and most major Federal-state programs" (Johnson 2006, 3), contributing an estimated $463 billion to the Social Security Trust Fund as of 2002 that they themselves can never access due to their unauthorized status. The National Immigration Law Center has made similar arguments (Fremstad 2006).

Proponents and opponents of immigration restriction have very different visions of what the balance should be in the identity-community trade-off. Anti-immigration proponents focus on how immigration, especially unauthorized immigration, threatens traditional notions of U.S. identity and U.S. well-being more broadly. Their opponents argue that immigrants, including the unauthorized, are already part of the United States and need to be legalized. This raises the question as to whether meaningful reconciliation in the two views is possible. In the following discussion of bills that Congress considered in 2006 and 2007 we see how these distinct views were formalized in specific legislation.

## The Intended and Unintended Politics of Recent Immigration Reform

In response to President Bush's call for immigration reform in January 2004, the first major bill that came out of the House of Representatives was HR 4437, the Border Protection, Antiterrorism, and Illegal Immigration Control Act of 2005, sponsored by Representative James Sensenbrenner (R-Wisconsin), then chairman of the House Judiciary Committee, and thirty-five co-sponsors. It was introduced on December 6, 2005, and was approved December 16, 2005, by a vote of 239 to 182. Its emphasis was on enhancing border security. It authorized the building of a 700-mile, double-layer fence across the 2,000-mile border between Mexico and the United States. It also required the mandatory detention of all non-Mexican unauthorized immigrants arrested in the United States. It set mandatory sentences for those convicted of smuggling unauthorized immigrants and for reentering the United States without proper documents after a deportation. Moreover, the legislation made it a felony to be in the United States without proper documents or to assist, encourage, direct, or encourage someone to attempt to enter or remain in the United States without proper authorization. It made a conviction of drunk driving a deportable offense as well. H.R. 4437 also established very clear guidelines that employers had to follow to verify the immigration status of workers and specified fines for employers who violated them; prison sentences were mandated for employers who were found to be repeat violators. Absent from H.R. 4437 were any proposals to either legalize unauthorized immigrants currently in the United States or establish a temporary guestworker program.

S. 2611, the Comprehensive Immigration Reform Act of 2006, was broader in scope and in many ways more consistent with President Bush's call for immigration reform. Senators John McCain (R-Arizona) and Edward Kennedy (D-Massachusetts) had been pursing immigration reform for quite some time. This new bill, finally introduced by Arlen Specter (R-Pennsylvania), then chairman of the Senate Judiciary Committee, had six co-sponsors: five Republicans, Sam Brownback (R-Kansas), Lindsay Graham (R-South Carolina), Chuck Hagel (R-Nebraska), John McCain, and Mel Martinez (R-Florida), and one Democrat, Edward Kennedy. S. 2611 was introduced on April 7, 2006, and was passed by the Senate on May 25, 2006, by a vote of 62 to 36 with important amendments proposed by Senators Martinez and Hegel.

Like H.R. 4437, this bill addressed border enforcement. It authorized the building of 370 miles of triple-layer fencing on the U.S.-Mexican border and the hiring of an additional 1,000 Border Patrol agents that year and another 14,000 by 2011. (There were 11,300 agents working for the Border Patrol in 2006.) Similar to the House bill, it required employers and subcontractors to electronically verify any new employees. Interestingly, it declared English the official language of the United States.

What was most different from H.R. 4437 was that this bill allowed the legalization of unauthorized immigrants who had been in the United States for at least five years, had not been a public charge, had paid $3,250 in fines and fees, had paid any back taxes, and had committed to learn English. Such people would become eligible for status as legal permanent residents in six years. After five additional years and further review, they could apply to become citizens. Unauthorized immigrants who had been in the United States for more than two but less than five years had to return to a "point of entry" and file a formal application to return. If the application was approved, such individuals would receive legal authority to work in the United States and later become eligible to apply for permanent legal residency. Those who had been in the United States for less than two years were required to leave the country. This bill also created a special guestworker program for approximately 1.5 million immigrant farm workers, who could, in time, earn legal permanent residency. It approved 200,000 new temporary guestworker visas per year. Finally, it doubled the number of H1-B skilled worker visas from 65,000 to 115,000.

Normally, when the House and Senate have two distinct versions of a bill, the leadership of each body appoints members to a conference committee. This was expected in this circumstance as well. Representative Dennis Hastert (R-Illinois), however, former speaker of the House of Representatives, chose not to allow the House to participate in such a committee. Rather, he decided that it would be best for the House to conduct a set of national hearings throughout the country to sense the pulse of the nation on this legislation. Sensenbrenner, a critical negotiator, said that "The president is not where the American people are at. The Senate is not where the American people are at. Amnesty is wrong because it rewards someone for illegal behavior. And I reject the spin that the senators have been putting on their proposal. It is amnesty" (quoted in Swarns 2006b, A1). Not to be outdone, Senator Arlen Specter decided to hold his own set of hearings as well.

From July 5 to September 1, 2006, various subcommittees of the House held hearings in twenty-two different cities around the country. An additional eleven hearings were held in Washington, D.C. These hearings were alleged to be one-sided from the very beginning. Among their formal titles were "Border Vulnerabilities and International Terrorism," "Should We Embrace the Senate's Grant of Amnesty to Millions of Illegal Aliens and Repeat Mistakes of the Immigration Reform and Control Act of 1986?" "Expanding the Border Fence: Its Impact on the Flow of Drugs and Aliens," "Is the Federal Government Doing All It Can to Stem the Tide of Illegal Immigration?" and "Examining Views on English as the Official Language" (American Friends Service Committee 2006).

Senator Specter was much more modest in his hearings. That same summer of 2006, he held three, in Philadelphia, Miami, and Washington, D.C. Their titles were "Comprehensive Immigration Reform: Examining the Need for a Guest Worker Program," "Contributions of Immigrants to the US Armed Forces," and "Examining the Need for Comprehensive Immigration Reform, Part II" (American Friends Service Committee 2006).

Sensenbrenner and his supporters were soon criticized for trying to use immigration as a wedge issue in the upcoming 2006 election (Navarette 2006). Representative Jim Kolbe (R-Arizona) was quoted as saying, "They [the hearings] are deliberately planned. A lot of Republicans are listening to a very shrill part of their base who are very loud about this issue, and they believe that this translates into votes in the base" (quoted in Swarns 2006a, A1). A spokesman for the House Judiciary Committee said that over sixty representatives asked for hearings in their districts (Swarns 2006a).

Although a compromise between H.R. 4437 and S. 2611 was never reached, Congress passed the Secure Fence Act of 2006 in September by overwhelming majorities in both chambers. The bill has five major sections.

- The first part requires the Secretary of Homeland Security to increase the use of personnel and technology such as unmanned aerial vehicles, ground-based sensors, satellites, radar, and cameras to secure the borders.
- The second recommends establishing more checkpoints, all-weather access roads, and vehicle barriers.
- The third part of the bill is the most noteworthy. It requires the secretary of Homeland Security to construct 700 miles of doubly reinforced fencing as of May 2008 and to implement a comprehensive surveillance system by May 2007.
- The fourth section requires the secretary to conduct a study of the feasibility of reinforcing surveillance and security in the U.S. border with Canada.

• The final section requires the secretary to evaluate the personnel and training needs of U.S. Customs and Border Protection within thirty days of the enactment of the law and to submit a report related to this assessment within sixty days.

President Bush signed the bill into law on October 26, 2007.

The use of immigration as a wedge issue did not work for the Republicans in the 2006 elections. New Democratic majorities gained control of both the House and Senate. Not surprisingly, the Comprehensive Immigration Reform Act of 2007, S. 1348, also known as the Secure Borders, Economic Opportunity and Immigration Reform Act of 2007, was soon introduced in the Senate. After months of hearings and debates, however, the bill was not enacted.

On March 22, 2007, Representatives Jeff Flake (R-Arizona) and Luis Gutierrez (D-Illinois) introduced a comprehensive bill entitled the Security Through Regularized Immigration and a Vibrant Economy (STRIVE) Act of 2007 (H.R. 1645), which aimed to legalize undocumented immigrants and create a more expansive guestworker program with a path to citizenship. To qualify to become legal, immigrants would have to pay a $2,000 fine and back taxes, and to pass background and security checks. If after six years immigrants had learned English and U.S. civics, avoided criminal convictions, and the head of the household had left and reentered the United States legally, they could become legal permanent residents and then citizens (Gaouette and Watanabe 2007). It would also increase penalties for crimes committed by immigrants and institute a biometric system for employers to verify the legal status of workers (Swarns 2007).

Under H.R. 1645, undocumented immigrants would be able to pay in-state college tuition and, over time, these students would become eligible for citizenship. The guestworker provisions would allow up to 400,000 low-skilled workers into the country annually. Their temporary visas were for three years with an option to renew for another three and the ability to petition for permanent residence after five.

On March 28, 2007, the White House pushed three new guestworker programs. The first would grant legal status to certain undocumented immigrants with Z visas, which would be renewable and require a fee of $2,000 every three years. Those granted a Z visa would be allowed to apply for green cards after a period of time. The two other programs would use Y visas to admit foreign workers and eventually allow them to apply for green cards; one of these was aimed at low-skilled workers. The administration proposed to set the cap on Y visas based on the needs of the market. Each year, the proposals would double the number of green cards issued while also restructuring the criteria for awarding cards. The programs would also eliminate the visa lottery. The proposals also called for mandatory verification for new workers, without specifying a system for that verification. Each proposal also included substantial fines for employers and proposed giving the Department of Homeland Security authority to cross-check records of the Social Security Administration.

Another piece of legislation, S. 1083, the Securing Knowledge Innovation and Leadership Act (SKIL Bill), proposed to increase the legal immigration of scientific, technology, engineering, and mathematics (STEM) workers into the United States by increasing the quotas on the H-1B visa, eliminating green card caps for certain advanced-degree holders, and streamlining the processing of employment-based green cards. Senator John Cornyn (R-Texas), introduced the bill on April 10, 2007. Representative John Shadegg (R-Arizona), introduced a similar bill in the House, H.R. 1930, on April 17, 2007. Neither made it out of their judiciary committees.

What is clear in the politics of each piece of legislation is that neither the Democratic or Republican leaders in Congress nor the White House could put together sufficiently stable coalitions across chambers to support comprehensive immigration reform. There was neither the will nor the skill to attain a new equilibrium in the identity-community trade-off.

## New Risks to the Identity-Community Trade-off

The preceding discussion can be understood as further evidence of the identity-community trade-off that continues to characterize so much of anti-immigrant politics in the United States. Despite the failure of Congress to reach a meaningful compromise, history suggests that the U.S. polity will, ultimately, again expand to include more of its people than it did previously.

But there are a number of new risks to this traditional evolution of the identity-community trade-off. Interestingly, these are challenges to both those who argue that U.S. identity is currently under siege and those who are confident that the brightest future for the United States is an ever-expanding community that embraces immigrants, including most of the unauthorized. The risks come from both domestic and transnational developments. In fact, a new term, *intermestic*, is sometimes used to refer to the way that the simple distinctions between international and domestic interests may no longer apply.

No one anticipated that on March 25, 2006, at least 500,000 people, and by some estimates 1,000,000, would march in downtown Los Angeles. The Los Angeles protest was in large part organized by Jesse Díaz, a doctoral candidate in sociology at the University of California–Riverside, and Javier Rodríguez, a journalist. Among the reasons for the success of the original Los Angeles march was that a coalition of church, immigrant rights organizations, and labor unions, combined with a call by several well-known Spanish radio show hosts, to have a major demonstration (Watanabe and Gorman 2006). When these numbers were surpassed on May 1, 2006, by an estimated 1,200,000–2,000,000 marchers in over sixty cities in forty-four different states (Cano 2006), it became apparent that an unprecedented mechanism of civil protest characterized immigration politics in the United States. The general understanding had been that the unauthorized and their supporters were not likely to protest publicly out of concern for their safety and thus were not easily mobilized. These assumptions were proven wrong (Cano 2006).

A second risk facing any new equilibrium in the identity-community trade-off is related to the growing influence of Latinos as voters in the United States. Despite having many noncitizens within their adult population and their being registered to vote at rates noticeably lower than either whites or African Americans, Latinos can be pivotal contributors to the winning margins of victory when there are certain kinds of splits within other segments of the electorate. This has occurred in several states, especially in California, to the advantage of the Democratic Party, and in Florida, to the advantage of the Republican Party (Fraga and Ramírez 2003/04, 2004).

Some Republicans, such as Senator Chuck Hagel (R-Nebraska), worry that gaining repute as the anti-immigrant party will alienate Latino voters from the Republican Party, citing what has happened to the Republican Party in California since Proposition 187 (Fraga and Ramírez 2003). By one estimate, Latinos only gave 29 percent of their votes to Republican congressional candidates in 2006, down from the 31 percent President Bush received in 2000 and the estimated 40 percent he received in 2004. Lionel Sosa, a close advisor to President Bush and Karl Rove on the development of their Latino strategy, said in reaction to the risk the Republican Party took in appearing as anti-immigrant, "We as a party got the spanking we needed" (quoted in Lovato 2007).

A third risk in the politics of the identity-community trade-off is related to the way that state and local governments seem to have taken immigration into their own hands. In summer 2006, many states and cities passed their own laws and ordinances to restrict further unauthorized immigration. A report of the National Council of State Legislatures in summer 2006 indicates that through early July thirty states had enacted fifty-seven laws directly related to unauthorized immigrants. Among the laws enacted where those that (Jones 2006):

- Prohibited the awarding of state contracts to businesses that knowingly hired unauthorized workers (Colorado).
- Fined employers with state contracts who do not fire workers who are known not to have appropriate documents (Louisiana).
- Required public employers and government contractors and subcontractors to verify the work status of all new employees through a federal program (Georgia).
- Authorized the training of seventy state troopers to arrest unauthorized immigrants (Alabama).
- Prohibited unauthorized immigrants from receiving state services such as adult education, child care, in-state tuition, and punitive damages in civil lawsuits (Arizona).
- Prohibited the use of unauthorized immigrants on state projects (Pennsylvania).
- Prohibited businesses from deducting the costs of salaries and benefits for unauthorized workers from their taxable revenue (Texas).
- Sent troops to the Mexican border (Arizona, Arkansas, California, Connecticut, Delaware, Kentucky, Minnesota, Montana, New Jersey, New Mexico, New York, North Carolina, South Dakota, Tennessee, Texas, Virginia, Wisconsin).

A number of cities have passed similar ordinances. Hazelton, Pennsylvania, which has experienced a sizable increase in Latino immigrants over a short period of time, enacted an Illegal Immigration Relief Act, which denied licenses to businesses that employ illegal immigrants, fined landlords $1,000 for each illegal immigrant discovered renting their properties, and required city documents to be in English only (Scolforo 2006). The Dallas suburb of Farmers Branch on November 15, 2006, passed ordinances that fined landlords who rented to unauthorized immigrants $500 per tenant per day, gave police authority to seek certification to act as agents of the Department of Homeland Security, and declared English the official language of the city (Blumenthal 2006). In Escondido, California, the city council gave landlords ten days to evict unauthorized immigrants and made landlords subject to "fines up to $1,000 a day, six months in jail, [and] suspension of their business license" (Moscoso 2006, A3). Each of these actions can be understood as a direct response to the perceived unwillingness and inability of the national government to do its job. State and local governments now act on the basis of how they do or do not see their interests served in any new equilibrium to the identity-community trade-off.

There are also risks grounded in the transnational nature of the identity-community trade-off. Clearly, a consensus has been attained on enhancing border security. Massey (2006), however, helps us to understand a counterintuitive consequence of the previous efforts to further secure the border that are likely to be replicated. Tougher enforcement reduces the return migration of unauthorized immigrants because it is harder for them to return to the United States. The result is more unauthorized immigrants in the United States, leading to even greater calls for enforcement, leading to more undocumented having even greater incentives to remain in the United States. The United States is thus "locked into a perverse cycle" regarding immigration policy (Massey 2006).

Remittances are generally understood to benefit receiving families, communities, and countries. It is estimated that in 2003, Mexico received $13.3 billion from workers in the United States, the largest remittances of any country. According to Roberto Coronado, economic analyst of the Federal Reserve Bank of Dallas, El Paso Branch, this amount is about 140 percent of foreign direct investment in Mexico and about 71 percent of oil exports (Coronado 2004). Interestingly, the Mexican state of Zacatecas initiated a program in 1993 that matched the dollars invested in infrastructure programs; as of 2002, approximately $40 million had been invested in 788 projects in a number of its municipalities (Coronado 2004). It is hard to argue that remittances are not beneficial to Mexico.

What would be the impact on Mexico and Central America if remittances fell because of the increased deportation of unauthorized workers? It seems likely that hardship and demands for government support for lower-income families and communities would increase. If Mexico were unable to meet these demands, political instability could result, only increasing the incentives to move to the United States.

## The Future of Anti-Immigrant Politics in the United States

The position taken in the identity-community trade-off is fundamentally driven by how much confidence the individual has in the integrative capacity of the current U.S. nation-state. Arguments about illegality, security, cultural dilution, cost, labor competition, and racism are, at their core, reflections of low confidence in the capacity of the U.S. nation-state. Huntington's (2004) entire analysis derives from his fear that the

American creed is under such threat that the country is forced to reify its past as an Anglo, Protestant, and English-dominant society.

This is in contrast to the characterization of the American creed offered by Schlesinger (1991), in which, defending against what he characterizes as multicultural critics, he argues that central to the U.S. capacity to accommodate difference is its valuing of self-critique. It is this self-critique that is the key to understanding how much the United States can accommodate the multiculturalism, internationalism, and immigration that have always been part of its history (Fraga and Segura 2006). Roberto Unger and Cornel West refer to this confidence in the U.S. capacity to accommodate and integrate new populations as the "religion of possibility" in U.S. society (1998, 10). Immigrants, perhaps especially the unauthorized, judge that coming to the United States is worth the risks that they incur, probably based in large part on their hopes and dreams of what is possible in the United States. Although these dreams may never be fulfilled fully and can at times be shattered, they are grounded in an understanding of the unlimited possibilities of accommodation and integration in the United States.

The recent politics of immigration reform in the United States will again require that the nation make a difficult judgment regarding the identity-community trade-off. It does seem to be the case that the consistent majorities in favor of comprehensive reform, if properly mobilized and led, should be able to overcome the passionate voices of those on both sides of the immigration debate. At this writing, it is unclear whether either the Republican nominee, Senator John McCain, or the Democratic nominee, Senator Barack Obama (D-Illinois), will be that leader should one of them be elected president of the United States. Whatever the future holds, without a doubt, the contours of the future of the United States will be significantly determined by what this new balance in the identity-community trade-off will be.

# PART V

# IMMIGRANTS' POLITICAL OPPORTUNITY STRUCTURES BEYOND THE STATE

In previous chapters in this volume, Marco Martiniello (chap. 3) and Lorraine Minnite (chap. 4) call for greater attention to transnationalism in understanding immigrants' political behavior; the chapters in Part V respond. In chapter 13, Eva Østergaard-Nielsen takes a bottom-up approach to this issue, looking at how Turkish and Kurdish immigrants to Western Europe balance mobilization around issues in their new countries against mobilization around issues in their country of origin. In chapter 14, Gallya Lahav takes a top-down approach to the question of movement across borders, examining the attitudes of EU political elites regarding immigration policy and immigrant incorporation. Both chapters suggest that, although democratic states try to channel the political demands that immigrants can make on them, candidates' incentives to garner immigrant voters' support push these states into acknowledging immigrants' foreign policy demands. Thus, even as states try to set limits on their new populations, immigrants push back on states.

Lahav's surveys of members of the European Parliament show that they increasingly agree that immigration is a salient issue, that current immigration flows are at about the right level (as of 2004), and that the European Union should have common policies regarding immigration and immigrant incorporation. Yet she also finds, compared with 1992, less EU parliamentary support for immigrant rights and more support for national (rather than supranational) control over immigration policy. EU parliamentarians differ by country, party, and ideology; nevertheless, despite theoretical and political reasons to believe that political elites are working toward European cooperation on immigration policy, there are important constraints and limits. Lahav explains this perhaps surprising result and points to the paradox of increasing consensus on immigration or intake policy in parallel with persistent or even increasing *dis*sensus with regard to immigrant or integration policy.

Østergaard-Nielsen's chapter reveals the internal challenges of states in trying to do what Lahav says they want to do—set limits on immigration and immigrant rights. Their difficulties arise partly because "migrant political participation and identification at the local and transnational levels is not a zero-sum game." Immigrants seek not only socioeconomic integration, political rights, and antidiscrimination policies in the countries to which they migrate but also intervention in the political affairs of, or within the international community on behalf of, their homelands. The Netherlands, Germany, and Denmark have tried to offer migrants responses to the former set of demands while foreclosing action on the latter. Yet the political incentives of native-born politicians work against this strategy; German political parties, for example, highlight their support for Turkey in an effort to attract Turkish-origin German voters, much as U.S. political parties increasingly try to woo Latino voters.

U.S. political parties also get tangled up in internal conflicts over immigration policy and integration policies in ways that Luis Fraga (chap. 12) has shown and that we (Jennifer Hochschild and John Mollenkopf, chap. 19 in this volume) develop further. That is, they seek both to woo Latino voters and to control the border against "too many" Latin American immigrants. So do and will European parties as more and more immigrants and their descendents attain citizenship and suffrage, and make demands based on their concern about their countries of origin as well as their domestic needs. European politics will probably become even more complex than U.S. politics on this subject because European states must engage with EU-level governance; a multitude of immigrant groups with different origins and goals; an active transnational advocacy network; and greater contiguity with neighboring states that might have distinct circumstances, politics, and incentives. In comparison, even the cross-cutting pressures within the two-party U.S. political system look simple to navigate.

# CHAPTER THIRTEEN

# The End of Closet Political Transnationalism?

The Role of Homeland Politics in the Political Incorporation of Turks and Kurds in Europe

*Eva Østergaard-Nielsen*

In the Danish local elections in the early 1990s, a Turkish-origin candidate was listed for the Social Democratic Party in one of the Copenhagen constituencies. He was running in an area with a high concentration of migrants, especially Turkish-origin migrants, who had gained the right to vote in local elections more than a decade earlier. Then, as now, the support for the Social Democratic Party, which was in government up through the 1980s, was high among Turkish-origin voters. Still, to help out the candidate, party officials offered to invite a prominent Turkish social democrat from Turkey to boost the campaign. This offer was, however, immediately rejected by the candidate. As he explained, his Turkish voters in Copenhagen were not social democrats in Turkey. On the contrary, in terms of Turkish politics they were supportive of mainly right-wing nationalist or religious parties. And, although they would vote for the Social Democratic Party in Denmark because of its policies toward migrants, they would most likely distance themselves from a candidate standing next to a Turkish social democrat.

This anecdote stems from one of my first interviews with Turkish- and Kurdish-origin local politicians in Europe. It is highlighted as an example of the main point of this chapter—how homeland political identification and practices among Turks and Kurds intersect with their political incorporation in their countries of residence. The Danish Turkish-origin social democrat's dilemma is not a unique event. Homeland political interest in Turkish politics by Turkish and Kurdish migrants has not gone away with time and been replaced with immigrant political concerns over the situation in the country of residence. The understanding that migrant political participation and identification at the local and transnational levels is not a zero-sum game has been demonstrated on both sides of the Atlantic (Østergaard-Nielsen 2001; Levitt 2003; Guarnizo, Portes, and Haller 2003). This, however, is just a starting point for further inquiry into how a transnational view of migrants' political identification and agency may contribute to a more holistic understanding of their local political incorporation.

In the case of Turkey and Turkish migrants, transnational political identification and activities of migrants are important for a whole host of reasons. The very presence of more than 3 million Turks within the European Union further sensitizes the receiving countries, especially Germany, to bilateral and multilateral relations with Turkey. This sensitivity is reinforced by mobilization and lobbying among Turks and Kurds related to the domestic and foreign policy of Turkey (Østergaard-Nielsen 2003d). This chapter, however, does not focus on the extent to which Turkish or Kurdish migrants have influenced the domestic or foreign policy of their countries of residence or on the extent to which some of these political movements are perceived to constitute a security threat. Instead, it analyzes how Turkish- and Kurdish-origin migrants negotiate homeland political issues in their dealings with the political institutions of their country of residence.

This dimension of migrant homeland political orientation is relevant because migrants and migrant descendants have become an integral part of the political landscape throughout the European Union. Turkish and Kurdish migrant associations have long acted as representatives for the various ethnic, religious, and political groups of these migrant collectives. Turkish-origin voters have become important constituencies for political parties in Europe. Countries granting local voting rights to third-country nationals have a long-standing experience with electoral participation of migrants and migrant-origin representatives in local government. Moreover, with growing rates of naturalization, even countries with an exclusive policy on political rights for non-EU citizens, such as Germany, now have considerable Turkish-origin constituencies. The number of Turkish-origin political candidates and representatives has also grown. Such migrant representatives are attractive for political parties because having a migrant-origin candidate on the list signals an inclusive policy toward migrants. More important, such a candidate has the potential to attract votes from the co-ethnic, co-national, or co-religious migrant-origin voters. This chapter illustrates how homeland political identification is not just of a matter of interest to the relationship between migrants and their country of origin. The extent to which and ways in which homeland politics matter to Turks or Kurds enters into the equation of their relationship with their resident-country political institutions.

The following pages briefly outline the relationship between the Turkish-origin groups in Europe and their country of origin, Turkey, and then focus on two central dimensions of their local and homeland political orientation and mobilization. The first concerns the extent to which interest in transnational politics is durable over time and is relevant for also second- and third-generation migrant Turks and Kurds. In this context, we should evaluate homeland political orientation and engagement among migrants over time and generations, not just in terms of whether there is less or more of it, but we should also identify qualitative changes in the political identification and participation of Turks and Kurds as they maneuver in an increasingly complex and multilevel institutional and political environment.

The next section discusses the extent to which homeland political issues are included or excluded in processes of local political participation of Turks and Kurds. The term *closet transnationalism* refers to situations in which migrants tone down their identification with the homeland because of exclusionary demands for national commitment (Joppke and Morawska 2003). It has been argued that migrant political transnationalism is no longer something that migrants have to keep away from the local or national political arena of their countries of residence (Joppke and Morawska 2003). Yet, as the introductory anecdote indicates, political identification with homeland politics does not always translate easily into the political life in the country of residence.

At the time of my interviews, little was known about the homeland political identification and practices of Turkish migrants in Copenhagen. This was in part because homeland political agendas were rarely put forward by the Turkish migrants themselves and in part because of the limited political and institutional space granted to migrant political transnationalism related to the homeland within the host-country political system (Østergaard-Nielsen 2002). But has homeland politics become more accepted since then? To what extent does the attitude to homeland politics differ in various EU member states? To what extent are migrants from Turkey expected to participate as migrants focused on migrant political issues and not as Turks or Kurds interested in Turkish politics?

The final section briefly comments on how the case of the Turks and Kurds compares to other major migrant collectives in Europe, points out some of the remaining gaps in the current research field, and raises the issue of how migrant political transnationalism enters into recent debates and policies on migrant incorporation.

These discussions point to already-existing answers and identify possible further paths of inquiry that may complement them. They do so by rereading and updating my previous research on the transnational political mobilization of Kurds and Turks in four EU member states (Germany, the Netherlands, Denmark, and the United Kingdom). The analysis presented here is not a systematic comparison of these case studies (Østergaard-Nielsen 2001, 2002) but, instead, uses examples from especially the Danish, German, and Dutch research to illustrate the general arguments.

Just a few words on some of the central concepts used throughout this chapter—Turks and Kurds mobilize around a series of issues. One set of issues relates to their situation in their country of residence, referred to as *immigrant politics*. This includes issues of socioeconomic integration, political rights, problems with discrimination and racism, and the role of Islam in public space. Another area of mobilization has to do with the country of origin, referred to as *homeland politics*. This includes both direct intervention in the political affairs of the homeland and lobbying the host government or other relevant political actors on issues related to the country of origin. In the case of Turkey, issues of human rights, democratization, ethnic rights for Kurds, and religious rights for both Sunnis and Alevis have been on the agenda of migrant associations (Østergaard-Nielsen 2003d).[1]

This chapter highlights how immigrant political and homeland political issues overlap and intertwine and are at times inseparable. Moreover, they do not correspond to a dichotomy between local and transnational political participation. It is not that the immigrant political is local and the homeland political is transnational, per se. At the level of associations, immigrant politics can take on a transnational dimension, sometimes institutionalized through cross-border federations of migrant associations, and also take place through lobbying Europe-wide supranational or intergovernmental institutions. The transnational politics of migrants is, in other words, not necessarily homeland political. Meanwhile, homeland politics can take the same transnational dimension of networking and lobbying across borders, but can at the same time be very local to local. A recent study has noted a rise in hometown associations among Turks and Kurds in EU member states that strengthen local ties to their village of origin through social economic and political practices (Çaglar 2006).

## Turkey and the Turks and Kurds abroad

Turks and Kurds (from Turkey) constitute one of the largest migrant collective within the European Union. Following processes of guestworker recruitment and subsequent family reunification, as well as the continuous arrival of asylum seekers and irregular migrants, more than 3.5 million Turkish citizens and former Turkish citizens reside in EU member states. More than two-thirds (~2.4 million) live in Germany.[2] The forty-year time span between now and the heyday of Turkish guestworker recruitment in the 1960s means that at least three generations of Turks now live within the European Union. Indeed, by no means all Turkish citizens abroad have migrated. Approximately 614,000 Turkish citizens have been born in Germany alone.[3] The ethnic, religious, and socioeconomic differences among migrants from Turkey make any generalizations we could make about them difficult to sustain. Turkish citizens or former citizens living within the European Union may be Sunni or Alevi Muslims, identify themselves as Kurdish or another ethnic subgroup, be university trained, or be self-employed or, indeed, unemployed.[4] A more nuanced view of this group is often subdued in debates on migrant incorporation and political participation, in which the Turkish migrant collective has a high profile.

As in the case of other migrant groups, it is difficult to underestimate the significance of low-cost travel and electronic means of communication, and the availability of homeland media for Turkish migrants' ability to stay in touch with their homeland. Turks and Kurds in Europe can follow events in Turkey with the flick of the TV remote control or by reading one of the many Turkish newspapers that are widely available throughout Europe. They can log on to the Internet and seek and exchange information or express their opinion in blogs or chat fora.

Moreover, the Turkish governments has taken a series of measures to forge or strengthen ties with the Turks and Kurds abroad over the last decade and a half. From a set of policies aimed at catering for the guest workers and their families abroad until their return, a more recent set of policies are based on the realization that Turkish citizens and their descendants are a permanent feature of European societies and polities—and EU-Turkish relations. Like in the case of a series of other countries of emigration, the rationale behind these outreach policies is to foment the social capital upgrading of its citizens abroad and attract continued economic and political support (Bauböck 2003b; Østergaard-Nielsen 2003b). Among the various policies employed is allowing dual citizenship so that Turks can take up the citizenship of their country of residence without having to give up their Turkish passport. This was later followed by the introduction of a special pink card giving those Turkish citizens who had to give up their Turkish citizenship in order to naturalize abroad more rights in Turkey. In this way the Turkish government encourages the naturalization and political engagement of emigrants and their descendants in their countries of residence. In terms of political rights, Turkey has not managed to implement long-distance voting rights for its citizens abroad, although this has been on the agenda for more than two decades. Meanwhile, Turkey has also set up a consultative council for dialog between key policymakers and Turks abroad on both how Turkey may help solve the problems that its citizens experience abroad and how Turkish overseas citizens may contribute to the Turkish economy from afar.[5] It has recently been argued that Turkey should and could play a greater role in facilitating the integration of its citizens abroad (Erzan and Kirişci 2006).

Although the Turkish outreach policies have been interpreted as attempts to establish a pro-Turkish lobby inside Europe, research on Turkish and Kurdish migrant collectives in Europe indicate that there is no reason to overestimate the effect of these policies (Østergaard-Nielsen 2003d). Both first- and second-generation leaders of migrant associations often harbor a fairly cynical view of the extent to which Turkey has assisted them from afar, and they certainly do not want to be seen as a fifth-column representative of the Turkish state. Nonetheless, a number of associations are aligned with Turkish foreign policy and have helped put forward issues, such as the Armenian issue or the EU accession of Turkey, to the policymakers of their country of residence.[6]

Somewhat more complex is the impact of other political actors, such as parties and movements of various political, ethnic, and religious persuasions, which seek to mobilize economic and political support among the Turks and Kurds abroad. The success of these movements varies, but especially Kurdish and Sunni Muslim networks have come under intense scrutiny by both the countries of reception and origin. Indeed, the work of Turkish or Kurdish nonstate actors and opposition parties among the migrant collectives in Europe has been one of the main incentives for the Turkish state also to engage in its outreach policies. But, again, it is important to emphasize that the political and civic landscape of local and transnational Turkish associations and networks is not a remote controlled reproduction of the political situation in Turkey. Different political, religious, and ethnic movements and associations have reacted in various ways and with various levels of intensity to events and attempts of mobilization from Turkey (Østergaard-Nielsen 2003d).

## The Durability of Transnational Identification, Belonging, and Political Orientation among Turks and Kurds in Europe

The transnational lens on the political mobilization and participation of migrants has gained favor in European research on Turks and Kurds (Faist 2000; Koopmans and Statham 2003; Østergaard-Nielsen 2003d). Criticism of the transnational take on migration is abundant: it is not new, it is not representative for the whole migrant collective, and it is not durable.[7] The latter issue is highly relevant to the case of Turks and Kurds in Europe, given the high number of migrant or refugee descendants. Has interest in Turkish politics declined over the years? Are the children and grandchildren of Turkish or Kurdish migrants less interested and engaged in the politics of their homeland than their parents? Or are there other differences over time or between generations that we need to take into account when framing and carrying out research on the transnational dimension of political incorporation?

It is important to emphasize the lack of data on homeland political orientation and mobilization of migrants. So far the research field has been dominated by qualitative studies that sample on the dependent variable; that is, they study migrant transnationalism where it manifests itself, leaving behind the question of how widespread these practices are (Portes 2001). The predominance of qualitative over quantitative studies means that there is little in the way of surveys that indicate the differences among levels of transnational political orientation over time or between first- and second-generation migrants. Instead, there are studies using different migrant collectives or different states of residence and origin as independent variables to explain different levels of transnational political engagement (Østergaard-Nielsen 2001, 2003c; Guarnizo, Portes, and Haller 2003; Koopmans and Statham 2003).

A recent survey of the 'Euro-Turks' in Germany and France show a declining sense of affiliation with Turkey over the generations. Whereas approximately 50 percent of the first generation feels more closely affiliated with Turkey than its country of residence, only around 25 percent of the second generation Turks (defined as those born in Germany or France) feel that way (Kaya and Kentel 2005). Yet, at the same time, the results indicate that the identification of the second generation is somewhat ambiguous—the marginally largest group of respondents among the second generation feels equally affiliated with both the country they are born in and Turkey, leaving only around one-third of the respondents identifying mainly with Germany or France. Moreover, the closer identification with Germany or France does not really translate into a greater interest in German or French politics.[8] The study does not correlate interest in Turkish politics with birthplace, but the overall survey results indicate that Turks are not as interested in Turkish politics as is sometimes assumed in political debates. Approximately 40 percent of the Turks in Germany (and 50 percent of the Turks in France) was "not at all" or "not really interested" in Turkish politics and around one-third does not have a clear affiliation with any Turkish political party (Kaya and Kentel 2005). Still, that does leave more than one-third of the respondents in the "very interested" in Turkish politics categories and two-thirds that identify with a Turkish political party even though they were living or even had been born abroad.

In addition to trying to look at quantitative changes in transnational identification and engagement over time and between various generations of migrants, it is important to explore the qualitative differences. One tendency over the last decades is for Turkish and Kurdish associations, especially those having a stronger presence of second-generation migrants, to integrate the homeland political and migrant political dimensions of their outlooks and activities. Generally, there has been a trend toward an increasing focus on immigrant political issues among Turkish and Kurdish associations in Europe. Many associations are founded with this purpose in mind. Even associations originally born out of a transnational link with a political actor in Turkey tend to focus on the situation in the countries of residence. But, as mentioned, this immigrant political engagement may coexist alongside homeland political issues, and moreover, in some cases the two dimensions become inseparable. For example, the Kurds have linked their campaigns for recognition of their cultural rights in Germany, Denmark, and the Netherlands with their situation of discrimination in Turkey. Their pamphlets, seminars, and demonstrations have highlighted how Kurds have the right to be treated as Kurds (and not Turks) in their country of residence and that such recognition would send an important signal to the Turkish authorities. Similarly, a religious minority such as the Alevis may include references to their situation of long-standing discrimination in Turkey when trying to advocate more rights for Alevis in Germany, Denmark, and the Netherlands. Sunni Muslims have pointed to the parallels between the headscarf issue in Turkey and in Germany or, indeed, France (Østergaard-Nielsen 2003d).

Beyond ethnic and religious groups, another interesting example is the support and lobbying by European-based Turks and Kurds for EU membership for Turkey. Migration and the presence of a large collective of Turks in EU member states play an important role in the Turkish EU accession negotiations. The argument, repeatedly brought forward by major Turkish federations in Europe over the last decade, is that the entry of Turkey into the European Union would facilitate the integration of Turkish citizens or former citizens already living within the European Union. Beyond their automatic transition from third-country citizens to EU citizens, the inclusion of their country of origin would send an important symbolic signal. As argued by the head of the Turkish Community in Germany (Türkische Gemeinde in Deutschland, TGD), the support by German policymakers for the EU accession of Turkey is helpful for the integration and coexistence of German Turks in Germany because "many German-Turks have interpreted the rejection of their homeland as a snubbing of themselves" (Kolat 2003). These examples illustrate how homeland politics is no longer a long-distance relationship in the case of Turkey but may form an integral part of the migrant political advocacy campaigns of the Turks and Kurds within the European Union.

Following the same line of thinking, it is important to emphasize that identification with Islam or with a Turkish or Kurdish political movement is no longer transnational by default. The institutionalization of a number of religious, ethnic, or political movements in the countries of residence makes identifying with them less homeland-oriented than was true for the parent's generation. For a migrant to identify with or join these movements may, rather, be a reactive marker to distinguish themselves from the wider society of the country of residence informed by their experience of discrimination and exclusion (Schiffauer 1999). Membership in an ethnic, religious, or political association or network of residence may also be based on the social or religious services or the local political representation that these associations provide for the local community of Turks or Kurds (Ehrkamp 2005). The fact that these associations are linked transnationally with the homeland or kindred associations and movements in other countries is not irrelevant, but it can be secondary and not enter into the day-to-day functions of the associations. Thus, identification with or membership in a transnational homeland political network may be performed locally in the neighborhood.

Finally, it is worth exploring further the extent to which especially second- and third-generations Turks and Kurds are between the homeland and host-country only. The changing agendas of Turkish and Kurdish associations indicate that they are increasingly mobilized by or linked with wider issues of democratization and human rights, environment, and gender instead of the national political parties or movements favored by their parents' generation. Moreover, observers of other Muslim groups note that the second generation may identify with wider Islamic movements and solidarity with other Muslim groups elsewhere and that this can also inform local political participation. For instance, recent election results in Britain have shown how the second-generation Bangladeshi and Pakistani Muslims, to a much greater extent than the first generation, were disappointed with Labour because of the British involvement in the Iraq war (Bodi 2005).

We must add to this that the spaces and institutions for migrants' identification and political engagement also include the European dimension or international and transnational organizations. The bulk of the homeland political activity continues to take place at the local or national level. Yet, increasingly, European institutions, such as the European Parliament and the European Council, are also on the receiving end of Turkish and Kurdish homeland political and transnational political engagement. The central and vocal position of EU institutions on EU accession of Turkey, as well as related issues of the Turkish human rights record, the Kurdish issue, the Armenian issue, and the Cyprus conflict, has cemented their relevance as targets for homeland political lobbying of European-based Turks and Kurds.[9] Thus, the triadic framework of host country, homeland, and migrants (Sheffer 1986) is no longer sufficient to analyze processes of political identification and practices that go beyond national institutions and movements.

## Political Opportunity Structures and Transnational Networks among Migrant Associations in Europe

It has been suggested that, whereas the first generations of migrants were closet transnationalists subject to the exclusionary demands of their home and host states regarding their national commitments, today public discourse and political opportunity structures are much more tolerant of diversity and facilitate multilevel identification and political participation (Shain 1999; Joppke and Morawska 2003). The European experience of Turkish and Kurdish migrant political transnationalism seems to deviate from this observation in some respects.

The setup of the European Union entails the promotion of overlapping political membership for its citizens. Nevertheless, although more member states have allowed dual citizenship over the last decade, issues of dual national allegiance for third-country nationals are still contested in some EU member states (Faist 2007; Østergaard-Nielsen 2008). The signature campaign of the Christian Democratic Union during 1999 against the proposal of the Social Democratic–Green government coalition to allow dual citizenship is a case in point. At the time, it was argued that dual citizenship was the institutionalization of dual loyalties, a pathway to parallel societies and thus a threat to German national identity (Østergaard-Nielsen 2003d). Moreover, cross-border political mobilization along political, ethnic, and religious lines often sits uneasily in European debates on modes of migrant incorporation. In the case of the Turks and Kurds, acceptance of diversity seems to stop when this diversity manifests itself in political agency along homeland political agendas. Indeed, it is especially the political dimension of migrant transnationalism, the extent to which migrants support a political cause, movement or party outside their country of residence, that remains controversial in the relationship between these associations and the political institutions and actors in their country of residence.

Given the differences in citizenship and migrant-incorporation regimes in the various European countries, several studies have examined the significance of different resident-country political contexts on migrant homeland political activities, including those of the Turks. These studies argue that exclusive citizenship and migrant incorporation regimes, such as in Germany, serve to strengthen homeland political orientations and organizations among Turks and Kurds. In contrast, the Dutch multicultural inclusive regime may lessen homeland political activities because third-country citizens can vote in local elections in the Netherlands and migrant associations are actively included in institutionalized platforms for dialog with policy-makers (Abadan-Unat 1997).[10] For instance, one comparative quantitative empirical survey of the extent to which migrant transnational claims-making features in the host-country national press argues that there is more homeland political activity in Germany than in the Netherlands and that homeland politics in the Netherlands is more included in the political system (Koopmans and Statham 2003). But the impact of national political opportunity structures was less clear-cut in my comparative study of Turkish and Kurdish transnational and homeland political engagement in Germany and the Netherlands. In addition to a "more/less" type of evaluation of the amount of homeland politics, this study uncovered how differences in access to politics impact the particular ways in which migrant transnational political activities are formulated and communicated. Also, the host-country political institutions and actors stood out in this study as strong mediators of transnational political activity (Østergaard-Nielsen 2001). There is no doubt that the study of migrant transnational political practices needs to be located within their particular political institutional context.

Yet, because the research also included research on the transnational networks, it revealed how transnational practices are not only a function of the type of citizenship and the national political opportunity structures. Indeed, the main point of migrant transnational political networks is that they are unbounded by their national context and able to draw on resources from associations or other political actors elsewhere. The landscape and genealogy of transnational political organizations, many of which now also, or even foremost, serve as migrant political associations, stand out as very similar in Germany and the Netherlands (and Denmark), illustrating the importance of migrants' transnational networks back to their country of origin and, not least, among organizations in Germany, the Netherlands, and Denmark. Local associations are linked up through an increasingly institutionalized infrastructure of national and Europe-wide federations with varying types of ties to the homeland. Through these networks, associations pool resources and exchange information on both immigrant and homeland political issues. They hold joint festivals and political meetings or coordinate their campaigns (Østergaard-Nielsen 2001). Thus, comparative studies of the relationship between national political opportunity structures and migrant homeland political practices have limitations. Citizenship and political opportunity structures are key elements in the political universe of migrants, but so are their transnational networks and resources.

One of the main challenges arising from this is how to methodologically deal with the transnational in the local and the local in the transnational. Studies of migrant homeland political mobilization and participation, therefore, need to rid themselves of the most basic elements of methodological nationalism (Wimmer and Glick-Schiller 2002) and employ a methodology that allows for an unbounded understanding of migrant transnational and homeland political networks and participation.

Another main point, to return to the issue of closet transnationalism, is that it is important not to conflate those political opportunity structure open to migrant political participation with the opportunity for homeland political lobbying and claims-making. Even though the multicultural Dutch migrant-incorporation regime aimed to include and promote dialog with the migrant collective, these channels were by no means open to dialog on homeland political issues. Migrants from Turkey were supposed to participate as migrants, or to some extent as Muslim migrants, but not as Turks or Kurds. Thus, contrary to the claim that more-inclusive Dutch structures would incorporate transnational homeland political claims-making, there was, in the case of several Turkish or Kurdish groups, a schizophrenic system in which the homeland political activities took place more outside the Dutch political system of dialog with migrant associations. Alongside different models of migrant political incorporation, there can exist quite similar attitudes to migrants' transnational homeland political mobilization (Østergaard-Nielsen 2001).

Indeed, in the Netherlands, Germany, and Denmark, there was an explicit censoring of homeland political agendas and engagement in the context of migrant political participation.[11] Although some homeland political agendas were more controversial and unwelcome than others, there were numerous examples of host-country political actors urging Turkish and Kurdish associations to focus on migrant political issues and not the politics of Turkey.[12] Significantly, public funding for migrant associations also tends to be earmarked for immigrant political activities. In the case of Denmark, the guidelines for government funding for migrant associations makes clear that such funds cannot be used for anything even remotely homeland-related, such as "festivals in relation to national or religious holidays[,] ... closed arrangements or activities that collect money" (Østergaard-Nielsen 2002). That migrant associations are being funded to do immigrant political activities and not homeland politics is neither surprising nor controversial. It is difficult to imagine that any host country would fund a particular homeland political network or its activities in the context of immigrant political incorporation. Consequently, this invites migrant associations to tone down any homeland political agenda or affiliation in their dealings with public authorities. They do not want to appear to have an explicit homeland political affiliation so as not to hamper their opportunities for public funding. This is particularly the case with Turkish associations supporting right-wing nationalist or religious parties in Turkey. Such Turkish (and, to a lesser extent, Kurdish) migrant associations usually emphasize that they are "not political," by which they usually mean in the context of Turkish politics. As one head of a Turkish association in Copenhagen with a strong sympathy for the Turkish right-wing Nationalist Movement Party explained during an interview, it is important to stress that the activities of the association are cultural and not political because "Otherwise you often get misunderstood and then you don't get any funding." (Copenhagen, 2000)

Still, the exclusion or toning down of homeland political issues is also a frequently mentioned concern of the Turkish migrant federations themselves, especially those that try to bridge several religious, ethnic, and political groups. Homeland politics, as mentioned in several interviews, is best kept at arm's length because it divides the migrant associations and drains collective efforts to improve migrant political issues. For instance, in the case of the Turkish Consultative Body (Inspraak Organen Turken; IOT) in the Netherlands, made up of representatives from Turkish migrant associations, it was specifically mentioned in the statutes that homeland politics could not be discussed if one of the member associations was against it. Similarly, in Denmark, one of the major migrant political federations interviewed, the Federation of Ethnic Minority Organisations (Paraplyorganisationen for Etniske minoriteter; POEM), made it clear that it will have nothing to with "the politics of other countries." (Copenhagen, 2000)

## Homeland Politics at the Ballot Box

Homeland politics is also an ambiguous asset at the ballot box in the countries of residence. As already mentioned, migrant-origin candidates are attractive to political parties for a whole host of reasons, including their ability to attract the migrant vote. The concentration of migrants in certain urban areas means that Turkish-origin candidates have a higher chance of making it past the post there. Especially in electoral systems in which voters have the option of voting for a particular candidate, migrant-origin candidates have been noted to attract a high number of such votes, sometimes upping their ranking on the party list and securing their seat in local government. This is not to say that Turks automatically vote for Turks only. Yet the relationship between the Turkish-origin candidate and the migrant collective is often honed during election campaigns. Pamphlets are sometimes also produced in Turkish, and Turkish political candidates hold meetings with Turkish migrant associations on their own initiative, the initiative of their political party, or the initiative of the Turkish association itself. Similarly, the Turkish media, widely followed by the Turks abroad, tends to tune in on the Turkish-origin candidates, who in turn may use in particular the European-based Turkish press as a venue for their campaign.

On the surface, homeland politics is rarely welcomed or considered relevant for the relationship between parties and Turkish-origin voters. Time and time again, political party executives and policymakers in Germany, the Netherlands, and Denmark have stressed that they want to dialog on migrant politics and not homeland politics with their Turkish- or Kurdish-origin constituents. Migrant-origin candidates themselves emphasize that they are not running on a homeland political platform. Yet the reality on the ground is somewhat more complex. Diaspora politically driven lobbying and block-voting, as has been identified in the United States (Huntington 1997; Shain 1999), is not common in Europe or among the Turkish origin voters. Still, especially in Germany, where the Turkish-origin voters number around 600,000, German political parties are aware that their policies toward Turkey are, if not defining, then not irrelevant for their relationship with Turkish-origin voters. In particular, the issue of the EU accession of Turkey has become as much an issue of domestic politics as foreign policy because of its significance for the Turkish citizens (and also former citizens) living within the European Union.

In recent elections, political parties in Germany have highlighted how their policies toward Turkey are attractive to Turkish-origin German voters.[13] This is especially the case for the Social Democratic Party, which enjoys the support of the majority of Turkish-origin German voters. Indeed, the Turkish vote has been referred to as the "secret weapon of Schröder" (Wüst 2003:29). Leaders of the Social Democratic Party have stressed their support for the EU accession of Turkey in federal electoral campaigns. Likewise, Turkish-origin social democratic candidates have highlighted this issue. At the rallying website of two social democratic Turkish-origin candidates in the 2005 federal electoral campaign, the main paragraph informs voters that the Social Democratic Party has "consistently strived to achieve the beginning of the negotiations for Turkey's EU membership," whereas the opposition parties, as well as the recently formed and rival Left Party, is against the admission of Turkey to the European Union.[14]

Meanwhile, the Greens and the Christian Democratic Union have low support among the Turkish-origin voters (Wüst 2003) and their policies on Turkey have not been helpful in ameliorating this relationship. The Greens, who are otherwise advocates of very inclusive migrant-incorporation policies, took a very critical stance on the Turkish human rights deficit and, in particular, the handling of the Kurdish issue up through the 1990s, which was difficult to stomach for more conservative, pro-Turkish voters. Indeed, the dilemma of maintaining a critical stance on Turkey while not distancing their Turkish-origin voters led to the implosion of their Turkish membership association in the mid-1990s and the establishment of a new association in which homeland politics was taboo (Özdemir 1997). At the other extreme, the conservative Christian Democratic Union continues to turn off Turkish-origin voters with its emphasis on assimilatory incorporation policies. In terms of Turkey, their lack of attention to the human rights situation and the Kurdish issue up through the 1990s was welcomed by their limited number of Turkish-origin supporters, but their critical rhetoric toward Muslim immigrants and, in particular, their opposition to the EU accession of Turkey have been real obstacles.[15]

Although homeland politics is secondary, and often marginal, compared to immigrant political issues, there is usually coherence between the homeland political views of the candidates of Turkish or Kurdish origin and the Dutch, German, or Danish political parties for which they are running. The majority of Turkish- and Kurdish-origin candidates have been drawn to center left or left-wing parties with a political program more attractive to migrant collectives. That the Social Democratic Party in Germany has also been less critical of Turkey and in favor of EU membership for Turkey is a further plus. But when there is a significant conflict of opinion or identification in terms of Turkey or Turkish-EU relations, this may lead to the Turkish-origin candidate and the party going separate ways.

On the one hand, the political party may be weary of the homeland political views of their Turkish-origin candidate. During the 1990s, there were several instances when Turkish-origin candidates were screened and filtered out before they were allowed to run for office (Østergaard-Nielsen 2001). More recently, in the Dutch electoral campaign of 2006, the socialists excluded one Dutch-Turkish candidate and the Christian

Democrats excluded two Dutch-Turkish candidates because of their denial of the Armenian genocide of 1915. This view is contrary to the official policy of these Dutch parties. The decision provoked strong criticism both in Turkey and among Turkish organizations in the Netherlands.[16] On the other hand, migrant-origin candidates may opt out by themselves. For instance, the pro-Kurdish line of (especially) parties to the left of the social democrats has deterred some Turkish candidates who do not agree. In one instance, a Turkish-origin leader of the local chapter of the pro-Turkish Association for Promotion of the Thoughts of Atatürk declined the invitation to run for the Greens because she could not endorse the party line on Turkish domestic policy regarding the Kurdish issue.

This last example also illustrates how, from the point of view of the migrant-origin candidates themselves, homeland politics is a double-edged sword because it both attracts and deters voters. None of the candidates or representatives interviewed was unaware of the homeland political issues and their representation among the Turkish-origin voters. But successful Turkish and Kurdish candidates, as in the example of the social democrat in Copenhagen mentioned at the beginning of the chapter, try to keep homeland political issues or an affiliation with a particular homeland political Turkish association or political party in Turkey at bay. For instance, a Turkish-origin candidate for the senate in Berlin explained during an interview that he had difficulties in going to Turkish organizations because they would not have anything to do with the Green Party, which they perceived as "the anti-Turkish pro-Kurdish party" (Østergaard-Nielsen 2003). Little by little the doors opened for him, and whenever someone brought up the Kurdish issue he would say, "We are in Berlin, in Germany, we are not in Turkey; we should not keep what is happening in Turkey a secret but I have not come to talk about that. I have come to talk about Berlin, about Kreutzberg, about your problems." In another instance, a Turkish-origin candidate for the social democrats in Aarhus, Denmark, worked with Turkish migrant associations of all political and religious persuasions during his campaign in the local election in the late 1990s. Once he had come into office, he organized joint meetings in which these associations met and had the opportunity to leave aside their different homeland political persuasions and find common ground on immigrant political issues (Østergaard-Nielsen 2002).

We might suppose that second-generation political candidates would be less inclined to enter into debates on homeland political issues. And indeed, among the candidates interviewed, it is especially in this group that political candidates reject the issue of Turkish politics altogether as irrelevant to their political role in Denmark, the Netherlands, or Germany. But there are important exceptions.

In the case of one of the most high-profile second-generation Turkish-migrant politicians in Germany, Cem Özdemir, homeland politics was difficult to avoid. Indeed, Özdemir had an intense relationship with the Turkish media and Turkish politics during his time in the German Bundestag. As the first Turkish "guestworker child" in the Bundestag, he had a high profile in Turkish-German relations. By his own account, he, somewhat paradoxically, had to learn about Turkish politics while in the process of becoming a German policymaker (Özdemir 1997).

After being elected, Özdemir had only a brief honeymoon with his parents' country of origin. Although his occasionally critical stance on Turkish domestic and foreign politics was more moderate than in the case of some of his Green Party colleagues, his criticism was not well received in Turkey. He also took a very openly critical attitude toward the attempts of the Turkish government, political parties, and media to influence Turkish citizens abroad. Consequently, the Turkish media launched severe attacks on him and even called him a traitor and a back-stabber (Necef 2001; Østergaard-Nielsen 2003d). Özdemir has since become a deputy in the European Parliament for the Greens, where his political priorities include not only issues of migrant integration and EU-Turkish relations but also wider foreign political issues of human rights and U.S.–Middle Eastern relations.[17]

## Concluding Remarks

The case of Turks and Kurds illustrate how the homeland political orientation of migrants may intersect with their local political incorporation. Judging by the rapidly growing scholarship on migrant transnational political mobilization and participation in Europe, the Turkish and Kurdish migrants' continued interest in homeland politics is not exceptional.[18] Like the Kurds, a range of diaspora political groups, such as Sri Lankans and Somalis, engage in the intrastate conflicts or regional disputes of their countries of origin (Kleist 2007; Orjuela 2007). Likewise, migrant groups with a comparable migration trajectory to the Turkish migrants, such as Moroccans, have become important stakeholders in the processes of democratization and development in their countries of origin (Lacomba 2004; Lacroix 2005; Østergaard-Nielsen 2007). Yet only further more systematic research will establish to what extent the Kurdish and Turkish cases are representative for other migrant collectives in terms of how migrants negotiate their homeland political engagement in the process of their local political incorporation into their country of residence. In that respect, it is worth restating that, even among different political associations of Turks and Kurds, there are significant differences in processes of mobilization, types of claims-making, and the extent to which homeland political issues are brought forward in the local and national political fora of the country of residence. In part, this is because different political associations draw on different sets of transnational resources beyond the local context; in part, this is because some homeland political issues are more palatable in the political context of the receiving country than others.

Further studies of these phenomena need to take into account how perceptions of homeland politics are not fixed but are subject to change over time, both in the countries of residence and among the migrants themselves. Regarding the former, it seems relevant to explore how recent trends in migrant-incorporation regimes influence the homeland political claims-making of migrants. Broadly speaking, there has been a rupture in current thinking on how to manage migrant incorporation in several northern European countries. For some observers, the concept of multiculturalism has been seriously challenged by the rise of anti-immigrant sentiment and parties in countries such as the Netherlands and Denmark. For others, it is not the general concept that is at fault but a lack of coherent policies to help (especially) second-generation migrants find their feet in their societies of residence. Overall, a strengthened link among national identities, values, and membership has been identified in the policies on and practices of citizenship and migrant incorporation in a range of EU member states (Joppke and Morawska 2003; Brubaker 2001). These convergences of migrant-incorporation policies render the juxtaposition of the exclusive assimilationist Germany versus the inclusive multicultural Holland, mentioned in comparative studies of migrant political transnationalism, less clear cut. It is therefore relevant to further consider whether and how these public policy shifts influence the perceptions of and policies on homeland political and transnational mobilization and practices of migrants.

Alongside the task of identifying how recent trends in migrant incorporation regimes change the perceptions of homeland political engagement of migrants, it is worth noting that some migrant transnational engagement is more welcome than others. Cutting across national contexts, there are, very generally speaking, two quite opposite perceptions of the challenges and opportunities that migrant transnational engagement in homeland politics may offer. On the one hand, there are warnings of the particularist and extremist tendencies within the politicization of migrants and their descendants. Fueled by events such as 9/11 and the London bombings in July 2005, there is a particular focus on political extremism among second-generation Muslims and nationalist diasporas, and there are warnings of the worst-case domestic and international security threat that these groups and their transnational networks may pose (Kaldor, Anheier, and Glasius 2003; Huntington 2004; Leiken 2005b). This type of transnational political orientation is viewed as leading to a fragmentation of the polity in the receiving country and the sustaining of conflict in the country of origin. On the other hand, there is growing recognition of the transnational orientation of migrants and diasporas as a resource. Migrants' transnational networks and practices can work toward development and the democratization of their countries of origin and can constitute an important bridge between their countries of origin and residence (Nyberg-Sørensen, van Hear, and Engberg-Pedersen 2002; de Haas 2006; Østergaard-Nielsen 2007). These two sets of perceptions and their related policies are part of the same picture. European governments and societies are witnessing a concern with how to steer clear of long-distance nationalism or religious extremism and to foster a local and transnational citizenship along more cosmopolitan lines among migrant populations.

By no means are all Turkish- and Kurdish-origin migrants in Europe interested in Turkish politics, and only a fraction translates its interest into active membership in homeland political networks or other forms of political action. Still, the heterogeneous landscape of Turkish and Kurdish transnational networks in Europe means that they have featured in both sets of debates. The more radical and extremist transnational networks are perceived as a security threat, whereas other, more human rights–based and reformist organizations and networks have been noted for their efforts to strengthen civil society and the processes of democratization in Turkey. More generally, the very presence of the sizable number of Turkish citizens or Turkish-origin European citizens within the European Union is recognized as an important feature of Turkish-EU relations.

This chapter has illustrated how the transnational identification and engagement of Turks and Kurds is not just a matter of their long-distance relationship with Turkey but also plays into to their local political incorporation in their countries of residence.

The evaluation of the ways in which homeland political interest intersects with local political participation should not just focus on the scope and intensity of the extent to which Turks or Kurds are still interested in Turkish politics. It is equally relevant to identify the ways in which such homeland political affiliation changes over time and is informed by not only political events in Turkey but also the local and wider international political context. Although some issues and movements have stayed remarkably unchanged over the last decades, most political objectives and forms of mobilization and participation have transformed over time as migrants, refugees, and especially their descendants become more rooted in their local context. In particular, issues such as Turkish-EU relations and the local and international politics of Islam blur the boundaries between migrant and homeland political issues and render a distinction between the local and the transnational more difficult to sustain. Thus, the term *homeland politics* may have become too narrow to capture the transnational identification of (especially) second generation migrants, who may categorize their wider engagement in terms of the wider region, religion, or human rights and democratization.

The case of Turks and Kurds within the European Union demonstrates how transnational political engagement may coexist with political incorporation in the country of residence. Interestingly, recent elections in (especially) Germany indicate that political parties are realizing that their policies toward Turkey are not irrelevant to their growing Turkish-origin political constituencies. Yet they also highlight the boundaries and thresholds for homeland politics within the host-country politics. Across European states, some national gatekeepers still want Turkish migrant associations and political candidates to assimilate politically as migrants and to keep homeland political agendas and practices out of the host-country political system. Migrant associations and political representatives display a complex range of responses, spanning from keeping homeland political issues at bay from lack of interest to a more instrumental and selective inclusion of Turkish politics when it is not in conflict with their local political interests. On the national or local political scene, homeland politics has only partly come out of the closet, and it is still an ambiguous asset in their local political incorporation.

Among the broader lessons learned from the Kurdish and Turkish case is that the understanding of local political incorporation is enriched by including the wider transnational context. Turkish and Kurdish homeland political engagement may be influenced but is not dictated by the political opportunity structures in the country of residence. Homeland political activists may choose other discursive or physical venues for their claims-making and draw on transnational networks and resources. To the extent that migrants, refugees, and sometimes their descendants continue to be mobilized by homeland political issues, they challenge an assimilatory and locally bounded understanding of migrant political incorporation. There is, therefore, an important policy task involved in dealing with the mechanisms of inclusion and exclusion of migrant transnational political engagement in Europe. Alongside this, there is academic work to be done in clarifying overlapping concepts of the local and transnational participation and gathering new and preferably comparative data on how migrants, especially the second generation, negotiate their complex and multilevel transnational political environment.

# CHAPTER FOURTEEN

# Organizing Immigration Interests in the European Union

Constraints and Opportunities for Supranational Migration Regulation and Integration

*Gallya Lahav*

Assuming that immigrant incorporation is affected by host-country reception and policy environments, attitudinal and institutional norms reveal how Europeans reconcile their diverse interests around migration. Moreover, they provide key insights about how democratic societies may accommodate immigrant groups in their midst—a question driving the rationale of this book. In a global era of new security threats, western democracies are increasingly caught between their political and security pressures to protect their borders and their rights-based and global market norms—what has elsewhere been described as "the migration-security-rights trilemma" (Lahav 2005, 1). On the one hand, the realist pursuit of state sovereignty to protect national territory has envisioned more protectionist approaches to migration and border control. On the other hand, global economic imperatives of open markets, trade, and tourism, coupled with societal interests concerning civil liberties, social cohesion, democratic values, and constitutional guarantees, have promoted liberal norms and inclusionary practices. The role of foreigners and ethnic minorities in the terrorist attacks of 9/11, 3/11, and 7/7 have raised further concerns that open economic borders and liberal immigrant policies, the very hallmarks of Europe's "embedded liberalism" (Hollifield 1992; Sassen 1996) are increasingly at odds with the core responsibilities of liberal states and democratic governments to provide security for their citizens and resident foreigners.

Nowhere are these tensions and contradictions more profound than in the European Union, where nation-states have been pressured to reconcile their national impulses of protectionism with communitarian demands for more cooperation. The momentum toward European integration has exposed the incongruities between efforts to control the movement and treatments of people with that of promoting open borders, a free market, and liberal standards. The construction of Europe, in attempting to manage issues such as immigration collectively, brings to the fore the existing diversity of cultures and political traditions in the region, particularly in dealing with concepts that are so close to the core of identity—questions of "us" versus "them" (foreigners).

The drive toward building a common Europe is linked to immigration in two ways: institutionally and attitudinally (Lahav 2004a). First, institution-building and consolidation present all sorts of political contests: between national and supranational forces; between political parties, and between national group actors. These conflicts fundamentally involve how Europe should be organized. They channel and frame the entire immigration debate—already deeply laden with issues of sovereignty. The second component of European integration that influences migration thinking is related to the psychological and normative processes that buttress the construction of any new community: the identification of in-groups and out-groups. The conflict of identifying with one's nation versus with Europe as a whole is indeed real and impacts the politics of inclusion and exclusion. The creation of Europe requires a redrawing of the categories insiders and outsiders (foreigners) that often rests on the expansion of citizenship rights and inclusive norms. This attitudinal component of European integration is particularly sensitive to questions of national identity, citizenship, and immigrant integration.

Given these factors, how may immigration issues be organized in a supranational Europe whose members represent diverse cultural experiences, different ideological convictions, and different party affiliations? Has the construction of Europe reorganized long-standing ideological and national cleavages with regard to perceptions of immigration and ethnic minorities? To what degree has the drive toward European integration opened up new opportunities for managing migration and migrant incorporation? Drawing on broad policy developments and attitudinal norms reflected primarily by members of the European Parliament (MEPs), this chapter provides answers to these questions from a neo-institutional standpoint. It broadly assesses EU responses to these cross-pressures as they relate to both immigration control and immigrant policies in a Europe of changing boundaries.

## Theoretical Overview: Toward a Common and Comprehensive European Union Immigration Policy

Although immigration is traditionally construed as a two-fold dilemma involving questions of intake and challenges of incorporation, each European country has defined the issue and its approach rather differently.[1] The variations in policy approach underscore the multidimensionality of the issue, the diversity of the populations involved, their conditions of access to the host country, their legal status there, and the ensuing rights they have acquired. There are, of course, indelible differences in the perceptions of countries that derive from historical, cultural, economic, and political affinities and from the important privileged relations that each country has with different immigrant groups. National variations in the numbers and compositions of immigrants create diverse domestic interests and contexts (see table 14.1). For the most part, the data reveal attitudinal patterns that derive from national factors such as socioeconomic indicators, immigration experiences (e.g., being traditional receiving or emigration countries), immigrant numbers (especially non-EU foreigners), and public opinion (Lahav 2004b).

**Table 14.1** Foreign and Muslim populations in European Union countries, 1990s

| Country | Total population (in thousands) | Foreign population | | | | Muslims | |
|---|---|---|---|---|---|---|---|
| | | Number (in thousands) | Total percentage | EU foreigners (%) | Non-EU foreigners (%) | Number (in thousands)[a] | Percentage |
| Austria | 8,040 | 728.2 | 9.0 | n.a. | n.a. | 300 | 3.7 |
| Belgium | 10,143 | 910 | 9.0 | 5.5 | 3.6 | 370 | 3.6 |
| Denmark | 5,251 | 223 | 4.3 | 0.9 | 3.3 | 150 | 2.9 |
| Finland | 5,117 | 69 | 1.4 | 0.4 | 1.0 | 20 | 0.40 |
| France[b] | 56,577 | 3,597 | 6.4 | 2.4 | 4.0 | 4,000–5,000 | 8.0 |
| Germany | 81,817 | 7,173 | 8.8 | 2.2 | 6.6 | 3,040 | 3.7 |
| Greece | 10,465 | 155 | 1.5 | 0.4 | 1.0 | 370 | 3.5 |
| Ireland | 3,626 | 117 | 3.2 | 2.0[c] | 1.2[c] | n.a. | n.a. |
| Italy[d] | 54,780 | 1,095.6 | 2.0 | 0.2[c] | 1.8[c] | 700 | 1.23 |
| Luxembourg[e] | 419 | 142.8 | 34.1 | 27.3[c] | 6.8[c] | 38 | 9.0 |
| Netherlands | 15,494 | 726 | 4.7 | 1.2 | 3.5 | 696 | 4.5 |
| Portugal | 9,921 | 169 | 1.7 | 0.4 | 1.3 | 15 | 0.15 |
| Spain | 39,742 | 499 | 1.3 | 0.6 | 0.7 | 300–400 | 0.06 |
| Sweden | 8,837 | 531 | 6.0 | 2.0 | 4.0 | 250–300 | 3.11 |
| United Kingdom | 56,652 | 1,992 | 3.4 | 1.4 | 2.0 | 1,406 | 2.45 |

*Sources*: Eurostat (1999), reporting on 1997 figures, unless noted otherwise; OECD, SOPEMI (1992, 1999).

[a] Maréchal (2002), cited in Buijs and Rath (2002).

[b] OECD (1992), reporting 1990 figures.

[c] Eurostat (1994), reporting 1992 figures.

[d] OECD (1999), reporting 1996 figures.

[e] Eurostat (1999), reporting 1996.

*Note*: OECD and Eurostat data are derived from population registers of foreigners, except for France (from census), Portugal and Spain (from residence permits), and Ireland and the United Kingdom (from the Labour Force Survey). Figures do not add up to totals due to the differences in reports. n.a., no data available.

The nature of the immigration debate has become more complicated at the EU level because it reflects and magnifies the problems that each nation has internally confronted in regards to the issue (Lahav 2004a). The problem at the EU level is about the harmonization of national trends and the reorganization of political contestation. With the completion of the single market, citizens of any of today's twenty-seven member countries are no longer foreigners in the other twenty-six. Formulating a common policy involves deciding which outsiders require visas to enter the European Union and ensuring that illegal immigrants, drug traffickers, smugglers, and terrorists do not profit from the elimination of borders. It also raises traditional concerns about social welfare policies, citizenship rules and rights, integration strategies, asylum histories, and race relations—issues particularly subject to national and partisan ideological sensibilities and resistant to supranational delegation (Lavenex and Wallace 2005; Geddes 2000). Indeed, developments at the EU level have been suggestive of the controversies and limitations that remain concerning institutional dilemmas about transferring powers and implementation strategies from the intergovernmental pillar (the Justice and Home Affairs, JHA, Council) to the supranational communitarian level.

Notwithstanding, since the 1990s, the pressures for systematic collaboration on issues of immigration and asylum have been inescapable. By the turn of the twenty-first century, there were reasons to expect the emergence of a European immigration regime.[2] Several signs of convergence suggested possibilities for harmonization and cooperation at the EU level. First, global structural changes blurred the lines between the traditional immigration countries and emigration countries of southern Europe (Lahav 2004a, 144) Convergence among European countries has also been driven by international learning (Weil and Crowley 1994), a reluctant acceptance of policy limitations at the national level (Butt Philip 1994), a narrowing in the range of treatment of populations (Heisler 1992), and the force of European integration (Schnapper 1994; Lavenex and Uçarer 2002).

Second, European national debates exposed elusive differences among mainstream political parties. Domestic politics revealed that partisan lines were increasingly blurred, obscuring ideological differences (Schain 1988; Freeman 1979; Messina 1989; Simon 1989). Major immigration policy reforms granting (and restricting) rights to foreigners became associated as much with right-wing coalitions as with left-wing governments (Hammar 1985; Guiraudon 2002). The growing tendency of immigration politics to straddle the ordinary liberal-conservative divide had created "strange bedfellow" coalitions on reforms (Zolberg 2000) and party dealignments—making it possible to envision ideological consensus and the conflation of the two-dimensional space of migration (Money 1995).

Third, the salience and consolidation of new security issues such as terrorism, ethnic conflict, and migration on the post–Cold War agenda (Wæver et al. 1993) shifted migration-related issues from the predominantly technical domain of low politics (i.e., economic and social questions) to what international relations scholars refer to as high politics (i.e., issues pertaining to political and national integrity and security) (Koslowski 2001; Huysmans 1994). Within the context of the European Union, the securitization of immigration suggested that political elites could be more motivated than previously to escape to Europe in an effort to resolve domestic immigration-related dilemmas and to expand their capabilities (Lavenex and Uçarer 2002; Bigo 2001; Guiraudon 2003; Lahav and Messina 2005). The securitization of migration after 9/11 further blurred EU boundaries between internal and external threats (Bigo 2001), elevated immigration to the status of a "meta-issue" (Faist 2002, 11), and gave more impetus to European cooperation on immigration.

Certainly, the intense interest in transferring immigration policy to the EU level has been based on the assumption that whatever divisions existed earlier in the 1990s could be politically surmountable. Several policy developments since the Amsterdam Treaty and Tampere Council resolutions (in 1999) have reflected converging norms in that direction. The expanding jurisdiction of EU institutions over policy on immigration, asylum, refugees, and border security have placed a critical emphasis on finding common approaches to immigration management (for more detailed institutional analyses, see Guild and Harlow 2001; Lavenex and Wallace 2005; Geddes 2003; Guiraudon 2003). The transfer of immigration from the first to the third pillar of the European Community, as mandated by Title IV of the Amsterdam Treaty, significantly advanced the emergence of a common immigration policy. With the ratification of the Amsterdam Treaty in 1999, matters relating to "asylum, visas, immigration and controls at external borders" were brought under European Community procedures during a five-year transitional period, which commenced in May 2004.[3] The proliferation of European initiatives since (e.g., Nice and Seville) represented serious interest in cooperation among the EU member states, limited by a growing—but uneven—harmonization in the migration field.

Against the backdrop of increasing Europeanization and securitization of migration, how far can the EU member states go in pursuing a common approach that balances national security interests with immigrant integration and civil rights for the ethnically diverse populations of Europe? On balance, what can institutional and attitudinal developments in the European Union tell us about European norms regarding immigration and immigrant minorities? The following section examines empirical developments at the EU level and assesses substantive implications for immigration regulation and immigrant integration.

## Empirical Developments

### Institutional and Policy Cooperation

Migration questions have loomed large in European politics in response to changing borders of the European Union, and they have been caught in institutional conflicts that remain between the proponents of intergovernmental (state-centric) and supranational (communitarian) decision making (Lavenex and Wallace 2005). Although many such policies have been particularly sensitive to national impulses, the momentum toward European integration has increased the demand for EU competence in areas such as migration (Geddes 2000; Guiraudon 2003; Lahav 2004a) and security (Walker 2004).

To a large degree, the 9/11 attacks merely provided the necessary political impetus for European policymakers to address some of these long-standing concerns.

Referring to 9/11 events as "an assault on our open, democratic and multicultural societies," the member states of the European Union joined their transatlantic partners in calling for cooperation (Council of Europe 2001, 1). Acting with unprecedented speed, the European Council met in an extraordinary session on September 20–21, 2001, and adopted a detailed and ambitious plan of action to combat terrorism, based on a "coordinated and comprehensive approach" that fundamentally included migration regulation (Council of Europe, 2001 1; see also, Pastore 2005).[4] Central to the European response to the catastrophic events of 9/11 was the seemingly hasty strategy formulated by the JHA Council that September "to harness all the measures already adopted at the EU level...." and "to speed up the process of creating an area of freedom, security and justice...." (JHA Council, doc. 12156/01, 1).

Although the comprehensive approach to migration control became urgent after 2001, it is important to place these developments in the historical context of European integration efforts. The pursuit of "a balanced and comprehensive approach" to include migration control was rooted in earlier efforts (going back to the 1970s) such as the TREVI group, when migration was related to the fight against terrorism, human trafficking, drug smuggling, and organized crime. Although the 1992 Maastricht Treaty included an agreement to cooperate on migration and asylum, the 1999 Tampere Council was first to place a common migration and asylum policy on the top of the political and security agenda. These initiatives toward a comprehensive approach were institutionalized after the adoption of the Amsterdam Treaty, which cut across the first and third pillars of the European Union to establish a coherent program for EU action in law enforcement and judicial cooperation. With the formal creation of an "area of freedom, security and justice," (AFSJ) launched by the 1997 Amsterdam Treaty, these issues were carefully distributed across the three pillars of the European Union. Thus, the relationship between national sovereignty and EU competence entered a new phase with sensitive areas such as asylum and policing shifting from exclusively national competence to common legally binding EU law and policy. As part of the comprehensive strategy, the Tampere presidency Conclusions (1999) further established benchmarks that would lead to the culmination of the EU Charter of Fundamental Rights (Uçarer 2003, 306).

Despite its roots in intergovernmental security communities (such as the TREVI group), the pursuit of the comprehensive approach advocated by Tampere and embraced more intently after 9/11 exhibits several important novelties. The Tampere agenda was original in its focus on both the root causes of migration and the development of a European Neighborhood Policy (ENP), thereby externalizing migration as well. The search for a comprehensive approach put a premium on policies that would include both external and internal control strategies (including immigrant integration). In this way, a comprehensive policy approach significantly conflated two dimensions of the immigration equation: immigration control and immigrant strategies. That is, the momentum toward a common immigration policy at the EU level, although growing, upset the well-balanced equilibrium that had existed between the traditionally discreet components of immigration policy until the early 1990s, when the epistemic communities of immigration policy and immigrant policies were more separate (Hammar 1985; Sassen 1996; Lahav, Messina, and Vasquez 2007).

Clearly, a changing equilibrium was evident before 2001, but it has been increasingly manifest in institutional reforms to streamline and consolidate what were once separate axioms of the migration equation. The most radical institutional changes in that direction were captured by the formalization of an AFSJ that would pursue a comprehensive approach along those three principles. The Treaty of Amsterdam laid out the EU objective of a vast area of justice and home affairs (AFSJ) "to provide citizens with a high level of safety within an area of freedom, security and justice by developing common action among the member-states in the field of police, judicial cooperation and criminal matters *and* by preventing and combating racism and xenophobia" (Article K.1, Amsterdam Treaty signed on 2 October 1997). In this way, the European Union institutionalized its comprehensive approach based on the articulation of the three concepts seen to be central to civil liberties and the protection of vulnerable members of the community.

The creation of an AFSJ under a loose singular body reflected serious efforts to institutionalize a comprehensive approach to migration cooperation by including all aspects of immigration and immigrant policies. These led to the development of a common response to immigration and asylum seekers, the joint management of external borders, increasing coordination of national police forces in the fight against crime, the harmonization of national criminal and civil law, the creation of specialized EU bodies such as Europol and Eurojust and, most important, an issue that is one of the major concerns of the citizens of the European Union—security.

The new treaty also shifted some national-laden models of immigrant integration to the EU level (Geddes and Guiraudon 2004). Article 13 of the new treaty granted the European Community new powers to combat discrimination on the grounds of sex, racial or ethnic origin, religion or belief, disability, age, and sexual orientation. Among the new European Community laws or directives enacted in the area of antidiscrimination since the Treaty of Amsterdam and that came into force in 1999 are the Racial Equality Directive (2000/43/EC) and the Employment Equality Directive (2000/78/EC). Council Directive 2000/43/EC implements the principle of equal treatment between individuals irrespective of racial or ethnic origin, and Council Directive 2000/78/EC establishes a general framework for equal treatment in employment and occupation.

The transfer of such issues, long entrenched in national political and juridical systems and intrinsically imbued with state sovereignty, under a common EC/EU treaty has been heralded as one of the most revolutionary changes since the launching of the Single Market program (Monar 2005; Walker 2001–2002). Since 1999, the JHA Council has been the fastest-growing policy area in the European Union (Walker 2004). This remarkable expansion includes the adoption of well over two hundred legislative measures, involving nearly forty bodies, and the proliferation of meetings from four times per year to every month. The Secretariat of the European Council itself reportedly dedicates roughly 40 percent of its meetings and workload directly or indirectly to matters related to the AFSJ (Monar 2005). Justice, freedom, and security policies have witnessed an almost threefold increase in spending, from around 0.5 percent in 2006 to a projected 1.3 percent in 2013, forecast in the "2007–2013 Financial Framework for the EU" adopted in April 2005 by the College of Commissioners (European Commission 2004c; see also Vandermosten 2006).[5]

Although these sweeping developments may seem exaggerated to some, there is no doubt that they are most dramatic in the sense that the JHA Council has moved the European Union on a massive scale into areas that had for decades remained an essential preserve of national sovereignty. The Hague Program (adopted in November 2004) set a new five-year plan to strengthen the AFSJ further. It also committed the JHA Council to share more competence with the other European institutions, such as the Commission (Uçarer 2001), the Parliament, and the European Court of Justice (ECJ).[6] Most important, although The Hague Program emphasized the threat of terrorism at the same time that it noted the prominence of migration, it notably launched migrant integration issues on the agenda. Rather than seeking merely fair treatment of foreigners, the program called for their full integration as members of European society and outlined eleven Common Basic Principles for Immigrant Integration Policies to those ends (van Selm 2005).

Nonetheless, the enormous strides on questions of immigration control (e.g., policing, Europol; the Schengen Information System, SIS, for information exchange; foreign policy and judiciary cooperation; and migration and asylum regulation) overshadow the limited progress in harmonization of immigrant policies. Despite some notable efforts to place migrant integration concerns on the EU agenda (e.g., European Commission 2003a, 2004a), these initiatives have been far more controversial and rhetorical.[7]

The security logic of a comprehensive approach has tended to favor external security policies over internal policies of integration, such as labor policies, social welfare systems, religious practices, and civic rights (Chebel D'Appollinia 2007, 224). Even when EU institutions are focusing on internal policies, security dimensions dominate the policy logic. These include increased identity checks, more stringent conditions for issuing residence and work permits, new automated systems for the registration of foreigners, reduction of categories of individuals who may not be deported, closer monitoring of foreigner accommodations, limiting of rights of appeal, broadening of the category of potential deportees, and tougher penalties for assisting the illegal migration and employment of foreigners. These security biases are exemplified by the most recent return directive passed by JHA ministers and adopted by the European Parliament concerning the incarceration and banning of undocumented migrants from eighteen months to five years (European Parliament 2008). This legislation, which is a step toward a European immigration policy aims to encourage the voluntary return of illegal immigrants but otherwise lays down minimum standards for their treatment.

Although the European Union has been fiercely trying to coordinate the efforts of national governments by launching strategies against poverty, discrimination, and social exclusion, progress has been slow. Notably, whereas immigration and asylum policies are increasingly yielding to a common and coordinated EU framework, integration policies still largely remain outside of EU competence (particularly, that of the Commission). Although the development of a comprehensive migration policy has been increasingly institutionalized at the EU level, the persistence of divergent interests on immigrant integration, in fact, may fit closer with the intergovernmental types of cooperation that have prevailed up to now (Geddes 2003). As the next section shows, although broad policy developments on the ground reinforce trends toward policy harmonization at the EU level, attitudinal norms reflect important national and ideological impediments to a comprehensive approach, particularly with regard to immigrant integration policies.

## Attitudinal Developments: Toward Cooperation?

The policy developments already discussed compel us to examine attitudinal patterns along the two distinct immigration dimensions (intake and integration) of immigration regulation in the European Union. Given the changing policy environment, what do underlying attitudinal patterns and cleavages reveal about the prospects for migration cooperation and migrant integration in the Europe?

The evolution and impact of multilevel political interests in the European Union can be discerned by gauging attitudes of MEPs, European elites, who, in addition to holding distinct national loyalties, represent different party affinities, political cultures, and immigration experiences.[8] Given the expansive role of the European Parliament as a significant policy actor, with acquired policy competence over immigration and asylum-related issues since 2004, the attitudes of these decision makers provide an important cross-cultural, cross-ideological measure of European elite thinking. Furthermore, given that the European Parliament is the only supranational institution directly elected by the peoples of Europe, how decision makers organize and reconcile their diverse interests on the immigration front may tell us much about the nature of an integrated Europe at the beginning of the twenty-first century. Comparing original survey data on MEPs from 1992 to 2004, we can test some assumptions about the European Union as an opportunity structure for migration regulation.

Broadly speaking, longitudinal data on MEP perceptions of immigration resonate with that of public opinion (Lahav 2004a, 2004b). They reveal considerable attitudinal accord on broad policy goals such as European integration and common immigration rules. By the 1990s, European publics (over 70 percent) and MEPs (90 percent) were in very strong agreement with the notion that EU member states should follow common rules in matters of immigration. Both the public and elites across party and country lines agreed (1) that immigration problems were greater then ever before, (2) that immigration was one of the most controversial issues on the political agendas, and (3) that they wanted immigration controlled. They were also highly pessimistic about the future resolution of the issue.

This general consensus broke down, however, on the particulars (Lahav and Messina 2005). Attitudes toward institutional competence over such a common immigration policy as well as control over immigrants' status were rather polarized. The broad attitudinal agreements that emerged hid the fact that there were also significant divisions that remained among and between the elites and the public with regard to issues of immigrant integration. They differed in terms of the definitions of the problems, their preferences for immigration levels and privileged immigrant groups, and the structure and content of a common immigration policy. They also fundamentally diverged with regard to issues of immigrant rights (see Lahav 2004b for an overview). In line with the institutional and policy developments already noted, substantial convergence—even if uneven—has occurred, signaling potential movement toward migration cooperation in some cases (but notably absent in others).

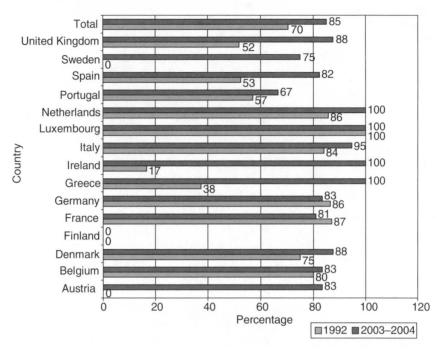

**Figure 14.1** MEP opinion by country on the importance of the immigration issue, 1992 and 2003–2004 (%). Based on the respondents who answered the question "How important do you think the immigration issue is in your country?" that this issue is "Important" or "Very important." N = 166 (1992); N = 147 (2003–2004). MEP, member of the European Parliament.

Among the great changes affecting immigration attitudes over time, the growing salience of immigration issues across Europe suggests a growing convergence over policy options. Indeed, there is little doubt that the MEPs, like the European public, view immigration-related issues as more salient in the current decade than in the previous one. As might have been reasonably anticipated in the light of the dramatic changes in the international and regional security environment since 9/11, the data represented in figures 14.1 and 14.2 reveal a significantly greater number (15 percent) of MEPs in 2004 identifying the issue of immigration as "very important" than did previously. As figures 14.1 and 14.2 also indicate, beneath the surface of this change in aggregate opinion are important differences in the distribution and continuity of MEP attitudes among the twelve original national delegations. Specifically, whereas the percentage of MEPs that identified the issue of immigration as "very important" remained relatively constant in Belgium, France, Germany, and Luxembourg between 1992 and 2004, the percentage endorsing this perspective changed rather significantly (i.e., between 10 and 83 percent) in Denmark, Greece, Ireland, Italy, the Netherlands, Portugal, Spain, and the United Kingdom. In every instance of significant change, MEP opinion shifted in a uniform direction—toward endorsing the view that immigration is a very salient issue (Lahav and Messina 2005).

The increase in concern about immigration among MEPs was especially great in the newer immigration countries of southern Europe and Ireland, which have witnessed

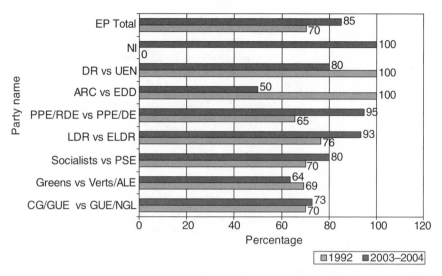

**Figure 14.2** MEP opinion by party on the importance of the immigration issue, 1992 and 2003–2004 (%). Based on the respondents across their party identification who answered the question "How important do you think the immigration issue is to your party?" that this issue is "Important" or "Very important." N = 164 (1992); N = 143 (2003–2004). ARC, Rainbow Group; CG/GUE, Left Unity–European United Left; DR, European Right; EDD, Europe of Democracies and Diversities; ELDR, European Liberal Democrat and Reform Party; EP, European Parliament; GUE/NGL, European United Left–Nordic Green Left; LDR, European Liberal Democrats; MEP, member of the European Parliament; NI, Non-Inscrits; PPE/DE, European People's Party–European Democrats; PPE/RDE, European People's Party–Republican Conservatives; PSE, Party of European Socialists; UEN, Union for Europe of the Nations; Verts/ALE, Group of the Greens–European Free Alliance.

not only higher rates of immigration during the past decade but a growing politicization of this issue, a trend that has further blurred the lines between the traditional countries of immigration (e.g., France, the United Kingdom, the Netherlands, and Belgium) and those of emigration (Lahav 2004a). Indeed, by 2004 only 3 percent of MEPs embraced the view that immigration was "not important," and among the MEPs within this small group, all derived from only four national delegations (Belgium, Finland, Portugal, and Spain).

These attitudinal shifts did not translate into any significant increase in support for restrictive immigration policies. Somewhat surprisingly, an upsurge in restrictive preferences did not, in the aggregate, manifest itself in the 2004 survey (Lahav and Messina 2005). As tables 14.2 and 14.3 illustrate, MEP opinions on the question of immigration restrictions changed relatively little between 1992 and 2004 because the percentages of parliamentarians who favored each of three respective options—increasing immigration, keeping immigration at current levels, and decreasing immigration—remained virtually constant over the period. Even so, the continuity in aggregate opinion masked important shifts in national and ideological preferences.[9] Thus, it is worth noting that, although there were some changes in preferences of immigration levels (and even in the unexpected direction), elite attitudes remain fairly constant (even if polarized) between 1992 and 2004. Approximately one-quarter of

**Table 14.2** MEP opinion by country on immigration restrictions, 1992 and 2003–2004 (%)

| Country | Increased | | Kept at present level | | Decreased | | Net change in "decreased" answers |
|---|---|---|---|---|---|---|---|
| | [1] 1992 | [2] 2003–2004 | [3] 1992 | [4] 2003–2004 | [5] 1992 | [6] 2003–2004 | ([6] − [5]) |
| Austria | n.a. | 25 | n.a. | 0 | n.a. | 75 | n.a. |
| Belgium | 11 | 25 | 56 | 75 | 33 | 0 | −33 |
| Denmark | 0 | 25 | 33 | 63 | 67 | 13 | −54 |
| Finland | n.a. | 50 | n.a. | 50 | n.a. | 0 | n.a. |
| France | 16 | 15 | 47 | 54 | 37 | 31 | −6 |
| Germany | 41 | 17 | 26 | 50 | 35 | 32 | −2 |
| Greece | 43 | 25 | 14 | 50 | 43 | 25 | −18 |
| Ireland | 0 | 0 | 83 | 67 | 17 | 33 | +17 |
| Italy | 32 | 40 | 45 | 47 | 23 | 13 | −10 |
| Luxembourg | 0 | 0 | 100 | 100 | 0 | 0 | 0 |
| Netherlands | 16 | 0 | 62 | 80 | 23 | 20 | −3 |
| Portugal | 17 | 0 | 83 | 100 | 0 | 0 | 0 |
| Spain | 44 | 46 | 44 | 54 | 11 | 0 | −11 |
| Sweden | n.a. | 50 | n.a. | 0 | n.a. | 50 | n.a. |
| United Kingdom | 15 | 7 | 75 | 57 | 10 | 36 | +26 |
| Total | 25 | 23 | 51 | 56 | 24 | 21 | −3 |

*Notes:* N = 167 (1992); N = 148 (2003–2004). Based on the question, "Should immigration in general be kept at its present level, increased, or decreased?" MEP, member of the European Parliament; n.a., no data available.

**Table 14.3** MEP opinion on immigration restrictions, by party, 1992 and 2003–2004

| Party[a] | Increase | | Decrease | | Net change in "decrease" answers |
|---|---|---|---|---|---|
| | [1] 1992 | [2] 2003–2004 | [3] 1992 | [4] 2003–2004 | ([4] − [3]) |
| CG/GUE vs. GUE/NGL | 60 | 71 | 0 | 0 | 0 |
| Greens vs. Verts/ALE | 60 | 57 | 10 | 0 | −10 |
| Socialists vs. PSE | 30 | 21 | 14 | 7 | −7 |
| LDR vs. ELDR | 21 | 8 | 29 | 15 | −14 |
| PPE/RDE vs. PPE/DE | 8 | 15 | 33 | 29 | −4 |
| EP average (all parties) | 24 | 22 | 24 | 21 | −3 |

*Notes:* N = 141 (1992); N = 108 (2003). Total does not equal 100% due to those who responded "Keep immigration at present level." CG/GUE, Left Unity–European United Left; ELDR, European Liberal Democrat and Reform Party; EP, European Parliament; GUE/NGL, European United Left–Nordic Green Left; LDR, European Liberal Democrats; MEP, member of the European Parliament; PPE/DE, European People's Party–European Democrats; PPE/RDE, European People's Party–Republican Conservatives; PSE, Party of European Socialists; Verts/ALE, Group of the Greens–European Free Alliance.
[a] 1992 party vs. 2003–2004 party.

MEPs was in favor of increasing immigration restrictions, one-quarter was against, and more than one-half was in favor of maintaining the status quo.

In light of the significant spike in the percentage of MEPs perceiving immigration to be a very important issue and the deterioration of the international security environment since 1992, we might have expected a higher percentage in 2004 favoring a

**Table 14.4** MEP identification of immigration problems and their linkage with other policy areas, 1992 and 2003–2004 (%)

| Issue linkages | 1992 | 2003–2004 |
|---|---|---|
| Integration | 35 | 47 |
| Citizenship | 4 | 12 |
| Race relations | 25 | 10 |
| Social welfare | 7 | 8 |
| Unemployment | 12 | 8 |
| Other | 15 | 8 |
| Crime | 1 | 7 |
| Education | 1 | 1 |
| Drug trafficking | 0 | 0 |

*Notes:* N = 167 (1993); N = 148 (2004). Responses to the question, "When you think of immigration problems, to which other area do you relate them *first*?" MEP, member of the European Parliament.

decrease in the overall levels of immigration. Instead, an increasing majority of MEPs (56 percent) supported the maintenance of current levels of immigration, suggesting that the debate over immigration intake may be more amenable to cooperation.

The relative satisfaction with immigration intake levels, despite the growing salience of the issue may be explained by issue linkage. As in 1992, and somewhat surprising given the post-9/11 climate, immigration issues did not seem to be linked to security and foreign policy in the minds of European parliamentarians. Instead, large pluralities of MEPs continued to link immigration with problems of immigrant integration or race relations in 2004, much as they did in 1992 In fact, when offered a choice of nine possible responses, almost one-half of all MEPs cited one issue, immigrant "integration," as the *first* area with which they linked immigration-related problems in 2004 (see table 14.4). The association of migration with integration concerns has prevailed over time, but it has increased significantly since the early 1990s.

The increasing proclivity to view the migration threat as a phenomenon associated to migrant integration and multiculturalism in Europe contrasts sharply with the case of the United States, which has tended to view immigration-related questions through the prism of physical security and border control (Lahav forthcoming). For the most part, the order-disrupting changes within Europe stem from the challenge of incorporating the predominantly nonwhite, non-Western, and often non-Christian immigrant populations into the white and nominally Christian societies of Western Europe (Heisler 2001). References to "immigration problems" in Europe are often synonymous with the problem of unskilled, non-Christian, nonwhite migrants or asylum seekers from the third world (Lahav 2004a, 115). These predilections are manifest in public opinion as well. Immigration in Europe has been popularly framed as a phenomenon that imperils the quality of life (Alexseev 2005, 66–67; Huysmans 2000, 752); Tsoulaka 2005). As Sjef Ederveen and colleagues (2004, 82) have demonstrated, more than one-half of all respondents in nineteen EU countries view ethnic minorities as posing some level of cultural and economic threat (see also Lahav, Messina, and Vasquez 2007).[10]

These preoccupations with immigrant and minority integration may explain why EU policymaking related to migration and security showed a more serious upsurge in the post-2004 period than following September 11, 2001. The murder of Theo van Gogh, Dutch filmmaker, by an Islamic extremist on November 2, 2004 was shocking to those who considered that his murderer had actually been born and raised in the Netherlands (and held dual Dutch and Moroccan nationality). The Madrid train bombings on March 11, 2004, and the July 7, 2005, bombings of the London Underground indeed fomented the perception that Islam was a threat to the European social and political system.

Given the central role of immigrant integration concerns in a new security order, what are the prospects for immigrant integration and rights? According to the longitudinal MEP data, support for the extension of immigrant rights declined and the restriction of immigrant rights increased over the decade. A large majority of traditionally socially conscious, MEPs continued to support the extension of immigrant rights (63 percent), but this proportion declined dramatically from the previous decade (from 77 percent in 1992). Conversely, whereas in 1992 only 4 percent of MEPs expressed the sentiment that immigrant rights should actually be restricted (nearly all of them from the European Right (DR), a radical right party), a decade later, despite the absence of the DR party, this figure had more than tripled to 13 percent and included members from all parties (see table 14.5).

Nevertheless, the percentage of those advocating maintaining the status quo increased from 1993 to 2004, a shift that may be explained in part by the objective expansion of immigrant rights in the period between our two surveys (Niessen, Peiro,

**Table 14.5** MEP opinion regarding immigrant rights, by party group, 1992 and 2003–2004 (%)

| Party[a] | Extended | | Leave | | Restrict | | Net change to "extended" answers |
|---|---|---|---|---|---|---|---|
| | [1] 1992 | [2] 2003–2004 | [3] 1992 | [4] 2003–2004 | [5] 1992 | [6] 2003–2004 | ([2] − [1]) |
| CG/GUE vs. GUE/NGL | 90 | 100 | 10 | 0 | 0 | 0 | 10 |
| Greens vs. Verts/ALE | 100 | 91 | 0 | 9 | 0 | 0 | −9 |
| Socialists vs. PSE | 97 | 82 | 3 | 13 | 0 | 5 | −15 |
| LDR vs. ELDR | 60 | 46 | 33 | 38 | 7 | 15 | −24 |
| PPE/RDE vs. PPE/DE | 62 | 42 | 37 | 38 | 2 | 19 | −20 |
| ARC vs. EDD | 67 | 25 | 33 | 50 | 0 | 25 | −42 |
| DR vs. UEN | 0 | 80 | 33 | 0 | 67 | 20 | 80 |
| NI | 0 | 25 | 100 | 25 | 0 | 50 | 25 |
| EP total | 77 | 63 | 19 | 24 | 4 | 13 | −14 |

*Notes:* N = 159 (for 1992); N = 139 (2003–2004). Responses to the question, "What should be done about the rights of immigrants?" ARC, Rainbow Group; CG/GUE, Left Unity–European United Left; DR, European Right; EDD, Europe of Democracies and Diversities; ELDR, European Liberal Democrat and Reform Party; EP, European Parliament; GUE/NGL, European United Left–Nordic Green Left; LDR, European Liberal Democrats; MEP, member of the European Parliament; NI, Non-Inscrits; PPE/DE, European People's Party–European Democrats; PPE/RDE, European People's Party–Republican Conservatives; PSE, Party of European Socialists; UEN, Union for Europe of the Nations; Verts/ALE, Group of the Greens–European Free Alliance.

[a] 1992 party vs. 2003–2004 party.

and Schibel 2005). If so, part of the drop-off in the percentage of MEPs supporting the extension of immigrant rights may have been driven by the perception that
immigrant rights were already at historically high levels in 2004 and, thus, did not
require further expansion (Lahav, Messina, and Vasquez 2007). More important, the
widening distribution of opinion on whether to increase or decrease rights among
MEPs signaled an increase in issue polarization among elites (see table 14.8, later in
the chapter). Furthermore, although the ideological differences remained in the same
direction, the polarizations became more intense, as indicated by the increasing ideological distance (a mean of 3.71 vs. 6) between the left and right.

Broadly speaking, the salience of migrant integration issues in Europe has generated mixed results for policies related to immigrant rights. For example, in the most
positive cases the emphasis on migrant integration has induced governments and
politicians to reconsider how Islam may become a European religion (Klausen 2006).
In this vein, although French President Jacques Chirac enjoyed an overwhelming
political victory in the National Assembly for his proposed law prohibiting Muslim
headscarves in schools, ironically one of the sole opponents against the bill came
from Jean-Marie Le Pen, a member of the anti-immigrant Front National, who feared
subsequent restrictions on Christians (Klausen 2005, 1).

The trends toward EU harmonization hide some important disagreements and ambivalence that exist and, in some cases, have intensified over the decade (even beyond
numbers and rights of immigrants). It explains why, despite notable distribution
of attitudes toward institutional competence, as regional integration proceeds, there
is more inclination to delegate immigration regulation to national oversight than
before (see Lahav and Messina 2005); see tables 14.6 and 14.7. The unexpected shift
of MEP opinion (12 percent) over time in favor of placing immigration regulation
in the hands of national governments perhaps signals the greater responsiveness of
governments to their respective national electorates. Clearly, many of these electorates have indicated their ambivalence toward EU competence over migration policy
(Commission of the European Conmmunities, Eurobarometers numbers 45–50). As
tables 14.6 and 14.7 reveal, partisan/ideological differences among MEPs also continue to prevail despite growing support for a common immigration policy.

Finally, although across the board, there seems to be a more restrictionist impulse
towards immigrant rights, political divisions also continue to distinguish opinion in
this policy area and in the ideological order found previously. Consistent with previous results, one of the largest polarizations found on immigration attitudes emerged
with regards to policies on incorporation and immigrant rights (table 14.8).

## Conclusion: Some Comparative Perspectives

This chapter provides a broad neo-institutional portrait of national and ideological
factors underlying immigration policy developments within the European Union.
The empirical data presented here provides a standpoint from which to evaluate
the nature of political contention about immigration in an emergent supranational
space. Assuming that attitudinal and policy developments provide a paradigm for the
broader political context of norms governing immigrant integration strategies, does

**Table 14.6** MEP opinion by country on where the responsibility for regulating immigration policy should reside, 1992 and 2003–2004 (%)

| Country | National governments | | EU, with member-state veto option | | EU institutions on the basis of majority vote | | Net change in "national governments" answers ([2] − [1]) |
|---|---|---|---|---|---|---|---|
| | [1] 1992 | [2] 2003–2004 | [3] 1992 | [4] 2003–2004 | [5] 1992 | [6] 2003–2004 | |
| Austria | n.a. | 33 | n.a. | 17 | n.a. | 50 | n.a. |
| Belgium | 10 | 33 | 20 | 0 | 70 | 67 | 23 |
| Denmark | 25 | 75 | 50 | 13 | 25 | 13 | 50 |
| Finland | n.a. | 50 | n.a. | 0 | n.a. | 50 | n.a. |
| France | 29 | 45 | 33 | 30 | 38 | 25 | 16 |
| Germany | 43 | 41 | 24 | 29 | 33 | 29 | −2 |
| Greece | 13 | 25 | 50 | 25 | 38 | 50 | 13 |
| Ireland | 0 | 33 | 50 | 0 | 50 | 67 | 33 |
| Italy | 20 | 21 | 16 | 21 | 64 | 58 | 1 |
| Luxembourg | 33 | 33 | 67 | 67 | 0 | 0 | 0 |
| Netherlands | 31 | 20 | 31 | 40 | 38 | 40 | −11 |
| Portugal | 29 | 67 | 57 | 0 | 14 | 33 | 38 |
| Spain | 16 | 6 | 47 | 19 | 37 | 75 | −10 |
| Sweden | n.a. | 25 | n.a. | 50 | n.a. | 25 | n.a. |
| United Kingdom | 46 | 64 | 21 | 18 | 33 | 18 | 18 |
| Unknown | n.a. | 0 | n.a. | 100 | n.a. | 0 | n.a. |
| Total | 27 | 39 | 31 | 21 | 42 | 40 | 12 |

*Notes:* N = 158 (1992); N = 142 (2003–2004). Based on responses to the question, "Who should be responsible for regulating immigration policy?" EU, European Union; MEP, member of the European Parliament; n.a., no data available.

**Table 14.7** MEP opinion by party on where the responsibility for regulating immigration policy should reside, 1992 and 2003–2004 (%)

| European Party Group[a] | National governments | | EU, with member-state veto option | | EU institutions on the basis of majority vote | | Net change in "national governments" answers ([2] − [1]) |
|---|---|---|---|---|---|---|---|
| | [1] 1992 | [2] 2003–2004 | [3] 1992 | [4] 2003–2004 | [5] 1992 | [6] 2003–2004 | |
| PPE/RDE vs. PPE/DE | 22 | 48 | 43 | 26 | 35 | 26 | 26 |
| LDR vs. ELDR | 29 | 29 | 35 | 14 | 35 | 57 | 0 |
| Socialists vs. PSE | 32 | 26 | 26 | 28 | 42 | 46 | −6 |
| Greens vs. Verts/ALE | 8 | 18 | 17 | 9 | 75 | 73 | 10 |
| CG/GUE vs. GUE/NGL | 0 | 30 | 30 | 30 | 70 | 40 | 30 |
| All party groups | 27 | 39 | 32 | 22 | 41 | 39 | 12 |

*Notes:* N = 140 (1992); N = 118 (2003–2004). Responses to the question, "Who should be responsible for regulating immigration policy?" CG/GUE, Left Unity–European United Left; ELDR, European Liberal Democrat and Reform Party; GUE/NGL, European United Left–Nordic Green Left; MEP, member of the European Parliament; LDR, European Liberal Democrats; PPE/DE, European People's Party–European Democrats; PPE/RDE, European People's Party–Republican Conservatives; PSE, Party of European Socialists; Verts/ALE, Group of the Greens–European Free Alliance.
[a] 1992 party vs. 2003–2004 party.

**Table 14.8** Ideological means of MEP policy positions, 1992 and 2004

|  |  | 1992 | 2004 |
|---|---|---|---|
| Should immigration levels increase or decrease? | Increase | 3.47 | 3.18 |
|  | Decrease | 5.24 | 5.61 |
| Common immigration policy | Disagree | 4.16 | 5.46 |
|  | Agree | 5.17 | 4.39 |
| Who should regulate immigration? | National governments | 5.03 | 5.08 |
|  | EU | 4.22 | 4.08 |
| Should immigration rights be extended or restricted? | Extended | 3.84 | 3.71 |
|  | Restricted | 5.9 | 6 |

*Sources:* Lahav (1992); Lahav and Messina (2005).

*Notes:* Values are means of ideological self-placement, based on a scale of 1–9, where 1 refers to the extreme left, and 9 represents the extreme right. N = 167 (1992); N = 148 (2004). EU, European Union; MEP, member of the European Parliament.

the European Union represent an opportunity structure or constraint for the management of immigration and immigrant incorporation?

The surprising obstacles to cooperation noted in this chapter reflect important schisms that remain with regard to immigration and immigrant regulation, and that also inform the EU comprehensive approach to migration management, embodied in the AFSJ. Although my conclusions here remain tentative, given the sample size of elites and the limited statistical testing possible, the attitudinal data are suggestive of uneven prospects for policy cooperation, especially in the area of immigrant rights, strategies of integration, and institutional authority.

Despite substantial movement to Europeanize migration and to adopt a comprehensive approach based on the intersection of security, freedoms, and liberties, there are a number of anomalies and attitudinal divisions worthy of note. On the one hand, the data show increasing agreement among elites (and the public) regarding the salience of immigration; in 2004, MEPs were nearly unanimous that immigration is a "very important" issue. They also continued to seek a common immigration policy. On the other hand, consensus on this question masked important divisions on other dimensions, polarizations that, in some cases, have become more entrenched even as Europe moves ever closer to a common immigration policy. Most surprising in this was the shift since 1992 in favor of national (vs. supranational) competence on immigration policy, which reflects the persistence of nationalist impulses among elites (see tables 14.6 and 14.7).

As illustrated previously, a more nuanced analysis reveals the stubborn ideological and national orientations impeding cooperation. Although across the board there seems to be a more restrictionist impulse toward immigrant rights, political divisions remain most pervasive in this policy area (even if in the predictable ideological order). Elite attitudes are also polarized on the subject of immigration restrictions (although constant between 1992 and 2004). Nonetheless, to the extent that a majority of MEPs prefer the status quo for immigration intake, that dimension of policy regulation— consistent with policy developments—has become less salient and more amenable to harmonization. More than ever, MEPs express satisfaction with the current flows (see tables 14.2 and 14.3), an indication that the challenges of immigration intake may be abating in Europe. These are encouraging signs that reflect the tremendous strides toward communitarizing immigration policy in the post-Amsterdam/Tampere period of the late 1990s and since the earlier survey.

These trends should be considered in light of the growing salience and protectionism with regards to immigrant integration, one of the chief immigration-related concerns raised since the early 1990s. Clearly, there is less support for immigrant rights than there was a decade earlier. The decline in support for immigrant rights follows what we may have expected given the trade-offs in rights that people are willing to make under the increasing security threat and growing salience of immigration issues (Lahav 2005). These reservations regarding immigrant rights corroborate the previous observations that policies dealing with integration matters (i.e., education, acculturation, language, and welfare) often derive from nationally laden models of citizenship and belonging and are less amenable to harmonization (Lahav 2004a, 220). Indeed, although there has been some success with regard to EU antidiscrimination legislation, there is clear evidence of a disjuncture between the immigration and integration policies adopted at the EU level and national paradigms (Geddes and Guiraudon 2004). The persistence of national and ideological influences on immigrant policies means that cooperation may be dependent on their linkage to other policy domains, such as foreign affairs or welfare policies (Lavenex and Uçarer 2002; Geddes 2003).

Generally speaking, the divisions give some credence to a two-dimensional space occupied by the immigration issue, in which policy on intake or control is marked by consensus but immigrant policy is characterized by more dissonance and partisan competition (Money 1995). This dichotomy suggests that immigration politics at the EU level may be less about traditional redistributive conflicts and more about questions of identity and sovereignty (Lahav 2004a; McLaren 2001)—areas most resistant to EU competence. More important, the analysis of policy and attitudinal developments reveal that despite the move to conflate immigration regulation in a comprehensive approach at the institutional level (e.g., the JHA Council), attitudinal patterns remain distinct and contentious.

How do we explain these apparent incongruities? As informed by the research findings, one possible answer is that, even as MEP opinion regarding the salience of immigration was converging during the decade, this convergence was not propelled, as the prevailing wisdom might presume, by a closer association between immigration and security issues (Lahav, Messina, and Vasquez 2007). The failure to link immigration issues to security over time coincides with policy developments and suggests caution about attributing causal antecedence to cooperation. In contrast to the predominant U.S. preoccupation with immigration as linked to security and external (border) controls, European responses have been more preoccupied with internal control, including migrant integration (Lahav forthcoming). When MEPs acknowledge the salience of immigration issues, doing so may reflect their concern about the deterioration of the cultural, economic, political or social environments of their countries. As in-depth interviews reveal, even when security *is* a major concern among MEPs, there appears to be significant variance in the cultural meaning of the concept.[11] The impact of domestic-political environments in shaping policy outcomes, as neo-institutionalists have long argued (March and Olsen 1984) is formidable in generating different migration concerns and patterns of contestation (Guiraudon and Lahav 2006).

Second, cooperation may mask important differences that stem from ideological and national interests around the nature of immigration problems—and particularly about strategies toward immigrant integration. As some research has shown, the longer immigration remains on the political agenda, the more politicized it becomes, as parties scramble to differentiate themselves from one another (Lahav 2004a, 214). Indeed, one of the most important conclusions to be derived from the earlier data is the impact of national phases of immigration. There is a temporal sequence to immigration politics. During the early stages of the immigration experience, there is a tendency to find cross-party consensus to defuse the issue. As the immigration debate invariably becomes salient, parties increasingly struggle to differentiate themselves and break the mainstream consensus. Thus, the longer a country has been receiving immigrants, the more divided elite opinion becomes. Attitudes toward immigration often reflect the different phases of immigration cycles among the EU countries, and these factors may condition party dynamics. Not only does this finding hold important implications for the central and Eastern European countries of the recent EU enlargement, but it reminds us that, despite the growing salience of immigration across countries, the issue is politicized quite differently.[12]

Third, the resistance to immigrant integration policies at the EU level—even as Europe is forging ahead toward a comprehensive program—is not surprising, given the salience of immigrant integration for the European public agenda and the critical differences that remain on that issue. Minority integration has been linked to a strong welfare tradition in Europe, and integration is thus the core of the nation-state project. Unlike the U.S. model, which lacks a federal integration policy (except for resettled refugees), the entrenchment of strong European welfare states precludes the possibility that legal or even, in some cases, illegal residents of a country will be excluded from the full range of nationally available welfare benefits (e.g., schooling, health care, and income support) (van Selm 2005). Moreover, Muslims have been perceived as an internal risk in Europe rather than as an external risk factor linked to international relations, as in the United States. The social integration of migrants has emerged as a top domestic priority for the European public, feeding the fear of an internal threat—a burning topic that reemerged with the 2004 Dutch murder and the 2005 riots in France.

Finally, the salience and politicization of the integration dimension of the immigration equation is equally logical given that most European countries have zero-migration rhetoric already in place (and predominantly accepted, as illustrated by the MEPs reactions presented here) for non-EU migrants while promoting the mobility of intra-Europeans for growing markets. In contrast to the United States, where mobility has been rather high (with 6 percent of the population reported to change countries every year), in Europe it has been more static (Council of Europe 2004). Only 2 percent of EU citizens live and work in an EU country that is not their country of origin—a cause of great concern to European policymakers (Claude-Valentin 2004).[13] Furthermore, although in Europe the majority of foreigners are third-country nationals (TCNs; i.e., third-world-origin, non-white, non-Christian populations) (see table 14.1), the ratio of non-EU to EU foreigners barely changed from 1993 to 2004, an indication of very low level of mobility within the European Union (Council of Europe 2004). Due to their low fertility rates and high rates of aging, most European countries have experienced demographic crises resulting from below-replacement population levels. Finally, in the face of these demographic aging trends and a steep and unabated decline in the size of national labor forces, replacement migration has emerged as a controversial solution to save the welfare net (United Nations 2001).

The proclivity to view immigration-related questions through the prism of internal security and control in the European Union has important political and policy implications, offering mixed results for immigrant incorporation. The preoccupation with internal migration control in Europe, linked as it is with organized crime, terrorism, and Islamic fundamentalism, has meant that over time the object of cooperation and control has become less about borders and more about the flows of migrants as an ongoing process (Gammeltoft-Hansen 2006) and the surveillance of movement (Lyon 2004; Salter 2008). Reinforcing their law enforcement proclivities, European countries have adopted "a strategy of policing foreigners rather than an immigration policy" (Council of Europe 2004, 41) or an immigrant policy.[14]

The recent European Parliament legislation on the incarceration of illegal migrants epitomizes this bias. Yet the conflation of the immigration equation in an age of increasing security has generated a momentum toward comprehensive reforms that favor immigration control policies (where attitudes are more moderate and stable) over immigrant integration or rights policies (which are more divisive). Clearly, intra-European policy goals have lurched toward the exclusion of immigrants in some contexts and their inclusion in other aspects (Favell 2001). As the broad policy developments and empirical attitudinal data outlined here demonstrate, important biases persist even as EU policy harmonization proceeds. The EU political space provides important opportunities to harmonize immigration policies, even as critical constraints to cooperation in areas of immigrant integration remain. Despite, and perhaps because, political contestation in Europe largely focuses on issues of immigrant integration, this policy area is most resistant to European cooperation and competence.

# PART VI

# IMMIGRANTS' POLITICAL RESOURCES AND STRATEGIES

Individual migrants and immigrant groups are neither passive recipients of native-born politicians' actions nor helpless victims of extant political institutions and practices. Earlier chapters in *Bringing Outsiders In* have already pointed to immigrant agency. At a theoretical level, Jennifer Hochschild and John Mollenkopf (chap. 2), Marco Martiniello (chap. 3), and Lorraine C. Minnite (chap. 4, all in this volume) insist that incorporation is a two-way street of influence and change. At an empirical level, Luis Fraga (chap. 12), Eva Østergaard-Nielsen (chap. 13), Mollenkopf and Raphael Sonenshein (chap. 6), and Reuel Rogers (chap. 7, all in this volume) have attended to immigrants' actions in local, national, or transnational structures. The chapters in part VI focus our attention even more fully on the resources, strategies, and purposes that immigrants bring to the political opportunity structures that they face.

Individuals and organizations must both make a crucial choice—whether to forge an identity as a component of mainstream society or to champion ethnic difference as a core element of a political claim. Joining the mainstream (which Minnite, chap. 4 in this volume, calls "absorption") allows the group and its members to take advantage of the opportunities and pathways that native-born citizens already enjoy, but it can come at the cost of submerging cherished manifestations of the newcomers' culture and enabling political elites to neglect distinctive needs. Conversely, creating a political persona that revolves around an ethnically or nationally based identity can help a marginalized group define itself as a stakeholder in the political fray; but it can also earn that group, and even members who do not participate in its assertiveness, a reputation as fractious, problematic, and threatening. In addition, it can make coalitions with other small groups difficult to develop and sustain.

As with the other topics in this book, that choice is not made free of constraints set by established paths of action. In chapter 15, Tariq Modood, in fact, identifies five state-driven channels for dealing with the cultural diversity that immigration brings: the decentered, liberal, republican, federated, and plural states. Each type has strong and weak forms. Modood argues that the plural state most facilitates ethno-religious political mobilization. In such a state, epitomized by Great Britain, "there is a recognition that social life consists of individuals and groups, and that both need to be provided for in the formal and informal distribution of powers." Furthermore, in the plural state, immigrant incorporation is more than assimilation, since it reformulates the state just as the state reshapes immigrants. That process precludes the problems of state monoculturalism.

In chapter 16, Sandro Cattacin ponders whether immigrant ghettos are really blights on the city and detriments to immigrant advancement. He argues that, in fact, immigrant fulcrums within cities can help people build foundations for mainstream political integration, should they choose to seek it eventually. Concentrated populations, even if they live in poverty, can organize and protect themselves from harmful elements of the dominant value system. Concentration also makes it easier for social service and health-care agencies to help the people most in need. Cattacin realizes that he is arguing against the grain, but he asserts that at least some features of a polity that the majority takes to be problematic can, with appropriate organization, skill, and perspectives, eventually facilitate inclusion—albeit not on a very linear path.

Whether immigrants choose to be mobilized along ethnic or religious lines—or in some other way or not at all—depends in part on their resources and their values or beliefs. Modood makes this point, and in chapter 17, Janelle Wong and Adrian Pantoja develop it. They seek to understand different levels of political inclusion across groups within a single nation by examining why members of various immigrant groups in the United States become naturalized citizens at unequal rates. They find that, even controlling for characteristics such as education and income, an individual's national origin is associated with the decision to naturalize. So is "embeddedness" in the United States. Wong and Pantoja try to explain their findings and, in the process, make it clear that we cannot assume either that immigrants are mostly like those of native parentage or that all immigrants are mostly alike in the political arena.

Finally, in chapter 18, Richard Alba and Nancy Foner examine differences in immigrant-origin candidates' election to political office in the United States, Great Britain, France, Germany, and the Netherlands. They focus on immigrants whose groups are large and dubiously incorporated, on the grounds that these are the people for whom inclusion is both most important and most difficult. They find that, although legal, electoral, and party structures in each country mediate electoral success, the attitudes and policies of states toward integration are just as important. The range "from the multiculturalism of Britain to the assimilationist republicanism of France" shapes what immigrants can aspire to in that country and the strategies that they should choose.

We come full circle, in short, from a focus on institutional opportunity structures and deeply embedded political practices to a focus on the perhaps more malleable realm of values, norms, immigrants' identities, and individual or group choices—and back again. That is no surprise; bringing outsiders in requires both that outsiders seek to come in and that insiders permit them to do so. The interesting questions lie in the terms on which inclusion is negotiated, the conditions in which it fails or is rejected, and the consequences for all concerned. These chapters begin, but do not come close to ending, the effort to answer those questions.

# CHAPTER FIFTEEN

# The State and Ethno-Religious Mobilization in Britain

## Tariq Modood

The migration into western democratic nation-states of the last few decades has seen an assertive politics in several countries on the part of the migrants and second-generation immigrants, explored here with particular reference to Britain. Of course, migrants and members of minorities do not have to participate in politics as migrants or as minorities; they may even eschew such categorization and the exoticness that implies, and certainly they may participate in politics in a variety of ways typical of nonmigrants. My concern here, however, is ideologies of identity and mobilization that have been present under certain racialized conditions prevailing in Britain and that have made certain kinds of politics possible.

Let me begin by briefly considering how states may be constituted by different types of conceptions of the individual, community, and the state. How a state or a citizenry responds to the claims of migrants, even which kinds of claims can be seriously and legitimately made by migrants and others, depends on the extent to which people believe that individuals, (ethnic) groups, and the nation-state form coherent unities, are the bearers of ethical claims, and can be integrated with one another. Five ideal types, marking five possible ways in which people may respond to the contemporary challenge of diversity consequent on immigration, can be distinguished: the decentered state, the liberal state, the republic, the federation of communities, and the plural state.[1] The purpose of the typology is to identify the kind of state self-image that has facilitated ethno-religious political mobilization. It may be characterized as the plural state, but it is better understood through its comparison and contrast with the other types. These other types, traces of which and advocates for which can be found in Britain as well as elsewhere, help to clarify some of the relevant, important characteristics of the British state and political culture or, at least, some representations of it. This chapter thus reflects a certain degree of Anglo-centrism.

My focus is on Britain but not merely descriptively but also in terms of developing an analytical frame that illuminates and explains Britain. Hence, Britain is not just one case illustrating some lawlike generalization or model. Nor does it display some kind of exceptionality or stand outside all comparative analytical endeavors. My hope is that the analytical frame deployed here can be the basis of comparative work but with the expectation that considerable revisions, adjustments, and extensions will be necessary before it is adequate for other national cases.

## Cultural Identity and the State: Five Ideal Types

### The Decentered State

Some theorists describe the present condition of the world as *postnational* or *postmodern.* Among the many things meant by this term is the assertion that, due to factors such as migration and the globalization of economics, consumption, and communications, societies can no longer be constituted by stable collective purposes and identities organized territorially by the nation-state. In its most radical version, this view rejects not only the possibility of a politically constituted multiculturalism but also the idea of a unified self per se:

> If we feel we have a unified identity…it is only because we construct a comforting story or "narrative of the self" about ourselves.…The fully unified, completed, secure and coherent identity is a fantasy. Instead, as the systems of meaning and cultural representation multiply, we are confronted by a bewildering, fleeting multiplicity of possible identities, any one of which we could identify with—at least temporarily. (Hall 1992a, 277).

The radical multiple self has a penchant for identities but prefers surfing on the waves of deconstruction to seeking reconstruction in multiplicity. It is post-self rather than a multi-self. Even in less radical versions, the self is no more connected to one location/society/state than another, any more than the typical consumer is connected to one producer or the goods of one country. Reconciled to multiplicity as an end in itself, its vision of diversity is sometimes confined to personal lifestyles and cosmopolitan consumerism; more significantly, its vision of multiculturalism does not extend to the state, which is expected to wither away.

Contemporary postnational scenarios envisage that the nation-state will increasingly decline as a focus of personal identity and loyalty as individuals identify with like-minded people across borders, based on lifestyles, cultural consumption, peripatetic careers, diasporas, and other forms of transnational networks, including those based on political hope, such as antiglobalization or the *ummah* as global Muslim consciousness. National citizenship will continue to decline in value as many of the conditions that it has in the past secured—such as security, rights, and economic well-being—can only be secured at a supra-national level, such as the European Union, or international level such the General Agreement on Trade and Tariffs (GATT) or the Kyoto agreement on environmental protection.

## The Liberal State

In contrast, the liberal theorist expects the integrity of individuals (although not necessarily of large-scale communities) to survive the social changes that are in motion. Individuals may temporarily become disoriented, bewildered by the multiplicity of identities, and temporarily decentered, but the liberal theorist confidently believes they will soon recenter themselves. Lifestyles in their neighborhoods may change as people of exotic appearance, large families, and pungent-smelling foods move in. The old residents and the new have to adjust (perhaps gradually, certainly repeatedly) their sense of self, community, and country as these changes occur, but the liberal theorist contends that no major political project other than the elimination of discrimination is required to achieve this. The state exists to protect the rights of individuals, but the question of recognizing new ethnic groups does not arise because the state does not recognize any groups. Individuals relate to the state as individual citizens, not as members of the group; the state is group-blind, it cannot "see" color, gender, ethnicity, religion, or even nationality. In the parlance of North American political theorists (it is certainly easier to see the United States, as led by some recent political theory and jurisprudence, than any European state as approximating to this liberal ideal; Sandel 1996), the just state is neutral between rival conceptions of the good. It does not promote one or more national cultures, religions, ways of life, and so on. These matters remain private to individuals in their voluntary associations with one another. Nor does the state promote any syncretic vision of common living, of fellow-feeling between the inhabitants of that territory other than the legal entitlements and duties that define civic membership.

## The Republic

The ideal republic, like the liberal state, does not recognize groups among its citizenry. It relates to each citizen as an individual. Yet, unlike the liberal state, it is amenable to one collective project—itself. More precisely, it is itself a collective project that is not reducible to the protection of the rights of individuals or the maximization of the choices open to individuals. The republic seeks to enhance the lives of its members by making them a part of a way of living that individuals could not create for themselves; it seeks to make the individuals members of a civic community. This community may be based on subscription to universal principles such as liberty, equality, and fraternity; to the promotion of a national culture; or, as in the case of France, to both. In a republic, the formation of public ethnicity, by immigration or in other ways, is discouraged and there is a strong expectation for, even pressure on, individuals to assimilate to the national identity. In such a situation, any call for public recognition by minority ethnic and religious groups could hardly get off the ground. Where there appear to be efforts by some ethnic or religious groups to create collective identities in the public space, negative responses by the state, such as the banning of the wearing of the symbols of identity in state schools seems reasonable (Kastoryano 2005; Laborde 2005).

## The Federation of Communities

In contrast to the first three responses to multicultural diversity, this option is built on the assumption that the individual is not the unit (or at least not the only unit) to which the state must relate. Rather, individuals belong to and are shaped by communities, which are the primary focus of their loyalty and the regulators of their social life. Far from being confined to the private sphere, communities are the primary agents of the public sphere. Public life, in fact, consists of organized communities relating to one another, and the state is therefore a federation of communities and exists to protect the rights of communities.

As with all of the ideal types listed here, we can think of both a more radical or extreme version of the model and a more moderate version that balances the rights of communities with the rights of individuals, including the right to exit from communities. The *millet* system of the Ottoman Empire, in which some powers of the state were delegated to Christian and Jewish communities, which had the power to administer personal law within their communities in accordance with their own legal systems, is an example of this model of the multicultural state and has occasionally been invoked in Britain as an example to emulate. The *millet* system offered a significant autonomy to communities but did not offer equality between communities or any conception of democratic citizenship. The problem with this system of political organization, therefore, is not that it is unable to give suitable cognizance to the call for recognition by minority ethnic and religious groups but, rather, that it is likely to remain an unattractive proposition to many in contemporary Europe unless a democratic variant can be devised. The system of pillarization in the Netherlands and Belgium, a moderate version of this type of institutionalized communal diversity within a democratic framework, may be favored by some but has become extremely unpopular, especially in the Netherlands, precisely on the grounds that it fosters separate communities without a sense of being members of a common citizenry.

## The Plural State

In the plural state, again an ideal type for which there are strong and weak forms, there is a recognition that social life consists of individuals and groups, and that both need to be provided for in the formal and informal distribution of powers—not just in law but in representation in the offices of the state, public committees, consultative exercises, and access to public fora. There may be some rights for all individuals (as in the liberal state) but mediating institutions such as trade unions, churches, neighborhoods, immigrant associations, and so on are also encouraged to be active public players and fora for political discussion and may even have a formal representative or administrative role to play in the state. The plural state, however, allows for, indeed probably requires, an ethical conception of citizenship, not just an instrumental one (as in the federation-of-communities conception). The understanding that individuals are partly constituted by the lives of families and communities fits well with the recognition that the moral individual is partly shaped by the social order constituted by citizenship and the public, which amplifies and qualifies, sustains, critiques, and reforms citizenship.

If the state should come to have this kind of importance in people's lives, it is most likely that they will, as in a republic, invest emotionally and psychologically in the state and its projects. The most usual form of this emotional relationship is a sense of national identity. In an undiluted form, national identity, like most group identifications, can be dangerous and certainly incompatible with the accommodation of minorities. On the other hand, assuming a plurality of identities and not a narrow nationalism, the plural state (unlike the liberal state) is able to offer an emotional identity with the whole to counterbalance the emotional loyalties to ethnic and religious communities, which should prevent the fragmentation of society into narrow, selfish communalisms. Yet the presence of these strong community identities will be an effective check against monocultural statism.

For the plural state, the challenge of contemporary mass immigration is the integration of transplanted cultures, heritages, and peoples into long-established yet ongoing historic national cultures, heritages, and so on. It is about creating a cultural synthesis in both private and public spaces, including in education and welfare provision. Above all, proponents of this new multiculturalism are anxious to find new ways of extending, reforming, and syncretizing existing forms of public culture and citizenship. This is not about decentering society or deconstructing the nation-state; rather, it is concerned with integrating difference by remaking the nation-state. In contrast to common political parlance, *integration* here is not synonymous with *assimilation*. Assimilation is something that immigrant or minorities must do or have done to them, whereas integration is interactive, a two-way process—both parties are an active ingredient and so something new is created. For the plural state, then, multicultural diversity means re-forming national identity and citizenship (Modood 2007).

## Britain: Ethnic Mobilization Discourses in a Plural State/Civil Society

It is because Britain approximates, or under certain political circumstances and leadership approximates, the ideal of a plural state that there has been considerable immigrant political assertiveness and that public discourse and policy have so easily converted migrants into ethnic minorities (the New Commonwealth primary migration from the West Indies and the South Asian subcontinent occurred mainly in the 1950s and 1960s, and a discourse of multiculturalism and ethnic minorities emerged in the 1970s). It is a commonplace observation that Britain, like its European neighbors, is an old country and not as hospitable to immigrants as, say, Canada, the United States, and Australia, countries that have been historically constituted by immigration. Yet, in relation to some groups of immigrants, Britain, in particular such cities as London, has been remarkably receptive and self-transformative. This is related to the British approximation to the plural state. More specifically, ethnic minority political mobilization in Britain began with a set of factors that enabled it to reach a degree of ideological assertiveness, prominence, and civic impact in a limited period of time that seems to be without parallel in continental Europe, even in countries such as France and (the former West) Germany, where the population that in British discourse is called *ethnic minority* is larger, both in relative and absolute terms. It is shaped by a set of opportunity structures constituted by the following:

- The British imperial connection, felt by many migrants, especially the incomers who arrived between the 1940s and the 1980s, and politically acknowledged by at least some white Britains.
- The British identity and sense of having a right to be in Britain.
- Automatic British citizenship and franchise among postcolonials from the day of arrival (later qualified).
- Large-scale antiracist struggles elsewhere in the English-speaking world, especially in the United States, in which the notions migrants and hosts were absent but which were borrowed or emulated, creating a confidence and assertiveness that, among migrants-as-guests, would be regarded as intolerable by hosts.

Hence, there is real sense that these groups were not just economic immigrants but former colonials moving to the metropolis. Partly through institutional fact (e.g., the free entry and automatic British citizenship on the day of arrival) and partly through their subsequent politics (their attitude), it is fair to say that what we are talking about is something in between a country-to-country movement and a movement from an outlying province of an empire to its ruling capital (Ali, Kalra, and Sayyid 2005; Hickman 2005). Neither is a satisfactory description of the phenomenon. The fact that it was not pure immigration but entry into a country on which migrants had a moral or political claim stands out when we compare it to migration to continental Europe or North American countries in the same period (descriptions of the mighty United States as an invisible empire notwithstanding). The British imperial legacy bequeathed a racialized character to this immigration and an automatic citizenship—a racism and an egalitarianism—that has some parallels with other core-periphery migrations, especially the French and Dutch cases, but that make it quite distinctive (Joppke 1996).

In most of the respects just mentioned, the West Indians, who thought of themselves as culturally and politically British in the way that New Zealanders arriving in England in the 1950s would have done so, took the lead in forging a minority political discourse and assertiveness that South Asians gradually assimilated into, adapted for their own use, or used as a point of departure to develop a less racial dualist (black-white) and more ethnic pluralist orientation. Once this minority assertiveness is part of a political culture and regarded as legitimate, perhaps even necessary to demonstrate a certain group dignity, then it can take forms that owe nothing to the original source. They can take, for example, the form of the Muslim campaign against *The Satanic Verses*, which to many observers initially bore no relation to anti-racism but has increasingly come to be seen in that light (Modood 1990, 2005b).

British ethnic relations, then, have been characterized by a high level of political mobilization, but have been constituted by different ideas and ideologies, including those that contradict official policy frameworks and are motivated by a resentment of misrecognition and the search for recognition (Taylor 1994). The political opportunities structure has been initially and strongly shaped by postcolonial and U.S. conceptions, producing a race-relations framework embodied in official discourse, laws, and policies. It has been a framework, however, that has encouraged and been responsive to ethnic minority challenges. Thus, the framework has been and continues to be modified over time and is at least partly shaped by ethnic minority political mobilization, and it includes efforts to redefine race, ethnicity, racism, discrimination, and, ultimately, British citizenship.

My suggestion is that there seem to have been six aspects or ideological orientations to ethnic minority political mobilization in Britain (Modood 2005a): (1) racial equality and antidiscrimination, (2) political blackness—unity of the other, (3) political blackness—racial identity, (4) ethnic and religious identities, (5) parts of Britishness, and (6) transnational ideologies. The first five aspects follow a rough chronological order, at least in terms of their emergence. They coexist as different tendencies at any one time in debate with and perhaps in open or implicit contestation with one another, informing the perspective of rival organizations or of rival groupings within the same organization or confusedly mixed up with one another. Individuals or groups may seek to combine some of the five orientations, but not only is there a rough chronology in the series in terms of emergence, there is one in the expansion of the types of mobilization and also in terms of relative ascendancy. The sixth aspect is a recurrent feature that takes different forms at different times.

## Racial Equality and Antidiscrimination

The post–World War II New Commonwealth immigration was led by the West Indians, some of whom, or their relatives, had voluntarily fought for Britain during the war and who hoped to better themselves while responding to invitations to assist in the economic reconstruction of the mother country. They were soon joined by large numbers of Indian and Pakistani young men, who too had a British Imperial connection, although a much less developed sense of British identity; instead, their identities revolved around tightly organized lines of kinship, custom, religion, language, postimperial nationhood, and so on—all of which gave them a clear and confident sense of not being British even while having an admiration for the former ruling power (this sentiment being at least as common as any residual anticolonialism) (Hiro 1991).

By the end of the 1950s, it was clear that racism against "coloured immigrants" was widespread and capable of erupting into violence and that popular pressure for stemming this immigration was building up. It was resisted originally by an internationalist antiracism, the core belief of which was that race as a biological concept had been scientifically destroyed (Montague 1964). There were no races because human beings were all the same under differently colored skins. *Racial equality,* then, meant that a person should not be excluded from any of the benefits of British citizenship and participation in British economic and social life that their talents and education allowed, just because they were not white.

## Political Blackness: The Unity of the Other

As racial equality consciousness developed in the 1960s, similar struggles in the United States and Southern Africa were influential in developing thinking in Britain. Racial equality discourse might have been aspiring toward color-blindness, but as these political contestations went on the racial black-white dualism became central to the antiracist discourse and the ways in which the oppressed mobilized against their oppression.

Hence, in the United States, the idea of historically excluded individuals claiming the citizenship that was theirs by right of U.S. nationality was joined by the idea of a black collective agency. In particular, for some young Northern urban black political leaders (Carmichael and Hamilton 1967; Cleaver 1968), the identity of being black implied the urgent need to unite as a distinct political force and not simply in a color-blind way with white liberals; to unite not so much as a pressure group to achieve limited political goals but to become a political community (in the way that nationalists conceive of a nation as a political community or that socialists used to conceive of a self-conscious class as a political community).

Some West Indian, Asian, and African intellectuals and activists began in the late 1960s or early 1970s to describe themselves as "black" (Banton 1987) and to theorize racialized populations, the white people's "other," in Britain and across the globe, past and present, as a singular collectivity standing in a particular relationship to other collectivities such as capital and labor. The message was that nonwhites suffered a distinct form or forms of exploitation and oppression not recognized within socialist or liberal critiques of British society or international capitalism and so needed to theoretically and politically define themselves in contrast to other collectivities, not just as new members of preexisting British groups and institutions (Sivanandan 1985).

The biggest influence of this new antiracism, as perhaps in the United States, was to give new currency, assertiveness, and dignity to the label *black,* that is, to the creation of a positive black identity. Although this has proved to be a major development in British race relations and in shaping ethnic minority political mobilization, it was not without its own internal difficulties.

## Political Blackness: Racial Identity

*Black* could be taken as a political racial identity in two different senses: a race, in the sense that a population has been conceived as a race by white people, which may have nothing more in common than how white people treat them; or a race in the sense of a similar physical appearance (being black), a similar territorial origin, a common history and so on, in short, not just as a subordinated population but as a people. The development of this racial identity in the United States became much more than just a political construct—it became a racial-ethnic-cultural pride movement. It was a movement by and for people of African roots and origins in the enslavement of African peoples in the New World, as symbolized in the slogan "black is beautiful." The celebration of the positive elements of the black diasporic African heritage of struggle and of the achievements of the contemporary bearers of that heritage became integral to the meaning of *black* as it was picked up across the world, including in the United Kingdom (Gilroy 1993).

But this created a serious incoherence in the meaning of *black* as a positive political identity (Modood 1994). On the one hand, it was a nonethnic term referring to a movement of resistance to racial subordination and, therefore, in aspiration, fully including Asians. On the other hand, it referred to a black diasporic African ethnicity and therefore by definition excluded Asians even though they were the numerical majority of nonwhites in Britain. That for many years this contradiction was not noticed or not thought problematic by advocates of political blackness—which included the majority of Asians involved in antiracism as a political movement for most of the 1970s and 1980s—enabling it to become the hegemonic minority discourse of the 1980s and accepted as such by the political classes (Hall 1992a; Ali 1991) reflects at least two things about this period.

First, although there were critiques of political blackness by radicals, who bemoaned the way that it was picked up by mainstream discourse and politics (Sivanandan 1985; Gilroy 1990), they were not primarily responsible for the demise of political blackness as a hegemonic presence. The fundamental problem for political blackness came from the internal ambivalence mentioned earlier, namely whether blackness as a political identity was sufficiently distinct from an ethnic pride movement and could mobilize without blackness. Second, this black identity movement, in a growing climate of opinion favorable to identity politics of various kinds, was successful in shifting the terms of the debate from color-blind individualistic assimilation to questions about how white British society had to change to accommodate new groups. But its success in imposing a singular identity on or making a singular identity out of a diverse ethnic minority population was temporary (probably at no time did a majority of Asians think of themselves as part of a positive black identity; Modood et al. 1997, 294–97). What it did was pave the way for a plural ethnic assertiveness as Asian groups borrowed the logic of ethnic pride and tried to catch up with the success of a newly legitimized black public identity.

## Ethnic and Religious Identities

Not only have British ethnic minorities not united under a single identity capable of mobilizing them all, but the number of identities that generate an intensity of commitment and a community mobilization grows all the time. Its not just black and Asian; the latter, although generally accepted by South Asians as a public identity, is quite thin and does not have the capacity to mobilize that Pakistani, Bangladeshi, and Indian do—or, better still, Sikh, Muslim, and Hindu. One proud, much proclaimed identity often gives way to another within a few years. Many passionate Pakistanis of the 1980s became dedicated Kashmiris in the 1990s (Ellis and Khan 1998).

Of course, much of this is to do with context and, in particular, what an individual feels he or she needs to react against. Pakistanis were blacks when it meant a job in a racial equality bureaucracy, Asians when a community center was in the offing, Muslims when the Prophet was being ridiculed, and Kashmiris when a nationalist movement back home had taken off and blood was being spilt. These identities are pragmatic moves as well as defining the field in which moves are made. Moreover, although the salience of these identities is context-dependent and requires appropriate champions, nevertheless a minority will respond to some forms of exclusion or inferiorization and not to others. The ones it will respond to are those that relate in some way to its own sense of being (Modood 1990; reproduced in 2005b). This sense of being is not atemporal and can change, but it does mean that neither the oppressor nor the oppressed is totally free to set the terms of a reactive identity—the oppression must speak to the oppressed, it must reach a sense of self that, if not in some sense authentic, is at least internalized.

So, part of the answer as to which identity will emerge as important to a group at a particular time lies in the nature of the minority group in question. That the Caribbeans have mobilized around a color identity and the South Asians around religious and related identities is not chance, nor it is just a construction; rather, it is based on something deeper about these groups. That many Muslims in their anger against Salman Rushdie's *The Satanic Verses* found a depth of indignation, a voice of their own, in a way that most had not found in relation to events and in mobilization in previous decades cannot be explained just in terms of issues to do with political leadership, rivalries, or tactics (Lewis 1994). Certainly, some individuals and organizations exploited the situation, but they could not have done so if there was not a situation to exploit (Modood 1990, 2005b).

In one important way, however, the context has changed over the last couple of decades, and this has influenced which minority identities have emerged and the ways in which they have developed. Minority ethnicity, albeit white ethnicity, has traditionally been regarded in Britain as acceptable if it was confined to the privacy of family and community and did not make any political demands. Earlier groups of migrants and refugees, such as the Irish or the Jews in the nineteenth and the first half of the twentieth century, found that peace and prosperity came easier the less public they made their minority practices and identity. Perhaps for non-European origin groups, whose physical appearance gave them a visibility that made them permanently vulnerable to racial discrimination, the model of a privatized group identity was never viable. Yet, in addition, we must acknowledge the existence of a climate of opinion quite different from that experienced by the earlier Irish or Jewish incomers.

In the last couple of decades, the bases of identity formation have undergone important changes, and there has come to be a minority assertiveness. Identity has moved from that which might be unconscious and taken for granted because it is implicit in distinctive cultural practices to conscious and public projections of identity and the explicit creation and assertion of politicized ethnicities. This is part of a wider sociopolitical climate that is not confined to race and culture or nonwhite minorities. Feminism, gay pride, Quebecois nationalism, and the revival of Scottishness are some prominent examples of these new identity movements that have come to be an important feature in many countries in which class politics has declined. Identities in this political climate are not implicit and private but are shaped, instead, through intellectual, cultural, and political debates and have become a feature of public discourse and policies, especially at the level of local government (cf. Young 1990; Taylor 1994; Kymlicka 1995). The identities formed in such processes are fluid and susceptible to change with the political climate, but to think of them as weak is to overlook the pride with which they may be asserted, the intensity with which they may be debated, and their capacity to generate community activism and political campaigns.

This politics of identity assertiveness, although initially taken up by racial and ethnic identities, from the 1980s onward was taken up by religious groups, initially by Sikhs and later, and most notably, by Muslims. In this way, the presence of organized minority religious communities is not simply diversifying ethnicity and religion in Britain but giving it an increased policy importance. This has, of course, become particularly obvious in relation to Muslims after September 11, but it was apparent much earlier (Modood 2005b). Paul Statham (1999) analyzed political claims-making in relation to race relations and multiculturalism as reported in the *Guardian* newspaper over a random six-week period. He found that nearly one-half of all claims were made by organizations with *Muslim* or *Islamic* in their title, thus showing that some groups had achieved a high level of autonomous organization on the basis of identities that at that time contradicted the categorization of them by the British state. It would be no exaggeration to say that many multiculturalists are dismayed by the emergence of Muslim consciousness. They took it for granted that multiculturalism would be respectful of secularism; although in general they believe that to require minority identities to confine themselves to the private sphere is oppressive, they believe religious identities to be an exception (Yuval-Davis 1992; Saghal and Yuval-Davis 1992). They never intended the recognition of difference to be extended to Muslims; for them, Muslim identity is a bastard child of British multiculturalism. Religious identity developments, then, challenge normative definitions of what should be public and private in a way that, even though deepening multiculturalism, has thrown multicultural advocacy into disarray (Modood 2005b and 2007).

Although Muslims have now become the most visible and politicized minority group, and this in due course turns out to have been indicative of a new phase in minority stigmatization and mobilization, this should not obscure another current development, the fifth ideological orientation.

## Parts of Britishness

Stuart Hall, among others, has argued that from the mid- to late 1980s "a significant shift has been going on (and is still going on) in black cultural politics" (Hall 1992a, 252). Not only does this entail a recognition of a diversity of minority identities, "a plural blackness," it also entails an understanding that ethnic identities are not pure or static. Increasingly ethnicity or blackness is less often experienced as an oppositional identity than as a way of being British (although the current position of Muslim identity, subject as it is to various global crises, is something of an exception at the moment). This inevitably challenges existing conceptions of Britishness (Gilroy 1987) and feeds into a wider public emphasis on the plural and dynamic character of British society and talk of "rebranding Britain" (Leonard 1997), a discourse that was taken up by the New Labour government, which came into power in 1997. Of course, the whole issue of British identity is now a topic of national debate in the wake of the rise of Scottishness and the new devolved constitutional arrangements. But it is worth noting that among those who first raised the issue of British identity and the need to remake it were minority intellectuals such as Stuart Hall, Bhikhu Parekh, and Paul Gilroy, and racial egalitarians have put the need to rethink a new inclusive Britishness as critical to the prospects for racial equality (Commission on Multi-Ethnic Britain [CMEB] 2000).

One of the most significant antiracist political mobilizations in recent years has been the campaign in the late 1990s to have the police find and prosecute the murderers of the black teenager Stephen Lawrence. Although not (yet) achieving its goal, the campaign achieved a national media prominence and a virtually unprecedented sense of shame among what is termed "middle England," and it led to significant legislation and institutional reform (Macpherson 2000). Although perhaps not so much supported among the white working classes, the campaign created a multiracial movement that evokes memories of the liberal protests of the 1960s, the Anti-Nazi League in the 1970s, and other antiracist demonstrations at which white faces were in a majority. It sharply contrasts with an earlier campaign, the demand to find and bring to justice the arsonists of a fire leading to the death of thirteen black teenagers and injuries to another thirty in 1981 in Deptford, South London. When a campaign march brought central London to a standstill, there was hardly a white face among the marchers (Phillips and Phillips 1998). The contrast shows how much has changed in twenty years. It also suggests that some of the liberal ideas of cross-racial solidarity of the Martin Luther King era are still alive. This history, then, has both cyclical and linear features. The British identity espoused by the 1948 Windrush hopefuls may be irrecoverable, but it may be that a new British identity is evolving that makes more sense to them than some of the politics in the period between then and now.

Another major campaign in which the concerns of a stigmatized minority community were shared by the political mainstream is the Iraq War. Again, this can be illustrated by reference to a street demonstration. In February 2003, London saw one of the biggest political demonstrations ever. It was reported that 2 million people joined this protest march, and although only a small fraction were Muslims, one of the three organizations that jointly called the march was the Muslim Association of Britain. This leads to the sixth ideological feature of ethnic minority mobilization.

## Transnationalism

We need to recognize the transnational influences made possible by cheap transportation and electronic communication. The Khalistani Sikh nationalist movement in Punjab in the 1980s was facilitated by the diasporic support it received, especially in the United Kingdom and North America, which, among other things, enabled the news that the Indian state was trying to suppress to almost instantaneously reach the entire world. Transnationalism can be an important feature of identity too. Just as this was true of pan-Africanism or pan-blackness in the earlier part of this story, it is true today with some British Muslims, especially those who are younger and better educated. The concept *ummah,* the global community of Muslims, has been politically embraced and reinterpreted as global victims, and the oppression in Palestine, Bosnia, Chechnya, Afghanistan, and Iraq has been used as an occasion to heighten a Muslim political identity, which is sometimes explicitly hostile to national identities and ethnic affiliations (Sayyid 2000). Just as advocates of political blackness seek to unite all nonwhites despite more specific ethnic identities, so, similarly, some Muslims are intolerant of ethnic minority identities. They argue that a toleration of ethnic diversity is a policy of divide and rule against Muslims because it blinds Muslims to their real numbers and power by placing them in small ethnic groups, usually in competition with one another for limited resources (Muslim Parliament of Great Britain 1992). (In this and other respects, the logic and rhetoric of political Islam can be seen as similar to political blackness; Modood 2005b.)

Muslim transnationalism, at the levels of sentiment, ideology, and organization, has perhaps been continually present, but it has increased since the Iranian Revolution of 1979; it first became most evident in Britain during the *Satanic Verses* affair at the end of the 1980s and subsequently has come to the fore in a way that no one would have predicted. The politics of being Muslim in Britain and, more generally, the West has, inevitably, come to be dominated by 9/11 and its aftermath. The military and civil liberties aspects of the war against terrorism, even more so than at the time of the *Satanic Verses* affair, have seen a vulnerable and besieged group assert itself publicly and at times defiantly. The majority of British Muslims, while condemning the terrorist attacks on the United States, opposed the bombing campaign in Afghanistan and the invasion of Iraq. A significant minority of Muslims, however, voiced support for the Taliban, even for Osama bin Laden, and some seemed to have gone to Afghanistan to fight for the Taliban (Modood 2005b). The terrorist aspects of *ummah*-ic internationalism were even more dramatically illustrated by the London bombings of 7/7 and the abortive bombings of 7/21. The fact that most of the individuals involved had been born or brought up in Britain, a country that had given them or their parents a refuge from persecution, fear, or poverty and that had given them freedom of worship, seems to have led many to conclude that multiculturalism has failed—or, worse still, to blame it for the bombings (Modood 2007).

It has been argued that some Muslims have become especially susceptible to extremist *jihadi* ideologies because of their racialized marginal position in British society and because the second and third generations feel as alienated from their parents' and grandparents' culture and Islam as they do from mainstream British society. In this cultural identity crisis, a simplified Islam and the closed circle of a cult gives them a sense of meaning and belonging (Akhtar 2005; Abbas 2006). Although there may be something correct in this, it cannot explain away the politics—the discourses and actions of jihadi militants are a response to various political situations in the Muslim world and to the involvement of the British state in some of those situations, especially the invasion of Iraq.

## Mobilization and Political Integration

It is of some significance that the two minority groups that have been most politically active, or at least disproportionately visible—the African-Caribbeans and the Pakistanis—are among the most economically disadvantaged and feel the most "picked on." This is surely indicative of the general phenomenon that it is the powerless that need to resort to visible politics and demonstrations in the streets. As a result, such groups become more talked about, and even though this often can be in negative terms as troublemakers, this kind of public presence is in itself sometimes a kind of legitimation of their presence in the country, a form of integration. They do not necessarily make many friends, but they become accepted as part of the political landscape. They also secure, and can become dependent on, a disproportionate share of public-sector jobs.

Conversely, more prosperous minorities do not need to enter politics in a confrontational mode or before they have a strong middle-class base. Using measures such as ownership of small and large businesses, income from employment, entry into prestigious universities, and entry into prestigious professions, we find that the most prosperous and upwardly mobile minorities are the Hindus and the Chinese (Modood 2005b). These two groups have virtually no political profile. Wealthy Hindus, together with other wealthy Asians, court politicians by inviting them to community and social functions, donating to party coffers, and (I believe) quietly building up networks of influence and patronage, mainly beyond the gaze of research. It is, therefore, unclear to what extent this activity might be at the level of the individual (in the same way as nonminorities organize politically) or ethno-religious networks. What is public, however, is how the party leaderships have started publicly praising and courting Asian businesspeople (the Asian business sector has in the last quarter century produced more than its share of millionaires and multimillionaires).[2]

It could be said with some justification that the less politically visible minorities benefit from the political environment created by the more assertive; without the work done by the assertive minorities and the opportunity offered to the less politically active minorities to contrast themselves with the assertive minorities, all ethnic minorities would have less opportunity and influence. This might be so, but the price that the assertive minorities pay can be quite high. There is no doubt that African-Caribbeans and Muslims are regarded as difficult groups—although in quite different ways—and this means that there may be contexts in which they must be seen to be not excluded, but this is at the price of being nonmodel minorities. Political engagement can be a form of integration for marginal groups; indeed, some forms of conflict (including confrontations such as the Brixton riots and the Rushdie affair) can have positive political effects. But if a group is not able to manage and moderate its public identity, it risks heightening, not lessening, its stigmatization. A judicious amount of conflict can be advantageous; it can open doors and achieve conceptual or policy shifts. But too much confrontation can mean that the minority is not perceived as an ally that the mainstream can do give-and-take business with.

Ethnic minority mobilization, no less than the rest of politics, requires judgment as to when and how much to demand, and when to compromise and cut a deal. Events such as the Brixton riots and the Rushdie affair burst on British politics with the "shock of the new/alien" (rhetorical expressions like "I don't know what country I am living in anymore" were typical). To judge their impact on social mobility is, from the side of minority activism, to evaluate what political advantage, if any, the political leaders of the relevant minorities were able to extract from what *prima facie* seem to be unredeemably negative episodes. This is the situation that Muslim political leaders and spokesperson find themselves in since the London bombings of July 2005, although perhaps damage limitation may be a more realistic goal than the extracting of political advantage. In any case, the current crisis can be used to achieve political integration as result in the increased marginality of Muslims.

## Challenges and Revisions to Liberal Citizenship

Muslims now dominate the minority mobilization space and Islamism has emerged as (to use a phrase that Charles Taylor once used of liberalism) "a fighting creed"

(Taylor 1994, 62), but this should not obscure that at, least to date and in relation to domestic matters, Muslim assertiveness has drawn considerably on the underlying discourses of multicultural equality (Modood 2005b; Modood 2007). Indeed, this assertiveness has taken different forms. Muslims, of course, have not simply manifested a single political position; there are principally three: a human rights appeal, a social equality agenda, and a group autonomy approach (a kind of Muslim power analogous to black power discourse). This should not surprise us, for these are indeed the three principal options in contemporary Anglo-American equality politics (Modood 2005b, 165–66).

Nevertheless, the ethnic minority politics described here has four implications for liberal citizenship, stemming from the fact that it takes the concept of equality beyond and into conflict with liberal citizenship. Recall that liberal citizenship is based on a public-private identity distinction that prohibits the recognition of particular group identities so that no citizens are treated in a more or less privileged way or divided from one another. First, most of ethnic minority politics is clearly a collective project and includes collectivities, not merely individuals. Second, ethnic minority politics is not color-blind. These two implications are relatively straightforward.

The third implication, however, has been less appreciated—ethnic minority politics takes race (and we could make the same point with the related politics of gender and sexual orientation) beyond being merely an ascriptive source of identity or category. Race is of interest to liberal citizenship only because people cannot choose their race and so should not be discriminated against on the basis of something over which they have no control. But if equality is about celebrating previously demeaned identities (e.g., an individual's taking pride in his or her blackness rather than in accepting it merely as a private matter), then what is being addressed in antidiscrimination, or promoted as a public identity, is a *chosen* response to the individual's ascription. (Exactly, the same applies to sex and sexuality. We may not choose our sex or sexual orientation, but we choose how to politically live with it. Do we keep it private or do we make it the basis of a social movement and seek public resources and representation for it?)

Now Muslims, a religious group, are using this kind of argument and making a claim that Muslim identity, just like certain forms of racial identity, should not just be privatized or tolerated but should be part of the public space. In their case, however, they come into conflict with an additional dimension of liberal citizenship—secularism, the view that religion is a feature, perhaps uniquely, of private identity and not public identity. This is the fourth implication of ethno-religious assertiveness for liberal citizenship.

Many classical liberals and some multiculturalists may respond by arguing that black and Asian (and female and gay) are ascribed unchosen identities, whereas being Muslim is about chosen beliefs, and that Muslims therefore need or ought to have less legal protection than the other kinds of identities. This is sociologically naïve or a political con. The position of Muslims in Britain today is similar to the other identities of difference as Muslims catch up with and engage with the contemporary concept of equality. No one chooses to be or not to be born into a Muslim family. Similarly, no one chooses to be born into a society where to look like a Muslim or to be a Muslim creates suspicion, hostility, or failure to get the job you applied for. How Muslims respond to these circumstances, however, will vary. Some will organize resistance, whereas others will try to stop looking like Muslims (the equivalent of blacks' passing for white). Some will build an ideology out of their subordination; others will not, just as a woman can choose to be a feminist or not. Again, some Muslims may define their Islam in terms of piety rather than politics; just as some women may see no politics in their gender, whereas for others their gender will be at the center of their politics.

Hence, although it might surprise U.S. readers, debates about migrant politics, multiculturalism, and ethno-religious equality in Britain and Europe generally increasingly involve debates about secularism (Modood, Triandafyllidou, and Zapata-Barrero 2005). This takes the postimmigration politics of accommodation into deep waters and is stimulating a backlash across Europe, not just from the nationalist right but across the political spectrum, not just from advocates of *laïcité* but also from erstwhile champions of multiculturalism (though the proclamations of the death of multiculturalism are premature: Meer and Modood, forthcoming). Some vigorous assertions of secularism belie the fact that mainstream European secularism is not ideological but an evolving compromise between organized religion and liberal democratic polities. Of course, such compromises are not static and vary from national context to national context, very much along the lines of the five ideal state types discussed at the beginning of this chapter. Nevertheless, it means that the institutional accommodation of some Muslim claims for political recognition, power-sharing, and resources is possible and, indeed, is taking place to some extent (Modood and Kastoryano 2005). As long as we are not wedded to inflexible concepts of liberalism and secularism, there is no reason to panic (Modood 2007).

This chapter's most important implication for the general study of immigrant political incorporation is to highlight the significance of political ideas and political discourses. The deployment and development of these discourses can reflect political assertiveness and lead to political conflict, but they can also lead to political integration. They are likely to be part of a broader climate of opinion, especially the contemporary "uprising" of subordinate identities such as female, gay, black, and minority nationalism, and one discourse can give rise, however unintentionally, to another. Whether political assertiveness and mobilization take place depends on the type of immigration, the reception status, and the relationship between culture, identity, and the polity in question. In relation to these three variables, in the British case:

- the type of immigration was postcolonial (rather than merely economic or of refugees)
- the status was of quasi-citizenship ("subjects of the Crown") with easy access to full citizenship, at least for the first few decades (rather than, say, guest workers) but in a context of racism and racialization
- yet with some official encouragement to maintain distinct group identities (rather than to repudiate them in favor of republican assimilation), for the orientation of national politics was sufficiently pluralist (rather than one of the other ideal types presented in the early part of this chapter).

How these variables worked in practice also depended on the socioeconomic and human capital profile of the migrants and the (latent) identities, solidarities, and enmities that they brought with them. The single most important point is that (post-) immigrant politics exists within a contested normative context—and the context extends to the framing and conceptualization of the politics. In my view, the normative political framing best suited for realizing the egalitarian ideals of the contemporary post-immigration settlements is civic multiculturalism (Modood 2007).

# CHAPTER SIXTEEN

# Differences in the City

## Parallel Worlds, Migration, and Inclusion of Differences in the Urban Space

*Sandro Cattacin*

The city attracts diversity: different ways of life, different trajectories, and different socioeconomic positions. Its anonymity promises liberty and attracts people who are searching for new opportunities. The city simultaneously combines the promise of indifference toward diversity (as outlined by Simmel 2001 [1900]) and of a possible social ascension, thereby particularly attracting people on the move. Cities draw both the elite of the "creative class" (Florida 2004) and the poor of society in search of a better future. In this sense, the city, par excellence, attracts migrants.

Traditionally, urban sociology has analyzed how migrants become included in urban life in two major ways. The first approach, made by social hygienists, adopted a cultural explanation. It underlined the perversity of self-exclusionary mechanisms among people who did not adopt a bourgeois way of life in the city (e.g., Mearns 1883) and promoted a negative vision of bad neighborhoods, segregated spaces, and ghettos. In short, immigrants concentrated in and formed stigmatized areas. Although not really liberated from the social hygienist prejudices, Georg Simmel (2001 [1900]) added an alternative explanation. For him, people living in segregated areas of the city were simply unable to leave their peasant background behind and chose to reproduce living conditions similar to those of their former peasant world in their urban neighborhoods. Lacking human, economic, and social resources, yet still needing communitarian relationships or some kind of mechanic solidarity, they were unable to seize the perspectives and potential of freedom offered by the city.

Park (1928) introduced a structural element that explained segregated spaces in terms of the territorial constitution of a city rather than the choices of the migrants themselves. The environment of the city organized itself in a functional way and put migrants and poor people in its less attractive areas. A dynamic of exclusion related to socioeconomic positions led the rich to take up the best places in the city and to confine the poor to the segregated spaces. Antisegregation policies, then, became the political way of fighting against a systematic exclusion; this policy choice is still the principal response to segregation in many of today's cities (Häußermann 1995).

These analyses of the Chicago School reached a turning point with the rediscovery of urban communities as self-regulated spaces of solidarity. William Whyte's *Street Corner Society* (1943) reflected this rediscovered point of view. Whyte interpreted the culturally homogeneous urban spaces occupied by lower socioeconomic-status people not only as risk areas but also as producing reciprocity and potentially stabilizing the city.[1] Segregated spaces, in fact, might have better social cohesion (and more social control) than other places, increasing people's capacity to survive, ontologically speaking, from both material and psychological points of view.[2] From the material point of view, more homogeneous communities can more easily exchange services in a nonmonetary economy. Psychologically speaking, neighbors do not systematically challenge one another's identity and neighborhood homogeneity facilities the recognition process of each person's identity. In the same logic, Herbert Gans (1962, x) started with the analyses of low-income population, which led him to analyze neighborhoods. Gans (1962, 252) in fact, discovered other values than the middle-class ones in Boston's West End, what he called a working-class subculture. He underlined the internal solidarity links in the neighborhood, which are at the origin of a subculture, and that the inhabitants were not chosen by the neighborhood but, being aware of the qualities of living in West End, chose to settle there.

This interpretation leads me to think, along with Michael Dear and Steven Flusty (2001), that spaces with a concentration of people with a low socioeconomic status are not problematic as such. In contrast to the Chicago School's interpretation, they can have a stable organization even with ever-changing populations, criminality, and violence. These new urban spaces also allow the intervening bodies in the social and health-care sectors to focus on their users.

## From Segregated Neighborhoods to Aggregated Neighborhoods?

Why not ghettos? This admittedly provocative question leads me to reconsider the internal dynamic of neighborhood formation in modern cities. In democratic and open societies organized around individualistic values, plural ways of living, and flexible organization, ghettos might play a different role than they did in the past, a role less focused on external exclusion or segregation and more focused on an internal re-appropriation of sense by the inhabitants of these places.[3] In other words, although Simmel did not see segregated spaces as serving a positive function and the Chicago School wanted to dismantle them, it may well be that their existence today can still contribute something positive and that trying to get rid of them would create more problems than benefits. To explore this hypothesis, this chapter examines the current transformation of urban space toward more homogenous aggregations of social groups. This transformation can be explained by external forces to neighborhoods and through a process of internal self-organization.

From an external contextual point of view, significant societal changes have led me to believe that such a communitarian transformation of the city is a consequence of the pluralization of society and the more flexible economy, both of which threaten social identity and cohesion, and at the end of the day must be re-created by individual efforts. The phenomena of individualization and economic flexibility thus complicate the integration of the whole society. As many authors have shown, this complexity has consequences for a growing number of people who are poorly included, whether economically or socially (see, for example, Castel 1995; Paugam 1991). And the more complexity and exclusion in people's everyday lives, the more research on identity as stabilizing communities is increasing. In contrast to Richard Sennett (1998), we think along with Zygmunt Bauman (2000) that flexibility and individualization transfer the search for values and identity to the private sphere. Through the search for identity and values, anarchic forms of communitarianism appear, grouping all kind of lifestyles. Whereas the general population is not subjected to these anarchic forms of communitarianism because they have been emancipated, since the 1970s, from the old group-building communities like churches and trade unions, people with migrant or ethnic backgrounds stabilize themselves in the face of the challenges of adapting to the city and the threat of complexity by forming communities with others of the same migrant or ethnic background.

Let us shift to the internal view explaining homogenous neighborhoods. Migration to the city—even of undocumented migrants—cannot be stopped because it represents a flow of people from contexts with fewer opportunities to those with more. From the social point of view, migration means basically that the old ties are weakened and that new ties have to be rebuilt in the new context of migration (Sayad and Fassa 1982). We can begin by positing that the social aggregation of migrants in urban spaces reflects a social logic. From the point of view of the internal organization, three main arguments support this idea. First, these urban spaces protect identities from the continuous challenge by the dominant value system in modern society. Second, the people and institutions in these spaces have a strong capacity to solve concrete problems through their self-organization. Finally, the extent to which they can realize this self-regulating potential depends on whether the other inhabitants of the city and their political representatives recognize that city neighborhoods—even those in which poor and politically marginal populations are concentrated—do in fact have a positive role to play. This recognition can open doors for more effective public policy interventions.

## Aggregated Neighborhoods as Opportunity-Seeking

Although aggregated neighborhoods are still constrained and shaped by various economic, legal, social, and racial inequalities, these areas still have a material and symbolic value for the people living in them. First, they are the entry point for many migrants to the city. They find people they know and communities that can help them and sustain their first steps toward economic and social integration into city life. In particular, undocumented migrants depend on such neighborhoods because they gain a feeling of security (Achermann and Chimienti 2005). Even in smaller cities without segregated spaces, people with the same roots and socioeconomic backgrounds can be found living or meeting near common spaces such as the railway stations, restaurants, and clubs.[4]

At first glance, these concentrations could seem problematic. In fact, taking a dynamic view, these places not only provide communitarian accommodations that lessen the negative impact of migration, but they provide a base from which the immigrant can take steps outside the neighborhood. In other words, migrants into the city find not only a warm and loyal surrounding but also an island from which they may exercise exit and voice (Hirschman 1970). Although exit might mean the migrants' returning to their home country after a failed migration project, it can also mean that they have moved to a new neighborhood that helps them belong to a new community. A voice strategy could mean that, having stabilized their position in the neighborhood, migrants find ways to achieve upward mobility. Aggregated neighborhoods can, thus, be the starting point or the end point of a migrant's history. They give migrants a chance to feel their way into a better life. Others have observed that residence in homogeneous but socially disqualified neighborhoods can, in some cases, help the inhabitants to avoid being confronted by external stigmatization, thus protecting their self-esteem; Paugam, for instance, describes this as "organized marginality" (2000, 129).

## Aggregated Neighborhoods as Protection from the Dominant Value System

Identities, particularly immigrant identities, are under stress. There is a twofold logic to this process. First, participation in a flexible economic system of weak identities and strong personalities challenges people who are searching for solid value orientations (Sennett 1998). Immigrants are well suited to a flexible economy because the migration process itself has already required them to compromise their identity. In contrast to the Fordist economy, the new flexible economy no longer compensates for the immigrants' lack of social integration by workplace-related community-building activities. Instead, this must come from where they live. Immigrants thus look on residential communities as identity-stabilizing places (Fibbi and Cattacin 2002).

Second, the pluralization process that has accelerated since the 1960s has weakened the pressure on immigrants to acculturate. As members of societies in which differentiation is increasing not only in magnitude but in the extent to which it is socially accepted, immigrants, like others, have options in choosing where they want to belong. In this market of identities, people may have weaker individual identities, but they are also obliged to use new ways of developing collective identities in order to exist and survive (Amselle 2000). If normality means living in a social space that does not require any affiliation, or if liminality is the norm (Bauman 2000), migrants' stabilizing their identity can represent a survival strategy (Szakolczai 1994).

Aggregated neighborhoods become places in which people with fragile identities, threatened by daily experiences of discrimination or stigmatization, can stabilize their identities through meeting people like themselves. That means, clearly, that the production of identity is not a simple reproduction of an old cultural framework but the creation of an urban identity that combines elements of reference and recognition inside groups. Identities that seem to be culturally determined are, in fact, constructed in a new context. They are, as Fredrik Barth (1969) suggests, open to change. And if they do not change, we have to understand this as a strategy of stabilization of fragile identities. The community in a modern society is nothing more than an archipelago of security—but it is not a finite determination of lifelong belonging.

Aggregated Neighborhoods as Problem Solvers

As Amitai Etzioni (1993) argued, urban spaces can be the starting point for communitarian self-help initiatives. The question is whether neighborhoods with large immigrant communities have developed this capacity. My hypothesis is that areas that have more freedom to act are more able to solve their own problems. The large cities in North America provide many examples of this ability to act, but it is less clear that the segregated spaces of European cities are legitimate places for political contestation (Donzelot, Mével, and Wyvekens 2003). Why do such differences continue to exist between the New and Old World cities? Probably because Europe has made the programmatic choice to fight poverty with a large welfare state that does not tolerate highly disadvantaged situations (Cattacin 2006). Only after the 1980s, when shifting economic and societal models began to limit the welfare state (Cattacin and Lucas 1999), did Europe start to realize that neighborhood poverty is an inevitable part of urban reality. In contrast, immigration countries such as the United States have used community-centered, not state-centered, means for developing social solidarity and do not charge individual failures to the society as a whole.[5]

Today we can discern a weakening of both models. The European model has been weakened by the apparent financial crisis of the welfare state and the related difficulties in pursuing redistribution policies. If European social policies share any common ground at the city level, it is the lack of an alternative model to antisegregation policy. Without resources and without ideas, European cities are working on a short-term logic of trouble-shooting that has no real prospects of succeeding. Riots and anomie are therefore the logical consequences (Donzelot 2006).

The end of generalized economic growth has also shown the limits of communal self-help efforts arising within immigrant neighborhoods. In the current economic dynamic, the correlation between poverty and spatial segregation mean that aggregated neighborhoods of low-status people have limited resources for mobilization. They risk being subjected to what Loïc Wacquant (2006) has called a process of "hyper-ghettoization," characterized by a loss of self-regenerating resources. Even though Wacquant may be overdramatizing the urban dynamics of the United States (and Europe) and underestimating the capacities of the communities, he nevertheless makes the point that the capacity for neighborhood mobilization is conditioned by material resources and that social capital depends on economic capital (see also Bagnasco 1999). Neighborhoods must have a minimal level of both dimensions if people and groups are to survive. Even if it is easier to meet people and find a job in city neighborhoods, sprawling city spaces and edge cities still confront us with neighborhoods without identity and in danger of anomie (Garreau 1991).

## Recognizing the Potential
## of Aggregated Neighborhoods

If we accept the argument that cities in modern societies need places in which people with a low socioeconomic status not only can live but can develop stable identities and self-organize their common resources as a starting point for social and economic integration, this is not the same as saying that we need ghettos as such, but only that we should not underestimate the clear positive functions that such places can have for our societies. To try to combat or eliminate such places means to follow a romantic view of a harmonious multicultural—and unattainable—society. It means seeing cities in a way that ignores their continuous dynamic of migration and reorganization (Donzelot 2006, 77).

Antisegregation policies that seek forcibly to blend the elements of urban society risk destroying the self-regenerating resources that society produces in more homogeneous spaces, even in low-income neighborhoods. Accepting that we live in a divided but pluricultural society—rather than in a homogeneously multicultural one—in which differences between neighborhoods are the norm implies that we need to find a way of using these differences as resources, not as problems. To use the fact that neighborhoods are different as a resource, we have to accept these differences, not to denigrate them. In other words, we have to find ways in which poor and immigrant neighborhoods can react to threats and troubles autonomously and deal with them (Donzelot and Estèbe 1994).

Recognizing the positive potential of neighborhood differences begins with acknowledging the suffering and collective identity formation that takes place within marginal neighborhoods, which in turn leads to a public embrace of groups that now are neither visible nor accepted. This "struggle for recognition" (Honneth 1994) allows immigrants and poor people to exist in dignity, but it also demands that the rest of society accept this dignity (as Taylor 1994 highlighted). This can even be expressed by social indifference toward the existence of different life worlds. But if we want to use these neighborhood differences to advance the project of producing an innovative urban society, we must find new ways to reinforce their positive elements. This is a question of the governance of the city.

## Governing Difference

Before analyzing how urban spaces can be organized so that density and difference enable people to be innovative and engage in democratic conflict resolution, we need to understand that the governance of cities today is a multifaceted dynamic in which local government plays a role but probably no longer a predominant one. In the face of this condition, local governments need to be open to innovation and change and to adopt urban development policies that are sensitive to difference. They need to develop new policy instruments that are adapted to an accelerated pace change in the city.

Nowadays, researchers highlight the fact that local authorities are in a much better position than national authorities to deal with the plurality of society and to apply concrete and appropriate measures to urban problems (Kazepov 2005). Even though the city is still the best level for governing differences and responding to social challenges, the actors of governance are many and varied. In particular, the local state is not the center of governance anymore but only one producer of decisions among others.

Indeed, deindustrialization, migration, and accelerated economic changes have challenged city authorities. Given the long-term urban development planning that took place in 1970s and the conservative stabilization that arrived in the 1980s, the last twenty years have confronted us with the resurgence of uneven growth and policy demands for reducing regulation and restructuring the old social welfare states. In the field of urban planning, it was the search for more liberty in planning cities that was formulated as the answer to the lack of urban innovation and development (Campos Venuti 1990). In this newly "splintered" city (Graham and Marvin 2001), governance takes place within a networked pattern of relatively independent organized worlds.

In such a network, the function of the city government is to guarantee basic infrastructure. The main actors are investors and anarchically formed into continuously changing communities. Urban life-world subcultures, such as those of immigrants, are generally organized through services and initiatives that the local state neither plans nor provides. For instance, the world of undocumented migrants is characterized by self-help and social service networks that the local state may acknowledge, or at least tolerate, but does not operate. When the local state is in the ambivalent position of knowing that undocumented migrants need a service, such as health care, but cannot easily deliver it officially, it accepts the existence of alternative health services. Without them, the local state would have to act in a way that might contradict its legal or political imperatives (not to serve those who are not formally eligible for them). By accepting this ambiguity, it facilitates the basic right to health care. Similar circumstances govern the worlds of drug abuse (Cattacin, Lucas, and Vetter 1996) and homelessness (Thelen 2006). Without parallel services—for the parallel worlds of urban existence—city problems would increase to point of crisis.

The networks that produce these services—and, in a sense, partial rights—arise through the self-organization of advocacy and solidarity groups. Access to what amounts to basic services is guaranteed if an individual belongs to a specific group. This production of partial (and informal) rights outside the sphere of the state transforms the logic of citizenship (Bauböck 2003a). De facto citizenship—as distinguished from the de jure citizenship of the old system—has become a variety of rights, which are realized in a city and to which access is given by different laws and societal actors. We can call this multifaceted new urban citizenship societal citizenship. As Engin Isin seems to suggest:

> Rather than merely focusing on citizenship as legal rights, there is now agreement that citizenship must also be defined as a social process through which individuals and social groups engage in claiming, expanding or losing rights. Being politically engaged means practicing substantive citizenship, which in turn implies that members of a polity always struggle to shape its fate. This can be considered as the sociological definition of citizenship in that the emphasis is less on legal rules and more on norms, practices, meanings and identities. (2000, 3)

This new citizenship is based not only on rights given by the state and societal actors but also by each person's multileveled affiliation with local, national, and even international or supranational rights. Even if the local state is still the main reference for people living in the city and, in particular, for immigrants in precarious situations, it still has to deal with these multiple affiliations, legacies, and constraints. Consequently, if city government aims to rule in a hierarchical, top-down manner, this (almost impossible) mission is doomed to failure. It can succeed only by working in tandem with all kinds of civil society organizations to make decisions and provide services.

Cities are thus moving from a hierarchical model of governance to a heterarchical model with many centers of decision making. If city governments recognize many different actors as producers and seek to combine their resources, they can enable these actors to integrate themselves horizontally, creating synergies among service producers and even solidarity within the city. This can take many forms, as studies of alternative ways of organizing social and health-care services have demonstrated (Blanke, Evers, and Wollmann 1986; Cattacin et al. 1999; Battaglini, Cattacin, and Tattini 2001a, 2001b). Attitudes may be tolerant or indifferent; organizational relationships can be based on exchange or coalitions. The key point is that the actors involved recognize that they all have relevant roles in the creation of a workable urban society.

Only capacity-building policies can really address the issues in disadvantaged neighborhoods, in the sense of creating new (and autonomous) resources. As Jacques Donzelot outlined in his work on the "animator state" (Donzelot and Estèbe 1994), only a shift from a paternalistic to a capability-building approach facilitated an improvement in the living conditions of the French *banlieux*. The new urban development policies for these areas promoted a kind of self-governance that involved giving power to the powerless, although we might wonder whether this was planned by an animator state or just an accidental side effect. This policy was discontinued in the 1990s as a result of financial cutbacks, not because the policy had failed. As many authors have pointed out, living conditions there degenerated once again as a consequence. In other words, incorporating the poorest people requires that they have some possibility of developing their own resources—an opportunity they generally take. Such an investment strategy falls within Amartya Sen's (1992) analyses of building capabilities.

What concrete instruments permit urban policy to be sensitive to differences and to pay particular attention to building up the capabilities of migrants? The increasing heterogeneity of urban societies increasingly reflects, as Stephen Graham and Simon Marvin (2001, 405) argue, the more general dynamics of societal pluralization. In the politics of urban policy in Europe, the last few years have witnessed an increasing awareness that local authorities urgently need to grapple with the differences that shape the contemporary urban environment. To "manage our co-existence in shared spaces," as Patsy Healey defines *planning*, we must above all acknowledge that "Population groups, differentiated by criteria of age, gender, class, dis/ability, ethnicity, sexual preference, culture and religion, have different claims on the city for a full life and, in particular, on the built environment" (1997, 3). Sandercock (1998, 2000) further argues that the following three factors led to a significant change in the agenda of urban planning: transnational migrations, postcolonialism, and the rise of civil society. These phenomena strengthen the idea that the cities of today are "cities of difference" (Fincher and Jacobs 1998). This means that, unlike the current modern planning paradigm, the new one should be based on the active involvement of groups representing such differences.

Following this logic, James Holston suggests that the new paradigm of urban planning should be based on what he calls "insurgent citizenship" (1995). In other words, the new-built environment should result from a participatory political process in which new identities, such as those of immigrants, homeless people, and sexual minorities, are empowered to confront the dominant culture (and its institutionalized powers).

In my view, three aspects are fundamental to the challenge of an urban citizenship:

- Promote urban diversity. This concerns urban policies that seek to attract different groups of people. We might call this "difference sensitive city-marketing." Urban environments should be planned partly in terms of the groups that will be solicited to settle down in them. In particular, if the city recognizes that immigrants are important to its future, it will recognize and accept migrants and invite them to participate in the construction of the city. For instance, Zurich and London think of urban development as a combination of demographic dynamics, quality of life for all inhabitants, and a tolerant climate (see, for London, Morphet 2007).
- Integrate diversity into urban development. The instruments that cities use to construct space should integrate difference in a sensitive way. Sensitivity toward diversity is crucial in the sphere of housing. In fact, housing policies help determine which groups can inhabit the city. They should take steps to counter the current trend, in which market mechanisms "bring about a tougher segregation" (Häußermann 1995, 90) and thus block the development of resources in these neighborhoods. A way to work against degrading neighborhoods is the development of concrete social policies that open social mobility to all inhabitants of a city. That means, in concrete terms, improving social rights and the use of these rights for marginalized groups and giving them possibilities and the resources for self-governance.
- Empower groups of difference to participate in the urban planning process. It is obvious that the poor and immigrant populations of low-status neighborhoods need to participate in the urban planning and problem-solving activities aimed at these neighborhoods and, indeed, the city as a whole.

When combined, these elements will enable city government to integrate differences as a key element of urban policy. A way to include differences in the planning process could be the creation of councils that reflect the communities living in a city and include representatives that are not citizens. This can be done in specific institutions such as hospitals (e.g., with the councils created in the Bradford Teaching Hospital; see Cattacin and Renschler 2008), through activities of empowerment in the management of schools (as in Berlin; see Beer, Deniz, and Schwedler 2007), or through councils in cities such as the Community Relations Council in Belfast (Murtagh, Murray, and Keaveney 2007).

## Aggregated Neighborhoods?

This chapter develops the idea of the neighborhoods as aggregations of people sharing certain traits (not just immigrant origin and socioeconomic characteristics) that not only should and could but presently are playing a positive role in the integration of immigrants into European (and doubtless U.S.) society. This dynamic lies at the heart of contemporary urban development. Such neighborhoods not only have an often-underestimate potential for self-regulation and stabilization, but in many instances they are delivering on that potential. They could do much more if urban policy sought to build on that capacity rather than working against it. The history of ghettos in the twentieth century was that their closure was enforced from the outside, but today we can promote them as open spaces. As Donzelot (2006) argues, the city has to be open and closed at the same time. The modern city has to help aggregated neighborhoods develop self-sustaining initiatives while avoiding the error of promoting ghettos. Finding the equilibrium between helping aggregated neighborhoods realize their potential and also enabling those who wish to move upward and outward from them cannot be achieved through state-centered planning; we need difference-sensitive governance constructed by local authorities.

# CHAPTER SEVENTEEN

# In Pursuit of Inclusion

## Citizenship Acquisition among Asian Immigrants

*Janelle Wong and Adrian D. Pantoja*

For immigrants in the United States, the acquisition of U.S. citizenship is a critical prerequisite for political inclusion because naturalized citizens enjoy many of the same rights and privileges afforded to individuals born on U.S. soil, including the right to vote and hold elective office (with the exception of the presidency). For much of history of this country, race (which was often synonymous with national origin) was the key factor determining who was eligible for admission into the country and eligible for citizenship. "Whiteness" became the legal moniker dividing those who were eligible for inclusion in the national community from those who were not.

Perhaps no other nonwhite immigrant group has been as profoundly impacted by racially exclusive immigration policies as Asians, who were the primary targets beginning with the Chinese Exclusion Act of 1882. That legislation barred Chinese immigration explicitly on the basis of national origin. Ironically, the exclusion of Chinese immigrants came at a time when the nation was seeking to bring African Americans into the political community through the abolition of slavery and the passage of the Reconstruction Amendments (Johnson 2004). In 1917, Congress further restricted immigration by creating the racialized Asiatic barred zone, which excluded all immigrants from Asia. Interestingly, Latin American immigrants were not subjected to these exclusions, even after the 1924 National Origins Act, which essentially shut off most immigration from Asian countries for over forty years.

Not unrelated to restrictive immigration legislation, immigrants from Asia faced legal barriers to becoming citizens throughout much of U.S. history. The right to naturalize was predicated on an individual's racial categorization. In *In re Au Yup*, an immigrant from China, Au Yup, petitioned a federal court in California to naturalize and become a U.S. citizen. The judge denied his petition because he was "of the opinion that a native of China, of the Mongolian race, is not a white person within the meaning of the act of congress" and therefore ineligible for citizenship.[1]

This and other judicial decisions barring Asians from citizenship on the basis of race harken back to the 1857 *Dred Scott v. Sandford* decision, in which blacks were denied citizenship solely on the basis of their race (Johnson 2004). Racial restrictions on naturalization were not lifted until the mid-twentieth century. Chinese were allowed to become citizens in 1943, Filipinos and Indians from South Asia could become citizens in 1946, and it was not until 1952 that other Asian groups were granted the right to naturalize (Chin et al. 1996). Although Asian immigrants became active in the U.S. political system through challenging racially restrictive legislation in the courts, their democratic participation in the United States was curtailed severely by the legacy of racial barriers to becoming full citizens.

Immigration from Asia rose dramatically after the passage of the Immigration Act of 1965, which opened immigration to all groups regardless of race or national origin. Between 1921 and 1960, Asian immigrants were less than 4 percent of all immigrants admitted. After 1965, Asian immigration surpassed all other groups except Latin Americans. Immigration has made Asian Americans one of the fastest growing minority groups in the United States and transformed the community into one that is majority foreign-born. Data from the November 2004 Current Population Survey show that, although the majority of Asian-origin adults in the United States were citizens through birth or naturalization, a significant proportion (nearly one in every three) were noncitizens during that election cycle (figure 17.1). Becoming naturalized citizens, then, represents an important barrier to Asians' ability to take part in U.S. elections and find inclusion into the U.S. political system.

Even though national origin is no longer a criterion for political inclusion, a cursory look at the naturalization patterns reveals national origin to be an important

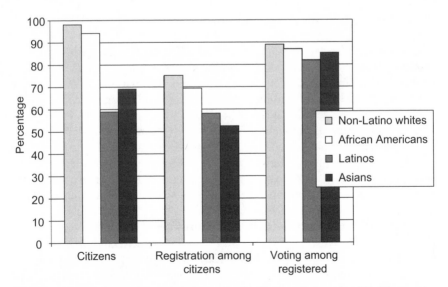

**Figure 17.1** Rates of citizenship, registration, and voting for four ethnic groups (%). All categories include those over 18 years old only. The African American category includes all who identified as "black alone or in combination." The Asian category includes all who identified as "Asian alone or in combination."
*Source:* U.S. Bureau of the Census, Current Population Survey, November 2004, tables 02-3-2, 02-6-1, 02-10.

factor shaping the acquisition of U.S. citizenship. Among the Asian immigrant population, there is considerable diversity and variation in terms of naturalization rates. Filipino and Chinese immigrants have some of the highest rates of naturalization, whereas Indian, Cambodian, and Laotian immigrants have some of the lowest (Ong and Nakanishi 2003). Is this variation simply the result of differences in sociodemographic characteristics such as age, education, income, and English proficiency, as is commonly believed (Ong and Lee 2001; Ong and Nakanishi 2003), or is Asian naturalization driven by other factors unique to their migration experience?

We seek to answer this question by drawing on data from the 2000–2001 Pilot National Asian American Political Survey (PNAAPS). The data set includes a total of 1,218 adults of the top six Asian American national origin population groups residing in the Los Angeles, New York, Honolulu, San Francisco, and Chicago metropolitan areas.[2] The Asian population in these metropolitan areas represents 40 percent of the Asian population in the United States. The telephone survey took place between November 16, 2000, and January 28, 2001. Respondents were randomly selected using random-digit dialing at targeted Asian zip code densities and listed-surname frames. Selection probability for each national origin sample is approximate to the size of the 1990 census figures for the national origin population in each metropolitan area.[3] The sample consists of 308 Chinese, 168 Korean, 137 Vietnamese, 198 Japanese, 266 Filipino, and 141 South Asians. When possible, the respondents were interviewed in their preferred language (English, Mandarin Chinese, Cantonese, Korean, or Vietnamese). Respondents of Japanese, Filipino, and South Asian descent were interviewed in English.

## Immigrant Naturalization

The requirements for naturalization in the United States today are relatively straightforward. Any legal immigrant admitted to the United States can become a citizen by filling out an Application for Naturalization Form N-400, if he or she is at least eighteen years old and has lived continuously in the United States for at least five years or three years if married to a U.S. citizen. The residency requirement is shortened to two years for legal permanent residents who are in the U.S. military. In addition, a prospective citizen must have a rudimentary knowledge of the English language, basic knowledge of U.S. history and government, be of good moral character, and not be a public charge. Finally, before becoming U.S. citizens, individuals are required to take an oath of allegiance to the United States. Children under eighteen who accompany their parents to the United States automatically become citizens when their parents naturalize (U.S. Department of Homeland Security 2004).

In practice, however, an immigrant must go through a series of bureaucratic hurdles even before he or she can take the English and U.S. history exams. The simple act of filing out an application can be daunting because minor errors on Form N-400 can result in a returned application. This is a minor inconvenience compared to having the application or any of the accompanying documents (fingerprints, photographs, application fee, photocopy of Permanent Resident Card, and other documents depending on special circumstances) lost in the piles of applications that the Immigration and Naturalization Service receives daily. Of course, sometime prior to or during the application process, an immigrant must have taken some steps toward learning the English language and learning U.S. history and civics. Fear that either exam will be too difficult can discourage prospective applicants (Grebler 1966; Cornelius 1981; Pachon 1987). In fact, among Mexican immigrants, fear of failing the English or U.S. history exam was the most common reason given why they were delaying the application process (Pachon and DeSipio 1994).

Other accounts of the naturalization process based on interviews with immigrants reveal that the motives behind the naturalization process are as varied as the reasons why individuals forgo the process or become discouraged while going through the process (Ramirez 1979; Alvarez 1987; North 1987; Jones-Correa 1998). These studies, based on intensive interviews, present a rich and complex understanding of the naturalization process, yet they are limited in their ability to make generalizations or isolate the relevant factors stimulating citizenship. To address this methodological shortcoming, much of the present scholarship on immigrant citizenship acquisition is informed by data drawn from randomly administered surveys and analyzed through quantitative techniques (for a review of early works, see DeSipio 1987).

Quantitative studies on immigrant naturalization largely emphasize the power of economic and cultural assimilation in shaping the naturalization decision (Bernard 1936; Grebler 1966; Garcia 1981; DeSipio 1987, 1996; Ong and Nakanishi 2003). In other words, as immigrants become more economically mobile and culturally embedded in the host country, they become citizens, either for instrumental reasons (to secure and advance their economic status or sponsor relatives for immigration) or affective reasons (stronger feelings of attachment and loyalties to the host country). Although the motives for acquiring citizenship vary across individuals, the socioeconomic and demographic predictors used by scholars to predict naturalization are largely similar. Study after study finds that naturalization is primarily shaped by education, age, income, length of residency, English language ability, and other variables capturing economic resources and cultural identification with the United States (Alvarez 1987; Grebler 1966; Garcia 1981; DeSipio 1996).

Some studies augment the so-called economic and cultural assimilation framework with the country of origin and host-country destination characteristics, called contextual factors (Portes and Mozo 1985; Portes and Curtis 1987; Yang 1994a, 1994b; Aguirre and Saenz 2002). These include an immigrant's proximity to the nation of origin; the per capita GNP, literacy rates, level of urbanization, and regime type of the nation of origin; and the immigrant's contact with Anglo populations in the United States. Most recently, scholars have also considered the impact of transnational ties in shaping the naturalization decision (Yang 1994b; Jones-Correa 1998, 2001b; Pantoja 2005). *Transnational ties,* as applied to immigration, are typically defined as "the process by which immigrants forge and sustain simultaneous, multi-stranded social relations that link together their societies or origin and settlement" (Basch, Schiller, and Blanc 1994, 7). The effects of immigrant ties to the country origin on naturalization remain an open question because some find it dampens naturalization (Yang 1994b; Pantoja 2005) whereas others find the opposite effect (Jones-Correa 2001b).

Despite the renewed interest in immigrant naturalization, the theoretical frameworks advanced by scholars were largely developed from the migration experiences of Latin Americans, in particular Mexican immigrants (Alvarez 1987; Pachon 1987; DeSipio

1987, 1996). Only a handful of studies include non-Latino immigrants in their analyses (Liang 1994; Yang 1994a, 1994b, 2002). Interestingly, these latter comparative works find that even when the study controls for a host of factors, country of origin, or national origin, differences in naturalization persist. In fact, some studies find country of origin to be the strongest predictor of naturalization (Bueker 2005). The significance of this finding can be interpreted two ways. First, the traditional predictors used do not go far enough in explaining why some groups have higher rates of naturalization, suggesting other factors need to be considered. Second, detailed examinations of particular immigrant national origin groups are warranted to isolate the predictors relevant to their migration experiences. It may be the case that the direction, magnitude, and significance of selected variables vary considerably across national origin groups. We might expect this because the propensity to naturalize is likely to depend on a range of factors, including economic and political conditions unique to particular sending countries.

From this brief review, we can conclude that much of the present scholarship on immigrant naturalization in the United States revolves around Mexican and other Latin American immigrants and that a consensus has emerged in support of the economic mobility thesis and cultural assimilation thesis as measured by socioeconomic and demographic predictors such as age, education, length of residency, and language use. Although scholars may be tempted to generalize from findings based on the experience of Mexican and other Latin American immigrants, we argue that to do so may lead to inaccurate conclusions. First, Latin Americans are distinct from immigrants from many other parts of the world because the majority comes from places that are geographically proximate to the United States. Such close proximity may lead to different patterns of naturalization due to the relative ease of travel, cultural flows, and circular migration. Further, although some Latin American migrants arrive from communist regimes such as Cuba, most research in this area is based on the experiences of Mexican migrants. The Mexican Constitution was modeled in part on the U.S. Constitution, and similar to the U.S. model, the Mexican government is a federal system with a president and a bicameral legislature. We know much less about the naturalization patterns of migrants who come from communist states such as China or Vietnam. Further, Latin American migrants share a Romance language and Christian tradition with many in the United States. Many from Asia do not share the linguistic or religious origins of most Americans. For these reasons, we must question the extent to which the experience of Latin American migrants applies to people from other parts of the world. To what extent do the economic mobility thesis and cultural assimilation thesis apply to Asian immigrants?

Immigrant political incorporation does not end once the migrant acquires U.S. citizenship (see Jennifer Hochschild and John Mollenkopf, chap. 2 in this volume). Newly naturalized citizens are also expected to voice their political preferences through voting and participation in other political activities. Recent works on immigrant political incorporation, specifically electoral participation, provide compelling evidence debunking the robustness of traditional socioeconomic and demographic predictors (Cho 1999; Ramakrishnan 2005). In particular, among Asians, traditional theories of political participation do not adequately explain their participation in politics (Lien, Conway, and Wong 2004). More significant are the social networks that immigrants develop in the host country that are a source of political socialization. If socioeconomic status does not adequately explain patterns of political participation among Asians, it may be the case that these same predictors have a minimal, or at least a differential, impact on Asian naturalization rates as a result of their unique migration and socialization experiences.

## Asian Americans and Naturalization

Data from the PNAAPS confirm findings from previous studies and highlight the substantial variation in naturalization rates across Asian origin groups (Ong and Nakanishi 2003). Filipino immigrants in the survey exhibit the highest rates of naturalization, followed by Vietnamese and Chinese. In contrast to other Asian immigrants, lower rates of naturalization characterize those from South Asia (India and Pakistan), Korea, and Japan (figure 17.2). This pattern runs counter to the socioeconomic mobility hypothesis, given the high levels of educational attainment and incomes of Indian, Korean, and Japanese immigrants. How, then, do we explain these group differences? Can they be explained by other migration-related factors?

We next consider the general determinants of Asian naturalization. We augment the socioeconomic model with a political behavior model, a minority community

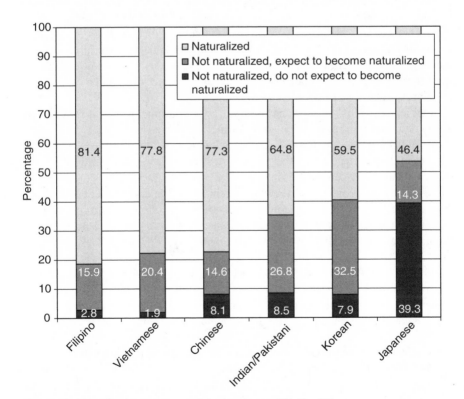

**Figure 17.2** Naturalization rates among Asian immigrants (%). N = 676.
*Source:* Pilot National Asian American Political Survey (PNAAPS).

and immigration status model, and a civic engagement model. This approach emphasizes the individual characteristics discussed by Hochschild and Mollenkopf (chap. 2 in this volume).

The civic engagement model represents a departure from previous works on immigrant naturalization, which assume that citizenship is primarily pursued for economic benefits and not for political rights (Borjas 2002). This assumption is reinforced by early studies on Latino political behavior demonstrating that foreign-born Latino citizens participate in electoral politics at rates lower than their native-born counterparts (DeSipio 1996). More recent works counter this assumption by observing that noncitizens desire to be active in politics and that those who are civically engaged are more likely to pursue naturalization (Barreto 2005; Pantoja and Gershon 2006).

Building on these works, we hypothesize that Asian immigrants who are civically engaged are more likely to become U.S. citizens *ceteris paribus*. The variables— Political Interest, Religiosity, Member of a Community Organization, and Strong Partisan—are grouped into the civic engagement model. We group this set of variables together because each is a measure of engagement in U.S. civic life (Putnam 2000). Robert Putnam describes political interest as a "critical precondition" of more active forms of involvement (2000, 35). He also identifies attachment to the parties as a key measure of civic engagement (2000, 37). Like political interest, strength of partisanship is a powerful predictor of more active types of participation, such as voting. He asserts that "churches provide an important incubator for civic skills, civic norms, community interests, and civic recruitment" (Putnam 2000, 66). He further claims that religiosity (often measured by attendance at religious services) is one of the most important correlates of civic engagement. Finally, organizational membership is a direct measure of civic engagement.

Variables falling into the minority community and immigration status model are closely tied to notions of ethnic identity formation in the United States and migration-related variables. Theories of pan-ethnicity most clearly inform our research in this area in that we hypothesize that those with stronger senses of identification with the pan–Asian American group will naturalize at higher rates.

Pan–Asian American ethnicity has been defined as "the development of bridging organizations and solidarities among several ethnic and immigrant groups of Asian ancestry" (Espiritu 1992, 14). The term *Asian American* is a political term that grew out of the Asian American Movement in the 1960s. According to Yen Le Espiritu:

> Although broader social struggles and internal demographic changes provided the impetus for the Asian American movement, it was the group's politics—confrontational and explicitly pan-Asian—that shaped the movement's content. Influenced by the internal colonial model, which stresses commonalities among "colonized groups," college students of Asian ancestry declared solidarity with fellow Asian Americans....Rejecting the label "Oriental," they proclaimed themselves "Asian American." (1992, 30)

In the 1960s, the term *Asian American* signified a recognition that, despite their distinct languages, religious backgrounds, economic well-being, and cultural traditions, many people of Asian origin identified with one another due to their shared histories of exclusion and migration. Espiritu and Michael Omi (2000, 53) assert that, despite very real differences between distinct national origin groups, at times Asian Americans have come together under the banner of Asian American identity to make political claims. We believe that those who have a strong identity with Asian Americans as a group (measured by whether respondents identify as Asian American and believe that Asian Americans share a common culture) will naturalize at higher rates than those who do not because they will be more likely to see citizenship as a means to consolidate and express group political power. For similar reasons, we include experience with discrimination in the model.

Based on past research (Uhlaner 1991), we hypothesize that experience with discrimination further serves to develop a sense of linked fate with others who fall into the same social category and that those who have experienced discrimination will become citizens in order to empower themselves to challenge racial prejudice. But because many Asian Americans in the United States arrived in the last three decades (Lien, Conway, and Wong 2004), we must also consider the possibility that the meaning of the term *Asian American* is different for contemporary immigrants compared to the mainly U.S.-born activists of the 1960s. Thus, it may be that attachment to Asian Americans as a group has little to do with why people become citizens. Further, experiences with discrimination could even lead an individual to retreat from citizenship if he or she felt unwelcome or alienated from the majority population in the United States.

Within this model, we include other variables that can be considered to be migration-related factors, such as language use (Language Segregation), years lived in the United States, ties to the home country, and participation in home-country politics. We include the first two variables as measures of U.S. cultural integration. Previous research suggests that high scores on these measures are associated with higher rates of naturalization (Bernard 1936; Grebler 1966; Garcia 1981; DeSipio 1987, 1996; Ong and Nakanishi 2003). The last two measures have to do with connections to the country of origin. One theoretical perspective posits that strong ties to the country of origin will drive down naturalization rates because the sense of having divided loyalties to two countries makes it difficult for immigrants to take an oath of allegiance to the United States (Jones-Correa 1998). But, as previously noted, evidence for this hypothesis is mixed. This set of variables is theoretically distinct from the minority community variables, but for the purpose of parsimony and presentation, we include the two sets of variables in the same model.

Following traditional social science research on political participation (Verba, Schlozman, and Brady 1995), all the models include six measures of socioeconomic status and demographic background that serve as control variables. These variables are Education, Income, Age, Marital Status, Gender (female), and Homeowner(ship). Although we group these control variables together, it is important to recognize that these variables may also measure substantive processes that are central to the study of naturalization and incorporation. For example, homeownership indicates an economic (and perhaps psychological) attachment to U.S. society and culture. Similarly, higher levels of education (especially if a good portion took part in the United States) may signify a greater degree of socialization into U.S. culture.[4]

Dummy variables are used to isolate the following Asian national origin groups: Chinese, Korean, Vietnamese, Filipino, South Asian (Indian and Pakistani), with Japanese immigrants as the reference group. Distinguishing between distinct national origin groups is critical because previous research contends that national origin is the single most important influence on naturalization (Bueker 2005). What is less clear is why national origin matters for citizenship.

Table 17.1 offers three multivariate models. The first is a demographic model with the national origin groupings. The second adds the civic engagement variables, and the third includes the minority community and migration status variables. The dependent variable is a dummy measure of naturalization (0 = not a citizen; 1 = naturalized citizen). The sample in all analyses included foreign-born respondents living permanently in the United States for at least five years.

Perhaps the most striking finding in each model is the significance of the national origin group membership even after we have controlled for many other predictors. We return to this finding later. Among the demographic controls, only age and home-ownership are significantly and positively related to Asian naturalization. The fact that education and income have no effect on naturalization suggests that socioeconomic resources are not significant influences on Asian immigrants, as they are on other immigrant groups such as Latinos.

Among the civic engagement variables only strong partisanship exerts a significant influence on Asian naturalization. Historically, political parties were the main source of political integration for immigrants. Although they no longer wield the same influence, it may be the case that closely identifying with the political parties captures a desire on the part of Asian immigrants to become active in politics. Having a meaningful voice in politics requires voting in elections, which requires being a U.S. citizen.

Finally, among the minority community variables, it is no surprise that length of residency exerts a powerful influence of naturalization. Research on Latino naturalization consistently finds length of residency to be among the strongest factors shaping the naturalization calculus (Garcia 1981; Portes and Curtis 1987; Pantoja and Gershon 2006). Also significant is the development of a pan-ethnic consciousness. Individuals who believe people of Asian descent in the United States have a great deal in common culturally are more likely to pursue naturalization. This is consistent with our expectations regarding the formation of a pan-ethnic community and the pursuit of political empowerment.

We also observe that being active in the politics of the home country is associated negatively with naturalization. This finding is consistent with a recent study on Dominican immigrants by Pantoja (2005). The negative effect of participation in home-country politics on naturalization may be driven by two factors: (1) political participation abroad is driven by a deep affection for the home country, which may lead these individuals to devalue U.S. citizenship because its pursuit also entails a high level of affection and commitment to the United States, and (2) among those who are politically active abroad, acquiring U.S. citizenship may be perceived by home-country kin and politicians as a betrayal of the homeland. After all, these individuals will have greater contact with politicians from the home country, individuals who for personal or strategic reasons are likely to hold and transmit strong feelings of patriotism and nationalism.

**Table 17.1** Determinants of Asian naturalization: Logistic regression

| | Socioeconomic model | | Civic engagement model | | Minority community and immigration status model | | Average change |
|---|---|---|---|---|---|---|---|
| | C | SE | C | SE | C | SE | |
| **Ethnicity**[a] | | | | | | | |
| Chinese | 1.61** | 0.53 | 1.77** | 0.55 | 4.00** | 0.90 | 0.41 |
| Korean | 1.02* | 0.53 | 0.70 | 0.57 | 1.99** | 0.84 | 0.22 |
| Vietnamese | 2.79** | 0.60 | 2.92** | 0.63 | 4.77** | 0.93 | 0.32 |
| Filipino | 1.98** | 0.54 | 1.71** | 0.57 | 2.90** | 0.85 | 0.29 |
| Indian/Pakistani | 1.41** | 0.57 | 1.20** | 0.60 | 2.85** | 0.88 | 0.23 |
| **Demographic information** | | | | | | | |
| Education | 0.06 | 0.08 | 0.07 | 0.09 | 0.08 | 0.11 | 0.06 |
| Income | 0.05 | 0.17 | −0.07 | 0.17 | −0.23 | 0.20 | −0.07 |
| Age | 0.03** | 0.01 | 0.03** | 0.01 | 0.02* | 0.01 | 0.20 |
| Married | −0.25 | 0.26 | −0.30 | 0.27 | −0.01 | 0.31 | 0.00 |
| Female | −0.05 | 0.22 | 0.01 | 0.23 | 0.16 | 0.27 | 0.02 |
| Homeowner | 1.28** | 0.25 | 1.20** | 0.26 | 0.93** | 0.30 | 0.15 |
| **Other information** | | | | | | | |
| Political interest | | | 0.06 | 0.12 | −0.20 | 0.15 | −0.09 |
| Attends religious services | | | 0.10 | 0.08 | 0.20** | 0.10 | 0.13 |
| Member community organization | | | 0.19 | 0.35 | 0.33 | 0.41 | 0.04 |
| Strong partisan | | | 0.20** | 0.08 | 0.20** | 0.09 | 0.13 |
| Experienced discrimination | | | | | 0.03 | 0.14 | 0.01 |
| Language segregation (high value = English) | | | | | 0.31 | 0.25 | 0.15 |
| Years lived in United States | | | | | 0.15** | 0.03 | 0.54 |
| Pan-Asian American identity | | | | | 0.12 | 0.27 | 0.02 |
| Asian Americans share common culture | | | | | 0.31** | 0.15 | 0.15 |
| Ties with home country | | | | | −0.02 | 0.08 | −0.02 |
| Active in home country politics | | | | | −1.38** | 0.53 | −0.29 |
| Constant | −2.97** | 0.75 | −3.20** | 0.82 | −7.20** | 1.29 | |
| Chi-square | 78.7 | | 84.39 | | 160.78 | | |
| df | (11) | | (15) | | (22) | | |
| Probability > chi-square | p < .000 | | p < .000 | | p < .000 | | |
| Sample size[b] | 492 | | 475 | | 456 | | |

*Notes:* Analysis based on logistic regression (STATA). Ordered logit analysis with three-category dependent variable measuring (1) naturalized, (2) not naturalized but expect to become naturalized, and (3) not naturalized and do not expect to become naturalized produced very similar results. Dependent variable is a dummy measure of naturalization (0–1). * indicates $p < 10$; ** indicates $p < 0.05$. C, coefficient; df, degrees of freedom; SE, standard error.

[a] Excluded category is Japanese.

[b] Sample includes only foreign-born who have lived in the United States for at least five years. When mean values are substituted for missing observations, the substantive results remain the same.

Despite these findings, it is important to note that multivariate analysis reveals that, among those Asian Americans in the PNAAPS sample, activity in home-country politics is not related to voter turnout. Further, activity in politics related to the home country is positively associated with participation in nonelectoral political activities for this group. Finally, we must be cautious in making assumptions about the causal direction of the relationship between transnational ties and citizenship acquisition. It may be that those individuals who do not care to or are unable to become citizens maintain the strongest connections with the country of origin. Thus, we can conclude that the process of attaining U.S. citizenship may exhibit a unique relationship with activity in homeland politics. It cannot be assumed that those who participate in homeland politics do so at the expense of participation in all types of U.S. politics (Wong 2006).

In the full model (minority community and migration status), we find limited support for the claim that socioeconomic resources drive naturalization among Asians immigrants. In contrast, we do find an association between some key indicators of embeddedness in the United States, such as homeownership, attendance at religious services, strong partisanship, and length of residence, which lend some support to the acculturation and civic engagement models of naturalization. Still, results from the multivariate analysis suggest that gaps in rates of naturalization persist between different Asian national origin groups, even after taking into account socioeconomic variables, civic engagement measures, and factors related to minority and immigration status. These findings draw attention to the need for a more nuanced approach to understanding Asian naturalization that includes attention to group histories and other variables not measured in standard surveys (including this one). In other words, we must take into account two critical elements of the model presented by Hochschild and Mollenkopf (chap. 2 in this volume): characteristics of the groups and, perhaps even more important, immigrants' repertoires of action. We next offer some speculations on why these groups have divergent patterns of naturalization.

## Persistent National Origin Differences in Naturalization

A critical set of variables not measured in the PNAAPS survey has to do with the economic conditions in the countries of origin and group histories in the United States. Japanese immigrants are the least likely to naturalize. Immigration from Japan to the United States peaked between 1900 and 1910 and came to a halt in 1924, with the passage of the Immigration Act of 1924. After World War II, immigration from Japan rose and remained steady at its present rate of approximately 5,000 per year (Toji 2003, 75). Japanese were once the largest Asian-origin group in the United States, making up over 50 percent of all Asian-origin people in 1960 (Takaki 1995, 36). But by 2000 Japanese were the sixth-largest group and the group that included the smallest proportion of immigrants (30.2 percent) (Toji 2003, 76). The Japanese-origin population in the United States exhibits the highest average income of any group, including non-Latino whites.

Yet, despite this resource advantage, as well as the existence of a long history of Japanese settlement in the United States, Japanese immigrants do not naturalize at high rates. One explanation for this may be due to the historical economic prosperity and the high standard of living in Japan. Following their defeat in World War II and the U.S. occupation, Japan experienced rapid economic development, described by many observers as "the Japanese economic miracle" (Murphey 2001, 413). Rhoads Murphey (2001) contends that production and income growth in Japan from 1950 to 1975 was faster than those measured in any country in history and that during that time incomes tripled. The economy faltered badly in the 1990s, but has since recovered (Koll 2005).

Although most Japanese (80 percent) live in crowded urban areas, they also live in a society with nearly no poverty, violent crime, or unemployment (Murphey 2001, 415) The literacy rate and life expectancy in Japan are the highest in the world. Because a single party has ruled Japan since 1955, critics question whether Japan constitutes a true democracy (Onishi 2005). Nevertheless, Japan boasts the oldest constitutional democracy in Asia and free elections. Japanese immigrants in the United States may not feel an urgent need to become United States citizens because they can enjoy a high standard of living and a stable government if they ever wish to return to Japan. (Japan does not allow dual citizenship—nor do any of the other Asian countries in this study).

Further, naturalization data from the U.S. Department of Homeland Security show that in 2004 10 percent of Japanese immigrants who naturalized were categorized as having "Executive and managerial" occupations—the highest proportion of executives of any of the groups included in this study. Many of these executives and managers are probably associated with transnational corporations. Such individuals probably lead advantaged lives in both the United States and Japan and do not feel that U.S. citizenship is an advantage. In addition, from 1994 to 1999, Japan was the leading sender of students to the United States (Open Doors 2005). Japanese students make up approximately 8 percent of all foreign students in the United States (Open Doors 2005). It follows that a significant proportion of Japanese may come to the United States as students and others come on temporary visas without plans to stay permanently and attain citizenship.

In contrast to Japanese migrants, Filipino and Chinese migrants both exhibit high rates of naturalization. We contend that having a large proportion of people working in professional occupations and having a long history of settlement in the United States partially accounts for higher rates of naturalization among Chinese and Filipinos compared to other national origin groups but that the political economies of the countries of origin also influence naturalization patterns for these two groups in the United States. Chinese and Filipinos are the two largest groups of Asians in the United States.[5]

Both of these groups also have a long history in the United States. Chinese immigration to the United States can be traced to the late 1840s, and migrants from the Philippines began to arrive in large numbers in the early 1900s. Although both groups have a long history in the United States, immigrants make up a substantial proportion of the contemporary Chinese (47 percent) and Filipino (50 percent) populations. Thus, another characteristic shared by the two communities is that they include people whose families settled in the United States many generations ago as well as a large number of newcomers.

Class composition is another shared trait among Chinese and Filipino immigrants. Many immigrants from China and the Philippines are professionals, although both groups also include a large number of people who struggle at the bottom of the economic hierarchy as restaurant workers, garment factory workers, and as workers in other low-wage occupations. Economic polarization is especially evident in the Chinese population. Two streams of migration flow into the United States from the "professionally trained" and "family reunification" preference categories embedded in post-1965 immigration policy. Because many of the original immigrants from China were from poor rural backgrounds, their relatives who arrive as part of the family-reunification program and settle in the United States are likely to come from similar circumstances. Nevertheless, a growing number of immigrants are professionals who are allowed to immigrate under policies that seek to increase the number of technical and high-skilled workers in the United States (Ong, Bonacich, and Cheng 1994; Lai and Arguelles 2003). Among immigrants admitted in 2004, 30 percent of those from the People's Republic of China and 27 percent of those from the Philippines arrived under the professional skills category. During the ten years that followed the passage of the 1965 Immigration Act, almost one-half of all immigrants from China were professionals (e.g., scientists, doctors, and engineers), and this trend toward professional occupational status in the migrant stream continues (Takaki 1995, 44). The Filipino community includes a large number of undocumented immigrants (De la Cruz and Agbayani-Siewert 2003, 48), and some members of the community struggle economically, such as World War II veterans who fought with the U.S. troops but never received full veterans' benefits. Over the past three decades, however, the United States has recruited a large number of Filipino nurses and doctors to compensate for domestic labor shortages. Ronald Takaki reports that in the 1970s "one-fifth of the 20,000 nurses who graduated from school in the Philippines came to the United States" and that "the flow of Filipino doctors has been even greater" (1995, 60). One vestige of the colonial relationship between the Philippines and the United States is that many residents in the former U.S. territory speak English, and as a result, schools in the United States have also been recruiting teachers from the Philippines (De la Cruz and Agbayani-Siewert 2003, 50).

A critical mass of people (large population) and connections to an established community (long history of settlement) lead to higher rates of naturalization because both are likely to imbue Chinese and Filipino immigrants with a sense of community and belonging in the United States. Professional occupational status probably endows many Chinese and Filipinos with the resources, skills, and social connections that that they need to negotiate the naturalization bureaucracy. All three factors may act in concert to catalyze Chinese and Filipinos toward naturalization.

Indians from South Asia actually make up the largest proportions of high-skilled professional workers (according to Department of Homeland Security data), and the group also sends the most students to the United States (Open Doors 2005). There were 80,466 students from India studying in colleges around the United States in 2004–2005. Again, many international students may not have plans to become U.S. citizens. Further, although the Indian population in the United States includes a large number of professionals on average, the group tends to exhibit more transnational ties to its home country than other Asian groups (Mishara 2006). Sangay Mishara

(2006) finds that, in fact, those Indians that take part in more transnational activities are also less likely to naturalize in the United States. Interestingly, transnational ties do not drive down other types of political activities (such as signing petitions, calling members of Congress, working on campaigns, and donating to candidates or causes) in this group.

Although other Asian national origin groups share specific demographic traits with Chinese and Filipinos, such as a relatively high rate of professional occupational status (Indians) or a long history in the United States (Japanese), economic and political conditions in the countries of origin must also be considered. In 1978, Deng Xiaoping, Chinese Communist Party leader, instituted major economic reforms aimed at dismantling the centrally planned economy. In the wake of these reforms, China focused on growing its export-oriented industries, and from the late 1970s to 2000, China experienced dramatic economic growth. Between 1978 and 1990, the Chinese GDP grew at nearly double-digit rates, and although GDP growth rate declined each year from 1990 to 1999, in no year was growth below 6 percent (Tan 2003). In the last two decades, multinational corporations have raced to China. Economic liberalization has been accompanied by a reduction in poverty, increased literacy rates, and improved health care (Murphey 2001, 399).

The astounding rise of China as a world economic power has translated into better opportunities for many of its people, but rapid economic expansion has not been without its challenges. We argue that these challenges have helped to push Chinese immigrants to naturalize in the United States at relatively high rates. Personal freedom has increased in China, but democratization has been slow (Ma 2002). Anecdotal evidence suggests an increase in applications for citizenship immediately after the Chinese government attack on peaceful demonstrators in Tiananmen Square in summer 1989.[6] Not unrelated to its economic growth, China has experienced the largest rural-to-urban transition in history. Ligang Song and Yu Sheng (2005, 110) report that from 1979 to 2003 the population growth in urban areas increased over 200 percent. In contrast, the national population growth was 30 percent during the same period. Urban dwellers were just 18 percent of the national population in 1978, but made up 41 percent in 2003. Even long-term urban residents have found themselves marginalized. Cai Fang and Dewen Wang (2005) claim that, beginning in the late 1990s, downsizing of state-owned firms caused massive unemployment in the cities. Pensions and health insurance do not continue for workers who are fired or retire early. Finally, urban sprawl has reduced the availability of usable land for farming and agriculture, resulting in a lack of jobs and land for rural inhabitants (Song and Sheng 2005, 111). Immigrants from China who recognize or have escaped these potential hardships may well be pushed to naturalize and become U.S. citizens.

Like many other Asian nations, the Philippines boasts a growing economy. Yet the growth rate of the country has been much slower than in other counties in Southeast Asia. Scholars attribute this fact to economic mismanagement, lack of infrastructure, and a series of natural disasters (Tan 2003). The Asian currency crisis that began in 1996 devastated the Filipino economy; following the crisis, the peso lost 40 percent of its value in a matter of months (Tan 2003, 93). In terms of social health indicators, the Philippines has not been able to translate its high rates of education (95 percent of the country is literate, and primary education is nearly universal) into a higher standard of living for its residents. As recently as 2000, the Philippines exhibited a high malnutrition rate for children under five (32 percent, compared to 14 percent in China), and underemployment is a serious problem. As a result, out-migration to the United States and other Asian countries has been massive. According to Tan (2003) some 86,000 Filipinos were working in other Asian countries in the late 1980s. After Ferdinand Marcos was forced from power in the 1980s, the country experienced political liberalization and brief periods of stability in the 1990s, but political unrest has plagued the country in more recent history. Unfavorable economic and political conditions probably provide positive incentives for Filipinos to make the United States their permanent home and, along with the other factors discussed, explain their relatively high rates of naturalization.

Another group that exhibits a high rate of naturalization is Vietnamese immigrants. Compared to their Chinese and Filipino counterparts, Vietnamese are much more recent arrivals, with fewer economic resources. In 1990, 25 percent of all Vietnamese-origin people in the United States were living in poverty, compared to 14 percent of the Asian-origin population as a whole (Chuong and Ta 2003, 72). Vietnamese also lagged behind other Asians in terms of educational achievement and income. Vietnamese made great gains in all of these areas between 1990 and 2000 (Park 2003), but gaps in socioeconomic status between Vietnamese and most other Asian-origin groups remain.

What, then, explains the high rates of naturalization among the Vietnamese immigrant population? They are the only group in our study to initially arrive as refugees to the United States. Harry Kitano and Roger Daniels report that "In all, from April 1975 to September 1984, more than 700,000 Southeast Asians were admitted to the United States" (1995, 150). Today, they represent the fifth largest Asian-origin group in the United States. Because most Vietnamese migrants arrived in the United States as political refugees with no intention of returning permanently to their country of origin, it is not surprising that they exhibit high rates of citizenship. Their naturalization patterns and migration experiences parallel those of Cubans.

In contrast to Chinese and Filipinos, people of Korean origin constitute a much smaller population in the United States, with a more recent history of large-scale settlement. Small numbers of Korean immigrants arrived in the United States in the early 1900s to work as laborers along with even smaller numbers of Korean political exiles and students. Up until 1950, the total Korean population in the United States remained steady at 10,000 (Chang 2003). It has grown at a steady rate over the past three decades, but with just 1.2 million people in the United States identifying as Korean (alone or in combination with another group affiliation) in 2000, Koreans still represent a relatively small share of the U.S. and Asian American population. Organizations and political elites may not expend scarce resources to target smaller populations for political mobilization, and low rates of mobilization are not likely to translate into high rates of naturalization. Other factors may also account for Korean migrants' lower naturalization rates. In recent decades, Koreans benefited from the strong, relatively stable (with the exception of the Asian currency crisis) economy of their country (Tan 2003). Thus, Korean immigrants may not feel compelled to naturalize in the United States to ensure escape from a treacherous economy. In addition, public opinion polls suggest that Koreans' hold the most negative attitudes toward the United States of all Asians (Kim 2003). These views may drive down naturalization rates among migrants.

Attention to the interaction of group histories, characteristics, and political economies in the countries of origin helps to explain the differential rates of naturalization among various Asian national origin groups. The analysis of the survey data shows that socioeconomic resources, political behavior, and factors related to minority status and migration alone cannot account fully for the group differences. Other variables not measured in the survey, such as historical migration trends, political and economic context in the country of origin, and aggregate demographics may also contribute to the variations in naturalization rates among different Asian groups. Finally, although we did not focus on local context in this analysis, research by scholars such as Gianni D'Amato (chap. 5 in this volume) suggest that attention to local context could further explain the different rates of naturalization between Asian groups.

## Conclusion

Naturalization and citizenship are especially important steps in the political integration and incorporation process for Asian immigrants. Throughout much of U.S. history, U.S. laws have systematically excluded people of Asian origin from naturalizing on the basis of race, beginning with a 1790 law that restricted naturalization to free white individuals. In 1922, the Supreme Court held that an immigrant from Japan was ineligible for citizenship because he was "clearly of a race that [was] not Caucasian and therefore entirely outside of the zone on the negative side" (*Takao Ozawa v. United States*).[7] The following year, Bhagat Thind, an immigrant from India, was denied his application for citizenship because the Court ruled that he was nonwhite (Haney-López 1996). The decisions in these cases served as precedent until the mid-1900s, when Congress liberalized the naturalization laws restricting migrants deemed nonwhite from attaining citizenship. The historical legacy of racial exclusion from citizenship for people of Asian origin in the United States ensures that "citizenship remains one of the most crucial legal and political categories around which the exercise or denial of democratic rights turns" (Gotanda 2001, 82).

Although national origin is no longer the de jure basis for political inclusion, national origin has become the de facto basis for inclusion. Clearly, not all groups who are eligible for U.S. citizenship naturalize at the same rate. Such variation was long believed to be due to differences in socioeconomic resources. One major finding in our analysis was that socioeconomic resources have little association with rates of naturalization among Asian immigrants. In contrast, the degree to which immigrants are embedded in their communities and civically engaged—indicated by homeownership, attendance at religious services, length of residence, and beliefs that Asians as a pan-ethnic group sharing a common culture—are associated with naturalization among Asian Americans. Yet, even after taking into account a host of potential influences on naturalization, the national origin differences in naturalization rates persist. Thus, recognizing the role of specific group histories, potential interactions between key variables, and the political and economic forces shaping ethnic group formation is an important first step toward gaining a better understanding of these group differences and of political incorporation more generally.

This observation has important implications for future research on immigrant political incorporation and mobilization. To best understand the differences between distinct national origin groups in terms of citizenship and other types of civic engagement, researchers need to take a closer look at the historical and macroeconomic forces that shape migration patterns for particular groups of immigrants. As predicted by the model of political incorporation introduced by Hochschild and Mollenkopf (chap. 2 in this volume), these forces create unique political incorporation pathways for each immigrant group. Some of these forces can be captured using individual-level survey data or other quantitative sources, but the research presented here also suggests that an approach that goes beyond individual resources (socioeconomic status) to capture more of the larger context of migration will provide a much richer explanation of why differences in rates of political mobilization and incorporation exist across groups.

Since 1965, Asian Americans, like previous European immigrants, have had the power of choice. Individuals who are eligible for U.S. citizenship can choose to pursue or forgo naturalization. The decision to become a U.S. citizen is not without costs, financial or psychological, and unlike previous immigrations, U.S. urban political machines are no longer actively naturalizing, courting, and mobilizing immigrants. Rather than subsidizing the costs of naturalization and political integration, the current of U.S. politics appears to be moving in the opposite direction. Presently, noncitizens face a politically hostile environment (see Luis Fraga, chap. 12 in this volume). They have a harder time obtaining social welfare benefits, receiving an education, or speaking a language other than English (Jones-Correa 1998). In short, the stakes involved in naturalization are intensifying.

Whether Asian American communities and organizations are capable of transforming Asian immigrants into Asian American citizens remains an open question. The 2006 marches for immigrant rights may have helped spur Asian naturalization despite the fact that Asian immigrants in the current debate over immigration reform received very limited attention from policymakers, pundits, and the popular press. The absence of Asian immigrants in the debate is somewhat surprising given that one out of every four immigrants in the United States originated from Asia. Further, few acknowledge that at least one out of every ten foreign-born Asians is without documents and that people from Asia make up the second largest group (behind Latinos) without documents (12 percent) (Passel and Cohn 2008). The recent debates over immigration are perhaps even more important for Asians than Latinos because a majority of them are immigrants and because their population size requires an even greater proportion of citizens and voters if they are to be politically relevant. Because the political fortunes of Asian Americans rest in the hands of a new and diverse generation of Asian immigrants, we can anticipate that Asian Americans will not be sitting idly on the sidelines of this important debate.

# CHAPTER EIGHTEEN

# Entering the Precincts of Power

## Do National Differences Matter for Immigrant Minority Political Representation?

*Richard Alba and Nancy Foner*

The 2005 riots in the French suburbs brought to the fore in a dramatic way our need to better understand how immigrants and their descendants are integrated into European societies and how European patterns compare with those that have developed in the United States. The riots also made clear the need to revisit comparative perspectives that have been prominent in the scholarly literature. Much of the comparative literature that looks at immigration in Europe and the United States has focused on the political sphere, particularly state policy regarding immigrants and immigration. A frequent concern is the question of convergence—whether parallel political, demographic, economic, social, and cultural forces are leading liberal democratic states in a common direction in the face of contemporary mass immigration.

In some ways, we argue, the answer is yes. There is no denying a number of trends toward convergence, particularly when it comes to state policies in several key areas, most notably citizenship and the recognition of distinctive cultural practices. Yet a convergence view offers only a partial—and indeed a limited—picture. As has often been pointed out, important country-specific differences continue to shape the policy responses to immigration in Europe and North America. We are not yet living in a postnational world; it is too early to declare the end of historically rooted national distinctions (Howard 2005, 716; Judt 2005).

But there is another problem that comes from putting so much emphasis on convergence, as many cross-national immigration studies do. Because convergence theorists (and, indeed, many other comparative analysts) focus so heavily on official government policies or on the representations of these policies in political discourse, they tend to tell a story of increasing immigrant inclusion. They risk missing, or at least seriously underplaying, the way historically rooted and durable social, political, and economic structures and arrangements create varying levels of barrier to immigrants and their descendants in different societies.

In developing this argument, we take as our focus an aspect of the political arena that has to do with actual political practices—the ability of immigrant-origin politicians to be elected to office. Surprisingly, this topic has received little attention in the literature on cross-national comparisons even though it is clearly critical for the integration of immigrants and their children—and indeed for their ability to influence the policies that shape their lives in such important ways. Our review of the evidence reveals some cross-national contrasts in the extent to which politicians from new immigrant groups have been able to gain elected office. Among the factors involved are the nature of the legal and electoral systems and party structures in each country, which create different kinds of opportunities and obstacles for electoral success. These political structures sometimes coincide with and sometimes depart from the different integration models of the societies, ranging from the multiculturalism of Britain to the assimilationist republicanism of France, which themselves constitute yet another factor that must be considered.

We begin this chapter with a discussion of the arguments put forward for convergence as well as the limits of a convergence approach for understanding immigrant political incorporation, especially when it comes to the ability to get elected. With this as background, we discuss why we have chosen to focus on the issue of electoral success—why, in short, the election of co-ethnics matters for immigrant minority communities. We then examine how successful new immigrant groups actually have been in this endeavor in Europe and the United States, focusing on local and regional levels, where the first manifestations of success can be expected. We subsequently proceed to a discussion of the factors accounting for the differences, with an emphasis on long-standing structural features in different countries that are involved. In our conclusion, we discuss the implications of our analysis for the convergence approach.

In the analysis, our focus is on five major countries of contemporary immigration: the United States, Britain, France, Germany, and the Netherlands. All five have received huge numbers of immigrants in the post–World War II decades and represent a range of different national integration regimes and political systems. Admittedly, we are constrained by the availability of studies on the political representation of major immigrant populations. Nevertheless, the range of variation in integration models and in the legal and institutional structures among these five is quite substantial. As already noted, the integration models range from multiculturalism to a strict assimilationism; the citizenship regimes range from absolute *jus soli* for the second generation in the case of the United States to, until 2000, *jus sanguinis* with limited naturalization in Germany; and the political systems range from a first-past-the-post competition between the candidates of two parties in the United States to multiparty systems with proportional representation in the Netherlands. Thus, our examination provides a suitable test of the hypothesis that national systems matter when it comes to immigrant electoral success.

There are, of course, limits to such a cross-national approach. Among other things, it does not get at the complexities of local variations among regions and cities within each country—something we point to along the way but are not able to systematically explore here. Moreover, we have had to rely on what are, admittedly, limited available data on immigrant-origin politicians. Thus we view this piece as a first necessary step in a long-term investigation.

## What Are the Arguments for Convergence?

A common theme in the cross-national literature comparing the effects of, and response to, immigration in European countries and the United States is that a convergence process is undercutting national distinctiveness. The increasingly important role of the European Union has meant that EU-instituted laws and policies, including some concerning immigrants and immigration, now pertain to all member states. Moreover, the recent period of mass immigration coincides with the rise of new globalizing forces. As one scholar puts it, modern-day transportation and telecommunication, among other changes, have led to "convergent modes of social and cultural transformation associated with the globalizing of cultural forms" (Vertovec 2004, 977). In an era of the "McDonaldization" of food tastes and consumption and the "Levi-ization" of clothing styles, it is not surprising that political as well as cultural studies are exploring cross-country convergences.

The basic thrust of convergence approaches is the argument that, over time, Western Europe and North America have become increasingly similar in terms of state policies relating to immigrants, in particular, policies toward citizenship, cultural practices, and welfare benefits (e.g., Freeman 1995b; Joppke and Morawska 2003; Soysal 1994; Weil 2001). In explaining this growing convergence, the emphasis is on shared domestic pressures and societal structural features as well as mutual borrowing or emulation. Convergence theorists point to the inherent principles or internal logic of liberal democracies in the context of mass immigration; the emergence, particularly within Europe, of transnational and postnational norms and rules that undermine the system of nation-states; and the need to cope with similar sets of problems arising from immigration, including the need to integrate immigrants into each society and provide them and their children with adequate housing, jobs, and education.

Consider citizenship policies, which have become more alike in Europe and the United States in recent years. In much of continental Europe before World War II, *jus sanguinis* (the principle that birthright citizenship can only be acquired through blood ties) was prevalent, so that many children of immigrants remained foreign even if they had spent all their lives in the country. In contrast, in the United States, *jus soli* (or birthplace citizenship) has been the dominant principle applied in an automatic and unqualified form whereby citizenship is conferred at birth on all children born in the country. The dominance of *jus sanguinis* over *jus soli*, it has been argued, was a logical development in many continental European nations when they were countries of emigration seeking to maintain links with their citizens abroad, just as in settler societies like the United States *jus soli* was useful in integrating immigrants of diverse origins into a new nation (Brubaker, 1992; Castles and Davidson 2000, 85). Not surprisingly, France, a country of large-scale immigration since the late-1800s, differed from its neighbors in having developed a more expansive political citizenship in the late nineteenth century based on *jus soli*—automatic citizenship at birth to the third generation (*double droit de sol*) along with easy access to citizenship for the second generation at the age of majority (Weil 2002).

Convergence theorists emphasize that the massive post–World War II immigration in Europe and the United States has brought the two sides of the Atlantic closer together in citizenship law, with continental European countries moving in a U.S. direction to make it easier for long-settled immigrants and their children to acquire citizenship.[1] By now, the majority of Western European countries provide *jus soli* citizenship to the second generation, although it occurs "not only automatically at birth [as it does in the United States], but also under conditions of residency or through voluntary acquisition, both of which are presumed to entail socialization" (Weil 2001, 30). Germany is a notable example of the shift away from descent-based citizenship to birthplace citizenship. Since a new citizenship law went into effect in 2000, provisional birthright citizenship is granted to members of the second generation if at least one parent has lived legally in Germany for eight years; individuals must decide by their twenty-third birthday whether to keep German citizenship or the nationality of their parents. In several European nations (e.g., Denmark and Sweden), a person born in the country to foreign parents can acquire citizenship at the age of majority after fulfilling certain residency requirements (Weil 2001, 30). In France, citizenship for a member of the second generation is acquired passively—it is automatically granted at age eighteen unless an individual rejects it. At the end of the twentieth century, of the major Western European immigration countries, only Austria and Switzerland still applied the *jus sanguinis* principle strictly—although procedures were in place by which the second generation (and immigrants) could naturalize after a certain residence period (Castles and Davidson 2000, 92–93).

Several factors have been put forward to account for the overall trend away from ethnic to civic-territorial principles, among them the influence of democratic values, the stabilization of political borders (which include the majority of nationals), and the shared experience of immigration (Weil 2001). Patrick Weil's (2001) argument is that a commitment to democratic values has forced states with restrictive acquisition rules to modify them, the old rules having been recognized as being incompatible with modern democratic norms and as impeding the integration of the second and third generations. Most *jus sanguinis* countries, as Stephen Castles and Alistair Davidson note, have realized that "exclusion from citizenship is problematic, leading to social marginalization, political exclusion, conflict and racism" (2000, 94).

Another kind of convergence has been noted—a move toward "de facto multiculturalism" in liberal immigrant-host states—a term Christian Joppke and Ewa Morawska use to describe how western democratic states have allowed "immigrants *qua* immigrants to find recognition and protection for their distinctive cultural practices" (2003, 8). The relevant measures range from the protection of rights to pragmatic concessions in the interest of public health or security. In liberal immigration-host states, Joppke and Morawska claim, de facto multiculturalism has become a "pervasive reality" (2003, 8). Only a few states, such as Canada, have adopted multiculturalism as official policy—the deliberate and explicit recognition and protection of immigrants as distinct ethnic groups—and Joppke and Morawska (2003, 10) argue that official multiculturalism has come under pressure everywhere but the de facto variety is much more widespread. In his magnum opus on convergent tendencies in rich democracies, Harold Wilensky lists the increasing openness of modern governments to minority group claims as one of nine such tendencies. The convergence, he argues, is toward the "American multicultural model" in the context of "a four-decade revival of massive migration from poor to rich countries and continuing in-dustrialization" (Wilensky 2002, 679).

Convergence perspectives typically insist on looking beyond the stated national models of multiculturalism or assimilation to the actual programs and policies as implemented. Indeed, Joppke and Morawska contend that academics have become captive of "political surface rhetoric" in their frequent contrasts of French assimila-tionism and Anglo-Saxon multiculturalism, ignoring the growing similarities in in-tegration approaches. Thus, despite the hard-line assimilationist ethos in France and what is often portrayed as a multicultural United States and an even more explicitly multicultural Canada, the "integration requisites" of liberal states inevitably lead to many similarities in policies at the local level (Joppke and Morawska 2003, 7–8).

Convergence around de facto multiculturalism is seen as developing out of the very ideologies of liberal democratic states—there is a reluctance to impose "particular cul-tural forms on their members" owing to "a procedural commitment to basic civic rules" as well as guilt about colonial pasts (Joppke 1998, 290). It has been suggested that policy emulation or borrowing may also operate. As Western European countries have come to see immigrants as a permanent presence, some have adopted, in modi-fied form, integration policies from across the Atlantic (Cornelius and Tsuda 2004, 17; Wilensky 2002).

Perhaps most important, de facto multiculturalism is viewed as a response to the need to develop strategies to maintain social order and promote social integration in the face of large-scale immigration. As Martin Schain (1999) argues, the French state has become involved in a de facto politics of multicultural recognition at the local level, driven by the need to find ethnic interlocutors or intermediaries and sounding boards for its policies. Indeed, he notes the irony that French governmental agencies are involved in the development of ethnic organizations and ethnic consciousness at the very time that such action should have been precluded by the reaffirmation of the republican model (Schain 1999, 210; see also Kastoryano 2002, 81, 100, 105). Particularly striking is the 2005 French government announcement of the creation of a foundation "for the work of Islam in France" that will support the construction and maintenance of mosques and the training of imams (Klausen 2005, 40).

Likewise, according to Patrick Ireland, by the early 2000s, many progressive Ger-man, Dutch, and Belgian policymakers were drawn to liberal multiculturalism; ethnic associations were seen as fulfilling an instrumental function, aiding immigrants' cul-tural and social integration while at the same time ensuring equality of opportunity (Ireland 2004, 223). Even in the 1970s and 1980s when Germany proclaimed it was not a country of immigration, consultative foreigners' auxiliary councils emerged in many cities to facilitate immigrant integration. For example, the Essen foreign-ers' auxiliary council lobbied for various multicultural policies such as hiring more translators and personnel familiar with immigrants' homelands and expanding eth-nic radio programming (Ireland 2004, 69–71).

In both France and Germany (as in the Netherlands, the United States, and Can-ada) educational programs in the home-country language have been supported in many locales. In Germany and France, at least in the past, this was to keep open the option of (and to facilitate) returning to the homeland; more recently in these two countries it has been to enable immigrants to acquire the domestic language more easily. Monolingualism may be a basic principle of the state in France, Germany, and the Netherlands, but outside of school, these countries have been forced to introduce language services to take account of immigrant needs in communicating with courts, bureaucracies, and health services (Castles and Miller 2003, 249).

Convergence perspectives are capturing an important aspect of policy changes that are bringing the countries of Western Europe and the United States closer together in many ways. Yet it is more accurate to speak of *relative* convergence because significant national differences remain. Even when it comes to citizenship—for which there is undeniably a degree of convergence—some European countries continue to have less liberal citizenship policies than others (see Howard 2005). And, when we turn to electoral politics, it is the country-specific differences—not the convergent trends—that stand out.

## The Role of Electoral Politics

Unsurprisingly, given the historical recency of many immigrant flows, a great deal of research on immigrant group political participation has focused on forms that do not require citizenship and thus do not directly involve electoral influence and success (Chung 2005). Under the spell of social movement theory, attention has focused especially on ethnic and other organizations that exert influence on political actors or are such actors themselves (e.g., Hooghe 2005). The claims made in political arenas by such organizations on behalf of immigrants have also been an important subject for research (Koopmans and Statham, 2000b; Koopmans 2004).

However, we argue here that electoral successes by immigrant minorities should still be regarded as the gold standard against which other forms of political participation should be measured. We focus here, in particular, on the ability of minority candidates to be elected to office, and we do so for four reasons.

First, election to political office is a direct measure of minority integration into the mainstream in the same sense that entry by minority individuals into high-status occupations is. It is an indication of a diminishment, however modest, in differentials in life chances that exist between the majority and minority (Alba and Nee 2003). Where immigrant minorities are not represented in elected office or are only minimally so, they evidently experience very unequal life chances in the attainment of such highly esteemed and powerful positions as mayor, city councilor, and parliamentarian.

Second, the occupation of elected political office by members of an immigrant minority gives the group a voice in decisions that can directly affect it. This is the case whether the office is part of the national government or a local one. As Nathan Glazer and Daniel Moynihan (1970 [1963]) observe, immigrant and ethnic groups are concentrated spatially, located typically in specific cities and even in specific neighborhoods; and because most government decisions have ramifications that are spatially differentiated, they have varied effects on different population groups. Thus, a group that is unable to achieve some degree of electoral representation has little or no ability to influence such decisions in its favor. Indeed, majority group politicians may believe that they can impose unfavorable decisions on such a group with impunity.

**Table 18.1**  Population data for immigrant-origin groups (%)

|  | Percentage of population | Percentage of electorate | Source |
|---|---|---|---|
| France (Maghrebins) | ~5.1 | 2.7 | Tribalat (2004); our estimate, FQP |
| Germany (Turks) | 3.1 | 1.0 | Bundesbeauftragte (2004); *Der Spiegel* (2005) |
| Great Britain (nonwhites, including mixed) | 7.9 | ~6.6 | 2001 census |
| Netherlands (ethnic minorities) | 8.8 | n.a. | Institute for Migration and Ethnic Studies (2004) |
| United States (Hispanics) | 12.5 | 7.4 | 2000 census |

*Notes: Immigrant origin* includes first and subsequent generations. n.a., no data available.

The 2005 German election offers a telling example because the Christlich Demokratische Union (CDU; Christian Democratic Union), which expected to win, took a strong position against the entry of Turkey into the European Union. In a country where individuals of Turkish origin make up 3 percent of the population (see table 18.1), this position might have been expected to call forth an ethnic vote against the party that might have been decisive in a closely contested election. But only 600,000–700,000 Turks had become German citizens (this figure includes individuals who were too young to vote; see Ataman 2005). The limited power of the ethnic electorate was visible prior to the election in the tiny representation of the group in the Bundestag—at that time, only two out of more than six hundred deputies. Thus, the ability of Turks to punish native German politicians who staked out positions hostile to the group and its interests seemed limited.

Third, elected politicians usually play a powerful role in many of the routine decisions of government, which are often formally made by civil servants, such as the awarding of contracts. They also typically exert influence on the hiring of individuals to occupy public offices that are exempt from civil-service regulations; indeed, such offices may be regarded as part of the "patronage" that is the spoils of electoral victory and is to be doled out to supporters. Thus, when a group fails to achieve electoral success, it typically loses out when such offices are distributed. By contrast, groups that achieve electoral success can use it as leverage to raise the socioeconomic position of many group members and, perhaps eventually, of the group itself. The Irish in the United States offer a compelling historical example; they used their leadership of Democratic Party political machines that ruled many U.S. cities a century ago to bring about massive municipal employment of their co-ethnics (Erie 1988; Waldinger 1996).

These first three reasons are based on tangible rewards that groups can attain through the electoral success of their members, but the fourth reason is more symbolic. The legitimacy of a political system, especially a democratic one, ultimately depends on its ability to give representation to different groups in the population. This would seem all the more true when the boundaries between groups are prominent and correlate with structures of inequality so that the boundaries effectively mark a societal cleavage. If immigrant minorities are unable to achieve significant electoral representation, then their attachment to the dominant institutions and norms of a society may well ultimately come into question and they are likely to define themselves, and be defined by others, as not just distinct from but in opposition to the native majority (Portes and Zhou 1993). Whereas the lack of electoral representation is likely to reinforce a sense of outsider status, the ability of a group to elect its own can nurture and strengthen a sense of identification with, and allegiance to, the society and its institutions, including the rules, procedures, and values of the political system, and indeed can itself be a source of pride.

The analysis we present here focuses on the ability of candidates from immigrant minority groups to be elected to local and regional offices. This seems a suitable restriction given the historical recency of the large-scale immigrations we consider. We would expect a priori that the degree of underrepresentation would be less at lower levels of the political system, where immigrant concentrations in particular regions might guarantee some degree of representation. Moreover, there is likely to be a lag between subnational and national electoral success because politicians typically begin their careers at the local level and it takes longer to build up the kind of support, resources, and influence necessary to attain nationwide (as opposed to local and regional) offices. Thus, electoral success at subnational levels is, at this stage, a better test of immigrant group political incorporation.

## Cases

We begin the empirical part of the chapter with a brief discussion of the groups we consider and a presentation of the most basic demographic data about them (see table 18.1). As noted earlier, we rely extensively (but not entirely) on extant studies about electoral representation, and this fact helps to determine the groups we can consider. But, in general, we aim to examine the representation of what can be called the "large and problematic" immigrant populations (Alba 2005; Lucassen 2005), *problematic* here meaning that the successful incorporation of these populations is seen to be in doubt. Our definition of the populations includes not only the immigrant generation but also subsequent ones, since citizenship is usually much more common among the second and third generations, whose members are therefore more likely to be voters.

In France, we focus on the Maghrebins, which generally refers to the at least nominally Muslim immigrants from Algeria, Morocco, and Tunisia; the term excludes the so-called *pied noirs,* the former European colonists who moved to metropolitan France in huge numbers after Algeria achieved independence in 1962, and the North African Jews, who were treated by French colonial authorities in a very different way from Muslims (Alba and Silberman 2002). Based on the work of the demographer Michèle Tribalat (2004; see also Simon 2003), we place the Maghrebin percentage of the French population at approximately 5.1 percent (see table 18.1). the group's proportion in the electorate is smaller than this (2.7 percent) because the first generation has been reluctant to naturalize (Sayad 1987); however, the great majority of the French-born generations hold French citizenship (Weil 2002).

In Germany, the group we examine is the Turks, the largest and most socially salient of the immigrant groups in the country. Our estimate of the group's proportion of the population (3.1 percent) includes an estimate of the number of Turkish-origin German citizens, generally given as in the 600,000–700,000 range (Ataman 2005; see table 18.1). The low proportion of Turks in the German electorate (1 percent) is a consequence of what were until recently stringent citizenship laws, which only began to be relaxed in the mid-1990s (Diehl and Blohm 2003).

In Britain, studies have typically focused on nonwhites, a population overwhelmingly derived from postcolonial immigration, especially from the Caribbean (i.e., West Indians) and the South Asian subcontinent (e.g., Indians and Bangladeshis). The British census gives a direct measurement of the proportion these groups form of the population (the 7.9 percent listed in table 18.1 includes individuals who describe themselves as "mixed," on the presumption that most racially mixed individuals would be socially recognized as nonwhite). Because members of these groups were recognized as British or Commonwealth citizens with full voting rights on their arrival in Britain, they form a percentage of the electorate almost as large as their percentage of the population.

In the Netherlands, ethnic minorities (the groups tallied in table 18.1 at 8.8 percent) include non-European immigrants and their descendants. These groups are heterogeneous in origin—some of them represent postcolonial migrations (e.g., the Surinamese) and others represent guestworker immigration (e.g., Turks and Moroccans). The immigrant groups form different portions of the electorate with respect to local and national elections. In 1985, the Netherlands gave immigrants with five years of residence the right to vote in local elections; the right to vote in national elections remains reserved for Dutch citizens.

Finally, in the United States, we consider Hispanic groups because the best record of electoral outcomes exists for them. Immigrants from Latin America currently make up approximately one-half of the U.S. foreign-born and 12.5 percent of the total population (see table 18.1). The situation is complicated by the fact that some Hispanic families have resided in the United States for a century or more, and because one of the important groups, Puerto Ricans, is not an immigrant group in a strict sense of the term. Nevertheless, the great majority of contemporary Hispanics are immigrants or descended from immigrants who have entered the United States since 1950. Indeed, because a large fraction of contemporary Hispanics, perhaps as much as a quarter, is composed of undocumented immigrants, the electoral weight of the group (7.4 percent) is considerably below its population percentage, as table 18.1 shows.

## Electoral Success at the Local and Regional Levels

Electoral success may be the gold standard, but immigrant origin groups generally have had a hard time achieving it in mainstream elective bodies. Nowhere does their electoral representation approach the proportion of immigrant minorities in the population, especially when the second generation is taken into account, although it varies across the five national situations we consider here.

**Table 18.2** Immigrant representation on state and local legislatures

| | Political entity | Immigrant representation (%) | Source |
|---|---|---|---|
| France (Maghrebins[a]) | Municipal councils, after 2001 elections in cities with populations of 50 thousand or more (Lyon, Marseille, and Paris excluded) | 3.3 ($N = 4,365$) | Geisser and Oriol (2001) |
| | Marseille, 2001 | 4.0 ($N = 101$) | Geisser and Kelfaoui (2001) |
| | Paris, 2006 | 3.0 ($N = 163$) | our tally |
| Germany (Turks) | *Landtage* (state parliaments), 2005 | 0.4 ($N = 1,841$) | our tally |
| | City councils, 2005 | 0.7 ($N = 3,032$) | our tally |
| Great Britain (nonwhites) | Local councils, 2001 | 2.6 ($N = 21,156$) | 2001 census of Local Authority Councillors |
| | London boroughs, 2001 | 10.6 ($N = 2,033$) | 2001 census of Local Authority Councillors |
| Netherlands (ethnic minorities) | Councils of all cities, late 1990s | 1.5 ($N = 10,000$) | van Heelsum (2002) |
| | Councils of six large cities, late 1990s | 13.4 ($N = 261$) | van Heelsum (2002) |
| | Amsterdam, late 1990s | 24.4 ($N = 45$) | van Heelsum (2002) |
| United States (Hispanics) | State senates (upper houses), 2005 | 3.2 ($N = 1,856$) | NALEO (2006) |
| | State assemblies (lower houses), 2005 | 3.2 ($N = 5,409$) | NALEO (2006) |

*Notes:* [a] Limited as far as possible to North Africans of Arab or Berber (i.e., Muslim) origins. NALEO, National Association of Latino Elected and Appointed Officials.

Our data (shown in table 18.2) are less than ideal because we have depended for the most part on existing studies, which are sometimes for city councils, sometimes for regional bodies (state legislatures in the United States and *Landtage* in Germany), and in one case for both. It does, nevertheless, emerge that Germany, the one country for which we have both city and regional data,[2] presents the worst record of immigrant group electoral success at the subnational level. Apart from the basically powerless foreigner councils in a number of German cities, Turks have had little success in gaining elected office; in 2005, only 0.4 percent of the members of various *Landtage* was of Turkish origin, and the figure was 0.7 percent for the city councils of the fifty largest cities. In the *Landtage,* Turkish representation is about one-eighth of the proportion of the group in the population; on the city councils, it lies between one-quarter and one-fifth. As noted earlier, German citizenship law has, until recently, been unusually restrictive, and therefore Turks make up a small portion of the electorate. Given these facts, Turkish underrepresentation appears to be not so extreme.

There is a suggestion in the variations among the *Landtage* that Turks have fared better than the aggregate figures indicate in some cities with large concentrations of the group. In fact, all the Turkish regional parliamentarians are found in two city-states: Berlin and Hamburg. This fact also means that in larger *Länder* with large immigrant populations, such as Baden-Württemberg and North Rhine-Westphalia, Turkish representation in the *Landtage* is nil. Klaus Geiger and Margret Spohn's (2001) account, based on interviews with immigrant-origin parliamentarians, makes clear that these politicians are so rare in legislative bodies in Germany that they have tended to be treated as outsiders by their colleagues and seen as representing the interests of foreigners rather than Germans.

France has also been identified as a country where immigrant minorities, especially groups such as the Maghrebins from former colonies, have had great difficulty in attaining electoral success at the local level. Romain Garbaye (2005), for instance, has drawn this conclusion from a comparison of Lille and Birmingham. The lack of immigrant political representation has also been cited as a factor behind the 2005 riots of second-generation youth in the *banlieues* (e.g., *The Economist* 2005; Gordon 2005). But, in the aggregate, the French situation does not appear exceptional. In their survey of cities (which excludes the three largest), Vincent Geisser and Paul Oriol (2001) found that politicians of Maghrebin origin represented 3.3 percent of city councilors, a percentage that was more than half the North African share of the population. This figure, moreover, was a substantial rise from the low level attained in the 1995 election. Yet putting matters in this way may risk overstating North African electoral success because the cities that Geisser and Oriol considered, all with populations of 50,000 or more, include many of the immigrant-rich suburban municipalities that surround the major cities of the country, such as Paris and Lyon.

Where French immigrant minorities may face the greatest barriers is in the large cities; here perhaps is where the mechanisms of exclusion described by Garbaye (2005) best apply. Two such cities are represented in our data: Marseille, which was analyzed by Geisser and Schérazade Kelfaoui (2001), and Paris, which we have tabulated as of 2006. The very limited representation in Marseille of Muslim politicians, the category of focus for Geisser and Kelfaoui, is striking. Not only is this category broader than that of the Maghrebins (it includes some sub-Sarahan African groups as well), but the city houses very large immigrant populations and has fostered a political culture that, in deviation from national French norms, has been *communitairiste* (giving explicit political and policy recognition to immigrant and ethnic communities) (Geisser and Kelfaoui 2001, 55). Probably because of this politics, Marseille was widely noted as the one place in France that remained peaceful during the 2005 riots. Yet Maghrebin representation in Marseille is no different than, on average, in other French cities. The same statement holds for Paris.

Relative to the sizes of immigrant groups in their populations, Great Britain and the Netherlands appear to have lower aggregate rates of immigrant group representation on city councils than does France. For instance, the 1.5 percent of Dutch city councilors who in the late 1990s belonged to visible immigrant minorities is quite low compared to the minority percentage of the Dutch population. These aggregate figures, however, fail to capture the extent to which immigrant minorities in Britain and the Netherlands have been able to win office in cities with large immigrant concentrations, in contrast to the situation in France. Because immigrant origin populations are concentrated geographically in both countries, this may be the more relevant test.

In London boroughs, 10.6 percent of the local councilors in 2001 were ethnic minorities, with Asians dominant. Indeed, in all forty local authorities in England and Wales where the white population constituted less than 90 percent of the total (fifteen outside of London and twenty-five London boroughs), the Asian community achieved a position close to parity. In eleven local authorities (including seven in London), the proportion of Asian councilors *exceeded* the proportion of Asians in the population (Le Lohé 1998). In the Netherlands as of 1998–2002, migrant-origin councilors were roughly one-quarter of the council in Amsterdam, below the 38 percent of ethnic minorities in the city population but still a very significant proportion. Immigrant minorities achieved high levels of representation on the councils of several other large cities, such as Rotterdam, where 17 percent of the councilors in 1998–2002 were of migrant origin, compared with 30 percent of the residents (van Heelsum 2002).

The U.S. data (as in Germany) refer to regional legislatures, those of the fifty states; to our knowledge, no systematic data are available for the city level.[3] At the state level, the electoral representation of Hispanics is superior to that of Turks in Germany, and in the aggregate it is approximately one-fourth of what we would expect if the population proportion were the sole determinant. Probably the single most important factor accounting for this discrepancy is the relatively low rate of citizenship among Latin American immigrants (compared to, say, Asian immigrants) in the United States; the Hispanic rate results partly from low rates of naturalization (see, e.g., Portes and Rumbaut 1996) and partly from the high rates of unauthorized status among Mexicans and Central and South Americans.

The situation in the major gateway cities of the United States is less clear-cut than in Britain and the Netherlands, partly because of the lack of systematic data. Nevertheless, there are indications that Hispanics have begun to gain political office in many of them. In 2005, three of the mayors in the top ten U.S. gateway central cities were Hispanic; in another three cities, the main challenger in the prior mayoral election was Hispanic. This statement includes the mega-gateways Los Angeles and New York; Antonio Villaraigosa, mayor of Los Angeles, is Mexican American, and Fernando Ferrer, a second-generation Puerto Rican, was the main challenger in the 2001 New York City mayoral election. In one major U.S. city, Miami, one immigrant group, Cubans, has attained a degree of political influence that is unmatched, to our knowledge, among all the major cities in the five countries under study—by the end of the twentieth century, six of the thirteen Miami-Dade commissioners were Cuban Americans, as was the mayor (Grenier and Pérez 2003, 98). We see the impact in the Miami-Dade school system where, for example, all students, including native English speakers, are expected to become bilingual (Stepick et al. 2003). But in New York, where more than one-third of the population is foreign-born and more than one-half is of immigrant stock, the city council remains in the control of native-origin politicians, with only six out of fifty-one members from immigrant communities in 2006.[4]

## How Can These Differences Be Explained?

This analysis—limited, we grant, by the extent and quality of the existing data—suggests a four-tier resumé of the basic findings. On the lowest tier, based on overall immigrant group electoral representation, is Germany. On the highest is the Netherlands, where immigrant minorities are represented by substantial delegations on the city councils of large cities, such as Amsterdam and Rotterdam. In between are France, Britain, and the United States, where immigrant groups have achieved some success in subnational elective bodies but with numbers generally well below population percentages. There is still a notable difference among the three—in Britain and the United States, immigrant-origin politicians have achieved an electoral weight in cities with large immigrant concentrations that they still lack in France (e.g., London and Los Angeles compared with Marseille). Along with this weight comes the chance to govern, which has been denied them so far in major French cities.

What accounts for these differences? Social and political institutions in each society—often conceptualized as political opportunity structures—play a large role. These include citizenship and voting laws as well as the nature of the electoral system. At the same time, institutional arrangements that structure opportunities for achieving electoral office are rooted in state policies that reflect particular national integration models, paradigms, and discourses. More than this, these integration models can make elites more or less amenable to minority group mobilization efforts and thus have an effect on immigrant minorities' access to and success at the polls.

To begin with, there is the basic ability to vote. Immigrant-origin politicians typically depend heavily on support from co-ethnics in order to gain office, and thus they do better when immigrant minorities can take part in elections. This is largely a matter of citizenship law. Germany has had the most restrictive citizenship law, and policies were even stricter when members of the current adult second generation were born and growing up. The first relaxation came in the mid-1990s, when Germany made the requirements for the second generation less rigorous and removed official discretion in the approval of citizenship applications. The effects of the 1999 law granting provisional citizenship to second-generation children will not be fully felt among adult members of the second generation for two decades. Turks who are now of voting age were legally foreign at birth and had to undergo a naturalization procedure to acquire German citizenship, something many did not do. Germany, in addition, does not accord local voting rights to noncitizens from outside the European Union. Consequently, Turks make up only about 1 percent of the voters and have therefore attained very limited representation among elected officials. The Dutch case reveals that a common explanation in Germany for Turkish isolation—namely, that the Turks prefer to remain apart and establish a "parallel" society—is inadequate because in the Netherlands Turks have emerged as the most politically active of the immigrant populations (see Fennema et al. 2001).

The German situation is in marked contrast to, say, Britain, with its long history of birthright citizenship as well as a liberal citizenship regime for the overwhelming majority of immigrants who arrived in the 1950s and 1960s. As sovereign subjects from colonies or former colonies, Asians and Caribbeans came as formal citizens with full voting rights. Certainly, the considerable electoral success of ethnic minorities at the local level in Britain has a lot to do with this fundamental fact.

Moreover, of the four European countries in our study, Germany alone does not allow dual citizenship, which no doubt decreases the voting pool by discouraging naturalization. (After 2000, German authorities even attempted to denaturalize some

Turks who resumed their Turkish citizenship after obtaining the German one.) Indeed, members of the second generation must decide by the age of twenty-three whether to retain German nationality or the nationality of their parents, a requirement that will depress the number of the second generation eligible to vote. Although the United States naturalization oath requires the renunciation of other citizenships, U.S. law has "evolved in the direction of increased ambiguity or outright tolerance in favor of dual nationality"—in practice pursuing a "don't ask, don't tell" policy (Jones-Correa 2001b, 1012). Similarly, in the Netherlands, although officially immigrants cannot keep prior citizenships when they naturalize, there are numerous exceptions to the policy, resulting in a de facto common practice of allowing naturalized citizens to maintain their prior citizenships (Howard 2005, 709).

Citizenship need not be a requirement to vote. The Netherlands stands out among the five countries examined here for having introduced local voting rights in 1985 for noncitizen foreign residents with at least five years residence—which explains why non-European immigrant minorities there have attained a considerable degree of local representation.[5] In the United States, where states and municipalities decide who is eligible to vote, no major immigrant city allows noncitizen voting rights, which clearly has hampered immigrants' ability to elect co-ethnics to local offices. In France, as Garbaye (2000, 288) notes, first-generation immigrants do not, as a rule, have the right to vote and have traditionally played little role in French electoral politics.

The advantages and disadvantages of different electoral systems for immigrant representation are not clear in our data on electoral success. Systems involving party lists, such as found in France, Germany, and the Netherlands, would seem to offer advantages because parties can include some immigrant minorities on their lists without suffering electoral disadvantage. But there may be little incentive for them to do so unless there are substantial votes to attract. And, as has been noted in the Dutch case, placement on the party list can be an issue because there the lower a candidate's position on the list, the less the chance of being elected (see Rath 1988a).

First-past-the-post systems, such as are found in Britain and the United States (and in France for election to the Assemblée Nationale)—with single-member districts, in which voters can cast one vote each and the candidate with the most votes wins—can facilitate the entry of immigrant minorities into elected office by allowing immigrant candidates to challenge native-born ones in electoral districts with heavy immigrant representation. There may even be a contagion effect in heavily ethnic minority areas; if one party selects an ethnic minority candidate in a constituency, other parties may feel pressure to name ethnic candidates as well (Bird 2004). The down side is that immigrant electoral success depends on a residential concentration of ethnic minority voters that coincides with constituency boundaries—in other words, on residential segregation (Martiniello 2000). As has been observed for Britain, few ethnic minorities are selected as candidates outside of areas with sizable minority communities (Sagger and Geddes 2000).

In the case of the United States, two legal aspects of electoral districting may play a role. First, and fundamentally, electoral districts are based on resident population, not numbers of voters. This may create some advantages for large immigrant minorities, who fully occupy a district despite low citizenship rates. In addition, the Voting Rights Act of 1965, designed to eliminate formal barriers that southern states had created to obstruct the African American vote, favors the creation of electoral districts where minorities are at least competitive and has been used to help immigrant minorities. Another factor that affects Hispanic representation is the long presence of major Hispanic groups in the United States, namely Mexicans and Puerto Ricans. Thus, Hispanics had achieved some political voice even before the latest waves of immigration greatly increased their numbers (Skerry 1993).

The structure of the party system, particularly as it shapes candidate recruitment and the selection process, is also involved in electoral success. In Britain, the ward-based system of local candidate selection in the Labour Party, as Garbaye (2004) contends, reinforces the advantages of the single-member district system in the context of high ethnic minority concentration. It has allowed minorities to get a foot in the door by giving the ward-level party organization the ability to designate candidates. In addition, procedures exist to appeal to higher levels of the party in cases of conflict over the choice of candidates. By contrast, the party system in major French cities (Garbaye presents Lille as representative of a large number of medium-range and large French cities) gives less power to the neighborhood level in the selection of candidates. In Lille, the selection of candidates by the dominant Socialist Party has usually been made consensually in favor of local notables or incumbents, thereby reinforcing a feeling of powerlessness and inaccessibility for outsiders (Garbaye 2000, 296; 2005, 32). Geisser and Kelfaoui (2001) tell the revealing story of a successful Maghrebin politician in Marseille—during the late 1990s the only Maghrebin on the city council—who in 2001 was forced off the party list of candidates at the direction of national Socialist Party headquarters; however, after vigorous local protest, she was placed back on, although in a lower position.

Then there is the role of national political ideologies or integration models, which have their roots in particular national traditions that developed in the past. There may well be a move to de facto multiculturalism as some convergence scholars suggest, yet pronounced differences remain in the integration models in different countries. Moreover, such models are not simply a matter of political rhetoric that is belied by actual practices. In fact, integration models, and the policies that flow from them, can influence political opportunities in a number of ways. Not unexpectedly, the three countries that have provided the most scope for immigrant-origin politicians in mainstream offices—Britain, the Netherlands, and the United States—have been the most willing to acknowledge immigrants as ethnic minorities with distinct needs and cultural rights. This recognition has played a role in the provision of voting rights to immigrants in Europe and, perhaps most notably in the United States, the acceptance of ethnicity as a basis for political claims and campaigns. Moreover, as Ruud Koopmans and Paul Statham note, "migrants and minorities have greater access to the political system where they are officially recognized and their organizations facilitated, and where their claims can refer to existing legal frameworks for equal opportunity, anti-discrimination, and cultural rights" (2000c, 38).

In the Netherlands, for example, the granting of local voting rights to foreign residents in the mid-1980s was an extension of minority policies promoting equality before the law and the notion that individuals should not be disadvantaged by foreign citizenship (Entzinger 2003, 65). (The multicultural policies that held sway in the Netherlands in the 1980s, in turn, reflected an earlier era of pillarization, in which each major religious group was officially recognized by the state and had its own institutional arrangements, including schools, newspapers, and trade unions; Entzinger 2003; Lijphart 1968.)

In Britain and the United States, state models of multiculturalism or ethnic pluralism reinforced the effects of the electoral, political, and party systems in providing scope for ethnic minority candidates. Whether the British policy of state-supported multiculturalism (along with extensive and progressive race relations legislation) was a product, as Joppke (1999b, 225) suggests, of the British historical model of pluralism in dealing with empire and various ethnicities within Britain or, as Adrian Favell (2001) contends, of the long-held British conception that the individual should be protected from the state, the fact is that it helped foster political mobilization along ethno-racial lines and legitimated ethnic minority claims to political office (Koopmans and Statham 2000b, 221).

In the United States, urban ethnic politics has a long-standing legitimacy, dating back to the nineteenth century when the Irish were able to infiltrate and take over the helm of big-city Democratic Party politics by mobilizing the ethnic vote (Erie 1988). The efforts of today's Latino and Asian politicians to gain local office by wooing the ethnic vote are generally viewed as a natural ethnic succession. Successful attempts by African Americans to win office in the wake of the civil rights movement have also provided a model for immigrant-origin politicians to follow. In the post–civil rights United States, it has become widely accepted that ethno-racial minorities—mainly blacks and Latinos, who together make up approximately one-quarter of the U.S. population—should be represented in important political bodies.

In contrast, the ways in which France and Germany have defined foreigners and their integration into the state have hindered ethnic minorities' ability to gain elected office. Germany held on to the guestworker model for much of the postwar period and insisted it was not a country of immigration—giving rise to what one journalist refers to as the "you're a guestworker, so you'll be going home" model (Kramer 2005, 41). As Geiger and Spohn (2001) observe, even German politicians at the national level tend to view their immigrant-origin colleagues in terms of their original nationalities and to question their ability to represent German constituencies. France, with its strong assimilationist principles, does not even officially recognize ethnic groups and has been loathe to accept group-specific approaches, which may be an added barrier that immigrant-origin groups have to face in gaining access to the mainstream through political office. Indeed, republican principles provide a basis for objecting to the very notion that immigrant-origin politicians are needed to include the views and interests of these constituencies.

## Conclusion

As we note at the outset, this chapter is a first comparative look at the success of immigrant minorities in achieving electoral representation. Our review of the data for France, Germany, Britain, the Netherlands, and the United States indicates, we believe, the value of such exercises, even if they are limited of necessity by the studies that are available.

Yet, preliminary though it may be, our analysis suggests major limits for convergence theories, which focus mainly on national laws and policies and give less attention to such factors as institutional structures that shape the concrete opportunities faced by immigrant minorities in different countries and particular national ideologies or models of immigration integration. In terms of the success of immigrant-origin politicians in gaining elective office, we find substantial differences among the five countries we have examined; and arguably these differences are not likely to erode in the near future.

This conclusion can be questioned insofar as we have found citizenship law and voting rights to be a major axis differentiating countries in terms of immigrant minority electoral success. Consequently, some might contend that increasing convergence with regard to citizenship law will soon undercut the key national differences that emerged in our study. The case of Germany stands out in large part because of the barriers posed by its citizenship laws through the mid-1990s. Now that, since 2000, provisional *jus soli* citizenship is granted to the large majority of the second generation, will its electoral pattern not converge with those in France, Britain, and the United States? We grant that it might, but no conclusion is justified as yet. The 1999 law that makes *jus soli* citizenship possible requires individuals to choose by the age of twenty-three between German citizenship and that of their parents, and we will not know how this choice turns out for some time. Germany, moreover, strongly discourages dual citizenship, so the choice may prove difficult for many second-generation Turkish Germans. At the other end of the spectrum, the Netherlands has promoted an unusual degree of immigrant electoral success by granting the right to vote in local elections to resident immigrants since 1985. It is not apparent to us that other countries will emulate the Netherlands in the near future.

The case of France, which has a *jus soli* citizenship regime for the second generation, demonstrates that other factors in addition to citizenship law (an area of convergence) are in play when it comes to immigrant electoral success. Although France has a middling level of local and regional representation of immigrant minorities in elected offices, their political weight in cities of dense immigrant group concentration is quite modest. In France, both the model of integration preferred by the political elite—republicanism—and the standard practices of the party system seem to work against immigrant representation on elected bodies. The republican model makes it very difficult for political actors to deliberately sponsor the careers of immigrant-origin politicians as a way of diversifying the political elite, as the uproar over the appointment of the first Maghrebin prefect reveals. The party system also seems to allot a low preference to immigrant-origin politicians at election time, as Garbaye (2000) and Geisser and Kelfaoui (2001) point out for the cases of Lille and Marseille, respectively.

In short, national differences matter and are likely to continue to matter when it comes to immigrant minorities' ability to enter the precincts of power in Western European countries and the United States. It remains for additional studies to further develop our analysis of these national differences—and the factors accounting for them—in the light of future elections and as immigrant minorities expand their political influence, albeit at what is bound to be an uneven pace in different countries.

# PART VII

# THE ROAD AHEAD

By this point, *Bringing Outsiders In* has viewed immigrant political incorporation through various lenses—in local arenas, within and across countries, in supranational organizations, and across national boundaries. The authors have examined particular groups, distinct characteristics of groups and individuals, and an array of political opportunity structures. We have considered how and why immigrants seek to become incorporated or reject incorporation, at least on the terms being offered—and we have considered how and why those terms are generous, inclusive, rigid, or hostile. In chapter 19, Jennifer L. Hochschild and John Mollenkopf justify the basic transatlantic comparison, and draw out some common themes from this plethora of perspectives. They end, appropriately, with observations about the political complexities of immigrant political incorporation and—no surprise here—a call for more study of this fascinating and urgent topic.

# CHAPTER NINETEEN

# Understanding Immigrant Political Incorporation through Comparison

*Jennifer L. Hochschild and John H. Mollenkopf*

About 200 million individuals, approximately 3 percent of the world population, live outside the country where they were born. Over 100 million migrants live in the more developed regions of the world, including 9 million in Northern Europe, 22 million in Western Europe, 6 million in Canada, and 38 million in the United States. Proportionally, 9 percent of the residents of Northern Europe, 12 percent of those in Western Europe, 19 percent of those in Canada, and 13 percent of residents of the United States are immigrants (United Nations 2006). (These figures include refugees displaced by conflict as well as possibly short-term economic migrants.) If we include their children born in these host countries (the second generation), the figures are roughly twice as high. The global number of migrants more than doubled between 1970 and 2002 and continues to rise (United Nations 2002). As international migration flows increase, so do the benefits and complexities for governments, native populations, and migrants themselves.

The political puzzles generated by high levels of immigration may be even more difficult to solve than the economic, cultural, and security puzzles. At any rate, they must take priority because economic, cultural, and security policies cannot be promulgated and implemented unless sufficient political forces are mustered. Immigrants should also make politics a priority (although they usually do not). After all, immigrants will be successfully incorporated into their host countries only after they have enough involvement and influence in decision making that they can help shape relevant policies and feel as though they are actors, not just acted upon. So politics matters—but, for reasons discussed in this book, even supporters of incorporation, in widely different countries, find it hard to bring outsiders in satisfactorily.

Western liberal democracies enthusiastically promote the free or only slightly restricted movement of information, capital, and goods and services—but not of people. Membership is simply too important for any government to relinquish control over who leaves and (especially) enters its territory. Clearly, control is never perfect, the composition of the population of a country is never ideal, and any sort of immigrant population will bring both benefits and costs. But every competent and rational state will seek to control its borders, attain the right balance of residents' skills and loyalties, and maximize the benefits of immigration while minimizing its costs.

The systematic comparison of immigrants' political incorporation is just beginning, in part because the direct involvement of recent immigrants in Western European and United States politics is itself just beginning. Nevertheless, we can integrate the chapters in this volume by comparing cases across several dimensions. We begin by focusing on the basic comparison between North America and Western Europe. Next we identify themes shared across the chapters as well as some deep disagreements among the authors. We conclude by identifying political and policy dilemmas, all of which need more attention from both scholars and activists.

## Historical Trajectories of Immigration on Both Sides of the Atlantic

Despite variations among histories and political dynamics of host countries and despite differences among immigrants themselves, actors on both sides of the Atlantic will need to address similar political and policy dilemmas over the next few decades. Let us consider first the considerable differences between North American and European immigration and then the even more substantial similarities.

### Differences

The two continents initially appear to be more unlike than like in their relationship to immigration. Canada and the United States both conceive of themselves as nations of immigrants. Although the United States was built partly by excluding some (Smith 1997), it was also built by including many others, particularly the descendents of white European immigrants. For example, immigrants made up about one-quarter of the Northern army in the Civil War, contributing vitally to its victory. Conversely, European nation-building has often focused on erecting a political boundary around a settled group defined as a nationality through historical, cultural, and geographical terms. In short, the United States and Canada are immigrant societies, whereas the Western European states are societies with immigrants (the analogy is to Ira Berlin's (2000) distinction between "slave societies" and "societies with slaves").

Both self-images are too simple, of course. In the North American cases, the conception of a country of immigrants ignores the millions of Indians who already lived in what Europeans labeled America, the hundreds of thousands of Africans brought as slaves, the thousands of Hispanics who became residents of the United States through conquest or treaty, and the untold numbers of Asians who were prohibited from permanent residence. In the European cases, the idea of historically rooted populations ignores centuries of immigration into Western Europe by colonial subjects and migration within it by the Roma, Jews, and others. Nevertheless, as Peter Schuck (chap. 11 in this volume) puts it, the political identity of the United States "is founded on...a set of civic ideals...accessible, in principle, to all humanity," one of which is "openness to newcomers." In contrast, "the unity of most other states is based on sturdy...commonalities such as language, religion, and ethnicity" (see also Huntington 1981).

Another obvious and significant difference between the two continents is the scale of the polity. The United States is so huge that it has had many distinct immigration stories at the same time. In the nineteenth century, Africans involuntarily immigrated into the South while Europeans desperately sought to migrate into the cities of the North; Mexicans acquired U.S. citizenship in the Southwest whether they wanted it or not; and Asians experienced voluntary immigration, contract labor, and exclusion in rapid succession in the West. Roughly the same story could be told for Canada. If we treat the European Union as a single political entity, then it too operates on the same large geographical and political scale and it too has many simultaneous immigration narratives: Poles and Estonians to Sweden and Germany, North Africans to Italy and France, Jamaicans and South Asians to England, and so on. But the European Union is not (yet?) a single state and no extant European country comes close to the scale and complexity of the U.S. or Canadian experience of immigration.

The smaller size of European countries has important implications for immigrant political incorporation. An obvious one has to do with language. Americans are (unnecessarily) concerned about the possibility that residents might speak a language other than English (Citrin et al. 2007; Schildkraut 2005), whereas Europeans work hard to learn several languages so that they can switch among them as needed. In addition, non-EU migrants in European countries face a complicated system of national laws and regulations that restrict their freedom of movement but also sometimes enhance their ability to organize and engage with an array of political bodies.

Thus as Richard Alba and Nancy Foner (chap. 18), Gianni D'Amato (chap. 5), Christian Joppke (chap. 8), Gallya Lahav (chap. 14), Marco Martiniello (chap. 3), Michael Minkenberg (chap. 10), and Eva Østergaard-Nielsen (chap. 13) all show, we must understand variation across the many relatively small countries of Europe to make sense of the overall patterns of immigrant political incorporation or exclusion on that continent. Conversely, with the exception of actions by occasional renegade states and assertive towns, the United States has a national policy with regard to immigration and to the legal status of various categories of immigrants. Canada, similarly, offers a huge space and many lower-level governments all under the umbrella of essentially the same immigration regime.

A third difference between the continents is their experiences in the past few centuries with regard to slavery. The United States was a slave society for the first two-thirds of its history, whereas since the 1600s European states have had a social structure resembling a caste system but no domestic enslavement. The profound legacy of slavery in the United States affects immigrant political incorporation in several ways. White (and black) citizens all understood that approximately one-seventh of the population was not intended to partake of Schuck's "set of civic ideals speaking in universal terms and accessible, in principle, to all humanity." As a result, immigrants still face the question of whether to try to join the dominant race, with all of its obvious advantages, or to ally with the subordinated race for reasons of identification and political commitment. In addition, African Americans' history over the past half-century provides a powerful model of resistance to oppression and more or less successful insistence on incorporation into the mainstream. In short, as Reuel Rogers (chap. 7) and Lorraine Minnite (chap. 4) both argue, the United States has a highly salient template for efforts to incorporate minority or disadvantaged ethnic groups, which most European states lack.

Finally, countries on each side of the Atlantic have distinctive political features. Many European states have the bureaucratic remnants of an old colonial system, a parliamentary legislative structure, an electoral system of proportional representation, parties that originally developed on the basis of class appeals, a history of state-sponsored religious institutions, and a plethora of transnational organizations. In the European Union, Europe also has a robust structure of cross-national governance and partial integration. Conversely, the United States has had *jus solis* citizenship laws since inception, strong and independent executives in the presidency and state-level governorships, two catch-all political parties and a first-past-the-post district-based electoral system, and a complicated system of federalism. (Canada shares some features of each system.) As most chapters in *Bringing Outsiders In* show, these elements of the political structure all affect immigrants' opportunities and strategies for seeking political incorporation.

## Similarities

Despite differences that prohibit easy comparisons within and across the continents, North American and Western European states share relevant important characteristics. Aristide Zolberg's framework is useful here. He argues that U.S. immigration policy has always been shaped by two independent interests, "one pertaining to the…effects of immigration on material conditions, the other for political conditions. [They] can be represented by cross-cutting axes, each with positive and negative poles" (Zolberg 2006, 19). The chapters in *Bringing Outsiders In* suggest that this typology holds for other countries as well as for the United States.

The continuum of political conditions runs from hostility to immigration and immigrants to various incorporative strategies; it maps roughly on to the dynamic of incorporation and nonincorporation that we discuss in chapter 2. At the negative pole, a substratum of virulent nativism probably always persists on both continents. But as Minkenberg (chap. 10) shows, the political impact of nativism and the degree to which it connects with more mainstream concerns vary. Sometimes political parties or actors effectively mobilize anti-immigrant sentiment; the U.S. Know Nothing Party of the 1850s, eugenicists of the 1920s, and Minutemen of the present have distinct features, but they bear a family resemblance to Jean-Marie Le Pen's Front National in France, Jörg Haider's Freedom Party in Austria, and Christoph Blocher's Swiss People's Party (SVP; Schweizerische Volkspartei). And on both continents, as many scholars (e.g., Luis Fraga, chap. 12) have noted, economic hard times, concern about job loss among disadvantaged native minorities, racism, religious antagonism, and cultural anxiety all enable hostility to immigrants or particular subsets of immigrants to enter the mainstream political arena (See also Higham 1992; Espenshade and Hempstead 1996; Fetzer 2000). That hostility may result in exclusion, stringent quotas, segregation, or expulsion (Ngai 2004).

At the positive pole of the continuum of political conditions lie efforts to incorporate immigrants into the host society through the means and stages discussed in chapters 2 and 3. Such efforts cannot be taken as a given, as the examples of European guest workers, African American slaves, Chinese contract workers, and Mexican braceros all suggest. Some national or more local governments and organizations, however, make genuine and extensive efforts at inclusion—ranging from efforts at Americanization (Pickus 2005), through liberal neutrality and endorsement of individual freedom of choice, to multiculturalist support for group-based political and policy space. As D'Amato (chap. 5) and Joppke (chap. 8) point out, schools are an especially important arena in which nations try to sort out their incorporative strategies (see also Hochschild and Scovronick 2003; McDonough and Feinberg 2003); political parties and civic organizations also play this role [see Rogers (chap. 7), Sandro Cattacin (chap. 16), and John Mollenkopf and Raphael Sonenshein (chap. 6)].

The analyses in *Bringing Outsiders In* also address, although less directly, Zolberg's second continuum of material conditions. Its negative pole is represented by efforts to exclude or exploit immigrant workers, or at least to prevent them from displacing native-born workers, whether low- or high-skilled. No nation discussed in this book keeps immigrants out of the labor force any longer, with the exception of a few categories of refugees or asylees. Nevertheless, residential segregation, job discrimination, and poor educational opportunities may keep immigrants or their children from becoming competitive workers; Rogers (chap. 7); Tariq Modood (chap. 15); Joppke (chap. 8); Fraga (chap. 12); and Duyvendak, Pels, and Rijkschroeff (chap. 9) all speak to those concerns.

Efforts by countries on both sides of the Atlantic to ensure that immigrants generate more economic benefits than burdens demonstrate the positive pole of the continuum of material conditions. Americans imposed head taxes and public charge payments in the nineteenth century to discourage steamship companies from transporting unemployables. The United States simultaneously encouraged or required Africans, Chinese, and Mexicans to do necessary jobs that free-born European American natives were unwilling to do. Employers now lobby for H1-B visas for high-skilled workers while working more quietly to ensure that undocumented workers are still available for essential low-skilled jobs. European nations designed guestworker programs and permitted citizens of colonized nations to immigrate to fill the needs for low- and high-skilled workers, respectively. European policies are changing in part because many leaders now perceive that their country will gain the most economic benefit from immigrant workers who are politically assimilated, reunited with their families, and better educated.

The chapters in *Bringing Outsiders In* suggest two further points of comparison that supplement Zolberg's two axes. The first focuses on the level of centralization in political decision making about immigration and immigrants. The United States has wrestled with this issue for over two centuries, even while the absolute number of immigrants and the foreign-born proportion of the population have varied dramatically. As population ratios rose, fell, and rose again (see figure 19.1), the legal regulation of immigration has followed a fairly straight, if highly contested, trajectory. In one of its earliest acts, the federal government made "free white persons" eligible for naturalized citizenship in 1790. For the next four decades, states provided the only regulation of immigration; although making no effort to control the number or national origins of immigrants, they sought to protect themselves from public charges

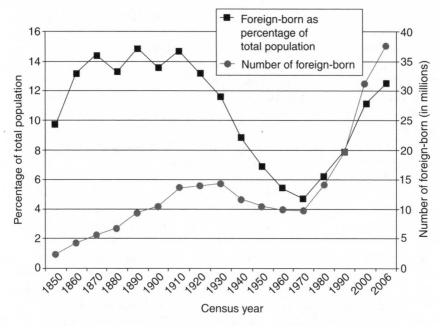

**Figure 19.1**  Number of foreign-born and proportion of U.S. population, 1850–2006.
*Source:* Migration Policy Institute, http://www.migrationinformation.org/datahub/charts/final.fb.shtml.

and to exclude criminals. After a series of judicial decisions, laws and counterlaws, and political confrontations and maneuvers, in 1876 the Supreme Court prohibited state head taxes and declared immigration to be in the hands of the federal government. At that point, Congress began, and has never ceased, to regulate the amount of immigration, to create various immigrant statuses, and to control the origins and presumed quality of immigrants (Zolberg 2006; Tichenor 2002; King 2000).

Several centuries later, Western Europe appears to be following the same path. With regard to immigration policy, decision making has moved from no control to decentralized control and may be moving toward centralized regulation at the EU level (European Commission 2007; Europa: Activities of the European Union 2007, 2008). That is, during the twentieth century, each nation in Western Europe developed its own laws with regard to countries of origin, number of immigrants, categories of immigration status, quality control for immigrants, and immigrant integration policies. By now, as Lahav (chap. 14) reports, most members of the European Parliament agree on the need to move toward consistent policies across member nations; some are in place and others are being developed. Lahav (chap. 14) shows that member states are unlikely to relinquish control of immigration policy to a central authority soon, but she also provides good reasons to expect it eventually.

An analogy is plausible, then, between states in the United States and member nations of the European Union. It took decades for the U.S. federal government to get states and localities to (mostly) relinquish control over immigration policy and policies toward immigrants, even after the federal courts and legislature had spoken. If the analogy holds, European nations will eventually follow suit, although the process may never be complete on either side of the Atlantic.

Finally, consider the actions of immigrants themselves. In both continents, many follow the scripts laid out for them by the host country. They work hard, care for their families, become citizens, participate politically in conventional ways if at all, learn the host-country language, follow its laws, generally keep their religious beliefs out of the public domain, and otherwise assimilate to their assigned roles. The rewards of a little social and economic upward mobility and a modicum of political voice come often enough that the prospect of a better life induces additional millions of people to move to these nations.

But the few immigrants who do not follow the script get most of the scholars', media's, and politicians' attention. Some on both continents try to become incorporated at a faster pace or deeper level than the host country wants—seeking votes for noncitizens, easier pathways to naturalization, amnesty for the undocumented, asylum for distressed relatives, public funds for schools or religious organizations, and public endorsement of religious prescriptions. Others resist the host-country incorporative efforts—retaining loyalty to their country of origin at the expense of the receiving country, eschewing the host-country language, and asserting their right to manage their family or community by religious rather than secular law. And a few violently resist incorporation in the name of religion, nationalism, or political ideals.

Immigrants' choices, as well as the ways in which native-born political leaders evaluate and respond to them, vary of course by country. Both sets of actions also vary along the dimensions laid out in chapter 2 in our model of immigrant political incorporation. Cattacin (chap. 16), Martiniello (chap. 3), Modood (chap. 15), Østergaard-Nielsen (chap. 13), and Wong and Pantoja (chap. 17) together provide a wide, although inevitably incomplete, array of representations of those actions and reactions in particular cases. Determining further how immigrants' political behavior does, and does not, follow or change that of native-born residents, and why that behavior ranges from eager assimilation to angry rejection, will keep a lot of scholars and political activists busy for decades.

## Shared Themes, Disparate Judgments

Comparisons of the structural conditions and historical trajectories across countries and even continents is thus illuminating, if not yet theoretically cohesive. In parallel fashion, comparison of various authors' arguments in *Bringing Outsiders In* demonstrates shared themes as well as sharp disagreement.

### Structures and Agency

A central issue for our authors is the old chestnut—the relationship between structure and agency. All agree that structures matter, that political action must be understood within an institutional context, and that immigrants and other political actors are not merely automatons responding to their context. Behind that general concurrence, however, lie illuminating differences, even disputes.

*Which* structures matter? In D'Amato's (chap. 5) portrayal, Swiss cantons and regions are the prime movers in granting citizenship to immigrants, whereas the national government is almost entirely reactive. Similarly, Rogers (chap. 7), Mollenkopf and Sonenshein (chap. 6), and Alba and Foner (chap. 18) focus on local electoral systems and political party configurations to explain political coalitions and voting results. In contrast, Wong and Pantoja (chap. 17) merge city-specific data in the United States on the unstated but plausible assumption that immigrants' place of residence does not much affect whether they become U.S. citizens. Unlike all those authors, Cattacin (chap. 16) downplays formal political institutions in favor of a focus on investors, neighborhood organizations, ethnic service providers, and other civic or private associations. Martiniello (chap. 3) bridges all of these differences by providing a useful typology of structures, including the level of government, the distinction between state and nonstate political activity, and even the role of transnational linkages.

*How much* do structures matter? Rogers (chap. 7), Mollenkopf and Sonenshein (chap. 6), D'Amato (chap. 5), and Alba and Foner (chap. 18) accomplish the bulk of their explanatory task by focusing only on political institutions. But for Lahav (chap. 14); Duyvendak, Pels, and Rijkschroeff (chap. 9); and Schuck (chap. 11), explanatory variables are not institutions but rather public attitudes, officials' ideology and partisanship, normative "notions of citizenship" (Schuck's term), and policy choices and outcomes. Joppke (chap. 8), Fraga (chap. 12), Minkenberg (chap. 10), and Modood (chap. 15) also depict ideologies, ranging from racial identity politics to liberal individualism, as crucial to any explanation of immigrant political incorporation. Moving in the other direction, Østergaard-Nielsen (chap. 13) warns against "methodological nationalism" because even so powerful a structure as the nation-state does not explain transnational political activity. And Minkenberg observes that "electoral system type...seems only marginally relevant," whereas "the cultural context of each country" shapes the impact of right-wing organizations across an array of European nations (chap. 10).

On the other side of the structure/agency divide, how should we analyze the immigrants' actions? Although all the authors concur that immigrants have room to maneuver within structures and common practices, the authors vary in the degree to which immigrants' agency is a central focus. Perhaps they also disagree implicitly on how much freedom of action immigrants really have. Cattacin (chap. 16) makes the strongest claim—immigrants have de facto citizenship by virtue of their consumption of city services. Modood (chap. 15) shows how immigrants' self-concepts change over time in ways that come close to determining their political activity and reception; Schuck (chap. 11) shows how immigrants' social and economic activity can shape their political actions. Even authors who focus on structures as explanatory variables, such as Rogers (chap. 7), Alba and Foner (chap. 18), and Mollenkopf and Sonenshein (chap. 6), imply engagement by immigrants in the political arena through their attention to coalitions, voting, and election to office. In contrast, Fraga (chap. 12), Lahav (chap. 14), and Minkenberg (chap. 10) have little to say about immigrants' agency because their chapters address how immigrants are treated by native-born citizens. Immigrants may not be passive recipients, but in these chapters, they are more acted on than acting.

## Liberal Individualism and Multiculturalism

Another old chestnut—the state's underlying normative strategy for immigrant political incorporation—is a second central theme in the chapters of *Bringing Outsiders In*. Most authors agree that what Joppke (chap. 8) calls state neutrality and state-supported multiculturalism are the primary alternatives. Roughly speaking, state (or liberal) neutrality treats immigrants as individuals who are essentially interchangeable from a policy perspective; conditional only on their immigration status, they have the same rights, constraints, relationship to the state, and political standing. In contrast, multiculturalism treats immigrants as members of cohesive groups that are each to be treated by policymakers in particular ways; the state has a distinct relationship with Muslims or Latin American immigrants that is different from (although perhaps parallel to) its relationship with Christians or European migrants.

Although the chapters agree on this basic distinction, they vary on how to understand and interpret it. Joppke (chap. 8) and Duyvendak, Pels, and Rijkschroeff (chap. 9) display the most direct conflict. Joppke (chap. 8) endorses the U.S. policy of separation of church and state, arguing that Muslims are, perhaps ironically, more effectively incorporated in a society that keeps religion in the private realm than in European nations that publicly support religious organizations. In his words, "multicultural policies have failed to bring about the socioeconomic mainstreaming of migrant ethnics." Duyvendak, Pels, and Rijkschroeff (chap. 9) claim, however, that the problems of multiculturalism in the Netherlands stem from too little of it rather than too much. In their view, it was the lack of sustained commitment by the government to multicultural policies in the political and cultural arenas that made the whole multicultural experiment fail.

Other chapters contribute to this debate. Modood (chap. 15) and Cattacin (chap. 16) both endorse public support for the development of group identities and organizations, the former in order to respond to racialization by the state and the latter as a means of group empowerment in homogeneous urban ghettos. But Schuck (chap. 11) comes down on the same side as Joppke (chap. 8). He argues that the state is and should be in the business of fostering its own dominant culture, leaving minority cultures to thrive or not in the private sphere, as their members prefer. Østergaard-Nielsen (chap. 13) notes, although she does not necessarily endorse, the recent turn toward assimilationism.

Some authors find the stark distinction between state neutrality and state-sponsored multiculturalism too simple to depict the actual process by which outsiders are brought in. Cattacin (chap. 16) claims that "we live in a divided but pluricultural society—rather than in a homogeneously multicultural one." Modood (chap. 15) points to a "plural blackness," by which he means "recognition of a diversity of minority identities." Joppke (chap. 8) points out that liberal neutrality has another antagonist in addition to multiculturalism, which he calls "national particularism." Schuck (chap. 11) describes affirmative action in a way that moves it outside state neutrality but not quite into multiculturalism. Alba and Foner (chap. 18), among others, point to the differences between French republicanism and other forms of universalistic liberalism. Lahav (chap. 14) finds that partisan and ideological differences within nations—from Green parties on the left to conservative parties on the right—give more analytic purchase on the views of members of the European Parliament than do differences in broad national philosophy. Minnite (chap. 4) points our attention away from any form of incorporation at all, toward "reversals and disincorporation" of immigrant groups. She also shows how essential it is to distinguish among minority groups in thinking about this issue. D'Amato's (chap. 5) observation that Rousseauean republicanism might require cultural homogeneity suggests further tensions down the road even in relatively pacific Switzerland.

### Predictions about Immigrant Political Incorporation

Not all chapters in *Bringing Outsiders In* indulge in prescription or prediction, but enough do to constitute a third overarching theme. Some fear for the future of immigrant political incorporation. D'Amato (chap. 5) articulates the possibility, indeed likelihood, of "future conflict between the partisans of the (national) rule of law and supporters of (local) popular sovereignty." The immediate issue is whether Swiss citizens should have the right to vote on naturalization laws or to make judgments on candidates for naturalization, as Blocher's SVP proposed. Even assuming resolution of that particular question, D'Amato (chap. 5) has no confidence that the underlying contest has been defused. Minkenberg (chap. 10) reinforces D'Amato's concern about radical European right-wing parties and movements. He highlights the violence of xenophobic social movements as well as the craven inclination of political parties to incorporate radical right parties, thus "granting them new legitimacy." Radical right parties and movements vary in their strength within as well as across European nations, but overall Minkenberg finds a substantial change from a few decades ago when political officials shunned and largely shut out radical right-wing actors and movements. Duyvendak, Pels, and Rijkschroeff (chap. 9), ironically, see in the celebrated "progressive monoculture" of the Dutch public not a solution to the difficulties of immigrant political incorporation but rather a "defensive and contorted reaction to ethno-cultural diversity." Wong and Pantoja (chap. 17) see a double bind for immigrants to the United States; "presently, noncitizens face a politically hostile environment," but at the same time "the costs of naturalization are intensifying and falling entirely on the immigrant and his or her community." Minnite (chap. 4) is pessimistic about whether incorporative tendencies can outweigh the pressures toward disincorporation or rejection of assimilation.

But other authors in *Bringing Outsiders In* are less pessimistic, or are even optimistic, about the trajectory of immigrant political incorporation. After detailing the many forms of hostility to immigrants, especially the undocumented, Fraga (chap. 12) predicts that "the U.S. polity will, ultimately, again expand to include more of its people than it did previously." Schuck (chap. 11) believes that such expansion is already underway; the "inclusive [U.S.] naturalization regime has produced impressive numerical results," and "by almost any definition… immigrants are rapidly integrating into U.S. life." Rogers (chap. 7) shows the many ways in which coalitions between native- and foreign-born minority groups can go wrong, but he also points to one successful alliance. In Hartford, Connecticut, "the at-large system of elections…encourages politicians to downplay identity-based politics…, which in turn minimizes intergroup conflict and facilitates alliance building across racial and ethnic lines." Cattacin (chap. 16) argues that homogeneous and even isolated immigrant neighborhoods "not only should and could but presently are playing a positive role in the integration of immigrants into European (and doubtless U.S.) society." And Modood (chap. 15) assures us—albeit with a stringent caveat—that "there is no reason to panic."

## Political and Policy Issues

All the chapters in *Bringing Outsiders In* end on a more or less tentative note. They draw the standard scholarly conclusion that "more research is needed," but many also reveal deep uncertainty with regard to the basic direction of incorporation. They are right to do so; there are no recipes or certainties here. Each country makes different choices in dealing with immigrants, and new leadership or changes in circumstances lead many states to change their choices over time, sometimes abruptly. The target population itself is not stable: immigrants from different nations present distinct demands, needs, and values; the proportion of immigrants from different nations shifts rapidly; immigrants move back to their countries of origin; and countries of origin change their relationship to migrants and host countries.

Regardless of the target population or political regime, the policy issues themselves are numerous. They include regularizing the status and future of undocumented immigrants (Fraga, chap. 12); bringing immigrants into electoral politics (Wong and Pantoja, chap. 17); redesigning political opportunity structures to give immigrants genuine political voice (Rogers, chap. 7; Alba and Foner, chap. 18; Mollenkopf and Sonenshein, chap. 6; Martiniello, chap. 3); developing and coordinating supranational policies toward immigrants and immigration (Lahav, chap. 14); controlling native-born residents' hostility to and violence against immigrants, and vice versa (Minkenberg, chap. 10; Modood, chap. 15; Fraga, chap. 12); enabling advocacy groups and religious or civic organizations to integrate immigrants into communities (Duyvendak, Pels, and Rijkschroeff, chap. 9; Cattacin, chap. 16); figuring out the implications of transnational sentiments and legal statuses (Østergaard-Nielsen, chap. 13); enhancing the quality of schools, jobs, and neighborhoods (Joppke, chap. 8); dealing effectively but not excessively with security concerns (Schuck, chap. 11), managing relations between central and more local governments (D'Amato, chap. 5; Lahav, chap. 14), and striving to prevent alienation and radicalization among poor, isolated, rejected, or ideologically motivated youth (Minnite, chap. 4; Østergaard-Nielsen, chap. 13; Modood, chap. 15; and Cattacin, chap. 16). And that is only a partial list.

Despite the urgency and importance of these issues, we conclude this book by raising the level of abstraction from particular concerns to their underlying political conundrums. As Fraga (chap. 12) points out, both the left and right face normative and partisan complexities—as do immigrants themselves. Liberal democratic countries will need to somehow manage these ideological and political complexities so they can address urgent cultural, economic, political, and moral policy concerns over the next few decades.

**Table 19.1** Views on desirable trajectories for immigration, and proportion of population that is foreign born, in selected western nations, 2003 (%)

| Country | Proportion of population that is foreign-born | Views on immigration | | |
| | | Increase levels of immigration "a lot" + "a little" | Keep levels of immigration the same | Reduce levels of immigration "a little" + "a lot" |
| --- | --- | --- | --- | --- |
| Switzerland | 23.1 | 6 | 50 | 44 |
| Canada | 18.7 | 30 | 39 | 31 |
| Germany | 12.9 | 4 | 23 | 73 |
| United States | 12.6 | 11 | 32 | 56 |
| Sweden | 12.0 | 12 | 31 | 57 |
| Austria | 11.4 | 7 | 30 | 63 |
| Netherlands | 10.7 | 4 | 27 | 70 |
| Great Britain | 8.9 | 6 | 16 | 78 |
| France | 7.8 | 8 | 27 | 66 |
| Norway | 7.6 | 8 | 22 | 70 |
| Denmark | 6.3 | 10 | 39 | 50 |
| Spain | 5.3[a] | 10 | 37 | 54 |

*Sources:* For foreign-born population, Organisation for Economic Co-operation and Development (OECD 2007, table A.1.4); for views on immigration, Zentralarchiv für Empirische Sozialforschung an der Universität zu Köln (ZACAT), which includes the multination International Social Survey Programme (ISSP), 2003, http://zacat.gesis.org/webview/index.jsp.

*Note:* For some countries, the survey included noncitizen respondents, so the table probably overestimates voters' support for more immigration.

[a] For 2001.

## Why Does Immigration Rise in Democratic Polities?

Underlying all of this complexity is a central puzzle for democratic theory—for several decades, most western countries have had high and rising levels of immigration even though a majority of their populations consistently want immigration to stabilize or decrease. That public sentiment has been apparent since the early 1960s, when survey researchers first asked about immigration. Table 19.1 shows the pattern for 2003, the most recent year for which we have comparable data in North America and Europe. With the notable exception of Canada, barely one-tenth of the population of any of these countries favors increased immigration, and one-half or more of the residents, except in Canada and Switzerland, want a decrease. Respondents' level of support for sustained or increased immigration bears no apparent relationship to the foreign-born population share in their country (although the subsequent rise in support for the Swiss right-wing SVP is presumably related to its very high proportion of nonnative-born residents.)

Governments also pursue the opposite of what most voters want over a long period of time on a few other policies; the best example is free trade. But such policies are unusual, volatile, and always subject to political challenge and the possibility of a populist revolt. Therefore, governments tend to be defensive about immigration. They are vulnerable to nativist pressures and make a big show of hostility to illegal immigration—while continuing to admit large numbers of immigrants and to turn a relatively blind

**Table 19.2** Relative approval of immigration among supporters of the two largest political parties in selected western nations, 2003 (%)

| Country | Increase immigration "a lot" + "a little," + "remain the same" | | | |
|---|---|---|---|---|
| | Largest party on the left | Percentage | Largest party on the right | Percentage |
| Austria | SPÖ (Social Democratic) | 35 | ÖVP (Austrian People's Party) | 31 |
| Canada | Liberal | 72 | Conservative | 62 |
| Denmark | Social Democratic | 56 | Liberal | 49 |
| France | PS (Socialist) | 49 | UMP (Union for a Popular Movement) | 21 |
| Germany | SPD (Social Democratic) | 33 | CDU/CSU (Christian Democratic Union/ Christian Social Union) | 22 |
| United Kingdom | Labour | 26 | Conservative | 14 |
| Netherlands | PvdA (Labour) | 39 | CDA (Christian Democratic) | 22 |
| Norway | Labour | 29 | Progress | 5 |
| Spain | PSOE (Socialist Workers) | 50 | PP (People's) | 39 |
| Sweden | SAP (Social Democratic) | 43 | M (Moderates) | 26 |
| Switzerland | Social Democratic | 73 | SVP (Swiss People's) | 25 |
| United States | Democratic | 49 | Republican | 34 |

*Source:* Zentralarchiv für Empirische Sozialforschung an der Universität zu Köln (ZACAT), which includes the multination International Social Survey Programme (ISSP), 2003, http://zacat.gesis.org/webview/index.jsp.

*Note:* Most respondents in both columns chose "remain the same" rather than "increase." For some countries, the sample size for respondents identifying with even the two largest parties is small, so these figures are not completely reliable.

eye to the undocumented. Immigrants are simply too important to the economy, demographic health, and thus fiscal health of host countries to be excluded even if they could be. Nevertheless, immigration policy and policies toward immigrants rest on a shaky foundation from the perspective of any political party seeking to win election, and this political weakness has consequences for all immigration-related policies.

## Ideological Conundrums

Political preferences with regard to immigration and immigrants are unusually not well aligned with typical partisanship. Both the left and right are internally divided, which makes for strange coalitions and tensions.

### Problems for the Left

Within the context of popular distaste for immigration, native-born leftists in most western nations are more welcoming to or at least tolerant of immigrants than are native-born rightists. Table 19.2 shows that members of left-wing parties are consistently, if modestly, more favorable toward immigration.

These figures accord with our general understanding of left and right ideologies. Social democratic (in the European context) and liberal (in the U.S. context) activists tend to be more oriented toward the international arena and less isolationist. (The present U.S. political configurations with regard to Iraq, and earlier with regard to Vietnam, are historical anomalies.) They tend to be more culturally flexible or cosmopolitan in their commitments, if not necessarily in their behaviors, and they sympathize with the desire to escape poverty and oppression that drives many to leave their home country. In recent years, European (and increasingly U.S.) leftist support for Palestinians in the Middle East has augmented sympathy for Muslim immigrants.

Leftists also believe in respecting cultural differences and honoring group identities, often through explicit public policies of multiculturalism. But they can be dismayed by the beliefs of many immigrants, who are frequently culturally and religiously conservative. Leftists disagree profoundly with many immigrants' gender practices, their treatment of children (especially daughters), and their views on homosexuality. Especially but not only in Europe, leftists are insistently secular, so they may be uneasy about immigrants' religious commitments and practices. Duyvendak, Pels, and Rijkschroeff (chap. 9) are the most explicit about this dilemma, but it arguably underlies many of the other chapters *of Bringing Outsiders In* as well.

Leftist political actors also worry that low-skilled immigrants will take jobs from low-skilled native-born workers. As Rogers (chap. 7) makes clear, that dilemma is especially acute when the threatened native-born workers are disproportionately ethnic minorities, such as black descendents of slaves in the United States. So the left endorses at least some immigration but has many concerns about actual immigrants.

## Problems for the Right

Political actors on the right also face ideological and partisan dilemmas. Rightists tend to be unenthusiastic about immigration for reasons that are the mirror image of the left: they are more isolationist, more culturally and politically nationalist, more concerned about the rule of law and legal status, and more inclined to rely on international markets than on migration to alleviate worldwide poverty. But rightists' views on gender and parental roles, homosexuality, and religiosity accord much more with the views of many immigrants than do leftists' views. Social conservatives are also more sympathetic to some immigrants' desire to bring religious values and practices into the public realm. Rightists, then, resist immigration but have a lot in common with a high proportion of actual immigrants.

The right faces additional dilemmas with regard to immigrant political incorporation. As Minkenberg (chap. 10) and Fraga (chap. 12) show, conservatives tend to be especially exercised about illegal immigration, but they also sometimes manage or own businesses that depend on undocumented immigrants' labor power and acquiescence to low wages and difficult working conditions. Industries of this sort, such as a restaurant owners' association or a construction trades association, can often be a potent national interest group. Conservatives might prefer regularizing the status of undocumented immigrants to maintain a stable workforce and to discourage casual and widespread acceptance of illegality. Regularization would also eliminate the hypocrisy of the government spending tax revenues on border protection while employers hire workers who have foiled that protection. But conservatives find it unpalatable to publicly endorse amnesty for undocumented immigrants in the United States or to be equivalently "soft" on undocumented immigrants in Europe.

The right faces an even deeper predicament regarding the ultimate goal of immigration policies and policies toward immigrants. Conservatives tend to be "national particularists" (in the phrase of Joppke, chap. 8), meaning that they endorse a strong version of unilateral assimilationism or liberal neutrality among individuals that Schuck (chap. 11) argues for and Modood (chap. 15) and Cattacin (chap. 16) worry about. But some conservatives are also nativists—and demonstrating hostility toward immigrants is not a good strategy for persuading them to assimilate. It is not easy for a political party or organization seeking to unify the right to reconcile these various contradictory impulses.

## Immigrants' Choices

Immigrants also get caught up in normative and political conundrums, which surely affect them more deeply. Should immigrants ally with conservatives, who may hold similar cultural values and provide employment but who may also oppose further immigration, want to exact a stiff price for incorporation, and flirt with xenophobia? Or should they ally with leftists, who oppose and even scorn some of their cultural or religious values but who might help them enact their cultural preferences, provide more social services, or support their access to the labor market?

The right strategy for building coalitions with other immigrants and disadvantaged groups is just as unclear, as Rogers (chap. 7) demonstrates. Should immigrant groups ally with other immigrants including refugees, undocumented, or temporary workers even if they come from a different part of the world and face different legal liabilities? Or should they seek to form coalitions with native-born residents of the same nationality or even of the same broad social class in the hopes of avoiding competition over jobs and tension over status and resources? Other questions: Should immigrants aim to enter their new polity as individuals or as members of an ethnic group? Can they retain ties to their countries of origin while becoming a citizen of the host country; should they ally with co-religionists across national borders; should they permit or encourage their children to become fully-fledged Germans, Dutch, or Americans?

Variants of these questions have always faced migrants, as a rich literature of histories and memoirs shows. But some issues and options are new or have attained a new urgency in this era of easy international travel, stateless organizations willing to use violence to attain their ends, and host countries increasingly nervous about security and national unity. For instance, Muslim immigrants might ponder how they can stay committed Muslims without being drawn into international radicalism, whereas migrants from former colonies might wonder how they can take advantage of their linguistic and cultural ties while avoiding demeaning ethnic stereotypes. And even the old questions that previous generations of migrants grappled with have no settled answers, as Østergaard-Nielsen (chap. 13), Martiniello (chap. 3), Modood (chap. 15), Wong and Pantoja (chap. 17), Cattacin (chap. 16), and Fraga (chap. 12) make clear.

## Policy Choices

These cross-cutting political and ideological commitments not only make life complicated for party leaders; they also make it even more difficult to address political, cultural, and economic problems. Like the partisan dilemmas, policy complexities contribute to our authors' high level of uncertainty about the eventual success of immigrant integration.

### Economic Policies

Western nations face low birth rates and the retirement of native-born workers born during the baby boom. The native-born population also will not take certain jobs (especially dirty jobs) unless those jobs pay relatively well. This means that all the countries discussed in *Bringing Outsiders In* must balance their need for immigrant workers to compensate for these circumstances with the need to regulate migrant flows, reduce unemployment, and control public dependency. They appear unable to get this balance right for very long.

Nations have experimented with various strategies: short- and long-term guest-worker programs, higher and lower overall quotas, ignoring and cracking down on low-skilled undocumented immigrants, raising and lowering the number of slots for highly skilled immigrants, enhancing and limiting public services, expanding and contracting educational and language programs, and encouraging workers to move to underdeveloped parts of the nation and concentrating them in major cities.

No single set of choices may be "right" over the long term for maintaining the balance between too many and too few workers of a given skill level. At best, a country can hope to adopt intelligent policies designed to solve actual problems in the short term rather than pursuing narrowly partisan or broadly ideological ends that have little to do with genuine economic needs or powerful market forces. With luck, skill, and appropriate advocacy and care, those policies need not sacrifice the immigrants themselves for actual or perceived national imperatives.

### Cultural Policies

Western nations must also balance the need for national integrity and unity against the attractions of diversity, fresh ideas and energies, and freedom for individuals and groups to remake themselves. Here, too, they may not be able to find just the right balance or maintain any balance for long. As the chapters in *Bringing Outsiders In* show, here too host countries have tried an array of policies: liberal neutrality, multiculturalism, national particularism, republican universalism, affirmative action, energetic assimilationist efforts, regional or national homogeneity, separatism, pillarization, transnationalism, supranational legislation and regulation, and others.

All these policies have virtues and flaws as well as exceptionally passionate advocates. Moreover, analysts and political activists, such as the authors in *Bringing Outsiders In,* disagree even on what the virtues may be or whether overcoming the flaws requires a more intense application of the same policies or a shift to a different one. A nation must not expect stable solutions; rather, it should aim for reasonable strategies that solve actual problems in the relatively short run. This seems obvious but can be rare; politicians and advocates often generate polarization in cultural arenas in lieu of adopting pragmatic compromises around cultural values.

## Political Incorporation

Finally, political systems must balance between too much and not enough openness to new constituents, demands, and activists. Political parties are always attuned to the immediately forthcoming election and compelled to respond to their current electoral base. But in order to thrive, they must also look to the longer-term future and appeal to new interests. That conundrum explains why, as Fraga (chap. 12) points out, the U.S. Republican Party (and the Democratic Party to a lesser degree) is split between wanting to restrict immigration and punish illegal immigrants and seeking to appeal to the huge group of potential Latino voters. It similarly explains why, as Minkenberg (chap. 10) depicts, European parties vacillate between excluding and including right-wing xenophobes.

Policymakers face a slightly different dilemma from political parties. Elected and appointed officials need stability and predictability to make and implement policies, but they must also accommodate major demographic shifts that inevitably change their tasks, especially in gateway cities and rapidly changing small towns. As Joppke (chap. 8), Cattacin (chap. 16), and Østergaard-Nielsen (chap. 13) point out, that conundrum plays out primarily in the institutions that have the least control over their circumstances and are closest to the most vulnerable native-born and immigrants: schools, poor neighborhoods, religious organizations, social service agencies, healthcare providers, and criminal justice systems. Policymaking may lose coherence; in the United States, some local jurisdictions have adopted harsh regulations against undocumented immigrants, whereas others nearby work strenuously to incorporate immigrants in ways that benefit all residents through programs of bilingual and adult education or new training for police and social service workers.

Central governmental officials must also balance domestic needs and pressures with those of the international or intergovernmental arena. Transnational links among countries or the relationship between national and EU-level parliaments will inevitably involve multifaceted political negotiations, as Østergaard-Nielsen (chap. 13) and Lahav (chap. 14) describe. Once again, a search for ideal, or even stable, solutions may well be a waste of effort. The more appropriate goal is to try to steer the polity toward accommodating new groups without excessively disrupting old alliances.

Immigration has helped to drive the development of North American countries and has changed European ones—how could it not? It is an exciting, powerful force with the potential to benefit the movers, the stayers, and the receivers. Whether for better or worse, immigration also provokes difficulties that cut across party lines and disrupt old coalitions, requiring governments to constantly adjust established policies and invent new ones. Involving immigrants themselves is essential to designing any successful strategy, but their incorporation into political voice and decision making is itself one of the problems to be solved. How political officials deal with the movement and engagement of people over the next few decades will be just as important as how they deal with the movement and use of money, ideas, goods, and boundaries.

## "More Research Is Needed"

Like most scholars, we succumb to the siren song calling for more research; as D'Amato (chap. 5), Martiniello (chap. 3), and Minnite (chap. 4) all point out, the political dimension of immigrant incorporation has been a relatively neglected topic for analysis. We close with a few questions for the next round of research.

What causal factors best explain population shifts, individual and group interactions, political encounters, and policy choices? Our chapters 1 and 2 point to a state's political opportunity structure, historical pathways, geography and physical scale, employers' and workers' incentives, and self-image as determinants of immigration policy. The other authors have added more causal variables: local political activism, supra-national organizations, transnational ties, ideology and partisanship, civic and religious organizations, public opinion, public policies, immigrants' political mobilization, racial and religious identities, relations with native-born minorities, and perhaps others. Two additional candidates for explanatory force are demography itself (the nature, direction, and speed of population movements across borders) and economic imperatives (including the balance between manufacturing and service in a country, its embeddedness in the global economy, the dynamics of labor markets, and immigrants' skills). All these factors matter, but an explanation involving a dozen or more causal forces lacks analytic bite, to put it mildly. So we need theories and evidence identifying the few most crucial levers of change that contribute to bringing outsiders in. Our model of incorporation in chapter 2, along with the presentations by Martiniello (chap. 3) and Minnite (chap. 4), begin that process, but we are all far from a parsimonious and comprehensive explanatory model.

Second, we need to know more about how public preferences affect immigration and immigrant policies in purportedly democratic countries. When does nativism rise into a significant political force or into violence? When and how do political parties resist or coopt xenophobia, and when do they incorporate or even galvanize it? When is hostility aimed at particular groups, and when is it aimed at immigration itself? Conversely, how and why does a nation emerge from influential nativism into an era of welcoming all or some immigrants? What role do business executives, religious leaders, local elites, and interest groups play? When, how, and why do states so often ignore public preferences with regard to immigration?

Third, how do immigrants' capacities and actions intersect with the political opportunity structure? When and how do immigrants form successful alliances, and when do they conflict with one another or with minority (or majority) groups in the host country? How do immigrants change the politics and policies of the host country? What effect does their exodus have on their countries of origin, and how do those countries change their relationship to the host countries?

We also need to refine our concepts for understanding immigrants themselves. How, if at all, is race or ethnicity like religion? Is it appropriate to compare African Americans or Hispanics with French Muslims or British Sikhs? Americans believe, based on their experience, that it is much easier for individuals to change their religion than their race; Europeans often believe, based on their experience, that religion is as central to individuals' identity as is race, and is less likely to be subject to change. In Britain, religious discrimination is understood and treated legally as a form of racism; in France, the term *race* is largely unacceptable; in the United States, some believe that substituting the term *ethnicity* evades the real subject of racial hierarchy. How do these various choices and valences affect immigrant political incorporation?

Moreover, other identities may matter more to many immigrants, despite academics' preoccupation with race and religion. Perhaps immigrants think of themselves primarily as workers or family members, or as representatives of a particular town or region. Do migrants from within the European Union connect more with native-born residents of the host country or with fellow immigrants from countries on other continents? More generally, when does a model based on identity or affiliation explain more than a model based on rational self-interest or mobilization by strategic political actors (Varshney 2003)?

Finally, is immigrant political incorporation too complex or contingent ever to be amenable to systemic explanation? Had Pim Fortuyn not been murdered (by an animal rights activist), would multicultural policies be different in the Netherlands? Had Al Gore become president in 2000 rather than George W. Bush, would U.S. policies with regard to 12 million undocumented immigrants differ? Had the attacks on New York City; Washington, D.C.; Madrid; and London not succeeded (or had there been more attacks or attacks elsewhere), would nations now treat Muslim immigrants differently?

Surely contingency and particularity matter, but this book is predicated on the belief that analysts need and can develop a few broad powerful theories of how outsiders can become insiders. We have many small models of immigrant political incorporation, often developed for a particular group or location, but few broad theories capable of assimilating all of the research. This book moves toward that goal by multiple comparisons and by locating immigrant incorporation within wider understandings of political opportunity structures. We trust that *Bringing Outsiders In* moves readers toward a more generic model of immigrant political incorporation—but plenty of work remains for the next book.

# Notes

## 1. Setting the Context

1. Europeans prefer the term *integration* or *incorporation*, but these mean pretty much the same thing as *assimilation*, at least as understood by Alba and Nee (2005).

2. To put it another way, approximately one-third of the foreign-born residents of the United States are Mexican; in addition, approximately one-half of them are undocumented, or illegal (Passel 2004). Mexican Americans have higher birth rates than Anglo or African Americans, so their share of the overall population is increasing.

3. Comparable data are not available on reading scores in the United States, but a very small share of immigrants reach high levels of proficiency.

4. http://zacat.gesis.org/webview/index.jsp. Some survey evidence points in the opposite direction, suggesting grounds for public support for immigrants' incorporation. Just over half of European, three-fifths of American, and two-thirds of Canadian respondents to the 2003 ISSP agreed that "immigrants improve [Country's] society by bringing in new ideas and cultures." And despite their concern about jobs, one-third of European respondents thought immigrants help their country's economy (about the same proportion as those who thought immigrants harm the economy); a plurality of Americans and a large majority of Canadians concurred (analysis of ZACAT data).

5. The immigrant 1.5 generation is the group that are children when they and their parent immigrate.

6. By no means do all immigrants to the United States enjoy high social status. Only 13 percent of native-born residents of the United States have less than a high school education, but 60 percent of immigrants from Mexico and 48 percent of those from Central America are equally poorly educated. Their household incomes are, not surprisingly, disproportionately low (Pew Hispanic Center 2008, tables 22, 32).

7. "At the lower end of the educational spectrum, 13 percent...of the second generation have less than a high school education compared with 32 percent...of the foreign born and 11 percent...of the third-and-later generation" (Migration Policy Institute 2006).

## 3. Immigrants and Their Offspring in Europe as Political Subjects

1. During the 1970s, a group of Molluccans "rail-jacked" a train in the Netherlands and took the passengers as hostages. In Belgium, the United Kingdom, and France, urban riots involving migrants or subsequent generations have been analyzed in political terms (e.g., the Brussels riots in 1991 and in 1997; the 2001 riots in Bradford, Oldham, and Burnley; and the unrest in various French *banlieues*, popular suburbs, in the 1980s, 1990s, and November 2005 and 2007). In July 2005, British Asian- and

West Indian citizens carried out the London terrorist attacks. In August 2006, the British secret services uncovered a terrorist plot seeking to blow up planes flying from the United Kingdom and the United States. Although it is difficult to know whether the actors involved saw these events as political, their potential political impact was strong.

2. For detailed data on the acquisition of nationality and on voting rights of third-country nationals in Western Europe, see Bauböck (2006, 106–12).

3. See http://www.ssb.no/english/subjects/00/01/20/vundk_en/ (accessed 3 March 2008).

## 4. Lost in Translation?

I thank Jim Johnson and anonymous reviewers for *Perspectives on Politics*, Susan Clarke, David Kettler, Frances Fox Piven, and the editors of this volume for their comments and criticisms on earlier versions of this chapter. All errors and shortcomings are my own.

1. Although it has become commonplace to assert that the scholarship on immigrant political incorporation is thin, there are many exceptions. Analysts do connect the different ways nation-states regulate migration flows across borders (their immigration policies) with the regulation of immigrants after they have arrived (their immigrant or citizenship policies). See, for example Zolberg (2006); Freeman (1995a); Joppke (1998); Hollifield (2004); Aleinikoff (2001); Andersen (2008).

2. *Racial Politics in American Cities* (Browning, Marshall and Tabb 2003), now in its third edition, presents case studies testing the minority group model in Los Angeles, Philadelphia, New York, Chicago, San Francisco, Atlanta, New Orleans, Birmingham, Baltimore, Miami, and Denver. See also Keiser and Underwood (2000) for further updates.

3. Because cities have always been the site of immigrant politics, urban scholars are well positioned to take up the study of immigrant political development. An earlier generation studying an earlier migration gave us the foundational theories of ethnicity and the political machine. That urban scholars have only now begun to theorize about the political incorporation of the post-1965 wave of immigrants (following such precursors as Brackman and Erie 1994; Jones-Correa 1998) is due to long-standing theoretical preoccupations with a major investment in research on the urban political economy and to a formalism equating politics with the performance of electoral-representative institutions and the behavior of government.

4. Jones-Correa (2005, 75) argues that *political incorporation* is difficult to define because the question presupposes that scholars can agree on the meaning of *politics*. This is no doubt true, but the problem is made worse by inattention to definitions of *incorporation*.

5. But, see DeSipio (2000) for a discussion of models of immigrant incorporation that differ somewhat from models of minority group incorporation.

6. There is a small but growing literature on alien voting rights in the United States. See, for example, Raskin (1993); Hayduk (2006). Critics charge that noncitizen voting will only "devalue" citizenship (Schuck 1998, 163–75).

7. de la Garza and DeSipio (1993) suggest that regular voting be permitted and voting records evaluated for evidence of good citizenship once an immigrant meets the five-year residency requirement for naturalization. They note that those seeking citizenship are tested on their knowledge of what makes a good citizen while at the same time being prevented from demonstrating it.

8. For sociological critiques of assimilation theory as applied to the post-1965 wave, see Portes and Zhou (1993); DeWind and Kasinitz (1997); Perlmann and Waldinger (1997); Alba and Nee (2003). For a defense, see Morawska (1994).

9. Cross-national research on migration, mostly concerning the integration of immigrants in Europe, has yielded important insights into how state institutional arrangements and discourses on membership pattern the strategies and participation of migrants in their host societies (see, for example, Soysal 1994). But this research still has less to say about the local response and, therefore, has not been integrated into studies of U.S. immigrant political incorporation.

10. Browning, Marshall, and Tabb (2001), themselves, address the issue of reversals and conclude that the era of the black-white biracial coalition as a vehicle of political incorporation for African Americans may, indeed, be over. Their consideration of what could replace it, however, simply tinkers with their original formulation by addressing the possibility of multiracial coalitions and coalitions that represent black interests without including black partners.

11. The academic literature on transnational social spaces is new, but the concepts transnationalism and social space, combined most effectively in the work of Thomas Faist (2000), are not. Hollifield notes,

"...the postwar international order created new legal spaces (rights) for individuals and groups" through the recognition of the principles of asylum, *norefoulement,* and rights across borders in international law—the U.N. Charter, the Universal Declaration of Human Rights (1948), the Convention on the Prevention and Punishment of the Crime of Genocide (1948), and the Convention Relating to the Status of Refugees (1951). Hollifield (2004, 891–92).

12. The notion of social space draws on the urban sociology of Henri Lefebvre (1991) and his argument that groups cannot constitute themselves outside social space; they cannot recognize themselves or others unless they produce a space for their experience. Social space allows for group identity and differentiation to emerge, and for bonds with others to develop. There is ample evidence of transnational community in the United States (see Basch, Glick Schiller, and Szanton Blanc 1994; Smith and Guarnizo 1998; Levitt 2001; Smith 2006).

13. For one effort to build mobilization into an analysis of immigrant voting patterns, see Ramakrishnan and Espenshade (2001).


## 6. *The New Urban Politics of Integration*

This chapter is a substantially revised version of a paper co-authored with Mark Drayse and Ana Champeny, "Race, Ethnicity, and Immigration in the 2005 Mayoral Elections in Los Angeles and New York," presented at the 2006 Annual Meeting of the American Political Science Association, Philadelphia.


## 7. *Political Institutions and Rainbow Coalitions*

I thank the editors of this volume and an anonymous reviewer for their helpful suggestions for improving this chapter. Thanks also to Lauren Ammons, Michael McGee,and Johnathan Weber for their fine research assistance.

1. For exceptions, see Joyce (2003); Mollenkopf, Olson, and Ross (2001); Jones-Correa (2000); Key (1949).

2. This may explain why New York—with its fifty-one district-based City Council seats—has avoided the mass riots that have consumed minority neighborhoods in other big cities (see Mollenkopf and Sonenshein, chap. 6 in this volume; Mollenkopf, Olson, and Ross 2001).

3. Differences in language, nationality, culture, generation, and history can and often do complicate relations among African Americans and immigrants from Asia, Latin America, and the Caribbean.

4. Despite the fact that nonwhites now constitute a comfortable 59 percent majority of the city population, whites nonetheless make up almost one-half of the active eligible voters and hold one-half of the City Council positions (Logan and Mollenkopf 2003).

5. African Americans have registered stronger negative feelings about recent Republican mayoral incumbents than their Afro-Caribbean counterparts (Logan and Mollenkopf 2003). African Americans also have a historically deeper and longer attachment to the Democratic Party than Caribbean-born blacks do (Rogers 2006).

6. For a brief schematic account of how political institutions and elites shape the political choices and actions of immigrants, see Hochschild and Mollenkopf (chap. 2 in this volume).

7. Numerous studies show that group identity can be heightened or primed by cues in the political environment (e.g., Huddy 2003; Conover 1988). New York electoral institutions create just such a context for voters and political leaders.

8. For a discussion and analysis of the racial polarization in the 1993 New York mayoral contest, see Kaufmann (1998, 2004).

9. As in New York City, homeownership rates are higher in Afro-Caribbean enclaves than in African American neighborhoods.

10. For a discussion of the calculations that lead party leaders to resist the political mobilization of new minority groups, see Fraga, chap. 12, and Minkenberg, chap. 10 in this volume.

11. The older and mostly male white leaders of the Republican Party might have seen in Airey-Wilson's campaign an opportunity to reinvigorate the atrophying party and appeal to the growing nonwhite immigrant constituencies in the city.

12. City records show that there were roughly 45,000 registered voters in Hartford in 2005.

13. Recent scholarship has found that political learning within a deliberative civic context is more achievable when participants encounter one another on equal terms (e.g., Walsh 2007; Oliver and Mendelberg 2000).

## 8. Successes and Failures of Muslim Integration in France and Germany

1. Summarizing a survey by sociologist John R. Logan of Brown University.

2. See the interesting observation by Martin Marty that fundamentalism can be found especially in "religions of the book," in which there is a "single divine scriptural revelation"; these include Judaism, Christianity, and Islam (Marty 2002, 13122). For a counterpoint, see Statham et al. (2005), who find that illiberal group demands, as rare as they are among minority groups in Western Europe today, are almost exclusively raised by Muslims. For a reappraisal of specifically Islamic difficulties with liberalism, see Joppke (forthcoming-b).

3. In September 2005, the provincial government of Ontario withdrew its proposal to use *shariah* law. For a detailed legal account of the issue, see the government-commissioned report by the former attorney general of Ontario, Marion Boyd (2004). The report favored the (qualified) use of *shariah* law simply because, on the basis of existing legislation, Christians and Jews were already allowed to use religious law to settle family matters, so excluding Muslims from this amounted to discrimination.

4. For an interesting critique of drawing continuity between John Locke's idea of toleration and contemporary state neutrality, see Gray (2000). Gray's rejection of liberal neutrality as a viable response to today's cultural difference rests on a problematic notion of "deep diversity," which is said to consist of "different kinds of ethical life" and to be different from mere "pluralism of lifestyles and personal ideals" (2000, 329). The difference between the two types of diversity is unclear.

5. A notable exception to the general acceptance of *laïcité* by French Muslims is the iconic leader Tariq Ramadan, who, rather than openly rejecting *laïcité*, prefers to remain silent about it. Among his many publications, see Ramadan (2004).

6. See especially Rau's (2004) speech occasioned by the 275th birthday of Lessing.

7. For an overview of the interest of Western European states in creating a moderate Islam, see Haddad and Golson (2007).

8. German court ruling 1 BvR 1783/99.

9. Federal Administrative Court ruling BVerwGE 99,1.

10. Federal Constitutional Court ruling 2 BvR 1436/02, 13.

11. Ibid., 20.

12. For an informative overview of various strands of Islamism, see ICG (2005).

## 9. A Multicultural Paradise?

1. "The Multicultural Drama" is the title of a widely discussed national newspaper article published by respected journalist Paul Scheffer on February 29, 2000, available at: www.nrc.nl/W2/Lab/Multicultureel/artikelen.html

2. We use the term *integration policy* in a neutral sense to refer to measures taken by government vis-à-vis certain categories of migrants and minorities residing in the Netherlands. The label *integration policy* actually came into vogue only in the 1990s in reference to individual migrants' participation in mainstream society and institutions. Prior to that, official documents used the terms *categorical policy* and *minorities policy*.

3. In the Netherlands, the minimum educational level deemed necessary for an individual to qualify for the labor market is fixed at graduation from the intermediate or higher level of secondary education or having reached the second level of intermediate vocational education.

4. *Pillarization* was the division of Dutch society into religious and ideological segments, each of which has its own schools, societies, political parties, broadcasting organizations, newspapers, hospitals, during the first half of the twentieth century. This vertical differentiation runs through all the social classes and included a Roman Catholic pillar; a Protestant pillar, which was further subdivided internally; and a neutral or secular pillar.

5. Bloemraad (2006) also shows how culturally distinct groups in Canada took advantage of laws meant to level differences between Anglophone and Francophone Canadians to promote their own linguistic and cultural distinctiveness.

## 10. Anti-Immigrant Politics in Europe

I thank Susana Galán (Barcelona) and Katrin Lüth (Frankfurt/Oder) for their assistance in locating and compiling material for this chapter.

## 11. Immigrants' Incorporation in the United States after 9/11

1. In this poll, 57 percent said immigrants one hundred years ago were "hard-working people who respected our democratic principles, were involved in the community and worked to learn English." Only 29 percent gave this response for immigrants who had arrived here in the last ten years.

2. In truth, the term *assimilation* serves as well as *integration* or *incorporation,* once we recognize that they all refer to essentially the same tortuous process.

## 12. Building through Exclusion

I thank Jessica Flores, Stanford University, and Ann Frost, University of Washington, for their invaluable research assistance.

1. Smith (1997, 6) uses the term *liberal.*

2. Smith refers to this as "democratic republican[ism]" (ibid.).

3. The concept *linked fate* comes from the work of Michael Dawson (1994). Although Dawson develops the term to refer to African Americans, it can also be applied to the general U.S. sense of peoplehood.

4. Smith (1997, 6) uses the term *inegalitarian ascriptive elements.*

## 13. The End of Closet Political Transnationalism?

A preliminary version of this paper was presented at the roundtable Between Host and Homeland: Europe and the Politicization of Second-Generation Diasporas, organized by the International Center for Migration, Ethnicity and Citizenship at the New School University and the Program on Citizenship and Security at the World Policy Institute, New York, May 13, 2005. I am grateful for the funding from the Mellon Foundation, kindly secured by the editors of this volume, and to Ciğdem Öztürk for her research assistance in updating facts and figures on Turkey and Turkish-Kurdish migrants in Europe. Some of the arguments and examples presented here have been published elsewhere.

1. For a more detailed presentation of this classification of migrant transnational political practices, which also includes the terms *emigrant politics, Diaspora politics,* and *trans-local politics,* see Østergaard-Nielsen (2003c).

2. See information on the Ministry of Foreign Affairs in Turkey website, http://www.mfa.gov.tr/MFA/ForeignPolicy/MainIssues/TurksLivingAbroad. Although it is not specified, these figures appear to include not just current holders of Turkish passports but also former Turkish citizens who have naturalized in their countries of residence. For instance, the figure for Turkish citizens given by the German federal statistical office was 1,764,318 on December 31, 2004, which does not include those Turks who have already naturalized.

3. See http://www.destatis.de/basis/e/bevoe/bevoetab10.htm.

4. For a more detailed description of the various ethnic, religious, and political groups among Turks and Kurds, see Østergaard-Nielsen (2003d).

5. For a more detailed description and evaluation of Turkish outreach policies, see ibid.

6. See, for instance, the press releases (in Turkish or German) on the website of one of the major Turkish federations in Germany, the Turkish community in Germany (www.tgd.de). Although the issue of migrant integration dominates, there are also press releases to the German press issued during 2004–2006 supporting the accession of Turkey to the European Union and defending the Turkish position on the issue of the recognition of the genocide of Armenians.

7. For discussions of such criticism, see Portes (2001); Vertovec (2004).

8. *Political integration,* defined by Kaya and Kentel (2005) as support for a political party in the country of settlement, is correlated much more with social class than with generation. Forty-six percent of second-generation Turks in Germany (compared to 55 percent of first-generation immigrant Turks)

do not feel affiliated to any German party at all, whereas the difference between the highest (25 percent) and lowest (almost 68 percent) social status groups identified by Kaya and Kentel (2005) is much higher.

9. Another set of international actors, international nongovernmental organization (NGO) networks similarly constitute an important platform for Turkish and Kurdish transnational political activities (Østergaard-Nielsen 2003c).

10. It has also been observed, however, that a multicultural incorporation regime, as in Holland, can contribute to a transnational homeland political orientation because of the resources and space given to the institutionalization of ethnic and religious organizations (Vertovec 1996).

11. The exception was the United Kingdom, where the London-based research displayed a remarkable willingness among both local and national policymakers to discuss the issue of Cyprus, the Kurds, and the EU accession of Turkey during meetings with the Turkish- and Kurdish-origin London constituencies (see Østergaard-Nielsen 2003a).

12. Please note that some homeland political agendas are more welcome than others. For instance, Kurdish movements distancing themselves from the PKK (Partiya Karkerên Kurdistan; Kurdistan Workers' Party) have had widespread access to key Dutch, German, and especially Danish policymakers. Similarly, the Alevis, a religious minority in Turkey, have enjoyed the attention of central German political actors also on homeland political issues (Østergaard-Nielsen 2003d).

13. For a more detailed description of how homeland political issues have featured in the relationship between German political parties and their Turkish membership associations during the 1990s, see Østergaard-Nielsen (2003d, 90–98).

14. See http://www.tuerken4spd.de.

15. In response to this, their Turkish membership organization, German-Turkish Forum (DTF), which emphasizes the common conservative outlook of the Christian Democratic Union and the Turkish-origin voters, has posted a policy paper on the Christian Democratic Union's position on Turkey that somewhat carefully tries to bridge the stance of the CDU and that of the potential Turkish supporters; see "Leitsätze für eine Türkeipolitik der CDU," http://www.dtf-online.de/home1.htm.

16. In the Turkish press, this incident was traced back to the intervention and strength of the Armenian lobby in the Netherlands; see Todays Zaman (2006). For other comments, see *International Herald Tribune* (2006); *NRC-Handelsblad* (2006).

17. See http://www.oezdemir.de/index.php?id=498.

18. Elsewhere I have discussed how the Turkish case compares to that of Mexicans in the United States (Østergaard-Nielsen 2003d) and how the studies of migrant transnational political practices differ across the Atlantic (Østergaard-Nielsen 2003c).

## 14. Organizing Immigration Interests in the European Union

1. Whereas immigration intake is largely informed by immigration-control strategies, immigrant policies concern the conditions of migrants and ethnic minorities resident inside the territory (Hammar 1985). These policies may be direct or indirect, and they go beyond conceptions of multiculturalism or assimilation strategies. This axis includes residence, family reunion, naturalization and citizenship, discrimination, civic citizenship, and all aspects of equality, access, and rights.

2. An *international regime* is a set of beliefs, principles, norms, rules, and decision-making procedures around which actor expectations converge in a given area (Ruggie 1982; Krasner 1982).

3. At the end of the five-year transitional period, the European Parliament gained the right to be consulted on immigration legislation and the right of initiative was transferred to the Commission. Also, qualified majority voting (QMV) and codecision procedures regarding immigration and asylum became possible.

4. This coordinated and interdisciplinary approach specifically placed an emphasis on the following themes: "enhancing police and judicial cooperation; developing international legal instruments; ending the funding of terrorism, strengthening air security, prioritizing cooperation with the US, and coordinating EU's global action." Council of Europe (2001, 1). Consistent with these initiatives were the agreement with the ambassadors of the then-candidate countries to adopt law enforcement and judicial measures for cooperation (European Conference Declaration, 2001; see also press release by the Belgian EU presidency, 22/09/20019) and the highly supportive European Parliament resolution adopted on October 4 (Council of Europe doc. GMT (2001) Inf33).

5. Even though it remains the smallest budget of all the areas of financial perspectives compared to those still dominating traditional European Communities policies, under the headings of sustainable

development, economic competitiveness, and social cohesion, for examples (Liberatore 2005, 21), its relative change and substantive emphasis are considerable.

6. The program also notably delegated more policymaking authority to European institutions. Whereas previously only the JHA Council had the power to decide, the bodies now responsible for these issue areas include the Commission; the JHA Council, including twenty-seven ministers responsible for immigration in each member state; and the European Parliament. The Commission drafts and issues proposals, and submits them to the JHA Council and European Parliament, which together have decision-making power.

7. European Commission (2003a), on immigration, integration, and employment, defines the EU conception of integration and lays out policy goals, as did European Commission 2004a on the economic migration of third-country national (TCNs).

8. This section largely derives from data collected by the author on MEP attitudes in 1992–1993 and with A. Messina in 2004. For a detailed description of the original studies, see Lahav, 2004a; Lahav and Messina 2005). The first study, conducted in 1992–1993 with MEPs of the third assembly (1989–1994), coincided with the signing of the Maastricht Treaty (1992) but was before the European Union expanded to include Austria, Finland, and Sweden. The sample ($n = 167$ MEPs, or 32 percent of the total survey response; including follow-up interviews with fifty-four MEPs) was broadly representative of the then twelve country parliamentary delegations and the nine official party groupings, excluding the Independents in the European Parliament (Lahav 1997). The second survey repeated many of the questions posed by the first and expanded on them in an effort to take into account the changes in the international security environment and on the immigration front. It consisted of a survey sample ($n = 148$) that represented 24 percent of the 1999–2004 (fifth assembly) and interviews with fifteen MEPs.

9. In Belgium, Denmark, Greece, Italy, and Spain, for example, MEP attitudes on immigration restrictions considerably shifted in a more neutral direction between 1992 and 2004, whereas opinion among the Irish and British delegations changed more negatively over the decade. In contrast, and in keeping with the aggregate results, MEP opinion remained virtually unchanged in France, Germany, Luxembourg, the Netherlands, and Portugal. Most interesting for observers of the extreme-right actors in Europe, representatives from Austria and Sweden, two of the three newest members of the third EU expansion, ranked highest in preferring to decrease the level of immigration (75 and 50 percent, respectively).

10. In general, citizens in the least affluent member states (Greece, Czech Republic, and Hungary) are more inclined to perceive ethnic minorities as threatening than those in the most affluent countries. Among the major immigration-receiving countries, the perception of threat is highest in Belgium and the United Kingdom.

11. In the 1992 study, for example, Greek MEPs talked about immigration as a security issue in terms of Turkey, whereas French MEPS tended to link immigration to insecurity and crime.

12. *Issue salience* can be distinguished from *politicization*. Although the immigration issue may be politically charged, its salience or attachment/attention in the minds of ordinary citizens may be uneven. Issues such as immigration or abortion often spark public debate and intense divisions, but they usually do not rank high as salient issues (see Lahav 2004a, 81; see also Gimpel and Edwards 1999; Givens and Luedtke 2004).

13. This limited mobility and failure to promote a real European labor market prompted the European Commission to dedicate 2006 to the Year of Workers' Mobility and to initiate the European Mobility Bus Tour.

14. This has included increased identity checks, more stringent conditions for issuing residence and work permits, new automated systems for registration of foreigners, reduction of categories of individuals who may not be deported, closer monitoring of foreigner accommodations, limited rights of appeal, broadening of categories of potential deportees, and tougher penalties for assisting illegal migration and employment of foreigners.

## 15. *The State and Ethno-Religious Mobilization in Britain*

1. These five ideal types and the terms used to mark them are my own. Given the many different ways that terms such as *liberal* and *the plural state* are used, my ideal types do not necessarily correspond to how some others may use these terms. For a more developed statement see Modood (1998, reproduced in 2005b). For a related typology, see Commission on Multi-Ethnic Britain (CMEB 2000, 42–48).

2. See, for example, the *Sunday Times* (London) Rich List, available at http://www.timesonline.co.uk/section/0,2108,00.html.

## 16. Differences in the City

This chapter was conceived through discussions with Milena Chimienti; her comments were extremely helpful. Erik Verkooyen also contributed comments at the final stage.

1. What is different from Simmel's thesis here is that society and the state no longer think that equality is possible and seem to have accepted that inequalities cannot be solved, only limited.

2. This distinction between psychological and material ontological survival is introduced by Milena Chimienti (2009) as an addition to Giddens (1991).

3. Historically, the word *ghetto* refers to a segregated and closed space based on cultural differences (in religion or race), as the first Jewish ghettos created in Europe in the sixteenth century (the word stems from this reality in Venice at that time) or the Afro-American ghettos (see Nightingale 2003 on this issue). Here I go beyond this historical meaning and regard ghettos as homogeneous open spaces with a high concentration of people of similar and in general low socioeconomic status, or what I call aggregated neighborhoods.

4. Typically, in smaller European cities, homogenization of neighborhoods is rare, even with high numbers of migrants; but this does not mean that they are not organized in communities. In fact, instead of ghettos we find meeting places, shopping malls, and buildings, which permit daily contacts (see the studies in Hoffmann-Nowotny and Hondrich 1982).

5. See the normative debate between Barry and Kymlicka and Banting (Barry 1990, 2001; Kymlicka and Banting 2006) about these two ways of creating social solidarity: community recognition and redistribution (see also Fraser and Honneth 2003).

## 17. In Pursuit of Inclusion

1. In re AH YUP, Case No. 104 Circuit Court, D. California 1 F. Cas. 223; 1878 U.S. App. LEXIS 1593; 5 Sawy. 155; 17 Alb. Law J. 385; 6 Cent. Law J. 387; 24 Int. Rev. Rec. 164 April 29, 1878.

2. In terms of geographical distribution, the sample varied somewhat by national origin group.

3. The resulting national origin quota, however, is close to the 2000 results because of the oversampling of certain national origin populations.

4. Education outside of the United States was not associated with naturalization rates in our models.

5. Over 2.7 million people in the United States identify as Chinese (alone or combination with one or more other races). They are the largest Asian national origin group; Filipinos are the next largest group (2.4 million) (Barnes and Bennett 2002).

6. Interview with an immigration lawyer in Los Angeles, California, June 6, 2005.

7. *Ozawa, supra,* 260 US at 198.

## 18. Entering the Precincts of Power

1. We speak of continental Europe here because Britain had a different *jus soli* tradition and the large post–World War II immigration led to a move away from pure *jus soli* to a slightly more restricted form (Weil 2001).

2. We are grateful to Basak Kasim for the counts of German legislators with Turkish names.

3. The data on Hispanic elected officials come from the data series maintained by the National Association of Latino Elected Officials (NALEO), and we are grateful to Luis Fraga of Stanford University for generously sharing with us his summary tabulations from this database.

4. This does not include the substantial number of Puerto Rican and African American city councilors. By 2006, Puerto Ricans and African Americans were slightly overrepresented on the city council. Taken together, blacks and Latinos had achieved a level of representation on the city council almost proportionate to their numbers in the city population.

5. As of 2004, Belgium, Norway, Spain, Denmark, Sweden, and Ireland allowed noncitizens to cast ballots in local elections (Hayduk and Wucker 2004; Togeby 2005).

# References

Abadan-Unat, Nermin. 1997. "Ethnic Business, Ethnic Communities, and Ethnopolitics among Turks in Europe." In *Immigration into Western Societies: Problems and Policies,* edited by Emek Uçarer and Donald Puchala, 229–51. London: Pinter.

Abbas, Tahir. 2006. Introduction. In *The State We Are In: Identity, Terror, and the Law of Jihad,* edited by Aftab Ahmad Malik, xi–xix. Bristol: Amal Press.

Abegg, Bruno, and Verein Migrationsmuseum Schweiz. 2006. *Small Number—Big Impact: Swiss Immigration to the USA.* Zürich, Neue Zürcher Zeitung.

Achermann, Christin, and Milena Chimienti. 2005. *Migration, Prekarität und Gesundheit: Ressourcen und Risiken von vorläufig Aufgenommenen und Sans-Papiers in Genf und Zürich.* Neuchâtel: Swiss Forum for Migration Studies.

Achterberg, Peter. 2006. "Het einde van links en rechts: Realiteit of populaire mythe?" *Mens en maatschappij* 81 (1): 51–63.

Ackerman, Spencer. 2005. "Why American Muslims Haven't Turned to Terrorism." *New Republic* (December 12): 18–20.

Acuña, Rodolfo. 1996. *Anything but Mexican: Chicanos in Contemporary Los Angeles.* London: Verso.

Aguirre, Benigno, and Rogelio Saenz. 2002. "Testing the Effects of Collectively Expected Durations of Migration: The Naturalization of Mexicans and Cubans." *International Migration Review* 36 (1): 103–24.

Aizenman, Nureth Celina. 2006. "Immigration Debate Wakes a 'Sleeping Latino Giant.'" *Washington Post,* April 6, A01.

Akhtar, Navid. 2005. *Young, Angry, and Muslim.* Film. Channel 4, United Kingdom, October 24.

Alba, Richard. 2005. "Bright vs. Blurred Boundaries: Second-Generation Assimilation and Exclusion in France, Germany, and the United States." *Ethnic and Racial Studies* 28 (1): 20–49.

——. Forthcoming. *Blurring the Color Line: New Possibilities for a More Integrated America in the 21st Century.* Cambridge, Mass.: Harvard University Press.

Alba, Richard, and Victor Nee. 2003. *Remaking the American Mainstream: Assimilation and Contemporary Immigration.* Cambridge, Mass.: Harvard University Press.

Alba, Richard, and Roxane Silberman. 2002. "Decolonization Immigrations and the Social Origins of the Second Generation: The Case of North Africans in France." *International Migration Review* 36 (4): 1169–93.

——. Forthcoming. "The Children of Immigrants and Host Society Educational Systems: Mexicans in the United States and North Africans in France." *Teachers College Record.*

Aleinikoff, T. Alexander. 2001. "Policing Boundaries: Migration, Citizenship, and the State." In *E Pluribus Unum? Contemporary and Historical Perspectives on Immigrant Political Incorporation,* edited by Gary Gerstle and John Mollenkopf, 267–91. New York: Russell Sage Foundation.

Alesina, Alberto, and Edward Glaeser. 2004. *Fighting Poverty in the US and Europe: A World of Difference.* Oxford: Oxford University Press.

Alexseev, Mikhail. 2005. *Immigration Phobia and the Security Dilemma: Russia, Europe, and the United States.* New York: Cambridge University Press.

Ali, Nasreen, Virinder Kalra, and Salman Sayyid, eds. 2005. *A Postcolonial People: South Asians in Britain.* London: Hurst.

Ali, Yasmin. 1991. "Echoes of Empire: Towards a Politics of Representation." In *Enterprise and Heritage: Crosscurrents of National Culture,* edited by John Corner and Sylvia Harvey, 194–211. London: Routledge.

Alvarez, Robert. 1987. "A Profile of the Citizenship Process among Hispanics in the United States." *International Migration Review* 21 (2): 327–51.

Amer, Mildred. 2007. *Membership of the 110th Congress: A Profile.* Washington, D.C.: Congressional Research Service.

American Civil Liberties Union. 2004. "About the ACLU's Immigrants' Rights Project." August 6. Available at: http://www.aclu.org/immigrants/gen/1163res20040906.html.

American Friends Service Committee. 2006. "House and Senate Immigration Hearings—Summer 2006." Available at: http://www.afsc.org/immigrants-rights/hearing-dates-2006.html.

American Patrol. 2007. "American Patrol Reference Archive: Illegal Immigration Is a Crime." Available at: http://www.americanpatrol.com/REFERENCE/isacrime.html.

Amse, Anne Katrien, and Willem Faessen. 2000. "Allochtonen en hun woonsituatie." In *Allochtonen in Nederland.* CBS, 61–68. Voorburg: Centraal Bureau voor de Statistiek.

Amselle, Jean-Loup. 2001. *Branchements: Anthropologie de l'universalite des cultures.* Paris: Flammarion.

Andersen, Kristi. 2008. "Parties, Organizations, and Political Incorporation: Immigrants in Six U.S. Cities." In *Civic Hopes and Political Realities: Community Organizations and Political Engagement among Immigrants in the United States and Abroad,* edited by S. Karthick Ramakrishnan and Irene Bloemraad, 77–106. New York: Russell Sage Foundation.

Anderson, John. 2003. *Religious Liberty in Transitional Societies: The Politics of Religion.* Cambridge, UK: Cambridge University Press.

Anti-Defamation League. 1995. *The Skinhead International: A Worldwide Survey of Neo-Nazi Skinheads.* New York: Anti-Defamation League.

Anwar, Muhammad. 1994. *Race and Elections: The Participation of Ethnic Minorities in Politics.* Coventry, UK: Centre for Research in Ethnic Relations, University of Warwick.

Appiah, K. Anthony. 1997. "The Multiculturalist Misunderstanding," *New York Review of Books,* October 9, 30, 32.

Ataman, Ferda. 2005. "Türkische Wähler: Wo die CDU unter fünf Prozent liegt." *Der Spiegel,* September 13. Available at: http://www.spiegel.de/politik/deutschland/0,1518,374502,00.html.

Bade, Klaus. 2003. *Migration in European History.* Oxford: Blackwell.

Bagnasco, Arnaldo. 1999. *Tracce di comunità: Temi derivati da un concetto ingombrante.* Bologna: Il Mulino.

Baillet, Dominique. 2001. "Militants d'origine maghrébine et intégration." *Revue Cairn* 14 (1): 91–103.

Balibar, Étienne. 2001. *Nous, citoyens d'Europe? Les frontieres, l'état, le peuple.* Paris: La Découverte.

Banton, Michael. 1985. *Promoting Racial Harmony.* New York: Cambridge University Press.

——. 1987. "The Battle of the Name." *New Community* 14 (1–2): 170–75.

Barnes, Jessica, and Claudette Bennett. 2002. *The Asian Population: 2000,* by U.S. Bureau of the Census. Washington, D.C.: U.S. Department of Commerce.

Barone, Michael. 2002. "Race, Ethnicity, and Politics in American History." In *Beyond the Color Line: New Perspectives on Race and Ethnicity in America,* edited by Abigail Thernstrom and Stephan Thernstrom, 343–58. Stanford, Calif.: Hoover Institution Press.

Barreto, Matt. 2005. "Latino Immigrants at the Polls: Foreign-Born Voter Turnout in the 2002 Election." *Political Research Quarterly* 58 (1): 79–86.

Barry, Brian. 1990. "The Welfare State versus the Relief of Poverty." *Ethics* 100 (3): 503–29.

———. 2001. *Culture and Equality: An Egalitarian Critique of Multiculturalism*. Cambridge, UK: Polity Press.

Barth, Fredrik, ed. 1969. *Ethnic Groups and Boundaries: The Social Organization of Culture Difference*. London: Allen and Unwin.

Basch, Linda, Nina Glick Schiller, and Cristina Szanton Blanc. 1994. *Nations Unbound: Transnational Projects, Postcolonial Predicaments, and Deterritorialized Nation-States*. Langhorne, Pa.: Gordon and Breach.

Battaglini, Monica, Sandro Cattacin, and Véronique Tattini. 2001a. "Reconnaissance et coopération: Quelle institutionnalisation de l'associationnisme? (premiere partie)." *Associations transnationales/Transnational Associations* 1 (2): 60–73.

———. 2001b. "Reconnaissance et coopération: Quelle institutionnalisation de l'associationnisme? (deuxieme partie)." *Associations Transnationales/Transnational Associations* 1 (3): 130–56.

Baubérot, Jean. 2004. *Laïcité 1905–2005, entre passion et raison*. Paris: Seuil.

Baubock, Rainer. 2003a. "Reinventing Urban Citizenship." *Citizenship Studies* 7 (2): 139–60.

———. 2003b. "Towards a Political Theory of Migrant Transnationalism." *International Migration Review* 37 (3): 700–23.

———, ed. 2006. *Migration and Citizenship: Legal Status, Rights and Political Participation*. Amsterdam: Amsterdam University Press, IMISCOE Reports.

Bauman, Zygmunt. 2000. *Liquid Modernity*. Cambridge, UK: Polity Press.

BBC News. 2004. "US Opposes Oklahoma Headscarf Ban." Available at: http://news.bbc.co.uk/2/hi/americas/3585377.stm].

Beauftragte der Bundesregierung für Migration, Flüchtlinge und Integration. 2004. *Daten, Fakten, Trends: Strukturdaten der ausländischen Bevölkerung*. Bonn, Germany.

Beer, Ingeborg, Alev Deniz, and Hanns-Uve Schwedler. 2007. "Berlin: Urban, Social and Ethnic Integration—An Urban Policy Challenge." In *Migration and Cultural Inclusion in the European City*, edited by William Neill and Hanns-Uve Schwedler, 136–47. Houndmills, UK: Palgrave Macmillan.

Benhabib, Seyla. 2002. *The Claims of Culture: Equality and Diversity in the Global Era*. Princeton, N.J.: Princeton University Press.

———. 2004. *The Rights of Others: Aliens, Residents and Citizens*. Cambridge, UK: Cambridge University Press.

Bentley, Arthur F. 1908. *The Process of Government: A Study of Social Pressures*. Chicago: University of Chicago Press.

Bergeron, Claire, and Jeanne Batalova. 2008. "Spotlight on Naturalization Trends in Advance of the 2008 Elections." Migration Policy Institute. Available at: http://www.migrationinformation.org/USFocus/display.cfm?id=670.

Berlin, Ira 2000. *Many Thousands Gone: The First Two Centuries of Slavery in North America*. Cambridge, Mass.: Harvard University Press.

Bernard, William. 1936. "Cultural Determinants of Naturalization." *American Sociological Review* 1 (6): 943–53.

Bigo, Didier. 2001. "Migration and Security." In *Controlling a New Migration World*, edited by Virginie Guiraudon and Christian Joppke, 121–49. London: Routledge.

Bird, Karen. 2004. "The Political Representation of Women and Ethnic Minorities in Established Democracies: A Framework for Comparative Research." Academy for Migration Studies in Denmark (AMID) Working Paper Series. Aalborg, Denmark.

———. 2005. "The Political Representation of Visible Minorities in Electoral Democracies: A Comparison of France, Denmark, and Canada." *Nationalism and Ethnic Politics* 11 (4): 425–65.

Birenbaum, Guy. 1992. *Le front national en politique*. Paris: Balland.

Bjørklund, Tor, and Jørgen Andersen. 2002. "Anti-immigration Parties in Denmark and Norway: The Progress Parties and the Danish People's Party." In *Shadows over Europe: The Development and Impact of the Extreme Right in Western Europe*, edited by Martin Schain, Aristide Zolberg, and Patrick Hossay, 107–36. New York: Palgrave Macmillan.

Blanke, Bernhard, Adalbert Evers, and Hellmut Wollmann, eds. 1986. *Die Zweite Stadt: Neue Formen lokaler Arbeits—und Sozialpolitik*. Opladen: Westdeutscher Verlag.

Bloemraad, Irene. 2005. "The Limits of de Tocqueville: How Government Facilitates Organisational Capacity in Newcomer Communities." *Journal of Ethnic and Migration Studies* 31 (5): 865–87.

——. 2006. *Becoming a Citizen: Incorporating Immigrants and Refugees in the United States and Canada.* Berkeley: University of California Press.

Blumenthal, Ralph. 2006. "Texas Lawmakers Put New Focus on Illegal Immigration." *New York Times,* November 16. available at: http://www.nytimes.com/2006/11/16/us/16immig.html?_r=1& scp=1&sq=&st=nyt

Bobo, Lawrence, and Vincent Hutchings. 1996. "Perceptions of Racial Group Competition: Extending Blumer's Theory of Group Position to a Multiracial Social Context." *American Sociological Review* 61 (6): 951–72.

Böckenförde, Ernst-Wolfgang. 2001. "'Kopftuchstreit' auf dem richtigen Weg?" *Neue Juristische Wochenschrift* 54 (10): 723–28.

——. 2004. "Ver(w)irrung im Kopftuchstreit." *Süddeutsche Zeitung,* January 16, 2.

Bodi, Faisal. 2005. "Ties That No Longer Bind: A New Generation of Muslims Is Breaking with Labour." *Guardian,* May 5. available at: http://www.guardian.co.uk/politics/2005/may/05/election 2005.religion>

Borjas, George. 1999. *Heaven's Door: Immigration Policy and the American Economy.* Princeton, N.J.: Princeton University Press.

——. 2002. "Welfare Reform and Immigration." In *The New World of Welfare,* edited by Rebecca Blank and Ron Haskins, 369–90. Washington, D.C.: Brookings Institution Press.

Bowman, Karlyn. 2006. "Beyond the Beltway, Voters Are Tuning Out Abramoff Scandal," *Roll Call,* January 18.

Boyd, Marion. 2004. *Dispute Resolution in Family Law: Protecting Choice, Promoting Inclusion.* Report to the Attorney General of Ontario. Available at: http://www.attorneygeneral.jus.gov.on.ca/english/about/pubs/boyd.

Brackman, Harold, and Steven Erie. 1994. "Beyond 'Politics by Other Means'? Empowerment Strategies for Los Angeles' Asian Pacific Community." In *The Bubbling Cauldron: Race, Ethnicity, and the Urban Crisis,* edited by Michael Peter Smith and Joe Feagin, 282–303. Minneapolis: University of Minnesota Press.

Braun, Rudolf. 1970. *Sozio-kulturelle Probleme der Eingliederung italienischer Arbeitskräfte in der Schweiz.* Erlenbach-Zürich: E. Rentsch.

Breton, Raymond. 1964. "Institutional Completeness of Ethnic Communities and the Personal Relations of Immigrants." *American Journal of Sociology* 70 (2): 193–205.

British Council Brussels. 2005. *European Civic Citizenship and Inclusion Index.* Brussels, Belgium: British Council Brussels, Foreign Policy Centre and Migration Policy Group.

Broughton, David, and Hans-Martien ten Napel. 2000. *Religion and Mass Electoral Behaviour in Europe.* London: Routledge.

Browne, Anthony. 2005. "Dutch Unveil the Toughest Face in Europe with a Ban on the Burka." *The Times,* October 13.

Browning, Rufus, Dale Rogers Marshall, and David Tabb. 1984. *Protest Is Not Enough: The Struggle of Blacks and Hispanics for Equality in Urban Politics.* Berkeley: University of California Press.

——. 1986. "Protest Is Not Enough: A Theory of Political Incorporation." *PS* 19 (3): 576–81.

——. 1990. "Minority Mobilization in Ten Cities: Failures and Successes." In *Racial Politics in American Cities,* edited by Rufus Browning, Dale Rogers Marshall, and David Tabb, 8–30. New York: Longman.

——. 2001. "Taken In or Just Taken? Political Incorporation of African Americans in Cities." In *Minority Politics at the Millennium,* edited by Richard Keiser and Katherine Underwood, 131–56. New York: Garland.

——, eds. 2003. *Racial Politics in American Cities.* 3rd ed. New York: Longman.

Brubaker, Rogers. 1992. *Citizenship and Nationhood in France and Germany.* Cambridge, Mass.: Harvard University Press.

——. 2001. "The Return of Assimilation? Changing Perspectives on Immigration and Its Sequels in France, Germany, and the United States." *Ethnic and Racial Studies* 24 (4): 531–48.

Bruce, Steve. 2006. "Did Protestantism Create Democracy?" In *Religion, Democracy, and Democratization,* edited by John Anderson, 3–20. London: Frank Cass.

Bueker, Catherine. 2005. "Political Incorporation among Immigrants from Ten Areas of Origin: The Persistence of Source Country Effects." *International Migration Review* 39 (1): 103–40.

Buijs, Frank, and Jan Rath. 2002. "Muslims in Europe: The State of Research," Paper prepared for the Russell Sage Foundation. New York (October).

Bullock, Lorinda. 2006. "Misguided Debate over Undocumented Workers Ignores Larger Challenge." *Baltimore Times Online,* June 13. Available at: http://www.btimes.com/News/article/article.asp?NewsID=9045&sID=3.

Bundesministerium des Innern. 2006. *Verfassungschutzbericht 2006.* Bonn: BMI.

——. 2008. *Verfassungsschutzbericht 2008.* Bonn: BMI.

Buruma, Ian. 2006. *Murder in Amsterdam: The Death of Theo van Gogh and the Limits of Tolerance.* New York: Penguin Press.

Bush, George W. 2004. "President Bush Proposes New Temporary Worker Program: Remarks by the President on Immigration Policy." White House. January 7. Available at: http://www.whitehouse.gov/news/releases/2004/01/20040107–3.html.

*Business Week.* 2005. "Embracing Illegals: Companies Are Getting Hooked on the Buying Power of 11 Million Undocumented Immigrants." July 18. Available at: http://www.businessweek.com/magazine/content/05_29/b3943001_mz001.htm.

Butcher, Kristin. 2006. "Why Are Immigrants' Incarceration Rates So Low? Evidence on Selective Immigration, Deterrence, and Deportation." Unpublished MS. Wellesley College, Economics Department.

Butt Philip, Alan. 1994. "European Union Immigration Policy: Phantom, Fantasy or Fact?" *West European Politics* 17 (2): 169–191.

Çaglar, Ayse. 2006. "Hometown Associations, the Rescaling of State Spatiality and Migrant Grassroots Transnationalism." *Global Networks* 6 (1): 1–22.

Camarota, Steven. 2002. "Census Bureau: Over 100,000 Illegal Aliens from the Middle East; New Government Report Raises Concerns in Light of Terrorist Threat." Washington, D.C.: Center for Immigration Studies. Available at: http://www.cis.org/articles/2001/censusillegalsme.html.

——. 2006. "Dropping Out: Immigrant Entry and Native Exit from the Labor Market, 2000–2005." Washington, D.C.: Center for Immigration Studies. March. Available at: http://www.cis.org/articles/2006/back206.html.

Campos Venuti, Giuseppe. 1987. *La terza generazione dell'urbanistica.* Milano: Franco Angeli.

Cano, Gustavo. 2006. "Political Mobilization of Mexican Immigrants in American Cities and the U.S. Immigration Debate." September. Mexico-North Research Network. Available at: http://www.mexnor.org.

Cardwell, Diane, Jonathan Hicks, and Randal Archibold. 2005. "Ferrer Takes Defensive after Comments on Diallo Killing." *New York Times,* March 17, B7.

Carens, Joseph. 2000. *Culture, Citizenship, and Community: A Contextual Exploration of Justice as Evenhandedness.* New York: Oxford University Press.

Carmichael, Stokely, and Charles Hamilton. 1967. *Black Power: The Politics of Liberation in America.* New York: Random House.

Carrying Capacity Network. 2005. "Bush Administration Pushes for Illegal Alien Amnesty Again! Devastating Effects for American Workers, Taxpayers, and Citizens." February. Available at: http://www.carryingcapacity.org/alerts/alert0205.html.

Castel, Robert. 1995. *Les métamorphoses de la question sociale: Une chronologie du salariat.* Paris: Fayard.

Castells, Manuel. 1975. "Travailleurs immigrés et luttes de classe." *Politique aujourd'hui,* no. 3–4: 5–27.

Castles, Stephen. 1995. "How Nation-States Respond to Immigration and Ethnic Diversity." *New Community* 21 (3): 293–308.

Castles, Stephen, Heather Booth, and Tina Wallace. 1984. *Here for Good: Western Europe's New Ethnic Minorities.* London: Pluto Press.

Castles, Stephen, and Alastair Davidson. 2000. *Citizenship and Migration: Globalization and the Politics of Belonging.* New York: Routledge.

Castles, Stephen, and Godula Kosack. 1973. *Immigrant Workers and Class Structure in Western Europe.* London: Oxford University Press.

Castles, Stephen, and Mark Miller. 2003. *The Age of Migration: International Population Movements in the Modern World.* 3rd ed. New York: Guilford Press.

Cattacin, Sandro. 2006. "Migration and Differentiated Citizenship: On the (Post-)Americanization of Europe." Malmö, Sweden: Malmö University, School of International Migration and Ethnic Relations.

Cattacin, Sandro, and Barbara Lucas. 1999. "Autorégulation, intervention étatique, mise en réseau: Les transformations de l'état social en Europe (les cas du VIH/sida, de l'abus d'alcool et des drogues illégales)." *Revue française de science politique* 49 (3): 379–98.

Cattacin, Sandro, Barbara Lucas, and Sandra Vetter. 1996. *Modèles de politique en matière de drogue: Une comparaison de six réalités européennes.* Paris: L'Harmattan.

Cattacin, Sandro, Benito Perez, Isabelle Renschler, and Eléonore Zottos. 1999. "'État incitateur' ou 'deuxième ville': L'animation socioculturelle à Genève." *Revue suisse de science politique* 5 (2): 67–92.

Cattacin, Sandro and Isabelle Renschler. 2008. "Barrières d'accès à la santé. Réponses urbaines à l'exclusion." In *Auf der Kippe. Sur la corde raide, edited by* Christoph Conrad and Laura von Mandach. Zürich: Seismo, S. 141–48.

Center for American Progress. 2007. "Strange Bed Fellows? Anti-Immigration Organizations and Hate Groups." Special Presentation. October 18. Washington, D.C.

Center for Equal Opportunities and Opposition to Racism. 2004. "National Analytical Study on Racist Violence and Crime: RAXEN Focal Point for Belgium." Available at: http://www.eumc.eu.int/eumc/material/pub/RAXEN/4/RV/CS-RV-NR-BE.pdf.

Centlivres, Pierre, and Dominique Schnapper. 1991. "Nation et droit de la nationalité suisse." *Pouvoirs* 56:149–61.

Cerutti, Mauro. 1992. "Les communistes italiens en Suisse dans l'entre-deux-guerres." In *Centenaire Jules Humbert-Droz: Colloque sur l'internationale communiste, la Chaux-de-Fonds, 25–28 Septembre 1991: Actes,* edited by Fondation Jules Humbert-Droz, 213–40. La Chaux-de-Fonds: Fondation Jules Humbert-Droz.

——. 1994. "Un secolo di emigrazione italiana in Svizzera (1870–1970), attraverso le fonti dell'Archivio federale." *Studi e Fonti* 20:11–104.

——. 1995. "L'immigration italienne en Suisse dans le contexte de la Guerre froide." In *Pour une histoire des gens sans histoire: Ouvriers, exclues et rebelles en Suisse: 19e–20e siècles,* edited by Jean Batou, Mauro Cerutti, and Charles Heimberg, 213–31. Lausanne: Éditions d'en bas.

Chang, Edward Taehan. 2003. "Koreans: Entrepreneurs par Excellence." In *The New Face of Asian Pacific America: Numbers, Diversity, and Change in the 21st Century,* edited by Eric Lai and Dennis Arguelles, 57–66. San Francisco: Asian Week.

Chavez, Linda. 1991. *Out of the Barrio: Toward a New Politics of Hispanic Assimilation.* New York: Basic Books.

Chebel D'Appollonia, Ariane. 2007. "Immigration, Security, and Integration in the European Union." In *Immigration, Integration, and Security: America and Europe in Comparative Perspective,* edited by Ariane Chebel d'Appollonia and Simon Reich, 203–28. Pittsburgh: Pittsburgh University Press.

Chimienti, Milena. 2009. *Migration et Prostitution. Les ressources de l'agir faible.* Zurich: Seismo.

Chin, Gabriel, Sumi Cho, Jerry Kang, and Frank Wu. 1996. "Beyond Self-Interest: Asian Pacific Americans toward a Community of Justice; A Policy Analysis of Affirmative Action." Available at: http://www.aasc.ucla.edu/aascresources/policy/beyond.pdf.

Cho, Wendy Tam. 1999. "Naturalization, Socialization, Participation: Immigrants and (Non-)Voting." *Journal of Politics* 61 (4): 1140–55.

Chong, Dennis, and Reuel Rogers. 2005. "Racial Solidarity and Political Participation." *Political Behavior* 27 (4): 347–74.

Chung, Angie. 2005. "'Politics without the Politics': The Evolving Political Cultures of Ethnic Nonprofits in Koreatown, Los Angeles." *Journal of Ethnic and Migration Studies* 31 (5): 911–29.

Chuong, Chung Hoang, and Minh-Hoa Ta. 2003. "Vietnamese: Overcoming the Past and Building a Future." In *The New Face of Asian Pacific America: Numbers, Diversity, and Change in the 21st Century,* edited by Eric Lai and Dennis Arguelles, 67–72. San Francisco: Asian Week.

Citrin, Jack, and John Sides. 2006. "European Immigration in the People's Court." In *Immigration and the Transformation of Europe,* edited by Craig Parsons and Timothy Smeeding, 327–61. New York: Cambridge University Press.

Citrin, Jack, Amy Lerman, Michael Murakami, and Kathryn Pearson. 2007. "Testing Huntington: Is Hispanic Immigration a Threat to American Identity?" *Perspectives on Politics* 5 (1): 31–48.

Clarke, Susan. 2003. "Globalism and Cities: A North American Perspective." In *Globalism and Local Democracy: Challenge and Change in Europe and North America*, edited by Robin Hambleton, Hank Savitch, and Murray Stewart, 30–51. New York: Palgrave Macmillan.

——. 2005. "Splintering Citizenship and the Prospects for Democratic Inclusion." In *The Politics of Democratic Inclusion*, edited by Christina Wolbrecht and Rodney Hero, 210–37. Philadelphia: Temple University Press.

Claude-Valentin, Marie. 2004. *Preventing Illegal Immigration: Juggling Economic Imperatives, Political Risks, and Individual Rights*. Brussels: Council of Europe Publishing.

Cleaver, Eldridge. 1968. *Soul on Ice*. New York: Dell.

Cohen, Cathy. 1999. *The Boundaries of Blackness: AIDS and the Breakdown of Black Politics*. Chicago: University of Chicago Press.

Cole, David. 2003. *Enemy Aliens: Double Standards and Constitutional Freedoms in the War on Terrorism*. New York: New Press.

Collier, David, and James Mahon Jr. 1993. "Conceptual 'Stretching' Revisited: Adapting Categories in Comparative Analysis." *American Political Science Review* 87 (4): 845–55.

Commission of the European Communities. 2001. *Flash Eurobarometer 114: International Crisis*, Brussels. (November).

——(diverse dates). *Eurobarometer: Public Opinion in the European Community*, nos. 45–50. Brussels.

Commission on Multi-Ethnic Britain (CMEB). 2000. *The Future of Multi-Ethnic Britain: Report of the Commission on the Future of Multi-Ethnic Britain [Parekh Report]*. London: Profile Books.

Connelly, Marjorie. 2006. "In Polls, Illegal Immigrants Are Called Burden," *New York Times*, April 14, A16.

Conover, Pamela. 1988. "The Role of Social Groups in Political Thinking." *British Journal of Political Science* 18 (1): 51–76.

Cornelius, Wayne. 1981. "The Future of Mexican Immigrants in California: A New Perspective for Public Policy." Working Papers in U.S. Public Policy, no. 6. University of California, San Diego.

Cornelius, Wayne, and Takeyuki Tsuda. 2004. "Controlling Immigration: The Limits of Government Intervention." In *Controlling Immigration: A Global Perspective*, edited by Wayne Cornelius, Takeyuki Tsuda, Philip Martin, and James Hollifield, 3–50. Stanford: Stanford University Press.

Coronado, Roberto. 2004. "Worker Remittances to Mexico." *Business Frontier* 1. Available at: http://www.dallasfed.org/research/busfront/bus0401.html.

Cosman, Madeleine. 2005. "Illegal Aliens and American Medicine." *Journal of American Physicians and Surgeons* 10 (1): 6–10.

Council of Europe. 2001. "Conclusion and Plan of Action of the Extraordinary European Council Meeting on 21 Sept 2001." Council of Europe doc GMT (2001) Inf 31.

——. 2004. *Preventing Illegal Immigration: Juggling Economic Imperatives, Political Risks, and Individual Rights*, edited by Claude-Valentin Marie. Brussels: Council of Europe.

Crul, Maurice, George Groenewold, and Liesbeth Heering. 2007. "Conclusions." In *Research Report: TIES Survey in Amsterdam and Rotterdam*, edited by Maurice Crul and Liesbeth Heering, 133–43. Amsterdam: IMES.

Cruz, José. 1998. *Identity and Power: Puerto Rican Politics and the Challenge of Ethnicity*. Philadelphia: Temple University Press.

Dagevos, Jaco. 2007. "Arbeid en inkomen." In *Jaarrapport Integratie 2007*, edited by Jaco Dagevos and Mérove Gijsberts, 131–63. The Hague: Sociaal en Cultureel Planbureau.

Dagevos, Jaco, and Mérove Gijsberts. 2005. "De opkomst van een allochtone middenklasse in Nederland." In *Hier en daar opklaringen: Nieuwjaarsuitgave 2005*, 84–89. The Hague: Sociaal en Cultureel Planbureau.

——, eds. 2007. *Jaarrapport Integratie 2007*. The Hague: Sociaal en Cultureel Planbureau.

Dagevos, Jaco, Mérove Gijsberts, and Carlo Van Praag. 2003. *Rapportage minderheden 2003: Onderwijs, arbeid en sociaal-culturele integratie*. The Hague: Sociaal en Cultureel Planbureau.

Dagevos, Jaco, Roelof Schellingerhout, and Miranda Vervoort. 2007. "Sociaal-culturele integratie en religie." In *Jaarrapport Integratie 2007*, edited by Jaco Dagevos and Mérove Gijsberts, 163–92. The Hague: Sociaal en Cultureel Planbureau.

Dahl, Robert. 1956. *A Preface to Democratic Theory.* Chicago: University of Chicago Press.

D'Amato, Gianni. 2001. *Vom Ausländer zum Bürger: Der Streit um die politische Integration von Einwanderern in Deutschland, Frankreich und der Schweiz.* Münster: Lit.

D'Amato, Gianni, and Damir Skenderovic. Forthcoming. "Outsiders Becoming Power Players: Radical Right-Wing Populist Parties and Their Impact in Swiss Migration Policy." In *Right-Wing Extremism in Switzerland: An International Comparison,* edited by Marcel Niggli. Baden-Baden: Nomos.

Damon, Anjeanette. 2006. "Movement Could Build Political Momentum." *Reno Gazette Journal,* April 12. Available at: http://news.rgj.com/apps/pbcs.dll/article?AID=20060412/NEWS1-/604120353/1002/NEWS.

Dancygier, Rafaela. 2007. Fighting Neighbors or Fighting the State: The Political Economy of Immigrant Conflict in Western Europe. Ph.D. dissertation, Yale University.

Dawson, Michael. 1994. *Behind the Mule: Race and Class in African-American Politics.* Princeton: Princeton University Press.

Dear, Michael, and Steven Flusty. 2001. "The Resistible Rise of the L.A. School." In *From Chicago to L.A.: Making Sense of Urban Theory,* edited by Michael Dear and J. Dallas Dishman, 3–16. Thousand Oaks, Calif.: Sage.

de Haas, Hein. 2006. *Engaging Diasporas: How Governments and Development Agencies Can Support Diaspora Involvement in the Development of Origin Countries.* Oxford: Oxford University, International Migration Institute.

De la Cruz, Melany, and Pauline Agbayani-Siewert. 2003. "Filipinos: Swimming with and against the Tide." In *The New Face of Asian Pacific America: Numbers, Diversity, and Change in the 21st Century,* edited by Eric Lai and Dennis Arguelles, 45–50. San Francisco: Asian Week.

de la Garza, Rodolfo, and Louis DeSipio. 1993. "Save the Baby, Change the Bathwater, and Scrub the Tub: Latino Electoral Participation after Seventeen Years of Voting Rights Act Coverage." *Texas Law Review* 71 (7): 1479–539.

de la Garza, Rodolfo, Angelo Falcon, and F. Chris Garcia. 1996. "Will the Real Americans Please Stand Up: Anglo and Mexican-American Support of Core American Political Values." *American Journal of Political Science* 40 (2): 335–51.

Demant, Froukje. 2005. "Meer inpassing dan aanpassing: Over de culturele integratie van migranten in Nederland en Duitsland." *Migrantenstudies* 21 (2): 70–86.

Democracy Now. 2006. "Rep. Sheila Jackson Lee: Immigration Is the Civil Rights Issue of Our Time." April 4. Available at: http://www.democracynow.org/article.pl?sid=06/04/04/1419254.

De Muelenaere, Michel. 2004. "La guerre est ouverte pour la présidence du VLD." *Le Soir,* November 29.

de Silva, Ian. 2007. "Our Illegal-Alien Criminal Class." *Washington Times,* April 12. Available at: http://www.washtimes.com.

DeSipio, Louis. 1987. "Social Science Literature and the Naturalization Process." *International Migration Review* 21 (2): 390–405.

——. 1996. *Counting on the Latino Vote: Latinos as a New Electorate.* Charlottesville: University Press of Virginia.

——. 2000. "The Dynamo of Urban Growth: Immigration, Naturalization, and the Restructuring of Urban Politics." In *Minority Politics at the Millennium,* edited by Richard Keiser and Katherine Underwood, 77–108. New York: Garland.

——. 2001. "Building America, One Person at a Time: Naturalization and Political Behavior of the Naturalized in Contemporary American Politics." In *E Pluribus Unum? Contemporary and Historical Perspectives on Immigrant Political Incorporation,* edited by Gary Gerstle and John Mollenkopf, 67–106. New York: Russell Sage Foundation.

DeSipio, Louis, and Rodolfo de la Garza. 1992. "Making Them Us: The Political Incorporation of Culturally Distinct Immigrant and Nonimmigrant Minorities in the United States." In *Nations of Immigrants: Australia, the United States, and International Migration,* edited by Gary Freeman and James Jupp, 202–16. Melbourne: Oxford University Press.

de Valk, Helga, and Maurice Crul. 2007. "Education." In *Research Report TIES Survey in Amsterdam and Rotterdam,* edited by Maurice Crul and Liesbeth Heering, 43–64. Amsterdam: IMES.

DeWind, Josh, and Philip Kasinitz. 1997. "Everything Old Is New Again? Processes and Theories of Immigrant Incorporation." *International Migration Review* 31 (4): 1096–111.

De Winter, Lieven. 2005. "The Vlaams Blok: The Electorally Best Performing Right-Extremist Party in Western Europe." In *Political Survival of the Extreme Right*, edited by Xavier Casals, 93–125. Barcelona: Institut de Ciències Politiques i Socials.

Diehl, Claudia, and Michael Blohm. 2003. "Rights or Identity? Naturalization Processes among 'Labor Migrants' in Germany." *International Migration Review* 37 (1): 133–62.

Dokumentationsarchiv des österreichischen Widerstands, ed. 1993. *Handbuch des österreichischen Rechtsextremismus*. Vienna: Deuticke.

Donzelot, Jacques. 2006. *Quand la ville se défait: Quelle politique face à la crise des banlieues?* Paris: Seuil.

Donzelot, Jacques, and Philippe Estèbe. 1994. *L'état animateur: Essai sur la politique de la ville*. Paris: Editions Esprit.

Donzelot, Jacques, Catherine Mével, and Anne Wyvekens. 2003. *Faire société: La politique de la ville aux États-Unis et en France*. Paris: Seuil.

Downs, William. 2001. "Pariahs in Their Midst: Belgian and Norwegian Parties React to Extremist Threats." *West European Politics* 24 (3): 23–42.

Duyvendak, Jan Willem. 2004. *Een Eensgezinde en Vooruitstrevende Natie*. Amsterdam: Vossiuspers UvA.

Duyvendak, Jan Willem, Hans Boutellier, Henk-Jan Van Daal, and Marjan De Gruijter. 2004. *Zelforganisaties van Migranten: Aanvullend Bronnenonderzoek Verwey-Jonker Instituut*. T.K. 28689, 12 (2003–2004), 108–63. The Hague: SDU.

Dwyer, Christopher. 1991. *The Dominican Americans*. New York: Chelsea House.

*The Economist.* 2005. "An Underclass Rebellion—France's Riots." November 12, 24–26.

Ederveen, Sjef, Paul Dekker, Albert van der Hortst, Wink Joosten, Tom van der Meer, Paul Tang, Marcel Coenders, Marcel Lubbers, Han Nicolaas, Peer Scheepers, Arno Sprangers, and Johan van der Valk. 2004. *Destination Europe: Immigration and Integration in the European Union*. New Brunswick, N.J.: Transaction.

Ehrenzeller, Bernhard, and Paul-Lukas Good. 2003. *Rechtsgutachten zu Handen des Gemeinderates von Emmen betreffend das Einbürgerungsverfahren in der Gemeinde Emmen*. St. Gallen: Regierungsrat.

Ehrkamp, Patricia. 2005. "Placing Identities: Transnational Practices and Local Attachments of Turkish Immigrants in Germany." *Journal of Ethnic and Migration Studies* 31 (2): 345–64.

Eisinger, Peter. 1973. "The Conditions of Protest Behavior in American Cities." *American Political Science Review* 67 (1): 11–28.

Ellis, Patrica, and Zafar Khan. 1998. "Diasporic Mobilisation and the Kashmir Issue in British Politics." *Journal of Ethnic and Migration Studies* 24 (3): 471–88.

Entzinger, Han. 2003. "The Rise and Fall of Multiculturalism: The Case of the Netherlands." In *Toward Assimilation and Citizenship: Immigrants in Liberal Nation-States*, edited by Christian Joppke and Ewa Morawska, 59–86. New York: Palgrave Macmillan.

Erie, Steven. 1988. *Rainbow's End: Irish-Americans and the Dilemmas of Urban Machine Politics, 1840–1985*. Berkeley: University of California Press.

Erk, Jan. 2005. "From Vlaams Blok to Vlaams Belang: The Belgian Far-Right Renames Itself." *West European Politics* 28 (3): 493–502.

Erzan, Refik, and Kemal Kirişci. 2006. "Introduction." *Turkish Studies* 7 (1): 1–11.

Eskridge, William N. 1990. "Gadamer/Statutory Interpretation." *Columbia Law Review* 90: 609–81.

Espenshade, Thomas, and Katherine Hempstead. 1996. "Contemporary American Attitudes toward U.S. Immigration." *International Migration Review*. 30 (2): 535–70.

Espiritu, Yen Le. 1992. *Asian American Panethnicity: Bridging Institutions and Identities*. Philadelphia: Temple University Press.

Espiritu, Yen Le, and Michael Omi. 2000. " 'Who Are You Calling Asian?': Shifting Identity Claims, Racial Classification, and the Census." In *Transforming Race Relations*, edited by Paul Ong, 43–102. Los Angeles: LEAP Asian American Public Policy Institute and UCLA Asian American Studies Center.

Etienne, Bruno. 1989. *La France et l'Islam*. Paris: Hachette.

Etzioni, Amitai. 1993. *The Spirit of Community: Rights, Responsibilities, and the Communitarian Agenda*. New York: Crown Publishers.

Europa: Activities of the European Union. 2007. *Common Programme for the Integration of Non-EU Member Country Nationals*. Available at: http://europa.eu/scadplus/leg/en/lvb/l14502.htm.

Europa: Activities of the European Union. 2008. *Framework Programme on Solidarity and Management of Migration Flows for the Period 2007–2013.* Available at: http://europa.eu/cgi-bin/etal.pl.

European Monitoring Centre on Racism and Xenophobia. 2002. *EUMC Report on Islamophobia after September 11.* Vienna: EUMC.

——. 2003a. "Immigration, Integration and Employment." COM, 2003, 336 final.

——. 2003b. *Majorities' Attitudes towards Minorities in European Union Member States.* Report 2. Vienna: EUMC.

European Commission. 2004a. *Green Paper on Economic Migration of TCNs.* COM 2004, 811 final.

——. 2004b. *Racist Violence in 15 EU Member States: A Comparative Overview of Findings from the RAXEN NFP Reports 2001–2004.* Vienna: EUMC.

——2004c. Commission Communication of 10 February 2004: "Building Our Common Future—Policy Challenges and Budgetary Means of the Enlarged Union 2007–2013" *COM(2004) 101* final.

——. 2006a. *Migration and Asylum in Europe 2003.* Brussels: Centre d'étude de Gestion Démographique pour les Administrations Publiques (GéDAP) and the Berlin Institute for Comparative Social Research (BIVS).

——. 2006b. *Muslims in the European Union: Discrimination and Islamophobia.* Vienna: EUMC.

——. 2007. "Towards a Common European Union Immigration Policy." Available at: http://ec.europa.eu/justice_home/fsj/immigration/fsj_immigration_intro_en.htm.

European Conference. 2001. *Declaration of European Conference on Alignment Candidate Countries with Conclusions of the European Council.* October 20 (Brussels).

European Parliament. 2008. "Parliament Adopts Directive on Return of Illegal Immigrants." Available at: http://www.europarl.europa.eu/news/expert/infopress_page/018–31787–168–06–25–902–200. 18/06/2008.

Eurostat (Statistical Office of the European Commission). 1999. *Yearbook 1998–1999: A Statistical Eye on Europe, Data 1987–1997.* Luxembourg: Office for Official Publications of the European Communities.

——. 1994. Yearbook 1994: A Statistical Eye on Europe, 1992–1993. Luxembourg: Office for Official Publications of the European Commmunities.

Euwals, Rob. 2007. *The Labour Market Position of Turkish Immigrants in Germany and the Netherlands: Reason for Migration, Naturalisation, and Language Proficiency.* IZA Discussion paper no. 2683.

Evans, Jocelyn, and Gilles Ivaldi. 2002. "Les dynamiques électorales de l'extrême-droite européenne." *Revue Politique et Parlementaire* 104 (1019): 67–83.

Faist, Thomas. 2000. *The Volume and Dynamics of International Migration and Transnational Social Spaces.* Oxford: Oxford University Press.

——. 2002. "Extension du domaine de la lutte: International Migration and Security before and after September 11, 2001." *International Migration Review* 36 (1): 7–14.

——. 2007. "The Shifting Boundaries of the Political." In *Dual Citizenship in Global Perspective: From Unitary to Multiple Citizenship,* edited by Thomas Faist and Peter Kivisto, 1–23. Basingstoke: Palgrave Macmillan.

Falcón, Angelo. 1988. "Black and Latino Politics in New York City: Race and Ethnicity in a Changing Urban Context." In *Latinos and the Political System,* edited by F. Chris Garcia, 171–94. Notre Dame, Ind.: University of Notre Dame Press.

Fang, Cai, and Dewen Wang. 2005. "Demographic Transition: Implications for Growth." In *The China Boom and Its Discontents,* edited by Ross Garnaut and Lgang Song, 34–52. Canberra: Asia Pacific Press, Australian National University.

Fanning, Bryan, Jo Shaw, Jane-Ann O'Connell, and Marie Williams. 2007. *Irish Political Parties, Immigration and Integration in 2007.* Dublin: University College Dublin.

Favell, Adrian. 2001. *Philosophies of Integration: Immigration and the Idea of Citizenship in France and Britain,* 2nd ed. London: Palgrave.

Federation for American Immigration Reform (FAIR). 2005. "Illegal Immigration Is a Crime." Issue brief. Available at: http://www.fairus.org.

Feirabend, Jeroen, and Jan Rath. 1996. "Making a Place for Islam in Politics: Local Authorities Dealing with Islamic Associations." In *Muslims in the Margin: Political Responses to the Presence of Islam in Western Europe,* edited by Anwar Shadid and Pieter Sjoerd van Koningsveld, 243–58. Kampen: Kok Pharos.

Fennema, Meindert. 2000. "Legal Repression of Extreme-Right Parties and Racial Discrimination." In *Challenging Immigration and Ethnic Relations Politics: Comparative European Perspectives*, edited by Ruud Koopmans and Paul Statham, 119–44. Oxford: Oxford University Press.

Fennema, Meindert, Jean Tillie, Anja Van Heelsum, Maria Berger, and Rick Wolff. 2000. *Sociaal Kapitaal en Politieke Participatie van Minderheden*. Amsterdam: IMES.

——. 2001. "L'Intégration politique des minorités ethniques aux pays-bas." *Migrations/Société* 13:109–29.

Fennema, Meindert, and Wouter van der Brug. 2006. "Der Aufstieg Pim Fortuyns in europäischer und historischer Perspektive." In *Radikale Rechte und Fremdenfeindlichkeit in Deutschland und Polen: Nationale und europäische Perspektiven*, edited by Michael Minkenberg, Dagmar Sucker, and Agnieszka Wenninger, 74–101. Bonn: IZ Osteuropa.

Ferrari, Silvio. 1995. "The Emerging Pattern of Church and State in Western Europe: The Italian Model." *Brigham Young University Law Review* 1995 (2): 421–37.

Fetzer, Joel. 2000. *Public Attitudes toward Immigration in the United States, France, and Germany*. New York: Cambridge University Press.

Fetzer, Joel, and J. Christopher Soper. 2004. *Muslims and the State in Britain, France, and Germany*. Cambridge, UK: Cambridge University Press.

Fibbi, Rosita, and Sandro Cattacin, eds. 2002. *L'auto e mutuo aiuto nella migrazione: Una valutazione d'iniziative di self help tra genitori italiani in Svizzera; mit einer deutschen Kurzfassung der Studie im Anhang*. Neuchâtel: SFM/FSM.

Fincher, Ruth, and Jane Jacobs, eds. 1998. *Cities of Difference*. New York: Guilford Press.

Fisher, Stephen. 2002. "The Vlaams Blok in Flanders". EREPS report. Available at: http://www.politik.uni-mainz.de/ereps/download/belgium_overview.pdf

Florida, Richard. 2004. *The Rise of the Creative Class: And How It's Transforming Work, Leisure, Community, and Everyday Life*. New York: Basic Books.

Foerster, Amy. 2004. "Race, Identity, and Belonging: 'Blackness' and the Struggle for Solidarity in a Multiethnic Labor Union." *Social Problems* 51 (3): 386–409.

Foner, Nancy. 1979. "West Indians in New York City and London: A Comparative Analysis." *International Migration Review* 13 (2): 284–97.

Foner, Nancy, and Richard Alba. 2008. "Immigrant Religion in the U.S. and Western Europe: Bridge or Barrier to Inclusion?" *International Migration Review* 42 (2): 360–92.

Fraga, Luis, John Garcia, Rodney Hero, Michael Jones-Correa, Valerie Martinez-Ebers, and Gary Segura. 2006. "Redefining America: Results of the Latino National Survey." Paper presented at the Woodrow Wilson Center, Washington, D.C., December 6.

Fraga, Luis, and Ricardo Ramírez. 2003. "Latino Political Incorporation in California, 1990–2000." In *Latinos and Public Policy in California: An Agenda for Opportunity*, edited by David Lopez and Andrés Jiménez, 301–35. Berkeley: Berkeley Public Policy Press.

——. 2004. "Demography and Political Influence: Disentangling the Latino Vote." *Harvard Journal of Hispanic Policy* 16:69–96.

Fraga, Luis, and Gary Segura. 2006. "Culture Clash? Contesting Notions of American Identity and the Effects of Latin American Immigration." *Perspectives on Politics* 4 (2): 279–87.

*Frankfurter Allgemeine Zeitung*. 2005a. "Hier fühlten sich alle gekränkt." November 9, 3.

——. 2005b. "Interview with Emmanuel Todd." November 12, 39.

Fraser, Nancy, and Axel Honneth. 2003. *Redistribution or Recognition? A Political-Philosophical Exchange*. London: Verso.

Freeman, Gary. 1979. *Immigrant Labor and Racial Conflict in Industrial Societies: The French and British Experience, 1945–1975*. Princeton, N.J.: Princeton University Press.

——. 1995a. "Modes of Immigration Politics in Liberal Democratic States." *International Migration Review* 29 (4): 881–902.

——. 1995b. "Modes of Immigration Politics in Liberal Democratic States: Rejoinder." *International Migration Review* 29 (4): 909–13.

——. 2004. "Immigrant Incorporation in Western Democracies." *International Migration Review* 38 (3): 945–69.

Fremstad, Shawn. 2006. "The Economic and Fiscal Effects of the Senate's Comprehensive Immigration Reform Act of 2006." Los Angeles: National Immigration Law Center, September 26.

Frey, William. 2006. *Demographics in the '00s Decade: The Role of Seniors, Boomers and New Minorities.* Washington, D.C.: Brookings Institution.

Frey, William, and Kao-Lee Liaw. 2005. "Interstate Migration of Hispanics, Asians, and Blacks: Cultural Constraints and Middle Class Flight." Population Studies Center Report 05–575. University of Michigan.

Friesema, Paul. 1969. "Black Control of Central Cities: The Hollow Prize." *American Institute of Planners Journal* 35 (2): 75–79.

Gammeltoft-Hansen, Thomas. 2006. "Filtering Out the Risky Migrant: Migration Control, Risk Theory and the EU," AMID Working Paper Series 52/2006. Academy for Migration Studies in Denmark, Aalborg.

Gans, Herbert. 1962. *The Urban Villagers: Group and Class in the Life of Italian-Americans.* New York: Free Press of Glencoe.

———. 2007. "Acculturation, Assimilation and Mobility." *Ethnic and Racial Studies* 30 (1): 152–64.

Gaouette, Nicole, and Teresa Watanabe. 2007. "House Immigration Bill Offers Citizenship." *Los Angeles Times,* March 21, A1.

Garbaye, Romain. 2000. "Ethnic Minorities, Cities and Institutions: A Comparison of the Models of Management of Ethnic Diversity of a French and British City." In *Challenging Immigration and Ethnic Relations Politics: Comparative European Perspectives,* edited by Ruud Koopmans and Paul Statham, 283–311. Oxford: Oxford University Press.

———. 2004. "Ethnic Minority Local Councillors in French and British Cities: Social Determinants and Political Opportunity Structures." In *Citizenship in European Cities: Immigrants, Local Politics, and Integration Policies,* edited by Rinus Pennix, Karen Kraal, Marco Martiniello, and Steven Vertovec, 39–56. Aldershot, UK: Ashgate.

———. 2005. *Getting into Local Power: The Politics of Ethnic Minorities in British and French Cities.* Oxford: Blackwell.

Garcia, John. 1981. "Political Integration of Mexican Immigrants: Explorations into the Naturalization Process." *International Migration Review* 15 (4): 608–25.

Garreau, Joel. 1991. *Edge City: Life on the New Frontier.* New York: Doubleday.

Garson, Jean-Pierre. 2004. *Migration in Europe: Trends and Perspectives.* Washington, D.C.: Migration Policy Institute.

Gay, Claudine. 2006. "Seeing Difference: The Effect of Economic Disparity on Black Attitudes toward Latinos." *American Journal of Political Science* 50 (4): 982–97.

Geddes, Andrew. 1993. "Asian and Afro-Caribbean Representation in Elected Local Governments in England and Wales." *New Community* 20 (1): 43–58.

———. 1998. "Race Related Political Participation and Representation in the UK." *Revue europeenne des migrations internationales* 14 (2): 33–49.

———. 2000. *Immigration and European Integration: Towards Fortress Europe?* Manchester, UK: Manchester University Press.

———. 2003. *The Politics of Migration and Immigration in Europe.* London: Sage.

Geddes, Andrew, and Virginie Guiraudon. 2004. "The Emergence of a European Union Policy Paradigm amidst Contrasting National Models: Britain, France and EU Anti-Discrimination Policy." *West European Politics.* 27 (2): 334–53.

Geiger, Klaus, and Margret Spohn. 2001. "Les parlementaires allemands issus de l'immigration." *Migrations Société* 13 (77): 21–30.

Geisser, Vincent. 1997. *Ethnicité républicaine: Les élites d'origine maghrébine dans le système politique français.* Paris: Presses de Sciences Politiques.

Geisser, Vincent, and Schérazade Kelfaoui. 2001. "Marseille 2001, la communauté réinventée par les politiques." *Migrations Société* 13 (77): 55–77.

Geisser, Vincent, and Paul Oriol. 2001. "Les français 'd'origine étrangère' aux élections municipales de 2001." *Migrations Société* 13 (77): 41–53.

———. 2002. "Les élus d'origine étrangère aux elections municipales de mars 2001: Paris, Lyon et Marseille." *Migrations Société* 14 (83): 27–38.

Gellner, Ernest. 1981. *Muslim Society.* Cambridge: Cambridge University Press.

Gerstle, Gary, and John Mollenkopf, eds. 2001. *E Pluribus Unum? Contemporary and Historical Perspectives on Immigrant Political Incorporation.* New York: Russell Sage Foundation.

Giannakouris, Konstantinos. 2008. "Ageing Characterizes the Demographic Perspectives of European Societies." *Eurostat Statistics in Focus* 72:1–12.

Gibson, James, and Amanda Gouws. 2003. *Overcoming Intolerance in South Africa: Experiments in Democratic Persuasion.* Cambridge, UK: Cambridge University Press.

Giddens, Anthony. 1991. *Modernity and Self-Identity: Self and Society in the Late Modern Age.* Cambridge, UK: Polity Press.

Gijsberts, Mérove, and Lex Herweijer. 2007. "Allochtone leerlingen in het onderwijs." In *Jaarrapport Integratie 2007,* edited by Jaco Dagevos and Mérove Gijsberts, 102–31. The Hague: Sociaal en Cultureel Planbureau.

Gilbertson, Greta, and Audrey Singer. 2000. "Naturalization under Changing Conditions of Membership: Dominican Immigrants in New York City." In *Immigration Research for a New Century: Multidisciplinary Perspectives,* edited by Nancy Foner, Rubén Rumbaut, and Steven Gold, 157–86. New York: Russell Sage Foundation.

Gilroy, Paul. 1987. *There Ain't No Black in the Union Jack: The Cultural Politics of Race and Nation.* London: Hutchinson.

——. 1990. "The End of Anti-Racism." *New Community* 17 (1): 71–83.

——. 1993. *The Black Atlantic: Modernity and Double Consciousness.* London: Verso.

Gimpel, James, and James Edwards Jr. 1999. *The Congressional Politics of Immigration Reform.* Boston: Allyn and Bacon.

Giugni, Marco, and Florence Passy. 2002. "Entre post-nationalisme et néo-institutionnalisme: La structuration des débats publics en Suisse dans le domaine de l'immigration et des relations ethniques." *Revue suisse de science politique* 8 (2): 21–52.

——. 2003. "Staatsbürgerschaftsmodelle und Mobilisierung der Immigranten in der Schweiz und in Frankreich im Hinblick auf politische Gelegenheitsstrukturen." In *Migration und die Schweiz: Ergebnisse des nationalen Forschungsprogramms "Migration und interkulturelle Beziehungen,"* edited by Hans-Rudolf Wicker, Werner Haug, and Rosita Fibbi, 109–38. Zürich: Seismo.

——. 2006. "Influencing Migration Policy from Outside: The Impact of Migrant, Extreme-Right, and Solidarity Movements." In *Dialogues on Migration Policy,* edited by Marco Giugni and Florence Passy, 193–213. Lanham, Md.: Lexington Books.

Givens, Terri, and Adam Luedtke. 2004. "The Politics of European Union Immigration Policy: Institutions, Salience, and Harmonization." *Policy Studies Journal* 32 (1): 145–65.

Glazer, Nathan. 1993. "Is Assimilation Dead?" *Annals of the American Academy of Political and Social Sciences* 530:122–36.

Glazer, Nathan, and Daniel Moynihan. 1970 [1963]. *Beyond the Melting Pot: The Negroes, Puerto Ricans, Jews, Italians, and Irish of New York City.* 2nd ed. Cambridge, Mass.: MIT Press.

Göle, Nilüfer. 1996. *The Forbidden Modern: Civilization and Veiling.* Ann Arbor: University of Michigan Press.

Gordon, Milton. 1964. *Assimilation in American Life: The Role of Race, Religion, and National Origins.* New York: Oxford University Press.

Gordon, Philip. 2005. "On Assimilation and Economics, France Will Need New Models." Brookings Institution, November 9. Available at: http://www.brookings.edu/opinions/2005/1109france_gordon.aspx.

Goren, Paul. 2005. "Party Identification and Core Political Values." *American Journal of Political Science* 49 (4): 881–96.

Gotanda, Neil. 2001. "Citizenship Nullification: The Impossibility of Asian American Politics." In *Asian Americans and Politics: Perspectives, Experiences, Prospects,* edited by Gordon Chang, 79–101. Palo Alto, Calif.: Stanford University Press.

Graham, Hugh Davis. 2002. *Collision Course: The Strange Convergence of Affirmative Action and Immigration Policy in America.* New York: Oxford University Press.

Graham, Stephen, and Simon Marvin. 2001. *Splintering Urbanism: Networked Infrastructures, Technological Mobilities and the Urban Condition.* London: Routledge.

Gray, John. 2000. "Pluralism and Toleration in Contemporary Political Philosophy." *Political Studies* 48 (2): 323–33.

Grebler, Leo. 1966. "The Naturalization of Mexican Immigrants in the United States." *International Migration Review* 1 (1): 17–32.

Green, Simon. 2004. *The Politics of Exclusion: Institutions and Immigration Policy in Contemporary Germany.* Manchester, UK: Manchester University Press.

Greer, Christina. 2007. "Black Ethnicity: Political Identity, Attitudes, and Participation in N.Y." Ph.D. dissertation, Columbia University.

Grenier, Guillermo, and Lisandro Pérez. 2003. *The Legacy of Exile: Cubans in the United States.* Boston: Allyn and Bacon.

Grieco, Elizabeth. 2003. *English Abilities of the US Foreign-Born Population.* Washington, D.C.: Migration Information Source. Available at: http://www.migrationinformation.org/USFocus/display.cfm?ID=84#7

Grimm, Dieter. 2002. "Kann der Turbanträger von der Helmpflicht befreit werden?" *Frankfurter Allgemeine Zeitung,* June 21, 49.

Gsir, Sonia, and Marco Martiniello. 2004. *Local Consultative Bodies for Foreign Residents—A Handbook.* Strasbourg: Council of Europe Publishing.

Guarnizo, Luis, Alejandro Portes, and William Haller. 2003. "Assimilation and Transnationalism: Determinants of Transnational Political Action among Contemporary Migrants." *American Journal of Sociology* 108 (6): 1211–48.

Guild, Elspeth, and Carol Harlow. 2001. *Implementing Amsterdam: Immigration and Asylum Rights in EC Law.* Portland, Ore.: Hart.

Guiraudon, Virginie. 2000. *Les politiques d'immigration en Europe: Allemagne, France, Pays-Bas.* Paris: L'Harmattan.

——. 2002. "Including Foreigners in National Welfare States: Institutional Venues and Rules of the Game." In *Restructuring the Welfare State: Political Institutions and Policy Change,* edited by Bo Rothstein and Sven Steinmo, 129–56. New York: Palgrave.

——. 2003. "The Constitution of a European Immigration Policy Domain: A Political Sociology Approach." *Journal of European Public Policy* 10 (2): 263–82.

Guiraudon, Virginie, and Gallya Lahav, eds. 2006. *Immigration Policy in Europe: The Politics of Control.* Special issue, *West European Politics* 29 (2).

Guiraudon, Virginie, Karen Phalet, and Jessika ter Wal. 2005. "Monitoring Ethnic Minorities in the Netherlands." *International Social Science Journal* 57 (1): 75–87.

Gutiérrez, David. 1998. "Ethnic Mexicans and the Transformation of 'American' Social Space: Reflections on Recent History." In *Crossings: Mexican Immigration in Interdisciplinary Perspectives,* edited by Marcelo Suárez-Orozco, 307–40. Cambridge, Mass.: Harvard University Press.

Haddad, Yvonne Yazbeck, ed. 2002. *Muslims in the West: From Sojourners to Citizens.* Oxford: Oxford University Press.

Hajnal, Zoltan. 2005. "The Missing Rainbow: Understanding Inter-Minority Cooperation in Local Politics." Paper presented at the annual meeting of the Midwest Political Science Association, Chicago.

Hall, Stuart. 1992a. "New Ethnicities." In *'Race,' Culture, and Difference,* edited by James Donald and Ali Rattansi, 252–59. London: Sage.

——. 1992b. "The Question of Cultural Identity." In *Modernity and Its Futures,* edited by Tony McGrew, Stuart Hall, and David Held, 273–326. Cambridge, UK: Polity Press.

Halle, David, ed. 2003. *New York and Los Angeles: Politics, Society, and Culture—A Comparative View.* Chicago: University of Chicago Press.

Halman, Loek, Ruud Luijkx, and Marga van Zundert. 2005. *Atlas of European Values.* Leiden: Brill.

Hammar, Tomas, ed. 1985. *European Immigration Policy: A Comparative Study.* Cambridge, UK: Cambridge University Press.

Haney-López, Ian. 1996. *White by Law: The Legal Construction of Race.* New York: New York University Press.

Hansen, Randall. 2003. "Migration to Europe since 1945: Its History and Its Lessons." In *The Politics of Migration: Managing Opportunity, Conflict and Change,* edited by Sarah Spencer, 25–38. Oxford: Blackwell.

Harchaoui, Sadik, and Chris Huinder, eds. 2003 *Stigma: Marokkaan! Over Afstoten en Insluiten van een Ingebeelde Bevolkingsgroep.* Utrecht: FORUM.

Harding, Gareth. 2004. "Makeover for Flemish Far Right." *Washington Times*/United Press International, November 15. Available at: http://washingtontimes.com/upi-breaking/20041115-124213-7311r.htm

Häußermann, Hartmut. 1995. "Die Stadt und die Stadtsoziologie: Urbane Lebensweise und die Integration des Fremden." *Berliner Journal für Soziologie* 5 (1): 89–98.

Hayduk, Ronald. 2006. *Democracy for All: Restoring Immigrant Voting Rights in the United States.* New York: Routledge.

Hayduk, Ronald, and Michele Wucker. 2004. *Immigrant Voting Rights Receive More Attention.* Washington, D.C.: Migration Information Source, November 1. Available at: http://www.migration information.org/Feature/display.cfm?ID=265.

Healey, Patsy. 1997. *Collaborative Planning: Shaping Places in Fragmented Societies.* Houndmills, UK: Macmillan.

Healy, Patrick. 2005. "The 2005 Elections: Mayoral Race, Bloomberg Cruises to Re-Election Victory, Corzine is Winner in Costly New Jersey Race." *New York Times,* November 9, A1.

Heering, Liesbeth, and Susan ter Bekke. 2007. "Labour and Income." In *Research Report: TIES Survey in Amsterdam and Rotterdam,* edited by Maurice Crul and Liesbeth Heering, 65–80. Amsterdam: IMES.

Heinisch, Reinhard. 2003. "Success in Opposition—Failure in Government: Explaining the Performance of Right-Wing Populist Parties in Public Office." *West European Politics* 26 (3): 91–130.

Heisler, Martin. 1992. "Migration, International Relations and the New Europe: Theoretical Perspectives from Institutional Political Sociology." *International Migration Review* 26 (2): 596–622.

———. 2001. "Now and Then, Here and There: Migration and the Transformation of Identities, Borders and Orders." In *Identities, Borders, Orders: Rethinking International Relations Theory,* edited by Mathias Albert, David Jacobson, and Yosef Lapid, 225–48. Minneapolis: University of Minnesota Press.

Helbling, Marc. 2008. *Practicing Citizenship and Heterogeneous Nationhood: Naturalizations in Swiss Municipalities.* Amsterdam: Amsterdam University Press.

Heredia, Luisa. 2008. "Faith in Action: The Catholic Church and the Immigrant Rights Movement, 1980–2007." Ph.D. dissertation, Harvard University.

Hero, Rodney. 1992. *Latinos and the U. S. Political System: Two-Tiered Pluralism.* Philadelphia: Temple University Press.

Hickman, Mary. 2005. "'Ruling an Empire, Governing a Multinational State': The Impact of Britain's Historical Legacy on the Ethno-Racial Regime." In *Ethnicity, Social Mobility and Public Policy in the USA and UK,* edited by Glenn Loury, Tariq Modood, and Steven Teles, 21–49. Cambridge, UK: Cambridge University Press.

Hicks, Jonathan. 2006. "Black Leaders Fear the Loss Of a House Seat." *New York Times.* June 12, B1.

Higham, John. 1992. *Strangers in the Land: Patterns of American Nativism, 1860–1925,* 2nd ed. New Brunswick, N.J.: Rutgers University Press.

Hiro, Dilip. 1991. *Black British, White British: A History of Race Relations in Britain.* 2nd ed. London: Grafton Books.

Hirschman, Albert. 1970. *Exit, Voice, and Loyalty: Responses to Decline in Firms, Organizations, and States.* Cambridge, Mass.: Harvard University Press.

Höbelt, Lothar. 2003. *Defiant Populist: Jörg Haider and the Politics of Austria.* West Lafayette, Ind.: Purdue University Press.

Hochschild, Jennifer, and Reuel Rogers. 2000. "Race Relations in a Diversifying Nation." In *New Directions: African-Americans in a Diversifying Nation,* edited by James Jackson, 45–85. New York: National Policy Association.

Hochschild, Jennifer, and Nathan Scovronick. 2003. *The American Dream and the Public Schools.* New York: Oxford University Press.

Hoffmann-Nowotny, Hans-Joachim, and Karl-Otto Hondrich, eds. 1982. *Ausländer in der Bundesrepublik Deutschland und in der Schweiz: Segregation und Integration; Eine vergleichende Untersuchung.* Frankfurt: Campus Verlag.

Hollifield, James. 1992. *Immigrants, Markets, and States: The Political Economy of Postwar Europe.* Cambridge, Mass.: Harvard University Press.

———. 2004. "The Emerging Migration State." *International Migration Review* 38 (3): 885–912.

Hollifield, James, Valerie Hunt, and Daniel Tichenor. 2008. "Immigrants, Markets, and Rights: The US as an Emerging Migration State." *Journal of Law and Policy.*

Hollinger, David. 2005. *Postethnic America: Beyond Multiculturalism,* revised and updated ed. New York: Basic Books.

Holston, James. 1995. "Spaces of Insurgent Citizenship." *Planning Theory and Practice* 13:35–52.

Home Office (United Kingdom). 2002. *Secure Borders, Safe Haven.* White Paper. London: Government Printing Office.

Honneth, Axel. 1994. *Kampf um Anerkennung: Zur moralischen Grammatik sozialer Konflikte.* Frankfurt: Suhrkamp.

Hooghe, Marc. 2005. "Ethnic Organisations and Social Movement Theory: The Political Opportunity Structure for Ethnic Mobilisation in Flanders." *Journal of Ethnic and Migration Studies* 31 (5): 975–90.

Horowitz, Donald. 1985. *Ethnic Groups in Conflict.* Berkeley: University of California Press.

Howard, Marc Morjé. 2005. "Variation in Dual Citizenship Policies in the Countries of the EU." *International Migration Review* 39 (3): 697–720.

Huddy, Leonie. 2003. "Group Identity and Political Cohesion." In *Oxford Handbook of Political Psychology,* edited by David Sears, Leonie Huddy, and Robert Jervis, 511–58. New York: Oxford University Press.

Huntington, Samuel. 1981. *American Politics: The Promise of Disharmony.* Cambridge, Mass.: Harvard University Press.

———. 1996. *The Clash of Civilizations and the Remaking of the World Order.* New York: Simon and Schuster.

———. 1997. "The Erosion of American National Interests." *Foreign Affairs* 76 (5): 28–49.

———. 2004. *Who Are We? The Challenges to America's National Identity.* New York: Simon and Schuster.

Huysmans, Jef. 1994. "Migrants as a Security Problem: Dangers of 'Securitizing' Societal Issues." In *Migration and European Integration: The Dynamics of Inclusion and Exclusion,* edited by Robert Miles and Dietrich Thranhardt, 53–72. London: Pinter.

———. 2000. "The European Union and the Securitization of Migration." *Journal of Common Market Studies* 38 (5): 751–77.

Ignatiev, Noel. 1996. *How the Irish Became White.* London: Verso.

Ignazi, Piero. 2003. *Extreme Right Parties in Western Europe.* Oxford: Oxford University Press.

Immigration Counters. 2007. "The #1 Site for Real-Time Illegal Immigration Statistics." April 11. Available at: http://immigrationcounters.com.

Immigration's Human Cost. 2007. "Crime Victims of Illegal Aliens." April 13. Available at: http://www.immigrationshumancost.org/text/crimevictims.html.

International Crisis Group (ICG). 2005. "Understanding Islamism." Middle East/North Africa Report no. 37. Brussels, March 2.

———. 2006. "La France face à ses Musulmans: Emeutes, jihadisme et dépolitisation." Europe Report no. 172, Brussels, March 9.

*International Herald Tribune,* Europe. 2006. "Dutch Political Parties Scrap Candidates Who Deny WWI Massacre of Armenians Was Genocide." September 27. available at: http://www.iht.com/articles/ap/2006/09/27/europe/EU_POL_Netherlands_Armenian_Killings.php

Ireland, Patrick. 1994. *The Policy Challenge of Ethnic Diversity: Immigrant Politics in France and Switzerland.* Cambridge, Mass.: Harvard University Press.

———. 2004. *Becoming Europe: Immigration, Integration, and the Welfare State.* Pittsburgh, Pa.: University of Pittsburgh Press.

Isin, Engin, ed. 2000. *Democracy, Citizenship and the Global City.* New York: Routledge.

Itzigsohn, José, and Silvia Giorguli Saucedo. 2002. "Immigrant Incorporation and Sociocultural Transnationalism." *International Migration Review* 36 (3): 766–98.

Ivaldi, Gilles. 2002. "L'extrême-droite renforcée mais toujours isolée." In *Élections 2002: Quelles logiques.* Special issue, *Revue Politique et Parlementaire* 104 (1020–21): 133–49.

Jackson, Jesse. 2006. "'Sí Se Puede' Means 'We Shall Overcome.'" Rainbow/PUSH Coalition. May 3. Tribune Media Services.

Jacobson, Matthew Frye. 1998. *Whiteness of a Different Color: European Immigrants and the Alchemy of Race.* Cambridge, Mass.: Harvard University Press.

Jennings, James, ed. 1997. *Race and Politics: New Challenges and Responses for Black Activism.* London: Verso.

Johnson, Benjamin. 2006. "Written Testimony of Benjamin Johnson, Director, Immigration Policy Center, American Immigration Law Foundation." Committee on the Judiciary, United States Senate. July 12.

Johnson, James, and Melvin Oliver. 1989. "Interethnic Minority Conflict in Urban America: The Effects of Economic and Social Dislocations." *Urban Geography* 10 (5): 449–63.

Johnson, James, Jr., Walter Farrell Jr., and Chandra Guinn. 1997. "Immigration Reform and the Browning of America: Tensions, Conflicts and Community Instability in Metropolitan Los Angeles." *International Migration Review* 31 (4): 1055–95.

Johnson, Kevin. 2004. *The "Huddled Masses" Myth: Immigration and Civil Rights.* Philadelphia: Temple University Press.

Johnson, Kirk. 1993. "The 1993 Elections: Connecticut, Mayor Perry Is Denied a Fourth Term by Voters in Hartford." *New York Times,* November 4, B10.

Jones, Charisse. 2006. "States Try to Block Illegal Workers." *USA Today,* July 10, A1.

Jones-Correa, Michael. 1998. *Between Two Nations: The Political Predicament of Latinos in New York City.* Ithaca: Cornell University Press.

——. 2000. "Immigrants, Blacks, and Cities." In *Black and Multiracial Politics in America,* edited by Yvette Alex-Assensoh and Lawrence Hanks, 133–64. New York: New York University Press.

——. 2001a. "Institutional and Contextual Factors in Immigrant Naturalization and Voting." *Citizenship Studies* 5 (1): 41–56.

——. 2001b. "Under Two Flags: Dual Nationality in Latin America and Its Consequences for Naturalization in the United States." *International Migration Review* 35 (4): 997–1029.

——. 2002. "On Immigrant Political Incorporation." Paper presented at the Workshop on Immigrant Incorporation, Mobilization and Participation. Maxwell School of Syracuse University, December 6.

——. 2005. "Bringing Outsiders In: Questions of Immigrant Incorporation." In *The Politics of Democratic Inclusion,* edited by Christina Wolbrecht and Rodney Hero, 75–101. Philadelphia: Temple University Press.

——. 2008. "Immigrant Incorporation in the Suburbs: Differential Pathways, Arenas and Intermediaries." In *Immigration and Integration in Urban Communities: Renegotiating the City,* edited by Lisa Hanley, Blair Ruble, and Allison Garland, 19–48. Baltimore, Md.: Johns Hopkins University Press.

Joppke, Christian. 1996. "Multiculturalism and Immigration: A Comparison of the United States, Germany, and Great Britain." *Theory and Society* 25 (4): 449–500.

——, ed. 1998. *Challenge to the Nation-State: Immigration in Western Europe and the United States.* Oxford: Oxford University Press.

——. 1999a. "How Immigration Is Changing Citizenship: A Comparative View." *Ethnic and Racial Studies* 22 (4): 629–52.

——. 1999b. *Immigration and the Nation-State: The United States, Germany, and Great Britain.* Oxford: Oxford University Press.

——. 2004. "The Retreat of Multiculturalism in the Liberal State: Theory and Policy." *British Journal of Sociology* 55 (2): 237–57.

——. 2005. *Selecting by Origin: Ethnic Migration in the Liberal State.* Cambridge, Mass.: Harvard University Press.

——. 2007a. "Beyond National Models: Civic Integration Policies for Immigrants in Western Europe." *West European Politics* 30 (1): 1–22.

——. 2007b. "State Neutrality and Islamic Headscarf Laws in France and Germany." *Theory and Society* 36 (4): 313–42.

——. 2009. *Veil: Mirror of Identity.* Cambridge, UK: Polity Press.

——. Forthcoming. "Limits of Integration Policy: Britain and Her Muslims." *Journal of Ethnic and Migration Studies.*

Joppke, Christian, and Ewa Morawska. 2003. "Integrating Immigrants in Liberal Nation-States: Policies and Practices." In *Toward Assimilation and Citizenship: Immigrants in Liberal Nation-States,* edited by Christian Joppke and Ewa Morawska, 1–36. New York: Palgrave Macmillan.

Joppke, Christian, and Zeev Rosenhek. 2002. "Contesting Ethnic Immigration: Germany and Israel Compared." *Archives européennes de sociologie* 43 (3): 301–35.

Joyce, Patrick. 2003. *No Fire Next Time: Black-Korean Conflicts and the Future of America's Cities.* Ithaca: Cornell University Press.

Judt, Tony. 2005. *Postwar: A History of Europe since 1945.* New York: Penguin.

Junn, Jane. 2000. "Participation in Liberal Democracy: The Political Assimilation of Immigrants and Ethnic Minorities in the United States." In *Immigration Research for a New Century,* edited by Nancy Foner, Rubén Rumbaut, and Steven Gold, 187–214. New York: Russell Sage Foundation.

Justice and Home Affairs. *Conclusions adopted by the Council.* Document 12156/01, 25/9/2002.

Kalbir, Shukra. 1998. *The Changing Pattern of Black Politics in Britain.* London: Pluto Press.

Kaldor, Mary, Helmut Anheier, and Marlies Glasius. 2003. "Global Civil Society in an Era of Regressive Globalisation." In *Global Civil Society 2003,* edited by Helmut Anheier, Marlies Glasius, and Mary Kaldor, 1–33. Oxford: Oxford University Press.

Kasinitz, Philip, John Mollenkopf, Mary Waters, and Jennifer Holdaway. 2008. *Inheriting the City: The Children of Immigrants Come of Age.* Cambridge, MA: Harvard University Press.

Kastoryano, Riva. 2002. *Negotiating Identities: States and Immigrants in France and Germany.* Trans. Barbara Harshav. Princeton, N.J.: Princeton University Press.

——. 2005. "French Secularism and Islam France's Headscarf Affair." In *Multiculturalism, Muslims and Citizenship: A European Approach,* edited by Tariq Modood, Anna Triandafyllidou, and Ricard Zapata-Barrero, 57–69. London: Routledge.

Kaufmann, Karen. 1998. "Racial Conflict and Political Choice: A Study of Mayoral Voting Behavior in Los Angeles and New York." *Urban Affairs Review* 33 (5): 655–85.

——. 2004. *The Urban Voter: Group Conflict and Mayoral Voting Behavior in American Cities.* Ann Arbor: University of Michigan Press.

——. 2007. "Immigration and the Future of Black Power in U.S. Cities." *Du Bois Review* 4 (1): 79–96.

Kaya, Ayhan, and Ferhan Kentel. 2005. *Euro-Türkler: Tükiye ile Avrupa Birligi arasinda Köprü mü, Engel mi?* Istanbul: Istanbul Bilgi Üniversitesi Yayinlari.

Kaya, Bülent. 2005. "Switzerland." In *Current Immigration Debates in Europe: A Publication of the European Migration Dialogue,* edited by Jan Niessen, Yongmi Schibel, and Cressida Thompson, 383–98. Brussels: Migration Policy Group.

Kazepov, Yuri. 2005. "Cities of Europe: Changing Contexts, Local Arrangements and the Challenge to Urban Cohesion." In *Cities of Europe: Changing Contexts, Local Arrangements and the Challenge to Urban Cohesion,* edited by Yuri Kazepov, 3–42. Oxford: Blackwell.

Keiser, Richard, and Katherine Underwood, eds. 2000. *Minority Politics at the Millennium.* New York: Garland.

Kertzer, David, and Dominique Arel, eds. 2002. *Census and Identity: The Politics of Race, Ethnicity, and Language in National Census.* New York: Cambridge University Press.

Key, Vladimir O. 1949. *Southern Politics in State and Nation.* New York: Vintage.

Kim, Claire Jean. 2000. *Bitter Fruit: The Politics of Black-Korean Conflict in New York City.* New Haven: Yale University Press.

Kim, Seung-Hwan. 2003. "Anti-Americanism in Korea." *Washington Quarterly* 26 (1): 109–22.

King, Desmond. 2000. *Making Americans: Immigration, Race, and the Origins of the Diverse Democracy.* Cambridge Mass.: Harvard University Press.

Kitano, Harry, and Roger Daniels. 1995. *Asian Americans: Emerging Minorities.* 2nd ed. Englewood Cliffs, N.J.: Prentice Hall.

Kitschelt, Herbert. 2007. "Growth and Persistence of the Radical Right in Postindustrial Democracies: Advances and Challenges in Comparative Research." *West European Politics* 30 (5): 1176–206.

Kitschelt, Herbert, and Wolfgang Streeck, eds. 2004. *Germany: Beyond the Stable State.* London: Frank Cass.

Kivisto, Peter. 2003. "Social Spaces, Transnational Immigrant Communities, and the Politics of Incorporation." *Ethnicities* 3 (1): 5–28.

Klausen, Jytte. 2005. *The Islamic Challenge: Politics and Religion in Western Europe.* Oxford: Oxford University Press.

——. 2006. "Counterterrorism and the Integration of Islam in Europe." In *Watch on the West,* Foreign Policy Research Institute, no. 7 (1). Available at: www.fpri.org.

Kleist, Naua. 2007. Spaces of Recognition: An Analysis of Somali-Danish Associational Engagement and Diasporic Mobilization. Ph.D. dissertation, University of Copenhagen.

Kolat, Kenan. 2003. *Türken begrüssen Schöders Äußerungen zu Eu-Mitgliedschaft der Türkei. Türkische Gemeinde Deutschland,* January 12. Available at: http://www.tgd.de/index.php?name=News&file=article&sid=201&theme=Printer.

Koll, Jesper. 2005. "Japan Is Back, for Real This Time." *Far Eastern Economic Review* 168 (9): 11–16.

König, Matthias. 2003. Staatsbürgerschaft und religiöse Pluralität in post-nationalen Konstellationen. Ph.D. dissertation, University of Marburg.

Koopmans, Ruud. 1995. "A Burning Question: Explaining the Rise of Racist and Extreme Right Violence in Western Europe," FS III 95–101, WZB, Berlin.

———. 2004. "Migrant Mobilisation and Political Opportunities: Variation among German Cities and a Comparison with the United Kingdom and the Netherlands." *Journal of Ethnic and Migration Studies* 30 (3): 449–70.

Koopmans, Ruud, and Hanspeter Kriesi. 1997. "Citoyenneté, identité nationale et mobilisation de l'extrême droite: Une comparaison entre la France, l'Allemagne, les Pays-Bas et la Suisse." In *Sociologie des nationalismes,* edited by Pierre Birnbaum, 295–324. Paris: PUF.

Koopmans, Ruud, and Paul Statham, eds. 2000a. *Challenging Immigration and Ethnic Relations Politics: Comparative European Perspectives.* Oxford: Oxford University Press.

———. 2000b. "Challenging the Liberal Nation-State? Postnationalism, Multiculturalism, and the Collective Claims-Making of Migrants and Ethnic Minorities in Britain and Germany." In *Challenging Immigration and Ethnic Relations: Comparative European Perspectives,* edited by Ruud Koopmans and Paul Statham, 189–232. Oxford: Oxford University Press.

———. 2000c. "Migration and Ethnic Relations as a Field of Political Contention: An Opportunity Structure Approach." In *Challenging Immigration and Ethnic Relations Politics: Comparative European Perspectives,* edited by Ruud Koopmans and Paul Statham, 13–56. Oxford: Oxford University Press.

———. 2003. "How National Citizenship Shapes Transnationalism: Migrant and Minority Claims-Making in Germany, Great Britain and the Netherlands." In *Toward Assimilation and Citizenship: Immigrants in Liberal Nation-States,* edited by Christian Joppke and Ewa Morawska, 195–238. Basinstoke, UK: Palgrave Macmillan.

Koopmans, Ruud, Paul Statham, Marco Giugni, and Florence Passy. 2005. *Contested Citizenship: Immigration and Cultural Diversity in Europe.* Minneapolis: University of Minnesota Press.

Koslowski, Rey. 2001. "Personal Security and State Sovereignty in a Uniting Europe." In *Controlling a New Migration World,* edited by Virginie Guiraudon and Christian Joppke, 99–120. London: Routledge.

Kramer, Jane. 2005. "Difference." *New Yorker,* November 21, 41–42.

———. 2006 "The Dutch Model." *New Yorker,* April 3, 60–67.

Krasner, Stephen. 1982. "Structural Causes and Regime Consequences: Regimes as Intervening Variables," *International Organization,* 36 (2): 185–205.

Kraus, Neil, and Todd Swanstrom. 2001. "Minority Mayors and the Hollow-Prize Problem." *PS* 34 (1): 99–105.

Kriesi, Hanspeter. 1995. "The Political Opportunity Structure of New Social Movements: Its Impact on Their Mobilization." In *The Politics of Social Protest: Comparative Perspectives on States and Social Movements,* edited by J. Craig Jenkins and Bert Klandermans, 167–98. Minneapolis: University of Minnesota Press.

Kriesi, Hanspeter, Ruud Koopmans, Jan Willem Duyvendak, and Marco Giugni. 1995. *New Social Movements in Western Europe: A Comparative Analysis.* Minneapolis: University of Minnesota Press.

Kullberg, Jeanet. 2007. "Fysieke en Sociale Kwaliteit van Wonen in en Buiten Concentratiewijken." In *Jaarrapport Integratie 2007,* edited by Jaco Dagevos and Mérove Gijsberts, 192–229. The Hague: Sociaal en Cultureel Planbureau.

Kymlicka, William. 1995. *Multicultural Citizenship: A Liberal Theory of Minority Rights.* Oxford: Clarendon Press.

———. 2001. *Politics in the Vernacular: Nationalism, Multiculturalism and Citizenship.* New York: Oxford University Press.

Kymlicka, William, and Keith Banting, eds. 2006. *Multiculturalism and the Welfare State: Recognition and Redistribution in Contemporary Democracies.* New York: Oxford University Press.

Laborde, Cécile. 2005. "Secular Philosophy and Muslim Headscarves in Schools." *Journal of Political Philosophy* 13 (3): 305–29.

Lacomba, Joan. 2004. *Migraciones y Desarrollo en Marruecos.* Madrid: Catarata.

Lacroix, Thomas. 2005. *Les Réseaux Marocains du Développement: Géographie du Transnational et Politiques du territorial.* Paris: Presses de Sciences Politiques.

Lafleur, Jean-Michel. 2005. *Le transnationalisme politique: Pouvoir des communautés immigrées dans leurs pays d'accueil et pays d'origine.* Louvain-la-Neuve: Academia Bruylant.

Lahav, Gallya. 1997. "Ideological and Party Constraints on Immigration Attitudes in Europe." *Journal of Common Market Studies* 35 (1): 377–406.

——. 2004a. *Immigration and Politics in the New Europe: Reinventing Borders.* Cambridge, UK: Cambridge University Press.

——. 2004b. "Public Opinion toward Immigration in the European Union: Does It Matter?" *Comparative Political Studies* 37 (10): 1151–83.

——. 2005. "The Migration, Security and Civil Rights Trilemma in the United States and Europe." Discussion paper for the RSCAS, Schuman Center, European University Institute, October.

——. Forthcoming. "Immigration Policy as Counter-Terrorism: The Effects of Security on Migration and Border Control in the European Union." In *Counter-Terrorism and Its Consequences,* edited by Martha Crenshaw. New York: Russell Sage Foundation.

Lahav, Gallya, and Anthony Messina. 2005. "The Limits of a European Immigration Policy: Elite Opinion and Agendas within the European Parliament." *Journal of Common Market Studies* 43 (4): 851–75.

Lahav, Gallya, Anthony Messina, and Joseph-Paul Vasquez III. 2007. "The Immigration-Security Nexus: A View from the European Parliament." Paper prepared for the EUSA Tenth Biennial International Conference, Montreal, Canada, May 17–19.

Lai, Eric, and Dennis Arguelles. 2003. "Introduction." In *The New Face of Asian Pacific America: Numbers, Diversity, and Change in the 21st Century,* edited by Eric Lai and Dennis Arguelles, 1–4. San Francisco: Asian Week.

Laubenthal, Barbara. 2007. "The Emergence of Pro-Regularization Movements in Western Europe." *International Migration* 45 (3): 101–33.

Lavenex, Sandra. 2005. "Internationalisation as Externalisation: The Foreign Policy of European Immigration Control." Paper presented at the NYU EUI Conference on an Immigration Policy for Europe. Florence, Italy, March 13–15.

Lavenex, Sandra, and Emek Uçarer. 2002. *Migration and the Externalities of European Integration.* Lanham, Md.: Lexington Books.

Lavenex, Sandra, and William Wallace. 2005. "Justice and Home Affairs: Towards a 'European Public Order'?" In *Policy Making in the European Union,* edited by Helen Wallace, William Wallace, and Mark Pollack, 5th ed., 812–33. Oxford: Oxford University Press.

Lefebvre, Henri. 1991. *The Production of Space.* Trans. Donald Nicholson-Smith. Oxford: Blackwell.

Legomsky, Stephen. 2005. *Immigration and Refugee Law and Policy.* 4th ed. Westbury, N.Y.: Foundation Press.

Leighley, Jan. 2001. *Strength in Numbers? The Political Mobilization of Racial and Ethnic Minorities.* Princeton, N.J.: Princeton University Press.

Leiken, Robert. 2005a. "Europe's Angry Muslims." *Foreign Affairs* 84 (4): 120–35.

——. 2005b. "Europe's Mujahideen: Where Mass Immigration Meets Global Terrorism." Center for Immigration Studies, Washington, D.C. Available at: http://www.cis.org/articles/2005/back405. html.

Le Lohé, Michel. 1998. "Ethnic Minority Participation and Representation in the British Electoral System." In *Race and British Electoral Politics,* edited by Shamit Saggar, 73–95. London: Routledge.

Leonard, Mark. 1997. *Britain™: Renewing Our Identity.* London: Demos.

Leuthold, Ruedi, and Christian Aeberhard. 2002. "Der Fall Emmen." *Das Magazin, no. 20,* 18–31.

Levine, Richard, and Carlyle Douglas. 1981. "Hartford Speaks More Clearly on Second Try." *New York Times,* October 18, sec. 4, 5.

Levitt, Peggy. 2001. *The Transnational Villagers.* Berkeley: University of California Press.

———. 2003. "'Keeping Feet in Both Worlds': Transnational Practices and Immigrant Incorporation." In *Toward Assimilation and Citizenship: Immigrants in Liberal Nation-States,* edited by Christian Joppke and Ewa Morawska, 177–94. New York: Palgrave Macmillan.

Lewis, Bernard. 2003. *What Went Wrong? The Clash between Islam and Modernity in the Middle East.* New York: HarperCollins.

Lewis Mumford Center for Comparative Urban and Regional Research. 2002. *Separate and Unequal: The Neighborhood Gap for Blacks and Hispanics in Metropolitan America.* Albany: State University of New York Press.

Lewis, Philip. 1994. *Islamic Britain: Religion, Politics, and Identity among British Muslims.* London: I. B. Tauris.

Liang, Zai. 1994. "On the Measurement of Naturalization." *Demography* 31 (3): 525–48.

Liberatore, Angela, 2005. "Balancing Security and Democracy: The Politics of Biometric Identification in the European Union." EUI Working Paper RSCAS no. 2005/30. Badia Fiesolana, San Domenico di Fiesole (FI).

Lien, Pei-te. 2001. *The Making of Asian America through Political Participation.* Philadelphia: Temple University Press.

Lien, Pei-te, M. Margaret Conway, and Janelle Wong. 2004. *The Politics of Asian Americans: Diversity and Community.* New York: Routledge.

Lijphart, Arend. 1968. *The Politics of Accommodation: Pluralism and Democracy in the Netherlands.* Berkeley: University of California Press.

Lind, Michael. 1995. *The Next American Nation: The New Nationalism and the Fourth American Revolution.* New York: Free Press.

Linder, Wolf. 1998. *Swiss Democracy: Possible Solutions to Conflict in Multicultural Societies.* 2nd ed. Houndmills, UK: Macmillan.

Lobo, Arun Peter, and Joseph Salvo. 2005. *The Newest New Yorkers, 2000: Immigrant New York in the New Millennium.* New York: New York City Department of City Planning.

Logan, John, and John Mollenkopf. 2003. *People and Politics in America's Big Cities: The Challenges to Urban Democracy.* New York: Drum Major Institute for Public Policy and the Century Foundation.

Lovato, Roberto. 2007. "Will Latinos Continue Moving Democratic?" *Public Eye,* April 3. Available at: http://www.alternet.org/story/49924/.

Lübbe, Hermann. 2004. *Modernisierungsgewinner Religion, Geschichtssinn, direkte Demokratie und Moral.* Munich: Fink.

Lucassen, Leo. 2005. *The Immigrant Threat: The Integration of Old and New Migrants in Western Europe since 1850.* Urbana: University of Illinois Press.

Luther, Kurt Richard. 2003. "The Self-Destruction of a Right-Wing Populist Party? The Austrian Parliamentary Election of 2002." *West European Politics* 26 (2): 136–52.

Lyon, David. 2004. "Globalizing Surveillance: Comparative and Sociological Perspectives." *International Sociology* 19 (2): 135–49.

Ma, Ying. 2002. "China's America Problem." *Policy Review* 111 (February–March): 43–57.

Macchiarola, Frank, and Joseph Diaz. 1993. "Minority Political Empowerment in New York City: Beyond the Voting Rights Act." *Political Science Quarterly* 108 (1): 37–57.

MacDonald, Heather. 2004. "The Illegal-Alien Crime Wave: Why Can't Our Immigration Authorities Deport the Hordes of Illegal Felons in Our Cities?" *City Journal* (winter). Available at: http://www.city-journal.org/printable.php?id=1204.

Macpherson of Cluny, Sir William. 1999. *The Stephen Lawrence Inquiry.* London: Stationery Office.

Mahnig, Hans, and Andreas Wimmer. 2003. "Integration without Immigrant Policy: The Case of Switzerland." In *The Integration of Immigrants in European Societies: National Differences and Trends of Convergence,* edited by Friedrich Heckmann and Dominique Schnapper, 135–64. Stuttgart: Lucius & Lucius.

Mangaliman, Jessie. 2006. "Clergy Leading Call for Human Immigrant Laws." *San Jose Mercury News,* April 2, A1.

Mangaliman, Jessie, and Joe Rodriguez. 2006. "Immigrants Movement Growing: Many See New Chapter in Civil Rights Struggle." *San Jose Mercury News,* April 12, A1.

Manhattan Institute for Policy Research. 2005. "Earned Legalization and Increased Border Security Is Key to Immigration Reform According to Republican Voters: New Poll." October 17. Available at: http://www.manhattan-institute.org/html/immigration_pol_pr.htm.

Marable, Manning. 1994. "Building Coalitions among Communities of Color." In *Blacks, Latinos, and Asians in Urban America,* edited by James Jennings, 29–44. New York: Praeger.

March, James, and Johan Olsen. 1984. "The New Institutionalism: Organizational Factors in Political Life." *American Political Science Review* 78 (3): 734–49.

Marcus, Jonathan. 1995. *The National Front and French Politics: The Resistible Rise of Jean-Marie Le Pen.* London: Macmillan.

Maréchal, Brigitte. 2002. *A Guidebook on Islam and Muslims in the Wide Contemporary Europe.* Louvain-a-la-Neuve: Academia Bruylant.

Martiniello, Marco. 1992. *Leadership et pouvoir dans les communautés d'origine immigrée: L'Exemple d'une communauté ethnique en Belgique.* Paris: L'Harmattan.

——. 1993. "Pour une sociologie politique de la situation post-migratoire en Belgique." In *Migrations et minorités ethniques dans l'espace européen,* edited by Marco Martiniello and Marc Poncelet, 167–86. Brussels: De Boeck Université.

——. 1997. "Quelle participation politique?" In *La Belgique et ses immigres: Les politiques manquées,* edited by Collectif, 101–20. Brussels: De Boeck Université.

——. 1998. "Les immigrés et les minorités ethniques dans les institutions politiques: Ethnicisation des systèmes politiques européens ou renforcement de la démocratie?" *Revue européenne des migrations internationales* 14 (2): 9–17.

——. 2000. "The Residential Concentration and Political Participation of Immigrants in European Cities." In *Minorities in European Cities: The Dynamics of Social Integration and Social Exclusion at the Neighborhood Level,* edited by Sophie Body-Gendrot and Marco Martiniello, 119–28. London: Macmillan.

——. 2005. "The State, the Market and Cultural Diversity." In *Middle East and North African Immigrants in Europe,* edited by Ahmed Al-Shahi and Richard Lawless, 29–42. London: Routledge.

——. 2007. "Belges d'origine etrangère dans les systèmes politiques régional et communal bruxellois (1994–2000)." In *Bruxelles ville ouverte: Immigration et diversité culturelle au cœur de l'Europe,* edited by Pascal Delwit, Andrea Rea, and Marc Swyngedouw, 163–80. Paris: L'Harmattan.

Marty, Martin. 2002. "Religious Fundamentalism: Cultural Concerns." In *International Encyclopedia of the Social and Behavioral Sciences,* edited by Neil Smelser and Paul Baltes, 13:119–123. New York: Pergamon.

Massey, Douglas. 2006. "The Wall That Keeps Illegal Workers In." *New York Times,* April 4. Available at: www.nytimes.com/2006/04/04/opinion/04massey.

Massey, Douglas, Jorge Durand, and Nolan Malone. 2002. *Beyond Smoke and Mirrors: Mexican Immigration in an Era of Economic Integration.* New York: Russell Sage Foundation.

McAdam, Douglas. 1982. *Political Process and the Development of Black Insurgency, 1930–1970.* Chicago: University of Chicago Press.

McCaffrey, Angela. 2005. "Hmong Veterans Naturalization Act: Precedent for Waiving the English Language Requirement for the Elderly." *Georgetown Immigration Law Journal* 19:495–550.

McClain, Paula, and Steven Tauber. 2001. "Racial Minority Group Relations in a Multiracial Society." In *Governing American Cities: Interethnic Coalitions, Competition, and Conflict,* edited by Michael Jones-Correa, 111–36. New York: Russell Sage Foundation.

McDonough, Kevin, and Walter Feinberg, eds. 2003. *Citizenship and Education in Liberal-Democratic Societies: Teaching for Cosmopolitan Values and Collective Identities.* New York: Oxford University Press.

McKee, Clyde. 2000. "Mike Peters and the Legacy of Public Leadership in Hartford, Connecticut." In *Governing Middle-Sized Cities: Studies in Mayoral Leadership,* edited by James Bowers and Wilbur Rich, 27–46. Boulder, Colo.: Lynne Rienner.

McLaren, Lauren. 2001. "Immigration and the New Politics of Inclusion and Exclusion in the European Union: The Effects of Elites and EU on Individual-Level Opinions Regarding European and non-European Immigrants." *European Journal of Political Research* 39 (1): 81–108.

McMahon, Robert. 2006. "Interview with Tom Tancredo: Tough Immigration Reform Essential to Maintain U.S. Identity." Council on Foreign Relations. July 24. Available at: http://www.cfr.org/publication/11141/tancredo.html

McNickle, Christopher. 1993. *To Be Mayor of New York: Ethnic Politics in the City.* New York: Columbia University Press.

Mearns, Andrew. 1883. The Bitter Cry of Outcast London: An Inquiry into the Condition of the Abject Poor. London: J. Clarke.

Meer, Nasar, and Tariq Modood. Forthcoming."The Multicultural State We Are In: Muslims, 'Multiculture' and the 'Civic Re-balancing' of British Multiculturalism." *Political Studies.*

Mégret, Bruno. 1996. *L'alternative nationale. Les priorités du Front national.* Paris: Éditions nationales.

Meier, Kenneth, and Joseph Stewart. 1991. "Cooperation and Conflict in Multiracial School Districts." *Journal of Politics* 53 (4): 1123–33.

Meijnen, Wim, ed. 2003. *Onderwijsachterstanden in Basisscholen.* (NWO/BOPO Onderzoek.) Leuven: Garant.

Meinecke, Friedrich. 1919. *Weltbürgertum und Nationalstaat: Studien zur Genesis des deutschen Nationalstaates.* Berlin: R. Oldenbourg.

Meliss, Nadine, and Erik Magnus Sund. 2003. "Dänemark." In *Handbuch der Ausländer—und Zuwanderungspolitik: Von Afghanistan bis Zypern,* edited by Wolfgang Gieler, 119–28. Münster: LIT-Verlag.

Messina, Anthony. 1989. *Race and Party Competition in Britain.* Oxford: Clarendon Press.

——. 2006. "The Political Incorporation of Immigrants in Europe: Trends and Implications." In *The Migration Reader: Exploring Politics and Policies,* edited by Anthony Messina and Gallya Lahav, 470–93. Boulder, Colo.: Lynne Rienner.

Mexican American Legal Defense and Educational Fund. 2004. "MALDEF and LULAC Rebuke Samuel Huntington's Theories on Latino Immigrants and Call on America to Reaffirm Its Commitment to Equal Opportunity and Democracy." April 23. Available at: http://www.maldef.org/publications/pdf/MALDEF_LULAC_Statement.pdf.

Migration Policy Institute. 2006. "Migration Information Source: The Second Generation in the United States." Migration Policy Institute. Available at: http://www.migrationinformation.org/Feature/display.cfm?id=446#7.

Miles, Robert. 1982. *Racism and Migrant Labour.* London: Routledge and Kegan Paul.

——. 1986. "Labour Migration, Racism, and Capital Accumulation in Western Europe since 1945: An Overview." *Capital and Class* 28 (spring): 49–86.

Miles, Robert, and Annie Phizacklea. 1977. "Class, Race, Ethnicity and Political Action." *Political Studies* 25 (4): 491–507.

Miller, Gary. 2005. "How Much Do Illegal Aliens Cost U.S. Taxpayers?" July 12. Available at: http://www.house.gov/garymiller/IllegalsCost2005.html.

Miller, John. 1998. *The Unmaking of Americans: How Multiculturalism Has Undermined the Assimilation Ethic.* New York: Free Press.

Miller, Mark. 1981. *Foreign Workers in Western Europe: An Emerging Political Force.* New York: Praeger.

——. 1982. "The Political Impact of Foreign Labor: A Re-evaluation of the Western European Experience." *International Migration Review* 16 (1): 27–60.

——. 1999. "Political Participation and Representation of Noncitizens." In *Migration and Social Cohesion,* edited by Steven Vertovec, 187–202. Cheltenham, UK: E. Elgar.

Minkenberg, Michael. 1998. *Die neue radikale Rechte im Vergleich: USA, Frankreich, Deutschland.* Opladen/Wiesbaden: Westdeutscher Verlag.

——. 2000. "The Renewal of the Radical Right: Between Modernity and Anti-Modernity" in *Government and Opposition* 35 (2): 170–88.

——. 2001. "The Radical Right in Public Office: Agenda-Setting and Policy Effects." *West European Politics* 24 (4): 1–21.

——. 2002. "The New Radical Right in the Political Process: Interaction Effects in France and Germany." In *Shadows over Europe: The Development and Impact of the Extreme Right in Western Europe,* edited by Martin Schain, Aristide Zolberg, and Patrick Hossay, 245–68. New York: Palgrave Macmillan.

——. 2003a. "The West European Radical Right as a Collective Actor: Modeling the Impact of Cultural and Structural Variables on Party Formation and Movement Mobilization." *Comparative European Politics* 1 (2): 149–70.

——. 2003b. "The Politics of Citizenship in the New Republic." *West European Politics* 26 (4): 219–40.

Minkenberg, Michael. 2007. "Democracy and Religion: Theoretical and Empirical Observations on the Relationship between Christianity, Islam and Liberal Democracy." *Journal of Ethnic and Migration Studies* 33 (6): 887–909.

——. 2008. "Religious Legacies and the Politics of Multiculturalism: A Comparative Analysis of Integration Policies in Western Democracies." In *Immigration, Integration and Security: America and Europe in Comparative Perspective,* edited by Ariane Chebel d'Appollonia and Simon Reich, 44–66. Pittsburgh, Pa.: University of Pittsburgh Press.

Minkenberg, Michael, and Pascal Perrineau. 2005. "La Droite Radicale: Divisions et Contrasts." In *Le vote europeen 2004–2005.* edited by Pascal Perrineau, 77–103. Paris: Presses de Sciences Politiques.

Minkenberg, Michael, and Martin Schain. 2003. "The Front National in Context: French and European Dimensions." In *Right-Wing Extremism in the Twenty-First Century,* edited by Peter Merkl and Leonard Weinberg, 161–90. London: Frank Cass.

Minnite, Lorraine C. 2005. "Outside the Circle: The Impact of 9/11 on Immigrant Communities in New York City," In *Contentious City: The Politics of Recovery in New York City,* edited by John Mollenkopf, 165–204. New York: Russell Sage Foundation.

Mishara, Sangay. 2006. "Transnationalism and Citizenship: South Asian Immigrants in the U.S." Paper presented at the annual meeting of the Western Political Science Association, Albuquerque, New Mexico.

Modood, Tariq. 1990. "British Asian Muslims and the Rushdie Affair." *Political Quarterly* 61 (2): 143–60.

——. 1994. "Political Blackness and British Asians." *Sociology* 28 (4): 859–76.

——. 1998. "Multiculturalism, Secularism and the State." *Critical Review of International Social and Political Philosophy* 1 (3): 79–97.

——. 2005a. "Ethnicity and Political Mobilisation in Britain." In *Ethnicity, Social Mobility and Public Policy: Comparing the USA and UK,* edited by Glenn Loury, Tariq Modood, and Steven Teles, 457–74. Cambridge, UK: Cambridge University Press.

——. 2005b. *Multicultural Politics: Racism, Ethnicity and Muslims in Britain.* Minneapolis: University of Minnesota Press.

——. 2007. *Multiculturalism: A Civic Idea.* Cambridge, UK: Polity Press.

Modood, Tariq, Richard Berthoud, Jane Lakey, James Nazroo, Patten Smith, Satnam Virdee, and Sharon Beishon. 1997. *Ethnic Minorities in Britain: Diversity and Disadvantage.* London: Policy Studies Institute.

Modood, Tariq, and Riva Kaṣtoryano. 2005. "Secularism and the Accommodation of Muslims in Europe." In *Multiculturalism, Muslims and Citizenship: A European Approach,* edited by Tariq Modood, Anna Triandafyllidou, and Ricard Zapata-Barrero, 162–78. New York: Routledge.

Modood, Tariq, Anna Triandafyllidou, and Ricard Zapata-Barrero, eds. 2005. *Multiculturalism, Muslims and Citizenship: A European Approach.* New York: Routledge.

Mollenkopf, John H. 1992. *A Phoenix in the Ashes: The Rise and Fall of the Koch Coalition in New York City Politics.* Princeton, N.J.: Princeton University Press.

——. 2003. "New York: (Still?) The Great Anomaly." In *Racial Politics in American Cities,* edited by Rufus Browning, Dale Rogers Marshall, and David Tabb, 3rd ed., 115–41. New York: Longman.

——, ed. 2005. *Contentious City: The Politics of Recovery in New York City.* New York: Russell Sage Foundation.

——. 2008. "School Is Out: The Case of New York City." *Urban Affairs Review* 44 (2): 239–65.

Mollenkopf, John, David Olson, and Timothy Ross. 2001. "Immigrant Political Participation in New York and Los Angeles." In *Governing Cities: Inter-Ethnic Coalitions, Competition, and Conflict,* edited by Michael Jones-Correa, 158–80. New York: Russell Sage Foundation.

Monar, Jörg. 2005. "Justice and Home Affairs." *Journal of Common Market Studies* 43 (suppl. 1): 131–46.

Money, Jeannette. 1995. "Two-Dimensional Aliens: Immigration Policy as a Two-Dimensional Issue Space." Paper presented at the annual meeting of the American Political Science Association, Chicago.

Montagu, Ashley, ed. 1964. *The Concept of Race.* New York: Free Press of Glencoe.

Montejano, David. 1987. *Anglos and Mexicans in the Making of Texas, 1836–1986.* Austin: University of Texas Press.

Mooney, Margarita, and Deborah Rivas-Drake. 2008. "Colleges Need to Recognize, and Serve, the 3 Kinds of Latino Students." *Chronicle of Higher Education*. 54 (29): A37–A39.

Morawska, Ewa. 1994. "In Defense of the Assimilation Model." *Journal of American Ethnic History* 13 (2): 76–87.

Morphet, Janice. 2007. "Embracing Multiculturalism: The Case of London." In *Migration and Cultural Inclusion in the European City*, edited by William Neill and Hans-Uve Schwedler, 167–78. New York: Palgrave Macmillan.

Moscoso, Eunice. 2006. "Illegal Immigrant Laws Challenged." *Atlanta Journal—Constitution*, November 27, A3.

Moser, Urs, and Simone Berweger. 2003. *Lehrplan und Leistungen: Thematischer Bericht der Erhebung PISA 2000*. Neuchâtel: Bundesamt für Statistik.

Mudde, Cas. 2007. *Populist Radical Right Parties in Europe*. Cambridge, UK: Cambridge University Press.

Münz, Rainer. 2005. *Europe: Population and Migration in 2005*. Washington, D.C.: Migration Information Source. Available at: http://www.migrationinformation.org/feature/print.cfm?ID=402.

Murphey, Rhoads. 2001. *East Asia: A New History*. 2nd ed. New York: Longman.

Murtagh, Brendan, Michael Murray, and Karen Keaveney. 2007. "Participatory Citizenship through Cultural Dialogue." In *Migration and Cultural Inclusion in the European City*, edited by William Neill and Hans-Uve Schwedler, 88–100. New York: Palgrave Macmillan.

Muslim Parliament of Great Britain. 1992. *Race Relations and Muslims in Great Britain: A Discussion Paper*. London: Muslim Parliament.

*The Nation*. 2006. "Immigrants and Us." April 11. Available at: http://www.thenation.com/doc/20060424/editors.

National Association of Latino Elected and Appointed Officials (NALEO). 2006. "Newcomers Eager to Learn English Face Waiting Lines across the Nation." October 6. Available at: http://www.naleo.org.

National Council of La Raza (NCLR). 2006a. "Latino Organizations Express Disappointment That President Bush Signs the Secure Fence Act." News Release. October 26.

——. 2006b. "National Latino Organizations Express Concern about Recent Immigration Raids." News Release. December 21. Available at: http://www.nclr.org/content/news/detail/43451/.

——. 2006c. "NCLR Joins 'We Are America Alliance.'" News Release. May 11.

——. 2006d. "NHLA Launches 'It Starts with You' Campaign." News Release. September 29.

National Immigration Forum. 2007. "While Debate Rages, the Public Continues to Support Realistic Immigration Solutions." December 10. Available at: http://www.immigrationforum.org/documents/PressRoom/PublicOpinion/2007/PollingSummary0407.pdf.

Navarette, Ruben. 2006. "Commentary: Immigration Hearings 'Cynical and Cowardly.'" CNN.com. July 6. Available at: http://cnn.com/2006/US/07/06/navarrette.immigration/index.html.

Necef, Mehmet. 2001. "Renegades and the Remote-Controlled: The Turkish Debate on the National Allegiance of the Turkish Immigrants in Germany." In *Beyond Integration: Challenges of Belonging in Diaspora and Exile*, edited by Maja Frykman, 116–40. Lund: Nordic Academic Press.

Neidhart, Leonhard. 1970. *Plebiszit und pluralitäre Demokratie: Eine Analyse der Funktion des schweizerischen Gesetzesreferendums*. Bern: Francke.

*New York Times*. 2001. "Hartford's Latinos Revel in Securing Mayor's Office." November 18, A35.

Ngai, Mae. 2004. *Impossible Subjects: Illegal Aliens and the Making of Modern America*. Princeton, N.J.: Princeton University Press.

Niessen, Jan, Maria Jose Peiro, and Yongmi Schibel. 2005. *Civic Citizenship and Immigrant Inclusion*. Brussels: Migration Policy Group.

Nightingale, Carl. 2003. "A Tale of Three Global Ghettos: How Arnold Hirsch Helps Us Internationalize U.S. Urban History." *Journal of Urban History* 29 (3): 257–71.

Noel, Don. 1996. "Harsh Laws May Enfranchise an Ethnic Bloc." *Hartford Courant*, November 13, A17.

Norris, Pippa. 2005. *Radical Right: Voters and Parties in the Electoral Market*. Cambridge, UK: Cambridge University Press.

North, David. 1987. "The Long Grey Welcome: A Study of the American Naturalization Program." *International Migration Review* 21 (2): 311–26.

*NRC-Handelsblad.* 2006. "Politieke partijen en hun etnische uithangborden." October 7. available at: http://www.nrc.nl/opinie/hoofdartikelen/article1730561.ece/Politieke_partijen_en_hun_etnische_uithangborden**

Nyberg-Sørensen, Ninna, Nick van Hear, and Paul Engberg-Pedersen. 2002. *The Migration-Development Nexus: Evidence and Policy Options.* IOM Migration Research Series. Geneva: International Organization for Migration.

Odé, Arend. 2002. *Ethnic-Cultural and Socio-economic Integration in the Netherlands: A Comparative Study of Mediterranean and Caribbean Minority Groups.* Assen: Van Gorcum.

Oliver, J. Eric, and Tali Mendelberg. 2000. "Reconsidering the Environmental Determinants of White Racial Attitudes." *American Journal of Political Science* 44 (3): 574–89.

Oliver, J. Eric, and Janelle Wong. 2003. "Intergroup Prejudice in Multiethnic Settings." *American Journal of Political Science* 47 (4): 567–82.

Oliver, Melvin, and James Johnson. 1984. "Interethnic Conflict in an Urban Ghetto." *Research in Social Movements, Conflicts, and Change* 6: 57–94.

Ong, Nhu-Ngoc, and David Meyer. 2004. "Protest and Political Incorporation: Vietnamese American Protests, 1975–2001." University of California Irvine, Center for the Study of Democracy.

Ong, Paul, Edna Bonacich, and Lucie Cheng. 1994. "The Political Economy of Capitalist Restructuring and the New Asian Immigration." In *The New Asian Immigration in Los Angeles and Global Restructuring,* edited by Paul Ong, Edna Bonacich, and Lucie Cheng, 3–38. Philadelphia: Temple University Press.

Ong, Paul, and David Lee. 2001. "Changing of the Guard? The Emerging Immigrant Majority in Asian American Politics." In *Asian Americans and Politics: Perspectives, Experiences, Prospects,* edited by Gordon Chang, 153–72. Stanford: Stanford University Press.

Ong, Paul, and Don Nakanishi. 2003. "Becoming Citizens, Becoming Voters: The Naturalization and Political Participation of Asian Pacific Immigrants." In *Asian American Politics: Law, Participation and Policy,* edited by Don Nakanishi and James Lai, 113–33. Lanham, Md.: Rowman and Littlefield.

Onishi, Norimitsu. 2005. "In Japan, a Disconnected Democracy." *International Herald Tribune.* September 8. Available at: http://www.iht.com/articles/2005/09/07/news/japan.php

Open Doors. 2005. "Open Doors: Report on International Educational Exchange." Available at: http://opendoors.iienetwork.org/?p=69689.

Oppenheimer, Andres. 2006. "The Oppenheimer Report: Hispanics Should Say 'Gracias' to Anti-Latin Zealots." *Miami Herald,* April 13, 12A.

Organisation for Economic Co-operation and Development (OECD) 1992, 1999. *SOPEMI Report: Trends in International Migration.* Paris: OECD.

——. 2004. *Learning for Tomorrow's World: First Results from PISA 2003.* Paris: OECD.

——. 2006. "PISA 2006 Science Competencies for Tomorrow's World." Available at: http://www.pisa.oecd.org/dataoecd/30/62/39704344.xls.

——. 2007. "International Migration Data 2007." Available at: http://www.oecd.org/document/3/0,3343,en_2825_494553_39336771_1_1_1_1,00.html.

Orjuela, Carmilla. 2007. "War, Peace and the Sri Lankan Diaspora: Complications and Implications for Policy." In *Diasporas, Armed Conflicts and Peacebuilding in Their Homelands,* edited by Ashok Swain, 61–72. Uppsala: Uppsala University.

Østergaard-Nielsen, Eva. 2001. "Transnational Political Practices and the Receiving State: Turks and Kurds in Germany and the Netherlands." *Global Networks* 1 (3): 261–82.

——. 2002. *Politik over Grænser: Tyrkeres og Kurderes Engagement i det Politiske Liv i Hjemlandet.* Århus: Magtudredningen, Århus University.

——. 2003a. "The Democratic Deficit of Diaspora Politics: Turkish Cypriots in Britain and the Cyprus Issue." *Journal of Ethnic and Migration Studies* 29 (4): 683–700.

——. 2003b. "International Migration and Sending Countries: Key Issues and Themes." In *International Migration and Sending Countries: Perceptions, Policies and Transnational Relations,* edited by Eva Østergaard-Nielsen, 3–30. Basingstoke, Palgrave Macmillan.

——. 2003c. "The Politics of Migrants' Transnational Practices." *International Migration Review* 37 (3): 760–86.

——. 2003d. *Transnational Politics: Turks and Kurds in Germany.* London: Routledge.

———. 2008. "Dual Citizenship: Policy Trends and Political Participation in the European Union." Policy Paper for the European Parliament, Committee for Constitutional Affairs, Brussels.

Özdemir, Cem. 1997. *Ich bin Inländer: Ein Anatolischer Schwabe im Bundestag*. Munich: Deutscher Taschenbuch Verlag.

Pachon, Harry. 1987. "An Overview of Citizenship in the Hispanic Community." *International Migration Review* 21 (2): 299–310.

Pachon, Harry, and Louis DeSipio. 1994. *New Americans by Choice: Political Perspectives of Latino Immigrants*. Boulder, Colo.: Westview Press.

Pantoja, Adrian. 2005. "Transnational Ties and Immigrant Political Incorporation: The Case of Dominicans in Washington Heights, New York." *International Migration* 43 (4): 123–46.

Pantoja, Adrian, and Sarah Gershon. 2006. "Political Orientations and Naturalization among Latino and Latina Immigrants." *Social Science Quarterly* 87 (suppl.): 1171–87.

Park, Julie. 2003. The Socioeconomic Progress of Southeast Asian Immigrants across the United States. Ph.D. dissertation, University of Southern California.

Park, Robert E. 1928. "Human Migration and the Marginal Man," *American Journal of Sociology* 33 (6): 881–93.

Parliamentary Committee of Inquiry. 2004. *Bruggen Bouwen*, T.K. 28689, 11 2003–2004. The Hague: Sdu.

Passel, Jeffrey. 2004. *Mexican Immigration to the U.S.: The Latest Estimates*. Washington, D.C.: Migration Information Source. Available at: http://www.migrationinformation.org/feature/display.cfm?ID=208.

Passell, Peter, and D'Vera Cohn. 2008. *U.S. Population Projections: 2005–2050*. Washington, D.C: Pew Research Center.

Pastore, Ferrucio. 2005. "The European Union and the Fight against Terrorism." In *Is There a European Strategy against Terrorism? A Brief Assessment of Supra-National and National Response*, edited by Ferrucio Pastore, Jörg Friedrichs, and Alessandro Politi, 7–12. CeSPI Working Papers no. 12/2005. Rome: Centro Studidi Poliitica Internazionale.

Paugam, Serge. 1991. *La Disqualification sociale: Essai sur la nouvelle pauvreté*. Paris: Presses universitaires de France.

———. 2000. *Le Salarié de la précarité: Les nouvelles formes de l'intégration professionnelle*. Paris: Presses universitaires de France.

Peled, Yoav. 1992. "Ethnic Democracy and the Legal Construction of Citizenship: Arab Citizens of the Jewish State." *American Political Science Review* 86 (2): 432–43.

Pelinka, Anton. 2005. "Wenn Macht ohnmächtig Macht: Die rechtspopulisitsche FPÖ ist als Regierungspartei gescheitert." in *Das Parlament* no. 45 (November 7): 12.

Pels, Trees, and Marjan de Gruijter, eds. 2006. *Emancipatie van de tweede generatie: Keuzen en kansen in de levensloop van jonge moeders van Marokkaanse en Turkse afkomst*. Assen: Van Gorcum.

Penninx, Rinus. 1988. *Minderheidsvorming en emancipatie: Balans van kennisverwerving ten aanzien van immigranten en woonwagenbewoners, 1967–1987*. Alphen aan den Rijn: Samsom.

Penninx, Rinus, and Marcus Martiniello. 2004. "Integration Processes and Policies: State of the Art and Lessons." In *Citizenship in European Cities: Immigrants, Local Politics, and Integration Policies*, edited by Rinus Penninx, Karen Kraal, Marco Mariniello, and Steven Vertovec, 139–64. Aldershot, UK: Ashgate.

Penninx, Rinus, and Judith Roosblad, eds. 2000. *Trade Unions, Immigration, and Immigrants in Europe, 1960–1993: A Comparative Study of the Attitudes and Actions of Trade Unions in Seven West European Countries*. New York: Berghahn Books.

Perlmann, Joel, and Roger Waldinger. 1997. "Second Generation Decline? Children of Immigrants, Past and Present—A Reconsideration." *International Migration Review* 31 (4): 893–922.

Perrazzo, John. 2002. "Illegal Immigration and Terrorism." *Front Page Magazine*, December 18. Available at: http://www.frontpagemag.com/Articles/Printable.asp?ID=5147.

Perrineau, Pascal. 2005. "Does Lepenism Exist without Le Pen?" In *Political Survival of the Extreme Right*, edited by Xavier Casals, 21–34. Barcelona: Institut de Ciències Politiques i Socials.

Petaluma Argus-Courier. 2006. "Poll: Most Say Illegal Immigrants Are Criminals." April 12. Available at: http://www.arguscourier.com/news/news/lastweekquestion06412.html.

Pew Hispanic Center. 2006. "Hispanics in America: The Optimistic Immigrant." May 30. Available at: http://www.pewtrusts.org.

——. 2008. "Statistical Portrait of the Foreign-Born Population in the United States, 2006." Available at: http://pewhispanic.org/factsheets/factsheet.php?FactsheetID=36.

Pew Research Center. 2007. "Muslim Americans: Middle Class and Mostly Mainstream." Pew Research Center, Washington, D.C., May 22.

Phalet, Karen, and Iris Andriessen. 2003. "Acculturation, Motivation and Educational Attainment: A Contextual Model of Minority School Achievement." In *Integrating Immigrants in the Netherlands: Cultural versus Socio-economic Integration,* edited by Louk Hagendoorn, Justus Veenman, and Wilma Vollebergh, 145–73. Aldershot, UK: Ashgate.

Phalet, Karen, Claudia Van Lotringen, and Han Entzinger. 2000. *Islam in de Multiculturele Samenleving: Opvattingen van Jongeren in Rotterdam.* Utrecht: Utrecht University.

Phillips, Anne. 1995. *The Politics of Presence.* Oxford: Clarendon Press.

Phillips, Mike, and Trevor Phillips. 1998. *Windrush: The Irresistible Rise of Multi-racial Britain.* London: HarperCollins.

*Phyllis Schlafly Report.* 2001. "The Threat of Terrorism Is from Illegal Aliens." 35 (3). Available at: http://www.eagleforum.org/psr/2001/oct01/psroct01.shtml.

Pickus, Noah. 2005. *True Faith and Allegiance: Immigration and American Civic Nationalism.* Princeton, N.J.: Princeton University Press.

Pinderhughes, Dianne. 1987. *Race and Ethnicity in Chicago Politics: A Reexamination of Pluralist Theory.* Urbana: University of Illinois Press.

Pitkin, Hanna. 1967. *The Concept of Representation.* Berkeley: University of California Press.

PollingReport.com. 2008. "Immigration." January 31. Available at: http://www.pollingreport.com/immigration.htm.

Portes, Alejandro. 2001. "Introduction: The Debates and Significance of Immigrant Transnationalism." *Global Networks* 1 (3): 181–94.

Portes, Alejandro, and John Curtis. 1987. "Changing Flags: Naturalization and Its Determinants among Mexican Immigrants." *International Migration Review* 21 (2): 352–71.

Portes, Alejandro, Luis Guarnizo, and Patricia Landolt. 1999. "The Study of Transnationalism: Pitfalls and Promise of an Emergent Research Field." *Ethnic and Racial Studies* 22 (2): 217–37.

Portes, Alejandro, and Rafael Mozo. 1985. "The Political Adaptation Process of Cubans and Other Ethnic Minorities in the United States: A Preliminary Analysis." *International Migration Review* 19 (1): 35–63.

Portes, Alejandro, and Rubén Rumbaut. 1996. *Immigrant America: A Portrait.* Berkeley: University of California Press.

——. 2001. *Legacies: The Story of the Immigrant Second Generation.* Berkeley and New York: University of California Press and Russell Sage Foundation.

Portes, Alejandro, and Min Zhou. 1993. "The New Second Generation: Segmented Assimilation and Its Variants among Post-1965 Immigrant Youth." *Annals of the American Academy of Political and Social Sciences* 530 (1): 74–96.

Prantl, Heribert. 2005. "Mehr als nur ein Gewitter: Was die Rechtsaußen-Parteien Europas Verbindet und was sie Unterscheidet." *Das Parlament,* no. 45 (November 7): 1.

Preston, Julia. 2008. "Immigrant, Pregnant, Is Jailed under Pact." *New York Times,* July 20, A1.

Putnam, Robert. 2000. *Bowling Alone: The Collapse and Revival of American Community.* New York: Simon and Schuster.

——. 2007. "*E Pluribus Unum:* Diversity and Community in the Twenty-First Century; The 2006 Johan Skytte Prize Lecture." *Scandinavian Political Studies* 30 (2): 137–74.

Ramadan, Tariq. 2004. *Western Muslims and the Future of Islam.* Oxford: Oxford University Press.

Ramakrishnan, S. Karthick. 2005. *Democracy in Immigrant America: Changing Demographics and Political Participation.* Stanford: Stanford University Press.

Ramakrishnan, S. Karthick, and Irene Bloemraad, eds. 2008. *Civic Hopes and Political Realities: Community Organizations and Political Engagement among Immigrants in the United States and Abroad.* New York: Russell Sage Foundation.

Ramakrishnan, S. Karthick, and Thomas Espenshade. 2001. "Immigrant Incorporation and Political Participation in the United States." *International Migration Review* 35 (3): 870–909.

Ramakrishnan, S. Karthick, and Paul Lewis. 2005. *Immigrants and Local Governance: The View from City Hall.* San Francisco: Public Policy Institute of California.

Ramirez, Daniel M. 1979. "Legal Residents and Naturalization: A Pilot Study," October. Mexican American Legal Defense and Education Fund, Los Angeles.

Ramírez, Ricardo, and Luis Fraga. 2008. "Continuity and Change: Latino Political Incorporation in California since 1990." In *Racial and Ethnic Politics in California,* edited by Bruce Cain, Jaime Regalado, and Sandra Bass, vol. 3, 61–93. Berkeley: Berkeley Public Policy Press.

Raskin, Jamin. 1993. "Legal Aliens, Local Citizens: The Historical, Constitutional, and Theoretical Meanings of Alien Suffrage." *University of Pennsylvania Law Review* 141 (4): 1391–470.

Rasmussen, Søren. 2001. "Modstanden og det Nationale." In *Mødet med den Europæiske Jungle: National Strategi og Ientitet i Dansk Europapolitik 1945–2000,* edited by Den jyske Historiker, 96–112. Århus: Århus Universitet.

Rath, Jan. 1988a. "Mobilization of Ethnicity in Dutch Politics," in *Lost Illusions: Caribbean Minorities in Britain and the Netherlands,* edited by Malcolm Cross and Han Entzinger, 267–84. London: Routledge.

——. 1988b. "Political Action of Immigrants in the Netherlands: Class or Ethnicity?" *European Journal of Political Research* 16 (6): 623–44.

——. 1991. *Minorisering: De sociale constructie van "Etnische Minderheden."* Amsterdam: Sua Amsterdam.

Rath, Jan, Rinnus Pennix, Kees Groedendijk, and Astrid Meyer. 1999. "The Politics of Recognizing Religious Diversity in Europe: Social Reactions to the Institutionalization of Islam in the Netherlands, Belgium and Great Britain." *Netherlands Journal of Social Sciences* 35 (1): 53–70.

Rau, Johannes. *Frankfurter Rundschau,* January 23, 2004.

Renan, Ernest. 1993. *Che cosa è una nazione?* Rome: Donzelli.

Rijkschroeff, Rally, Jan Willem Duyvendak, and Trees Pels. 2004. *Bronnenonderzoek Integratiebeleid.* The Hague: SDU.

Rijkschroeff, Rally, Geert ten Dam, Jan Willem Duyvendak, Marjan de Gruijter, and Trees Pels. 2005. "Education Policies on Migrants and Minorities in the Netherlands: Success or Failure?" *Journal of Education Policy* 20 (4): 417–35.

Rimer, Sara, and Karen Arenson. 2004. "Top Colleges Take More Blacks, But Which Ones?" *New York Times,* June 24, A1.

Roberts, Geoffrey, and Patricia Hogwood. 2003. *The Politics Today Companion to West European Politics.* Manchester, UK: Manchester University Press.

Rogers, Reuel. 2004. "Race-Based Coalitions among Minority Groups: Afro-Caribbean Immigrants and African-Americans in New York City." *Urban Affairs Review* 39 (3): 283–317.

——. 2006. *Afro-Caribbean Immigrants and the Politics of Incorporation: Ethnicity, Exception, or Exit.* New York: Cambridge University Press.

——. n.d. "Institutions and Inter-Group Relations." Unpublished manuscript. Northwestern University, Department of Political Science.

Roller, Edeltraud. 1999. "Shrinking the Welfare State: Citizens' Attitudes towards Cuts in Social Spending in Germany in the 1990s." *German Politics* 8 (1): 21–39.

Rosenstone, Steven, and John Hansen. 1993. *Mobilization, Participation, and Democracy in America.* New York: Macmillan.

Roy, Olivier. 1992. *L'Échec de l'islam politique.* Paris: Seuil.

——. 2004. *Globalised Islam: The Search for a New Ummah.* New York: Columbia University Press.

Royce, Anya Peterson. 1982. *Ethnic Identity: Strategies of Diversity.* Bloomington: Indiana University Press.

Rucht, Dieter. 1994. *Modernisierung und neue soziale Bewegungen: Deutschland, Frankreich und USA im Vergleich.* Frankfurt: Campus.

Ruggie, John. 1982. "International Regimes, Transactions and Change: Embedded Liberalism in the Post-War Economic Order." *International Organization,* 36 (2): 379–415.

Rumbaut, Rubén, Roberto Gonzales, Golnaz Komaie, and Charlie V. Morgan. 2006. *Debunking the Myth of Immigrant Criminality: Imprisonment among First- and Second-Generation Young Men.* Washington, D.C.: Migration Information Source. Available at: http://contact.migrationpolicy.org/site/R?i=vhS06zFz8ttwehKjdrEprA.

Rydgren, Jens. 2004. "Explaining the Emergence of Radical Right-Wing Populist Parties: The Case of Denmark." *West European Politics* 27 (3): 474–502.

——. 2007. "The Sociology of the Radical Right." *Annual Review of Sociology* 33: 241–62.

Saggar, Shamit, ed. 1998a. "British South Asian Elites and Political Participation: Testing the Cultural Thesis." *Revue européenne des migrations internationales* 14 (2): 51–69.

——. 1998b. *Race and British Electoral Politics.* London: UCL Press.

Saggar, Shamit, and Andrew Geddes. 2000. "Negative and Positive Racialisation: Re-examining Ethnic Minority Political Representation in the UK." *Journal of Ethnic and Migration Studies* 26 (1): 25–44.

Sahgal, Gita, and Nira Yuval-Davis, eds. 1992. *Refusing Holy Orders: Women and Fundamentalism in Britain.* London: Virago Press.

Salins, Peter. 1997. *Assimilation, American Style.* New York: Basic Books.

Salter, Mark, ed. 2008. *Politics at the Airport.* Minnesota: University of Minnesota Press.

Sandel, Michael. 1996. *Democracy's Discontent: America in Search of a Public Philosophy.* Cambridge, Mass.: Belknap Press of Harvard University Press.

Sandercock, Leonie. 1998. *Towards Cosmopolis: Planning for Multicultural Cities.* New York: John Wiley.

——. 2000. "When Strangers Become Neighbours: Managing Cities of Difference." *Planning Theory and Practice* 1 (1): 13–30.

Santos, Fernanda. 2007. "Demand for English Lessons Outstrips Supply." *New York Times.* February 27, A1.

Sartori, Giovanni. 1970. "Concept Misformation in Comparative Politics." *American Political Science Review* 64 (4): 1033–53.

Sassen, Saskia. 1996. *Losing Control?* New York: Columbia University Press.

Sayad, Abdelmalek. 1987. "Les Immigrés Algériens et la Française." In *Questions de la nationalite, histoire et enjeux d'un code,* edited by Smain Lacher, 125–203. Paris: L'Harmattan.

Sayad, Abdelmalek, and Farinaz Fassa. 1982. "Éléments pour une sociologie de l'immigration." in *Travaux de science politique No 8.* Lausanne: Institut de Science Politique.

Sayyid, Salman 2000. "Beyond Westphalia: Nations and Diasporas—the Case of the Muslim *Umma.*" In *Un/Settled Multiculturalisms: Diasporas, Entanglement, Transruptions,* edited by Barnor Hesse, 33–50. London: Zed Books.

Schain, Martin. 1987. "The National Front in France and the Construction of Political Legitimacy." *West European Politics* 10 (2): 229–52.

——. 1988. "Immigration and Changes in the French Party System." *European Journal of Political Research* 16 (6): 597–621.

——. 1999. "Minorities and Immigrant Incorporation in France: The State and the Dynamics of Multiculturalism." In *Multicultural Questions,* edited by Christian Joppke and Steven Lukes, 199–223. Oxford: Oxford University Press,

——. 2006. "The Extreme-Right and Immigration Policy-Making: Measuring Direct and Indirect Effects." *West European Politics* 29 (2): 270–89.

Schain, Martin, Aristide Zolberg, and Patrick Hossay, eds. 2002. *Shadows over Europe: The Development and Impact of the Extreme Right in Western Europe.* New York: Palgrave Macmillan.

Scheepers, Peer, Mérove Gijsberts, and Evelyn Hello. 2002. "Religiosity and Prejudice against Ethnic Minorities in Europe: Cross-National Tests on a Controversial Relationship." *Review of Religious Research* 43 (3): 242–65.

Schiffauer, Werner. 1999. *Islamism in the Diaspora: The Fascination of Political Islam among Second Generation German Turks.* Working Paper no. WPCT 99-06.Oxford: Transnational Communities.

Schildkraut, Deborah. 2005. *Press One for English: Language Policy, Public Opinion, and American Identity.* Princeton, N.J.: Princeton University Press.

Schlesinger, Arthur. 1991. *The Disuniting of America: Reflections on a Multicultural Society.* New York: W. W. Norton.

Schmidt, Jochen. 2002. *Politische Brandstiftung: Warum 1992 in Rostock das Asylbewerberheim in Flammen aufging.* Berlin: Edition Ost.

Schnapper, Dominique. 1994. "The Debate on Immigration and the Crisis of National Identity." *West European Politics* 17 (2): 127–39.

Schrag, Peter. 2006. "Immigration: Will It Be the Hot Poker of 2006?" *Sacramento Bee,* April 26, A1.

Schuck, Peter. 1998. *Citizens, Strangers, and In-Betweens: Essays on Immigration and Citizenship.* Boulder, Colo.: Westview Press.

——. 2000. "Citizenship in Federal Systems." *American Journal of Comparative Law* 48: 195, 200–203.

——. 2003. *Diversity in America: Keeping Government at a Safe Distance.* Cambridge, Mass.: Belknap Press of Harvard University Press.

——. 2006. *Meditations of a Militant Moderate: Cool Views on Hot Topics.* Lanham, Md.: Rowman and Littlefield.

——. 2007a. "The Disconnect between Public Attitudes and Policy Outcomes in Immigration." In *The Politics of Immigration Reform,* edited by Carol Swain, 17–31. New York: Cambridge University Press.

——. 2007b. "In Diversity We (Sorta) Trust," *American Lawyer* 29 (December) 83–84.

——. 2007c. "Taking Immigration Federalism Seriously." *University of Chicago Law Forum,* 57–92.

Schuck, Peter, and Rogers Smith. 1985. *Citizenship without Consent: Illegal Aliens in the American Polity.* New Haven: Yale University Press.

Schuck, Peter, and John Williams. 2000. "Removing Criminal Aliens: The Pitfalls and Promises of Federalism," *Harvard Journal of Law and Public Policy* 22:367–464.

Schuck, Peter, and James Q. Wilson. 2008. *Understanding America: The Anatomy of an Exceptional Nation.* New York: Public Affairs Press.

Schuh, Sibilla. 1987. "Luciano und die Höhle der Elefanten—Selektionsdruck im Spannungsfeld zwischen zwei Welten." In *Fremde Heimat: Soziokulturelle und sprachliche Probleme von Fremdarbeiterkindern,* edited by Armin Gretler, Ruth Gurny, Anne-Nelly Perret-Clermont, and Edo Poglia, 223–39. Cousset: Delval

Sciolino, Elaine. 2007. "Immigration, Black Sheep and Swiss Rage." *New York Times,* October 8

Scolofo, Mark. 2006. "Hazelton Council Passes Ordinance against Illegal Immigrants." Associated Press. Available at: http://ap.org.

Scott, Joan Wallach. 2007. *The Politics of the Veil.* Princeton, N.J.: Princeton University Press.

Sen, Amartya. 1992. *Inequality Reexamined.* Cambridge, Mass.: Harvard University Press.

Sennett, Richard. 1998. *The Corrosion of Character: The Personal Consequences of Work in the New Capitalism.* New York: Norton.

Sensenbrenner, James. 2005. "Border Protection, Antiterrorism, and Illegal Immigration Control Act of 2005." United States House of Representatives, Dec. 15. Available at: http://thomas.loc.gov/cgi-bin/query/F?r109:1:./temp/.

Seper, Jerry. 2004. "Illegal Criminal Aliens Abound in U.S." *Washington Times.* January 26. Available at: http://www.washingtontimes.com.

Setzler, Mark, and Nick McRee. 2005. *Becoming Young Americans: The Acculturation and Civic Assimilation Patterns of Young Immigrants in the US.* Paper presented at the annual meeting of the American Political Science Association, Washington, D.C., September 1–4.

Shain, Yossi. 1999. *Marketing the American Creed Abroad: Diasporas in the U.S. and Their Homelands.* Cambridge, UK: Cambridge University Press.

Sheffer, Gabriel, ed. 1986. *Modern Diasporas in International Politics.* London: Croom Helm.

Shefter, Martin. 1986. "Political Incorporation and the Extrusion of the Left: Party Politics and Social Forces in New York City." *Studies in American Political Development* 1:50–90.

Silberman, Roxane, Richard Alba, and Irène Fournier. 2007. "Segmented Assimilation in France? Discrimination in the Labour Market against the Second Generation." *Ethnic and Racial Studies* 30 (1): 1–27.

Siméant, Johanna. 1998. *La Cause des sans-papiers.* Paris: Presses de Sciences Politiques.

Simmel, Georg. 2001 [1900]. *Philosophie des Geldes.* Cologne: Parkland Verlag.

Simon, Julian. 1989. *The Economic Consequences of Immigration.* Oxford: Basil Blackwell.

Simon, Patrick. 2003. "France and the Unknown Second Generation: Preliminary Results on Social Mobility." *International Migration Review* 37 (4): 1091–119.

Singer, Audrey, Susan Wiley Hardwick, and Caroline Brettell, eds. 2007. *Twenty-First Century Gateways: Immigrant Incorporation in Suburban America.* Washington, D.C.: Brookings Institution Press.

Sivanandan, Ambalavanan. 1985. "RAT and the Degradation of Black Struggle." *Race and Class* 26 (4): 1–33.

Skenderovic, Damir, and Gianni D'Amato. 2008. *Mit dem Fremden politisieren: Rechtspopulistische Parteien und Migrationspolitik in der Schweiz seit den 1960er Jahren.* Zürich: Chronos.

Skerry, Peter. 1993. *Mexican Americans: The Ambivalent Minority.* New York: Free Press/Macmillan.

Sleeper, Jim. 1993. "The End of the Rainbow." *New Republic,* November 1, 20–5.

Smith, Michael Peter. 2001. *Transnational Urbanism: Locating Globalization.* Malden, Mass.: Blackwell.

Smith, Michael Peter, and Luis Guarnizo, eds. 1998. *Transnational from Below.* New Brunswick, N.J.: Transaction.

Smith, Robert Courtney. 2006. *Mexican New York: Transnational Lives of New Immigrants.* Berkeley: University of California Press.

Smith, Rogers. 1997. *Civic Ideals: Conflicting Visions of Citizenship in U.S. History.* New Haven: Yale University Press.

Sniderman, Paul, and Thomas Piazza. 1993. *The Scar of Race.* Cambridge, Mass.: Belknap Press of Harvard University Press.

Sniderman, Paul, and Louk Hagendoorn. 2007. *When Ways of Life Collide: Multiculturalism and Its Discontents in the Netherlands.* Princeton, N.J.: Princeton University Press.

Soininen, Maritta. 1999. "The 'Swedish Model' as an Institutional Framework for Immigrant Membership Rights." *Journal of Ethnic and Migration Studies* 25 (4): 685–702.

Soininen, Maritta, and Henry Bäck. 1993. "Electoral Participation among Immigrants in Sweden: Integration, Culture and Participation." *New Community* 20 (1): 111–30.

Solomos, John, and Les Back. 1991 "Black Political Mobilisation and the Struggle for Equality." *Sociological Review* 39 (2): 215–37.

———. 1995. *Race, Politics, and Social Change.* London: Routledge.

Sonenshein, Raphael. 1993. *Politics in Black and White: Race and Power in Los Angeles.* Princeton, N.J.: Princeton University Press.

———. 2003a. "Post-incorporation Politics in Los Angeles." In *Racial Politics in American Cities,* edited by Rufus Browning, Dale Rogers Marshall, and David Tabb, 3rd ed., 51–76. New York: Longman.

———. 2003b. "The Prospects for Multiracial Coalitions: Lessons from America's Three Largest Cities." In *Racial Politics in American Cities,* edited by Rufus Browning, Dale Rogers Marshall, and David Tabb, 3rd ed., 333–56. New York: Longman.

———. 2004. *The City at Stake: Secession, Reform, and the Battle for Los Angeles.* Princeton, N.J.: Princeton University Press.

———. 2006. "Meet the New Boss." *Los Angeles Times,* August 27, M1.

Sonenshein, Raphael, and Mark Drayse. 2006. "Urban Electoral Coalitions in an Age of Immigration: Time and Place in the 2001 and 2005 Los Angeles Mayoral Primaries." *Political Geography* 25 (5): 570–95.

Sonenshein, Raphael, and Susan Pinkus. 2002. "The Dynamics of Latino Political Incorporation: The 2001 Los Angeles Mayoral Election as Seen in *Los Angeles Times* Exit Polls." *PS* 35 (1): 67–74.

———. 2005. "Latino Incorporation Reaches the Urban Summit: How Antonio Villaraigosa Won the 2005 Los Angeles Mayor's Race." *PS* 38 (4): 713–21.

Song, Ligang, and Yu Sheng. 2005. "Rapid Urbanization and Implications for Growth in China." In *The China Boom and Its Discontents.* edited by Ross Garnaut and Lgang Song, 105–27. Canberra: Australian National University, Asia Pacific Press.

Southern Poverty Law Center. 2001a. " 'Blood on the Border': With Racist Rhetoric Heating Up and the American Economy on Unsteady Legs, More Anti-Immigrant Violence Looms." Intelligence Report. Spring. Available at: http://www.splcenter.org/intel/intelreport/article.jsp?aid=230&printable=1.

———. 2001b. "In Their Own Words," Intelligence Report. Spring. Available at: http://www.splcenter.org/intel/inelreport/article.jsp?sid-174&printable=1.

———. 2007. "Close to Slavery: Guestworker Programs in the United States." Montgomery, Ala. Available at: http://splcenter.org.

Soysal, Yasemin. 1994. *Limits of Citizenship: Migrants and Postnational Membership in Europe.* Chicago: University of Chicago Press.

Spiro, Peter. 1994. "The States and Immigration in an Era of Demi-Sovereignties." *Virginia Journal of International Law* 35: 121–78.

———. 2008. *Beyond Citizenship: American Identity After Globalization.* New York: Oxford University Press.

Stasi Report. 2003. *Le Rapport de la Commission Stasi sur la Laïcité*. Reprinted in *Le Monde*, December 12, 2003.

Statham, Paul. 1999. "Political Mobilisation by Minorities in Britain: Negative Feedback of 'Race Relation'?" *Journal of Ethnic and Migration Studies* 25 (4): 597–626.

Statham, Paul, Ruud Koopmans, Marco Giugni, and Florence Passy. 2005. "Resilient or Adaptable Islam? Multiculturalism, Religion and Migrants' Claims-Making for Group Demands in Britain, the Netherlands and France." *Ethnicities* 5 (4): 427–59.

Statistics Canada. 2003. "Ethnic Diversity Survey." *The Daily*. (September 29). Available at: http://www.statcan.ca/Daily/English/030929/d030929a.htm.

Stepick, Alex, Guillermo Grenier, Max Castro, and Marvin Dunn. 2003. *This Land Is Our Land: Immigrants and Power in Miami*. Berkeley: University of California Press.

Stolberg, Sheryl. 2006. "After Immigration Protests, Goal Remains Elusive." *New York Times*, May 3, A1.

Stöss, Richard. 2005. *Rechtsextremismus im Wandel*. Berlin: Friedrich-Ebert-Stiftung.

Strudel, Sylvie. 1996. *Votes juifs: Itinéraires migratoires, religieux et politiques*. Paris: Presses des Sciences Politiques.

Sunier, Tijl. 2000. "Moslims in de Nederlandse Politieke Arena." In *Emancipatie en Subcultuur: Sociale Bewegingen in België en Nederland*, edited by Tijl Sunier, Jan Willem Duyvendak, Sawitri Saharso, and Fridus Steijlen, 138–57. Amsterdam: Instituut voor Publiek en Politiek.

Swarns, Rachel. 2006a. "Critics Say Politics Driving Immigration Hearings." *New York Times*, August 7, A1.

———. 2006b. "House Negotiator Calls Senate Immigration Bill 'Amnesty' and Rejects It." *New York Times*, May 27, A1.

———. 2007. "Bush Aides Pledge Work for Immigration Bill," *New York Times*, March 1, A5.

Swyngedouw, Marc, and Gilles Ivaldi. 2001. "The Extreme Right Utopia in Belgium and France: The Ideology of the Flemish Vlaams Blok and the French Front National." *West European Politics* 24 (3): 1–22.

Szakolczai, Arpad. 1994. "Thinking beyond the East-West Divide: Foucault, Patocka, and the Care of the Self." *Social Research* 61 (2): 297–323.

Takaki, Ronald. 1995. *Strangers at the Gates Again: Asian American Immigration after 1965*. New York: Chelsea House.

Tan, Gerald. 2003. *Asian Development: An Introduction to Economic, Social, and Political Change in Asia*. 2nd ed. Singapore: Eastern Universities Press.

Tarrow, Sidney. 1994. *Power in Movement: Social Movements, Collective Action, and Politics*. New York: Cambridge University Press.

Taylor, Charles. 1994. "Multiculturalism and 'The Politics of Recognition.'" In *Multiculturalism: Examining the Politics of Recognition*, edited by Amy Gutmann, 25–73. Princeton, N.J.: Princeton University Press.

Thelen, Lionel. 2006. *L'exil de soi: Sans-abri d'ici et d'ailleurs*. Bruxelles: Facultés Universitaires Saint-Louis.

Thompson, J. Phillip III. 2005. *Double Trouble: Black Mayors, Black Communities, and the Call for a Deep Democracy*. New York: Oxford University Press.

Thürer, Daniel. 1989. "Der politische Status der Ausländer in der Schweiz: Rechtsposition im Spannungsfeld zwischen politischer Rechtlosigkeit und Gleichberechtigung?" In *Festschrift für Ulrich Häfelin zum 65. Geburtstag*, edited by Walter Haller and Alfred Kölz, 183–204. Zürich: Schulthess.

Tichenor, Daniel. 2002. *Dividing Lines: The Politics of Immigration Control in America*. Princeton, N.J.: Princeton University Press.

Tillie, Jean. 1998. "Explaining Migrant Voting Behaviour in the Netherlands: Combining the Electoral Research and Ethnic Studies Perspective." *Revue européenne des migrations internationales* 14 (2): 71–95.

———. 2000. *De Etnische Stem: Opkomst en Stemgedrag van Migranten Tijdens Gemeenteraadsverkiezingen, 1986–1998*. Utrecht: Forum.

Todays Zaman. 2006. "Armenian Genocide Hinders Turkish-Dutch Candidates." September 28. available at: http://www.todayszaman.com/tz-web/detaylar.do?load=detay&link=36876**

Todd, Emmanuel. 1994. *Le destin des immigres: Assimilation et ségrégation dans les démocraties occidentales*. Paris: Seuil.

Togeby, Lise. 1999. "Migrants at the Polls: An Analysis of Immigrant and Refugee Participation in Danish Local Polls." *Journal of Ethnic and Migration Studies.* 25 (4): 665–84.

——. 2005. "The Electoral System and Representation of Minorities." Paper presented at the annual meeting of the American Political Science Association, Washington, D.C.

Toji, Dean. 2003. "Japanese: The Rise of a Nikkei Generation." In *The New Face of Asian Pacific America: Numbers, Diversity, and Change in the 21st Century,* edited by Eric Lai and Dennis Arguelles, 73–78. San Francisco: Asian Week.

*Toronto Star.* 2004. "Protest Rises over Islamic Law in Ontario," June 8.

Tribalat, Michèle. 2004. "Une estimation des populations d'origine étrangère en France en 1999." *Population* 59 (1): 51–82.

Truniger, Markus. 2002a. *Qualität in multikulturellen Schulen, QUIMS: Schlussbericht der Projektleitung über die zweite Phase (1999 bis 2001).* Zurich: ED.

——. 2002b. *Schulung der fremdprachigen Kinder und interkulturelle Pädagogik: Überprüfung der Umsetzung der Empfehlungen (Schuljahre 1999/2000 und 2000/01), Bericht zuhanden des Bildungsrats.* Zürich: ED.

Tsoulaka, Anastassia. 2005. "Looking at Migrants as Enemies." In *Controlling Borders: Free Movement into and within Europe,* edited by Didier Bigo and Elspeth Guild, 161–92. Burlington, Ver: Ashgate.

Turkenburg, Monique, and Mérove Gijsberts. 2007. "Opleidingsniveau en Beheersing van de Nederlandse Taal." In *Jaarrapport Integratie 2007,* edited by Jaco Dagevos and Mérove Gijsberts, 72–102. The Hague: Sociaal en Cultureel Planbureau.

Uçarer, Emek. 2003. "Justice and Home Affairs," In *European Union Politics,* edited by Michelle Cini, 294–311. Oxford: Oxford University Press.

——. 2001. "Sidekick No More? The European Commission in Justice and Home Affairs." European Integration Online Papers (EIOP), 5 (5), available at http://www.eiop.or.at/eiop/texte

Uhlaner, Carole. 1991. "Perceived Discrimination and Prejudice and the Coalition Prospects of Blacks, Latinos, and Asian Americans." In *Racial and Ethnic Politics in California,* edited by Byran Jackson and Michael Preston, 339–71. Berkeley: IGS Press.

Uitermark, Justus, Ugo Rossi, and Henk Van Houtum. 2005. "Reinventing Multiculturalism: Urban Citizenship and the Negotiation of Ethnic Diversity in Amsterdam." *International Journal of Urban and Regional Research* 29 (3): 622–40.

Uitterhoeve, Wilfried, ed. 2000. *Nederland en de anderen: Europese vergelijkingen uit het Sociaal en cultureel rapport 2000.* Nijmegen: SUN.

Unger, Roberto, and Cornel West. 1998. *The Future of American Progressivism: An Initiative for Political and Economic Reform.* Boston: Beacon Press.

United Nations. 2001. *Report of the Expert Group Meeting on Policy Responses to Population Ageing and Decline.* Population Division. New York: UN.

——. 2002. "International Migration Report 2002." Available at: www.un.org/esa/population/publications/ittmig2002/2002ITTMIGTEXT22–11.pdf.

——. 2006. "International Migration 2006." *Avilable at:* www.un.org/esa/population/publications/2006Migration_Chart/2006IttMig_chart.htm.

*University of California at Davis Law Review.* 2005. Symposium: Immigration and Civil Rights after September 11: The Impact on California. 38 (3): 599–1047.

U.S. Bureau of the Census. 2007. "Hispanics in the United States." Washington, D.C. Available at: http://www.census.gov/population/www/socdemo/hispanic/files/Internet_Hispanic_in_US_2006.pdf.

U.S. Commission on Immigration Reform. 1997. "Becoming an American: Immigration and Immigrant Policy." Available at: http://www.utexas.edu/lbj/uscir/becoming/fr-toc.html.

U.S. Department of Homeland Security. 2004. "A Guide to Naturalization." Form M-476. Citizenship and Immigration Services. Available at: http://www.ailc.com/services/natz/English.pdf.

——. 2005. "2004 Yearbook of Immigration Statistics." Office of Immigration Statistics. Available at: http://www.dhs.gov/xlibrary/assets/statistics/yearbook/2004/Yearbook2004.pdf.

——. 2007. "Trends in Naturalization Rates." Office of Immigration Statistics. Available at: http://www.dhs.gov/xlibrary/assets/statistics/publications/ntz_rates508.pdf.

——. 2008. "2007 Yearbook of Immigration Statistics." Office of Immigration Statistics. Available at: http://www.dhs.gov/xlibrary/assets/statistics/yearbook/2007/ois_2007_yearbook.pdf.

U.S. Department of Justice. 2003. "The September 11 Detainees: A Review of the Treatment of Aliens Held on Immigration Charges in Connection with the Investigation of the September 11 Attacks." Office of Inspector General. Available at: http://www.usdoj.gov/oig/special/0306/index.htm.

U.S. Government Accounting Office (GAO). 2005a. "Information on Certain Illegal Aliens Arrested in the United States." GAO-05-646R. Washington, D.C., May 9.

——. 2005b. "Information on Criminal Aliens Incarcerated in Federal and State Prisons and Local Jails." GAO-05-337R. Washington, D.C., April 7.

Vaca, Nicolas. 2004. *The Presumed Alliance: The Unspoken Conflict between Latinos and Blacks and What It Means for America.* New York: Harper Collins.

Vaes, Bénédicte. 2004. "La Societé Flamande Gangrenée par le Blok." *Le Soir,* October 9, 3.

Van Der Laan, Wendy, and Justus Veenman. 2004. "Onevenredigheid Qua Onderwijs, Arbeid en Inkomen." In *Onderzoek Integratiebeleid. Aanvullend Bronnenonderzoek Verwey-Jonker Instituut,* edited by Verwey-Jonker Instituut. The Hague: SDU, 13–40.

Vandermosten, René. 2006. "Migration as a Multi-Pillar Issue: An Insider's View." Paper presented at RSCAS, European University Institute, Florence, Italy, March 1.

Van der Veer, Peter. 2006. "Pim Fortuyn, Theo van Gogh, and the Politics of Tolerance in the Netherlands." *Public Culture* 18 (1): 111–24.

Van Donselaar, Jaap. 2005. "The Lonsdale Problem. Appearances Are Deceptive." Leiden University/Anne Frank House. Available at: http://www.annefrank.org/upload/downloads/Lonsdalesummary Eng02.doc.

Van Donselaar, Jaap, and Peter Rodrigues. 2004. "National Analytical Study on Racist Violence and Crime: RAXEN Focal Point for the Netherlands." Available at: http://www.eumc.eu.int/eumc/material/pub/RAXEN/4/RV/CS-RV-NR-NL.pdf.

Van Heelsum, Anja. 2000. "Political Participation of Migrants in the Netherlands." Paper presented to the International Metropolis Conference, Rotterdam, November 13–20.

——. 2002. "The Relationship between Political Participation and Civic Community of Migrants in the Netherlands." *Journal of International Migration and Integration* 3 (2): 179–99.

Van Kersbergen, Kees, and André Krouwel. 2003. "De Buitenlanderskwestie in de Politiek in Europa." In *Politiek in de Multiculturele Samenleving: Beleid en Maatschappij jaarboek 2003,* edited by Huib Pellikaan and Margo Trappenburg, 188–218. Amsterdam: Boom.

Van Praag, Carl,o and Jeannette Schoorl. 2007. "Housing and Segregation." In *Research Report TIES Survey in Amsterdam and Rotterdam,* edited by Maurice Crul and Liesbeth Heering, 31–42. Amsterdam: IMES.

van Selm, Joanne. 2005. "Immigration Is Becoming a Key Issue for Europe's Future," *European Affairs* (summer). Available at: http://www.europeanaffairs.org/current issue/2005 summer/2005 summer 08. pp.4 6.

Varsanyi, Monica. 2006. "Interrogating 'Urban Citizenship' vis-à-vis Undocumented Migration." *Citizenship Studies* 10 (2): 229–49.

Varshney, Ashutosh. 2003. "Nationalism, Ethnic Conflict, and Rationality." *Perspectives on Politics.* 1 (1): 85–99.

Veenman, Justus. 1994. *Participatie in perspectief: Ontwikkelingen in de sociaal-economische positie van zes allochtone groepen in Nederland.* Houten: Bohn Stafleu Van Loghum.

——. 1999. *Participatie in perspectief: Verleden en toekomst van etnische minderheden in Nederland.* Houten: Bohn Stafleu Van Loghum.

Veldboer, Lex, and Jan Willem Duyvendak. 2004. "Wonen en integratiebeleid: Een gemengd beeld." *Sociologische Gids* 51 (1): 36–52.

Verba, Sidney, Kay Lehman Schlozman, and Henry Brady. 1995. *Voice and Equality: Civic Voluntarism in American Politics.* Cambridge, Mass.: Harvard University Press.

Verhaar, Odile, and Sawitri Saharso. 2004. "The Weight of Context: Headscarves in Holland." *Ethical Theory and Moral Practice* 7 (2): 179–95.

Vertovec, Steven. 1996. "Multiculturalism, Culturalism and Public Incorporation." *Ethnic and Racial Studies* 19 (1): 49–69.

——. 2004. "Migrant Transnationalism and Modes of Transformation." *International Migration Review* 38 (3): 970–1001.

Veugelers, John, and André Magnan. 2005. "Conditions of Far-Right Strength in Contemporary Western Europe: An Application of Kitschelt's Theory," *European Journal of Political Research* 44 (6): 837–60.

Vigdor, Jacob. 2008. *Measuring Immigrant Assimilation in the United States.* New York: Manhattan Institute for Policy Research, May. Available at: http://www.manhattan-institute.org/html/cr_53.htm.

Viscusi, W. Kip, and Richard Zeckhauser. 2003. "Sacrificing Civil Liberties to Reduce Terrorism Risks," *Journal of Risk & Uncertainty* 26 (2/3): 99–120.

Wacquant, Loïc. 2006. *Parias Urbains: Ghetto—Banlieues—Etat.* Paris: La Découverte.

Wæver, Ole, Barry Buzan, Morten Kelstrup, and Pierre Lemaitre. 1993. *Identity, Migration, and the New Security Agenda in Europe.* London: Pinter.

Waldinger, Roger. 1986. *Through the Eye of the Needle: Immigrants and Enterprise in New York's Garment Trades.* New York: New York University Press.

——. 1989. "Race and Ethnicity." In *Setting Municipal Priorities, 1990,* edited by Charles Brecher and Raymond Horton, 50–79. New York: New York University Press.

——. 1996. *Still the Promised City? African-Americans and New Immigrants in Postindustrial New York.* Cambridge, Mass.: Harvard University Press.

Waldinger, Roger, and Mehdi Bozorgmehr, eds. 1996. *Ethnic Los Angeles.* New York: Russell Sage Foundation.

Waldinger, Roger, and Renee Reichl, 2006. *Second-Generation Mexicans: Getting Ahead or Falling Behind.* Washington, D.C.: Migration Information Source. Available at: http://www.migrationinformation.org/Feature/print.cfm?ID=382.

Waldrauch, Harald. 2003. "Electoral Rights for Foreign Nationals: A Comparative Overview of Regulations in 36 Countries." Paper presented at conference on Challenges of Immigration and Integration in the European Union and Australia, University of Sidney, February 18–20.

Walker, Martin. 2001–2002. "Post 9/11: The European Dimension," *World Policy Journal* (winter): 1–10.

Walker, Neil. 2004. *Europe's Area of Freedom, Security and Justice.* Oxford: Oxford University Press.

Walsh, Katherine Cramer. 2007. *Talking about Race: Community Dialogues and the Politics of Difference.* Chicago: University of Chicago Press.

Walters, Ron. 2006. "Hispanic Mobilization: Next Steps." *Chicago Defender,* April 19, A1.

Wanner, Philippe, and Gianni D'Amato. 2003. *Naturalisation en Suisse: Le Rôle des changements législatifs sur la demande de naturalisation; rapport.* Zürich: Avenir Suisse.

Watanabe, Teresa, and Anna Gorman. 2006. "More Than 500,000 Rally in L.A. for Immigrants' Rights." *Los Angeles Times,* March 25, A1.

Waters, Mary. 1999. *Black Identities: West Indian Immigrant Dreams and American Realities.* Cambridge, Mass.: Harvard University Press.

Waters, Mary, and Richard Alba. 2008. *The Next Generation: The Children of Immigrants in Europe and North America.* Cambridge: Harvard University, Department of Sociology.

Wattenberg, Ben J. 1991. *The First Universal Nation.* New York: Free Press.

Weil, Patrick. 2001. "Access to Citizenship: A Comparison of Twenty-Five Nationality Laws." In *Citizenship Today: Global Perspectives and Practices,* edited by T. Alexander Aleinikoff and Douglas Klusmeyer, 17–35. Washington, D.C.: Carnegie Endowment for International Peace.

——. 2002. *Qu'est-ce que un Français? Histoire de la nationalité française depuis la révolution.* Paris: Grasset.

——. 2004. "Lifting the Veil of Ignorance." *Progressive Politics* 3 (1): 17–22.

Weil, Patrick and John Crowley. 1994. "Integration in Theory and Practice: A Comparison of France and Britain." *West European Politics* 17 (2): 110–26.

We Need a Fence. 2007. "Illegal Immigration Is Out of Control." April 15. Available at: http://www.weneedafence.com/problem.asp.

White, William F. 1943. *Street Corner Society: The Social Structure of an Italian Slum.* Chicago: University of Chicago Press.

Widfeldt, Anders. 2000. "Scandinavia: Mixed Success for the Populist Right." *Parliamentary Affairs* 53 (3): 486–500.

Wihtol de Wenden, Catherine. 1988. *Les imigrés et la politique.* Paris: Presses de Sciences Politiques.

Wikan, Unni. 2002. *Generous Betrayal: Politics of Culture in the New Europe*. Chicago: University of Chicago Press.

Wilensky, Harold. 2002. *Rich Democracies: Political Economy, Public Policy, and Performance*. Berkeley: University of California Press.

Williams, Michelle. 2006. *The Impact of Radical Right-Wing Parties in West European Democracies*. New York: Palgrave Macmillan.

Wimmer, Andreas, and Nina Glick Schiller. 2002. "Methodological Nationalism and Beyond: Nation-State Building, Migration and the Social Sciences." *Global Networks* 2 (4): 301–34.

Wolfe, Alan. 2001. "Strangled by Roots." *New Republic*, May 28, 29–33.

———. 2004. *An Intellectual in Public*. Ann Arbor: University of Michigan Press.

Wong, Carolyn. 2006. *Lobbying for Inclusion: Rights Politics and the Making of Immigration Policy*. Stanford: Stanford University Press.

Wong, Janelle. 2002. "Thinking about Immigrant Political Incorporation." Paper presented at Workshop on Immigrant Incorporation, Mobilization and Participation, Maxwell School of Syracuse University, December 6.

———. 2006. *Democracy's Promise: Immigrants and American Civic Institutions*. Ann Arbor: University of Michigan Press.

*World Journal*. 2003. "Chinese Communities Vary Widely." trans. Michael Huang. June 20. Accessed at http://www.gothamgazette.com/citizen/jul03/chinese_demo.shtml.

Wüst, Andreas. 2003. "Das Wahlverhalten Eingebürgerter Personen in Deutschland." *Aus Politik und Zeitgeschichte* 2003 (52): 29–38.

Yang, Philip. 1994a. "Ethnicity and Naturalization." *Ethnic and Racial Studies* 17 (4): 593–618.

———. 1994b. "Explaining Immigrant Naturalization." *International Migration Review* 28 (3): 449–77.

———. 2002. "Citizenship Acquisition of Post-1965 Asian Immigrants." *Population and Environment* 23 (4): 377–404.

Young, Iris. 1989. "Polity and Group Difference: A Critique of the Ideal of Universal Citizenship." *Ethics* 99 (2): 250–74.

———. 1990. *Justice and the Politics of Difference*. Princeton, N.J.: Princeton University Press.

Yurdakul, Gökçe and Y. Michal Bodemann. 2006. "We Don't Want to Be the Jews of Tomorrow." *German Politics and Society* 24 (2): 44–67.

Yuval-Davis, Nira. 1992. "Fundamentalism, Multiculturalism and Women in Britain." In *"Race," Culture and Difference*, edited by James Donald and Ali Rattansi, 278–91. London: Sage.

ZACAT. Zentralarchiv für Empirische Sozialforschung an der Universität zu Köln. http://zacat.gesis.org/webview/index.jsp.

Zahner, Claudia, ed. 2005. *PISA 2003: Kompetenzen für die Zukunft, zweiter nationaler Bericht*. Neuchâtel/Bern: Bundesamt für Statistik.

Zaslove, Andrej. 2004. "Closing the Door? The Ideology and Impact of Radical Right Populism on Immigration Policy in Austria and Italy." *Journal of Political Ideologies* 9 (1): 99–118.

Zielbauer, Neil. 2002. "Poverty in a Land of Plenty: Can Hartford Ever Recover?" *New York Times*, August 26, A1.

Zolberg, Aristide. 2000. "The Politics of Immigration Policy: An Externalist Perspective." In *Immigration Research for a New Century: Multidisciplinary Perspectives*, edited by Nancy Foner, Rubén Rumbaut, and Steven Gold, 60–68. New York: Russell Sage Foundation.

———. 2006. *A Nation by Design: Immigration Policy in the Fashioning of America*. Cambridge, Mass.: Harvard University Press.

Zolberg, Aristide, and Long Litt Woon. 1999. "Why Islam Is Like Spanish: Cultural Incorporation in Europe and the United States." *Politics and Society* 27 (1): 5–38.

# Contributor Biographies

**Richard Alba** is distinguished professor of sociology at the Graduate Center of the City University of New York and co-author (with Victor Nee) of the award-winning book *Remaking the American Mainstream: Assimilation and Contemporary Immigration* (Harvard University Press, 2003). He continues to research the incorporation of immigrants and their children in North America and Western Europe.

**Sandro Cattacin** is a professor and director of the Sociological Department at the University of Geneva. His research fields are urban policies and social and health policies, in particular regarding marginal groups and migrants. He has taught at the universities of Zurich, Fribourg/CH, Constance, Neuchâtel, and Malmö. His recent publications concern migration and health, misanthropy, and migrant associations.

**Gianni D'Amato** is Professor for Migration and Citizenship Studies at the University of Neuchâtel and director of the Swiss Forum of Migration and Population Studies (SFM). His research interests are focused on the political consequences of mobilities. He has recently co-authored a study on radical right-wing populist parties and their impacts on migration policies in Switzerland, *Mit dem Fremden politisieren: Rechtspopulismus und Migrationspolitik in der Schweiz seit den 1960er Jahren* (Chronos Verlag, 2008).

**Jan Willem Duyvendak** is a full Professor Of Sociology at the University of Amsterdam. He studied sociology and philosophy in Groningen and Paris. Until 2003 he was director of the Verwey-Jonker Institute for Social Research and Professor of Community Development at the Erasmus University in Rotterdam. He has published in the areas of social movement mobilization (*The Power of Politics* [Westview Press, 1995]), sexuality, professionalism (*Policy, People, and the New Professional* [Amsterdam University Press, 2006]) and Dutch minority policies.

**Nancy Foner** is distinguished professor of sociology at Hunter College and the Graduate Center of the City University of New York. Her recent work on immigration has compared U.S. immigration today and a century ago, the immigrant experience in various U.S. gateway cities, and immigrant minorities in the United States and Europe. Her books include *From Ellis Island to JFK: New York's Two Great Waves of Immigration* (Yale University Press, 2000), *In a New Land: A Comparative View of Immigration* (New York University Press, 2005), and (as editor) *Across Generations: Immigrant Families in America* (New York University Press, 2009).

**Luis Ricardo Fraga** is associate vice provost for faculty advancement, director of the Diversity Research Institute, Russell F. Stark University Professor, and professor of political science at the University of Washington. He is coauthor of Multiethnic Moments: The Politics of Urban Education Reform (Temple University Press, 2006) and is coauthor (with Gary Segura) of "Culture Clash? Contesting Notions of American Identity and the Effects of Latin American Immigration," in *Perspectives on Politics* (June 2006). He is also completing the forthcoming coauthored book *Making It Home: Latino Lives in the United States* (Temple University Press). He is one of the co-principal investigators of the Latino National Survey, the first-ever state-stratified survey of Latinos in the United States.

**Jennifer L. Hochschild** is the Henry LaBarre Jayne Professor of Government at Harvard University, professor of African and African-American Studies, and Harvard College Professor. She holds a lectureship in the Harvard Kennedy School. Most recently, she is the co-author (with Nathan Scovronick) of *The American Dream and the Public Schools* (Oxford University Press, 2003) and (with Brenna Powell) of "Racial Reorganization and the United States Census 1850–1930: Mulattoes, Half-Breeds, Mixed Parentage, Hindoos, and the Mexican Race," in *Studies in American Political Development* (spring 2008). With two co-authors, she is currently working on a book titled *Blurring American Racial Boundaries: Skin Color, Multiracialism, Immigration, and DNA*.

**Christian Joppke** is a professor of politics at the American University of Paris. His most recent book is *Veil: Mirror of Identity* (Polity Press, 2009); he has also recently written *Selecting by Origin: Ethnic Migration in the Liberal State* (Harvard University Press, 2005) and co-edited (with Ewa Morawska) *Toward Assimilation and Citizenship: Immigrants in Liberal Nation-States* (Palgrave Macmillan, 2003). Currently he is writing a book on citizenship and immigration, to be published by Polity Press.

**Gallya Lahav** is associate professor of political science at the State University of New York at Stony Brook. She teaches and writes on international migration and European regional integration. In addition to numerous articles and chapters on migration politics, she is also the author of *Immigration and Politics in the New Europe: Reinventing Borders* (Cambridge University Press, 2004), co-editor (with Virginie Guiraudon) of *Immigration Policy in Europe: The Politics of Control* (Routledge, 2006), and co-editor (with Anthony Messina) of *The Migration Reader* (Lynne Rienner Publishers, 2007).

**Marco Martiniello** is research director at the Belgian National Fund for Scientific Research (FRS-FNRS). He teaches sociology and politics at the University of Liège and is the director of the Center for Ethnic and Migration Studies (CEDEM) in the same university. He is also member of the Executive Board of the European Network of Excellence IMISCOE (International Migration and Social Cohesion in Europe) and president of the Research Committee n°31 Sociology of Migration (International Sociological Association). His main research interests are migration, ethnicity, racism, multiculturalism, and citizenship as policy and political issues in the European Union and in Belgium with a transatlantic comparative perspective.

**Michael Minkenberg** is the current Max Weber Chair for German and European Studies at New York University. He has taught comparative politics at the universities of Göttingen and Heidelberg, at Cornell University, and at the European University Viadrina in Frankfurt (Oder). His research interests include the contemporary radical right; immigration, nationalism, and the politics of citizenship; and the relationship between religion and politics in western democracies. Among his recent publications is *The Radical Right in Europe: An Overview* (Verlag Bertelsmann Stiftung, 2008).

**Lorraine C. Minnite** is an assistant professor of political science at Barnard College, Columbia University, and a senior fellow at Demos: A Network of Ideas and Action. She is a co-author (with Frances Fox Piven and Margaret Groarke) of *Keeping Down the Black Vote: Race and the Demobilization of American Voters* (New Press, 2009), and she coordinates the New Americans Exit Poll project in New York City.

**Tariq Modood** is professor of sociology, politics, and public policy, and the founding director of the Centre for the Study of Ethnicity and Citizenship at the University of Bristol. His recent publications include *Multiculturalism: A Civic Idea* (Polity, 2007); (as co-editor with Glenn Loury and Steven Teles), *Ethnicity, Social Mobility and Public Policy in the US and UK* (Cambridge University Press, 2005); and (as co-editor with Geoffery Brahm Levey), *Secularism, Religion and Multicultural Citizenship* (Cambridge University Press, 2008).

**John H. Mollenkopf** is Distinguished Professor of political science and sociology at the Graduate Center of the City University of New York and directs its Center for Urban Research. His most recent book, with Philip Kasinitz, Mary Waters, and Jennifer Holdaway, is *Inheriting the City: The Children of Immigrants Come of Age* (Harvard University Press and Russell Sage Foundation, 2008). He is currently researching immigrant political incorporation in New York and Los Angeles and comparing the second generation in the United States and Europe.

**Eva Østergaard-Nielsen** is a Ramon y Cajal Fellow in the Department of Political Science at the Autonomous University of Barcelona. Her publications include *Transnational Politics: Turks and Kurds in Germany* (Routledge, 2003) and *International Migration and Sending Countries* (Palgrave, 2003), as well as several articles in international journals. Her current research focuses on the politics of migration and migrant incorporation in Europe, the role of migrants in development and democratization of their countries of origin, and transnational networks of civil society organizations.

**Adrian D. Pantoja** is an associate professor of political studies and Chicano studies at Pitzer College (Claremont Colleges). His research, which has appeared in numerous journals and edited volumes, revolves around the Latino population, immigration, public opinion, and voter behavior.

**Trees Pels** is head of the research group Multicultural Issues at the Verwey-Jonker Institute (Utrecht, Netherlands). Her main field of study is the socialization, education, and development of children of minorities. One of her recent books (co-edited with Maja Deković and Suzanne Model) is *Child Rearing in Six Ethnic Families: The Multi-Cultural Dutch Experience* (Edwin Mellen Press, 2006).

**Rally Rijkschroeff** has been research director of Verwey-Jonker Institute (Utrecht, Netherlands) since 1993. His extensive research experience includes evaluation studies on the participation and integration of immigrants in multicultural societies, (local) social policy, and strategic governance issues. He is actively involved in studies on disability issues, client organizations, and social activation.

**Reuel Rogers** is an associate professor of political science at Northwestern University. He is the author of *Afro-Caribbean Immigrants and the Politics of Incorporation: Ethnicity, Exception, or Exit* (Cambridge University Press, 2006). His current research explores how suburbanization is reshaping political attitudes and behavior among blacks.

**Peter H. Schuck** is the Simeon E. Baldwin Professor of Law, Yale Law School. His most recent books are (co-edited with James Q. Wilson) *Understanding America: The Anatomy of an Exceptional Nation* (Public Affairs, 2008); (co-authored with Richard J. Zeckhauser) *Targeting in Social Programs: Avoiding Bad Bets, Removing Bad Apples* (Brookings Institution Press, 2006); *Meditations of a Militant Moderate: Cool Views on Hot Topics* (Rowman & Littlefield, 2006); *Diversity in America: Keeping Government at a Safe Distance* (Belknap Press of Harvard University Press, 2003); *The Limits of Law: Essays on Democratic Governance* (Westview Press, 2000); and *Citizens, Strangers, and In-Betweens: Essays on Immigration and Citizenship* (Westview Press, 1998).

**Raphael Sonenshein** is professor of political science and public administration at California State University, Fullerton. He studies racial and ethnic politics in big cities, particularly Los Angeles. His most recent book is *The City at Stake: Secession, Reform, and the Battle for Los Angeles* (Princeton University Press, 2004). Sonenshein's current research is on urban coalitions in an age of immigration.

**Janelle Wong** is an associate professor of political science and American studies at the University of Southern California. She is the author of *Democracy's Promise: Immigrants and American Civic Institutions* (University of Michigan Press, 2006). Her current research focus is on how growing numbers of evangelical and Pentecostal immigrants are changing conservative political coalitions in the United States.

# Index

Page numbers followed by letters *f* and *t* refer to figures and tables, respectively.

# Index